Hollywood Musicals
You Missed

ALSO BY EDWIN M. BRADLEY
AND FROM MCFARLAND

*Unsung Hollywood Musicals of the Golden Era:
50 Overlooked Films and Their Stars, 1929–1939* (2016)

*The First Hollywood Sound Shorts,
1926–1931* (2005; paperback 2009)

*The First Hollywood Musicals:
A Critical Filmography of 171 Features,
1927 through 1932* (1996; paperback 2004)

Hollywood Musicals You Missed

Seventy Noteworthy Films from the 1930s

Edwin M. Bradley

McFarland & Company, Inc., Publishers
Jefferson, North Carolina

ISBN (print) 978-1-4766-7358-5
ISBN (ebook) 978-1-4766-3993-2

LIBRARY OF CONGRESS AND BRITISH LIBRARY
CATALOGUING DATA ARE AVAILABLE

Library of Congress Control Number 2020018828

© 2020 Edwin M. Bradley. All rights reserved

No part of this book may be reproduced or transmitted in any form or by any means, electronic or mechanical, including photocopying or recording, or by any information storage and retrieval system, without permission in writing from the publisher.

Front cover image: a crime queen-pin (Dorothy Burgess) shows off the much-coveted last man on Earth (Raul Roulien) in Fox's bizarre science-fiction musical *It's Great to Be Alive* (1933) (author's collection)

Printed in the United States of America

*McFarland & Company, Inc., Publishers
Box 611, Jefferson, North Carolina 28640
www.mcfarlandpub.com*

To Kathy, James, and Andrew

Table of Contents

Preface   1

1. Songs of the Dawn   5
2. They Don't Write 'Em Like That Anymore   41
3. A Hillbilly Sym-Funny   76
4. Where the Tenors and the Baritones Play   106
5. Invasion of the Opera Singers, or: End of an Aria   146
6. The Teenagers Are Restless   189
7. Big Stars, Short Memories   219

Chapter Notes   261
Bibliography   279
Index   283

Preface

Never mind the present—who needs to travel to *La La Land* or imagine a Beatles-free *Yesterday* when you can go *Flying Down to Rio*, book passage on a *Show Boat*, or love a *Footlight Parade*? You can take a deep dive into the Hollywood musical of the 1930s and not want to come up. The dawn of sound … *42nd Street* … pre–Code sass … Crosby, Astaire, and Eleanor Powell … Lubitsch, Berkeley, and Hermes Pan … Tin Pan Alley moving West … little Shirley tap-dancing with Bill Robinson … MacEddy-style romance … the invasion of swing … first glances at Judy and Mickey. Other decades can boast musicals with more patriotism, bigger bands, splashier color, pricier budgets, and rock 'n' roll. But with the Hollywood assembly line operating at peak efficiency, the period from Al Jolson's first audible syllable to the final tick of the clock of film history's greatest year remains, to these eyes, the greatest period for American musical cinema. There is still so much in the 1930s to write about, and it doesn't have to be about the same old faces and same old songs.

This book is a follow-up of sorts to my two other books specific to the nascent movie musical. The more recent, *Unsung Hollywood Musicals of the Golden Era* (2016), featured 50 films of 1929–39, mainly those with novelty angles—short-time leads, rising stars, "non-musical" performers, and production-related oddities. The idea was to spotlight less-heralded pictures at the expense of over-familiar studios and stars. In this volume, as in that one, you'll see less than the norm from Metro-Goldwyn-Mayer or Warner Bros., many of whose films have been written about widely and programmed frequently on Turner Classic Movies. What you do read here about some of the most famous performers of the 1930s cine-musical will relate, for amusement's sake, to films you might not expect from them. And you're going to get some Westerns—and like them.

The 70 films featured on these pages are selected not only because of the celebrity of the people in them, but also because of why they were made. The 1930s movie musical developed through tangents that reflected larger trends in film in general and the culture at large. A genre that didn't exist before Jolson opened his mouth to sing at Warners was defining itself throughout the decade. Stung by the public rejection of musicals created by the glut of them on the market in 1929–30, filmmakers sought to recover the lost audience for their songfests. This was accomplished most notably, in the consensus of film historians, by exploiting the uniquely cinematic qualities of the musical, by breaking through the confines of the traditional proscenium stage setting, as was done most spectacularly in the Busby Berkeley spectacles at Warner Bros. The likes of *42nd Street*, *Dames*, *Footlight Parade*, and the *Gold Diggers* series have been extensively documented and analyzed.

But as we will see throughout this book, the Hollywood studios pursued other angles and exploited other trends with their musicals. The movies did this initially by importing scores of actors and singers from other media—vaudeville, radio, and the legitimate theater—although this was the case in 1939 as well as 1929. They saw the value in precocious preteens who could sing or dance—not only Shirley Temple, Judy Garland, Mickey Rooney, and Deanna Durbin, but also Jane Withers, Bobby Breen, Mitzi Green, Sybil Jason, Gloria Jean, and even mini-skater Irene Dare—but Hollywood always has been attracted to budding talents. So what was specific to the 1930s?

We'll start by looking at some of the first "trendy" Hollywood musicals, those from the initial crop. Audiences thrilled by the novelty of song and dance as well as dialogue prompted the studios to overproduce musical films, and what was fresh and new in mid–1929 seemed passé by the summer solstice of 1930. In Chapter 1, we examine a group of pre–1934 features, many rarely viewed until recently. Many of those entries share a history of hectic production, uncertain release, and the ultimate audience rejection that forced the genre into a temporary near-hiatus.

In Chapter 2, we will look at the earliest efforts to glamorize the professional and personal lives of songwriters in the kind of biographical pictures that would become much more prevalent in the 1940s and 1950s. These experiments were necessitated by the lack of charisma when the real songwriters were set before the cameras—check out Rodgers and Hart, or even Johnny Mercer. But the need for box office results led to such inappropriate castings as Don Ameche as Stephen Foster, and Tyrone Power and Bing Crosby as max-fictionalized renderings of Irving Berlin and Gus Edwards, respectively.

Chapters 3 and 4 are related in showing how Hollywood exploited the growing popularity, fueled by radio airplay and population demographics, of Western and "hillbilly" music by featuring both countrified styles on screen, in both comedic and more respectful ways. This led to the rise of such stars as Gene Autry, Roy Rogers, Bob Burns, Pinky Tomlin, and, in a beloved novelty act with an unusual backstory, the Missouri-bred, Arkansas-linked hillbilly entertainers Weaver Brothers and Elviry. City slickers sneered at these pictures; non-sophisticates yearned for more.

Chapter 5 deals with efforts to make screen stars out of famous opera performers in the mid- to late 1930s, with mixed results at best. The popularity of these outsized voices (Grace Moore, Lawrence Tibbett, Gladys Swarthout, and others) didn't last long, but that didn't stop Hollywood from trotting them out, sometimes outrageously. The public might have delighted in the failures of these lofty personalities—which brought them down to "our" level—but these highbrow artists ended up getting more out of their cinematic transactions than did film-industry bean counters.

The impact of the swing music craze nationally is examined in the films chosen for Chapter 6. These pictures grew out of unease from youth audiences, who wanted to hear jazz and dance music with energy. For the most artistically respected purveyors of this style, such as Benny Goodman and Louis Armstrong, this brought unexpected exposure on the screen to listeners of all ages. But the most quantitatively successful big bandsman of the swing era in terms of that exposure was not who you might think it was.

For the seventh and final chapter, we take a slightly different path, as we demonstrate that big names didn't always score big at the picture paybox. Even as the major companies kept assigning their most gifted and/or popular stars to as many musicals as possible, this could be to the point of diminishing artistic and/or financial returns. Jolson, Crosby, Alice Faye, and Jeanette MacDonald and Nelson Eddy all made a stinker or two. We'll dig into some pictures those megastars might have wanted us to forget, even if some of them don't come off too poorly in retrospect.

Some of the title selections in this book could be described as random or quixotic, but again, the general idea was to stay away from pictures that have been excessively analyzed.

I could have included the Universal mega-musical *King of Jazz* in my chapter about recent early-sound rediscoveries, as it certainly has been "rediscovered," but what more would I add beyond what James Layton and David Pierce said about that film in their terrific book about it? I'd rather shed a little light on the still-little-seen *Are You There?* from the same year, or the later obscurities *It's Great to Be Alive, Mountain Music,* and *Fatal Lady*. Maybe, after reading about them here, you'll want to seek them out as well. On the other hand, although *Alexander's Ragtime Band* has been the subject of much previous scholarship, I found it impossible to write a chapter about 1930s composer biopics without including it. Same with including a Gene Autry example in a study of singing Westerns, although *The Phantom Empire* is a serial that has been examined at great length by devotees of both science fiction and the B Western.

A few other notes of explanation:

- Yes, there are three 1929 releases in a book about Hollywood musicals of the 1930s. However, all were playing in American theaters well into 1930, and I didn't deem it inappropriate to include them.
- All but one of the titles herein were viewed by the author. The exception was *Harlem on the Prairie* (1937), which has been included for the sake of completeness regarding the Westerns career of its star, Herbert Jeffries.
- I typically take a liberal definition of the term "musical." Based on the number of songs, who sings them, and their relationship to characterization or plot development, a handful of the titles here stretch that definition. For example, *Jazz Heaven* was widely advertised as a musical in 1929, although it may not qualify by current standards.
- Film titles marked with an asterisk (*) were featured in *Unsung Hollywood Musicals of the Golden Era*. Feel free to read more about them in that volume.
- Regarding the discography information, I have chosen to list only U.S.-released 78-rpm recordings made by people involved with the film at (roughly) the time of the film's initial release. Especially valuable in compiling these listings was the Online 78 rpm Discographical Project (78discography.com).
- The date at the start of each film entry usually is the general release date, although if I noticed a New York or Los Angeles premiere or some other kind of non-preview showing that was earlier, its date is shown instead.

Eric Hoyt's wonderful Digital Media History Library, which provides online access to important research material, particularly trade publications, has continued to be a godsend. It remains fascinating that even cursory examinations of such vintage publications reveal the wide differences in how films and film people were perceived in certain cultural or geographical quarters. "What the Picture Did for Me"—a feature of *Exhibitors Herald and Moving Picture World*, which became the *Motion Picture Herald*—reads like an internet message board in the diversity of comments by theater owners and managers about the artistic quality and commercial value (two not-always-mutual terms) of motion pictures in their locales. "WTPDFM" entries are replete with snide comments about movies that were mismatched to their audiences, as well as flowery praise of titles that, we know from hindsight, went nowhere. (Note to self: If you go into the theater biz, think twice about booking an opera picture in Beaver City, Nebraska.) The Digital Media History Library also yields fan magazine coverage that shows how star images were conceived and maintained, and it chronicles the interesting ways in which pictures were marketed. Another useful Internet site has been Newspapers.com, which is especially helpful in spotlighting coverage for mass audiences as opposed to that for inside-the-industry folks. The Internet Movie Database remains problematical in terms of accuracy, but it includes a lot of info, albeit much necessary to verify.

Some of the information in this book has been repurposed from my movie-themed blog, earlysoundguy.com. Chuck Anderson's comprehensive "Old Corral" website (www.b-westerns.com) has great information on series Westerns and their makers, and we thank Chuck for his personal assistance. Ancestry.com contains valuable records and family information that helped fill in some blanks. Thank-yous also must go to the late (and much-missed) Ron Hutchinson of the Vitaphone Project, the UCLA Film and Television Archive (Scott MacQueen and Mark Quigley), and the New York Museum of Modern Art Department of Film (the late Charles Silver). Richard Barrios and Ray Faiola read sections of the book and provided valuable feedback. Don Dahlstrom, my favorite at proofreading, did some more. Also thanks to Roy Blakey, the late Bill Cappello, Richard Finegan, Richard Koszarski, Boyd Magers, Ray Paredez, Paul Seno, OJ Sikes, and Wade Williams. I interviewed the now-deceased actress Dorothy Lee for my 1996 book, *The First Hollywood Musicals*, and some of her comments are included here.

As has always been the case, special gratitude goes to my wife, Kathy, and our sons, Andrew and James. Andrew sat through many of these films with me and aided in my research. He can take a break now.

1

Songs of the Dawn

The modest trade magazine with the boastful title *Inside Facts of Stage and Screen* had a strong opinion to offer in a below-the-masthead editorial of July 1930. Posting a pointed question with "And Now, What?" as the headline, the commentary writer had an oversized axe to grind with a certain tuneful entertainment:

> Despite dollars, time, energy, and industry, despite an unusual array of Broadway songsmiths, directors, writers, singers, dancers, comedians, and dance-masters; despite [T]echnicolor, [M]ulticolor, and any other kind of color; despite wide screens and fancy screens, publicity, exploitation, and ballyhoo, the new art form, the screen musical … has proven the most complete and unmitigated flop in the entire history of amusement.[1]

Given the state of the Hollywood musical by the middle of 1930, one cannot blame the journalistic overkill. The glut of singing and dancing films since the advent of sound had frayed public interest. The backlash from the formerly song-hungry audience happened quickly. According to the 1930 *Film Daily Year Book of Motion Pictures*, no fewer than four musicals appeared in the journal's annual 10-best poll for 1929. As selected by 327 of the "foremost critics and editors in the United States," Metro-Goldwyn-Mayer's *The Broadway Melody* came in at number two, RKO's *Rio Rita* at four, Warner Bros.' *Gold Diggers of Broadway* at five, and MGM's *Hallelujah!* at 10.[2] Additionally, Fox's fringe musical *The Cock-Eyed World* ranked number eight, albeit more due to its ribald comedy than its song interludes.

However, the *Film Daily* top 10 for 1930 boasted no song films, and the public didn't seem to mind their absence. Theater owners were putting up marquees reading "This Is Not a Musical" or "This Is Not a Revue," even if the attractions inside were precisely those. When the "And Now, What?" essay appeared, the folks at resource-rich MGM were about to dismantle *The March of Time*—a lavish revue, nearly complete but suddenly a financial gamble—into what would become pieces of filler for other films. Warner Bros. had been the first studio to bankroll a Broadway production—Cole Porter's *Fifty Million Frenchmen*—but now Porter's music was deemed anathema to audiences who were soon to get a same-titled but reworked comedy featuring low cavorters Ole Olsen and Chic Johnson, wasted in Technicolor. In another anti-musical horror story, the *Inside Facts* piece referred to Fox either changing the title of one of its unwanted musicals, so that note-wearied patrons might take it as an out-and-out comedy, or considering the less desirable but palatable label "comedy with songs." Now what, indeed!

Maybe it wasn't a surprise to that editorial writer when, only three years later, the screen musical returned in glory. But what if he were to learn that, 86 years after he'd put poison pen to paper, one of the biggest no-gos of that "unmitigated flop" period would become a triumph for the film industry? The digital restoration of Universal's 1930 Paul Whiteman–led Technicolor revue *King of Jazz* took close to five years before its premiere in May 2016 at the Museum of Modern Art in New York. The film—the one that brought Bing Crosby to Hollywood with Whiteman's band—existed in incomplete prints shown in revivals of the 1970s and issued on sketchy-looking VHS in the '80s and '90s. The restoring team located multiple versions around the globe to go with the original two-color camera negative (housed at UCLA) and reassembled the movie, restoring missing footage while returning the film to the running order intended by its director, Broadway visionary John Murray Anderson. *King of Jazz* was added to the National Film Registry, spurring the restoration, which was followed by an exhaustively researched book about the movie by historians James Layton and David Pierce. The attention culminated in a handsome 2018 release for *King of Jazz* on DVD and Blu-ray in the Criterion Collection prestige line, plus a 2019 airing on Turner Classic Movies. Universal has more classic restorations in store, we are told.

King of Jazz has been the most conspicuous rediscovery from the early sound era, but pre–1933 musicals also continue to pop up for broadcast on TCM and other outlets. Others, unshackled from archival limitations or grey-market mockeries, have been revived on home video without even having aired on cable television, as when Criterion included Paul Fejos' 1929 musical drama *Broadway* (see below) as an extra on a DVD/Blu release in 2012. In 2014, Warner Archive issued the Olsen and Johnson rarity *Oh, Sailor, Behave!** (1930) on DVD, and four years later, the Universal Vault DVD series yielded the George M. Cohan musi-comedy *The Phantom President* (Paramount, 1932). Some of the movies highlighted in this chapter have emerged from public-domain or legal oblivion for availability on commercial disc and YouTube. Other early talkie musicals survive but can be viewed only through archival visitation or rare screenings at film conventions, but at least they can continue to be enjoyed.

It's easy to lose yourself in this early period, as we see each of the major studios begin to develop their own musical personalities … and collective personality. Warner Bros. pre–Berkeley was the home of Jolson, Winnie Lightner, wall-to-wall underscoring, and Technicolor (in hues now mostly lost to us). RKO was the locale of lovely Bebe (as in Daniels), comics Bert and Bob (as in Wheeler and Woolsey), and forgotten secondary males (Hugh Trevor, Allen Kearns, Everett Marshall). Fox kept it homey and simple, slipping song numbers into the films of the romantic duo Janet Gaynor and Charles Farrell while force-feeding us El Brendel and J. Harold Murray. Paramount went upscale with Chevalier, Jeanette MacDonald, and the Lubitsch Touch when not descending with Jack Oakie and Helen Kane. MGM dazzled with its usual star power, in brightness and numbers. Then there were John Boles, Stanley Smith, Lawrence Gray, and Marjorie "Babe" Kane, who seemed to be everywhere around town. God love 'em all.

What will be the next *King of Jazz* for musicals mavens? Who knows? The current Holy Grail among early talkies is Warner Bros. Technicolor release *Gold Diggers of Broadway*, one of the biggest box office hits of 1929. The complete soundtrack exists, as does a sizable portion of the picture element, including most of the last two reels, which were donated to the British Film Institute in the 1980s. Thanks to discoveries made on both sides of the Atlantic, we can now see Nick Lucas' important "Tip-Toe Through the Tulips" production number and other excerpts—one of which, seconds long, was found not long ago in a kiddie toy projector. A little more of Winnie Lightner or Albert Gran never hurts.

There's always hope that someday, whether it's as we sit in a theater or on our couches, we will be able to see *Gold Diggers of Broadway* from beginning to end. Or maybe some recent dawn-of-sound restorations or preservations—*Follow Thru*, *The Vagabond King*, and *Viennese Nights* among them—that have not made it to home video at this writing. So when we ask "And now, what?" we do so out of hopeful anticipation, not with the indignant frustration of a blessedly inaccurate depths-of-1930 pundit.

Broadway
(Universal; May 27, 1929)

Director: Paul Fejos. Producer: Carl Laemmle, Jr. Presented By: Carl Laemmle, Sr. Scenario: Edward T. Lowe, Jr., Charles Furthman. Dialogue: Edward T. Lowe, Jr. Titles: Tom Reed. Based on the play by Philip Dunning and George Abbott (New York opening, September 16, 1926; 603 performances). Photography: Hal Mohr. Photographic Effects: Frank H. Booth. Editors: Maurice Pivar, Robert Carlisle, Edward Cahn. Sound: C. Roy Hunter. Art Directors: Charles D. Hall, Thomas F. O'Neill. Dance Direction: Maurice L. Kusell. Costumes: Johanna Mathieson. Synchronization and Score: Howard Jackson. Assistant Director: William J. Reiter. Running Time: 105 minutes. Technicolor sequence.

Cast: Glenn Tryon (Roy Lane); Evelyn Brent (Pearl); Merna Kennedy (Billie Moore); Thomas E. Jackson (Dan McCorn); Robert Ellis (Steve Crandall); Otis Harlan (Andrew "Porky" Thompson); Paul Porcasi (Nick Verdis); Marion Lord (Lil Rice); Leslie Fenton (Jim "Scar" Edwards); Arthur Housman (Dolph); George Davis (Joe the waiter); Betty Francisco (Maizie); Edythe Flynn (Ruby); Florence Dudley (Ann); Ruby McCoy (Grace); Rita Flynn (chorine); Edgar Dearing (club patron); John Kelly (masher at party); Gus Arnheim and His Cocoanut Grove Ambassadors.

Songs: "Bounce a Little Ball at Your Baby" [Tryon, chorus], "Broadway" [Tryon, Kennedy, chorus], "The Chicken or the Egg" [Tryon, chorus], "Hittin' the Ceiling" [Tryon, chorus, twice], "Hot Footin' It" [Arnheim band, danced by Tryon], "Sing a Little Love Song" [Tryon, Kennedy] (Sidney Mitchell, Archie Gottler, Con Conrad).

Home Video: Criterion DVD/Blu-ray.

The Story: At the Paradise Club in Manhattan, song-and-dance man Roy Lane performs with his singing partner and sweetheart, Billie Moore, who also is coveted by bootlegger Steve Crandall. Crandall shoots a rival gangster, "Scar" Edwards; the immediate aftermath of the murder is inadvertently witnessed by Roy and Billie, but Crandall swears Billie to secrecy. Not so easily silenced, Roy vows to kill Crandall if he harms Billie. Edwards' moll, Pearl, a dancer at the Paradise, has been spying on Crandall, and she kills him out of vengeance. Roy becomes a suspect, but police detective Dan McCorn rules that Crandall has committed suicide, clearing Pearl, Roy, and Billie.

Mid-major Universal uncharacteristically spent a cool $1.5 million to bring Philip Dunning and George Abbott's hit stage drama *Broadway* to the screen as a passion project of Carl Laemmle, Jr., the studio head's son, and Paul Fejos, the studio's most creative filmmaker. The younger Laemmle commissioned a huge art-deco nightclub set—70 feet high and a city block wide—which replaced the intimate speakeasy of the play and provided a locale for multiple production numbers set to six songs. *Broadway* has enough music to qualify as a musical, but the numbers are casually integrated into the storyline and the film is rooted more in the gangster movie tradition than in the backstage musical. Still, the mix is potent, inventively filmed and full of dramatic tension and slangy dialogue. This saga of love and vice and death in a Manhattan nightspot is now widely available for viewing on DVD and Blu-ray after decades of limited access.

Broadway is significant in the history of the early sound film less in its words or music and more in the ingenuity of its director. Fejos made movies in his native Hungary before coming to the U.S. to work as a bacteriologist for the Rockefeller Institute. In 1927, at age 30, he directed *The Last Moment*, a striking experimental film with suicide as its theme, which led to his signing by Universal. His first Hollywood feature was the 1928 part-talkie *Lonesome*, a charming study of "little" people living in the big city that reminded many of King Vidor's more-acclaimed *The Crowd*. A lonely working-class man and woman, played

In Universal's inventive *Broadway*, gun moll Evelyn Brent aims her gun at bootlegger Robert Ellis—and points the Hollywood musical toward realism.

by Glenn Tryon and Barbara Kent, meet by chance in the teeming metropolis of New York, then are separated and reunited within the space of 24 hours. Fejos' innovative use of such techniques as montage, superimposition, subjective images, and color tinting impressed critics as well as patrons. Fejos followed *Lonesome* with a more routine film, *The Last Performance* (1929), a silent thriller that he later admitted he'd made because he wanted to work with its star, Conrad Veidt. Unlike *Lonesome*, it was a money-loser.

Next came *Broadway*, termed as a prestige "Super-Jewel" production by the studio and advertised as the "first million-dollar talkie," costing even more than Universal's part-talking filming of *Show Boat*, in production just before. *Broadway* was based on the production by the famed theater impresario Jed Harris that ran for a year and a half in New York, toured worldwide, and significantly furthered the career of its original male lead, Lee Tracy. Universal paid a lofty $225,000 for the movie rights, and producer Laemmle, Jr., figured he had the right man to make it when Fejos emerged. Given the confines of the stage version, Fejos had some reservations. "*Broadway* is a very good play," he recalled in a 1960s oral history, "but the whole damn thing is happening in a tiny, little back room in a nightclub."[3]

The solution, as production began in December 1928, was to open things up and make the familiar new again, especially to those potential filmgoers who had seen the stage original. Fejos' cameraman was the resourceful Hal Mohr, whose credits included *The Jazz Singer* and Erich von Stroheim's *The Wedding March*. Fejos designed a 28-ton crane, built by a Los Angeles engineering firm, that was to give Mohr's camera greater fluidity than was seen heretofore in a talking picture. The self-propelled crane included a 25-foot boom supporting a camera platform that could travel from every conceivable angle at a speed of 600 feet per minute horizontally and 400 feet a minute vertically.[4] "You could stop it on a pinhead," Mohr recalled to historian Richard Koszarski decades later. "It was a miraculous piece of equipment."[5]

This "*Broadway* crane," which was said to cost $75,000 to build, would be used at Universal for years. For its debut, it was used most strikingly in the *Broadway* musical numbers, in which songs written by Con Conrad, Archie Gottler, and Sidney Mitchell were staged by Maurice Kusell and performed primarily by Glenn Tryon as Roy Lane, resident song-and-dance expert at the Paradise Night Club, and his chorines. Art director Charles D. Hall designed the $20,000 oversized nightclub set to accommodate the crane.[6] The set, described by the *New York Times* as "a compendium of New York," showcased 50-foot columns meant to resemble skyscrapers, "gigantic figures of cubistic form," a carved figure representing the "princess of pleasure," and vivid city street scenes painted on the curtain from which the nightclub performances emerge. The *Times* noted that Fejos, who made two trips to New York for select location shots, actually secured permission from the newspaper to take a panoramic view of Broadway from an elevator zooming to the top of the New York Times Building, but that the idea had to be abandoned because the cost of the elevator and the insurance for the stunt was prohibitive.[7]

The technique of shooting that did occur does justice to the artistic surroundings. After Tryon and the girls emerge from behind the curtain—which, in a nice touch symbolizing the film's grit, the camera pushes through instead of parting—and begin to sing each of their songs, Mohr takes the camera airborne, revealing the individual work of the performers, then glides around the club, as if to remind us that the happy music masks the offstage struggles of the figures below. The visuals of each performance yield to the backstage intrigue, with the music clearly in the background of the dialogue, then Fejos returns to each number as the songs conclude. Thus, nearly all the numbers are disallowed from existing on their own; we are constantly reminded of their function as temporal diversions. The lone exception is the finale, an uninterrupted two-strip Technicolor production number that follows the wrap-up of the story.

Even though the new version of *Broadway* necessarily truncated the play, critics agreed that the movie retained the flavor of the original. One new touch in Universal's version was a striking opening, in which a bare-chested, devilish reveler mockingly splashes hooch over miniatures of the New York skyline even before the credits begin to roll. The moral corruption of its characters having been implied, the story begins with Roy dreaming of fame with his singing partner and best girl. "I see our names in lights right now—Roy Lane … and Company … $200 for you and $500 for me," he tells Billie Moore. Played by Merna Kennedy, Billie is a good-hearted soul—"If I've ever seen a professional virgin, she's it," a jealous showgirl snaps—but her on- and off-stage stage partnership with Roy is imperiled by slick bootlegger Steve Crandall (Robert Ellis). Crandall is an unusually passionate crook, tenderly calling Billie his "little fella," then vowing that he'd "do murder for you."

Crandall's dispatching of rum-running rival "Scar" Edwards (Leslie Fenton) signals his downfall. When vigilant police detective Dan McCorn (Thomas Jackson) arrives to investigate, Crandall summons up all the bravado he can ("Should I have my pockets sewed up because there's a bull outside?"), but he's clearly spooked. Roy and Billie had witnessed the removal of Edwards' gunshot body from the Paradise, but Crandall has sworn Billie to secrecy and her false testimony temporarily clears him. Roy, however, is not so easily silenced, for he vows to kill Crandall if he harms Billie. Neither is Edwards' moll, Pearl (Evelyn Brent), who has been spying on Crandall as a dancer at the Paradise. Pearl confronts and then kills Crandall with a shot "through the old pump," as opposed to the one Crandall had put through Scar's back. The Paradise's hard-nosed proprietor, Nick Verdis (Paul Porcasi, reprising his stage role), attempts to make Roy a suspect, but McCorn wisely, if inaccurately, declares that Crandall has committed suicide. This clears Pearl and enables Roy and Billie to answer a booking agent's call for shows, beams Roy, "in Chambersburg and Pottsville next week." Remember, he adds, "we're all artists!"

Upon *Broadway*'s premiere in its titular locale in May 1929, *New York Times* reviewer Mordaunt Hall called the film "handsome entertainment, in which much of the drama in the original survives."[8] Jackson (1886–1967), who excelled in *Broadway* on Broadway, earned most of the critical acclaim for what would be the first movie in a lengthy career. His stone face and robotic but authoritative line-reading soon typecast the actor (usually billed with his middle initial of "E.") as a tough urban lawman in the likes of *Little Caesar* (1931) and *Mystery of the Wax Museum* (1933). Universal teamed Tryon (1894–1970) and Kennedy (1908–1944) twice more in 1929, in the comedies *Barnum Was Right* and *Skinner Steps Out*, although Tryon soon would abandon his acting career to become a producer-screenwriter, and Kennedy would retire early to marry Busby Berkeley. Also getting good notices for *Broadway* was Brent (1899–1975), a darkly attractive leading lady on loan from Paramount, but her career was soon to begin a slow decline.

The lofty expense to produce *Broadway* resulted in a loss of $421,000 for the studio.[9] Universal still thought enough of Fejos' work to assign him to another major musical, the Paul Whiteman starrer *King of Jazz*, and then to what was released in 1930 as *Captain of the Guard* [q.v.]. Neither project worked out for director or studio, and Fejos was replaced during the production of both films. For a time, there was talk that Fejos would resume his directorial career at MGM, but he eventually returned to Europe and never made another American film. *Broadway* was remade by Universal in 1942 with George Raft—playing a fictionalized version of himself in place of the Roy Lane role—and Pat O'Brien.

Meanwhile, the 1929 version was mainly seen only in washed-out bootlegs of the silent version, made for unwired theaters, that lacked synchronization with the extant soundtrack. The only American archival print of the film, which was housed at the Library of Congress (and was viewed by the author in 1994), looked good but lacked the color finale. That changed for the better in 2012 when the Criterion Collection series included *Broadway*, along with Fejos' *The Last Performance*, as extras on its DVD debut release of *Lonesome*. However, *Broadway* had to be made whole in a reconstruction created by incorporating the end of the silent version—with images of the final song number—with an unsynchronized soundtrack element discovered in a private collection. This shortcoming was remedied in 2016 when Universal digitally mated a reproduction from the original black-and-white camera negative with surviving color elements of the final number from the Hungarian National Digital Archive and Film Institute.[10] At last, Fejos' *Broadway* looks as close to intended as possible.

Jazz Heaven
(RKO; October 29, 1929)

Director: Melville W. Brown. Producer: William LeBaron. Associate Producer: Myles Connolly. Screenplay/Dialogue: Cyrus Wood, J. Walter Ruben. Story: Pauline Forney, Dudley Murphy. Photography: Jack MacKenzie. Editors: Ann McKnight, George Marsh. Art Direction: Max Rée. Sound: Hugh McDowell, Jr. Photographic Effects: Lloyd Knechtel. Running Time: 68 minutes.

Cast: Sally O'Neil (Ruth Morgan); John [Johnny] Mack Brown (Barry Holmes); Clyde Cook (Max

Langley); Joseph Cawthorn (Herman Kemple); Albert Conti (Walter Klucke); Blanche Friderici (Mrs. Langley); Henry Armetta (Tony); J. Barney Sherry (John Parker); Adele Watson (Miss Dunn); Ole M. Ness (Professor Rowland); Ray Cooke (telegram messenger); Kay Deslys (tenant); Sherry Hall (radio announcer).

Songs: "Someone" [Brown on piano, then sung by Brown and O'Neil, then played twice by Brown on piano, then sung (now with words) by O'Neil with Brown, then played by band at nightclub, then sung by Brown], "Come on In" [nightclub dancers] (Sidney Clare, Oscar Levant).

Working Title: *Boarding House Blues*.

The Story: In the shadow of Tin Pan Alley, aspiring songwriter Barry Holmes is so intent upon finishing his latest composition that he keeps his fellow apartment house tenants, and landlord Langley, up all nights. Barry meets Ruth Morgan, a neighbor, whose idle humming of the tune enables Barry to complete it, but stern Mrs. Langley evicts Barry, and the young man's piano is destroyed in an accident. Ruth is being pursued romantically by bickering music publishers Kempel and Klucke, but both men agree that Barry's tune, which doesn't have lyrics yet, is unready for the big time. Mr. Langley, a night watchman at a piano factory, allows Barry and Ruth to use a piano there after hours. The song "Someone" is inadvertently broadcast—and receives so many requests for subsequent airplay that Barry and Ruth, who have no idea they have made it on the air, are "discovered." The two also have fallen in love, although Kempel and Klucke attempt to keep them apart. Misunderstandings ensue, but only temporarily.

The RKO picture that introduced (read: bludgeoned us with) the song "Someone" was titled *Jazz Heaven* but had little to do with jazz, much less heaven. It was freely promoted as a musical comedy—even advertised as "Radio's Glorious New Melody Show"—although that description can be challenged given how we have come to define movie musicals. But the standards were murkier in 1929, and one cannot claim that this film's music—albeit pretty much just one so-called "glorious new melody," played and sung repeatedly—isn't important as a plot device. An otherwise insignificant piece of fluff, *Jazz Heaven* stands as a prime example of the early sound "theme song" craze gone awry.

For much of the silent era, folks had been writing theme songs for movies—to promote both the songs and the pictures to which they were sometimes tenuously attached—but such tactics escalated when audible voicings factored in. Film buffs long have laughed at the infamous example of the synchronized Norma Talmadge picture *The Woman Disputed* (1928) being graced with the song "Woman Disputed, I Love You," although the fact that the song was actually heard in the film has been … disputed. Stand-alone themes such as "Charmaine," from *What Price Glory?* (1926), "Diane" from *Seventh Heaven* (1927) or "Pagan Love Song" from *The Pagan* (1929) became genuine sheet-music favorites as their films' leitmotifs. When the technology allowed for full-fledged musical numbers, the theme song concept ramped up in volume, especially when one such tune, "Sonny Boy," as frequently and lugubriously sung by Al Jolson, was judged the highlight of the biggest-grossing picture of 1928, *The Singing Fool*.[11] Now, it seemed, every other movie had to have an integrated theme song—a trend that began to weigh heavily on cinematic storytelling in general, and retard the evolution of the filmed musical in particular. This led to an overabundance of stories with backstage settings (or random backstage scenes, so there would be an excuse for the singing) and awkward presentations of love songs in contrived locales. An example of the latter is an unbilled Russ Columbo singing "How Am I to Know?" from a prison cell as Charles Bickford and Kay Johnson are married on Death Row in Cecil B. DeMille's jaw-dropping MGM soaper, *Dynamite* (1929).

The theme song surplus was frequently acknowledged in the press. In a nationally syndicated column, the playwright and critic Robert E. Sherwood made fun of the problem:

Sally O'Neil and Johnny Mack Brown portray the couple brought together by music in RKO's *Jazz Heaven*.

> …Even the most adroit composers and lyricists can go just so far with theme songs and no farther. After all, one might say (hopefully), they can't continue indefinitely thinking up movie titles that slide as rhythmically into waltz time as *Ramona* did.
> …We now have every right to expect:
> "Man in the Iron Mask, I Love You."
> …"Gentlemen of the Press, I Love You."
> "A Connecticut Yankee in King Arthur's Court, I Love You."
> These will be sung by one of the leading players, whose voice doesn't photograph any too well but who looks cute when mouthing the words. The melodies will be repeated in every love scene throughout the picture—and not until you have had a chance to count the repetitions of the theme song do you realize how many love scenes there are in the average movie.[12]

By the middle of 1930, the overuse of extraneous/inappropriate music turned the public against musicals. But in the winter of 1929–30, RKO could tout its new *Jazz Heaven*—essentially a comedy about two lovers who are brought together by a song (singular)—as a "melody show" and make it work. RKO also could get away with casting Sally O'Neil and Johnny Mack Brown in a musical, even though neither could sing very well nor (in Brown's case) play the piano audibly before the camera.

The fledgling studio planned the film under the title *Boarding House Blues* with Sally Blane and Hugh Trevor in the leads, but it forsook those in-house actors for imports with brighter star power. RKO borrowed Brown (1904–1974) from MGM, where he had been playing decorative second leads. To many people in 1929, Johnny Mack (or John Mack, as he sometimes was billed) was known primarily as the All-American football halfback who led the University of Alabama to victory in the 1926 Rose Bowl game. That prestigious contest was played in Hollywood's back yard, and the movie folks took note. Metro cast Brown opposite Joan Crawford, Marion Davies, Norma Shearer, and Greta Garbo, and he held his own against Mary Pickford, who borrowed him to lend his thick Southern accent to her maiden talkie, *Coquette* (1929). JMB's cowboy stardom was a few years away. Meanwhile, O'Neil (1908–1968) had become famous with *Sally, Irene and Mary*, the 1925 MGM comedy that also boosted the careers of Crawford and Constance Bennett.[13] O'Neil's first role in an all-sound film was in the first full-color talkie, Warner Bros.' musical *On with the Show!*—in which, not surprisingly, the singing voice you might expect from a colleen born Virginia Louise Noonan from Bayonne, New Jersey, was dubbed. *Jazz Heaven* director Melville Brown and screenwriter J. Walter Ruben were transfers from Paramount, where they had collaborated on the Richard Dix-June Collyer romance *The Love Doctor* (1929).

The script by Ruben and Cyrus Wood does little to lessen the painfully obvious mismatch of Brown and O'Neil as a romantic pair, the Southern courtliness of Brown's songwriter character in uneasy contrast to O'Neil's urban forwardness in which "That's a fine way to talk, ya big bozo!" passes as love discourse. With music being the universal language, they are brought together by "Someone," the tune that he spends most of the film attempting to work out on his keyboard. We hear "Someone" in stages, as an instrumental, a semi-hummed version without words, and finally, a complete rendition, inadvertently broadcast to great acclaim on a national radio program. This accident enables the composer to get his song purchased by a duo of music publishers. These songsters, played by Joseph Cawthorn and Albert Conti, consider themselves adversaries for the affections of O'Neil's character, but her heart lies with her youngest suitor.

In something of an omen, *Jazz Heaven* opened in New York on the "Black Tuesday" of the stock market crash. Editor "Red" Kann of *Motion Picture News* dismissed it as "innocuous, pleasant and frothy … [it] won't leave any impression because it is such lightweight material."[14] Irene Thirer of the *New York Daily News* slyly noted that the throaty contralto she'd heard out of O'Neil's mouth a few nights earlier in the film *Broadway Scandals* had been replaced by a "full soprano." For the record, Thirer thought only the tones for "Someone" were someone else's, and she did praise *Jazz Heaven* for its fancy set design and "smooth directorial treatment."[15]

Only two people seem to have benefited from *Jazz Heaven* beyond its paydays. One was Joseph Cawthorn, a Broadway veteran of stereotypically German humor who had recently come to Hollywood to use his accented voice in talkies. Radio's very early musical *Street Girl* gave him an initial push, and good notices for *Jazz Heaven* prompted Cawthorn (1868–1949) to sell his home in New York and move permanently to Los Angeles on the strength of a long-term RKO contract.[16] Cawthorn is in full malapropping form in *Jazz Heaven*, greeting his publishing-house charges with "greetings and solutions" and fighting with Conti nearly as incessantly as we hear the serpentine theme song.

The other person for which *Jazz Heaven* was a real asset was its melodist, Oscar Levant. Levant (1906–1972) was new in Hollywood, having come from New York as an acting hopeful; he'd appeared for two years on Broadway in the play *Burlesque* and reprised his role in its film adaptation, *The Dance of Life* (Paramount 1929). But Levant could write the kind of music Hollywood needed so sorely at this point, and he found steady employment penning tunes for many early RKO pictures, among them 1935's *In Person* [q.v.]. After the death of his good friend George Gershwin, Levant achieved fame as a pianist and composer in the late 1930s and eventually established a career as an actor and acerbic TV talk host. The late

'20s-early '30s section of his career has been largely ignored, but the songwriting royalties must have been good, even if the songs sometimes weren't.

The Talk of Hollywood
(Prudence Pictures/Sono-Art World Wide; December 9, 1929)

Director: Mark Sandrich. Producers: Samuel Zierler, Harry H. Thomas. Story: Mark Sandrich, Nat Carr. Dialogue: Darby Aaronson. Photography: Walter Strenge. Editing: Russell Shields. Sound: George Osthmann, John Dolan. Art Director: Ernest Fegte. Production Manager: Frank Melford. Assistant Director: Harold Godsoe. Running Time: 70 minutes.

Cast: Nat Carr (J. Pierpont Ginsberg); Fay Marbe (Adoré Renée); Hope Sutherland (Ruth Ginsberg); Sherling Oliver (John Applegate); Edward Le Saint (Edward Hamilton); Gilbert Marbe (Reginald Witlock); John Troughton (James, the butler); William Crane (O'Flaherty); Al Goodman's "Follow Thru" Orchestra; The Leonidoff Ballet.

Songs: "No, No, Baby" [Fay Marbe, Goodman orchestra, danced by Gilbert Marbe], "Sarah" [Carr, Goodman orchestra, danced by Leonidoff Ballet], "They Say Good-Night in the Morning" [Fay Marbe, Goodman orchestra, Leonidoff Ballet] (Al Piantadosi, Jack Glogau); "Daughter of Mine" (Al Piantadosi, Nat Carr, Jack Glogau).

Home Video: Alpha DVD.

The Story: J. Pierpont Ginsberg, a successful producer of silent pictures, is filming his long-awaited first talkie, a musical drama called "Is Love a Sin?" He brags to the press: "If it ain't a Ginsberg, it ain't a talkie!" Ginsberg's daughter, Ruth, is in love with the mogul's lawyer, John Applegate, who asks her to marry him. Production delays—some of which involve his temperamental star, Adoré Renée—and technical glitches set back the production. Heavily in debt, Ginsberg must rely on funds provided by Applegate to finish the picture. Ginsberg shows "Is Love a Sin?" to potential distributors, but the preview screening results in disaster when a drunken projectionist plays the soundtrack discs out of order. However, one of the money men decides the film was intentionally played for laughs, and he gives Ginsberg a substantial contract to make more. Ginsberg gives his blessing to Applegate to marry Ruth.

Twenty-three years before audiences laughed with delight at the parody of the first talkies in *Singin' in the Rain*, they were groaning in dismay at *The Talk of Hollywood*. A story about a failing producer for a failing company as filmed by a real failing company, this forlorn indie comedy with music was meant to make fun of the talking-picture craze, only to become a joke unto itself—then and now.

Starring vaudeville comedian Nat Carr as the ridiculously stereotypical Jewish movie producer, *The Talk of Hollywood* was touted as the first cinematic satire of the talkies. That may not have been the case by the time the feature finally played in theaters, but it definitely would have been more novel at the time it was filmed, in May 1929 at the new RCA Gramercy studio in New York City.[17] The process was the sound-on-film Photophone system—a rival to the sound-on-disc Vitaphone format—so it was perhaps no accident that a key plot twist of the film had to do with the foibles of using Vitaphone-type record discs to synchronize with the picture. The script—penned by Carr and the film's director, Mark Sandrich—was filled with humor stemming from the fractured English and ethnic syntax spouted by Carr. The latter had been doing the Semitic thing for decades on the stage and in silents, in many of which he played unrelated but behaviorally similar characters named Ginsberg. The actor's act was deemed important enough to be preserved in a 1927 Vitaphone short, *Nat Carr, Character Comedian*.

Carr (1886–1944) plays the Ginsberg of *Talk* as a low-budget Samuel Goldwyn, with linguistic manglings such as "Talking pictures are only in their infantry" and "What's the use of crying over spent milk?" During a confab with reporters, he's willing to bring out some cigars only after being assured that the "advertising" is free. While making a mess called *Is Love a Sin?*, Ginsberg is beset by the kinds of occupational problems about which real producers in 1929 must have cringed. There's the picky screenwriter who cries, "I worked on that line for two days!"; a swishy leading man whose voice doesn't match his looks; an actress who stutters through an audition; and a black actor who Ginsberg claims doesn't talk enough like a "darkie." A fart joke is thrown in. None of it is very funny.

Then there's the film-within-the-film's leading lady, Miss Adoré Renée, played by a performer who rated her own opening-credits title card: "Presenting the International Star MISS FAY MARBÉ in her Talking Picture Debut." Adoré is supposed to be French; many people thought Marbe was a Gallic native, too. Actually she was American-born, allegedly from New York society, who made herself over as a Continental chanteuse and dancer in musical comedy. Her initial success came in Europe, and as the 1920s progressed, she made good on her home shores, notably in Jerome Kern's *Oh Boy!* She cuts up a bit with Carr via dialogue in her first talkie, but her singing and dancing in *The Talk of Hollywood* is confined to the movie's one extended musical sequence, a 15-minute cabaret scene in which Marbe performs two songs to the instruments of Al Goodman's "Follow Thru" Orchestra.[18] Her suggestive lyrics and dance are accompanied by ample energy, a comely smile, a skimpy dress, and a well-positioned ostrich feather.

Like its fictional counterpart, *The Talk of Hollywood* got made on a shoestring. It was the first talking production of Prudence Pictures (formerly Excellent Pictures), which had been inactive for a year before producers Samuel Zierler and Harry H. Thomas got busy making this picture. Marbe apparently was promised more than this one assignment by the producers, but when no further work came in the months after *Talk* was shot, she sued Zierler for $150,000 for breach of contract and other damages.[19] Sherling Oliver, a young Broadway actor cast as Carr's prospective son-in-law, had to have been disappointed as well, if only because his name was misspelled as "Sherline" in the opening credits. Al Piantadosi, who co-wrote the music in *Talk*, also wasn't happy; he complained that the songs were improperly showcased on screen and so declined to publish them himself.[20]

This was in December, when Zierler secured a tardy release for *The Talk of Hollywood* through the low-rent Sono Art company. (*Talk* would be the only film produced by Prudence Pictures.) But by the time the movie debuted in theaters in the first months of 1930, it seemed all the more stilted and out of date—and no one came away happy. The *Motion Picture News* reviewer thought *Talk* offered "Nat Carr and little else," and *Variety* savaged the picture as "Badder than bad. Best example of sound era on how a talker must not be made."[21]

As someone who wasn't precisely as advertised, off screen or on, Marbe (1899–1986) was a bit of a character, but that made the saucy, black-haired miss fit right in with Hollywood, no matter how poor the reviews for her first talkie. In February 1930, with *The Talk of Hollywood* in theaters, she journeyed to California to make herself better known in the movie world. She arrived amid publicity that she had insured her smile for $250,000. "Miss Marbe came to Hollywood for a vacation more than anything else," a syndicated columnist asserted. "But now film producers want to get her before the movie cameras."[22] Marbe and her dancer brother, Gilbert (who also appears in *The Talk of Hollywood*), headquartered at the upscale Roosevelt Hotel, and in April she was feted at the Montmartre café and in a series of parties that included such guests as Louis B. Mayer; director James Cruze and his actress wife, Betty Compson; the Duncan Sisters; and opera star Alice Gentle.[23]

Marbe motored around between stage dates in a conspicuous blue-and-white

Pierce-Arrow with a chauffeur decked out in the same hues. Ever on the alert for colorful behavior, the *New York Daily News* snidely elaborated further on her activities:

> A movie premiere is the one thing that Miss Marbe waits for. It is then that she can be seen. She makes it a point to drive up to the theatre at exactly 8:30, when the crowd is gathered on the sidewalk waiting to see the celebrities.
>
> At a recent premiere out there.... Marbe, according to plans, drove up to the theatre at exactly 8:30. Just then, there was an accident in the next block, and the crowd hurried away to see what was the matter. This upset Miss Marbe—but only for a moment. She ordered her chauffeur to keep driving around the block until the crowd returned.[24]

Ultimately, the only film work Marbe got after *The Talk of Hollywood* was an eight-minute Columbia performance short, *A Continental Evening* (1930), and one number in a *Voice of Hollywood* single-reeler for Tiffany. She was absent from American view within a few years, and her exposure abroad declined as well by the end of the decade. She won a mere $6,000 in her suits against Zierler and Prudence upon settlement in 1932, even after claiming that the producer's "coldness against her intentions" was the cause of the breach.[25]

Marbe taught voice and drama in New York City during the 1950s and public speaking classes in Connecticut and Florida schools until her 80s. In a newspaper interview near the end of her life, she was less inclined to be quoted about her showbiz dealings with Enrico Caruso, George Gershwin, Winston Churchill, and the Marx Brothers (to note a few names she dropped), and more about her teaching of "personality development" speaking and the compliments received from her students. But some of Norma Desmond seemed to have rubbed off, as the reporter indicated.

> For fifty years, from the 1920s, the theater and its celebrities were her existence.... The entertainer had many acquaintances, few close relationships. She never married.
>
> "Sex wasn't that important. A man wasn't that important. Marriage wasn't that important. I loved what I did. Can you understand that?"[26]

Similarly, Nat Carr's better days were passing as the '30s dawned. He followed *The Talk of Hollywood* by playing the lead in a 1930 Pathé two-reeler, *Two Plus Fours*, now better known as one of Bing Crosby's earliest films. From then on, it was small or bit flicker parts, especially as Hollywood sought to downplay overt ethnic humor, to supplement legitimate stage work (occasionally with his actor brother, Alexander Carr) and dates in what remained of vaudeville. Among the stage engagements was a 1932 pairing in which Nat Carr was billed second to the famed conjoined twins, Violet and Daisy Hilton. Carr died at 57 after what was reported as "several months' illness." Meanwhile, Mark Sandrich transitioned from his feature-length flop in *The Talk of Hollywood* to directing shorts (which in this case was a step up). He helmed comedies for RKO—among them the Oscar-winning three-reeler *So This Is Harris* (1933) and the musical feature *Melody Cruise** (1933)—before directing multiple Fred Astaire-Ginger Rogers dancefests, including the sublime *Top Hat*.

The Talk of Hollywood was quickly forgotten, although as late as 1932 it was playing in the hinterlands, now advertised as "a singing and dancing musical" in lieu of the outmoded satire-of-the-talkies angle. Long feared (or hoped) lost, the film was rediscovered in the 1980s. It has been played at festivals and purveyed on public-domain DVD in recent years as an "it's so bad, it's good" type of attraction. It also has become shorthand in illustrating just how perilous the talkie transition was, as if to verify that *Singin' in the Rain* was no exaggeration. An '80s British TV documentary showed an excerpt from *The Talk of Hollywood*—not-quite-accurately describing it as "a spoof short made by one of RKO's top directors"—in which Ginsberg learns that malfunctioning microphones have caused the loss of a day's shooting.[27] Three decades later, in 2018, a vintage-film buff billing himself as Charles Slater posted a short video called *A Vitaphonic Nightmare*, in which a *Talk of Hollywood* clip shows a sound-on-disc mishap in which Ginsberg's drunken projectionist carelessly breaks a record of a upcoming reel and substitutes another, creating a series of comic mismatches in sound and picture—and leading to the near-catastrophe that somehow saves the producer's career.

"Gee, that was an hour of torture!" one character says about watching Ginsberg's unfortunate movie within the movie. Not so with the whole of *The Talk of Hollywood*—it drags on for an hour and 10 minutes.

Captain of the Guard
(Universal; March 29, 1930)

Directors: John S. Robertson; Paul Fejos (uncredited). Dialogue and Titles: George Manker Watters. Screenplay: Arthur Ripley. Story: Houston Branch. Photography: Gilbert Warrenton, Hal Mohr. Editor: Milton Carruth, Ted J. Kent. Sound: C. Roy Hunter. Costumes: Johanna Mathieson. Running Time: 83 minutes.
Cast: Laura La Plante (Marie Marnay); John Boles (Rouget de l'Isle); Sam De Grasse (Bazin); James Marcus (Marnay); Lionel Belmore (Colonel of Hussars); Stuart Holmes (Louis XVI); Evelyn Hall (Marie Antoinette); Claude Fleming (magistrate); Murdock MacQuarrie (Pierre); Richard Cramer (Danton); Harry Burkhardt (Materoun); Otis Harlan (Jacques); George Hackathorne (Robespierre); DeWitt Jennings (priest); Harry Cording (Le Bruin); Ervin Renard (lieutenant); Stanley Fields (hangman).
Songs: "Can It Be?" [La Plante], "Carry On" [Boles, chorus], "For You" [Boles, three times], "Maids on Parade" [La Plante], "You, You Alone" [Boles, reprised twice by La Plante] (William Francis Dugan, Heinz Roemheld); "La Marseillaise" [Boles, reprised by Boles, chorus] (Claude Joseph Rouget de l'Isle); "Song of the Sword" [Boles] (Houston Branch, Charles Wakefield Cadman).
Working Title: *La Marseillaise*.
Disc: Victor 22373 ("For You"/"You, You Alone," John Boles).

The Story: In a France beset by rumors of impending revolution, Marie Marnay, the daughter of an innkeeper, and Rouget de l'Isle, her music teacher, fall in love ("For You," "You, You Alone"), to the dismay of royal spy Bazin, who wants Marie for himself. Rouget is commissioned as a captain in the Royal Hussars ("Song of the Sword"), but he promises to return to marry Marie. After her father is killed by royalists, Marie joins the revolutionists and becomes known as "The Torch." Bazin traps Rouget into unintentionally betraying Marie, and both lovers are imprisoned. While in custody, Rouget is inspired to write the stirring anthem "La Marseillaise." He renounces the king and gathers an army to march on Paris, to free Marie, and to launch a revolution.

"Of all the meteors that have flashed across the Hollywood skies," the fan magazine *Photoplay* gushed in the autumn of 1929, "none in history has scooted brighter and faster than John Boles."[28] The virile baritone that entertained Broadway audiences in the early '20s had been quieted for a few years after Boles first came to Hollywood to act, but now the movies sang as well as talked. After raising a voice to go with his attractive profile in the early operettas *The Desert Song, Rio Rita,* and *Song of the West,* Boles was inked by Universal to a long-term contract to make more. Boles' first "U" songfest was an ambitious period piece titled *La Marseillaise* and set to co-star studio mainstay Laura La Plante under the direction of Hungarian stylist Paul Fejos. But nothing went right on this seemingly promising production—at the cost of its director, its composer, its believability, its global exposure, and even its name. That we know this picture as *Captain of the Guard* instead is only a hint of its troubles.

Boles (1895–1969) was a key recruit in a new plan for success at Universal and its newly installed general manager, Carl Laemmle, Jr., son of the studio's founder and president. With the entrenchment of sound, the "little major" was turning up a collective nose at the modestly budgeted product that had long generated the bulk of its business in small-town America. The company's announcement early in 1930 that it was cutting its output of features by more than half in the coming year—from nearly 60 for the 1929–30 season down to 20 or so for 1930–31—meant the end of the trail for cowboy stars Hoot Gibson and Ken Maynard, whose contracts were not renewed.[29] Their quickie five-reelers were to be supplanted by fewer but more creative "prestige" pictures, some of which already were in production, with budgets at a heftily allotted $500,000 apiece, or so boasted studio publicity.[30] At the time Universal announced its new strategy, the Fejos-Boles-La Plante musical was just coming out, and the outlook was bright.

Universal had high hopes when production began near the end of 1929 on a story meant to depict the 1792 composing by Claude Joseph Rouget de l'Isle of the French national anthem, "La Marseillaise," a call to freedom amid the tumult of that country's revolution. Fejos seemed like the right man to bring it to life. He'd graduated from indie avant-garde films into two of Universal's most interesting, and most praised, early talkies: *Lonesome* (1928) and *Broadway* (1929) [q.v.], the latter a part-Technicolor musical melodrama. The great expense on *Broadway* resulted in a big money loss for the studio, but Fejos had the younger Laemmle in his corner.

Junior tabbed Fejos and Hal Mohr for another super-musical, *King of Jazz*, to star Paul Whiteman and his band. But disagreements over the script of that film led to a long delay in production, and director and cameraman were transferred to the Boles-La Plante project in August 1929. This provided the director with plenty of resources, including his camera crane and some 5,000 extras for a scene showing the Parisian mob battling the king's loyalists, plus the services of esteemed composer Charles Wakefield Cadman and well-known playwrights Houston Branch and George Manker Watters to create the music and story. However, Laemmle, Jr., didn't like Cadman's songs, and other composers were

Even two of Universal's top stars—Laura La Plante and John Boles—couldn't rescue the big-budget *Captain of the Guard* from failure.

brought in to write. The studio continued to give Cadman primary credit for the music, perhaps for contractual reasons, even if most of it was heard only incidentally in the final cut.[31]

Fejos also met with resistance, or he was perhaps himself resistant. He feuded with the younger Laemmle and asked for his release from the studio. On October 26, 1929, Fejos escaped serious injury after an apparent 88-foot fall from a scaffolding from which he was shouting instructions for the crowd scene. The incident forced Fejos' replacement as director by John S. Robertson, although Mohr remembered that the Hungarian may not have been so physically impaired after all.

> We were up on top of the Notre Dame set. We broke for lunch, and Paul stayed behind a little bit. I got out to the front of the studio to get lunch, and I heard this ambulance come flying in … back to the set. Paul had seemingly fallen down these steep steps on the back of the set. He was lying at the bottom of the steps without any visible scars or blood, no broken limbs. But apparently his back was thrown completely out of joint. You could never know if this was true or not, but that's when they put him in the hospital and that's when [Robertson] took the picture over.…[32]

Fejos had been unhappy with the futility of having to wait on *King of Jazz*, and he also was disappointed over being passed over to direct Universal's much-anticipated war saga *All Quiet on the Western Front*. Robertson received sole directorial credit on *La Marseillaise*, which was, as a trade publication reported, "practically remade" by him.[33] Universal's response was that the picture was redone because "it couldn't be ended" as the original director intended.

Universal's product was mainly intended for small-market theaters and not for major big-city houses, but to jump-start revenues, the company booked *La Marseillaise* at New York's A-list Roxy Theater as the first of its "Big Three Supers" for the season. The others were to be *King of Jazz*, which was filmed as an extravagant studio revue by Broadway director John Murray Anderson, and *All Quiet on the Western Front*. Whiteman heavily plugged *La Marseillaise* along with *King of Jazz* on his weekly *Old Gold* radio show for weeks prior to the former's late-March 1930 premiere. Having promoted him as "The Best Male Voice on the Screen," Universal was confident enough in Boles to announce him for two more musicals, *Gypsy Love Song* and *The Love Cavalier*, both to co-star his *King of Jazz* duet partner, Jeanette Loff, for its 1930–31 slate.

However, there were signs Universal was uneasy about *La Marseillaise*. The most obvious was the official changing of the film title to *Captain of the Guard* only days before its debut. The studio explanation, stated in full-page trade ads attributed to Laemmle the elder, was "because of the difficulty so many people had in pronouncing the French title. The smartest exhibitors in the world liked the original title for sentimental reasons, but when it came to box-office reasons, they unanimously preferred *Captain of the Guard*."[34] The name change also may have been related to in-house concerns over the historical accuracy of the Houston Branch-Arthur Ripley script, which made major alterations to the story of the real l'Isle. Indeed, the film premiered with a screen-filling title that seemed like an apology:

> "The French Revolution brought Liberty to the world, on the wings of 'La Marseillaise.' A story of that song is here set forth: Our justification for taking liberties with history is that fiction is the drama's function, not fact, but the soul of Rouget de l'Isle is here and the spell of his deathless song."

The Billboard's New York critic saluted *Captain of the Guard* as "interesting and entertaining, but other reviews—and viewer reactions—were more like *Variety*'s description of 'Universal's most pretentious release of the season.'"[35] A correspondent for the *Los Angeles Times*, a daily not known for hard-hitting reviews, called it "a feebly juvenile story poorly acted," and *Picture Play*, a fan magazine, was similarly nasty: "Bombastic and dull.... The pity of it is that even the French Revolution can be made silly in the wrong hands."[36]

Most observers agreed that Boles was OK, if a little overwrought, but that La Plante, a capable comedienne in the silents, was miscast as the heroine. She utters dialogue like "Am I not a royalist?" and "I'm not your leader—I'm only one of you!" as if she's just walked in from somewhere in Iowa. It also doesn't help that her likely dubbed voicings of some of the film's pedestrian original tunes seem too dainty for her character's crypto-feminism. She poses as a Joan of Arc-like figure, "The Torch," in a knockoff of secretive operetta battle heroes such as the one in *Song of the Flame*, a Broadway show-turned-1930 film with Bernice Claire as Russia's "The Flame." Or with a gender flip, like *The Desert Song*, the 1929 movie version of which had Boles as the rebellious "Red Shadow." Per the studio's blessing, La Plante (1904–1996) was on her way out at the "U" anyway, a cameo in *King of Jazz* her exit en route to free-lance work.

Early paybox returns justified the shaky outlook for *Captain of the Guard*. At the Roxy, it made nearly $100,000 its first week—about the average take for that house—before tailing off to a disappointing $70,000 its second week.[37] The numbers were worse a few weeks later on the Left Coast, where *Captain* grossed a mere $9,200 in its initial week at the Orpheum in Los Angeles.[38] Meanwhile, the disgruntled Paul Fejos wired New York writers and disclaimed any credit, except for the sequences showing the banquet of the Hussars, the march of the men of Marseillaise, and the battle scenes—which happened to be the best, and most praised, parts. "The rest," his missive, revealed in the press, was said to say, "is unknown to me."[39] We're not sure whether to blame Fejos (or Robertson) for Boles' histrionics—the actor was rarely known for underplaying—which are most annoying as his face contorts from an expression of inspiration to an appearance of discomfort as the idea for "La Marseillaise" strikes de l'Isle.

Although set in France, *Captain of the Guard* was kept out of that country by Universal after Alexandre Stein, the studio's chief in Paris, saw it in London and "made up his mind the historical liberties had ruined the pictures chances for France."[40] Among the chief concerns was said to be that de l'Isle's song was sung by Boles in English and not French. The film was shown in parts of Canada as *La Marseillaise*, but after audiences complained in Montreal, the title was changed back to *Captain of the Guard*.

The overall foreign grosses for *Captain of the Guard* were no embarrassment, but the film's poor domestic showing, coupled with its $729,000 negative cost, led to an overall money loss of nearly $272,000.[41] There was fallout over the setback: The two Boles-Loff starring musicals went unmade, as the public turned away from such films.[42] Universal did not release another musical until *Moonlight and Pretzels** and the independently produced *Myrt and Marge** debuted in 1933. Universal continued to make *Captain* available in its "Show-at-Home" 16 mm library, but only in a truncated silent version. Seven decades after its release, the silent emerged on the film collectors' grey market, but Universal retained a 35 mm show print of the sound release that has been shown at film festivals in recent years. We can now hear and see what got so many people up in arms, on and off screen, in 1930.

And of Universal's Boles-ian strategy regarding fewer but better films? *All Quiet on the Western Front* grossed nearly $1 million and won the Academy Award as best picture, but *King of Jazz* was a huge money-loser at $1.2 million. Universal brought back its cowboy shows. Still, *All Quiet* and *King of Jazz* remain among a group of truly memorable Universal features from 1930 and 1931, including *Dracula*, *Frankenstein*, and *Waterloo Bridge*. In retrospect, they made the failure of *Captain of the Guard* well worth tolerating.

Movietone Follies of 1930
(Fox; May 4, 1930)

Director: Benjamin Stoloff. Associate Producer: Al Rockett. Screenplay: William K. Wells. Photography: L. William O'Connell. Editor: Clyde Carruth. Sound: Joseph E. Aiken. Art Director: Stephen Goosson. Costumes: Sophie Wachner, Alice O'Neill. Musical Director: Arthur Kay. Dance Direction: Danny Dare, Maurice L. Kusell, Max Scheck. Assistant Director: Lew Breslow. Running Time: 72 minutes.

Cast: El Brendel (Axel Svenson); Marjorie White (Vera Fontaine); Frank Richardson (George Randall); Noel Francis (Gloria de Witt); William Collier, Jr. (Conrad Sterling); Miriam Seegar (Mary Mason); Huntley Gordon (Marvin Kingsley); Paul Nicholson (Bill Hubert); Yola d'Avril (Babette); J.M. Kerrigan (gateman); Betty Grable (chorine).

Songs: "Cheer Up and Smile" [Francis, chorus], "Doing the Derby" [ensemble], "Here Comes Emily Brown" [Richardson, White, chorus] (Jack Meskill, Con Conrad); "Bashful" [Brendel, White], "I Feel That Certain Feeling Coming On" [Brendel, Francis] (Cliff Friend, James V. Monaco); "Having a Ball" [chorus], "I'd Love to Be a Talking Picture Queen" [White, chorus] (Joseph McCarthy, James Brockman, James F. Hanley); "You'll Give In" [Brendel, White] (Joseph McCarthy, James F. Hanley).

Also Known As: *Fox Movietone Follies of 1930; New Movietone Follies of 1930.*
Alternate Titles: *Svenson's Big Night Out; Svenson's Big Party.*

The Story: Conrad Sterling is an errant Broadway playboy whose behavior earns the disfavor of his uncle and benefactor, Marvin Kingsley. Conrad is in love with Mary Mason, a kind-hearted showgirl. Conrad's valet, Axel Svenson, poses as a millionaire lumber magnate from Minnesota as he attempts to court one of Mary's fellow chorines, Gloria, while Vera Fontaine, another actress, also shows interest while cheating on egotistical actor George Randall. Mary comes to believe that Conrad is untrue to her, so to repair the relationship, he secretly hires the entire company of her show to stage a benefit for disabled war veterans at his uncle's Long Island estate. There, Axel is pursued by a maid, Babette, as well as Vera and the gold-digging Gloria. The benefit begins as Vera sings "I'd Love to Be a Talking Picture Queen." Axel, seduced backstage by Gloria, renders "I Feel That Certain Feeling Coming On." George and Vera go before the footlights in blackface for "Here Comes Emily Brown." Babette reveals Axel's real identity to Gloria, who "graciously" concedes the Swede to the unknowing Vera ("Bashful," "You'll Give In"). Uncle Marvin appears and threatens to cut off Marvin's inheritance if his nephew continues a relationship with Mary. Mary overhears Conrad's refusal of his uncle's demand and is convinced that Conrad loves her. Marvin is revealed as "Dodo," the mysterious "sugar daddy" of Gloria, and the show goes on ("Doing the Derby," "Cheer Up and Smile"). Conrad pairs with Mary, Vera with George, Gloria with Marvin, and—with the help of a $500,000 inheritance he unexpectedly receives from a distant relative—Axel ends up with Babette.

Movietone Follies of 1930 became an early victim of the public disfavor toward musicals in that pivotal year. The new film was envisioned as bigger and better than its titular predecessor, *William Fox Movietone Follies of 1929*, and boasted three performers from the studio's recent hit musical *Sunnyside Up*. But in the end, the 1930 edition was, as *Photoplay* declared, "just another revue."[43] It garnered so little confidence in the face of a tune-tired public that Fox rushed it through production and then changed its release title in many markets to emphasize the comedy angle. The latter is how this surprisingly enjoyable film should be most fondly remembered, for it was no small feat to make faux-Swede comic El Brendel into a chick magnet.

When the 1930 *Follies* was in the talking stages, there was little reason to think it couldn't match or exceed its studio's high notes. *William Fox Movietone Follies of 1929* had been a big deal, as a nearly plotless revue filled with elaborate production numbers—most notably one in which starlet Sue Carol introduced what would become a Charleston-like dance trend called "The Breakaway." It was an early experiment in the studio's Multicolor process and 70 mm "Grandeur" exhibition format, although both assets were not fully utilized for release. A spring '29 offering, these *Follies* (which, at this writing, existed only in fragmented audio) was a big moneymaker, and Fox assigned its director, David Butler, to make *Sunnyside Up*, the first musical for the studio's big romantic team of Janet Gaynor and Charles Farrell, for fall release. With a scenario and score by the De Sylva-Brown-Henderson creative trio complementing the Gaynor-Farrell allure, *Sunnyside Up* grossed more than $2 million and set up a trio of its supporting players—professional rube Brendel, wisecracking soubrette Marjorie White, and amiable tenor Frank Richardson—for better opportunities.

Each of the three had earned the boost. Brendel (1890–1964) had kicked around vaudeville since the early 'teens, often as part of a married-couple act with his wife, Flo Bert, and spouting trademark dialective quips such as "Yumpin' yiminy!" before making it to Broadway in 1921. Brendel, a native of Philadelphia, was not only un–Swedish (of German descent, actually) but an Ivy Leaguer (University of Pennsylvania) to boot. He came to silent movies despite their stilling of his speaking voice, but he made a strong impression as a German-American soldier in Paramount's war saga *Wings* (1927). Talkies re-established him as a Swede, and he brought down movie houses nationwide with his quip about "the lay of the land" in Fox's mega-grossing war comedy *The Cock-Eyed World* (1929). White (1904–1935) was a 4-foot-10 blonde who had performed since childhood in her native Canada and was another Broadway import. As Gaynor's best pal in *Sunnyside Up*, White (in her film debut) sang "It's Great to Be Necked" and stole scenes from the star. Richardson (1898–1962), also from Philadelphia, portrayed White's love interest in *Sunnyside Up* and introduced the song "Walking with Susie" in *William Fox Movietone Follies of 1929*. In between the two *Follies* pictures, Richardson appeared with Brendel and White in the mammoth cast of their studio's all-star revue, *Happy Days* (1930).

In January 1930, with *Sunnyside Up* raking in serious dollars in theaters and *Happy Days* about to open as Grandeur's first true showcase, Fox confidently announced its *New Movietone Follies of 1930* as the "most novel and stupendous production ... in its ... existence."[44] John Blystone, a comedy specialist who had just made the dramas *Thru Different Eyes* and *The Sky Hawk* for Fox, was announced as the director, with a cast led by White, John Garrick, Maureen O'Sullivan, Noel Francis, Walter Catlett, pop singer "Whispering" Jack Smith, and a chorus of 100 shapely dancers. (The youthful O'Sullivan had just filmed her celluloid debut in *Song o' My Heart*, Fox's failed attempt to make a film star out of Irish singer John McCormack.) There was no "William Fox" in the title of the new *Follies*, as the studio founder had gone bankrupt in the stock market crash and was forced to relinquish control of his company.

Even as Brendel was added to the cast, and other names were inserted and withdrawn, *Movietone Follies of 1930* (the copyrighted title) showed hints of unease prior to the start of shooting in early March, not least of which was the replacement of Blystone with a less-respected director, Benjamin Stoloff, who had cut his teeth on Fox silent Westerns but had least just helmed *Happy Days*. Initial reports from the studio were that all of Fox's two-score roster of songwriters would contribute, but most turned their talents elsewhere, including the popular Buddy De Sylva, Lew Brown, and Ray Henderson to the science-fiction musical *Just Imagine*. Plans to make *Follies* in Grandeur were nixed. Even as Stoloff climaxed the filming with the big ensemble number, "Here Comes Emily

Noel Francis (left) and Marjorie White inexplicably tussle over El Brendel in Fox's *Movietone Follies of 1930*.

Brown," with Richardson and White in blackface and a reputed dancing chorus of 125, the paybox returns on musicals were declining in general, boding not well for *Follies*. When shooting ended in early April, a trade publication noted that because "song-and-dance films seem on the wane, it is understood that final work will be rushed for as early a release as possible."[45]

Follies began theatrical play in middle and small markets in early May, with the biggest urban openings at the end of June. The results were not pretty. The New York City premiere run at the Roxy, abetted by a stage show featuring famed "shimmy" dancer Gilda Gray, drew a pan from a *Variety* writer who seemed to own a filter to tell the background of each audience member: "High school children and out-of-towners ... found plenty of chuckles ... [but the film] did not get over ... with the regular patrons."[46] Only Brendel—cast as a playboy's valet who masquerades as a millionaire lumber man at a society stage show—escaped critical brickbats. Typical was the response from *Exhibitors Herald-World*: "Brendel makes the trite plot and ancient gags at all bearable. The little Swede manages to make you laugh in spite of the poor material handed him."[47]

Fox grew panicky. For the Los Angeles opening on June 28 and many other West Coast engagements (and some in the East), the title of the film was changed to *Svenson's Wild Party*, naming it for Brendel's character and leaning its promotion more toward Brendel's and White's comedy and away from the ample musical content. In Scandinavian-laden Minnesota and Wisconsin, it appeared as *Svenson's Big Night Out*.

But the barn was locked too late. In May, Fox had announced, for the 1930–31 season, a production of *New Movietone Follies of 1931*, with Brendel, Lee Tracy, Dixie Lee, Richard Keene, Marie Saxon, *Ziegfeld Follies* beauty Claire Luce, and many others. That project quietly disappeared.

Because *Movietone Follies of 1930* exists in a 35 mm print in the UCLA Film and Television Archive, we can make up our minds about its worth 90 years later. It reveals itself as a fun little film with a few surprises. On the minus side are low-wattage performances by William Collier, Jr. (1902–1987) and Miriam Seegar (1907–2011) as the juvenile couple—a misbehaving playboy and the virtuous showgirl he loves over the objections of his stuffy uncle (Huntley Gordon).[48] Another disappointment is the integration of the music. This is a straight comedy for half of its 72-minute length, after which the action stops almost dead for the enactment of a revue planned by the playboy to win back his sweetie. There are seven numbers—four as part of the revue, three that occur backstage. Among them are White's charming, name-dropping rendition of "I'd Love to Be a Talking Picture Queen," in which she tells of intended alliances with Warner Baxter, Edmund Lowe, and Charles Farrell (all Fox he-men, conveniently). "How I'd love to be synchronized!" she exclaims. White also has a blackface duet with Richardson of "Here Comes Emily Brown," with a Southern horseracing motif, and Brendel and Noel Francis team nicely for "I Feel That Certain Feeling Coming On" as her character seduces his. (She thinks he's rich, remember?)

In her debut feature, Francis (1906–1959) makes a charming comedy partner for Brendel, and their byplay provides much of the kick in the mildly risqué script by erstwhile *George White's Scandals* writer William K. "Billy" Wells, now cinematically prolific. Francis' gold-digging Texan comes on to the duplicitous Swede on a couch while he's trying to cope with the effect of a jug of ice cubes on which he's just sat. "Something tells me that, deep down in your heart, your love is growing cold," she says. "Deeper down than that," is the poor fellow's reply. Later, after Francis learns her target's true lot, she not-so-graciously relinquishes him to the unknowing troupe mate played by White. "I had you all wrong! You've got a heart of gold!" White concedes emotionally. Francis' reply (her character feigning tears) is "I know it, but I can't help it!" Francis displays a pleasing contralto on the closing "Cheer Up and Smile" number, in which she taunts a chorus of prehistoric manservants into getting a life.[49] Sadly, the former Ziegfeld girl became stuck in the floozie/gun moll mold for most of her too-short career.

The reviewers in 1930 were right about Brendel: He is the best thing in the picture, if only because we can believe that he can get three women to chase him. Not only White and Francis, but also a fiery French maid played by Yola d'Avril, who's written so stereotypically that she lapses into her native tongue whenever she gets agitated. "The only lumber about him is his head!" is her best line in English—a reference to Brendel, of course. For once, El is playing a character with an IQ, and his romantic maneuverings show that he has a libido, too. "Oh, there's lots of things I go for/But they're no good on the sofa," he sings in "Bashful," in a rhyme that works, given his pretend diction.

Brendel was plenty busy in this period, most notably as the nominal lead/scene stealer in *Just Imagine* (1930). A less-impressive starring assignment in Fox's *Mr. Lemon of Orange* (1931) cast doubt on his ability to carry a picture, and he settled into what became a long vocation as a sidekick type in features, a top-billed player in shorts, and smaller roles in TV. He never lost that on-screen accent, and if he's a polarizing figure among film buffs today, they ought to check him out in *Movietone Follies of 1930* and re-evaluate.

Ladies in Love

(Chesterfield; May 15, 1930)

Director: Edgar Lewis. Producer: George R. Batcheller. Story and Screenplay: Charles Beahan. Photography: M.A. Anderson. Editor: James Morley. Sound: Lester E. Tope. Assistant Director: Melville Shyer. Running Time: 65 minutes.

Cast: Alice Day (Brenda Lascelle); Johnnie Walker (Harry King); Freeman Wood (Ward Hampton); Marjorie "Babe" Kane (Marjorie); James Burtis (Al Pine); Dorothy Gould (Patsy Green); Elinor Flynn (Mary Wood); Mary Carr (Mrs. Wood); Mary Foy (Mrs. Tibbs); Bernie LaMont (Frank Jones).

Songs: "My Big Boy" [Kane, reprised by band at party], "Oh! How I Love You" [Day, twice], "One Sweet Song" [Day, reprised by band at party] (Lester Lee, Charles Levison).

Working Title: *Hearts in Bondage*.

Home Video: Alpha DVD.

The Story: Piano teacher Harry King journeys from his small town in Vermont to visit his favorite radio singer, Brenda Lascelle, to convince her to perform "Oh! How I Love You," the song he's written for her. Having promised to marry snooty broadcast executive Ward Hampton, Brenda temporarily dismisses Harry's request, even though the Vermonter is posing as a millionaire. Marjorie Kane entertains the guests at a station party with the song "My Big Boy." Harry is reduced to working as a cook, but he is reminded by kind-hearted announcer Al Pine that "when you've hit the bottom, there's no place to go but up." Mary, Harry's gold-digging fiancée from back home, arrives to complicate matters, and Ward threatens to blacklist Brenda if she sings "Oh! How I Love You." With aid from Al and his girlfriend, Patsy, Harry hears his song played over the air and wins Brenda.

Even the smallest movie companies got caught up in the 1929–30 craze for musicals, and one of the few contributions by the obscure Chesterfield Motion Picture Corporation was *Ladies in Love*. Heading the cast were Alice Day and Johnnie Walker, two actors who had seen better roles in much better pictures.

Ladies in Love was one of two song films released by Chesterfield during the early sound wave. The other (now presumed lost) was *Love at First Sight*, which premiered in January 1930 and featured Norman Foster and the Paul Specht Orchestra. Its director, silent-film veteran Edgar Lewis, returned to the rented Tec-Art Studio in Hollywood in February to make *Ladies in Love*, which would be the last film in a megaphone career filled with Westerns and other action fare. Lewis' initial male lead was James Murray, the leading man of MGM's acclaimed 1928 drama *The Crowd*.[50] For reasons unknown, Murray was replaced by former Columbia leading man Walker, whose star was beginning to wane, even if he didn't know it.

The jut-jawed Walker (1894–1949) was best known for his roles in Fox's 1920 mega-hit drama *Over the Hill to the Poor House*, as the dutiful son who saves his kindly mother from a life of poverty, and in the 1926 Paramount actioner *Old Ironsides*, as War of 1812 hero Stephen Decatur. By the end of the '20s, he was in his mid–30s and having to prove himself all over again in talkies—and with a nasal New York accent. Walker, perhaps delaying the obvious but honestly intending to expand his creative repertoire, spent most of 1929 away from picture acting. He toured extensively as the star of a one-act playlet, *Gentleman George*, and unsuccessfully attempted to produce a talkie film with the Broadway actress Peggy Wood for an independent company.[51]

An emotive return to the screen had to pay the bills, and Walker went back to Columbia and was paired with Day in the Tin Pan Alley drama *The Melody Man* (1930). Walker was a second male lead in that picture as well as Frank Capra's *Ladies of Leisure* (1930), which starred a young Barbara Stanwyck. Walker got more to do in *Ladies in Love*, which for Day (1905–1995) was just another in a breakneck succession of roles at the majors and minors. She was a stunning blonde not known for singing abilities but teamed, nonetheless, with musical figures in 1929's *Is Everybody Happy?* (bandleader Ted Lewis) and *Little Johnny Jones* (singing comic Eddie Buzzell), plus the WB revue *The Show of Shows*. A former Mack Sennett bathing beauty and 1928 WAMPAS Baby Star, Alice was the elder of the movies' two Day sisters—but not as big a name as sibling Marceline.

Founded and operated by Broadway-based businessman George R. Batcheller, Chesterfield was better known for mysteries and action-type product. Newspaper ads for *Ladies in Love* played up serious angles for "The First Great Drama of Radio" and "A Sensational Drama of Life, Liberty, and the Reckless, Unending Pursuit of a Good Time." The screenplay was supplied by a big fish in a small pond: Charles Beahan, a corpulent former Cecil B. DeMille story editor who had lately co-written the Broadway adaptation of the popular novel *Jernagan*. Beahan would become known later for his tumultuous, sometimes violent marriage to Sidney Fox, co-star of the Bela Lugosi horror classic *Murders in the Rue Morgue* and the infamous RKO musical *Down to Their Last Yacht**. Fox's death in 1942, by an overdose of sleeping pills that may have been suicide, makes it retrospectively creepy to sample Beahan's stabs at comic dialogue in *Ladies in Love*. Consider these warnings from one character to another: "If you don't marry me, I might kill myself!" and "Scatter this harem, Casanova, or you'll be broadcasting your next announcement from a funeral parlor!" In the small markets where films like this played, patrons could figure that the hero's fiancée is going to turn out to be unfaithful because she smokes.

Ladies in Love is set at a New York City radio station where a hangdog rube from Vermont (Walker) tries to sell a song—and himself—to the outlet's resident singer (Day). Bona fide vocalist Marjorie "Babe" Kane (1909–1992) appears briefly as herself to sing with her baby-like "bo-peep" tones, but the official theme song—"Oh! How I Love You," which became a minor hit—is twice delivered by Day in what may not be her real voice. Day wasn't known for singing, and it wouldn't be too much longer before she'd cease being known for acting. She married a Hollywood stockbroker in 1930, gave birth to a child in 1931, and was out of pictures after 1932. Walker became a producer for the stage and occasional Hollywood shorts and features before dying of a heart attack too young at 55.

Ladies in Love was lauded by *Variety* as "well told and containing sufficient suspense and some action," but when it opened in New York City, a local critic noted that its accompanying feature on the bill, a revival of the Rudolph Valentino silent *Son of the Sheik*, got a much bigger hand from the audience.[52] It's inconsequential as a piece of filmmaking, but like many bottom-rung pictures, it gives bigger roles to small-part actors you'd barely see in major-studio flicks. In this case, it's James Burtis (1893–1939), who in his screen debut gets plenty of screen time as a comical station announcer—a change of pace from his bits as cops, hoods, soldiers, and reporters in more than 100 other 1930s movies. "Aren't you glad you're alive, folks?" is Pine's catchphrase for his listeners, which only adds to the screenwriter's preoccupation with mortality. If you haven't heard of two other secondary players, Dorothy Gould and Elinor Flynn, it's because they were scarcely seen in pictures other than this one. Flynn, whose character is the closest thing to a villainess in *Ladies in Love*, was a stage and radio player who was in rehearsals for a Broadway show when she perished, age 28, in a 1938 auto accident. Even director Lewis didn't last long past this film; he transitioned to acting bits before his death, also in 1938.

A much more familiar face in *Ladies in Love* is Mary Carr (1874–1973), who was known for portraying sympathetic elderly mothers in film. She had been paired with Johnnie Walker multiple times—she was his saintly mom in *Over the Hill to the Poor House*—so often that the two actors parodied their association in a 1930 short in Tiffany's *Voice of Hollywood* series. In that film, the two joke about Carr being mistaken for Walker's real mother as she presents him with food and underwear to pack away for an upcoming train trip. The short would have played well on the same theatrical bill as *Ladies in Love*.

Border Romance
(Tiffany; May 18, 1930)

Director: Richard Thorpe. Producer: Lester F. Scott, Jr. Story/Screenplay: John Francis Natteford. Photography: Harry Zech. Editing: Richard Cohoon. Musical Director: Al Short. Set Director: Ralph M. DeLacy. Sound: John Stransky, Jr. Running Time: 64 minutes.
Cast: Armida (Conchita Cortez); Don Terry (Bob Hamlin); Marjorie "Babe" Kane (Nina); Victor Potel (Slim); Wesley Barry (Victor Hamlin); Nita Martan (Gloria); J. Frank Glendon (Buck); Harry von Meter (captain); William Costello (lieutenant).
Songs: "The Girl from Topolobombo" [Kane, chorus], "My Desert Rose" [Terry], "Song of the Rurales" [von Meter, chorus, three times], "Yo Te Adoro (How I Adore You)" [Armida, Terry, reprised by Terry] (Will Jason, Val Burton).
Alternate Titles: *Down by the Rio Grande*; *Song of the Rurales*.
Home Video: Alpha DVD; Sinister Cinema DVD.

The Story: Brothers Bob and Victor Hamlin journey across the border into Mexico to go horse trading with their pal, Slim. When a Mexican attacks Victor in a saloon, Bob shoots the intruder dead and the three Americans flee to avoid capture by the local militia, the "rurales." After his horses are stolen, Bob attempts to find Buck, who had approached him about a possible sale. Bob is attracted to the lovely Conchita but must pursue Buck's girl, Gloria, to get to him. Meanwhile, Slim must fend off the advances of his old flame, Nina, to recover a lost bankroll. Bob takes Conchita into seclusion to protect her from harm. He battles Buck's men and surrenders to the rurales, who tell him that the man he killed in the saloon was a notorious bandit, El Gallo. Bob collects a reward—and wins Conchita.

In the song-happy months of early sound Hollywood, there were gangster pictures, war movies, society stories, aviation adventures, and sports tales with tunes shoehorned in. So there were also chaps in chaps doing pop on the prairie. Some came from the stage to celluloid, in operettas such as *Rio Rita* (1929) and *Song of the West* (1930) that fans of dyed-in-the-wool Westerns preferred to avoid. Others were originals—if not very original. An obscure early example of the musical Western is *Border Romance*, a 1930 entry from the independent Tiffany company.

The he-man singing voice in *Border Romance* belonged to Don Terry, a 27-year-old former Olympic boxer and Harvard football star who had made his first cinematic impact as a dramatic actor in Fox's 1928 crime drama *Me, Gangster*. The former Don Loker of Boston, Massachusetts, Terry (1902–1988) had come to California as a tourist, wanting to at least see stars without being one himself. One day, while lunching in Hollywood's famous Café Montmartre, Terry was handed a business card by Charles Francis Coe, who had just completed the screenplay for *Me, Gangster*. "I could not get into a studio," Terry recalled in an interview with *Photoplay* magazine. "Imagine my surprise when a man came over to me and asked if I was in pictures. I thought he was kidding, especially when he said I was just the type."[53]

Coe talked Terry into making a screen test, after which he was hired to play a poor kid who becomes a feared criminal and then goes up the river. But *Me, Gangster*, which was well received by critics, failed to register with the public, and its director, Raoul Walsh, took the same kind of heat for Terry's lack of impact as he would for his "discovery" of the similarly untried John Wayne in *The Big Trail* (1930). Terry was relegated to male decoration in Joan Crawford's first talkie, *Untamed* (1929), then to Tiffany fare. In *Border Romance*, he was placed with petite Mexican spitfire Armida (1911–1989), a teenaged protégé of youth star maker Gus Edwards, and former juvenile performer Wesley Barry. Neither Terry nor Armida were auto-sellable, and in many markets, the third-billed Barry (1907–1994) was advertised as the star. The operetta-style Western was helmed by indie-studio regular Richard Thorpe, who at the age of 34 already had more than 50 pictures on his directorial resume.

Although Tiffany aspired to loftier product—the Great War dramas *Journey's End* and *Woman to Woman*, for example—*Border Romance* was the kind of unpretentious picture that was bread and butter for the studio's clientele. Not surprisingly, Tiffany had a more-established cowboy star, Bob Steele, sing in some of his 1930 films, but they weren't as overtly musical as *Border Romance*. *Border* also is filled with the breezy comic relief that consumers expected to supplement the action—and, in Terry's and Armida's cases, vocalizing of the theme song "Yo Te Adoro (How I Adore You)." The two principals spend much of the film deciding if they will be a pair—she being the broadly indecisive one—with an expected happy ending.

The comic touch is supplied by gawky sidekick Victor Potel, who is shown complaining that he can't get a drink from a brook because "the horses got kind of careless in the water." In an even more censorable scene, Potel's character jumps into a lake for a swim, not immediately realizing that it is the locals' "ladies' day" and the water is populated by a group of virtually naked women. Prolific singer-comedienne Marjorie "Babe" Kane adds to the

A musical number by Marjorie "Babe" Kane provides a break from the action in *Border Romance*.

fun as Potel's overly aggressive girlfriend and offers one of the movie's four Will Jason-Val Burton songs. The unsympathetic types are adequately played by veteran heavies Harry von Meter and J. Frank Glendon, the former appearing in his only credited talkie role in a film career that began in 1912.

Variety's reviewer criticized *Border Romance* for a "disjointed story, choppily edited and bromidic dialog" but agreed that "a few meaty sequences and good bits of comedy make this the kind of entertainment second run and neighborhood trade will patronize."[54] Terry gives the male lead sufficient panache, even when his Boston accent (as in when he says "You *cahn't* be angry") distracts from the verisimilitude. *Border Romance* didn't do much to advance Terry's career, but he made a living with roles in "B" action pictures and serials, most notably as the title character in the chapter plays *Don Winslow of the Navy* (1942) and *Don Winslow of the Coast Guard* (1943). After World War II, Terry transitioned to the corporate world as an executive under his real name.

Ever busy with the indies, Thorpe made another Tiffany Western with songs, *Under Montana Skies*, later in 1930, but it had a non-singing lead in Kenneth Harlan, who was known to many as the star of the 1923 version of *The Virginian*. Instead, the primary vocalist was Nita Martan, who had a small role in *Border Romance* (and who had lately performed in MGM's starry musical *Chasing Rainbows*). After a few more years on Poverty Row, Thorpe "graduated" to A-grade and near-A features at MGM, among them *Night Must Fall*, *The Prisoner of Zenda*, and *Knights of the Round Table*. He sat in the director's chair well into the 1960s, by which time *Border Romance* had become a distant memory.

Kathleen Mavourneen

(Tiffany; June 20, 1930)

Director: Albert Ray. Screenplay: Frances Hyland, based on the play by Dion Boucicault. Photography: Harry Jackson. Editor: Arthur Roberts. Art Director: Hervey Libbert. Set Director: George Sawley. Running Time: 54 minutes.
Cast: Sally O'Neil (Kathleen O'Connor); Charles Delaney (Terry); Robert Elliott (Dan Moriarty); Aggie Herring (Aunt Nora Shannon); Walter Perry (Uncle Mike Shannon); Francis Ford (butler); Lydia Yeamans Titus (Fanny); Donald Novis (singer).
Songs: "Kathleen" [Delaney, twice, reprised by orchestra, then by chorus], "Mother My Own" [Delaney, reprised by Delaney, O'Neil] (James Brockman); "Come Back to Erin" [chorus] (Charlotte Alington Pye Barnard); "Garryowen" [danced by chorus] (trad.); "Killarney" [Novis] (Edmund Falconer); "Let Erin Remember the Days of Old" [chorus] (Thomas Moore); "A Little Bit of Heaven (Shure They Called It Ireland)" [Novis] (J. Keirn Brennan, Ernest R. Ball); "The Rakes of Mallow" [chorus] (trad.); "The Rocky Road to Dublin" [chorus] (trad.); "The Wearing of the Green" [chorus] (trad.).
Alternate Title: *The Girl from Ireland*.
Home Video: Alpha DVD.

The Story: Kathleen O'Connor sails to New York City from Ireland to stay with her Aunt Nora and Uncle Mike and reunite with her sweetheart, Terry, a plumber who declares his love for her by singing "Kathleen." Kathleen meets the local ward boss, Moriarty, who invites her and her friends to his fancy home on Long Island for a party in her honor. While Terry is distracted by a mishap created by the host, Moriarty proposes marriage to Kathleen, who accepts. On her wedding night, she watches in shock as her new husband shoots dead a man who accuses the politician of murder, but the episode is revealed as a dream. Kathleen rejects Moriarty's marriage proposal and returns to Terry ("Mother My Own").

In the early summer of 1929, Tiffany-Stahl promoted the impending release of *Kathleen Mavourneen* as its first 100 percent all-talking feature. But it would not be such, whether by design or happenstance, and now this creaky little film survives as little more than a primer on the popular Irish image at the end of the 1920s.

Film audiences of the time likely knew the name "Kathleen Mavourneen" as an old-time song from Ireland, written in 1839 and popular in the U.S. during the Civil War, or as an oft-revived play by Irish writer Dion Boucicault. The play concerns a peasant girl who is wooed by a rich landlord but decides to stay within her class after experiencing a dream about the alternative. The basic story was adapted into a handful of motion pictures, among them a 1919 Fox version that starred the very non–Irish Theda Bara. Tiffany's production of 1929–30 was headlined by one of Hollywood's quintessentially Irish-American actresses, Sally O'Neil. Petite, curly-haired O'Neil was easily typecast in the title role of what Tiffany touted as "a laughing love story with music." Given the strong popularity of Irish songs—which only grew as Irish immigrants filled American cities out into the hinterlands—an Irish movie musical seemed a natural.

Under director Albert Ray, the play *Kathleen Mavourneen* was updated to contemporary New York City and the peasant girl became a just-off-the-boat immigrant from the Ould Sod who is the object of the affections of a singing plumber (tune-dubbed Charles Delaney) and a moneyed politician (Robert Elliott). Delaney had some name value, and his first big break as a picture actor had come opposite O'Neil at MGM in *Frisco Sally Levy* (1927). The jaunty Delaney, publicized widely for his Navy stunt-flying duty in the Great War, had an open-faced, distinctly Irish look that appealed to viewers without distracting them from his usually-more-famous female co-stars. *New York Daily News* critic Irene Thirer praised him as "our idea of a leading man, who is just handsome enough and yet not too handsome."[55] Unfortunately, Delaney (1892–1959) was about to begin the long journey down from the majors, where he was paired multiple times at First National with Alice White, who was to blonds as O'Neil was to brunettes.

Kathleen Mavourneen was announced in the late spring of 1929,[56] and filming commenced that summer, but it wasn't released for nearly a year thereafter, until June 1930. The reasons for the delay are unclear, although judging from the adverse response the film would create, it's likely that its studio—its name now shortened to Tiffany after the departure of production head John M. Stahl—knew it had a stinker on its hands. The production troubles began early, as an experiment of using more than a half dozen dialogue writers proved unwieldy, and most of the script had to be rewritten.[57] A leadership vacuum at Tiffany after Stahl's abrupt exit in the fall of 1929 may have impacted the release. Some Irish-themed Hollywood pictures were criticized by Irish groups for stereotypical ethnic depictions—the Marie Dressler-Polly Moran comedy *The Callahans and the Murphys* (1927), which also featured O'Neil, was withdrawn from distribution by MGM and the early Colleen Moore musical *Smiling Irish Eyes* (First National, 1929) was banned in Ireland. But there seem to have been no concerted objections over this minor Tiffany release.

The eventual negative reviews for *Kathleen Mavourneen*—which *The Film Daily* called a "weak number plugging the Irish angle," while *Photoplay* readers were advised to "save your money"—must have been particularly disheartening for O'Neil.[58] She had remained busy in the months that her Tiffany film sat on the shelf, churning out no less than seven talkies that beat *Kathleen Mavourneen* to theaters. Among them were two musicals, Columbia's *Broadway Scandals* (1929) and Warner Bros.' *Hold Everything* (1930), plus RKO's fringe musical *Jazz Heaven* [q.v.]. O'Neil also appeared briefly with her actress sibling, Molly O'Day, in the all-star "Meet My Sister" song number from the 1929 Warners studio revue *The Show of Shows*. O'Neil had endured snippy comments about her figure from the likes of über-columnist Louella Parsons, who wrote in late 1929 that "Sally looked a little plumpish to me in her last pictures, and I don't know why.... Maybe it's the fault of the camera."[59]

What O'Neil could not have known was that her career was about to begin a slow decline, and her personal life was no brighter. In November 1929, the feds came after her, claiming she owed more than $1,000 in back taxes, and in 1930, O'Neil and O'Day both filed for personal bankruptcy.[60] In January 1930 came reports that a bullet was fired into one of the windows of a car in which the two sisters were sitting, from a car that allegedly followed the pair from home.[61] The same month *Kathleen Mavourneen* finally debuted, O'Neil was in vaudeville with O'Day in a failing two-act in which they sang, danced, and talked about how they got into pictures. The endeavor, tied in part to their recent joint appearance in the Columbia drama *Sisters*, must have seemed promising; the siblings were awarded an all-expenses-paid trip from Hollywood to New York without any advance look by the stage circuits. But the show flopped. "Badly and hastily slapped together" and "To say they were in vaude, is to profane the word," read reports from the East.[62]

In 1937, after years in American quickies, O'Neil went to England to appear in *Kathleen Mavourneen*, yet another filming of the Boucicault story, this time with an English cast and an Ireland setting, although the results were no more favorable. The actress returned to the theater but never regained footing in pictures, despite periodic reports of a comeback. She "retired" to Illinois, the home state of her industrialist husband, and was enjoying artistic activity as a painter when she died, reportedly of pneumonia, in 1968. By then, most of her Hollywood work had been forgotten.

The 1930 *Kathleen Mavourneen* surfaced early in the 21st century via public-domain video. As one might expect from a piece of entertainment from this era, the Irish characters are friendly but stereotypically portrayed as uncouth, insular, prone to conflict, and acutely sentimental. As cultured and gentlemanly the politician is, he's still from the clan, reminds the plumber: "Ah, the big Irish show-off! Why, three years ago, he was spilling soup down the front of his vest in the Automat. But now he must have a man stand behind him and spill it down his back!" Then there's this exchange between the romantic leads after he has sung her a love song:

> HE: "You see, colleen, there's no blarney at all, but just m'love comin' out into song."
> SHE: "Blarney or not, when you sing like that, it's almost convinced I am."
> HE: "Then let me sing it to you for the rest of your life. Ah, Kathleen, in all this world, there's nothin' means anything to me but you."
> SHE: "Terry, darlin,' when you talk like that, I could listen to you the whole night through!"

The sentimentality extends to the extended medley of old Irish melodies by a chorus gathered at a party, pop singer Donald Novis appearing amid the bunch to lead some of the singing.[63] "Let's have an Irish musical cocktail! We'll sing all the Irish songs we know!" he exclaims. And they do.

Are You There?

(Fox; November 30, 1930)

Director: Hamilton MacFadden. Story/Dialogue: Harlan Thompson. Photography: Joseph Valentine. Editor: Al De Gaetano. Sound: W.W. Lindsay. Art Directors: Stephen Goosson, Duncan Cramer. Costumes: Sophie Wachner. Musical Director: Arthur Kay. Dance Direction: Edward Dolly. Choral Direction: Frank Tresselt. Assistant Director: Sam Wurtzel. Running Time: 60 minutes.
Cast: Beatrice Lillie (Shirley Travis); John Garrick (Lord Geoffry Brent); Olga Baclanova (Countess

Helenka); George Grossmith (Duke of St. Pancras); Jillian Sand (Barbara Blythe); Lloyd Hamilton (hostler); Gustav von Seyffertitz (von Diddendorf); Nicholas Soussanin, Richard Alexander, Henry Victor (international crooks); Roger Davis (barber); Paula Langlen (page); Bo-Peep Karlin, Adele Cutler, Mary Carr, Lorraine Bond, Lucille Miller, Catherine Brown, Marbeth Wright, Bee Stephens (ensemble dancers); The Fox-Movietone Augmented Chorus.

Songs: "Bagdad Daddies" [Lillie], "Lady Detectives" [Lillie, Langlen, chorus], "Queen of the Hunt Am I" [Lillie, chorus] (Grace Henry, Morris Hamilton).

The Story: Shirley Travis, a London-based private detective, shows off various disguises as she leads her pupils in a dance number, "Lady Detectives," and reminds them to "always get your man." Lord Geoffry Brent asks if Shirley will help him and his fiancée, Barbara Blythe, wrest his father, the Duke of St. Pancras, from the money-grabbing Russian Countess Helenka. Helenka is secretly part of a gang of international crooks planning a holdup at the duke's country estate. Shirley visits the estate in the guise of Lady Diana Drummond, a famous big-game hunter and equestrian. The crooks seek to expose Shirley as an imposter at a fox hunt, but after being schooled by a friendly hostler, Shirley manages to catch the fox with her bare hands ("Queen of the Hunt Am I"). The duke suddenly decides that he will propose marriage to the countess at a party that night, so Geoffry pretends to make love to the Russian to create a scandal that will keep the duke from her permanently. The male crooks kidnap Shirley and, to keep her from the party, hold her captive, but the hostler follows on a motorcycle, and his unintentional gunshot into the villain's lair enables Shirley to escape. Posing as an acrobat, Shirley entertains the partygoers with a number ("Bagdad Daddies") set in an Arabian harem. The hostler and a gorilla help Shirley thwart the crooks, the estranged Geoffry and Barbara are reunited, and the duke decides that Diana/Shirley is his martial choice after all.

Beatrice Lillie was called "The Funniest Woman in the World," but when it came to breaking into Hollywood, the deadpan comedienne of Broadway and London stage fame might as well have been just off the train from Peoria. Her primary contribution to the early sound era was *Are You There?*—an offbeat musical comedy with a mainly international cast. This hour-long programmer generated no faith from its studio, which cut much of its music, withheld it from wide release and dumped it mainly in small towns where few could appreciate its quirky humor and one-of-a-kind leading lady.

The Canadian-born Lillie (1894–1989) was adored by the illuminati for her droll, deadpan humor, often conveyed by a mere voice inflection, an arched eyebrow, or the spacing of words in a line of dialogue. With close-cropped hair and angular features, she was a sophisticate who refused to be taken seriously; hence, the title of her autobiography, *Every Other Inch a Lady*, a reference to her reluctant status as the wife of a member of the English peerage. (Media coverage from her heyday often identified her as Lady Peel as well as her birth name.) Lillie's distinctive look was utilized in a series of highbrow revues on both sides of the Atlantic starting in the mid-'teens. She made her feature-film debut in 1926, but the MGM comedy *Exit Smiling* didn't make much of an impression, proving that to truly enjoy Lillie, one had to hear her.

In 1929, Lillie voiced her sentiments in the all-talking and -singing Warner Bros. revue *The Show of Shows*. She performed in two comedy sketches—one of which, "Recitations," teamed her with Frank Fay, Louise Fazenda, and Lloyd Hamilton in an amusing series of pretentious utterings that, when mixed together, told a completely different story than when spoken separately. The other sketch, "Beatrice Lillie and Her Boy Friends," was cut from the film prior to release, and when Warners released the deleted scene as a short subject, Lillie unsuccessfully sued the studio for breach of contract and $100,000. Her claim was that by presenting her as a one-reel-worthy comic, the company had damaged her reputation and "presented ... [her] to the world as a cheap and inconsequential performer."[64] In 1930, Lillie took what she hoped would be a cleaner stab at Hollywood, although, as she wrote in her autobiography, "once again, it was a movie that stabbed me."[65] Lillie returned to Hollywood in mid–March and was put to work on a Fox musical farce, *Are You There?*, as a crafty Sherlock Holmes–style detective with a gender twist.[66]

Fox initially announced David Butler, the maker of the studio's recent hit musical *Sunnyside Up*, to direct, and there were reports that comic Harry Langdon was to be signed for a key supporting role. Instead, Butler bowed out over objections over his co-directing, and the solo job went to Hamilton MacFadden, a less-movie-seasoned import from the New York stage.[67] The Langdon part was landed by Lloyd Hamilton, a well-known silent-era comic now fading and grown paunchy. Hamilton was a Yank, but the rest of the cast came from foreign soil: John Garrick, Jullian Sand (replacing Ireland's Maureen O'Sullivan), George Grossmith and Henry Victor from England; Olga Baclanova and Nicholas Soussanin from Russia; and Gustav von Seyffertitz of Germany. The *Are You There?* composers—former *Earl Carroll's Vanities* songwriters Grace Henry and Morris Hamilton—were American but new to films, the wife-and-husband duo having just been brought to Fox to write songs for *Movietone Follies of 1930* [q.v.].

Quirky comedienne Beatrice Lillie was a perennial hit on stage, but her first foray into talking films didn't fare so well.

Fox used the "something different" angle in promoting *Are You There?*—not only reminding middle America that this was a cast of outsiders, but also in spreading a not-so-comic-if-you-think-about-it yarn about Lillie driving down the wrong (left) side of Hollywood Boulevard because she forgot she couldn't drive as she had in London.[68] On the set, the cast was mostly at sea with American moviemaking technique. Lillie recalled that Grossmith, an actor, producer and playwright for nearly 40 years, "wandered around the studios, elevating his celebrated eyebrows in horror, complaining, 'My dear fellow, it is not *done*. It is just not *done* like that, I assure you.'"[69] For a stage-seasoned player like Lillie, not hearing the response to her comedy on the noiseless sets instead of the laughter from footlight galleries was disconcerting, and she told an interviewer, "Try to be comic for half a dozen spectators, grimly silent behind cameras.... Of course, a microphone can't throw things."[70]

By the time *Are You There?* wrapped in early June, musical films were beginning to disappear from vogue, and Fox responded by trimming three of the intended six songs from the final cut of the Lillie picture. Then it held back the film, and the publicized general release date went from September 28 to November 30 to December 14 to May 3 (1931) to ... when? Late in 1930, *Are You There?*—now being promoted as a straight comedy rather than a musical—was screened to test audiences and some trade journal reviewers, with mixed results. *Exhibitors Herald World* said it "unreels laughs after laughs" and called Lillie "smart-looking, clever and mirth-provoking.... Her personality and grace are registered superbly upon the screen."[71] But *Motion Picture News* unleashed its editor and publisher, "Red" Kann, to decry a lack of belly laughs: "The average audience won't know whether they went super-subtle on this or just muffed the works."[72]

Fox decided to limit the American release of the Lillie film to small theaters and skip the more-demanding major-city trade.[73] So instead of New York or Los Angeles viewers seeing a performer they might previously have watched in person, down-to-earth folks in such locales as Sedalia, Missouri; Massillon, Ohio; Coudersport, Pennsylvania; and Harlingen, Texas, were mystified by Beatrice Lillie on celluloid in the final weeks of 1930. *Are You There?* spread to theaters in Pittsburgh by the following March and in Cincinnati by August 1931. But by this time, it had been hammered to bits by *Variety* publisher "Sime" Silverman in a review that followed a one-day engagement in a New York City house. "Made so long ago it's too bad Fox could not have forgotten it forever," he wrote.

> A ridiculous talker ... so bad it looks and sounds as though made in England. But it was done by Fox in Hollywood and now appears to have been sent out where it can play ... for what salvage is possible.... It will be 20 years before a picture audience will commence to get Bee Lillie.[74]

It would take somewhat less time for U.S. audiences to "get" Lillie, who returned to the screen in a 1938 Bing Crosby musical for Paramount, *Dr. Rhythm*. Her final credit among a half-dozen movies was a prominent role in the 1967 musical *Thoroughly Modern Millie*. Meanwhile, *Are You There?* lost almost all of its negative cost of $430,000.[75]

So, to paraphrase Gertrude Stein, is there an *Are You There?* there? Fortunately, unlike so many early talkies, it has survived—a complete version of its theatrical print reposes at the Museum of Modern Art in New York—and (as viewed by the author) it plays quite favorably. MacFadden and scripter Harlan Thompson allow Lillie a goodly share of her deadpan expressions, raised eyebrows, and flute-like voice tones as Shirley Travis, an intrepid, "ultra-modern" London private detective. It plays to her strengths.

The opening of the film is particularly impressive. Shirley is apparently getting by enough to afford a lavish, futuristic private office (with art-deco sets by Steven Goosson, an Oscar nominee for the early Fox sci-fi musical *Just Imagine*, and Duncan Cramer). There is a television-type monitor with which Shirley can check on comings and goings, and a revolving door with which she can whisk in clients from the lobby. Shirley and six of her pupils show off their disguises—among them Napoleon, George Arliss, and Douglas Fairbanks types, and a Chinese sage—in a clever dance number, "Lady Detectives." Shirley then answers a round of telephone calls requesting her services. "No, madame, that's much too pure," she tells one caller, "I only take immoral cases." Lord Geoffry Brent (Garrick) visits, asking Shirley if she will help him wrest his father, the Duke of St. Pancras (Grossmith), from the money-grabbing clutches of a Russian countess named Helenka. Geoffry fears for the family estate, and rightly so, for the bogus countess is secretly part of a gang of international crooks planning a holdup at the estate. The leader of said gang (von Seyffertitz) happens to be perched with his minions on Shirley's roof, and he tosses a bomb inside. When the smoke clears, Shirley and Geoffry surrealistically continue their conversation as if nothing has happened.

Shirley agrees to visit the estate in the guise of Lady Diana Drummond, a famous big-game hunter and equestrian. At a party in her honor, "Diana" makes a Captain Spaulding–type dramatic entrance, preceded by footmen, an ostrich, a bagpiper, and a gorilla. The duke, a passionate huntsman himself, takes her into his study to talk shop. In typical Lillie-chat, the hunter lady brags about killing a huge tiger in Africa.

> "I suppose you used a 40–40 on the tiger," the duke asks.
> "Oh, nooo, nooo," Diana replies, oblivious to such weaponry, "a 50–50."
> "I haven't heard of a 50–50…"
> "Well, you see, it's like this: It's 50–50 if you get the tiger—or the tiger gets a-youuu."

The crooks know that the visitor isn't the real Diana, so they plot to get her involved in the upcoming big fox hunt. Shirley needs a lesson in horsemanship—and fast. In the stables, she finds a hostler (Hamilton) who professes he knows nothing about horses but is eager to help anyway. After an overnight lesson, Shirley is asked to lead the hunt atop a balky steed named Bullet. She is soon thrown from the horse, but as she rests against a tree, the exhausted fox jumps into her lap. The rest of the hunting party intervenes, and "Diana" is lauded for her skill at catching the fox with her bare hands. Giddily, she sings "Queen of the Hunt Am I" as the other hunters dance and sing along, though only Lillie fools with the high notes in her own inimitable way. It is the best exhibition of her vocal style in the space of 60 minutes.

Later, Shirley disguises herself as a Cockney nurse and gives Helenka (Baclanova, already struggling with the heavy accent that deprived her of talkie stardom) a violent "massage" as she looks for evidence that would implicate the countess. There is more briskly paced action as Shirley is kidnapped and held captive by the gang, but luckily saved by an amateurishly aimed gunshot from the hostler. This enables Shirley to show up on time for the film's final musical number, "Bagdad Daddies," in which she, while posing as an acrobat, is tossed around onstage—so passionately that you're supposed to know it's fake—by a pair of big, bare-chested "harem attendants." The thieves have planned a jewel holdup at the end of the song, but Shirley confuses them by jazzing up the tune a bit. The signal is made to begin the holdup, but the hostler and the gorilla knock cold two of the baddies and dump them on stage, and the plot is thwarted, Geoffrey and his fiancée (Sand) are reunited, and Shirley ends up with the fish-faced, fuddy-duddy duke. Maybe that's not such a happy ending.

In hindsight, *Are You There?* might have been even more interesting with its full complement of songs. One of the deleted numbers, a choral-and-dance presentation of the Russian folk tune "Advice to Lovers," is seen for a few seconds prior to the "Bagdad Daddies" finale. Also filmed, then cut, were "It Must Be the Iron in the Spinach," with which the captive Lillie annoys her kidnappers, and "You Can Always Count on Me," a romantic ballad sung by Garrick to Sand. The absence of the last might help to explain Sand's too-brief time on screen.

The story of *Are You There?* didn't quite end with its disappearance into the Fox vaults. It was unearthed in 1971 for a quote-unquote official New York premiere as part of historian Miles Kreuger's retrospective of early musicals at MOMA. Lillie, who had never seen the film, showed up and, in a sign of the mental troubles that would plague the rest of her life, marched onstage to a standing ovation and greeted the audience by exposing part of her breast and asking, "How do you like that?"[76] As for the onscreen diversion, a *New York Times* writer on hand was unimpressed, rationalizing any value of the film to Lillie's talent and "a patina that in the popular arts inevitably encourages a kind of silly, forgiving nostalgia."[77]

Actually, *Are You There?* has more than just nostalgia value; it's a neat piece of fun. It needs little apology for its amusing, sometimes even inventive, showcasing of an unusual performer too infrequently screened. It deserved to be seen by more people in 1930, and it's a pity it's not in wider circulation.

It's Great to Be Alive
(Fox; June 2, 1933)

Director: Alfred L. Werker. Associate Producer: John Stone. Adaptation: Paul Perez, based on the novelette *The Last Man on Earth* by John D. Swain. Dialogue: Arthur Kober. Screenplay Contributors: William Kernell, Donald W. Lee. Photography: Robert H. Planck. Editor: Barney Wolf. Sound: Alfred Bruzlin. Art Director: Duncan Cramer. Costumes: Royer. Music Director: Samuel Kaylin. Dance Direction: Sammy Lee. Assistant Director: Philip Ford. Running Time: 69 minutes.

Cast: Raul Roulien (Carlos Martin); Gloria Stuart (Dorothy Wilton); Edna May Oliver (Dr. Grace Prodwell); Herbert Mundin (Brooks); Joan Marsh (Toots); Dorothy Burgess (Al Moran); Emma Dunn (Mrs. Wilton); Edward Van Sloan (Dr. Wilton); Robert Greig (Perkins); Gloria Roy (Helen); Blanche Payson (oversized gangster); Toby Wing (kissing blonde); Edward Dillon (airplane mechanic); Julie Carter (girl); Florine McKinney (American ambassador); Betty Keeler ("Cheko" ambassador); Marguerite Warner (Dutch ambassador); Leonore La Hogue (Cuban ambassador); Elene Shannon, Beatrice Rossi, Margaret Rilling, Martha Reeves, Helen Pacino, Kathleen Oglivie, Mona Munro, Helene Friend, Mildred Lewis, Liana Galen, Florence Kitzmiller, Zaruhi Elmassian, Emilia Da Prato, Josephine Campbell, Mary York, Betty Baldrick, Lorraine Bridges, Beatrice Becker, Mildred Carroll, Willow Wray, Lois Woody, Eleanor Wells, Gelai Talata, Alice Towne (singers); Marjorie Seavey, Ruth Moody, Harriet Mathews, Loraine Marshall, Lucille House, Dorothy Compton ("Cheko" dancers); Margaret Nearing, Ruth Jennings, Sugar Geise, Dixie Dean, Sally Haines, Audrene Brier, Betty Bryson, Mildred Clare (Dutch dancers); Geneva Sawyer, Lucille Porcett, Patsy Lee, Peaches Jackson, Theo De Voe, Harriette Haddon, Marbeth Wright (Cuban dancers); Eva Sabenie, Lucille Miller, Gloria Fayth, Amo Ingraham, Edith Haskins, Sally Arden, Esther Brodelet, Bonita Barker (American dancers); Gwen Seager, Bee Stevens, Margaret Harding, Lee Bailey, Georgia Clarke (dancing pages).

Songs: "Good Bye Ladies" [Roulien], "I'll Build a Nest" [Roulien, Stuart, reprised by Roulien, then by Roulien, Oliver, chorus], "It's Great to Be the Only Man Alive" [Roulien], "Women! Women! Women!" [Roulien, Mundin], "World Congress" [Roulien, Oliver, McKinney, chorus] (William Kernell).

The Story: In 1933, handsome socialite Carlos Martin is engaged to marry Dorothy Wilton, the daughter of a scientist who is investigating the outbreak of masculitis, a deadly worldwide virus that affects males only. Before relinquishing bachelorhood for marriage, Carlos hosts a dinner for his many former sweethearts, to whom he reluctantly sings "Good Bye Ladies." Dorothy remains suspicious of Carlos' wandering eye toward women, especially the alluring "Toots," but Dorothy forgets her jealousy when he sings "I'll Build a Nest" to her during their engagement party. After the party, Carlos and the Wiltons' butler, Brooks, lament the complications of romance ("Women! Women! Women!"). A mistake by Brooks puts Carlos in Toots' bedroom, and Dorothy breaks the engagement. To get over his disappointment, Carlos takes off on a trans-Pacific flight, but he crashes and is marooned on a deserted island. In 1935, Dr. Grace Prodwell joins Dr. Wilton and other international experts in battling the masculitis plague. Prodwell leads a symposium of worldwide scientists, who pontificate in their own tongues as Prodwell humorously translates. By 1938, the virus has killed the world's male population—except for Carlos, who was assumed dead in the plane crash. Dr. Prodwell leads an unsuccessful effort to create a synthetic man. An aviatrix locates Carlos from the air and alerts Dr. Prodwell, but a group of female gangsters led by Al Moran captures him first and returns him to the United States. The gangsters decide to put Carlos up for auction and hide him in a luxurious apartment with many female servants ("It's Great to Be the Only Man Alive"), but officials thwart the scheme. Dorothy tries to reunite with Carlos, but their attempt to escape by air fails. Carlos' fate is to be decided by a League of Nations-type group, to which singing and dancing representatives of various countries—Cuba, Holland, Czechoslovakia, and the U.S.—make their cases to claim him in marriage ("World Congress"). Carlos reacts to the loss of his freedom by threatening suicide, so Dr. Prodwell rules that he be allowed to marry the woman of his choice—Dorothy.

Despite its modest intentions as a program filler, *It's Great to Be Alive* is among the most unusual of early songfests: a farcical science-fiction musical in which a key premise is realized when half the world is killed off in a medical epidemic. It also offers a rare-for-the-time Latino leading man, butch bootleggers, barbell-carrying chorines, garden-variety pre–Code innuendo ... and Edna May Oliver in a suit and tie. Audiences and reviewers of 1933 greeted this strange brew with mixed praise, perhaps depending on their tolerance for a 20-minute idea stretched to nearly 70. *It's Great to Be Alive* is another of those minor Fox musicals that sadly disappeared over the decades, but lately it has been unearthed, restored, and screened for classic-film devotees who can delight in its weirdness. This one did.

In the spring of 1933, when *It's Great to Be Alive* was filmed, the Hollywood musical was back, thanks to *42nd Street*—a monster hit that revived the genre with the promise that musical numbers would be better integrated into plots and thus more engaging to audiences. In other words, *Variety* quipped, the "melody will not be dragged in by the heels as before, but will be added to advance the plot."[78] More than 40 films with music were in production by spring, with nearly 30 more already slated for release during the 1933–34 season.[79] That meant that suitable material had to be found, and for cash-strapped Fox, that meant vocalizing properties that were already under studio control. *It's Great to Be Alive* was a remake of a 1924 Fox silent comedy, *The Last Man on Earth*, based on a novelette about a fellow (played on screen by Earle Foxe) who survives a global outbreak that kills the rest of the world's male population. The twist here was that *Alive* was also a redo of a Spanish-language musical comedy already produced by Fox, *El último varón sobre la Tierra*.

El último varón sobre la Tierra ("The Last Man on Earth") starred Raul Roulien, a Brazilian-born actor, tenor, playwright, and songwriter whom Fox was keeping busy in Spanish-language productions mainly derived from the studio's sound and silent films. Roulien had debuted in *Eran trece*, an alternate version of *Charlie Chan Carries On* (1931), and starred in *No dejes la Puerta abierta*, a foreign take on the Fox romantic comedy *Pleasure Cruise* (1933). Those films were made with Spanish-speaking casts, but Roulien also was placed in occasional English-language pictures, most notably the Janet Gaynor-Charles Farrell-George Gershwin musical *Delicious* (1931). Away from the camera, Roulien spent ample time learning to speak better English (according to studio publicity) and pursuing his passion for polo. He was key to the studio's flourishing effort to target foreign markets, as was José Mojica, the Mexican singer who had starred in English and Spanish versions of the musical *One Mad Kiss* (1930), and Fox announced plans in mid–1932 to make as many as 20 Spanish-language features featuring Roulien and Mojica.[80]

Under the direction of James Tinling for producer John Stone, and with Roulien and Rosita Moreno as the couple upon whose romance the world depends, *El último varón sobre la Tierra* was shot in the fall of 1932.[81] With musicals in America back in vogue a few months later, it seemed natural to try out the 26-year-old Roulien and his film—and, once translated, its songs by veteran composer William Kernell—in a "standard" talkie. Fox's judgment seemed to be verified in March 1933 when *El último varón sobre la Tierra* set box office records during a record-setting theatrical run in Madrid.[82] Roulien, it was hoped, could charm U.S. audiences as another accented import, France's Maurice Chevalier, already had, and Fox surrounded him with capable comic talents Oliver (as a mannish scientist who is central to stemming the epidemic), Herbert Mundin, and Robert Greig; fetching Joan Marsh; tough-gal Dorothy Burgess; and a newish ingénue in Gloria Stuart. Stuart, a 1932 WAMPAS Baby Star, was learning the acting ropes with constant work in minor features and a few of greater importance (John Ford's *Air Mail* and James Whale's horrific *The Old Dark House* and *The Invisible Man*). She landed the *Alive* role after Fox failed to secure Constance Cummings or Dorothy Jordan.

As unimportant as Stuart (1910–2010) considered *It's Great to Be Alive*, even in her dotage, she did remember her distaste for co-star Roulien's ingestive habits:

> My most unfavorite actor I ever knew was a man named Raul Roulien…. When Maurice Chevalier went back to Paris, all the studios scrambled to find a replacement, and Fox came up with Raul Roulien, from South America—who was addicted to garlic and red wine, and song. So I'm standing there, day in, day out … with a singer who has a yen for garlic and red wine. And it was just ghastly. Sorry, Raul![83]

With a familiar story masquerading as something new and different, *It's Great to Be Alive* was filmed in April 1933 with Stone again producing and Alfred L. Werker now the director. Werker's presence practically screamed "second-rate"—just before making *It's Great to Be Alive*, the B-specialist was assigned by Fox to reshape Erich von Stroheim's edgy *Walking Down Broadway* into an uncredited mediocrity retitled as *Hello, Sister!* IGTBA was another low-priority item from executive producer Sol Wurtzel's "B" unit, shot at Fox's older, newly reopened, second-string facility on Western Avenue in Hollywood, miles away from the newer, more prestigious "Movietone City" lot in Beverly Hills. Fox's minor films—ground out with efficient budgets of about $250,000—were more competent than flashy, but they kept the pipeline of product flowing to theater screens. In the case here, there was some flash—dance numbers choreographed by Sammy Lee and even some special effects, as when Oliver attempts to create a "synthetic man" and sees her creation go up in smoke.

"A man is never through with women until women are through with him," Roulien's playboy, Carlos Martin, is told by his wise butler (Greig) at the outset of the film, which shows the young man burning glam photos from the lovers he is about to forsake for pretty socialite Dorothy, played by Stuart. ("Yours without a struggle," reads the suggestive autograph on the photo of Stuart's main rival, Toots, played by Marsh.) Carlos, who loves Dorothy but is abjectly unready for monogamy, is consoled at his own engagement party by Dot's drunken servant (Mundin), with whom he sings "Women" while attempting to walk upstairs to bed. Too tipsy to reason, Mundin accidentally directs the young man to the bedroom of Toots, leading to a case of mistaken identity that prompts the main couple to break up.

Carlos is disconsolate enough to take his plane, "The Spirit of Dan Juan," on a flight across the Pacific, and it is from here that *It's Great to Be Alive* transitions from a slackly paced, Lubitsch-style romantic comedy into a less conventional low-comic fantasy. The pace quickens and years pass quickly as Carlos is marooned on a remote island while the rest of the globe deals with all the manly deaths. By the time Carlos is fought over as "the property of the world," we've seen a series of chases in which the hero is found (in a beard and loincloth) and lost and found again. In this new world, there are no males, but no loss of gender tropes—women gangsters dress like Al Capone, but there isn't even a genuine pre–Codey hint of lesbianism. Maybe not enough time has passed?

Despite the many unanswered questions, the film climaxes nicely with a production number—part spoken-sung and part sung—depicting the lone male's trial before a League of Nations-type group led by Oliver's Dr. Prodwell. Choruses from various nations make their cases for Carlos' hand through song and dance—there's a rumba-style bid from Cuba, and a Czech contingent brings in barbells to demonstrate that heavier and stockier girls are worthy, too. When Carlos threatens to do himself in—which, in a pre-artificial insemination era, would lead to the world's end—Prodwell swiftly confers with her colleagues and allows the man to marry his true sweetheart, thus allowing Dorothy to forsake her earlier insistence to Carlos that "I wouldn't marry you if you were the only man alive!"

And then it's over—in 69 minutes—although it's better to let yourself soak in the amusing afterglow of *It's Great to Be Alive* rather than think about it too deeply. What if Carlos and Dorothy can't procreate? And what if you've come to like any of the other male characters—who just ... disappear? Although the songs aren't particularly memorable, and modern viewers might find the film's attitudes patronizing, this is fast-paced, escapist fun with many touches that buffs should enjoy. A song number called "It's Great to Be the Only Man Alive" finds Roulien singing to a bevy of beautiful servants in which mobsters have set him up; one of the beauties is film-fan favorite Toby Wing, who leans in to kiss the camera in a subjective shot meant for the man's point of view.[84] And if you're a Monster Kid raised with the original Frankenstein and Dracula, how can you not enjoy the novelty of seeing the usually professorial Edward Van Sloan amorously referring to his screen wife (matronly Emma Dunn) as "Sugar"? Not surprisingly, the filmmakers had a bout with the Hays Office, which objected to the script's "overemphasis on sex" and "series of humorous but nevertheless, rather baldly suggestive events."[85] After a censor representative viewed a pre-release print, Fox was forced to make a number of cuts but left in a shot of Marsh's character dropping a key into the bodice of her dress as if to dare Roulien to find it.[86]

"It's Great to Be a Live Wire!" boasted ads for *It's Great to Be Alive*, which, not surprisingly, garnered wildly varying reactions in 1933. *The Hollywood Reporter* thought the first half made the film draggy, praised Oliver (1883–1942) as a "high spot," derided Roulien as "the world's greatest mugger," and, all in all, lauded it as "different" and "screamingly funny" in its central premise.[87] *The Film Daily* was strongly positive: "Bright, snappy entertainment with laughable dialogue, catchy tunes and pretty girls."[88] But the film tanked in New York and Los Angeles, the latter despite live opening-week appearances by Roulien and Mundin (1898–1939), and *Variety* dismissed it as "just a b.o. dud."[89] Reactions from exhibitors ran the gamut from "too silly" to "business very poor" to "patrons called it cute" and "good hot-weather picture."[90]

The New York Times criticized Roulien for his excessive "eye-rolling and shoulder-shrugging."[91] And an unbylined review from the *Philadelphia Inquirer* was even nastier:

> Mr. Roulien's performance, alas, creates no furore, nor is he even a particularly pleasant person to watch with his puffy cheeks, and his self-conscious manner, His speaking voice falls far less pleasantly upon the ear than did the early vocal efforts of John Gilbert. In all kindness, one would suggest that the Fox Company ... let Mr. Roulien go back to his roles in pictures made wholly for Spanish-speaking audiences.[92]

Roulien isn't as bad as all that, but his lack of pizazz is a problem for *It's Great to Be Alive*. Still, as the film began to hit theaters, Wurtzel and Stone announced plans for a second starring English-language musical for the actor,[93] but this was a rare piece of positive news during a key period for him. The Fox musical follow-up did not pan out, and Roulien signed up for what would be his most notable Hollywood film appearance, third-billed in RKO's *Flying Down to Rio* (1933). Unfortunately, in September 1933, while *It's Great to Be Alive* was in general release and *Flying Down to Rio* was being shot, Roulien's wife was killed in Hollywood after being hit by a car driven by John Huston, the screenwriter and future star director. In a case whispered to be unduly influenced by the defendant's actor father, Walter Huston, the parties settled in court in 1935. Roulien asked for $250,000 but received a reported $5,000.[94]

Rio was no triumph, either, for Roulien. His character was intended to be a rival of Gene Raymond for the affections of Dolores del Rio, but all three actors were overshadowed by the dazzling debut of the musical's secondary couple: Fred Astaire and Ginger Rogers. Roulien (1905–2000) eventually returned to Brazil to work as a television director, screen host, and journalist. When he died at age 94, it was not from masculitis, but pneumonia.

After a brief theatrical reissue in 1938, *It's Great to Be Alive* almost literally disappeared, with no television screenings in its future. However, the Museum of Modern Art in New York preserved the film from a rare nitrate print in its collection, and it was re-premiered there in July 2017 along with the silent *The Last Man on Earth*.[95] Of late, it has played to enthusiastic audiences on the classic-film convention circuit—including, in 2018, Capitolfest in Rome, New York, and Cinecon in Los Angeles. Had it been made by MGM, Warner Bros., or RKO—and thus likely televised at some point on TCM—*It's Great to Be Alive* might have become a cult favorite. Maybe it will become one yet.

2

They Don't Write 'Em Like That Anymore

"Now, you know the tune. But do you know who wrote it? Probably not. You see, that's the way it always is. You hear the songs, learn them and love them, but the man who created them is hidden behind that song. So now we're going to bring to you these great popular composers, so that you may meet the men who with their songs have given you so many happy moments."
—Norman Brokenshire, in *Melody Makers* with Sammy Fain, 1932

In the 1940s and '50s, the creators of the Great American Songbook became frequent fodder for Hollywood musicals. James Cagney as George M. Cohan! Cary Grant as Cole Porter! Robert Alda as George Gershwin! Mickey Rooney as Lorenz Hart! Movies about real-life songwriters were inevitable as, needing fresh material and feeding viewer-nostalgia pangs, studios turned to highly sanitized stories about famous and obscure men who happened to be gifted composers and lyricists. Bing Crosby biographer Gary Giddins has written half-seriously that, for their untruths about their subjects, especially regarding toned-down Jewishness and the straightening of complicated sexuality, these films merited a "special ring in hell."[1]

But in the 1930s, when these songsters were closer to their primes, or not long deceased, Hollywood was less inclined to mythologize them by name. This did not mean that the viewing public didn't know or care about Gershwin or Porter or even their lesser kin. Georgie Cohan was a true (and rare) equal-parts performer-writer hyphenate, so, even in career decline by the dawn of sound, he remained a person of interest. Duke Ellington and Paul Whiteman were songwriters who were more famous for performing. Irving Berlin didn't have to be a Cohan-like dynamo to be a luminary—he, as Jerome Kern famously said, *was* American music. In pre-rock era American pop, the song, as known by as composer, was generally considered more important than the performer of it. So even the less-heralded creators from Tin Pan Alley could gain non-movie followings via ample sheet music sales or dates on radio, where they could perform or discuss their works without having to be seen. Viewing the music men in the flesh only reminded audiences that they were mainly unexciting, plain, bookish types who cast their rhythmic spells despite their exterior lack of romance. New-media consumers might have asked, "How could this be?"

By safely relying on, or becoming mired in, backstage settings, early musicals immediately made the allure of American songwriters and songwriting into a reliable trope. The first audible fictional depictions of songsters revealed them as handsome, flashy, driven, even attractively amoral. In MGM's *Lord Byron of Broadway** (1930), this meant that the scribe played by Charles Kaley could build a career on hits inspired by his own life, or by exploiting tragedies of lost friends. Metro offered another young, ebullient womanizer in *Children of Pleasure* (1930), but only after converting his Semitic counterpart in the source play (*The Song Writer*, said to be inspired by Berlin's marriage to a WASP socialite) into an Irish American portrayed by Lawrence Gray. The deep thinker depicted by Phillips Holmes in Paramount's *Pointed Heels* (1929) agonizes whether to abandon his longhair composition in favor of stage-comedy pop that could fill his empty pocketbook and save his marriage (to Fay Wray ... thus, a worthy sacrifice). Meanwhile, Universal's *Moonlight and Pretzels** (1933) finds the pop poet played by Roger Pryor desperately pushing his next big show by telling a prospective financier that he has, in the can, "279 songs just to start with ... weather songs, moon songs, river songs, baby and mammy songs." The effort to make the fictional practice of songwriting interesting reached its most ridiculous with 1938's *Radio City Revels*, an RKO flop in which Bob "Bazooka" Burns plays a hick who can create tunes only when he's sleeping—greedy producers feverishly write down the notes and words he sings while reposing.

A looker such as Pryor could win professional favor on appearance alone, but this was at odds with the reality for tune scribes. This was evident long before the end of the first film-musical cycle, as the unfetching faces behind some of the world's most beautiful melodies turned out to be utilizable only in small doses. As part of their parade of vaudeville and opera performers, early Vitaphones trotted out *Joseph E. Howard, America's Popular Composer* and *Archie Gottler, His Songs Are Sung in a Million Homes* in one-reel shorts of 1928. In early 1930, Vitaphone teamed singing composer J. Fred Coots ("Doin' the Raccoon") and baseball pitcher-turned-stage tenor Waite Hoyt in a single-reel trifle; the pairing, originated in vaudeville, was short-lived and the movie, *A Battery of Songs*, was lost to posterity. For the 1929 two-reeler *Makers of Melody*, Paramount enlisted Richard Rodgers and Lorenz Hart to interact in framing material to renditions by Broadway actors of the duo's most famous songs. At one point in their recounting of their early days together, the two awkwardly joke about suicide seconds before being vocation- and life-saved by the inspiration to pen "I'll Take Manhattan." Given their lack of "it," *Makers of Melody* marked the first, and last, time Rodgers and Hart chatted in a scripted flicker.

Paramount also unearthed Charles K. Harris, the 62-year-old composer of "After the Ball," to be seen singing that Gay Nineties ballad in one of the studio's "Screen Songs" animated shorts. Harris, a year away from his death, smiles wistfully for the camera and asks, "Would you like to hear it? Well, I'm going to try and sing it to you. Of course, I haven't got a voice like Caruso, but the sentiment is still there!" He gamely croaks out a verse and the chorus before leaving it to his cartoon pals to bring the song home. In terms of time passed, seeing the Harris short upon its debut in 1929 would be akin to hearing Andrew Lloyd Webber recall "Memory" now—not really so far past. Harris was famous but not necessarily recognizable, so there was a true novelty factor for viewers, and his heyday seemed more distant at the outset of the Depression than the "Me" Decade of *Cats* would be in the Trumpian era.

Inclined to outsize, MGM shoehorned 10 composers and lyricists into *The Song Writers' Revue* (1930), which, publicity claimed, was inspired by a crap game of sorts on the studio lot in which staff songsters traded licks on the ivories.[2] Droll emcee Jack Benny, years away from easing into his vain and miserly radio persona, cajoles the participants into creating a popular tune on the spot from their on-stage pianos. "You don't need much of a vocabulary to write a song," Benny says as a challenge. The jumbled result, as reputedly assembled by Fred Fisher, Gus Edwards, the team of Arthur Freed and Nacio Herb Brown, and others viewed, unfortunately proves the host right. The 20-minute film is a fascinating novelty but reveals no hidden charisma among the songsmiths, some of whom show an uncertain display of spoken English that stands as a contrast to their mastery of music's universal language.

In 1932, the tiny Master Art Products company doubled down on the visual value of songwriters by debuting a series of "Melody Makers" one-reelers featuring Cliff Friend, Benny Davis, and Gus Edwards, among others, performing their own compositions. The series, which ran sporadically until 1935, led off by featuring future multiple-Oscar winner Sammy Fain at the piano for "Let a Smile Be Your Umbrella," and announcer Norman Brokenshire's introduction (which leads off this chapter) seemed to sum up the quandary in attempting to glorify regular-guy songsters.[3] That didn't stop Paramount from trying out a promising songster-to-performer duo in lyricist Mack Gordon and composer Harry Revel. The outgoing, corpulent Gordon, New York City-bred and originally an actor and singer in vaudeville, was the nominal front man; the quieter, English-born Revel retreated behind the piano. When the two weren't churning out melodies at a prolific rate, they were placed in small parts in features—*Sitting Pretty* (1933) and *Collegiate* (1936)—and, most notably, featured in their own one-reeler, *Hollywood Rhythm* (1934). The short is a promotional vehicle for the upcoming feature *College Rhythm*, with the composers assuring some of the latter film's principals (actors Jack Oakie and Lyda Roberti, director Norman Taurog, and dance director LeRoy Prinz appear) that their new songs will earn a passing grade. All that remains is Gordon and Revel to sweat out the completion of their latest score. With a pleasing tenor and ingratiating patter, Gordon might have represented a missed opportunity as a screen singer and comic (even with his avoirdupois). But, then, who would have written "Did You Ever See a Dream Walking?"?

Although real songwriters continued to cameo in shorts and features, it would have to be left to fictionalized depictions to make the real men appealing. One strategy was for studios to retreat into the distant past and go Euro. Unremembered now, Fox's semi-musical *Love Time* (1934) became known in its time as the program romance that ended the Hollywood career of German star Lilian Harvey—who refused to emote for it—and not for any entertainment value. Reviewers conceded Nils Asther his good looks but praised little else in his unrealistic portrayal of the sickly Franz Schubert.[4] MGM fared much better in 1938 with *The Great Waltz* [q.v.], a classical follow-up to its box-office-friendly impresario-bio *The Great Ziegfeld*, which won the 1936 Best Picture Oscar and sparked a trend toward show-business biopics in general. As a Hollywood conception of Austria's Johann Strauss II, Fernand Gravey was no William Powell.

Harmony Lane (1935) was a failed effort by a Poverty Row studio to bring to film the life of Stephen Foster—finally, one of our own. The first acknowledged feature-length personal tribute to a 20th century American music master didn't arrive until late in the decade, and the effort began with the Great One: Irving Berlin. *Alexander's Ragtime Band* (1938) was initially intended as a full-fledged biopic (the term "biopic" hadn't been invented) of the title song's revered creator, but it was ultimately based on an original story written by Berlin about a musician billed as Alexander. The project, two years in the making, began as an inspiration of 20th Century–Fox chief Darryl F. Zanuck to lift the Hollywood musical from the general perception that it was in the doldrums. This was partly because of a sluggish economy and competition from radio. But also there was, as *Variety* termed it, a glut of "clambake musicals"—big backstagers dependent more on flashy production values than book and characterization. As befitting a mogul, Zanuck thought the answer to the surfeit of spectacle was to make another one—but with the then-considered-novel aim of beginning (*Variety* again) "a cycle of pictures built around or using the title of pop tunes whose popularity has persisted over the years and which also lend themselves to dramatic treatment."[5] And who persisted more masterfully than Irving Berlin?

Despite its lack of new music, *Alexander's Ragtime Band* was a smash, and once Hollywood had put its toe in the water for the subgenre that would come to be known as "jukebox musicals," there was more splashing. Paramount issued two more songwriter-tribute prototypes before the 1930s closed. *The Star Maker* hedged, as had the Berlin picture, by casting a major star in a highly fictionalized version of its subject, but *The Great Victor Herbert* at least included someone answering to the name of Victor Herbert. In the decade's final days, Fox sought to duplicate its *Alexander* success by bringing out Don Ameche, one of the previous picture's stars, as Stephen Foster (or a facsimile thereof) in *Swanee River*.

Within three years, we'd get Cagney as Cohan, and the hellacious future was cast. Not surprisingly, the biggest proponent of American-composer musicals was Zanuck. As part of a swath of 1940s and '50s backstage biopics of figures from throughout showbiz, and frequently in league with his longtime colleague and producer George Jessel, Zanuck and 20th Century–Fox brought to the screens depictions of such tunesmiths as Ernest R. Ball (*Irish Eyes Are Smiling*), Joseph E. Howard (*I Wonder Who's Kissing Her Now*), Fred Fisher (*Oh, You Beautiful Doll*), Paul Dresser (*My Gal Sal*), and, inevitably, John Philip Sousa (*Stars and Stripes Forever*). These films eliminated or soft-played their subjects' ethnic ties as if, as Zanuck biographer George F. Custen has written, "all Americans sprang fully socialized from a small town in the Midwest."[6]

Here, we'll look at some of the trend-forming films, plus a trio of adjuncts: a Gilbert-and-Sullivan jukebox musical from Poverty Row and two RKO programmers in which one of the greatest of all songsmiths took stabs at non-cameo emoting. Johnny Mercer as a college boy? Only in the movies.

Harmony Lane
(Mascot/Republic; August 28, 1935)

and *Swanee River*
(20th Century–Fox; December 30, 1939)

Harmony Lane

Director: Joseph Santley. Producer: Nat Levine. Supervisor: Colbert Clark. Screenplay: Elizabeth Meehan, Joseph Santley. Story: Milton Krims. Photography: Ernest Miller, Jack Marta. Editors: Ray Curtiss, Joseph H. Lewis. Musical Director: Arthur Kay. Sound: Terry Kellum. Running Time: 84 minutes.

Cast: Douglass Montgomery (Stephen Foster); Evelyn Venable (Susan Pentland); Adrienne Ames (Jane McDowell); Joseph Cawthorn (Professor Henry Kleber); William Frawley (Edwin P. Christy); David Torrence (Mr. Pentland), Gilbert Emery (Mr. Foster); Lloyd Hughes (Andrew Robinson); Al Herman (Tambo); Cora Sue Collins (Marion Foster); James Bush (Morrison Foster); Florence Roberts (Mrs. Foster); Ferdinand Munier (Mr. Pond); Clarence Muse (Old Joe); Victor DeCamp (William Foster, Jr.); Edith Craig (Henrietta Foster); Mildred Gover (Delia); James B. Carson (proprietor); Rodney Hildebrand (Mr. Wade); Mary MacLaren (Mrs. Wade); Earl Hodgins (Bones); Hattie McDaniel (Liza); Wynne Davis (singer); The Famous Shaw Negro Choir [Frieta Shaw Ethiopian Chorus].

Songs: "Beautiful Dreamer" [Montgomery], "De Camptown Races" [Montgomery], "Come Where My Love Lies Dreaming" [female trio], "Lou'siana Belle" [minstrel chorus], "My Old Kentucky Home" [female chorus], "Oh! Susanna" [Montgomery, choruses], "Old Black Joe" [children's chorus], "Old Folks at Home" ("Swanee River") [Montgomery], "Why No One to Love?" [Frawley] (Stephen Foster);

"Didn't My Lord Deliver Daniel?" [Muse, Shaw choir] (trad.); "Every Time I Feel the Spirit" [Muse, Shaw choir] (trad.); "Give Me That Old Time Religion" [Muse, Shaw choir] (trad.).
Home Video: Alpha DVD.

The Story: In 1848 Pennsylvania, young composer Stephen Foster gains inspiration from hearing black spirituals in services led by Old Joe. Stephen is in love with Susan Pentland, whose name inspires a new composition, "Oh! Susanna." Stephen's father disapproves of his son's music and sends him away to work for his brother's steamship company. Susan marries Andrew Robinson, and a depressed Stephen falls into drink even though his career is starting to thrive. E.P. Christy, leader of a famous minstrel show, takes credit for Stephen's music after buying it for paltry sums. Stephen marries Jane McDowell, but she disapproves of minstrelsy and complains about their lack of funds. Stephen mourns the death of Old Joe, who inspires "Old Black Joe." Susan explains to Stephen that they were forced apart by Jane's influence, and Jane correctly accuses Stephen of still loving Susan. Stephen and Jane have a child, Marion, but the couple separate and Stephen moves to New York. Stephen's music falls out of vogue with publishers, and he is beset by financial and drinking problems. In 1863, Foster writes "Beautiful Dreamer" but, needing cash quickly, agrees to sell it for $25. Stephen's old music teacher, Kleber, and Christy arrange a benefit performance for their ill, impoverished friend. It comes too late for the dying Foster, who has one final meeting with Susan.

Swanee River

Director: Sidney Lanfield. Associate Producer: Kenneth Macgowan. Screenplay: John Taintor Foote, Philip Dunne. Photography: Bert Glennon. Editor: Louis R. Loeffler. Art Directors: Richard Day, Joseph C. Wright. Set Decorator: Thomas Little. Costumes: Royer. Musical Director: Louis Silvers. Dance Direction: Nick Castle, Geneva Sawyer. Sound: W.D. Flick, Roger Heman. Technicolor Director: Natalie Kalmus. Assistant Director: Aaron Rosenberg. Running Time: 85 minutes. Technicolor.
Cast: Don Ameche (Stephen Foster); Andrea Leeds (Jane); Al Jolson (Edwin P. Christy); Felix Bressart (Henry Kleber); Richard Clarke (Tom Harper); Chick Chandler (Bones); Russell Hicks (Dr. Andrew McDowell); George Reed (Old Joe); Diane Fisher (Marion Foster); George Breakston (Ambrose); The Hall Johnson Choir (choral ensemble); Al Herman (Tambo); Charles Trowbridge (William Foster); George Meeker (Henry Foster); Leona Roberts (Mrs. Foster); Charles Tannen (Morrison Foster); Clara Blandick (Mrs. Griffin); Nella Walker (Mrs. McDowell); Georgia Caine (Ann Rowan); Thaddeus Jones (Dan); Harry Strang (mate); Harry Tyler (pianist); Georgie Billings (office boy); James C. Morton, James Blaine (bartenders); Robert Homans (sheriff); Bruce Mitchell (jailer); Ruth Clifford (governess); Jesse Graves (servant); Daisy Lee Mothershed (maid); Hal K. Dawson (drunken man on riverboat); Robert Emmett Keane (drunken man in café); Edward Earle (master of ceremonies at Christy concert); Edward LeSaint (Jonathan Fry); Mae Marsh (Mrs. Fry); Bruce Warren (orchestra leader); David Newell, Harry Denny, Jean Houghton (guests); Lloyd Whitlock, Forbes Murray (critics); Claire DuBrey (angry woman in café); Herbert Rawlinson (Army officer in café); Harry Depp (dresser); William Newell (stage manager); Dora Clement (nurse); Wright Kramer (doctor); Arthur Rankin (clerk); Selmer Jackson (Army medical examiner); Gladden James (hotel clerk); Tom Seidel (bellboy); Cecil Weston (landlady); John Hamilton (doctor); Bert Moorhouse (attendant); George Magrill, Jack Perry, Billy Wayne (agitators); George O'Hanlon (ticket taker at Christy concert); Larry Steers (older man on riverboat); Les Clark (specialty dancer).
Songs: "De Camptown Races" [Jolson, chorus], "Here Comes the Heavin' Line" [Hall Johnson Choir], "Jeanie with the Light Brown Hair" [Ameche], "My Old Kentucky Home" [Ameche, Jolson, chorus, reprised by Fisher], "Oh! Susanna" [Ameche on piano, reprised by Jolson], "Old Black Joe" [Hall Johnson Choir], "Old Folks at Home" ("Swanee River") [Jolson, chorus], "Ring, Ring de Banjo" [Ameche, orchestra] (Stephen Foster).
Academy Award Nomination: Best Music, Scoring (Louis Silvers).
Home Video: 20th Century-Fox DVD.

The Story: Stephen Foster, a young man from Pennsylvania, courts Jane McDowell, a miss from Kentucky, whose father disapproves of Stephen's attempt to make a living from the *writing of popular songs. When Stephen's family experiences financial troubles, Stephen is asked by his father and brothers to take a job as a shipping clerk in Cincinnati. In desperation, Stephen sells the rights to his latest work, "Oh! Susanna," to minstrel-show impresario E.P. Christy for $15 and allows Christy to take the songwriting credit. Discouraged, Stephen nearly ends his romance with Jane, but Christy encourages him to write songs for the showman's productions under his own name ("De Camptown Races"). Foster goes on tour with the minstrels, and when Christy falls asleep during a performance in Chicago and cannot perform, Foster takes the stage himself to sing "My Old Kentucky Home." By 1852, that song and other triumphs allow Stephen and Jane to marry. To curry favor with Jane after a disagreement, Stephen is inspired to write "Jeanie with the Light Brown Hair." However, the Fosters' daughter, Marion, is born while Stephen is getting drunk in a saloon. The death of Uncle Joe, the McDowell family's faithful servant, prompts Stephen to pen "Old Black Joe." The Civil War breaks out, and Stephen attempts to join the Army, but is privately told he has a weak heart. As Stephen's drinking worsens, Jane leaves her husband, and he lives alone in obscurity, his creativity stilled, as a piano player in a New York City saloon. Stephen's music goes out of style as old-fashioned, and he is viewed in the North as a Southern sympathizer. Jane returns to Stephen and encourages him to write "Old Folks at Home." The song is to be debuted on stage by Christy and his men, but before the performance, Foster dies at home from a heart attack. Christy sings "Old Folks at Home" in tribute to his fallen friend.*

Might a dreary little offering from dinky Mascot Pictures stand as Hollywood's first "official" songwriter bio-musical? It well might.[7] But *Harmony Lane*—a remembrance of Stephen Foster, the composer long heralded as "The Father of American Music" despite his early death at age 37—is as low on accuracy as in budget. It stands, comparatively ignored, in the wake of 20th Century–Fox's costlier, starrier, and even more inaccurate Foster opus, *Swanee River*. The 85 minutes of *Swanee River* go down a little easier than the 84 of *Harmony Lane*, but one comes away making fewer excuses for the more-modest effort.

Swanee River set its course only four years after *Harmony Lane*, but it wasn't as if the public had tired of Stephen Collins Foster. Seven decades after his death, Foster remained a seminal figure in American culture with his inventory of sentimental, Southern-flavored songs. To 21st century sensibilities, the glorification of music strongly inspired by black spirituals with undertones of racial subjugation may seem incomprehensible, but it kept a powerful hold on society in the early decades of the 20th century. As Foster historian Ken Emerson has written, the composer "fascinated ... the Jewish immigrants and sons of immigrants who embraced and transformed" American popular song: "Not only did Foster symbolize the American identity they were eager to assimilate, but also, as the first American composer to support himself ... from the sales of his sheet music, Foster blazed the trail that eventually led to Tin Pan Alley."[8] The title that opens *Harmony Lane* is more succinct, citing Foster as "the man who wrote the songs which will ever live in our hearts."

The romanticizing of Foster wasn't confined to the creative community. In the Depression years, many living Americans could remember Foster's music when it was relatively new. His influence remained especially potent in the South, of course: Even though 20 or so of Foster's more than 200 compositions were expressly written for the minstrel shows that helped make his name, most of his other works were classical-inspired parlor songs. Kentucky made Foster's "My Old Kentucky Home" its official state song in 1928, and Florida did the same with his "Old Folks at Home" (aka "Swanee River") in 1935. To traditionalists in that region especially, this music evoked nostalgia for the era of slavery. No one could deny that the specifics of Foster's life—artistic success offset by under-appreciation, purported alcoholism, pennilessness, and, in 1864, earthly demise—made for potentially great drama on screen. It was another asset that his music was in the public domain, thus saving any company committing it to celluloid the customary performance costs.

Harmony Lane, the initial screen treatment of Foster's life, was one of the final productions of Mascot—and the first to go out under the trademark of Republic Pictures, the company into which Mascot was merged just before the film hit theaters. Director Joseph Santley and two other screenwriters unfortunately saw fit to add more drama than even Foster deserved. The script attributes his depression and death as much to a failed romance—a love triangle that seems to have no basis in history—as the perils of drink and unjust publishing-industry economics. The frustrated sweethearts are more than adequately played by Douglass Montgomery and Evelyn Venable. Montgomery (1907–1966), best known at this point for his pairings with the likes of Katharine Hepburn (in *Little Women*) and Joan Crawford (*Paid*), had just scored in Universal's *Mystery of Edwin Drood*. An actor of strong sensitivity, he works earnestly to overcome the script deficiencies in *Harmony Lane*. Mainly he is successful, although not so while in pasty makeup in the lachrymose final scenes as the dying protagonist. He doesn't sing well—as a pro like Lanny Ross, who was initially slated for the role, would have—but it doesn't matter much. The contrast between the two women in Foster's life—his demure, angelic lost love and his selfish, snooty wife (Adrienne Ames)—is depicted in terms too stark even for a standard screen bio.

Another problem: Santley presents too much of the music in fragmented, backgrounded form, an exception being an entertaining rendition of "Oh! Susanna." It begins as Foster works out the lyrics in his head (a process that the film shows him doing multiple

Mascot's ambitious *Harmony Lane* spotlighted Douglass Montgomery (upper left) as composer Stephen Foster and Joseph Cawthorn as Foster's mentor.

times) and is picked up by a series of ensembles—an American stage quartet, a group of slaves, students in Germany, a chanteuse in France—showing the spread of the song worldwide. The script also offers a tired theme of highbrow versus lowbrow music, as personified in a German-born professor, played by Joseph Cawthorn and based on Foster's real mentor, Henry Kleber, who implores Foster to write symphonies instead of popular fare.

On the plus side, William Frawley, as egotistical minstrel man E.P. Christy, whose shows most famously spotlighted Foster's music, gets to sing a little and provide some exuberance.[9] The film also benefits from a well-made montage of images depicting Foster's decline. This fictionalized Foster derives some of his ample guilt from his acknowledged debt to black folk, especially the aged Joe (Clarence Muse), the mentor and symbol of his people, to whom the youthful composer confesses to "trying to steal a song out of your hearts.... I owe you a lot more." When the older man dies, Foster writes "Old Black Joe" in tribute. For many moviegoers in 1935, much less in our day, this likely wasn't compensation enough.

Even for those who see Foster as an antebellum Benny Goodman, Elvis, or Eminem, crossing racial lines to popularize a music genre for the masses, *Harmony Lane* has not aged well. Mass-market reviewers noted that its appeal was generationally based: "Mae Tinée" of the *Chicago Tribune* noted that the younger generation would "pronounce it mawkish and curl a lip" while older folks would believe that "the tender music which recalls a flood memories makes up for deficiencies."[10] Compliments in African American newspapers were mainly confined to Clarence Muse's work. In its day, however, *Harmony Lane* garnered some praise, and not just because it was considered auspicious for an outfit like Mascot. Publications targeted to potential exhibitors were most laudatory, with *The Film Daily* praising "an outstanding production ... in authentic biography on the screen," "dramatic screen material in its purest form," and "one picture in a thousand."[11]

Even more effusive was Mo Wax, editor and publisher of the *Independent Exhibitors Film Bulletin*—a sheet, not coincidentally, targeted to owners of the same tier of theaters Poverty Row films were most likely to play. He wrote in a column:

> Viewing a film in the cold, unresponsive emptiness of a projection room is unfair and I usually avoid it. But, when I was asked in New York last week to look at *Harmony Lane,* my curiosity prevailed and I entered one of those tiny, two-by-four rooms ... where you sit at the very base of the screen, with a sound horn half way in one of your ears.
>
> But, I heard a man cry in that projection room! When the picture ended, he sat there, his handkerchief to his eyes, sobbing. He was, as far as I know, a veteran of countless film sob stories, but he wept like a woman over scenes on celluloid. *Harmony Lane* will do that to people![12]

Harmony Lane couldn't do much for Mascot, which, along with the original Monogram company and other small companies, was merged into Republic Pictures. Years later, Republic considered Foster still important enough—and PD-cheap musically—for a third screen biography, *I Dream of Jeanie*. Little-known Bill Shirley, Muriel Lawrence, and Eileen Christy played another highly fictionalized Foster and his two sweeties, but Shirley and the rest of the cast were upstaged by Ray Middleton's portrayal of E.P. Christy. This came out in 1952, and times would change soon (bye, bye, blackface). Not surprisingly, *Harmony Lane* has not fared well in retrospect. In his seminal 1982 book about Mascot, historian Jon Tuska not surprisingly dismissed one of the studio's most promising projects for its excessive "vulgar sentimentality" and reduction of Foster's life to "a series of song cues."[13]

One might say the same about the reductive song cues in *Swanee River*, but at least 20th Century–Fox toned down the sentiment as it turned up the visual quality from black-and-white to glorious Technicolor, and with one of the hottest leading men in Hollywood in 1939. Don Ameche, the new Stephen Foster, was already known for his roles in period musicals (*In Old Chicago, The Three Musketeers,* and *Alexander's Ragtime Band* [q.v.]) and the non-musical bio *The Story of Alexander Graham Bell*. Ameche (1908–1993) so ably played the telephone inventor that now it was said, by one fan-mag profiler, that "children who used to go to school to study history now go to the movies to study Ameche."[14] Watching Ameche play a mustached, debonair Foster points up the difference between him and Douglass Montgomery. One is a movie star with an external acting flair; the other is a character lead who plays more internally—think Tom Cruise versus Sean Penn. Ameche was paired with Andrea Leeds, who was borrowed by Fox from Samuel Goldwyn after her Oscar-nominated performance as the doomed wannabe actress in *Stage Door* (1937).[15] Her effective work in *Swanee River* did not lead to better screen opportunities; she got married shortly after filming and retired from acting at age 25.

In January 1939, David O. Selznick announced intentions to make *Swanee River* as a Foster bio.[16] Perhaps because Selznick had his hands full with *Gone with the Wind*, the project went to TCF, where chief Darryl Zanuck envisioned another pairing of *Alexander's Ragtime Band* lead Tyrone Power and director Henry King.[17] But it was Ameche instead of Power and Sidney Lanfield directing a screenplay credited to novelist John Taintor Foote and Fox mainstay Philip Dunne. Lanfield took his company of more than 100 actors and technicians to the Sacramento River region to shoot exteriors in August 1939. Hopes were high, as *Swanee River* was one of four Technicolor specials then in or near production for

Down-and-out music man Stephen Foster (Don Ameche) gets encouragement from colleague E.P. Christy (Al Jolson) in the Fox biopic *Swanee River*.

Fox, the others being *Hollywood Cavalcade* (Ameche with Alice Faye), *Drums Along the Mohawk* (Claudette Colbert-Henry Fonda), and *The Blue Bird* (Shirley Temple). The Foster bio was set to premiere at the end of the year, in competition with the proto-blockbuster *GWTW*.

The third co-star of *Swanee River* was Al Jolson, a natural choice to play the blackface showman E.P. Christy. In what would turn out to be his last major credited film role, Jolson (1886–1950) gets to lead three numbers, including the closing title song, and provide highlights with dialogue such as the in-jokey "If there's anything I hate in a man, it's an inflated ego!" Christy's presence at the tear-jerking but invented climax, after Foster's death, was pointed to as one of the film's historical fibs—the real minstrel man had thrown himself out a window two years prior. Another liberty was making Foster, with Ameche's light but pleasant baritone, a performer as well as song scribe. The actor sings "Jeanie with the Light Brown Hair," "My Old Kentucky Home," and "Ring, Ring de Banjo." Meanwhile, Felix Bressart, as Henry Kleber, and George Reed, as the slave who inspires "Old Black Joe," compare unfavorably to their livelier *Harmony Lane* counterparts. Foster's final important composition, "Beautiful Dreamer," is frequent in the underscoring but is not presented vocally.

Swanee River adopts the conventional view, propagated by Foster's surviving family, that he was an untutored genius who lapsed into disfavor partly due to the perception that he was firmly a Southern sympathizer during the Civil War. Modern scholars, however, believe that the composer's personal politics were more complicated and even pro–Union/anti-slavery. That the latter would be the actual attitude of the songwriter who did so much to mythologize the Old South would not do.[18] Even with its adherence to accepted truth and its matinee-idol star, however, *Swanee River* does not stint on footage of the hero's decline, although it wrongly attributes Foster's death to a weak heart and not the ravages of alcohol and/or squalor. This was in line with Zanuck's view, expressed in an intra-studio memo, that "we must fight every minute from letting this become a depressing story.... We must root for Foster—create a pull for the finish."[19]

Despite this soft-pedaling of Foster's alcohol problem, Zanuck and TCF were targeted by music teachers nationwide for even mentioning that personal shortcoming. Edwin N.C. Barnes, a Washington, D.C., educator who was executive secretary of the Stephen Foster Memorial Foundation, complained in one of an avalanche of letters sent to the studio: "Must the record of Foster's later years be used to smear both his name and his songs in the eyes of America's children?"[20] Zanuck might have responded that *Swanee River* had redeemed Foster by showing him drink-free in creating his final great work, the title song (aka "Old Folks at Home"), although this was historically inaccurate, as that song was birthed in 1851.

Swanee River did good business, even surpassing the opening returns in New York's Roxy theater of its storied predecessor *Alexander's Ragtime Band*; the New Year's Eve weekend business helped. Perhaps influenced by regency bias, *The Hollywood Reporter* lauded it as "about the best blending of story and song the sound screen has ever had."[21] *Variety* praised the "excellent color and showmanly [sic] presentation" but was un-enamored with the "cumbersome" story.[22] Not everyone was so impressed. The sage, exhibitor-minded *Harrison's Reports* unfavorably compared *Swanee River* to *Harmony Lane*, asserting that the newer movie had sacrificed the humanity of Foster's story in favor of a more technically lavish presentation. "I am not making this comparison to disparage Mr. Zanuck's efforts," opined *Harrison*'s editor-publisher P.S. Harrison, "but merely to show that lavish expenditure of money does not always mean better results."[23]

And, besides, *Swanee River* didn't make a man cry in a projection room!

Old Man Rhythm
(RKO; August 2, 1935)

and *To Beat The Band*
(RKO; November 8, 1935)

Old Man Rhythm

Director: Edward Ludwig. Associate Producer: Zion Myers. Screenplay: Sig Herzig, Ernest Pagano. Story: Lewis Gensler, Sig Herzig, Don Hartman. Additional Dialogue: H.W. Hanemann. Photography: Nicholas Musuraca. Editor: George Crone. Musical Director: Roy Webb. Song Numbers Staged By: Sam White. Dance Director: Hermes Pan. Art Director: Van Nest Polglase. Associate Art Director: Perry Ferguson. Sound: John Tribby. Music Recordist: P.J. Faulkner, Jr. Running Time: 76 minutes.

Cast: Charles "Buddy" Rogers (Johnny Roberts); George Barbier (John Roberts, Sr.); Barbara Kent (Edith Warren); Grace Bradley (Marion Beecher); Betty Grable (Sylvia); Eric Blore (Phillips); Erik Rhodes (Frank Rochet); John Arledge (Pinky Parker); Johnny Mercer (Colonel); Donald Meek (Paul Parker); Evelyn Poe (Honey); Dave Chasen (Andy); Joy Hodges (Lois); Douglas Fowley (Oyster); Margaret Nearing (Margaret); Ronald Graham (Ronald); Sonny Lamont (Blimp); Bill Carey (Bill); Tom Kennedy (college guard); Bess Flowers (secretary); Frank Edmunds (dancer); Lucille Ball, Virginia Reid [Lynne Carver], Jane Hamilton, Maxine Jennings, Kay Sutton (college girls); Carlyle Blackwell, Jr., Claude Gillingwater, Jr., Erich von Stroheim, Jr., Kenneth Howell (college boys).

Songs: "Boys Will Be Boys, Girls Will Be Girls" [Grable, Hodges, Poe, Bradley, Graham, Arledge, Kent, chorus], "Comes the Revolution, Baby" [Mercer, Poe, chorus; danced by Grable, Lamont], "I Never Saw a Better Night" [Rogers, Bradley, Mercer, Fowley, Arledge], "Old Man Rhythm" [Bradley, Grable, Nearing, Hodges, Graham, Mercer, Carey, Poe; danced by Lamont, Frank Edmunds; reprised by company], "There's Nothing Like a College Education" [Grable, Hodges, Arledge, Fowley, Nearing, Carey, Lamont, Mercer, Blore, Poe, chorus] (Johnny Mercer, Lewis Gensler).

Working Title: *Papa's in the Cradle*.
Home Video: Warner Archive DVD.

The Story: Fairfield College welcomes students for a new semester ("There's Nothing Like a College Education"), among them Johnny Parker, son of the co-owner of a New York doll manufacturing company. Word gets back to Johnny's father, John, Sr., that his son is spending more time on glamorous Marion Beecher than on his less-flashy longtime girlfriend, Edith Warren, or his studies. The elder Roberts is embroiled in a fight over majority control of his company with partner Frank Rochet, but he takes time out to enroll as a Fairfield freshman to monitor his son's studies and social life. John, Sr., is advised by fellow frosh Pinky Parker— whose father, Paul, is the doll company's business manager—to write a letter pretending that the doll company is bankrupt in order to fool Marion about Johnny's financial status. Although the letter is not sent, the company really does begin to fail, and Rochet and Paul Parker hasten to Fairfield to convince John, Sr., to leave college or give up the company. Marion threatens to leave school over her quarrel with the elder Roberts, but Johnny makes up with her ("I Never Saw a Better Night"). At a school dance ("Old Man Rhythm"), with Marion within earshot, the elder Parker pretends to agree to a buyout, without knowing the offer from Rochet is genuine. Marion, thinking Johnny is soon to be broke, leaves him, and John, Sr., saves his business.

To Beat the Band

Director: Ben Stoloff. Associate Producer: Zion Myers. Screenplay: Rian James. Story: George Marion, Jr. Photography: Nicholas Musuraca. Editor: George Crone. Musical Director: Alberto Colombo. Song Numbers Staged By: Sam White. Art Director: Van Nest Polglase. Associate Art Director: Perry

Ferguson. Sound: John Tribby. Music Recordist: P.J. Faulkner, Jr. Costumes: Walter Plunkett. Assistant Director: Kenny Holmes. Running Time: 67 minutes.
Cast: Hugh Herbert (Hugo Twist/Elizabeth Twist); Helen Broderick (Freeda McCrary); Roger Pryor (Larry Barry); Fred Keating (Fred Carson); Eric Blore (Hawkins); Phyllis Brooks (Rowena); Evelyn Poe (Barbara Shelby); Johnny Mercer (member of band); Ray Mayer (McCrory); Joy Hodges (Ruth Harper); The Original California Collegians (themselves); Sonny Lamont (dancer); Nick Condos (solo dancer); Ronald Graham (singer in Harper band); Torben Meyer (headwaiter); Willie Best (elevator operator); Monte Collins (morgue worker); Harry Holman (irked nightclub patron); Eddie Featherstone (man knocked down in nightclub); Virginia Reid [Lynne Carver] ("Miss America 1936").
Songs: "Eeny, Meeny, Miney, Mo" [Poe, Mercer, Graham, Collegians], "I Saw Her at Eight O'Clock" [Keating, Mercer, Poe, Collegians, Herbert, Brooks, Blore], "If You Were Mine" [Pryor, Collegians], "Meet Miss America" [Hodges, Mercer, Lamont, Graham, Collegians; danced by Contos], "Santa Claus Came in the Spring" [Pryor]; "What's the Use of Living?" [Graham] (Johnny Mercer, Matty Malneck).
Working Title: *If You Were Mine*.
Home Video: Warner Archive DVD.

The Story: Klutzy socialite Hugo Twist talks his upstairs neighbor, Larry Barry, out of a suicide leap over financial difficulties, then learns from his lawyer, Freeda McCreery, that he is about to inherit the $59 million fortune of his Aunt Elizabeth. The catch is that Hugo must marry a widow within three days; otherwise, the money will be awarded to bandleader Fred Carson and his players. Hugo is engaged to the beautiful, young Rowena, so Larry offers to help by marrying Rowena and then committing suicide so she will become a widow. Larry falls in love with Rowena ("Santa Claus Came in the Spring") and is reluctant to carry out his part of the bargain. Seeking a $1 million cut of the inheritance, Freeda informs Carson of the will, and he and his band shadow Larry to keep the latter from killing himself ("What's the Use of Living?"/"Eeny, Meeny, Miney, Mo"). Now deciding to seek the entire $59 million, Freeda tells Hugo's valet, Hawkins, she will pay him $10,000 to sway Hugo's attentions to Freeda, who really is a widow. Rowena and Larry pledge true love ("If You Were Mine"). At a nightclub concert, Hugo marries Freeda ("Miss America 1936"), then Elizabeth appears, saying her "death" was a ruse. Fred and band lose a big check, and Freeda is stuck with Hugo.

Johnny Mercer came to Hollywood in 1935 as a "triple threat"—songwriter, actor, and singer. The Southern gentleman began at RKO by appearing in a pair of low-budget musical comedies, *Old Man Rhythm* and *To Beat the Band*, that were enough to prove that his greatest talent was as a tunesmith. The man who became one of the greatest lyricists of his generation, or any other, proved to be just another guy in these two pictures—his only screen acting credits.

Mercer (1909–1976) was already starting to make a name for himself when RKO signed him in May 1935. He was known for his lyrics of such hits as "Pardon My Southern Accent" (reflecting his background in Savannah, Georgia), "Lazybones," and "If I Had a Million Dollars." In 1932, he won a "Youth of America" talent contest that led to a job as vocalist, lyricist, emcee, and sketch writer for Paul Whiteman's mega-popular band—a "utility fielder," as the versatile Mercer described himself.[24] Among his songwriting partners with the Whiteman unit was violinist Matt Malneck, who would figure into Mercer's early film career. With a 13-week RKO pact at a reported $750 per, Mercer welcomed the opportunity to settle down in one place for a while with his young wife.[25] But not everyone who registered with the public on the concert stage or via radio waves could click on the big screen, as Mercer was about to find out.

As talented as he was, Mercer wasn't going to start out at the top even within the RKO musical hierarchy. Instead of being assigned to one of the studio's prestigious Fred Astaire-Ginger Rogers pictures, he was placed under the charge of producer Zion Myers. Myers was a production associate on two Astaire-Rogers features, *The Gay Divorcee* and

Roberta, but he was a longtime comedy specialist, with past and future collaborators including Buster Keaton and the Three Stooges. Most inauspiciously, he wrote and directed a series of talking-dog two-reelers for MGM in 1929–31. Myers now had his own unit at RKO, and its first project, filmed in May and June of 1935, was *Old Man Rhythm*, another of those rah-rah college musicals.

With Mercer's lyrics set to music in five songs by Broadway and film veteran Lewis Gensler, *Old Man Rhythm* was sold as the return to the screen by Charles "Buddy" Rogers. The eternal "America's Boyfriend" had foresworn picture work two years prior in favor of Broadway roles and, subsequently, touring with his own dance band.[26] Rogers (1904–1999) had an underpowered tenor, but he was a legit musician who had cut his talkie teeth in musicals. If he was out of place in *Old Man Rhythm*, it was because he was, at 30, not exactly college age. Corpulent character man George Barbier played Rogers' father in the generation-gap story, and young talents Grace Bradley, Betty Grable, Barbara Kent, 270-pound dancer Sonny Lamont, and pop singers Joy Hodges and Evelyn Poe joined older funsters Eric Blore, Erik Rhodes, Donald Meek, and Dave Chasen in the cast for director Edward Ludwig.

Grable, then a vocalist for Ted Fio-Rito's band, had heretofore struggled for attention as glorified blond set decoration who could sing and dance a little. In 1935, she was known more as the girlfriend—and then the fiancée—of Jackie Coogan than for anything she did in *Old Man Rhythm* or any other picture. Chasen (1898–1973) was a vaudeville comic (and former pantomiming stooge of headliner Joe Cook) before retiring in 1936 to run the Los

Before he was renowned as one of America's greatest songwriters, Johnny Mercer was little more than a background player (far right) in RKO's *To Beat the Band*, with Roger Pryor (bottom left), Fred Keating (center) and Evelyn Poe.

Angeles restaurant that bore his surname. He's in *OMR* only to look goofy. Hodges (1915–2003), sang with multiple big bands and on Broadway but became best known as a key contact for Ronald Reagan in his quest to break into movies. Hermes Pan took time out from the Astaire-Rogers *Top Hat* to stage the dances for *Old Man Rhythm*, and somewhere among the co-eds was a blond background player named Lucille Ball.

Myers made do with what he had, which wasn't a lot, and that impressed the man from Savannah:

> The studio gave him only leftovers, and, suffering multitudinous setbacks in every department, he still kept cheerful while he watched his staff putting together one of the most old-fashioned college movies ever made. This in spite of the fact that he, or somebody, had been smart enough to have among the bit players and extras running around the campus both Lucille Ball and Betty Grable.[27]

With a character named "Colonel," Mercer was destined to make light of his geographic heritage, which he did in the opening number, "There's Nothing Like a College Education."[28] The tune, set aboard a train bound for the passengers' college, serves as a mini-primer of most of the characters, who sing joyously ... except for the carefree young man played by Mercer, who is plainly irked from having to end his slumber atop a luggage rack. Mercer's own penned words describe his fictional self as an "A" student in love-making because "I satisfy!" with Southern hospitality. There is, as you'd expect, some clever wordplay, here having to do with the terms "sprechen" and "checkin'" as they pertain to Yankee-style academia.

The Colonel's spoken output consists of a few uninspired wisecracks, so Mercer's only other highlights are in music that puts his off-the-cuff vocal style to good use. In "I Never Saw a Better Night," the focus of which is the discord of the central Rogers-Bradley romance, Mercer joins John Arledge and Douglas Fowley in pajamas as they serenade their respective tootsies in a dormitory courtyard before they are sent back to their room by a campus guard. Even better, Mercer joins his designated girlfriend, played by Evelyn Poe, in a duet, "Comes the Revolution, Baby," a bluesy love song that doubles as a gentle dig at campus political rebellion and gives the duo a modest dance showcase. Poe, a pint-sized, curly haired, 17-year-old pepperpot who required an on-the-set tutor for schooling, had only two feature-film credits, this and the follow-up Myers-Mercer musical, *To Beat the Band*. She was discovered in New York by songwriter Al Siegel, who had found Ethel Merman a few years before but didn't quite repeat that success with Poe. The Mercer-Poe section of the number yields to a kazoo chorus, in which various characters play household items as percussive instruments, and separate tap sets by Grable and, with floor-rattling somersaults, the rotund Lamont.

Despite its fun production numbers and brisk, breezy pace, *Old Man Rhythm* was no great accomplishment for RKO, relying on predictable comedy over a fellow of Barbier's age and physique as a beanie-wearing freshman—and thus, having violated senior-class edicts, having to push a peanut along a sidewalk with his nose. The film opened during the then-financially fallow summer season, and not always to its best advantage. In Beverly Hills at the end of August 1935, it was awkwardly paired with Noël Coward's mystical thinking-man's drama *The Scoundrel*. An extreme, but not uncommon, reaction to *Old Man Rhythm* was the one from *The Educational Screen*, which rated it "Absurd" with "No value," as a "senseless hodge-podge of endless jazz, cheap romance, dizzy dancing, and silly absurdities, laid in the craziest 'college' yet screened. It will be funny, stupid, or idiotic, according to intelligence and taste of the spectator."[29]

Still, RKO must have had some faith, for even as *Old Man Rhythm* was beginning playdates in August 1935, Myers was grinding out another value musical—with many of the same actors, including Mercer. "Hollywood was like a boom city in those days, and even I got better offers from other producers on the same lot the day after the picture opened," Mercer recalled. "But if Zion wanted me, I wouldn't desert him, and we did another picture right away before my RKO contract ran out."[30] Unfortunately, *To Beat the Band* showed Mercer less favorably than its predecessor, and Mercer was dismissed as a triple-threat man, his promise as a Hoagy Carmichael/Oscar Levant–type singing/instrumentalizing sidekick unfulfilled.

This time, Mercer's co-writer—of six pedestrian melodies—was Matt Malneck, as Gensler had moved on to Paramount as a producer. Portraying a horn player/vocalist in the orchestra helmed by Fred Keating, Mercer sings in three numbers—most conspicuously on "Eeny, Meeny, Miney, Mo" and "I Saw Her at Eight O'Clock"—but he has only a few words of solo dialogue as he runs around the big city with his bandmates. His character doesn't even have a name: In trade-review cast lists, he's billed as "Member of Band." Director Ben Stoloff's musical comedy puts the emphasis on comedy, as old pros Hugh Herbert and Helen Broderick have at it, supported by *Old Man Rhythm* alums Blore, Poe, Hodges, twinkle-toed Lamont, and standard-issue overaged juves Keating and Roger Pryor. (Buddy Rogers had returned to his band tours.) Herbert, borrowed from Warners, and Broderick, an Astaire-Rogers fixture, play the central roles, which means the film has no stars to sell it. *To Beat the Band* is not as snappy or endearing as *Old Man Rhythm* and is more firmly in the time-passer mold.

Despite his uneven use, Mercer garnered some recognition for his presence, and a writer for the fan-oriented *New Movie Magazine* called him "one of RKO's new finds."[31] He was out at RKO by the end of 1935, but not before making a key contact with Fred Astaire. Astaire came to Mercer needing lyrics to a song he'd written, "I'm Building Up to an Awful Letdown." Mercer did so, and the song became a moderate hit. Mercer returned to the movies—as a songwriter but not on screen—for good in 1936 when his words-and-music work "I'm an Old Cowhand (From the Rio Grande)" was made into a big hit by Paramount's Bing Crosby vehicle *Rhythm on the Range* [q.v.]. The multi-Oscared co-writer of "Moon River," "Days of Wine and Roses," "In the Cool, Cool, Cool of the Evening," "Hooray for Hollywood," and so many more, was off and writing.

Warner Archive issued *Old Man Rhythm* and *To Beat the Band* together on a single DVD in 2015. The Mercer angle was not indicated on the disc package cover, but grateful film musical lovers understood the connection.

The Girl Said No

(Grand National; July 12, 1937)

Director/Producer: Andrew L. Stone. Presented By: Edward L. Alperson. Screenplay: Betty Laidlaw, Robert Lively. Story: Andrew L. Stone. Photography: Ira Morgan. Editor: Thomas Neff. Art Director: Lewis J. Rachmil. Sound: William Wilmarth. Musical Director: Arthur Kay. Musical Advisor: Edwin Lester. Dance Director: Frank Moulan. Production Manager: Ray Heinz. Assistant Director: Alexis Thurn-Taxis. Running Time: 72 minutes.

Cast: Robert Armstrong (Jimmie Allen); Irene Hervey (Pearl Proctor aka Virginia Lee); Edward Brophy (Pick); Paula Stone (Mabel); Harry Tyler (Chuck); Richard Tucker (Charles Dillon); Gwili Andre (Gretchen Holman); Max Davidson (Max); Josef Swickard (Jonesy); Bert Roach (Sugar Plum); Horace Murphy (Joe); William Danforth (Howard Hathaway); Vera Ross (Beatrice Hathaway); Vivian Hart (Kitty); Frank Moulan (Mark); Allan Rogers (John); Arthur Kay (Adolph); Carita Crawford (Yum-Yum); Tudor Williams (Williams); Mildred Rogers (Peggy); Lester Dorr (Barnes); Carl Stockdale (Lockwood); Donald Kerr (doorman); Phil Dunham (café customer); Isabel La Mal (acting

teacher); Claire Rochelle (Miss Pringle); Rolfe Sedan (headwaiter); Rose Plumer (Fanny); Harry Semels (vocal coach); Wilbur Mack (dancing coach).
Songs: "Behold the Lord High Executioner" (from *The Mikado*) [Moulan, chorus], "For He's Gone and Married Yum-Yum" (from *The Mikado*) [Moulan, Hart, Crawford, Rogers, chorus], "The Flowers That Bloom in the Spring" (from *The Mikado*) [Rogers], "I'm Called Little Buttercup" (from *H.M.S. Pinafore*) [Ross], "I Am the Monarch of the Sea" (from *H.M.S. Pinafore*) [Moulan, Hart, Williams, chorus], "It Really Doesn't Matter" (from *Ruddigore*) [Danforth, Hart, Moulan, Ross], "The Magnet and the Churn" (from *Patience*) [Danforth, Hart, Williams, chorus], "Mi-ya Sa-ma" (from *The Mikado*) [Danforth, Ross, chorus], "Policeman's Song" (from *The Pirates of Penzance*) [Danforth, chorus], "Three Little Maids from School" (from *The Mikado*) [Crawford, Hart, Hervey], "A Wand'ring Minstrel I" (from *The Mikado*) [Rogers] (William S. Gilbert, Arthur Sullivan); "Rhythm in My Heart" [Hervey] (Val Burton, Will Jason).
Working Title: *Broadway Chiselers*.
Also Known As: *With Words and Music*.
Academy Award Nomination: Best Sound Recording (Grand National Sound Department, A.E. Kaye, sound director).
Home Video: Alpha DVD (as *With Words and Music*).

The Story: Racetrack bookie Jimmie Allen is smitten by dance hall hostess Pearl Proctor, who cons him out of a substantial sum of money despite the warnings of his pals Pick and Chuck. To exact revenge and pay his debts, Jimmie pretends to be a talent scout and promises to star Pearl in a Broadway show within 60 days in return for $500 in advance and 10 percent of her future earnings. Jimmie uses his professional connections with a theatrical producer, Charles Dillon, and his star actress, Gretchen Holman, to deceive Pearl about his show-business acumen. He arranges for Pearl to take singing and dancing lessons ("Rhythm in My Heart"), passes her off as a socialite who wants her name in lights, and hires members of a down-and-out Gilbert and Sullivan theatrical troupe—now running a lunch room—for a performance of "The Mikado." Not realizing their acting comeback is a sham, the grateful restaurant owners, the Hathaways, sell their business to raise funds, and Pearl quits her job to further her "career" while confessing her love for Jimmie. Although guilt-ridden Jimmie wants to stop the show and not take Pearl's money, his toadies fill the theater for the "Mikado" opening. With the police about to intervene, Jimmie halts the show and exposes the ruse, but the actors agree to finish the performance. The critics in attendance are impressed, Dillon promises to keep the production going, and Pearl agrees to Jimmie's marriage proposal.

Andrew L. Stone was the rare filmmaker who was really dedicated to bringing music to the masses, which he did often in a long career. And for Stone and those masses, some of the most beloved music was in the catchy melodies and witty wordplay of two Victorian-era Britishers, William S. Gilbert and Arthur Sullivan. You could even hail from London, Ohio, or London, Finland, to know and love Gilbert and Sullivan's distinctive brand of satirical light opera, and such concoctions as *The Mikado*, *H.M.S. Pinafore*, and *The Pirates of Penzance* were known, and performed, in every corner of the globe in the 1930s.

In America, those years were particularly kind to those shows. Broadway was the locale for Gilbert and Sullivan revivals that became annual and seasonal attractions as staged by producer Milton Aborn's Civic Light Opera Company, featuring actors—William Danforth, Vera Ross, Vivian Hart, Frank Moulan—who had trod the boards in Savoyard works for decades. That most-influential of theater critics, Brooks Atkinson of *The New York Times*, attempted to explain this enduring quality:

> In spite of their age and their innocence of modern spirit, the Savoy operas are loved with a passion rarely squandered on anything in the contemporary theatre. When the orchestra strikes up the overture..., it is a pleasure to watch faces in the audience; they are lighted with joy.... The popularity of Gilbert and Sullivan is genuine, satisfying a taste that nay be cultivated but that is perfectly sincere.[32]

But you couldn't hear G&S in a movie house—not until Stone came along in 1937 with a crowd-pleasing musical comedy, *The Girl Said No*, which pays affectionate tribute to Gilbert and Sullivan despite its Depression-era, American-city setting. Stone (1902–1999) had toiled in Hollywood for more than a decade but had not accomplished much of real note. The Oakland, California, native was a prop man at Universal before attracting the attention of Paramount head Adolph Zukor with an independently made two-reel drama, *The Elegy* (1927). Stone directed a handful of shorts and features (among them 1930's *Sombras de gloria*, a Spanish-language version of the indie musical *Blaze o' Glory*) and produced a series of comic trailers that were shown at theaters to accompany their prize drawings. Stone became known as an efficient filmmaker who, as he would describe it late in his life, believed that "directorial touches are a lot of crap…. The fact [is,] I could make films of quality for less money than the others."[33] He eschewed back projection, harsh lighting, process work, and even post-synching in favor of streamlining his works.

In 1936, Stone was signed as a director-producer-writer by Edward L. Alperson, who needed creative talent for his new Grand National Films. For his first feature credit as a producer, Stone targeted Gilbert and Sullivan fare, even though it was considered unfilmable for legal and financial reasons. Although there were no American copyrights to the music, its rights in the British Empire were strictly controlled by the shows' original producers, the D'Oyly Carte Opera Company, and no Hollywood company was inclined to make a movie that couldn't be shown in most of the Brit-civilized world. No matter: Stone built a story

In the charming Gilbert and Sullivan-meets-Damon Runyon comedy *The Girl Said No*, a bookie (Robert Armstrong, center) tries to sell a theatrical producer (Richard Tucker) on the talents of an aspiring singer (Irene Hervey).

set in the modern day that cleverly incorporated Gilbert-Sullivan works and cast Robert Armstrong, that reliable movie mug, and Irene Hervey, an underused starlet, as the leads.

Tough-guy Armstrong (1890–1973) had been King Kong's foil, of course. Hervey (1909–1998) was better known for her marriage to Allan Jones than for anything on screen. Grace Bradley was the originally signed tough-gal ingénue for *The Girl Said No*, but Hervey was asked to step in. Newly freed from servitude at MGM after four years of a seven-year commitment, she was tired of being cast as a society girl, which she would not be in Stone's picture. "And to think I nearly missed the part!" the actress told the *Los Angeles Times* in 1937.

> I had received my release from my contract at MGM. When I was offered the stellar role in *The Girl Said No*, I was the silly girl who said "no." Luckily, they gave me another chance.... I adore being a common, rather coarse girl. You see, I've been refined for four years, always the "nice" ingenue. Oh, this has been a wonderful year.[34]

Stone began Hervey's run of good fortune by shooting *The Girl Said No* in 17 business days in March and April 1937, at Grand National's facilities and others rented from Universal, for a paltry $76,000.[35] The tale of a New York racetrack tout putting on a faux musical show to avenge a slight by a taxi dancer was initially titled *Broadway Chiselers*, but the ultimate title stressed the romantic angle.

The instrument of the elaborate con, a washed-up group of aging Gilbert-and-Sullivan actors reduced to singing in a hash house, is presented as old hat, but the "Former Sensations of Broadway" are shown as worthy and relevant even in a cynical Depression-era world. "That's the trouble with these old hams; they don't know when they're washed up," a restaurant customer sneers as the troupers joyfully sing. But they actually do know, and their joy at believing they're being re-appreciated is palpable and touching. Upon acknowledging to Armstrong that she and her husband have told their restaurant to mark their return to the stage, one of the troupers explains that theirs is the lot of the actor: "That's the gamble we're taking.... We're turning back to a life we love. We've known great happiness in the theater, and we belong to it, all of us. And if the curtain falls and the show's a failure, then that's sort of the end of everything, isn't it?"

Stone ups the entertainment value by casting genuine New York G&S stage stars Danforth, Ross, Hart, and Moulan as the main singers, and the work of these dedicated Savoyards is so affecting that we are willing to suspend disbelief at the matronly Ross singing "Poor Little Buttercup." Stone fills out the cast with other veterans—Bert Roach, Josef Swickard, Max Davidson—who were likely as grateful for the work as the fictional actors. As Armstrong's chums, Edward Brophy and Harry Tyler are clearly in the Damon Runyon mode, right down to their characters' colorful nicknames. Hervey gets to show off her curves more than her vocalizing skills (which were dubbed), but she's convincing enough in a transition from "10-cent torso twister" to would-be society miss, even if she seems more comfortable in the latter guise. In this story, everybody's fooling everybody else, but "at least the elevator's on the up-and-up," concedes the con lady.

Given the modern setting, Stone doesn't stint on the Gilbert-and-Sullivan songbook, but the centerpiece is *The Mikado*, the duo's most famous work, with no less with six selections presented in the final reel as the bookie's scheme to enact revenge on the taxi dancer plays out. In prints shown internationally, Stone avoided the copyright problem by substituting from the operetta *Princess Ting Ah Ling*.[36] *Penzance*, *Pinafore*, *Ruddigore*, and *Patience* also are represented, but the milieu is unmistakably 1930s New York and not 1890s London or ancient Japan, nor any place where seas are ploughed. "It is odd that no one ever before has thought of it," wrote *Washington Post* critic Nelson B. Bell in a glowing review,

> I mean the adroit weaving into the warp and woof of a modern comedy-romance of Broadway bookmakers, theatrical producers and taxi-dancers of the imperishable music and tricky lyrics of the Gilbert and Sullivan operettas as has been done in *The Girl Said No*. This picture represents the most adept blending of past and present in the theater that these eyes and ears ever have encountered.[37]

The *Los Angeles Times* called *The Girl Said No* "one of the surprise pictures of the season," *Variety* lauded it as "amiable ... deserving of success," and the usually stingy *New York Times* praised it as Grand National's "brightest offering ... a most charming picture ... that takes on a nostalgic and indefinable pathos."[38] The film even earned an Academy Award nomination, for sound recording. Grand National thought so much of Stone's work that before the general release of *The Girl Said No*, the studio announced that he would direct and produce another musical. It was to feature selections from *Die Fledermaus* and to star Stuart Erwin (quite a combo!). But before that project could get off the ground, Stone turned around and signed a five-year contract to go back to Zukor and Paramount.[39]

With a lame-duck director and leads who hardly tripped off the tongue as household names, Grand National hit the Gilbert-and-Sullivan exploitation angle hard, and audiences responded. *The Girl Said No* was the rare indie production to gain a booking at New York's Radio Music Hall. And in 1939, when England's General Film Distributors made a Technicolor filming of *The Mikado* the first sanctioned G&S movie musical, *The Girl Said No* was hauled out to provide timely competition—and fill more than a few show dates.[40]

The reception for *The Girl Said No* inspired Stone to make grander musicals, though not immediately. At Paramount in 1938, he wrote and directed *Stolen Heaven*, a romantic drama with secondary music elements, and then also produced *Say It in French*, a light comedy that debuted the Hoagy Carmichael-credited "April in My Heart." Stone's next effort, much more vocally substantial, was 1939's *The Great Victor Herbert* [q.v.], another nod to a great catalog of composing work. *The Great Victor Herbert* is a more important film than *The Girl Said No*, but it isn't nearly as fun.

Alexander's Ragtime Band

(20th Century–Fox; August 5, 1938)

Director: Henry King. Associate Producer: Harry Joe Brown. Screenplay: Kathryn Scola, Lamar Trotti. Adaptation: Richard Sherman. Story: Irving Berlin. Photography: Peverell Marley. Editor: Barbara McLean. Sound: Arthur von Kirbach, Roger Heman. Art Directors: Bernard Herzbrun, Boris Leven. Set Decoration: Thomas Little. Costumes: Gwen Wakeling. Musical Director: Alfred Newman. Dance Director: Seymour Felix. Assistant Directors: Robert Webb, Henry Weinberger. Running Time: 106 minutes.

Cast: Tyrone Power (Roger Grant, aka Alexander); Alice Faye (Stella Kirby); Don Ameche (Charlie Dwyer); Ethel Merman (Jerry Allen); Jack Haley (Davey Lane); Jean Hersholt (Professor Heinrich); Helen Westley (Aunt Sophie); John Carradine (taxi driver); Paul Hurst (Bill Mulligan); Wally Vernon (himself); Ruth Terry (Ruby); Douglas Fowley (Snapper); Chick Chandler (Louie); Eddie Collins (Corporal Collins); Joseph Crehan (stage manager); Robert Gleckler (Eddie); Dixie Dunbar (specialty); Joe King (Charles Dillingham); Charles Coleman (head waiter); Stanley Andrews (Colonel Roberts); Charles Williams (agent); Jane Jones, Otto Fries, Mel Kalish (trio); Selmer Jackson (aide at radio station); Donald Douglas (patriotic singer); The King's Men (Army singers); Tyler Brooke, Arthur Rankin (assistant stage managers); Jack Pennick (drill sergeant); Cully Richards (band member); Charles Tannen (Dillingham's secretary); Lon Chaney, Jr. (photographer at *Come One Come*

All rehearsal); Paul McVey (stage manager); Edward Keane (Army officer); Edwin Stanley, Sam Ash (theater critics); Ralph Dunn, James Flavin (Army captains); Harry Tyler (Ship Café proprietor); Alberto Morin (restaurant manager); Edward Mundy (barker); Alexander Pollard (waiter); James C. Morton (bartender); Eleanor Wesselhoeft (Martha); A.S. "Pop" Byron (train conductor); Fred Santley (songwriter); Ron Wilson (piano player); Jack George (recital violinist); Carol Adams (hat check girl); Richard French, Robert Lowery, Joe Cunningham, Stanley Taylor (reporters); Kay Griffith, Lynne Berkeley (autograph seekers); Helen Ericson, Elizabeth Palmer, Dorothy Dearing (girls at recital); Harold Goodwin (military policeman); Rondo Hatton (barfly).

Songs: "Alexander's Ragtime Band" [Faye, band; reprised by Faye, chorus], "All Alone" [Faye], "Blue Skies" [Merman, club band; reprised by Faye, chorus], "Cheek to Cheek" [band on radio], "Easter Parade" [Ameche, chorus], "Everybody Step" [Merman, chorus], "Everybody's Doin' It Now" [Vernon, Dunbar, Faye, chorus], "For Your Country and My Country" [Douglas], "The Gypsy in Me" [Santley], "Heat Wave" [Merman, chorus], "I Can Always Find a Little Sunshine in the YMCA" [The King's Men], "In My Harem" [Haley, danced by Vernon, Chandler (deleted from release print)], "Lazy" [club band], "Marching Along with Time" [played by band over opening and end credits (number by Merman, chorus deleted from release)], "Marie" [band], "My Walking Stick" [Merman, chorus], "Now It Can Be Told" [Ameche, reprised by Faye, band], "Oh! How I Hate to Get Up in the Morning" [Haley, chorus], "Pack Up Your Sins and Go to the Devil" [Merman, chorus], "A Pretty Girl Is Like a Melody" [Merman], "Ragtime Violin" [trio, band], "Remember" [Faye], "Say It with Music" [Merman], "Some Sunny Day" [Ameche, chorus (deleted)], "That International Rag" [Faye, Haley, Chandler], "This Is the Life" [Vernon, band], "We're on Our Way to France" [chorus], "What'll I Do?" [chorus], "When I Lost You" [band], "When the Midnight Choo-Choo Leaves for Alabam'" [Faye, band] (Irving Berlin).

Also Known As: *Irving Berlin's Alexander's Ragtime Band.*

Academy Award: Best Music, Scoring (Alfred Newman).

Academy Award Nominations: Best Picture; Best Writing, Original Story (Irving Berlin); Best Art Direction (Bernard Herzbrun, Boris Leven); Best Film Editing (Barbara McLean); Best Original Song ("Now It Can Be Told," Irving Berlin).

Home Video: 20th Century–Fox DVD, VHS.

The Story: San Francisco violinist Roger Grant dislikes playing in Nob Hill classical recitals, even with the approval of snooty Aunt Sophie and Professor Heinrich. He moonlights in a ragtime band that secures a tryout at Dirty Eddie's saloon on the Barbary Coast. Without music to play, the band borrows sheet music, recently sent to saloon singer Stella Kirby by a friend in the East, for a new, Irving Berlin-penned tune, "Alexander's Ragtime Band." With Stella reluctantly fronting, the band makes a hit with the new song, which catapults bandleader Roger—now known as "Alexander." The expanded act achieves regional success ("Ragtime Violin," "That International Rag," "Everybody's Doin' It Now") as Alexander and Stella bicker over his playing Pygmalion to soften her brassy image. The band's piano player, Charlie Dwyer, shows his love for Stella by writing the song "Now It Can Be Told," but he realizes that Stella and Alexander are in love. Stella accepts an offer from Broadway impresario Charles Dillingham to move to New York as a solo ("This Is the Life," "When the Midnight Choo-Choo Leaves for Alabam'"), and the band dissolves. During the Great War, Alexander and bandmate Davey Lane enlist in the Army, and Alexander creates an all-soldier stage show ("Oh! How I Hate to Get Up in the Morning," "We're on Our Way to France"), which Stella, a star on Broadway, attends in New York. After the war, Alexander locates Stella, but he learns she is married to Charlie, now a prominent composer. Alexander re-forms his band with Davey to play jazz with vocalist Jerry Lane ("Say It with Music," "A Pretty Girl Is Like a Melody," "Blue Skies") in a Greenwich Village club managed by old friend Bill Mulligan. Charlie and Stella divorce amicably, as he knows Stella cannot truly love him. The band leaves for a tour in Europe as a lovesick Stella withdraws from public view ("Pack Up Your Sins and Go to the Devil," "What'll I Do?" "My Walking Stick," "Remember," "Everybody Step," "All Alone"). Alexander impulsively proposes to Jerry, but she declines, and the band returns to the U.S. to launch a radio program. Alexander reconnects with Charlie, and they resolve to find Stella. *Alexander's* orchestra presents a swing concert at Carnegie Hall ("Marie," "Easter Parade," "Heat Wave"). Stella stays away from the concert, but with the help of a music-loving taxi driver, she is tricked into listening on the radio and then goes on stage to sing "Alexander's Ragtime Band" as an affirmation of her and Alexander's love.

Theatergoers of 1938 were not going to be fooled by their neighborhood marquees, which listed the headliners of *Alexander's Ragtime Band* as Tyrone Power, Alice Faye, and Don Ameche. Folks knew the real star was Irving Berlin, even if they weren't privy to the film's original studio-sanctioned title, *Irving Berlin's Alexander's Ragtime Band*. This was not quite, as was advertised by 20th Century–Fox, "the greatest box office success ever produced," but it wasn't far off. At a time when only 30 to 40 Hollywood pictures per year were produced for more than $1 million, *Alexander* cost Fox just over $2 million—and grossed $3.6 million upon its initial release.[41]

This was an all-ages attraction, given that, as *Variety* declared in its official review of the film, "the Berlin repertoire taken from various musical shows, films and from the shelves of pop sheet [music] stores, comprise a symphony as familiar to the average man and woman as the faces of close friends."[42] Add a new-school swing angle to its repertoire of 29 songs, and *Alexander* was made to rejuvenate the movie musical. A fleeting visual reference to his writing of the title song was the only overt reference to Berlin in the narrative, but this was a biography without a bio, not just an account of the impact of Berlin's music but of the evolution of early 20th-century American pop.

Alice Faye, Don Ameche (at piano) and Tyrone Power form the love triangle in the lavish *Alexander's Ragtime Band*. Jack Haley (on drums) and Wally Vernon are at the flanks in this performance scene.

If Darryl Zanuck had had his way, it really would've been a saga of Berlin the man, not just of Berlin's music. Berlin (1888–1989) had written the score for *On the Avenue* (1937), and Zanuck wanted to involve him in another musical, one based on Berlin's life. The title of the nascent property seemed a natural, for "Alexander's Ragtime Band" was Berlin's first landmark hit. He had introduced the song at a Friars Club event, to a polite but unimpressive response, but the famous contralto Emma Carus took up the tune, turning it into a smash. The song garnered more than 2 million copies of sheet music sales in the year of its 1911 debut and turned ragtime into a national phenomenon. In the years ahead, Berlin gained his first experience with motion pictures, and not to his advantage. A highly publicized project, *Puttin' on the Ritz* (1930), debuted the jaunty title song and a pleasing "Alice in Wonderland" number, but audiences did not warm to the film's coarse, Jolsonesque lead, Harry Richman. The genuine Jolson sang a handful of Berlin works in *Mammy* (1930), but that picture lost money as well, and not until the Fred Astaire-Ginger Rogers RKO musicals *Top Hat* (1935) and *Follow the Fleet* (1936) did new Berlin music register on screen. Now, Berlin and Zanuck had to be mutually pleased.

In a deposition pertaining to a plagiarism lawsuit over the story rights for *Alexander's Ragtime Band*, Zanuck described the genesis of the film:

> I had been interested in doing the life story of Irving Berlin. Mr. Berlin objected for personal reasons. He did not feel that it would be proper or good taste to present his more or less colorful life on the screen. Of course that was a private and personal objection and I saw his point.
>
> …I thought of the idea of doing a picture called *Alexander's Ragtime Band*, which was the most popular song that Irving Berlin had written…. I told Mr. Berlin that the title … would be the basis for a tremendous musical and that we could, without violating his private life, invent a fictitious story but we could include certain definite incidents from his life….[43]

Berlin agreed to this in late 1936, and he, with screenwriter Richard Sherman, devised a tale, about a fictional musician-bandleader named "Mr. Alexander," for which Berlin would be Academy Award-nominated for Best Original Story. According to author Laurence Bergreen's detailed Berlin biography, *As Thousands Cheer*, which recaps the development of the film via research of TCF production files, Berlin submitted to Zanuck an unwieldly scenario of which the mogul definitely did not approve.[44] It located the introduction of "Alexander's Ragtime Band" not in Berlin's New York City but in New Orleans. "Alexander" endures an up-and-down career periodically fortified by occasional encounters with Irving Berlin, descends into obscurity as ragtime goes out of style, and ultimately finds renewed fame—and regains the love of his lost sweetheart—when he conducts his orchestra in a concert at Carnegie Hall. Zanuck wanted more of a "wow" factor: "Maybe our trouble is that we are trying to tell a phase of American musical evolution instead of a story about two boys and a girl. The story of these three is our main plot; the other, the important background."[45]

Zanuck might have thought the script lacked the drama of Berlin's actual life, which included the tragic early death of his first wife and the anti–Semitic prejudice that preceded his second marriage. For temperamental bandleader-violinist "Alexander"—portrayed by the Irish-American Power (1914–1958)—the only amorous complication, albeit a big one in the plot, was over the (wink-wink) pretty good chance of his ending up with the saloon singer-turned-Broadway star played by Faye.[46] Add Ameche in the third-wheel part, and you had the three stars of TCF's big period musical drama of the 1937–38 season, *In Old Chicago*. That film was directed by Fox favorite Henry King, who was especially adept at the studio's popular style of historical drama, and scripted by studio regular Lamar Trotti. Both reprised their duties for *Alexander's Ragtime Band*, which began shooting in September 1937, with Berlin a regular presence on the set, piano at hand. "Sometimes he'd just sit and watch," Faye recalled. "Sometimes he'd play and sing his songs to help me get their feeling."[47]

The finished script by Trotti and Kathryn Scola does allude to an important incident in Berlin's life, as Power's Alexander joins the Army and stages an all-soldier Broadway show similar to *Yip Yip Yaphank,* which Berlin created when a sergeant during the Great War (and for which he wrote the enduring "Oh! How I Hate to Get Up in the Morning," sung here by second lead Jack Haley). The Carnegie Hall finale is more out of the past of Paul Whiteman and his orchestra's legendary 1924 appearance at New York's Aeolian Hall that introduced Gershwin's "Rhapsody in Blue." But although the story was fictionalized, the songs were all from Berlin, who, Zanuck stated, had to buy up the old material he did not control.[48] No doubt Berlin's percentage-of-the-gross deal—reported as 10 percent—made that effort all the more affordable.[49]

Three songs—"Now It Can Be Told," "My Walking Stick," and "Marching Along with Time"—were written for the film. The "Marching Along with Time" number, delivered by the ever-dynamic Ethel Merman, was trimmed from the final release print, limiting its use to the opening credits as Alexander, in silhouette, conducts. "My Walking Stick" is punched across by Merman in male drag in a nightclub scene replete with baton-stick twirlers. As the primary love ballad, "Now It Can Be Told" is most central to the proceedings. Ameche's character, who has lost his heart to Faye's Stella Kirby, first soloes it at a rehearsal piano as she listens with introspection, but a reprise by Faye and the band moments later reveals truer emotions. Through a well-staged, economical series of facial gestures and other body language mid-song, Ameche dejectedly realizes that Power is her true love, and Power now knows it … now it *can* be told.

Small moments such as that counterbalance the march-of-time bigness of *Alexander's Ragtime Band.* For example, John Carradine plays a faintly malevolent cab driver, and although he's been enlisted to drive Stella to Carnegie Hall for a final-reel reunion with Alexander, one might think the future screen Dracula is more inclined to drive her to her doom. Power and Ameche are capable enough, although both actors might have been more convincing with a little more age—especially when the story touches on Alexander's personal decline after the war. There are some small moments—unexpectedly small, given his status as a respected actor—from Jean Hersholt as a professor who urges Alexander to ditch rag for the classics. The less Hersholt, the better, as too many musicals touched upon music-culture clashes, and this one rightly didn't dwell on that one.

It's more fun to read behind the brief passive-aggressive interaction of Faye's and Merman's characters, who both fancy Alex. Their differences are illustrated in an extended sequence that contrasts the rise of Alexander's postwar fortunes with the decline of Stella's career—the film alternates between upbeat numbers by backup songbird Merman ("My Walking Stick," "Everybody Step," "Pack Up Your Sins and Go to the Devil") as Alex's orchestra triumphantly tours Europe with downbeat songs from Faye's more modest locales ("Remember," "All Alone," "What'll I Do?"). Merman must have been reminded she wasn't back on Broadway, where, in the stage version of *George White's Scandals* in 1931, she was a star and Faye was a chorus girl to whom Merman kindly lent $10.[50]

Given all that's stuffed in, Merman gets a good bit to sing, with a tender (for her) rendition of "A Pretty Girl Is Like a Melody" a nice change of pace over her more characteristic deliveries. Not surprisingly, Berlin would provide Merman with her greatest success a decade later with her Broadway triumph in *Annie Get Your Gun.* Meanwhile, Faye transitions convincingly from a dolled-up "Queen of Ragtime" to an elegant leading lady in a role that mirrored the transition of her persona in Hollywood. No wonder the actress considered this her favorite part, although she was amused that, in a story spanning a quarter-century, she and her co-stars seemed not to age.

Fox built buzz on *Alexander* by press-previewing it auspiciously in Hollywood on May 24, 1938, before its general issue in August. On August 3, two days before the New York City premiere at the prestigious Roxy house, a reluctant Berlin took to a CBS microphone in that city to introduce a one-hour program about *ARB*: "A singer can speak with his voice. An actor can speak with his tongue in his cheek. But what can a songwriter say?"[51] The answer came in the show that followed, as hosted by Al Jolson and featuring appearances, from New York and California, by Eddie Cantor, Sophie Tucker, Darryl Zanuck (of course, in a chat with Louella Parsons), and many others. Faye, Merman, and Power presented songs and dialogue from the film. It was potent stuff for the masses, who were even more drawn in by strongly laudatory press reviews. "It is by no means a musical in the accepted film sense," opined *The Hollywood Reporter*. "Rather, it is the aggrandizement of the evolution of American popular music and a monument to Irving Berlin.... So perfectly are this film story and the music interwoven that it seems ... the songs themselves wrote the script."[52] Said *The New York Times*: "The picture simply runs roughshod over minor critical objection and demands recognition as the best musical show of the year."[53]

Alexander's Ragtime Band broke box office records in many cities, including New York, where its opening-day attendance at the Roxy cashed in at an all-time high with more than 29,000 patrons (the line began forming at 2:35 a.m.), and more than 600,000 in the first month.[54] A month into its national release, the film had made $1.2 million, nearly its negative cost, and by the end of August, "Now It Can Be Told" already ranked third nationally in sheet music sales while a revived "Alexander's Ragtime Band" was fifth.[55] *Alexander* the film ranked behind only Disney's record-breaking *Snow White and the Seven Dwarfs* in box office performance for 1938, and it became 20th Century–Fox's biggest grosser to date. The film was a standout in a year in which the production of traditional (read: comedic) musicals in Hollywood declined, but it helped establish a new pattern for "serious" song films.

Like an earlier mega-musical, *King of Jazz* (1930), *Alexander's Ragtime Band* makes the retroactive mistake of excluding African Americans from the creation of jazz, save for the brief appearance by an all-black band in a nightclub sequence midway through the film. Berlin didn't particularly like swing or jazz, but even he had to agree that Alfred Newman's Academy Award-winning musical direction gave his music a contemporary kick, even turning the ending reprise of the title role into a swing melody. Besides nominations for Berlin's story and original song "Now It Can Be Told," *Alexander* was an Oscar finalist for best picture, art direction, and editing. It started a new cycle in Fox songfests that placed music within dramatic contexts taken from the lives of real show people. Its immediate successors were *Rose of Washington Square* (a Faye-Power teaming based loosely on the career of Fanny Brice), *Hollywood Cavalcade* (a Faye-Ameche vehicle echoing Mack Sennett), and *Swanee River* [q.v.] (with Ameche as Stephen Foster).

Alexander's Ragtime Band was never forgotten, though, certainly not in 1944 by one Mrs. E. Marie Cooper Oehler Dieckhaus, a former St. Louis resident now of Casper, Wyoming. She sued TCF for plagiarism, contending that the studio had access to her unpublished novel *Love Girl* and adapted it into *Alexander*. (This was the case that necessitated the deposition from Zanuck.) A U.S. district judge actually ruled in the plaintiff's favor, granting Dieckhaus' request for an injunction against continued showings of the film, and ordering the studio to permit her to share in all of the picture's profits. But a federal appellate court reversed that ruling in 1946 by asserting there was no direct evidence that Fox had the access claimed.[56]

As if to celebrate that decision, 20th followed in 1947 with a major reissue of *Alexander*, which benefited from the novelty of seeing Faye, who was a few years into retirement from the movies, on the big screen. To promote the re-release, which extended to some U.S. markets well into 1950, Ty Power reprised his role in a *Lux Radio Theatre* broadcast of April 1947, opposite Dinah Shore, Al Jolson, Dick Haymes, and Margaret Whiting. In 1954, Fox dipped into the Berlin songbook again with a glossier Technicolor songfest, *There's No Business Like Show Business*, with Mitzi Gaynor, Marilyn Monroe, Donald O'Connor, and Johnnie Ray as song-and-dance siblings and, as their parents, Dan Dailey and ... Ethel Merman. Ethel's bigger part didn't spare the pans for an overstuffed, corny film that signaled the decline of the classic American film musical.

Six decades hence, 20th Century–Fox brought out *Alexander's Ragtime Band* on VHS and then DVD, proving the film's worth to modern audiences. Perhaps because it is a Fox property and thus not in heavy rotation on TCM, *Alexander's Ragtime Band* is under-recognized in the context of 1930s movie musicals. But it is the finest Berlin screen showcase of any decade—and arguably the apex of Fox song filmmaking.

The Star Maker
(Paramount; August 25, 1939)

Director: Roy Del Ruth. Producer: Charles R. Rogers. Executive Producer: William LeBaron. Screenplay: Frank Butler, Don Hartman, Arthur Caesar. Story: Arthur Caesar, William A. Pierce. "Suggested by the Career" of Gus Edwards. Contributor to Screenplay Construction: Walter DeLeon. Photography: Karl Struss. Editor: Alma Macrorie. Art Direction: Hans Dreier, Robert Usher. Set Decoration: A.E. Freudeman. Costumes: Edith Head. Sound: Charles Hisserich, Richard Olson. Musical Director: Alfred Newman. Vocal Arrangements: Charles Henderson. Music Assistant: Troy Sanders. Dance Director: LeRoy Prinz. Vocal Instructor for Linda Ware: Norman Winter. Conducting the Philharmonic Orchestra of Los Angeles: Walter Damrosch. Assistant Director: Hal Walker. Running Time: 94 minutes.

Cast: Bing Crosby (Larry Earl); Louise Campbell (Mary); Linda Ware (Jane Gray); Ned Sparks ("Speed" King); Walter Damrosch (himself); Laura Hope Crews (Carlotta Salvini); Thurston Hall (Mr. Proctor); Clara Blandick (Miss Esther Jones); John Gallaudet (Duke); Ben Welden (Joe Gimlick); Janet Waldo (Stella); Paul Stanton (Mr. Coyle); Billy Gilbert (stage father/steel worker); Joseph Crehan (Mr. Marlowe); Grace Hayle (rural mother); Johnnie Morris (newsboy); Harry C. Bradley (train conductor); Frank Faylen, Wally Maher, George Eldredge, Stanley Price (reporters); George Guhl, Jimmie Dundee, Max Wagner (piano movers); Ralph Sanford (doorman); A.S. "Pop" Byron (stage doorman); Allen Fox (photographer); Fritzi Brunette (Cutie's mother); Kenneth Wilson (Ken); Billy Simms (Spike); Donald Brenon (Judge); Danny Daniels (Blackie); Don Hulbert (Duck); Darryl Hickman (Boots); Dante DiPaolo (Turkey); John Andrews (Andy); Gloria Atherton (Curly); Dorothy Babb (Dottie); Tommy Batten (Bats); Mary Ellen Bergren (Ivories); Gene Collins (Dummy); Eugene Eberle (Whitey); Patsy McCarty (Patsy); Roland Dupree (Frenchy); Joe Geil (Red); Richard Humphries (Chicago); Jackie McGee (Lucky); Joyce Arleen (Toots); Marilyn Martin (Ginger); Patsy Lee Parsons (Cookie); Jean Ruth (Butch); Leon Tyler (Big Ears); Howard Smiley (Skipper); Jacqueline Ossia (Penny); Kay Tapscott (Marilyn McKay).

Songs: "I Can't Tell Why I Love You, But I Do" [kids], "If I Was a Millionaire" [Crosby, newsboys chorus, reprised by Crosby], "School Days" [Ware, Crosby, kids], "Sunbonnet Sue" [kids] (Will D. Cobb, Gus Edwards); "He's My Pal" [kids], "In My Merry Oldsmobile" [Crosby, kids] (Vincent Bryan, Gus Edwards); "By the Light of the Silvery Moon" [orchestra], "Look Out for Jimmy Valentine" [Crosby] (Edward Madden, Gus Edwards); "An Apple for the Teacher" [Ware, Crosby, kids], "Go Fly a Kite" [Crosby, newsboys chorus], "A Man and His Dream" [Crosby], "Still the Bluebird Sings" [Crosby, kids] (James V. Monaco, Johnny Burke); "I Wonder Who's Kissing Her Now" [Crosby] (William M. Huff, Frank R. Adams, Joseph E. Howard, Harold Orlob); "The Sidewalks of New York" [danced by newsboys] (James W. Blake, Charles Lawlor); "The Darktown Strutters' Ball" [Ware] (Shelton Brooks); Symphony No. 5 in C Minor [orchestra] (Ludwig van Beethoven); "Parla Valse"

[Ware] (Luigi Arditi); "Valse des Fleurs" ("Waltz of the Flowers") [Ware, orchestra] (Peter Ilyich Tchaikovsky).

Disc: Decca 2640A, Decca 3602A, Decca 25496 ("An Apple for the Teacher," Bing Crosby and Connee Boswell); Decca 2640B ("Still the Bluebird Sings," Bing Crosby with John Scott Trotter Orchestra); Decca 3602B ("School Days"/"Sunbonnet Sue"/"Jimmy Valentine"/"If I Was a Millionaire," Bing Crosby with the Music Maids and John Scott Trotter Orchestra); Decca 11022 ("Still the Bluebird Sings," Bing Crosby with John Scott Trotter Orchestra); Decca 11023, Decca 2641 ("A Man and His Dream"/"Go Fly a Kite," Bing Crosby with John Scott Trotter Orchestra).

The Story: Egotistical but underemployed New York songwriter Larry Earl frequents St. Mark's orphanage because he likes singing to the kids ("Jimmy Valentine") and because he's courting Mary, who is employed there. Mary agrees to marry Larry, who yearns to make the big time ("A Man and His Dream"). Walking along the street to apply for a dead-end job, Larry sees a group of newsboys singing and dancing ("The Sidewalks of New York") and is inspired to train them into a vaudeville act ("If I Was a Millionaire") but is constantly rejected. Mary persuades Proctor, a prominent theater owner, to give the act, Larry Earl and His Singing Newsboys, a tryout ("Go Fly a Kite"). Audiences like the act, and with the help of publicity man "Speed" King, Larry gets the idea to search for child talent all over the country via train. After a string of stage successes has made him famous, Larry hears the impressive voice of classically trained 14-year-old Jane Gray ("Parla Valse"). He doesn't think he can use her in vaudeville, but Jane demonstrates she can sing Larry's kind of music ("Darktown Strutters' Ball"), and he gets her opera singer mother, Carlotta, out of the way by sending her out on tour. Jane leads a big "School Days" number in Larry's newest show, but the production is cut short with the intercession of members of the Children's Welfare Society, who cite a new law prohibiting children from working past a certain hour. As a result, Earl's shows close nationwide. To keep Jane singing, Larry seeks the counsel of famous conductor Walter Damrosch, who hires the girl. As Larry and Mary watch, Jane sparkles before a Carnegie Hall audience with "Waltz of the Flowers," performed with the Los Angeles Philharmonic. As happy as he is with Jane's success, Larry frets over his own future and ponders quitting show business. But Speed acquaints Larry with the new medium of radio, which provide a new creative avenue. On a nationwide broadcast, Larry and kids perform "Still the Bluebird Sings," and he buys a national radio company.

What did Eddie Cantor, George Jessel, Eleanor Powell, Groucho Marx, Mae Murray, the Duncan Sisters, the Lane Sisters, and Walter Winchell have in common? They owed their careers, in at least part, to Gus Edwards. Edwards—the producer, composer, and sometime performer known as the one of the biggest talent scouts in showbiz—lent his name, money, and songwriting skills to series of popular children's vaudeville and radio revues from just past the turn of the century into the Depression Era. In the late 1930s, Edwards' recognition factor as a symbol of a bygone era made his life story of potential Hollywood interest. That the result became a Bing Crosby musical titled *The Star Maker* is its own interesting, if slightly sad, tale.

Edwards' compositions included such standards as "By the Light of the Silvery Moon," "In My Merry Oldsmobile," "Sunbonnet Sue," "Your Mother and Mine," and perhaps his most famous song, "School Days," the name of one of his shows spotlighting child performers—and more than a few future adult stars—whom his company recruited from all over the nation. By 1913, *Variety* reported, there were 62 Edwards-sanctioned "School Days" troupes crisscrossing the globe.[57] The German-born Edwards also wrote songs prolifically for the stage, including some editions of the *Ziegfeld Follies*. As vaudeville started to fade, Edwards (1879–1945) took his little troupers to radio, skipping nary a beat. He was pushing 50 when talkies came in, but he not only wrote most of the music for MGM's *The Hollywood Revue of*

1929, he also lent his presence as a singer and actor to much of that film, most memorably in leading the bizarre production number "Lon Chaney's Going to Get You, If You Don't Watch Out," a comic-scary, song-and-dance salute to the secretive Metro star. Edwards and his kids went on to appear in multiple short subjects out West, but now more grandfatherly than paternal, he eventually settled into a quiet life in his familiar New York City.

By 1938, Edwards had slowed down a lot, to the point of battling health problems, but he attracted the interest of Charles R. Rogers, who was back to producing films independently after stints as production head at Universal and RKO. In August 1938, piggybacking on the instant-hit status of Fox's semi-bio *Alexander's Ragtime Band* [q.v.], Rogers announced he had acquired the film rights to Edwards' life for a "special box office attraction" called *The Star Maker*. Early reports indicated that Edwards was set to collaborate with Rogers on the musical score and story development, and Rogers disclosed that he was in negotiations with Paramount to borrow the estimable Bing Crosby for the title role.[58] Rogers got Crosby, but only after signing with Paramount as a producer in December 1938.[59]

Rogers brought to his new employer (actually, one of his old ones, for a few of his indies had been released there)—and *The Star Maker*—his latest discovery. She was a 13-year-old soprano from Detroit named Linda Ware. Ware was already drawing comparisons to another golden-voiced, classically inclined teenager—Deanna Durbin, whose rise to fame Rogers had overseen at Universal. Even before the public was to hear the former Beverly Jane Stillwagon vocalize on screen, it came to know Ware because of press accounts of her atypical, nomadic background—the early death of her mother in Pennsylvania, time spent in an orphanage in Ohio, a budding career groomed while in the custody of an aunt and uncle in Michigan. As Ware told it to columnist Sheilah Graham years later, the aunt who freed Ware from the orphans' home spotted a newspaper blurb about MGM's search for a girl to play a young version of Jeanette MacDonald's character in *The Girl of the Golden West* (1938). Ware moved with her aunt to L.A., garnered no offers, and was about to return home when she signed with the same agent who had launched Durbin. Soon, she was placed under exclusive pact to Rogers.[60]

Perhaps to utilize Ware's talents ideally—and, more pertinently, to narrow the gulf between Edwards' Old World countenance and Crosby's modern air—*The Star Maker* story/script, credited to four writers, became something different than anticipated. Between the securing of Crosby and the start of shooting in April 1939, the film became an account of a fictional songwriter named Larry Earl, who sings his songs to kids in his fiancée's orphanage and, prompted by a chance incident on a city street, becomes a promoter-producer of young'uns of indeterminate time, place, and name.

Not only was this a "new" Gus Edwards—because, other than the catalog songs, it was hardly Edwards at all—it was a "new" Bing Crosby. For once, he was portraying a happily married man, hitched to his lady in the first reel. Larry's weakness isn't another woman, it's his impatience to get ahead, spurred by spendthrift ways and what his ever-patient wife deems a "problem child" attitude. There's nothing of Crosby's laid-back personality in this dynamic portrayal. "I'm going up like a rocket! I'll have kid acts all over the country!" he recklessly exclaims, willing to live on hope before his fledgling troupe even cinches its first real job. "I'll pick 'em up out of nowhere. I'll give 'em a stage name before they got a family name!" Mrs. Earl, as portrayed by starlet Louise Campbell in a nothing-burger role, nods tolerantly. Campbell was a more intelligent actress than shown here, with solid work opposite Fred MacMurray and Ray Milland in Paramount's *Men with Wings* (1938), but gigs like the Crosby job soon drove her back to the New York stage.[61]

Rogers and director Roy Del Ruth had some non–Crosby/Edwards treats in store for

Bing Crosby seals a deal with highbrow conductor Walter Damrosch as Ned Sparks and young Linda Ware look on approvingly in the (sort of) Gus Edwards bio *The Star Maker*.

the paying public before production on *The Star Maker* wrapped in July. One was the stunt casting of venerable conductor Walter Damrosch, the former New York Philharmonic director lately an NBC official and radio host, as himself. Another was the addition of professional sourpuss Ned Sparks to play Earl's press agent, who is somehow hired in spite of his hatred for children. Sparks' torturous reading of a bedtime story to a group of tykes is the comic highlight of *The Star Maker*, and the sardonic agent's declared "favorite pastime" of "throwing child actors downstairs, dimples and all … [doing] my heart good to hear 'em bounce" is a W.C. Fields sound-alike.

Another advance asset was a heavily promoted search for those tykes: A mob of 1,575 aspirants who auditioned in person for the film was whittled down to 40 or so who made the final cut. "Everybody is cast now, but I'm still waylaid at the studio gates every day by people with kids," dance director LeRoy Prinz said in a syndicated newspaper account. "I've had everything tried on me—threats, bribery, and tears."[62] Among the kids hired as the dancing newsboys chorus that began Earl's (and Edwards') success were Darryl Hickman, who became a prominent youth performer at MGM and elsewhere; Danny Daniels, before he was a top dancer and stage/film/TV choreographer; and Dante DiPaolo, a future actor, dancer, and choreographer … and husband of Rosemary Clooney, Crosby's *White Christmas* song-and-dance partner. DiPaolo, barely 13 when he tried out for *The Star Maker*, was instructed by Prinz not to change a thing when Crosby showed up to hear the lad sing "Stardust" for the fifth time in his five auditions. "Do it exactly that way because Bing really likes 'Star Dust,'" Prinz smartly advised DiPaolo, who told Gary Giddins.[63]

Paramount characteristically played up Ware's potential as a "sensational singing discovery" as the premiere neared for the girl, now age 14, in August 1939. She was handed a couple of orchestral classics to perform on screen, and, for variety's sake, the pop chestnut "Darktown Strutters' Ball" and "An Apple for the Teacher," one of four Jimmy Monaco-Johnny Burke songs penned for the movie. "Teacher" became the film's biggest commercial hit, as recorded by Crosby and Connee Boswell. Another of the new tunes, "A Man and His Dream," shows Crosby in *primo* voice for what is something of a theme song for this story. A further Crosby highlight is a plaintive rendition of the timeless "I Wonder Who's Kissing Her Now," an old song but not Gus Edwards'. There is plenty of Edwards music in the film, but it is mostly limited to the depictions of the Larry Earl revues instead of being integrated into the plot. "School Days," led by Bing in drab schoolmaster's garb, is presented in an audience sing-along format that firmly nods to its nostalgic status, and in 1939, theater patrons wouldn't have been shy about singing it back. The last of Crosby's 19 starring features in the 1930s, *The Star Maker* at least ranks among the better entries of his uneven output over the second half of the decade. His next release, *Road to Singapore* (1940), paired him with Bob Hope and pushed his career to a higher plain of popularity.

The returns for *The Star Maker* were favorable, and it opened to brisk late-summer business. *The Film Daily* went so far as to call it "far and away the best picture Bing Crosby has made to date."[64] Having showed her range on highbrow and lowbrow fare in her screen baptism, Ware was praised as well, even if commentators were not shy to put the brakes on lofty comparisons to Deanna Durbin. *The New York Times* sicced critic Frank Nugent on the picture, and he snottily dismissed Edwards as a "show-minded Pied Piper who used to swing around the old vaudevjlle circuits" and then doubled down: "…It is all, if Mr. Edwards will pardon us, too much like a Gus Edwards revue and far too much of that."[65]

Edwards himself must have winced at Paramount ads touting *The Star Maker* as "the thrilling, true-to-life story" of the impresario, although his reaction to the film seems to have gone publicly unreported. We do know that, on August 18, 1939, when a banquet was given in Los Angeles to commemorate Edwards' 60th birthday, a host of his protégés showed up—but Ware and Rogers, not Crosby, represented *The Star Maker* to the star maker.[66] We also know that Edwards continued to live sedately, health failing (with paresis a rumored cause), still accepting plaudits, before suffering a fatal heart attack at age 66. And that when Joan Edwards, before she became prominent on radio as a *Your Hit Parade* vocalist, sought advice from her Uncle Gus about her intended vocation, he warned her to "stay out of show business."[67]

One wonders if Linda Ware might have reacted to the same warning, for nothing that followed the *Star Maker* opening night quite lived up. Ware was busy with radio and personal appearance dates during the early '40s but made only one more movie, singing two unmemorable songs in a 1941 PRC crime drama, *Paper Bullets* (aka *Gangs, Inc.*). She endured more intrafamilial strife, as her long-estranged father attempted to re-enter her life; her response was that he "never so much as bought me an ice cream cone."[68] During World War II, Ware (1925–1975) married an Army Air Corps lieutenant, but they were divorced within a few years, and she was scammed out of the $185 she was to get for selling her engagement and wedding rings.[69] Ware continued a modest singing career that lasted almost up until her death in Las Vegas at age 50.

But think of it: For the little while she was a star, Ware represented another small victory for the great Gus Edwards.[70]

The Great Victor Herbert
(Paramount; December 6, 1939)

Director/Producer: Andrew L. Stone. Executive Producer: William LeBaron. Screenplay: Russel Crouse, Robert Lively. Story: Andrew L. Stone, Robert Lively. Photography: Victor Milner. Editor: James Smith. Art Direction: Hans Dreier, Ernest Fegte. Set Decoration: A.E. Freudeman. Costumes: Edith Head. Sound: Hugh Grenzbach, John Cope. Musical Director: Arthur Kay. Music Supervisor: Phil Boutelje. Score: Arthur Lange. Vocal Arrangements: Max Terr. Dance Director: LeRoy Prinz. Production Manager: Robert Stillman. Assistant Director: Stanley Goldsmith. Running Time: 91 minutes.

Cast: Allan Jones (John Ramsey); Mary Martin (Louise Hall); Walter Connolly (Victor Herbert); Lee Bowman (Dr. Richard Moore); Susanna Foster (Peggy); Judith Barrett (Marie Clark); Jerome Cowan (Barney Harris); John Garrick (Warner Bryant); Pierre Watkin (Albert Martin); Richard Tucker (Michael Brown); Hal K. Dawson (George Faller); Emmett Vogan (Forbes); Mary Currier (Mrs. Victor Herbert); James Finlayson (lamplighter); Sandra Lee Richards (young Peggy); Betty Bryson (ballerina); Billy Engle (cab driver); Jack Gardner, Josef Swickard (reporters); Arthur Stuart Hull (sultan); Gertrude Messinger (Barney's secretary); Bert Roach (backstage comic singer); Harry Tyler (man at parade); George Walcott (Denton); Fred Warren (piano player); Carroll Nye (man listening outside window); Larry Steers (man backstage at *Rose of the World*).

Songs (*sung in "bicycle" medley): "Absinthe Frappé" (from *It Happened in Nordland*) [orchestra at party], "Ask Her While the Band Is Playing"* (from *The Rose of Algeria*) [Martin], "March of the Toys" (from *Babes in Toyland*) [parade band], "Rose of the World" (from *The Rose of Algeria*) [Foster, Garrick, Jones, chorus], "Twilight in Barakeesh" (from *The Rose of Algeria*) [chorus, orchestra] (Glen MacDonough, Victor Herbert), "All for You" (finale of *The Princess Pat*) [Martin, Jones, chorus], "Kiss Me Again" (aka "If I Were on the Stage," from *Mlle. Modiste*) [Foster], "Neapolitan Love Song"* (from *The Princess Pat*) [Jones], "Thine Alone" (from *Eileen*) [Jones, Martin] (Henry Blossom, Victor Herbert); "I'm the Leader of Society"* (from *The Viceroy*) [Martin], "There Once Was an Owl" (from *Babette*) [Jones, Martin, chorus], "To the Land of My Own Romance" (from *The Enchantress*) [Foster, Garrick, Jones, chorus, twice] (Harry B. Smith, Victor Herbert); "Ah! Sweet Mystery of Life" (from *Naughty Marietta*) [Jones, Martin, chorus], "I'm Falling in Love with Someone"* (from *Naughty Marietta*) [Jones] (Rida Johnson Young, Victor Herbert); "How Did You Get That Way?"* (from *Angel Face*) [Martin], "I Might Be Your 'Once-in-a-While'"* (from *Angel Face*) [Martin], "Lullaby (Bye, Bye, Baby)" (from *Angel Face*) [Jones] (Robert B. Smith, Victor Herbert); "Al Fresco" [Martin sings to new lyrics as "I Am Beautiful"], "Punchinello" [chorus sings to new lyrics as "Happy Day"], "Yesterthoughts" [Martin, Jones, chorus sings to new lyrics as "Wonderful Dreams"] (Frank Loesser, Phil Boutelje, Victor Herbert); "Fleurette" [orchestra at party], "A Kiss in the Dark" (from *Orange Blossoms*) [chorus, reprised by Martin] (B.G. De Sylva, Victor Herbert); "Some Day" (from *Her Regiment*) [Jones, chorus] (William LeBaron, Victor Herbert); "Air de Ballet" [dancers], "Chang the Lover" (from *The Willow Plate*) [Richards], "I Love Thee, I Adore Thee"* (from *The Serenade*) [Jones] (Victor Herbert).

Working Titles/Also Known As: *The Gay Days of Victor Herbert*; *The Life and Melodies of Victor Herbert*; *The Life of Victor Herbert*; *Victor Herbert*.

Academy Award Nominations: Best Cinematography, Black and White (Victor Milner); Best Music, Scoring (Phil Boutelje, Arthur Lange); Best Sound Recording (Paramount Sound Department, Loren L. Ryder, sound director).

The Story: An inexperienced actress falters on stage during an opening-night performance of "Rose of the World," an operetta written and conducted by the famed composer Victor Herbert, but she rallies as the performance continues. After the show, Herbert explains to reporters the girl's story. Shown in flashback, 14 years earlier, Louise Hall is a small-town choir singer who is new to New York when she, by chance, sings a duet ("Ah! Sweet Mystery of Life") with gifted but egotistical operetta star John Ramsey. John takes a professional and personal interest in Louise. He invites Louise to a birthday party for Victor and convinces the composer to listen to her ("There Once Was an Owl"). Although impressed, Victor declines to cast her in his new show because she's not a name. John's agent, Barney Harris, and a jealous showgirl, Marie Clark, disparage Louise's abilities. Louise's hometown sweetheart, Dr. Dick Moore, visits her but she forsakes him in favor of John. Over Victor's concerns, Louise lands a leading role in the latest Herbert production once the composer learns she and John are now married. Barney warns John that his box office appeal will decline now that he has a wife, and he is proven correct, as Louise's career begins to overshadow his. John complains about being billed below Louise, but he relents when he discovers she has been trying to keep him top-starred. John and Louise welcome a daughter, Peggy. Louise decides to retire from the stage in deference to John, who has been relegated to second leads ("Some Day") behind tenor Warner Bryant. Louise and Peggy move to Switzerland before returning home, and Dick comes to New York to do important medical research regarding children and pneumonia. Louise becomes a voice teacher as she raises Peggy into her teens and John is forced into demeaning parts in obscure acting companies. Peggy shows talent ("Kiss Me Again") and impresses Victor, but John walks out on his family after an acrimonious Christmas celebration and is exiled by Barney to a tour of Australia. In 1914, Louise is convinced to make a comeback in a revival of one of her old shows with Bryant, as Victor is determined that operettas make a comeback in the ragtime era. When vocal problems sideline Louise, Peggy steps into her role, and the flashback ends as the action returns to the first night of "Rose of the World." When Peggy reveals her jitters, John takes the stage to help his daughter attain stardom ("To the Land of My Romance").

Buoyed by his resourcefulness with the Gilbert-and-Sullivan tribute *The Girl Said No* [q.v.], Andrew L. Stone emerged as a major-musical maker with a major-studio entry, *The Great Victor Herbert*, in 1939. Even as he utilized the songbook of Tin Pan Alley's first superstar, Stone made Herbert a peripheral character in a romance that co-starred one of Hollywood's most talented tenors in Allan Jones and a new-to-film actress-soprano from Texas who became a megastar herself—although it was on Broadway and not on the screen where Mary Martin clicked. Infrequently shown today, *Victor* was a popular attraction for Paramount in 1939, as patrons blissfully immersed themselves in the music of a master who was not so long gone and certainly not forgotten.

Just as he had grown up listening to Gilbert and Sullivan, Stone had loved the works of Herbert, the prolific Irish-American songwriter, conductor, and cellist whose repertoire covered traditional Euro-styled romantic operetta (*Babes in Toyland, Naughty Marietta, The Red Mill*); grand opera; orchestral compositions ("Irish Rhapsody"); and *Ziegfeld Follies* interpolations. If he had never written a note, Herbert (1859–1924) would have earned the everlasting gratitude of his brethren by co-founding ASCAP in 1914. In 1935, 11 years after Herbert was felled by a heart attack, Paramount began talk of a film about him, but no one could agree about how to present a life that was light on public drama. The project's original title, *The Life and Melodies of Victor Herbert*, promised more than it could deliver, as prospective writers grappled with how much of that life to portray.[71]

The making of the Herbert film may have been hastened by the occasion of Herbert's 80th-anniversary year, which also included a retrospective of his works at the New York World's Fair and the issuing of a 3-cent postage stamp depicting the composer. Scenarios by Benjamin Glazer and Gilbert Gabriel had been shelved, and it was left to Stone to enter as director and producer and decide the final focus. Penned by Russel Crouse and Robert Lively and based on a story by Stone and Lively, the script that was filmed set Herbert as sort of a kindly uncle to two singing lovers whose careers diverge in a *Star Is Born* manner—meaning his star eclipsed by hers. Stone seeks to deal with the lack of salaciousness in Herbert's life by not giving him a real personality and not imposing anything on him besides a wife (who is seen only briefly), a habit of working at a standing desk, and a birthday to celebrate.

Stone has it both ways in that—unlike Irving Berlin's treatment of himself in *Alex-*

Mary Martin is welcomed to the movies by the soon-to-depart Walter Connolly, a natural for the title role in *The Great Victor Herbert*.

ander's Ragtime Band—he doesn't feel inclined to pretend his subject doesn't exist, but he allows the viewer to see enough of Victor Herbert so as not to feel cheated by the film's title. It helped immensely that Stone cast an actor with a strong physical resemblance to Herbert—Walter Connolly, the portly, mustached character player known for supporting portrayals of cranky but good-hearted businessmen. If the Best Supporting Actor Oscar had existed when Connolly played Claudette Colbert's father in *It Happened One Night* (1934), Connolly would have been a shoo-in to be nominated. For Stone's film, Connolly's character needed only to have lifted his baton and been properly benevolent to succeed, for there was no intent to probe his subject's psyche.

In contrast to the opening disclaimer about the lack of historical accuracy in *Captain of the Guard* [q.v.], Stone waits until the end titles to provide a similar on-screen explanation: "No attempt has been made to depict in this picture the actual life of the immortal Victor Herbert…. A careful effort has been made, however, to preserve the character and mood of the great composer whose music serves as the inspiration for this picture." This text was added at the request of Ella Herbert Bartlett, the composer's daughter, who was functioning as an advisor on the project, and who was strongly protective of her father's reputation. If Stone and Paramount seemed particularly attuned to the concerns of Bartlett, it may have stemmed from her discontent at *Babes in Toyland* being made into a 1934 Laurel and Hardy romp by Hal Roach and with liberties taken in story and the Herbert music for the Jeanette MacDonald-Nelson Eddy vehicles *Naughty Marietta* (1935) and *Sweethearts* (1938) at MGM. The Herbert contingent was happy with Paramount's old-school choice for music director, Arthur Kay, a favorite conductor of the composer and, like Herbert, schooled in Germany.

The official title of Stone's movie was to be *The Gay Days of Victor Herbert*, but it was changed just before its premiere in early December after a complaint from Bartlett that it would be "libelous" and "damaging" to her father's reputation.[72] By this time, Stone had, in six weeks ending September 30, 1939, finished a production costing $780,000—his *Girl Said No* expenditure tenfold—and $37,500 over budget.[73] Some two-dozen Herbert melodies were featured, including excerpts from multiple operettas—with show titles slightly changed for the screen, as Paramount had purchased rights to the music, but not to the operetta settings.[74] This allowed Stone to take artistic license and present songs from different shows as in the same production, to the possible objections of Herbert devotees. *The Rose of Algeria*, a now-obscure 1909 stage offering, gets the most exposure, as excerpts from it make up the framing footage of the story. In addition to the tinkering with the original operetta performances, Frank Loesser, then a contract lyricist at Paramount, was enlisted to supply words to renditions of some Herbert instrumental pieces—with Ella Bartlett's blessing.

All three of the main actors in *The Great Victor Herbert* had something important to prove, Connolly (1887–1940) because of the chance to justify his improved billing and Jones (1907–1992) because he was coming off nearly a year and a half of inactivity at his former home, MGM. Competition squelched by that studio's go-to tenor, Nelson Eddy, was rumored as the reason. Martin hadn't even appeared in a film yet, but she was already famous for her star-making "My Heart Belongs to Daddy" mock-striptease number from her first Broadway show, Cole Porter's *Leave It to Me!* She had more at stake than either of her co-stars. Martin (1913–1990) had tested at MGM and Universal in 1936–37 but was found wanting; her nose was deemed too big or her chin declared too small, or she wasn't shapely enough. "Daddy" landed her a contract in Hollywood, but she couldn't be kept there. Martin was seen in nine films at Paramount between 1939 and 1943, which except for a couple of later cameos as herself and at least one early stint as an uncredited voice dubber, constituted her entire big-screen career. The movies failed to capitalize on the outsized stage personality of *Peter Pan* and *South Pacific*; on celluloid, she was just another singer—or, at least in the case of *The Great Victor Herbert*, a Jeanette MacDonald knockoff.

Stone cast Martin over the objections of studio head William LeBaron, and the director rehearsed extensively with her. Jones, Connolly and fellow cast member Jerome Cowan generously gave Martin advice on camera technique as filming progressed, and dance director LeRoy Prinz gave her a two-week crash course in ballet that made her feet bleed from under their slippers.[75] As Martin recalled in her autobiography about the lead-up to her screen debut:

> …For months, the makeup men had a field day. Using my same face, they made me up to look exactly like Jean Parker … and Jean Arthur…. Claudette Colbert … and Rosalind Russell … kinda. They even tried to make me look sexy. But most of the time, I just looked sick.[76]

Perhaps she was exaggerating this reminiscence, for the response to Martin in *The Great Victor Herbert* was encouraging. Bosley Crowther of *The New York Times* praised her for developing "unexpected resources in the role of an actress as well as that of a frivolous chanteuse, and a charmingly juvenile songstress."[77] In other words, she wasn't bad at all. But her singing of "A Kiss in the Dark" and other melodies aren't a match for what we're used to seeing from her; the hindsight is to our detriment. When Ethel Merman does Annie Oakley, it's Ethel Merman. When Mary Martin does a generic 1910 operetta soprano, she's a generic soprano. She's still charming, and Stone stuffs in as much Herbert as possible, most charmingly in a Martin-Jones medley sung during a bicycle ride through the country. Without the time-taking back projection Stone so disliked, the two actors trade situationally appropriate catchphrases from a variety of Herbertian sources. With his own charm and not much more to do than look Victor-ly, Connolly also engendered great praise, but he had little time to enjoy it. In May 1940, he died after a stroke at his Los Angeles-area home.

The *Times*' Crowther echoed the mixed thoughts of many professional reviewers in his overall view of the film as "a large and splendid ... tribute to the Irish genius.... If Victor Herbert were the sort of man we think he was, he is turning in his grave today. But his music ... is still inimitably superb, still the greatest show music that ever struck ... the Broadway sector."[78] *Variety* was more upbeat: "It is elaborately produced, visually effective.... With the advantages of Victor Herbert's superlative score, the film should please the musically inclined."[79] Even with the positive reviews, *The Great Victor Herbert*'s box office outperformed big-city press expectations as one of the 1939–40 season's most underrated releases, according to a survey by *Motion Picture Herald*.[80]

An unforeseen reason for the respect for *The Great Victor Herbert* was its unveiling of one of the season's most promising juvenile talents in 14-year-old Susanna Foster, cast as the offspring of Jones and Martin. She sings "Kiss Me Again" as a warm-up to her triumph on stage at the climax with "To the Land of My Romance." Foster's discovery was much belated, as the native of Minnesota had spent a year at MGM buried deep among its talent roster and without a shred of work, under her real name of Suzanne Larson. A project to be titled *B Above High C*, a peak singing level this prodigy could attain, was announced for her but went unmade. A new agent and voice teacher led Foster to Paramount, where she tried out for *The Star Maker* [q.v.] but lost out to Linda Ware.[81] But choreographer Prinz took note, and Foster won out for *The Great Victor Herbert* in a well-publicized teen-talent search for an unknown coloratura that purportedly sent studio execs to New York, London, and Paris.[82] They needn't have bothered to go so far. Foster (1924–2009) went on to co-star in *Phantom of the Opera* (1943) for Universal before retiring a few years later for marriage and a family.[83]

In what was perhaps Oscar's most competitive year, *The Great Victor Herbert* earned three Academy Award nominations, for black-and-white cinematography, sound recording, and scoring. Armed with a fresh Paramount contract, Stone continued to make musicals—he followed *Herbert* with *The Hard-Boiled Canary* (1941), a tuneful comedy reuniting Jones and Foster. Then came *Stormy Weather* (1943), an all-black Fox production with Lena Horne and Bill "Bojangles" Robinson; *Hi Diddle Diddle* (1944), an independent project via UA; and *Sensations of 1945* (1944), an indie that marked W.C. Fields' film finale. Stone worked closely with his then-wife, co-producer and film editor, Virginia Lively Stone, and became best remembered for a run of self-produced, gritty, location-realistic 1950s crime thrillers: *Highway 301*, *A Blueprint for Murder*, and *Cry Terror!* among them. The quest for realism prompted Stone to partially sink an ocean liner for *The Last Voyage* (1960) and to wreck a train on a burning bridge for *Ring of Fire* (1961).

Stone gained his lone Academy Award nomination for his original screenplay for *Julie* (1956), an MGM thriller. But he returned to musicals, the romantic melodies he had heard in his youth in California still echoing. Unfortunately, Stone hastened the end of his long career with the failure of two lavishly mounted composer biopics, *Song of Norway* (1970, about Edvard Grieg) and *The Great Waltz* (1972, on Johann Strauss II). At least after *The Great Victor Herbert*, he could go to his grave—which he did at age 97—knowing for certain he'd done right by his subject. Some of the proof came in the response from Herbert's family, for in 1940, the composer's son-in-law wrote to Stone about their reaction to his movie: "You may be interested to know that we are going to see *The Great Victor Herbert* for the third time…. It is a picture which grows on one and the more we see it the better we like it."[84] We can't help but feel the same.

3

A Hillbilly Sym-Funny

"STICKS NIX HICK PIX." Such read the now-famous headline—as outsized as *Variety* could make it—on July 17, 1935, in the lead story on the front page of the most widely read publication in show business. The cleverly rhyming lead-in was a tad misleading. The story below concerned the moviegoing preferences of rural audiences, but it was based only on an interview with a lone theater operator from Iowa. And it didn't really stress that the farm-and-country folk didn't turn out for pictures about people like themselves, more that they liked higher-class subjects—the likes of *The Barretts of Wimpole Street* and *The Scarlet Pimpernel*—more than one might expect. Still, that such a paper would consider "HICK PIX" as screamer material made a statement about the significance of rural-themed films and their mid–1930s viewership.

People had been watching pix set in the country practically since the advent of the medium, but what was different now was that they could have music—the kind that could be enjoyed by hicks and non-hicks alike. This resulted from the growth of two related, yet marginally different, strains of American music that emerged from similar roots but different geographic areas. Country music, then known as "hillbilly," originated in the South, primarily in Appalachia, during the 1920s, and Western music, or "cowboy," came out of the great expanse beyond the Mississippi River, mainly during the decades after the Civil War. Both styles were influenced by the folk ballads of England, Scotland, and Ireland. Eventually, they would come together in a genre termed "country western." Population trends fed the growth of hillbilly/country, as folks from the East moved West, especially to California and the West Coast, and Southern farm refugees filled growing cities both in that region and in labor-hungry Northern industrial locales. One could be from anywhere and claim "hillbilly" kinship, however, according to cultural historian J.W. Williamson, who in retrospect defined the term as: "rough, rural, poor but fruitful, blatantly antiurban, and often dangerous, but not necessarily hailing from the Southern Appalachians or even from any mountain."[1]

An important boost for hillbilly culture came from the advent and expansion of radio and sound recordings. The *National Barn Dance*, the first country radio program, began in 1924 in Chicago and was spun off a year later into the Nashville-based *Grand Old Opry*, the most famous country radio show. Other radio programs, the long-running country-store comedy *Lum and Abner* foremost among them, spotlighted rural values, and within their formats, city slickers were regularly outfoxed by the perceived simpletons. Propelled by the popularity of Mississippi-born "yodeling" vocalist Jimmie Rodgers and others, hillbilly and rural records represented 25 percent of the 65 million records sold in 1929.[2] This led to talent scouts scouring the country for people who could sing in the Rodgers style, especially in the wake of the singer's sudden death in 1933. The most famous to follow in Rodgers' path was Oklahoma's Gene Autry, who would in time transition from yodeling hillbilly singer to radio star to cinema icon.

The hillbilly craze continued unabated even as the Depression deepened. Folks may not have had the money to buy records or sheet music, but the radio was entertainment for free and the movies charged cheap. By 1934, it was plausible for Fox to insert a couple of hick-related song numbers into a mass-audience feature film—in this case, the Depression-themed comedy *Stand Up and Cheer!*—while knowing that viewers were clued in. After the government's new "Secretary of Amusement" (portrayed by Warner Baxter) calls for hillbilly tunes to please the huddled masses, he gets "Broadway's Gone Hill-Billy" (with vocalist Sylvia Froos leading a rope-twirling dance ensemble) and "She's Way Up Thar" (in which John "Skins" Miller sings to Stepin Fetchit about his mountain-based sweetheart).

Not surprisingly, however, it was the musical short subject that began the rural influence in motion pictures. Rodgers himself, the "Singing Brakeman," was captured by Columbia in a 1930 one-reeler that preserved renditions of "Waiting for a Train" and "T for Texas," helping to verify his posthumous christening as "The Father of Country Music." Frank Luther, a prolific composer and performer of early country and popular host of radio's *Hillbilly Heart Throbs*, made a series of low-budget shorts at Educational Pictures in 1934–35 with country/Western/nostalgic stories. Entries such as *Hillbilly Love*, *Mountain Melody*, and *Rodeo Day* were filled with music to compensate for bare-bones plotting. When Luther went on to his only feature film, it would be to star as an uptown radio tenor in the quickie *High Hat* (1936), with scarcely a hint of his work as a non-sophisticate. Although Rodgers died young (of tuberculosis) and Luther transitioned into other kinds of music, others were eager to step in to cater to small-town audiences who shared hillbilly values even if they weren't hillbillies themselves. Further fodder for small-towners came in the forms of the Cabin Kids, an African American quintet of children who were featured in 11 Educational musical comedies of 1935–38 before ending their film stint in Gene Autry Westerns.

The integration of hillbilly into pop culture was a double-edged sword. Snobby Coasters could use the term as a putdown of "white trash." After the 1930s, "hillbilly" declined in use in favor of the more neutral "country," at least until *The Beverly Hillbillies* became a 1960s TV sitcom hit to Americans everywhere. The guitar- and fiddle-centered rural music form stressed simple values of loyalty, family, and piety of which natives, turning the "hillbilly" slur on its head, could be proud—and with which even more-cultured folks could connect as nostalgia for simpler times in an age of economic upheaval and changing social traditions. As comic material for the movies, country types were parodied for their lack of education, sophistication, guile, or cleanliness, and the songs in many hillbilly musicals were, as written by Hollywood/New York craftsmen like Johnny Mercer and Sam Coslow, mere imitations of "pure" country. Although screen hicks were belittled and swindled by Northerners, they usually emerged victorious and unsullied, and if they could carry a tune as well as outfox their so-called betters, all the better to curry audience favor.

"Their" music was exploding. In August 1937, performers from eight Dixie states gathered for the annual Mountain Music and Dance Festival, touted by *Variety* as "the largest gathering of mountain music and folk dance 'artists' ever held in America."[3] (Note the doubting quote marks around "artists.") That event took place in Asheville, North Carolina, but the epicenter of 1930s-1940s hill tunery was Arkansas, the hardcore-country locale of *Lum and Abner*, Bob "The Arkansas Traveler" Burns, and the hillbilly trio Weaver Brothers and Elviry. Arkansas also was the setting of what one might call the *Citizen Kane* of 1930s cornpone film musicals—Paramount's way-over-the-top *Mountain Music* (1937), which co-starred actor/humorist/musician Burns. He played a mountain man who suffers amnesia whenever hit on the head, is suspected of murdering his brother, and is being pursued for marriage by big-mouthed Martha Raye ... not necessarily in the order of gravity.

The geographic inspirations for *Mountain Music* bought into Paramount hype. Especially elaborate, at least by Arkansas standards, was the promotion of the picture's Southern premiere in the state's resort town of Hot Springs—which was one of the on-screen locales. The manager of the local Malco Theatre outlet, one W. Clyde Smith, cooked up festivities that included a parade by Boy Scouts and a boys bazooka band, prizes for best-dressed couples at a costume party, a mock hillbilly wedding, and an "Old Fiddlers' Mountain Music" contest, all advancing screenings at a movie house that Smith adorned with a mock front meant to look like a cabin, composed of bark slabs and a railing fence at the edge of the street side. The guest list for the Hot Springs bash was topped by actual relatives of Bob Burns (as opposed to the actual Bob Burns). Smith's effort earned him a special bronze "Quigley Plaque" from the publishers of the trade publication *Motion Picture Herald*.[4] Marketing a hillbilly movie could be fun, and more than one theater manager around the nation was assigning his employees to don fake beards—or grow new ones—to mimic the country-cousin look.

Mountain Music was crazier and more endearingly stupid than another prominent hillbilly picture, Warner Bros.' *Swing Your Lady** (1938), the acknowledged *Heaven's Gate* of hick pix. *Swing Your Lady* hasn't aged well, as a professional-wrestling-themed musical comedy with Nat Pendleton and Louise Fazenda as lovey-dovey opposing grapplers. It has become best known as Humphrey Bogart's worst movie, but Bogart would find better things to do, and fortunately, so did the country movie subgenre. It moseyed into the 1940s as the market for its music grew in number and geography, propelled by modest song-filled comedies at sub-major Republic. Some of those Republics starred the Weavers and Elviry—who managed to escape from the ignominy of singing and acting in *Swing Your Lady*, as if to remind us something positive had come out of Bogey's folly.

Pigskin Parade
(20th Century–Fox; October 23, 1936)

Director: David Butler. Associate Producer: Bogart Rogers. Screenplay: Harry Tugend, Jack Yellen, William Conselman. Story: Arthur Sheekman, Nat Perrin, Mark Kelly. Photography: Arthur Miller. Editing: Irene Morra. Art Director: Art Peters. Set Decoration: Thomas Little. Costumes: Gwen Wakeling. Music Director: David Buttolph. Sound: Bernard Freericks, Roger Heman. Assistant Director: Ad Schaumer, Jack Temple. Technical Advisor: Victor M. Kelly. Running Time: 95 minutes.

Cast: Stuart Erwin (Amos Dodd); Patsy Kelly (Bessie Winters); Jack Haley (Slug Winters); Yacht Club Boys (themselves); Johnny Downs (Chip Carson); Betty Grable (Laura Watson); Arline Judge (Sally Saxon); Dixie Dunbar (Ginger Jones); Judy Garland (Sairy Dodd); Anthony [Tony] Martin (Tommy Barker); Fred Kohler, Jr. (Biff Bentley); Grady Sutton (Mortimer Higgins); Elisha Cook, Jr. (Herbert Terwilliger Van Dyck); Eddie Nugent (Sparks); Julius Tannen (Dr. Burke); Pat Flaherty (referee); Sam Hayes (radio announcer); Robert McClung (harmonica-playing country boy); Jack Murphy (usher); David Sharpe (messenger boy); Si Jenks (baggage master); John Dilson (doctor); Jack Stoney (police officer); George Y. Harvey (brakeman); Hal Seiling, Orville Mathews (football players); Ben Hall (young man in stadium); Al Klein (man in stadium); Charles C. Wilson (Yale coach); George Offerman, Jr. (Freddy); Maurice Cass (Professor Tutweiler); Jack Best (Professor McCormick); Douglas Wood (Professor Dutton); Charles Croker-King (Professor Pillsbury); Edward LeSaint (judge); George Herbert, Cyril Ring (professors); Alan Ladd, June Gale (students).

Songs: "The Balboa" [Garland, Dunbar, Yacht Club Boys, Downs, Grable, Haley, Kelly, chorus], "Hold That Bulldog" [cut from film but listed in opening credits]; "It's Love I'm After" [Garland], "T.S.U. Alma Mater" [chorus], "The Texas Tornado" [Garland, reprised by chorus], "You're Slightly Terrific"

3. A Hillbilly Sym-Funny

[Martin, Dunbar, chorus], "You Do the Darndest Things, Baby" [Haley, Judge] (Sidney D. Mitchell, Lew Pollock); "Down with Everything" [Yacht Club Boys, chorus], "Football Song" ("We Brought the Texas Sunshine Here with Us") [Yacht Club Boys], "We'd Rather Be in College" [Yacht Club Boys], "Woo! Woo!" [Yacht Club Boys, chorus] (Yacht Club Boys); "Fox Chase" [McClung] (trad.); "Oh! Susanna" [McClung] (Stephen Foster).
Alternate Title: *Harmony Parade*.
Academy Award Nomination: Best Supporting Actor (Stuart Erwin).
Disc: Decca 957 ("It's Love I'm After"/"You're Slightly Terrific," Tony Martin with Victor Young Orchestra).
Home Video: 20th Century–Fox DVD.

The story: Officials from Yale University decide to issue an invitation to the University of Texas for a game against Yale's mighty football team, but a clerical error directs the missive instead to tiny Texas State University (enrollment: 700). TSU, which hasn't won on the gridiron in two years, accepts the bid just as its new football coach, Slug Winters, and his sharp-tongued wife, Bessie, arrive at the school from New York. The bickering couple are greeted by student Chip Carson, TSU's athletics manager and publicity director; his girlfriend, Laura Watson; and singing-and-dancing students Tommy Barker and Ginger Jones. Texas State's chances to win are curtailed when the team's best player, Biff Bentley, is injured. On a "recruiting" trip to Arkansas, Bessie, Chip, and Laura discover Amos Dodd, a football-throwing hillbilly prodigy whom they enroll at TSU after falsifying his credentials. Amos' sweet-singing sister, Sairy, comes along to study music ("The Balboa"). To distract man-hungry co-ed Sally Saxon from Amos, Bessie convinces her husband to pretend to make love to Sally ("You Do the Darndest Things, Baby"). Sairy sings "The Texas Tornado" to send the team off to Yale for its showdown, and on the day of the big game, she entertains the crowd on the field with "It's Love I'm After." In the game, played in a blizzard, Bessie devises a last-second passing play that a shoeless Amos improvises into a long run for the winning touchdown. The TSU contingent celebrates with a reprise of "The Texas Tornado."

A box-office champion from the newly amalgamated 20th Century–Fox, the feel-good college musical *Pigskin Parade* was about more than just football, alma mater, and David versus Goliath. It also was one of those *Variety*-termed "hick pix" with two prominent backwoods characters—one that set the fixins for the first Academy Award–nominated hillbilly performance, and the other a mini-dynamo played by a teenager who would grow up to become one of Hollywood's greatest musical stars. Meet Stuart Erwin and Judy Garland—playing siblings from Arkansas who give *Pigskin Parade* that little extra kick.

The pair initially seemed like just two more components in a starless cast filled with Fox-rostered secondary players—Jack Haley, Patsy Kelly, Dixie Dunbar, Tony Martin, Arline Judge—and two college-student-attractive loan-outs—Betty Grable from RKO and Johnny Downs from Paramount. TCF had MGM to thank for the services of both Erwin and Garland, albeit for very different reasons. Slow-talkin' Erwin (1903–1967) had been playing unsophisticated but likable comic types on the screen since the dawn of sound, including a turn as a college gridder in the Paramount musical *Sweetie* (1929) that helped earn him his first long-term studio contract. Then, he was a lunkheaded lineman; now, after a routine loan from Metro to Fox, he was fitting right in as a simple-minded but strong-armed quarterback. "He has the only voice in Hollywood with the priceless quality of being funny without anything particularly funny to say," a fan magazine writer wrote of Erwin's oddly appealing California twang. "…His funnybone is in his throat."[5]

The backstory for Garland (1922–1969) was more complicated, as the little girl with the big voice was not yet considered ready for prime time, and her rental for *Pigskin Parade* amounted to an audition on the Fox dime. Now a solo act after years of performing with

Stuart Erwin and Judy Garland (center) play hillbilly siblings who shake up college football in *Pigskin Parade*, with (from left) Jack Haley, Patsy Kelly, Johnny Downs, and Betty Grable.

her sisters in vaudeville, and in occasional movie shorts, she attracted the attention of Metro czar Louis B. Mayer during a date with her sisters and was summoned to the studio for a screen test. She was immediately signed to a contract, but MGM had no immediate work for a 5-foot-zip, slightly chubby teen with regular-gal looks. She was too old to be Shirley Temple and too young to be Alice Faye. Forced to decide between two teen singers on their roster, MGM kept the straight-ahead pop of Garland over the operatic strains of Deanna Durbin, who was soon to create a sensation at Universal.[6] As *Pigskin Parade* went before the cameras in August and September 1936 for release in late October, Garland's home studio was about to learn if it had made the right call.

We don't see Garland or Erwin until the film is nearly half done, after the action takes a jaunt to the dregs of the Razorback State. Heretofore, we have seen obscure Texas State University—led by its wide-eyed football coach (Haley) and his deceptively game-savvy spouse (Kelly)—accidentally get invited to play against mighty Yale but lose its best player to injury. On a talent hunt to Arkansas, Kelly, Downs, and Grable encounter a taciturn, overalls-clad kid (played by Robert McClung) who seems to communicate best by playing a couple of numbers on his harmonica—the closest to what *Pigskin Parade* offers in actual hick music. The lad supplies his own sound effects, including dog barks, of a fox hunt, and then offers up "Oh! Susanna" as played through his nose.[7]

Eventually, the kid tells the visitors that the rural prospect they've come to recruit has been snapped up by none other than Yale! No matter, for Erwin's character shows them that he can throw muskmelons into a net held by his kid sister (Garland) from 50 yards away—

and we realize we are looking at the solution to TSU's personnel deficit. This is followed by some amusing exploitations of hick-comedy tropes: The new quarterback can throw well only while barefoot (he has the biggest feet in his county), he and his sister fail to recognize each other when out of their farm rags, she mistakes an ear-wash bottle brand for a fancy alias, and the Texas State folks sit through the big game at Yale wearing cowboy/cowgirl garb.

Garland is ninth-billed as Amos' sis, Sairy, who follows him to Texas State to study music. The teen's role was initially to encompass little more than a running gag in which Sairy would ask if she could do a song—as in "Why won't somebody listen to me sing?"—but consistently be told not to because no one thought she would be any good.[8] However, Garland's voice—astonishingly mature for a 14-year-old—was too good to be wasted, even as a mini-Judy Canova. This would explain the out-of-place rendition of a ballad, Sidney Mitchell and Lew Pollack's "It's Love I'm After," by Garland on the field as a warm-up for the climatic Big Game. The game itself was filmed by director David Butler on a 60-yard layout on the Fox backlot, with newsreel footage of a college game played in the snow matched in with the fictional action.[9]

More in the film's jolly mood are two Garland-led numbers—the dance showcase "The Balboa," and "The Texas Tornado," a rousing tune that's a Western tune in title only ... and, well ... for the guns shot off by some of the singers. The last of those numbers was filmed on the field in the Los Angeles Memorial Coliseum, and actress June Gale, then a bit player seated in the stadium, years later recalled its power: "The voice! The voice! I can hear it now, it was so remarkable."[10] In his own reminiscence, Butler agreed: "I'll never forget her because she had a tremendous voice ... a beautiful, wonderful voice."[11]

The outsiders from MGM aren't the only high scorers in *Pigskin Parade*. Haley and Kelly make a great team to lead a team: In a bit of gender-stereotype reversal, she spends time at home drawing up plays while hubby dons an apron to wash dishes. She taunts him with insults like "You haven't got a brain!" and thinks so little of the coach that she's willing to let him pitch woo to gold-digging student Judge to keep her away from Erwin. (It was a heart, not a brain, that Haley's Tin Man lacked when he and Garland were reunited in *The Wizard of Oz*.) Martin and Dunbar duet capably on a love song, "You're Slightly Terrific." Elisha Cook, Jr., impacts as the kind of tract-wielding student communist that college movies liked to make fun of; he boasts that school is merely a tool for the exploitation of the masses before his credentials are stolen to get Amos enrolled. Sprightly direction by Fox reliable Butler, the use of many University of Southern California students as extras, and location shooting at the L.A. Coliseum, the Rose Bowl in Pasadena, and nearby Occidental College give the film an energy that studio-bound sets might not have provided.[12]

Modern viewers may find the presence of the Yacht Club Boys as overaged students as so beyond belief as to be annoying, but the pop comedy quartet was a big draw and at least sought to explain its stunted academic status in a song, "We'd Rather Be in College" (they say they're there because they don't want to add to the jobless rate). And despite Garland's vocal show-stealing, some reviewers predicted the YCB-penned and -performed "Woo! Woo!" as the expected breakout hit of *Pigskin Parade*.[13] The Boys, in fact, began their collective career in the mid–1920s as one of those ubiquitous "collegiate" music acts, but the deceptively sophisticated, clever wordplay in their self-penned tunes, sung at breakneck speed, earned them a following that lasted well beyond their student-age years. In *Pigskin Parade*, they satirize higher-ed radicalism in the high-speed "Down with Everything," in which poor Elisha Cook is put through the philosophical and physical ringer.

With a "Cast Picked for Entertainment"—as Fox promos asserted, implying a lack of sure star power—this is a cinematic whole that exceeds the sum of its parts. "We don't say that *Pigskin Parade* deserves a Nobel prize or anything so solid, but it is good fun and almost everyone but the Yales should like it," praised *The New York Times*.[14] *Variety* also lauded the film but rightly questioned why it hadn't been released earlier in the fall for prime exploitation by "the Thanksgiving gridiron peak season."[15] Even at that, *Pigskin Parade* earned a hefty $900,000 at the box office.[16]

Despite his billing at the top of the cast list (because someone had to be there), Stu Erwin garnered the film's lone Academy Award nomination, in the newly established Best Supporting Actor category, but he lost the statuette to Walter Brennan's performance in *Come and Get It*. The lofty billing was a misnomer, anyway, for Erwin's Amos clearly is a supporting character in *Pigskin Parade*, and more of him might have been too much of a good thing. For exhibitors, anyway, the size of Erwin's role was no indicator of its popularity among viewers. In Jackson, Tennessee, for example, the proprietor of the State Theatre thought to use a newspaper ad for Erwin's next film to remind potential audiences of the actor's melon-hurling heroics:

> REMEMBER?
> *The Hilarious Football Hero of "Pigskin Parade?"*
> STUART ERWIN
> *Here He Is Again …*
> *In One of the Funniest Films You've Ever Seen!*[17]

The last part was suspect … said "funniest" was MGM's *All American Chump*, a programmer in which Erwin played yet another bumpkin … but one who also happened to be a math whiz who used his brains to become a champion at playing bridge. A closer look at Erwin on the whole would reveal that he was indeed more nuanced than credited, exuding more of an innocent quality than outright ignorance, although that didn't stop Fox from planting newspaper stories that the actor preferred outright looney roles. This might be why Erwin's biographer, Judy Cornes, has derided his only Oscar nomination—for "one of his most stereotypical roles"—as "short-sighted … typical of the movie industry's critical misapprehension of Erwin's entire career."[18]

Media reports that Fox sought to reunite the *Pigskin Parade* cast for a sequel proved untrue—it didn't help that most of the key players were pacted elsewhere.[19] But the film did fuel an appetite for more college musicals, with some being MGM's *Rosalie* (with Nelson Eddy somehow cast as a West Point cadet), Warners' *Varsity Show*, and Columbia's *Start Cheering*, plus the official/unofficial follow-up to *Pigskin Parade*, TCF's *Life Begins in College*, with the Ritz Brothers top-billed. The *Los Angeles Times* called the "rah-rah epidemic" in Hollywood "the biggest [trend] almost since the gangster days."[20] From the mid–1930s through the mid-'40s, Johnny Downs practically made a career out of college films with almost interchangeable titles: *College Holiday*, *College Scandal*, *College Rhythm*, *Campus Rhythm*, *Hold That Co-ed*, and *All-American Co-ed*.

Audiences loved *Pigskin Parade*—and Judy Garland. But the young actress—as perhaps any other 14-year-old would be—was dismayed at watching herself in her first feature:

> I thought I would look as beautiful as Garbo or Crawford, that makeup and photography would automatically make me glamorous…. When I saw myself on the screen, it was the most awful moment of my life. My freckles stood out! I was fat. I was *loud*—like I was singing to the third gallery at the Orpheum! I burst into tears…. I was ready to go back to vaudeville.[21]

Garland was recalling this in 1943, when she was older and thinner, much more famous but not much less insecure. By then, newspaper ads for reissue showings of *Pigskin Parade* almost universally boasted Garland and Betty Grable—the latter now riding high at Fox—as its stars. Given the lot that Garland made from a little in her debut feature, audiences likely were not disappointed by the bait-and-switch. In the short run, *Pigskin Parade* springboarded Garland to a key casting in the first of her big-time MGM musicals, *Broadway Melody of 1938*. In the long run, it gave birth to her legend.

Pinky Tomlin and the Melody Four: *With Love and Kisses*

(Ambassador-Conn-Melody; December 20, 1936)

Director: Leslie Goodwins. Producer: Maurice Conn. Associate Producer: Coy Poe. Screenplay: Sherman L. Lowe. Story: Al Martin, Sherman L. Lowe. Editorial Supervision: Martin G. Cohn. Photography: Arthur Reed. Art Direction: E.H. Reif. Sound: J.S. Westmoreland. Music Director: Edward Kay. Special Effects: Kenneth Peach. Running Time: 66 minutes.

Cast: Pinky Tomlin (Homer "Spec" Higgins); Toby Wing (Barbara Holbrook); Kane Richmond (Don Gray); Arthur Housman (Gilbert Holbrook); Russell Hopton (Flash Henderson); Jerry Bergen and Billy Gray (radio comedians); The Peters Sisters ("Red Star Cheese Sisters" trio); Chelito and Gabriel (dance duo); Fuzzy Knight (Butch); Kenneth Thomson (Draper); G. Pat Collins (Joe); Jack Ingram (Jack); Olaf Hytten (Dickson); Billy Benedict (hillbilly kid); Bunny Bronson (Jane); Bob McKenzie (Mayor Jones); Eva McKenzie (Mrs. Higgins); Bruce Mitchell (desk sergeant); Kernan Cripps (police officer); Si Jenks (Sheriff Wade); Minnie Cow and His Inspiration.

Songs: "Don't Ever Lose It Whatever It Is (That Made Me Fall in Love with You)" [Peters Sisters] (Pinky Tomlin, Paul Parks); "I'm Right Back Where I Started" [Tomlin] (Pinky Tomlin, Coy Poe); "Sittin' on the Edge of My Chair" [Tomlin] (Pinky Tomlin, Paul Parks, Coy Poe); "Sweet" [Wing, reprised by Tomlin, then by Wing] (Pinky Tomlin, Al Heath, Buddy LeRoux); "The Trouble with Me Is You" [Tomlin, twice] (Pinky Tomlin, Harry Tobias); "With Love and Kisses" [Tomlin] (Connie Lee).

Disc: Brunswick 7525 ("The Trouble with Me Is You," Pinky Tomlin with Russ Plummer Orchestra); Brunswick 7811 ("I'm Right Back Where I Started," Pinky Tomlin); Brunswick 7897 ("Sittin' on the Edge of My Chair"/"With Love and Kisses," Pinky Tomlin and His Music).

Home Video: Alpha DVD.

The Story: Down on the farm in Arkansas, Homer "Spec" Higgins gets inspiration for writing tunes by milking Minnie, the family cow, as he sings. While listening to a national radio show, he learns that popular singer Don Gray—to whom Spec had sent his song "Sittin' on the Edge of My Chair"—has claimed it as his own creation. Spec goes to New York to confront Gray, but Gray's publicity man, Flash Henderson, has the young man put in jail. Gray gets Spec released, then offers the newcomer a paltry $200 to buy the rights to, and credit for, the song. Thrown into jail again after punching Flash, Spec befriends alcoholic lawyer Gilbert Holbrook. Spec also attracts the attention of Gilbert's sister, nightclub singer Barbara Holbrook ("Sweet"), whom he had met briefly while she was traveling through Arkansas. Spec promises Barbara he will write a song about her. Draper, a racketeer-turned-music publisher, blackmails Gray into sharing the profits on Spec's songwriting. Spec agrees to the deal but insists he can't work properly without Minnie, who is shipped to New York to give Spec inspiration to write "The Trouble with Me Is You." Spec tells Barbara about his supposed financial windfall, and she assures him that Gilbert will negotiate a more equitable contract. Gray secretly plans to get rid of the cow, which is in Draper's apartment. Spec is nearly jailed—again—for filing a police report about the disappearance of the cow. With the police watching, Gilbert negotiates with Draper to cut Spec and Minnie in on 50 percent of the music ("With Love and Kisses").

Sing While You're Able
(Ambassador-Conn-Melody; March 20, 1937)

Director: Marshall Neilan. Producer: Maurice Conn. Associate Producer: Coy Poe. Screenplay: Charles R. Condon, Sherman L. Lowe. Story: Charles R. Condon, Stanley Lowenstein. Assistant Director: Henry Spitz. Editorial Supervision: Martin G. Cohn. Photography: Jack Greenhalgh. Art Direction: E.H. Reif. Sound: Glen Glenn. Music Director: Edward Kay. Running Time: 66 minutes.

Cast: Pinky Tomlin (Whitey Morgan); Toby Wing (Joan); Bert Roach (Blodgett); Suzanne Kaaren (Gloria); Sam Wren (Bennett); Monte Collins (Adams); Harry C. Bradley (C. William Williams); Mike ["Prince" Michael] Romanoff (Prince Boris); Fern Emmett (landlady); Rita Carlyle (Thelma); The [Three] Brian Sisters (Rita, Jane, and Dotty); Lane Chandler (Simpson); James Newill (radio singer); Harry Strang (Chatham); Elma Pappas (torch singer); Gladys Gale (Mrs. Van Dusen); Henry Roquemore (Mr. Van Dusen); Three Mountain Boys (hillbillies).

Songs: "I'm Gonna Sing While I'm Able" [Tomlin, twice] (Connie Lee, Paul Parks); "I'm Just a Country Boy at Heart" [Brian Sisters, Tomlin, Three Mountain Boys, reprised by Tomlin] (Pinky Tomlin, Connie Lee, Paul Parks); "Leave It Up to Uncle Jake" [Tomlin, reprised by Tomlin, Romanoff, chorus] (Paul Parks, Connie Lee, Al Heath, Buddy LeRoux); "One Girl in My Arms (Is Worth a Million in My Dreams)" [Newill] (Harry Tobias, Roy Ingraham); "You're My Strongest Weakness" [Tomlin, reprised by Tomlin, Wing] (Coy Poe, Buddy LeRoux, Al Heath).

Also Known As: *Swing Brother Sing*; *Swing Is the Thing*.

Disc: Brunswick 7849 ("I'm Just a Country Boy at Heart," Pinky Tomlin and His Music).

Home Video: Alpha DVD.

The Story: The Williams Toy Company radio show is floundering in the ratings, and owner C. William Williams is urged by his general manager, Bennett, and top salesman, Adams, to shake up the product. When their car breaks down while traveling through Arkansas, Williams and his daughter, Joan, are assisted by a farmer, Whitey Morgan, and when they hear him sing, Williams signs Whitey to a radio contract. On his bus trip to the big city, Whitey thwarts a robbery attempt. Whitey falls in love with Joan, but she sees him only as a way to avoid her fiancé, Bennett. On the eve of Whitey's radio debut, Bennett has him kidnapped by hoods who dump him in a river. Whitey makes it to the studio on time, but chilled after his fall, he loses his voice and cannot perform. Doctors fear that Whitney may never perform again, but he realizes he can sing again after performing "I'm Gonna Sing While I'm Able." Whitey secures work through an agent, Blodgett, at a costume party honoring a foreign prince at which Joan and her father happen to be guests. Joan grows closer to Whitey as the two duet on "You're My Strongest Weakness." Whitey is dispirited when he overhears Joan's friend Gloria talk about how Joan has been using him. With aid from the prince, Whitey's song "Leave It Up to Uncle Jake" becomes a national hit, and Whitey saves the Williams company from financial ruin by giving the company the rights to the song. Whitey remains lovesick and returns to his farm ("I'm Just a Country Boy at Heart"), but he and Joan make amends.

Thanks for Listening
(Ambassador-Conn-Melody; October 21, 1937)

Director: Marshall Neilan. Producer: Maurice Conn. Screenplay: Rex Hale, Joseph O'Donnell, Stanley Roberts, based on the short story "Don't Fall in Love" by John B. Clymer. Assistant Director: Henry Spitz. Dialogue Director: Charles Gerson. Editorial Supervision: Martin G. Cohn. Photography: Jack Greenhalgh. Art Direction: E.H. Reif. Sound: Glen Glenn. Music Director: Bakaleinikoff. Dance Director: Edward Court. Running Time: 63 minutes.

Cast: Pinky Tomlin (Homer Tompkins); Maxine Doyle (Toots); Aileen Pringle ("Lady" Lulu Broderick); Claire Rochelle (Trixie Broderick); Henry Roquemore (Utah Pete); Rafael Storm (Maurice); Beryl Wallace (Gloria Bagley); The [Three] Brian Sisters (Sally, Irene, and Mary); George Lloyd (Champ);

[Robert] Elliot "Jonah" Jones (Gabriel); Charles Prince (sheriff); Charlotte Treadway, Grace Field (ladies); Benny Burt (stuttering man).

Songs: "I Like to Make Music" [Tomlin, Roquemore, Jones], "In the Name of Love" [Tomlin] (Connie Lee, Al Heath, Buddy LeRoux); "Listen to Me" [Brian Sisters] (Connie Lee); "The Love Bug Will Bite You (If You Don't Watch Out)" [Tomlin, reprised by Brian Sisters] (Pinky Tomlin).

Working Title: *Don't Fall in Love*.

Disc: Brunswick 7849 ("The Love Bug Will Bite You," Pinky Tomlin and His Music).

Home Video: Alpha DVD.

The Story: Homer Thompkins is a singing, guitar-playing music teacher in a hotel in the divorce capital of Reno, Nevada, where his sweetheart, Toots, is a manicurist. The guests there would rather unburden their concerns to Homer than employ him as a music teacher ("In the Name of Love"). "Lady" Lulu Broderick, a gang leader posing as a wealthy English woman, sets up Homer in an office as a "professional listener." Homer sings "The Love Bug Will Bite You (If You Don't Watch Out)" to a pair of newlyweds who register at the hotel. Lulu—who is in cahoots with her daughter Trixie, boastful actor Maurice, and ex-prizefighter "Champ"— uses Homer's business to obtain information on his clients. One bit of news pertains to the location of a lucrative gold mine owned by townsman "Utah" Pete. Homer gets wise to the operation and intentionally reveals the location of an abandoned quarry to throw off the criminals. Homer is reunited with Toots and intends to realize his dreams of marrying Toots and becoming a duck farmer.

Swing It Professor

(Ambassador-Conn-Melody; November 15, 1937)

Director: Marshall Neilan. Producer: Maurice Conn. Associate Producer: William Berke. Screenplay: Nicholas H. Barrows, Robert St. Clair. Story Suggested By: Connie Lee. Assistant Director: Henry Spitz. Editorial Supervision: Martin G. Cohn. Photography: Jack Greenhalgh. Editor: Richard G. Wray, Martin G. Cohn. Art Direction: E.H. Reif. Sound: Glen Glenn. Music Director: Bakaleinikoff. Dance Director: George Grandee. Running Time: 59 minutes.

Cast: Pinky Tomlin (Professor Artemis J. Roberts); Paula Stone (Teddy Ross); Milburn Stone (Lou Morgan); Mary Kornman (Joan Dennis); Gordon [Bill] Elliott (Randall); Pat Gleason (Toby); Garner, Wolf, and Harkins [The Three Gentle Maniacs] (students); The Four Squires [Lou Butterman, Jack W. Smith, Harry S. Powell, Glen T. Peters] (club band); Ralph Peters (Beaver); George Cleveland (dean); Harry Depp (trustee); Harry Semels (Angelo); The Four Singing Tramps [Fred Harder, Tom Clark, Art Moore, Bob Snyder] (tramps); George Grandee (dance director); Billy Gray (gangster).

Songs: "I'm Richer Than a Millionaire" [Tomlin, Four Singing Tramps], "I'm Sorta Kinda Glad I Met You" [Tomlin, reprised by Kornman, then by Tomlin, Paula Stone], "Old-Fashioned Melody" [Tomlin, reprised twice by Tomlin, Paula Stone, Four Squires], "Swing for Dear Brownell" [Gentle Maniacs] (Connie Lee, Al Heath, Buddy LeRoux); "Chi mi frena in tal momento" (sextet from *Lucia di Lammermoor*) [Four Singing Tramps] (Gaetano Donizetti).

Working Title: *Gentlemen Must Live*.

Home Video: Alpha DVD; Sinister Cinema DVD.

The Story: At Brownell University in small-town Illinois, music professor Artemis J. Roberts sings to music student Joan Dennis about his disdain for swing music in favor of traditional tunes ("Old-Fashioned Melody"). His views cause his forced resignation from the school, and Artemis cannot find new work because of the high demand for swing musicians. He temporarily falls in with a band of hoboes ("I'm Richer Than a Millionaire") and works as a street musician in New York. There, Artemis meets Lou Morgan, a racketeer embroiled in an intense rivalry with fellow crook Randall. Lou installs Artemis as the frontman of his nightclub to showcase the swing singing and dancing talents of Lou's girlfriend, Teddy Ross.

Joan arrives at the club after having followed Artemis to the big city. Randall, mistakenly thinking Artemis is a feared underworld figure called "The Professor," attempts to bribe the young man into buying his friendship. Complications ensue as Artemis and Teddy become attracted ("I'm Sorta Kinda Glad I Met You"), Lou and Joan are smitten, Randall seeks revenge on Artemis, and Artemis begins to think swing music isn't so bad after all.

In 1936, a Poverty Row operator named Maurice Conn decided to take the filmmaking techniques of his company's modest Westerns and other action films and apply them to pop musicals. Low-budget musicals had been made in Hollywood since the dawn of sound, but no one before Conn had produced a series of non-singing-cowboy musicals centered around a single star. Conn signed a popular, young singer-songwriter, Pinky Tomlin, to headline four 1936–37 song films targeted to appeal to small-town and rural audiences, just as his actioners were. The stories—which strongly featured country and/or Western themes—were generally liked by patrons of 80 years ago, and they can continue to be enjoyed, as long as your expectations aren't unreasonably high. However, these films' over-ambitiousness pushed Conn's independent company toward financial ruin.

At age 30 or thereabouts, the two central figures in the series had big dreams despite their unpretentious beginnings. New Hampshire-born Conn (1906–1973) served as assistant to Mascot Pictures President Nat Levine before going out on his own in 1934. He produced features under multiple imprimaturs—Ambassador, Conn, and Melody Pictures, or a combination of the first two of those names—and made sure his directors made pictures with a minimum of wasted effort or resources. For the Ambassador label, Conn put out action dramas and B-Westerns headlined by Kermit Maynard, the lesser-known brother of cowboy star Ken Maynard. Under the Conn brand, there were adventure quickies starring youthful Frankie Darro and handsome Kane Richmond. These efforts—which each cost in the very economical neighborhood of $10,000 to make—employed experienced craftsmen behind the camera and time-tested players in front of it, and were generally considered above the usual Poverty Row standard.

Then there was Melody Pictures, Conn's production label for his musicals, which he established in April 1936 when he announced the quartet of

With hits such as "The Object of My Affection" and "The Love Bug Will Bite You (If You Don't Watch Out)," Pinky Tomlin was better known as a singer and composer than as a movie actor.

Tomlin features for the 1936–37 season.[22] Also announced were four semi-Western adventures, based on works by famous author James Oliver Curwood and starring Kermit Maynard, and six Darro-Richmond "Sport-o-Stunt" action pictures. Conn intended to film all these at the Talisman on Sunset Boulevard—formerly a production base for Monogram Pictures (which was just merged into the new Republic Pictures)—and release them through states-rights exchanges, among them his own Chelsea Pictures.

The Melody projects were built around Truman "Pinky" Tomlin (1907–1987), a lanky, bespectacled redhead born in Arkansas and raised on a farm in Oklahoma. He earned his nickname because he sunburned easily because of his fair complexion. Tomlin first gained national attention in 1934 after he submitted "The Object of My Affection," a song he'd written, to bandleader Jimmie Grier. The Grier band's recording, with Tomlin on vocals, became a huge hit—and the most famous among Tomlin's many compositions. Tomlin's light drawl and aw-shucks disposition conformed to his farm-boy image, but his innocence masked a keen mind—he'd studied geology and law at the University of Oklahoma. And he quickly learned how to play the game in Hollywood as a kind of counter-intuitive hipster whom mothers also could love.

Tomlin sang and played guitar regularly on the widely popular radio show starring Eddie Cantor—who dubbed Tomlin "Public Swingster No. 1"—and played supporting roles in features. Among his earliest films, issued in 1935, were MGM's *Times Square Lady* and Fox's *Paddy O'Day** (his love interest in the latter was played by a young Rita Hayworth, née Cansino). Billed in the *Times Square Lady* opening as "Pinky Tomlin of Durant, Oklahoma," he sang "The Object of My Affection" and "What's the Reason (I'm Not Pleasin' You)?" to a cow as box-office insurance for top-billed Robert Taylor and Virginia Bruce, who soon impacted his life away from the screen. Tomlin bought a spacious ranch in the San Fernando Valley, next to the one owned by Taylor. Rapidly acknowledged as one of the movie colony's most eligible bachelors, Tomlin was linked in the fan mags to Bruce (plus Alice Faye and the future Hayworth ... not bad for a country boy). The Melody Pictures deal was not only intended to expand Tomlin's screen time as an actor, but also to showcase more of his music, much of which was also credited to his manager, Coy Poe, whom Conn hired as an associate producer as part of the package.

The female lead for the first two Melodies—*With Love and Kisses* and *Sing While You're Able*—was Toby Wing, a stunning blonde heretofore better known for her looks, seemingly captured as often by nightclub photographers as by the motion picture camera, than for her acting ability. In decorative chorus-girl bits mainly at Paramount and Warner Bros. (where she stood out in the "Young and Healthy" number in *42nd Street*), Wing (1915–2001) was earning more fan mail than players who got to speak substantive dialogue, and her list of reported suitors ranged from Jackie Coogan to Maurice Chevalier to Franklin D. Roosevelt, Jr. Leslie Goodwins, a British-born director making his debut in features after years in comedy shorts, shepherded the cast through the shooting of *With Love and Kisses* in October and November 1936, during which an unexpected—or maybe totally expected—thing happened: Tomlin and Wing got engaged. In mid–November, with the film just wrapped, its stars announced they were planning a March 1937 wedding. The announcement at a Hollywood party came as the event's emcee was shyly whispered the news by the couple, then a band celebrated by playing "The Object of My Affection."[23] Before long, news came that Tomlin had presented Wing with a hefty diamond ring as the two departed on a personal-appearance tour to support *With Love and Kisses*, which opened in December.[24]

Conn exploited Tomlin's ties to the Eddie Cantor program, which in January 1937 featured the actor singing "The Trouble with Me Is You," one of the selections from *With Love and Kisses*. Exhibitor-targeted ads for the film tagged this as "advertising you can't buy … box office is written all over it." Conn was happy enough with the potential of his musicals that he decided to spend more on all of his upcoming pictures. He said he had surveyed his franchise holders across the country before projecting a 1937–38 season schedule of 28 to 36 features, double or more the number of the previous season, at an estimated total production cost of $1.1 million.[25] These were heady plans for a 30-year-old entrepreneur who had started his solo filmmaking operation not long before with a mere $1,000 in his pocket. As Conn told a trade publication in a January 1937 interview:

> As a result of my survey, the bulk of my program next season will be 75% musical and melodrama. To that end, our production budgets will be raised and standardized at a $40,000 minimum and a $100,000 maximum.
>
> …The simplest way to insure the success of a picture, or at least to minimize its chances for failure, is to make it exactly what it is intended to be. A Western should be just that…. A melodrama should be melodrama; a comedy, comedy; a drama, drama…. It has long since been proven that it is impossible to please everyone, but by aiming a picture at a definite type of audience, you will come out with a winner in the vast majority of cases.[26]

With Love and Kisses established the heartland-friendly Tomlin-Conn plot formula in which an innocent simpleton is exploited by citified evils. In *WLAK*, it was an Arkansas farmer and aspiring songwriter traveling to New York, having his melody stolen, being thrown into jail twice (and nearly a third time), and getting ripped off by a crooked music publisher who buys his melodies for a mere few hundred dollars apiece.[27] Rural audiences could laugh at themselves, too. Tomlin's character can't stay on rhythm unless he's milking his family cow, which is brought to the city, and inside a swanky apartment, to spur her owner's inspiration. (Hence, the film's ad boast: "He Turned Broadway Into a Barnyard!") As in other hick musicals of the time, there's a reference to the country craze—when Tomlin asks a radio studio secretary for help, she assumes the worst and tells him, "There are 321 hillbilly auditions ahead of you." Later, Tomlin accidentally orders radishes at a fancy restaurant when he picks a random foreign word out of the menu. Trade reviews gave *With Love and Kisses* respectable reviews, tossing around adjectives such as "pleasing" and "unpretentious" and deeming it suitable fare for family and neighborhood theaters as well as rural houses.[28]

In publicity for the film, Conn further emphasized Tomlin's regular-guy nature by noting that he was such a fiend for the sedate card game of rummy that he played it with the electricians on the set whenever *With Love and Kisses* was between takes.[29] Another fabricated press release called Tomlin's twang "a menace to the American slanguage" and compared it to Jimmy Durante's distinctive speech. As Tomlin wrote years later, this kind of promotion ignored his more-cerebral qualities:

> It didn't bother Maurice Conn Productions that their "uneducated actor who never took a music lesson" could compose and score four films. They simply ignored my duties as composer and went on issuing backwoods background publicity. They were trying to promote me as a successor to Will Rogers…. I did what I could, within limits, not to destroy my credibility as a country boy. The best lines I ever heard about actors and education came from Hermione Gingold. She said: "I got all the schooling any actress needs. That is, I learned to write enough to sign contracts."[30]

The second Tomlin-Conn collaboration, *Sing While You're Able*, entered production in mid–February 1937, with Wing as a socialite who becomes an object of the affection of a certain four-eyed Arkansas farmer. But not all the news was upbeat for what *Melody* called its "swinging, singing new love team." In the last week of January, Tomlin and Wing called off their engagement, with a report quoting her as saying, "We talked it over and decided marriage at this time might interfere with our separate careers."[31] Whispers at the time hinted that the romance was a studio concoction, and Tomlin admitted as much in his autobiography.[32]

Some of the cast members were different from *With Love and Kisses*—and there was a new director, the once-great silent filmmaker Marshall Neilan (who would helm the rest of the series)—but this follow-up was pretty much the same movie. Neilan was at the tail end of a once-great career behind the camera, but the same man who had once been Mary Pickford's director of choice was reduced to the quickies because of his alcoholism. Still, Neilan brought his Tomlin films in on time and on budget. His musical numbers in *Sing While You're Able* are nothing special, although the young Brian Sisters trio makes a pleasant complement to Tomlin on "I'm Just a Country Boy at Heart," which they sing while Tomlin whistles periodically as his character packs his bags for the city. *Sing While You're Able* even features a couple of action scenes—fisticuffs complete with music cues heard in the program Westerns with which Conn was more comfortable. The Tomlin-Conns are replete with character actors taking a break from sidekick- or heavy-type roles in oaters; among them are Fuzzy Knight, Lane Chandler, Jack Ingram, Harry Strang, and future cowboy stars James Newill and Gordon "Wild Bill" Elliott.

There are some other unusual names in these pictures. In *Sing While You're Able*, Michael Romanoff, the supposed Russian prince who lately had been exposed as a con artist, plays an actual foreign noble who helps our hero build a career. "Mike" (as his name appears in the credits) had done better acting work as a professional imposter and would fare better still in future decades as a Beverly Hills restaurateur. *Sing While You're Able* marked Romanoff's movie acting debut, as well as the debut in features for the Brian Sisters, a threesome of adolescent harmony siblings cast to provide youth appeal for family audiences attracted to the Tomlin-Conn films. The Idaho-bred Brians—Betty, Doris, and Gwen—were initially mentored by singer Connee Boswell and performed specialties in more than a dozen Hollywood titles from the mid–1930s through the mid '40s. Like Tomlin, they were typecast as country girls—they sang "How 'Ya Gonna Keep 'Em Down on the Farm (After They've Seen Paree)?" in their initial film, the Hal Roach short *Our Gang Follies of 1936* (1935). They enjoyed an encouraging professional relationship with Tomlin, with whom they worked again in *Thanks for Listening*. Among the sisters' other credits were *New Faces of 1937** at RKO and *Kentucky Moonshine* [q.v.], *Sally, Irene and Mary* (1938), *Little Miss Broadway* (1938), and *Tin Pan Alley* (1940) at 20th Century–Fox. Another interesting name was Robert Elliot "Jonah" Jones, who plays a Tomlin sidekick in the third series entry, *Thanks for Listening*. Jones was an influential jazz trumpeter who much later won a Grammy and played with Lionel Hampton, Cab Calloway, and many others.

By the time *Thanks for Listening* was being shot in August and September 1937, Conn was spending significantly more on his musicals than he had on his initial action films. The production values didn't necessarily show it in *Thanks for Listening*, although there seemed to be more care in devising a script with an interesting angle.[33] This time, Tomlin is out West, not in a big city but in the little-big divorce haven of Reno, Nevada, playing a hotel music teacher who becomes the unwitting accomplice of blackmailers as a "professional listener." The crooks, led by a fake socialite played by former silent star Aileen Pringle, want the listener, whom they install in an office, to find out information on a gold mine through his soothing social technique.

A modern viewer might be surprised to learn that professional listening—a business at which clients could unburden to a listener with understanding and confidentiality—actually was a thing in 1937. For, say, $3 per hour and $2 per half hour, in cities big and small, a talker could unwind about romance or business or loneliness, all without the listener keeping records or casting aspersions ... psychology without the psychologist. In *Thanks for Listening*, Tomlin's character is advertised as "Dr. Homer Tompkins, P.L.," with slogans such as "Dr. Tompkins Can Make You Forget Yourself" and "The Professional Listener Will Make You LIVE-LOVE-LAUGH." Among Tompkins' customers are an older lady who misses her estranged husband, a stage mom who wants someone to hear her daughter's accordion playing, and a stuttering foreigner whom Tomlin exiles to a dictaphone with the promise that he will listen to the man's halting speech once the recording can be speeded up. Another patron is a conniving spouse played in a rare credited film appearance by noted beauty and sometime actress Beryl Wallace, longtime mistress of showman Earl Carroll.[34] To emphasize the gentle parody of the conversation trend, the youthful Brian Sisters show up briefly to sing "Listen to Me."

"Listen to Me" is one of only four songs featured in *Thanks for Listening*. Thankfully, one of the other three is the popular, and still very charming, "The Love Bug Will Bite You," a Tomlin composition sung by Tomlin. ("Love Bug" is probably better known now for its rendition by Spanky, Buckwheat, and company in the beloved short *Our Gang Follies of 1938*.) The other tunes were contributed by Connie Lee, Al Heath, and Buddy LeRoux, who wrote songs for all of the Tomlin-Conn musicals, but close Tomlin associate Coy Poe, whose interest in Melody Pictures had been bought out by Conn, was notably absent from the credits for *Thanks for Listening*. Assembly-line brunette Maxine Doyle makes scant impact as Tomlin's leading lady in a picture that, despite its plot novelty, is a step below its two predecessors. Doyle became better known as the female lead opposite Bela Lugosi in the Republic serial *S.O.S. Coast Guard* (1937), after which she married its co-director William Witney.

The last of the Tomlin-Conn musicals, *Swing It Professor*, turned out to be the best of the four, although for once (or maybe because) there were no hillbillies, cows, or cowboys. The cast was upgraded (especially from the weak roster in *Thanks for Listening*), and the premise—built around the syncopated-music craze and wrapped in a gangster story—was reliably funny for the intended audience in the neighborhoods and sticks. Tomlin plays a displaced college music teacher from Illinois who loses his gig because he can't dig swing. This time, he has two romantic options—a demure pupil (Our Gang alumna Mary Kornman) and a savvy nightclub hostess (Paula Stone). An attractive blonde from the singing-and-dancing Stone family, Paula represented a major upgrade for Conn but must have swelled the budget. The chief gangster (played by Paula's cousin Milburn Stone, later of *Gunsmoke*) is given a life-changing lesson in poultry raising by country girl Kornman. Tomlin's small-time academe spends the film being misread: He's threatened with a beating by highbrow hoboes if he dares to sing swing for his supper, but then somehow intimidates legit menaces—a competing band of New York toughs led by Bill Elliott—into thinking he's a Mister Big from Chi-town. A surprise ending, acknowledged by Tomlin's character to the audience at the finish, bridges the big-town/small-town gulf. It was an upbeat way to close the series, even if there were patrons who wanted still more of these Pinky Tomlin pictures.

Swing It Professor opened in November 1937, and Conn had high enough hopes—or, considering what was to come, enough of a sense of desperation—to preview it in a prestigious Los Angeles theater, the Paramount. There, it was paired with a prestige Paramount musical, *High, Wide and Handsome*. A *Motion Picture Herald* reviewer on hand acknowledged that this was a brave move for an indie such as Conn: "Naturally, and it was probably expected, there were quite a few walkouts.... Yet the applause upon conclusion of the preview indicated that those who remained regarded the preview favorably."[35] *The Film Daily* added to the favorable press for *Swing It Professor* by praising it as a "light, pleasant offering, full of fun."³⁶

By this time, Conn's plans for 1937–38 had already been downsized from 28–36 planned releases to a mere 16, and they did not include more Tomlin titles. Instead, it was announced in the trades that the mogul had signed pop singer Gene Austin ("My Blue Heaven") for four to six "outdoor musicals" with military or crime settings, and Conn sought to pair tenor Donald Novis and ingénue Grace Bradley in a more traditional musical to be called *Sweethearts in Swingtime*.³⁷ It was becoming apparent that Conn was in financial trouble. In November 1937, less than two weeks after the *Swing It Professor* screening in L.A., his company filed for bankruptcy as two of its creditors, one of which was a film laboratory, sought control of the negatives of its films—the potentially popular *Professor* among them—that they held as security on a $50,000 promissory note.³⁸ The $50,000 was a serious undervaluing even of such cheaply made properties, but Conn had few options. Conn Productions suspended filmmaking operations after the first of the new year, although a federal judge allowed its founder to remain in charge. None of the 1937–38 titles so optimistically announced were made. By June 1938, *Variety* reported that Maurice Conn was to retire Ambassador Pictures and Conn Productions, with Melody Pictures having long since passed from the scene.³⁹ Conn re-emerged as a producer for 20th Century–Fox, Monogram, and Eagle-Lion, but his best days were past.

Pinky Tomlin had plenty of alternatives to Conn's quickies, and even as *Swing It Professor* was touring theaters, he was in competition with himself in the Republic cornpone musical comedy *Down in "Arkansaw"* [q.v.]. He continued in movies into the '40s while leading his own orchestra on tours nationwide, but he eventually tired of the show-business grind. Tomlin operated a successful oil company in Beverly Hills, hosted a 1950s L.A. television show titled *Music Is My Beat*, and quietly raised a family. Somewhere on the internet is a clip of Tomlin as a contestant on the Groucho Marx-hosted game show *You Bet Your Life* in 1958.⁴⁰ Tomlin, now an oil executive, is introduced under his real first name but soon revealed (in an obvious setup meant to come off as surprising) as Pinky, and his ensuing rendition of "The Object of My Affection" prompts Marx to lament—this being early in the rock 'n' roll era—that they don't write 'em like Pinky did anymore. Most of the audience for that show likely agreed.

Tomlin lived long enough to see a revival of "The Object of My Affection," in the 1973 hit movie *Paper Moon*, and to write an autobiography, named for that song, published six years before his death. In the book, Tomlin wrote that in life "there are only three essentials: work to do, someone to love and something to hope for."⁴¹ It was a philosophy in tune with the modest but virtuous characters he played on screen, and never did we get to see so much of them as in Maurice Conn's little time-fillers.

Mountain Music

(Paramount; June 18, 1937)

Director: Robert Florey. Producer: Benjamin Glazer. Assistant Director: Russell Matthews. Screenplay: John C. Moffitt, Duke Atteberry, Russel Crouse, Charles Lederer, based on the *Hearst's International-Cosmopolitan* magazine story by MacKinlay Kantor. Photography: Karl Struss. Editor: Eda Warren. Art Directors: Hans Dreier, John Goodman. Set Direction: A.E. Freudeman. Sound: Phil G. Wisdom, Don Johnson. Dance Director: LeRoy Prinz. Musical Director: Boris Morros. Orchestrations: Victor Young. Vocal Supervisor: Al Siegel. Running Time: 76 minutes.

Cast: Bob Burns (Bob Burnside); Martha Raye (Mary Beamish); John Howard (Ardinger Burnside); Terry

Walker (Lobelia Shepardson); Rufe Davis (Ham); George ["Gabby"] Hayes (Grandpappy); Spencer Charters (Justice Sharody); Charles "Slim" Timblin (Shep); Jan Duggan (Ma); Olin Howland (Pappy); Fuzzy Knight (Amos); Wally Vernon (Odette Potts); Cliff Clark (medicine show doctor); Goodie Montgomery (Alice); Rita La Roy (Mrs. Lovelace); Georgia Simmons (Ma Shepardson); Arthur Hohl (prosecuting attorney); Miranda Giles (Aunt Effie); William Burress (Minafee); Buster Brodie (Snuffy); William "Red" Donahue (hillbilly chased and kicked by mule); Jack Clifford (guard); Walter Soderling (court clerk); Jim Toney (juror); Edmund Elton (judge); Sam Ash (assistant prosecuting attorney); Dick Rush (police officer); Charles Arnt (hotel manager); Louis Natheaux (Mr. Lovelace); Charles Judels (orchestra leader); Don McKinney (bellboy); Hal K. Dawson (hotel clerk); Eddie Tamblyn (bellhop); Laura Treadwell (manager's wife); Florence Gill (woman with chicken voice); Virginia Dabney (Edna); Paul Kruger (attendant); Elsa Christian (Lady Godiva); Lew Kelly (mailman); Terry Ray [Ellen Drew] (Helen); Robert St. Angelo (chef); Harvey Parry (busboy); Ward Bond, Wally Maher (G-men); Harvey Karels, Jolane Reynolds, David Robel, Charles Teske (adagio dancers); Jimmy Conlin (medicine show shill); Spec O'Donnell (Monotony youth); Jerry Tucker (kid); Priscilla Moran (girl); "U–No," a mule (himself).

Songs: "Beat on This Box" ["jailbirds" band], "Can't You Hear That Mountain Music?" [hillbilly chorus, reprised by Raye, Burns, chorus], "Good Morning" [Raye, reprised by Raye, Vernon]; "Thar She Comes" [hillbilly chorus, reprised by Raye, Burns, chorus] (Sam Coslow); "If I Put My Heart in My Song" [Raye] (Sam Coslow, Al Siegel); "Mama Don't Allow No Music Played in Here" [Davis] (trad.).

The Story: In the mountains of Arkansas, the Burnsides and Shepardsons have been feuding for 75 years, but the impending wedding of Bob Burnside and Lobelia Shepardson figures to ease tensions ("Can't You Hear That Mountain Music?"). Woman-shy Bob is marriage bait because he owns a diamond mine, but he has an odd affliction: He suffers amnesia whenever he's hit in the head. Bob knows that his brother Ardinger is Lobelia's true love, and he cuts short the wedding ceremony by riding away on a mule. However, the local authorities are led to believe that Ardinger has killed his brother to inherit the mine. In the nearby city of Monotony, Mary Beamish is a singer in a show run by local theater owner Odette Potts ("Good Morning"). Mary attempts to make Bob her beau to show her friends that she can land a man ("If I Put My Heart in My Song"). Because of his quirk, Bob alternates between adoring Mary, when he's amnesiac, and forgetting who she is; at times he thinks he's "Hamilton W. Lovelace." Bob and Mary check into a Hot Springs hotel, but their plans to elope are scuttled when they meet the wife of the real Lovelace. Mary is drafted into substituting for an injured dancer at a hotel dinner show that turns out disastrously. Thrown out of the hotel, Bob and Mary are convinced by Lobelia to return home, where Ardinger is on trial for murder, and Mary must weigh Bob's love for her against his clearing his brother's name. The matter is righted in court, and the Burnside-Shepardson feud is settled ("Thar She Comes").

Mountain Music must be seen to be believed. It wasn't the first hillbilly movie of the 1930s, but it may have been the best—whatever distinction that brings. There is no critical consensus on the "best" part, as this music-laden comedy—a big box-office success—has hardly been seen, much less written about, in recent decades. Its visibility has not been helped by its lack of legacy star quality. But as a weird hybrid of cornpone satire, backstage humor, and courtroom shenanigans, it's stupid in an endearing way.

Paramount was crazy like a fox in casting two actors untried as leads, for Martha Raye and Bob "Bazooka" Burns were in a brief spell as the hottest comedy pair in filmdom. In scarcely more than a year after being signed separately by the studio, they had played support together in two Bing Crosby musicals, *Rhythm on the Range* (1936) [q.v.] and *Waikiki Wedding* (1937), and appeared (but not together) in the radio revue *The Big Broadcast of 1937* (1936) [q.v.]. *Mountain Music* was meant as routine fare, but the studio spinning the two actors into their own vehicle made plenty of sense. Burns (1890–1956) had kicked around show business for more than 20 years—some of it in a blackface act. After guest stints with Rudy Vallee and Paul Whiteman in 1935, Burns suddenly rose to fame on Crosby's *Kraft*

Music Hall radio show as a homespun, drawling comic philosopher with humorous commentaries on his mythical relatives back in Van Buren, Arkansas. He earned his nickname from the homemade novelty instrument he played, supposedly invented with a couple of gas pipes and a whiskey funnel.

Sometimes accompanied by his bazooka, Burns had broken into Hollywood playing bits, usually uncredited and mainly at Fox. At Fox, he is supposed to have met Will Rogers, who encouraged him to "keep a-goin' at somethin'. Take any offer you can get."[42] Rogers did not live to see Burns become his folk-multimedia successor, similarly juggling radio work, film roles, personal appearances, and a syndicated newspaper column. Burns' column, headlined "Well, I'll Tell You," appeared mainly in small markets and was doled out in compact doses of dialect-ridden prose, as in the example below, reproduced in its entirety and meant to convey the Ozark sage's bemused attitude about the picture business:

> In most professions like bein' a doctor or lawyer, people go to school for years and then they expect to open up an office and start in gradually and finally build up a pretty good business, but out here in Hollywood it's different. There's been so many cases where a person got a good picture and made a success overnight and they've jest kinda gotten to be an impatient lot.
>
> The other day on the set where we are makin' *Mountain Music*, we were usin' a bunch of children and I happened to notice a little red-headed boy walkin' up and down with a worried look on his face, and I says, "What's the matter, sonny—you look worried," and he says, "Yes, I was jest thinkin'," he says, "I'm 4 years old today and what have I got to show for it?"[43]

Here's a shotgun wedding for you, as Bob Burns prepares to get hitched to Terry Walker in the forgotten hillbilly hit *Mountain Music*.

Burns (or his ghost writer) must have rolled his eyes at those who achieved the early success that had eluded him, perhaps even Raye, who was barely into her 20s but already hot stuff. Born into a vaudeville trunk, Raye (1916–1994) was a band vocalist before being "discovered" by director Norman Taurog, who was looking for a comic actress for his Western sendup *Rhythm on the Range*. The raucous, rubbed-faced Raye was matched with Burns in a secondary romance behind top-billed Crosby and Frances Farmer, and what studio publicity touted as "America's fastest-growing comedy team" was born.

Raye had little time to reflect on her sudden notoriety. She was shuttled from film to film in 1937, was fulfilling a weekly radio commitment with none other than Al Jolson, and was enduring the first of her seven marriages, a tumultuous four-month union with makeup man Hamilton "Bud" Westmore. There were snide remarks by fan-mag scribes that this plain Jane had "gone elegant." In fact, Raye was pretty good about putting up a front about her self-assurance. "Two years ago … nobody paid any attention to me. I was just another singer," she told syndicated columnist Jack Stinnett in the summer of 1937. "Now I'm supposed to know all the answers. I don't, but I'm supposed to … that's what makes me nervous."[44]

Filming of *Mountain Music* began in March. Not far in, there was a disagreement over the script—credited to four writers (among them the future prize-winning producer and librettist Russel Crouse) and based on a magazine story by Iowa-born MacKinlay Kantor, the Pulitzer Prize-winning novelist. Producer Benjamin Glazer responded by discharging director Charles Riesner. The unlikely-seeming replacement, on a single day's notice, was Robert Florey, the French-born filmmaker whose background as an avant-garde stylist belied his placement in mainly routine Hollywood fare such as the Bela Lugosi chiller *Murders in the Rue Morgue* and the early musical flop *The Battle of Paris*.* Part of Florey's atypical style in *Mountain Music* is his frequency of close-ups on the bearded, weather-beaten mountaineer faces. In an unexpected admission, Florey would reminisce years later that *Mountain Music* was one of his favorites among his movies.[45]

Young contractees John Howard and Terry Walker were handed roles as the second-tier couple, but more notable was the exhaustion of Hollywood's supply of simpleton types: George "Gabby" Hayes, Fuzzy Knight, Olin Howlin, and *Tobacco Road* stage headliner Charles "Slim" Timblin. The backwoods milieu of *Mountain Music* was strengthened even more with bits by "Barnyard Nightingale" Florence Gill, better known for her impressions of chickens and other poultry in Disney cartoons and occasional live-action fare, and the man-and-mule vaudeville act William "Red" Donahue and "U–No." *Mountain Music* also was what a prominent trade called "a bonanza for hillbilly virtuosi," as "bearded Bachs" from the musicians union who could play Jew's harps, zithers, bazookas (of course), and other countrified instruments were summoned to Maribou Lake and the Lasky Ranch in Los Angeles for location shooting.[46]

Some of those instruments are heard as the story opens with an Arkansas shotgun wedding that prompts some of Sam Coslow's words-and-music content, followed by a tableau evocative of a *Hee-Haw* episode: lazy, long-bearded, slow-talkin' fellas in overalls sprawled over hammocks with hound dogs at their sides. After some inter-familial feuding in which nobody gets killed, Burns is given a medicine-show setup to talk about his bald Uncle Fud and homely Aunt Sophie. The fictional Bob, a family black-sheep because he works and bathes and somehow has enough smarts to run a diamond mine, suffers from amnesia whenever he is hit in the head or doused with water (actions signaled by his odd little dance and a few transitory notes from an off-screen bazooka). This keeps him careening between knowing who he is and, when out of his head, courting Raye's man-hungry miss, whom he espies initially by pressing his face, child-like, against the front window of her house, just before she sings Coslow and Al Siegel's "If I Put My Heart in My Song."

Raye's ensuing performance of a difficult adagio dance brought her unwelcome criticism when, according to a story spread by a prominent New York City columnist, she kicked visitors off the set of *Mountain Music*. This gave mag writers even more fodder for their high-hat narrative: Raye closed the set for filming of the dance not because she was an egotist but because "she didn't want a lot of people watching her land on her anatomy," conceded *Modern Screen*, which snidely added: "Touches of elegance, though, are reflected in a new town car, a chauffeur, and six fur coats."[47]

The second half of *Mountain Music* surrenders some of its satirical potential by moving from the mountains to theater and hotel stages and, finally, to a crazy courtroom sequence during which Bob must clear his brother for his own murder, but the stars' chemistry keeps things moving. A running gag concerns Bob's first exposure to civilization, as when his first trip in an elevator evokes the fearful comment "Hey, wait a minute—this room's movin'!" This kind of thing convulsed audiences in 1937, as did a sequence in which Bob puts his head up U-No's rear while trying to push it across a river.[48] "From here, it's hard to tell which is the jackass!" comments a grizzled onlooker.

Besides her perilous apache, Raye offers less-dangerous vocalizations of not only "If I Put My Heart in My Song" but also the hit "Good Morning," which is repeated in styles ranging from country to scat and in an odd number in which Raye and supporting comic Wally Vernon are dressed in baby-girl garb. (As we said, this is a movie best seen to be believed.) Decades later, "Good Morning" became known to baby boomers as the familiar jingle used in TV commercials for Kellogg's Corn Flakes, and Coslow received a sizable fee from the cereal company for many years as a result.[49]

As much as *Mountain Music* benefited Burns and Raye, it may have done even more for a player much less frequently seen: Rufe Davis, a nightclub comic from Oklahoma appearing in his first feature.[50] Davis (1908–1974) got a huge career boost on the strength of one song number, the folksy "Mama Don't Allow No Music Played in Here," in which he presented an array of musical-instrument impressions and other sound effects, among them a motorboat and the otherwise-absent bazooka. Word-of-mouth about Davis' work was so good that he was billed third in some print ads, and Paramount quickly signed him to do a similar novelty number ("Sound Effects Man") in another comedy feature (*This Way, Please*). He had a lengthy career in film, including many B-Westerns, and television, as a regular on the '60s sitcom *Petticoat Junction*.

But people didn't just like Davis, they liked his movie. According to Paramount, *Mountain Music* drew 150 percent above standard box-office business in 18 key national markets—for what showmen would call a "freak" picture. Said showmen were mainly delighted to have it in their houses. "We don't have Bank Night any more in Texas," a theater operator in that state reported to *Motion Picture Herald*, referring to the popular lotto franchise, "but thank the Lord we have Paramount."[51] "Let's have another 'Hillbilly Opry'; it's a great box office tonic," added a correspondent from Montana.[52] From rural Illinois: "Three cheers ... for this one. They liked it, and, oh boy, the business this will do."[53] But it wasn't just those theater men in the wide-open spaces who saw a boost in biz. "One of the 'nuttiest,' 'screwiest' features I have ever witnessed. There isn't anything to it, but it kept our audience in a continued roar of laughter," went an account from New Jersey.[54]

There was some high-falutin' resistance to this low-culture lollapalooza: *Mountain Music* was termed "inferior" and "half-witted" by the *Chicago Tribune* scribe billed as "Mae Tinèe" and dismissed as "the most unalluring picture yet" by *Variety* columnist Cecelia

Ager.[55] But reviews were mainly positive once the film opened in June 1937, and there were immediate calls for a follow-up. Paramount obliged … sort of. It announced yet another Burns-Raye love match in a comedy to be called *The Arkansas Traveler* (one of Burns' other nicknames), but the studio instead paired Raye with a new comic contractee, Bob Hope, in *College Swing* and *Give Me a Sailor*. Raye would become nearly as famous as Hope for her tireless work entertaining wartime service members, although baby boomers would remember her better for late-life denture-cream commercials. Raye and Burns were teamed one more time by Paramount, but back as the secondary couple, in a Dorothy Lamour-Ray Milland musical comedy, *Tropic Holiday* (1938).

Burns moved on to RKO, where in *Radio City Revels* (1938) he appeared in another musical as another rube with another psychological quirk—this one being the ability to write hit songs in his sleep. He continued to make movies, talk on the radio, and invest in California real estate, the last doing most to make him rich. His former countrymen in the real Van Buren grew tired of his schtick and sometimes complained about it, and Burns parted ways with Paramount for good in the early '40s over his plaint that a proposed movie would be too demeaning to folks back home. However, service folk thought enough of his novelty instrument that they nicknamed the U.S. Army's hand-held anti-tank rocket launcher the "bazooka."

In his final years, Burns lived in a sprawling ranch in the San Fernando Valley, where visitors were greeted by an automated driveway gate that opened automatically as a spoken recording welcomed them to the place, along with a fanfare of bazooka music.[56] Ol' Bob never forgot where his grits were buttered.

Kentucky Moonshine
(20th Century–Fox; May 13, 1938)

Director: David Butler. Associate Producer: Kenneth Macgowan. Screenplay: Art Arthur, M.M. Musselman. Story: M.M. Musselman, Jack Lait, Jr. Additional Dialogue and Comedy Songs: Sid Kuller, Ray Golden. Photography: Robert Planck. Editor: Irene Morra. Art Directors: Bernard Herzbrun, Lewis Creber. Set Direction: Thomas Little. Costumes: Royer. Sound: Alfred Bruzlin, Roger Heman. Music Director: Louis Silvers. Vocal Supervisor and Music Arranger: Jule Styne. Running Time: 85 minutes.

Cast: The Ritz Brothers [Harry, Jimmy, Al] (themselves aka The Slack Brothers); Tony Martin (Jerry Wade); Marjorie Weaver (Caroline); Slim Summerville (Hank Hatfield); John Carradine (Reef Hatfield); Wally Vernon (Gus Bryce); Berton Churchill (J.B.); Eddie Collins ("Spats" Swanson); Cecil Cunningham (landlady); Paul Stanton (Mortimer Hilton); Mary Treen ("Sugar" Hatfield); Francis Ford (Grandpa Hatfield); Frank McGlynn, Jr. (Clem Hatfield); The Brian Sisters (specialty trio); Clarence H. [Hummel] Wilson (attorney); Jan Duggan (nurse); Si Jenks, Theodore Lorch (buckboard drivers); Irving Bacon (hotel clerk); Olin Howland (Tom Slack); Carroll Nye, Tom Hanlon (radio announcers); Allen Wood (bellboy); Freddie Walburn (kid in rafters); Paddy O'Flynn, Lester Dorr, Wally Maher, Robert Lowery, Sherry Hall, Dick French (reporters); Jack Gargan, Milton Kibbee (photographers); Jack Norton (drunk); Guy Wilkerson (hillbilly).

Songs: "Moonshine Over Kentucky" [Martin, Brian Sisters; reprised by Martin, Ritz Brothers], "Reuben, Reuben, I've Been Swingin'" [Ritz Brothers], "Sing a Song of Harvest" [Weaver, Brian Sisters, chorus] (Lew Pollack, Sidney D. Mitchell); "Kentucky Opera" [Ritz Brothers] (Jule Styne, Sid Kuller, Ray Golden); "Swinging I Pagliacci" [Martin] (Jule Styne, Ruggiero Leoncavallo); "The Old Oaken Bucket" [Weaver] (Samuel Woodworth, George Kiallmark).

Also Known As: *Moonshine Over Kentucky*; *Three Men and a Girl*.
Home Video: 20th Century–Fox DVD.

The Story: Swing bandleader-singer Jerry Wade's radio show, "Sunshine Time," is losing steam in the ratings, and Jerry proposes to sponsors that a dose of home-grown "hillbilly" *talent will attract listeners. After hearing of Jerry's plan to go to Kentucky to scout talent, down-on-her-luck New York actress Caroline and three sibling vaudeville actors she has befriended make plans to head to the Bluegrass State ahead of time to pretend to be yokels and get "discovered." She raises the money for the trip by sweet-talking a fellow boarding house resident, "Spats" Swanson. After arriving and narrowly escaping a skirmish between two feuding families, Caroline and the boys ("Reuben, Reuben, I've Been Swingin'") attract the attention of Jerry and his announcer, Gus. Jerry and Caroline fall in love. Caroline ("Sing a Song of Harvest") and the boys ("Kentucky Opera") perform on a special Wade broadcast from Kentucky and are invited to New York to appear on the show. Hours before the first broadcast in New York, Spats shows up and threatens to expose the fakery to the media, and a contrite Caroline reacts by writing a parting letter to Jerry and planning a train trip to Chicago. The brothers confess their trickery to Jerry, who rushes to the train station to find Caroline. He leaves that night's broadcast in the hands of the trio, who turn it into a comedy show, but Jerry, now reunited with Caroline, reappears to lead the final number, "Moonshine Over Kentucky."*

The Ritz Brothers are polarizing figures among film buffs, who retroactively regard them with the respect akin to the Three Stooges (meaning sizable) or Mitchell and Durant (not so much) within the realm of Golden Age low-comic teams. Some find it repellent that this trio of mugging, eye-crossing, face-contorting siblings graduated from being sidemen for top-rank musical stars to headlining their own movies. But *Kentucky Moonshine*, one of their first starring pictures, is a pretty good example of their ... uh, art.

Like so many others, the Ritzes—New Jersey-born Al (1901-1965), Harry (1907-1986), and Jimmy (1904-1985)—honed their high-energy comedy-with-music act in vaudeville. In large part because of their physical resemblance to each other, the brothers derived much of their humor from working as a unit rather than adopting separate personalities. At times it was hard to tell the Ritzes apart, although with his rubber face and penchant for snappy quips, youngest brother Harry was the unquestioned ringleader of the act, and he has been cited as a major influence on greats such as Jerry Lewis, Sid Caesar, and Mel Brooks. In retrospect, the siblings seem derivative of another brother act, the Three Stooges, but in their day, the Ritzes were considered more important than the Stooges.

With the right material, much of it created by Harry, the Ritzes could be very funny—even in the movies audaciously so, as in their devastating parody of Alice Faye, with Harry in womanly garb, in their shared 1937 vehicle, *On the Avenue*. By this time, the brothers were well into their feature career—which began in another Faye starrer, *Sing, Baby, Sing* (1936)—as 20th Century-Fox support. After further successes for the brothers in the likes of *One in a Million* (1936) and *You Can't Have Everything* (1937), the studio thought it time to spin them off into their own fare. Their first headlining film, *Life Begins in College* (1937), grossed a solid $1.5 million, prompting follow-ups.[57]

Kentucky Moonshine was considered important enough to be assigned to a top TCF director, the reliable if unspectacular David Butler (*Sunnyside Up*, *Pigskin Parade*, multiple Shirley Temples). As the title indicates, the Ritzes go barefoot and cockeyed as guys from Brooklyn who pose as hill folk in the Bluegrass State to get "discovered" by the host (Tony Martin) of a swing-music radio show. With Martin sporting a one-shot moustache and still working on a screen image beyond that of Mr. Alice Faye, only the Ritzes earned above-the-title billing. (Martin knew what to expect, this being his fifth shared credit with the Ritzes.) The female lead was Marjorie Weaver, a pleasant, pretty brunette who was getting good roles at Fox after being stuck in Warner Bros. bits. Cast as a New York singer who joins the Ritzes on their heartland trek, Weaver (1913-1994) actually was from Kentucky, raised in Louisville. *Kentucky Moonshine* began as a hillbilly story commissioned by TCF production head Darryl F. Zanuck for the talents of contract actors Joan Davis, Jack Haley, and Wally Vernon, but only Vernon ended up in the finished product.[58]

Kentucky Moonshine mines much of its humor from culture-clash stereotypes. The radio host wants genuine country talent for his ratings-challenged show because there have been too many showbiz "hillbillies from Brooklyn," and his soap-company sponsors agree to his plan because their research proves that people who like swing (those hipsters!) don't like soap. (So does that mean hillbillies do?) The Ritzes spend most of the film pretending to be confounded by modern conveniences such as elevators, bathtubs, flashbulbs, and electronic media (Martin: "I'd like to put you in radio." Harry: "Does it hurt?"). Studio publicity held that the brothers required time to prepare for their roles by putting dirt under their fingernails to be more effective mountaineers, and scarcely more believably, that they developed "acute skin poisons" from wearing the fake long beards they had to use in playing mountaineers.[59]

Not all of the gags in the film are based on pretending to be a hick. When the show's announcer (Vernon) holds up an "applause" cue during a broadcast down home, the literacy-challenged audience responds with silence. And in an obligatory scene in which the brothers encounter feuding mountain families, a clan patriarch (Slim Summerville) is asked by his tomboy daughter, "Hey, paw, what do you want for dinner? Fried chicken or pork chops?" Paw and Harry simultaneously reply: "Both!" The cultural/ethnic differences in dining on fried chicken versus pork chops were not lost on viewers, even if they didn't know the Ritzes were Jewish.

Martin's character is scouting for authentic mountain music, not the Brooklynized type. For the sake of mass-audience entertainment, this was not the type aired in *Kentucky Moonshine*, which showcases three songs by Tin Pan Alley tunesmiths Lew Pollack and Sidney Mitchell. Weaver presents the pastoral "Sing a Song of Harvest," which is more of how a Yankee songwriter might envision a country ballad than the real thing. "Reuben, Reuben, I've Been Swingin'" is a boisterous mix of country and would-be swing, with the Ritzes singing, dancing, playing hillbilly instruments, and doing animal imitations. "Moonshine Over Kentucky" is performed twice, the second time in the Ritz-dominated finale, which takes place during the course of a radio broadcast but which is full of gags that only could be enjoyed seen and not heard. These include the brothers' burlesques of various radio attractions (Rudy Vallee, Professor Quiz) and the "Snow White" story as told by Walt Disney.

Some viewers might find annoying another section of the song in which the Ritzes mimic the style and dress of the kiddie harmony trio The Brian Sisters, which had sung "Moonshine Over Kentucky" earlier in the film. One wonders what the little girls thought of those guys making fun of them, however good-natured. Another number in *Kentucky Moonshine* is "Kentucky Opera," contributed by Fox-hired Ritz gag writers Sid Kuller and Ray Golden and future songwriting great Jule Styne, then a vocal coach at Fox who was uncredited in *Kentucky Moonshine*. There also is a swing version of the prologue from *I Pagliacci*, sung by Martin, who made that number part of his nightclub act and repeated it on screen in the 1951 RKO musical *Two Tickets to Broadway*.

Director Butler liked the Ritzes as entertainers, but they tried his patience on the *Kentucky Moonshine* set.[60] The brothers insisted on not being made to sing while barefooted while in their guise as hicks, so they were fitted with rubber feet. Another disagreement grew over which of the brothers would stand in the middle during a song number—Butler rightly wanted Harry, as clearly the funniest of the trio. After *Moonshine* wrapped, Darryl Zanuck had to talk Butler into doing a second picture with the Ritzes, which turned out to be *Straight, Place and Show* (1938)—in exchange for his getting a plumier assignment on *Kentucky* (1938), which bore no relationship at all to *Kentucky Moonshine*.

The same theater patrons who enjoyed small doses of the Ritzes responded positively to seeing more of their zaniness, and *Kentucky Moonshine* was a popular attraction in the late spring and summer of 1938. Individual theater ballyhoo consisted of untold numbers of locals having to don long beards and pretend to be the brothers. Another promotion, conducted by multiple theaters that showed *Kentucky Moonshine*, was even more of a dare for patrons, as chronicled by this account in a newspaper in small-town East Liverpool, Ohio:

> The management advertised … that any man or woman coming barefooted would be admitted without charge. At first [customers] were timid …, then someone took his shoes off in front of the theater and walked in. They tried checking shoes at the door, but still they came, so the rules were changed so that you had to come to the theater in your bare feet.
>
> The customers solved this by checking their shoes in the fire station across the street and in various restaurants and hiding them in the alleys. Some left them in their cars.
>
> It really worked out well and the management reported no complaints of trodding on tender toes.[61]

A particular favorite of patrons everywhere was the very timely parody of Disney's *Snow White and the Seven Dwarfs*, which features Harry Ritz as the Evil Queen/Witch. *Snow White* went into national release in February 1938, during the filming of *Kentucky Moonshine* (which lasted from mid-January through the end of March), so it must have seemed like a natural for sendup. The Disney film set box office records—by 1939, it would become the highest-grossing feature of all time—so *Kentucky Moonshine* benefited greatly from audience familiarity. Ritz brothers or no, the film was named one of 1938's top box office performers by *Harrison's Reports*. "It's field day for the Ritz Brothers, who sing, dance and clown to make this a rollicking laugh fest," cheered *The Film Daily* in a typically representative review.[62] *New York Times* reviewer Frank S. Nugent admitted that he was in the minority in an audience that cheered for the film, but he glumly gave *Kentucky Moonshine* its due while deciding that "nothing is wrong with the Ritzes … except that there are three too many of them."[63]

The material was good for the Ritzes in *Kentucky Moonshine* … but was it entirely original material? Possibly not. In October 1938, Hollywood trade publications reported that 20th Century-Fox was being sued by writer Howard J. Green and songwriters Ned Washington and Sammy Stept for $1,050,000 on plagiarism charges.[64] According to TCF legal records, the three claimed that *Kentucky Moonshine* was based on a script they'd written, "Nitwit's Holiday," and submitted to Fox. A similar accusation, settled for a mere $300, was lodged by writer Ralph Spence, who noted to Fox the similarities between the *Kentucky Moonshine* script and one he'd co-authored about a radio station janitor—played by comedian El Brendel in a 1934 Vitaphone two-reeler named *Radio Scout*—who was sent to Kentucky to find hick music talent.[65] TCF's assertion was that *Kentucky Moonshine* co-writer Art Arthur, a former columnist for the *Brooklyn Daily Eagle*, got his inspiration from hearing the proprietor of a New York nightclub complain that his so-called "hillbilly" performers were actually from Brooklyn.[66] The degree of sameness in these cases is interesting, but given the national thirst for country-oriented movies at this point, such similarities can't be assumed as intentional.

Kentucky Moonshine was one of the cinematic highlights of the Ritz Brothers' collective career, even if it didn't have the budget of an Alice Faye or Janet Gaynor film at Fox. With few exceptions, the quality of their starring films declined as they were relegated to TCF's "B" unit and producer Sol Wurtzel, prompting Harry Ritz to quip, "Things have gone from bad to Wurtzel."[67] In 1939, the studio-performer relationship had declined enough that the Ritzes left Fox, only to go to even less elaborate films at Universal. But if they continue to be ill-regarded today—and that's very much a matter of opinion—no one need blame *Kentucky Moonshine*.

Down in "Arkansaw"
(Republic; October 8, 1938)

and *Jeepers Creepers*
(Republic; October 27, 1939)

Down in "Arkansaw"

Director: Nick Grinde. Associate Producer: Armand Schaefer. Screenplay: Dorrell McGowan, Stuart E. McGowan. Photography: Ernest Miller. Editor: William Morgan. Supervising Film Editor: Murray Seldeen. Musical Director: Cy Feuer. Music Arranger: Dave Torbett. Art Director: John Victor Mackay. Costumes: Irene Saltern. Production Manager: Al Wilson. Assistant Director: George Blair. Running Time: 65 minutes.

Cast: Ralph Byrd (John Parker); Weaver Brothers [Leon and Frank] and Elviry (Abner, Cicero, and Elviry Weaver); June Storey (Mary Weaver); Pinky Tomlin (Pinky); Berton Churchill (Judge); Guinn Williams (Juble Butler); Walter Miller (Marks); Gertrude Green (Elsie); Selmer Jackson (Edwards); Arthur Loft (Turner); Ivan Miller (Lewis); John Dilson (Graves); Al Bridge (Jake); Karl Hackett (Wilkins); Chester Gunnels, Gloria Rich (specialty acts).

Songs: "The Arkansas Traveler" [Weavers] (Sanford C. Faulkner); "The Farmer Is Not in the Dell" [Tomlin] (Walter Kent, Eddie Cherkose); "In the Heart of the City That Has No Heart" [Weavers, band] (Thomas S. Allen, Joseph M. Daly); "Lulu Walls" [Weavers] (trad.).

Home Video: Grapevine Video DVD.

The Story: Pine Ridge, Arkansas, makes national headlines when the federal government seeks to build a dam that will force the mountain villagers to vacate their land. Abner Weaver and his wife, Elviry, and their cousin, Cicero, are prominent in their refusal to comply. Abner and Elviry announce the engagement of their daughter, Mary, to townsman Juble Butler. Government agent John Parker and his friend Pinky are sent to Pine Ridge to force the residents to accept the federal subpoenas ("The Farmer Is Not in the Dell"), which they attempt to do by pretending to stage a talent contest for a fake record company. The Weavers win the contest ("Lulu Walls") and are served with the court documents, but refuse to cooperate, although Mary and Parker become attracted to each other. Parker's efforts are secretly undercut by construction boss Marks, who is in league with the local power company, which will go out of business if the dam is built. Marks stages a dynamite accident that he hopes will turn the hill folk away from the government men; after several townspeople are injured, the dam project is postponed. While the case is litigated, Parker attempts to win the hillbillies' favor by exposing them to sophisticated life by taking them to a fancy nightclub ("In the Heart of the City That Has No Heart") and convincing them of the wonders of prefabricated housing. Elviry and the other women of the town convince the menfolk to vote to sell their land. After Juble is shot, Parker is blamed, but Marks and his cohort Jake are rightfully exposed. The dam project begins anew, the hillbillies move to their new locale, and Mary and Parker are married.

Jeepers Creepers

Director: Frank McDonald. Associate Producer: Armand Schaefer. Screenplay: Dorrell McGowan, Stuart E. McGowan. Photography: Ernest Miller. Editor: Ernest J. Nims. Supervising Film Editor: Murray Seldeen. Musical Director: Cy Feuer. Art Director: John Victor Mackay. Costumes: Adele Palmer. Production Manager: Al Wilson. Assistant Director: Phil Ford. Running Time: 69 minutes.

Cast: Weaver Brothers [Leon and Frank] and Elviry (Abner, Cicero, and Elviry Weaver); Roy Rogers (Roy); Loretta Weaver (Violey); Thurston Hall (M.K. Durant); Maris Wrixon (Connie Durant); Johnny Arthur (Peabody); Lucien Littlefield (Grandpa); Billy Lee (Skeeter); Bud Geary, Ralph Sanford, Joe McGuinn, Robert S. Wilke, Dirk Thane, Bill Wolfe, Curley Dresden (men).

Songs: "Jeepers Creepers" [Rogers; reprised by Weavers, Hall, Wrixon, Rogers, chorus] (Johnny Mercer, Harry Warren); "In the Good Old Summertime" [Weavers, band] (Ren Shields, George Evans); "In the Shade of the Old Apple Tree" [Weavers] (Harry Williams, Egbert Van Alstyne); "Listen to the Mockingbird" [Rogers, Lee] (Alice Hawthorne); "The Little Brown Jug" [Weavers, Rogers, chorus] (R.A. Eastburn); "Some Folks Do" [Weavers, chorus] (Stephen Foster); "S-A-V-E-D" [Weavers, chorus], "Wait for the Wagon" [Weavers, chorus] (trad.).

Also Released As: *Money Isn't Everything.*

The Story: In the peaceful mountain village of Pineville, mayor and justice of the peace Abner Weaver leads his town in church on a Sunday morning ("S-A-V-E-D"). He cites the negative headlines of the day in encouraging his fellow citizens to donate food to striking coal miners. The strike is against the United Coal Owners Association, whose president, banker M.K. Durant, is visiting the area but would rather go fishing than to church. Durant is taken into custody by Pineville's sheriff, Roy, for creating a fire hazard, and the banker and his daughter, Connie, are each sentenced by Abner to a day of hard labor. While wielding a pickaxe in punishment, Durant discovers a rich vein of coal on the Weavers' property, and he conspires to use the new find to fill the void left by the strike. Abner refuses Durant's offer to buy the Weaver property, but Durant sends his men to mine the land anyway. He distracts the villagers with a fancy party at a big-city hotel, where the Weavers perform "In the Good Old Summertime." Although Abner's daughter Violey pines for Roy, he would rather court Connie ("Jeepers Creepers"), and Abner's spinster sister, Elviry, hankers for Durant's secretary, Peabody. Durant reveals he has acquired the title to the Weaver homestead by paying back taxes; he offers to pay the family for the lost land, but Abner declines. The townspeople grow disenchanted with the presence of the coal workers, who violate tradition by working on Sunday, but a hayride temporarily smooths things over ("Little Brown Jug," "Wait for the Wagon"). A drunken worker causes a road accident that kills the grandfather of Abner's nephew, Skeeter. When the country folk demand justice, the miners engage them in a gun battle, and a forest fire breaks out. The blaze traps Durant in his overturned car, but he is saved by Skeeter, who brings word to townspeople who rescue the banker. A thankful Durant announces he will settle the strike and give the Weavers back their land, and the principals celebrate by singing "Jeepers Creepers."

Long before the Clampetts laid eyes on their bubblin' crude, the Weavers—more specifically, the Weaver Brothers and Elviry—reigned as pop culture's first family of hillbilly. Leon (1882–1950) and Frank Weaver (1891–1967) were real siblings from rural Missouri—a bespectacled straight man and his silent-as-Harpo partner—who teamed with Leon's wife, singer-comedienne June Petrie Weaver (1891–1977), to become famous in vaudeville and radio as Abner, Cicero, and Elviry. The three were signed by Republic Pictures in 1938 to make what became a series of 11 popular song-and-dance comedies, the first two of which were *Down in "Arkansaw"* and *Jeepers Creepers*. Dismissed by reviewers, these pictures were targeted at simple folk but could be appreciated by all, and it is no accident that the

Weavers' humor influenced such countrified cut-ups as Minnie Pearl, Judy Canova, and the gang from *Hee-Haw*.

The Weavers' fast-paced live shows, chock-full of corny, Ozarkian humor and novelty musicianship, took them and their stock company from modest American stages to tours around the world. The trio transitioned to the airwaves via the nascent Grand Ole Opry and then, inevitably, to motion pictures, where, constricted by plotting, they weren't thought to be as funny as when viewed live. To see the original "Arkansaw Travelers" in the flesh was to see Abner preside as a drawling, fatherly master of ceremonies introducing cowboy choruses and clog dancers. A grinning, pantomiming Cicero would be adorned in a spinning bow tie while playing drums and percussion (including washboards, rake handles, handsaws, and cymbals attached to his knees), and hard-boiled "sister" Elviry would sing with gusto and lead a colorfully costumed "chorus of maidens." She also liked to interact with the audience. On a given night, this tough talker might respond to a heckler who would, say, call for Cicero to come out, with, "You're going to get Cicero all right—but you won't until I'm through!"

Despite Elviry's bluster on stage, the Weaver collective was so sturdy that it survived the potentially touchy situation of June divorcing Leon in mid-career and marrying Frank, apparently without so much as a professional hiccup. A clearer on-the-job hazard came when the Weavers made their debut in pictures at citified Warner Bros. in support of Humphrey Bogart in the misguided mountain musical comedy *Swing Your Lady**. When Bogart wasn't seen walking through his role as a pro wrestling promoter, Louise Fazenda and Nat Pendleton held center stage as wince-worthy romancing grapplers, and future "Blondie" Penny Singleton and future President Ronald Reagan (in a small role) weren't enough help. Absented from the stinkeroo central story, the Weavers sang two numbers for atmosphere in the early-1938 release but escaped the withering criticism of it. Fortunately, down-home Republic was looking for acts, so the Weaver three became a more natural fit there before year's end.

The Weavers had to settle for second billing in their maiden Republic production, as the credits for *Down in "Arkansaw"* were headed by handsome action man Ralph Byrd, who had lent his jutting jaw to serial success in the studio's *S.O.S. Coast Guard* (1937) and *Dick Tracy* (1937), the latter of which led to a sub-career playing the famed comic-strip lawman. Directed by longtime B-movie craftsman Nick Grinde, *Arkansaw* set the template for the Weavers' Republic programmers, in which insular but kindly rural people triumph over threats to their culture from worldly sources. In this instance, the threats are the building of a dam by the government in a mountain village and the interference of the local power company in the project. The Weavers lead the town in its resistance to the modernization, although Elviry has the regional disadvantage of being a woman and Cicero apparently can speak only in bird sounds.

Without everyday conveniences—such as automobiles, telephones, radios, or motion pictures—to enjoy, the locals cherish their music, and much of what there is in *Down in "Arkansaw"* purports to be authentic: a square dance reel with a string band and various percussive utensils; a short interlude by longtime Weavers collaborator "Cousin" Chester Gunnels on the bones, a traditional folk instrument; and a couple of numbers led by Elviry. The chestnut "In the Heart of the City That Has No Heart" is performed in a nightclub where Byrd has taken the gussied-up mountaineers to coax them into civilizing; the song, a cautionary tale of a girl's despoiling by the bright lights, is meant as the Weavers' suspicious response. The "spontaneous" spoken byplay among the Weavers during the number is the film's best indication of what the clan's live act must have been like, and it shows the

"Bones" player Chester Gunnels leads a specialty number in Republic's folksy *Down in "Arkansaw."* Leon "Abner" Walker is immediately to Gunnels' left, and brother Frank (aka "Cicero") is the curly haired player second from the right.

strong personality of Elviry, who is typically smarter than she appears in these modest pictures.

More lighthearted in *Down in "Arkansaw"* is Arkansas-born Pinky Tomlin, back as a secondary player in pictures after his run of starring musical programmers at Melody Pictures (see above). He sings a new comic tune, the nursery-rhyme variation "The Farmer Is Not in the Dell," when not terrifying sheltered mountain children by making chicken squawks over his portable microphone. *Down in "Arkansaw"* doubles down on the culture-clash humor with a scene in which the mountain folk are befuddled by gadgets in a modern prefab home. Cicero pulls a radio away from the wall to find out where its noise is emanating, and a hillbilly mom attempts to put her dirty-faced son in the washing machine she has just learned about. But this is a Republic picture, and it wouldn't be so without a serious climactic conflict replete with gunplay, a fistfight, and a right-over-might victory. Byrd ends up with the Weavers' knockout-blond daughter (June Storey), which is less of a surprise than the fact that Abner and Elviry could have conceived her. Storey was borrowed from Fox for this picture, but advance publicity from Republic made it clear that she fit right in at her new outdoor-picture-minded studio by emphasizing her hobby of "collecting hunting trophies and her collection … is the envy of many big game hunters."[68]

Variety dismissed *Down in "Arkansaw"* as "lightweight" and "implausible," with "laughs … few and far between."[69] But a theater owner from Iowa perhaps better reflected the public view of the film when he said for posterity: "It seems these type pictures do more business than the biggest box office hits of the season."[70] So, within a few months,

Republic brought back most of the behind-the-scenes crew to join the now-first-billed Weaver Brothers and Elviry in a new musi-comedy. The title of *Jeepers Creepers* was borrowed from the hit song penned by Johnny Mercer and Harry Warren for the 1938 Warner Bros. musical comedy *Going Places* [q.v.], in which Louis Armstrong debuted the tune by singing it to a horse. Also lent, because it was now firmly part of the popular culture, was the song itself—performed by the Weavers' handsome, new romantic lead: Roy Rogers. Yes, that Roy Rogers.

Rogers (1911–1998) was just beginning his immortal career as a singing cowboy star, having earned that status after stepping in temporarily for Gene Autry while the latter was in a contract dispute with Republic. When *Jeepers Creepers* was being filmed in September 1939, Rogers had already been seen in nine starring B-oaters made in scarcely more than a calendar year, but the studio at this point still thought it prudent to keep him busy in other kinds of roles. As sheriff of a mountain town where Abner Weaver is the mayor and justice of the peace, Roy becomes attracted to a visiting socialite (Maris Wrixon) and is flirted with by a local miss played by June/Elviry's real daughter, Loretta.[71] Loretta tries to win over Roy by wearing shoes to church, which means she isn't going to get very far, and when the lawman's attention isn't affixed to the prettier and wealthier of the two misses, it is diverted to a dispute over coal discovered on the Weaver homestead. *Jeepers Creepers* is nominally a musical comedy, but a drunken driving-induced fatality, a forest fire, and general white-collar dishonesty clutter up matters before the requisite happy conclusion.

There is significantly more music in *Jeepers Creepers* than *Down in "Arkansaw,"* and it is not just mere scene-setting. It is shown as integral to country culture, most importantly as part of the townspeople's religious faith—the cornerstone of their philosophical and social lives. *Jeepers Creepers* opens during a Sunday church service in which the parishioners sing (and spell out key words) the gospel standard "S-A-V-E-D":

> Some people go on weekdays to D-A-N-C-E.
> They go to church on Sunday to show their H-A-T.
> Some people dab their faces up with P-A-I-N-T.
> And then they laugh at us because we're S-A-V-E-D.

Abner leads the service by reading from the day's headlines of unsaved folks in trouble—one of the banners, ominously, warns "War Rages in Europe" (this is 1939, after all)—before exhorting his people to setting a godly example close to home by supporting striking coal miners. An antagonist in the strike, a big "coal man" portrayed by Thurston Hall, is later brought before justice Abner and "bailiff" Elviry, and she reminds the grumpy visitor that "a man that sings can't be ornery 'cause singin' makes you shine on the inside like soap and water does on the outside." Music is a frequent unifying force in the film—the townspeople and the roughneck strike breakers put aside their differences temporarily at a hayride where they sing the familiar tunes "Little Brown Jug" and "Wait for the Wagon." Bashful Roy makes a forceful attempt for Wrixon's affection with a rendition of the title song—no sense wasting it on his steed. In a departure from his super-chaste persona of his cowboy pictures, he even steals a kiss from his girl. "Jeepers Creepers" is reprised at the finish in a joyous resolution of the story that pleases the rural and city interests. Even Hall joins in, after being reminded by Mayor Weaver, "You can't sing and feel bad at the same time!"

Jeepers Creepers even reinforces its populist message in the guise of its youngest character, a little boy played by Billy Lee. Near the end, Hall's character finds himself in an overturned car during an oncoming forest fire and reliant on the aid of the boy, whose grandfather has just been killed through the negligence of one of the coal man's minions.

"I need help, sonny! I can't get out of here!" cries the capitalist. "Not even with all your money?" replies the boy, who ought to be grieving enough to not think of class differences. "I guess I had that coming," says Hall. "...You mean you'd go through that fire for me?" Responds Lee, perhaps a tad too authoritatively to be convincing: "Mister, this ain't no time to hold a grudge!" True to the movie's religiosity, Abner prays for the town's deliverance from the fiery catastrophe, and the Almighty responds by making it rain up a storm. Such melodramatics were prime fodder for the sticks; so was the film's stance on labor and management, a trait that the *Variety* reviewer saw fit to warn theater owners about. "Film has a strong labor angle, designed to please the common folk," the weekly's writer stated.[72] Said commentator might have warned readers that Elviry had let her guard down enough to pair up with Hall's prissy assistant, played by milquetoast Johnny Arthur.

No matter, for the Weavers were enough of a screen draw to sign a contract extension with Republic after *Jeepers Creepers*. They continued their series there until 1943; thereafter, with vaudeville all but dead, they spent more time in their native locale of Springfield, Missouri. Among the later of their 11 features at Republic were *Grand Ole Opry* (1940), which introduced country music greats Roy Acuff and Uncle Dave Macon to pictures, and *Arkansas Judge* (1941), which reunited the Weavers with Roy Rogers. The success of the Weavers' films led RKO to sign hick radio comics Lum and Abner for their own series, and Republic secured singer-comedienne Judy Canova to make more rural-themed movies.

Although the Weaver Brothers and Elviry are little remembered, their brand of humor never has gone away, not even in a more cynical modern world. As the historian Don Creacy has written, "The Weavers' movies had a simple but important message for the people who had suffered through the Great Depression and endured the hardships of [World War II]: Hard work and honesty will lead to better times; don't forget to laugh and sing along the way; and while you're at it, help people, don't hurt them."[73]

4

Where the Tenors and the Baritones Play

Hillbilly musicals were becoming a specific category in the Depression era, but way out West, spurred by similar influences, the cowboy was also finding voice to revitalize a stagnant genre. This did not happen overnight. Right out of the talkie transition, Hollywood Westerns took time for occasional, mainly incidental song numbers by leading cowpokes, but early efforts were short on creativity and half on heart. In discussing endeavors such as these, we exclude higher-budget, major-studio Broadway adaptations like *Rio Rita* (1929) and *Song of the West* (1930), which were not as much Westerns as operettas set in the West, and odd one-offs like MGM's *Montana Moon* (1930), which paired the very un-cowgirlish Joan Crawford with handsome Johnny Mack Brown, not yet having found his calling as a cowboy hero.

Heroes from bread-and-butter oaters were un-sonically buoyant. Western series star Ken Maynard warbled a tune in a Tiffany "Voice of Hollywood" variety short of 1930, then was shown singing and playing guitar in some of his own B vehicles at Universal, as early as the part-talking *Parade of the West*. Maynard's compatriot Bob Steele impressed his many fans when he showed off his tenor in his first all-talkie, *Near the Rainbow's End* (1930). Steele's studio, Tiffany, dared to offer a newly minted singing cowboy in 1930's *Border Romance* [q.v.], although Don Terry didn't catch on as a Western stud. A Pathé release of 1930, *Pardon My Gun*, stopped the action involving white-hatted Tom Keene dead in its tracks to throw in a lengthy song, dance, and trick-roping vaudeville show that included singer-comedienne Mona Ray, eccentric dancer Al "Rubber Legs" Norman, and Abe Lyman and His Orchestra. It was all earnest, but awkward. Even future cowboy icon John Wayne was shown vocalizing in four 1933–35 quickies, but he was dubbed, hinting at his lack of a future as a baritone or tenor.[1]

Whether made by minor units at major studios or by completely independent entities, Westerns fell victim to the woeful economy, and even though they were cheap to make (even in the later '30s, one could be filmed for $10,000 or less), fewer of them were released in America during 1933 and 1934 than at least since the early '20s.[2] By 1935, the Poverty Row Western had grown stale, the same basic stories being presented in picture after picture, still popular though in need of a burst of personality and imagination to enthrall a loyal audience. The personality turned out to be Gene Autry, no great looker but already a prominent "hillbilly" recording artist. The imagination came from Nat Levine, founder and president of modest Mascot Pictures. Their signal collaboration was *The Phantom Empire*, a 12-chapter serial that influenced the futures of three film genres—science fiction, the Western, and the musical—especially as the first "official" singing Western.

Audiences rapidly warmed to musical Westerns—not just for the music, but for the nostalgia of real cowboys singing around campfires or while riding horses on the open prairie, a victory of American individualism without the classist stigma attached to their hillbilly brethren. Like hillbilly, Western music was derived from British Isles folk, but with a touch of Mexican flair prompted by geography. If employed, instruments were simple and portable—fiddles, guitars, harmonicas—and backing choruses numbered no more than a handful of voices. These musical practitioners found the cowboy label more desirable than the hillbilly brand; it was more romantic to dress as a cowboy than as a mountaineer. But the two divergent styles were never far apart, for, as country historian Anthony Harkins has written,

> the cultural divide between hillbilly and cowboy was easily crossed because country music iconography had always occupied a middle ground between mountains and plains.... By the mid–1930s, then, country singers still sang about cabins in the mountains, but they now referred to the Rockies, not the Cumberlands, and the Kentucky Ramblers of the *National Barn Dance* became the Prairie Ramblers.[3]

Cowboy numbers tended, especially in B Westerns, to complement the action without interfering with it, and they were usually short enough so youthful patrons could sit through them without squirming. Outside of the movie business, 1930s cowboy music would become more sophisticated by the jazz-influenced "Western swing" popularized by Bob Wills and others, but its impact would not be felt on film until well into the 1940s, so when you heard a cowboy song in a cowboy picture before then, it was usually basic stuff. Song sequences comfortably reflected the emotions of otherwise stoic heroes who might seem silly airing thoughts of love, tribulation, or environmental contentment via spoken word. To those who didn't want their cowboy heroes to get too mushy with their women, courting by song was a pleasing compromise. Given the roster of plot reversals the cowhand could endure, his rationale for singing could be shaky, as one decades-later commentator stated in jest: "Them bandits have beaten my mother, ravished my girl, burned down my house, killed my cattle and blinded my best friend. I'm goin' to get 'em if it's the last thing I do. But first, folks, I'm going to sing you a little song."[4]

The singers were deemed sillier when their tones were too refined. Among the many Autry successors, guileless, naturalistic talents such as Roy Rogers—who became Autry's chief "rival" in the 1940s—and Tex Ritter lasted with fans, while voice-trained, citified types like Smith Ballew, Fred Scott, and Dick Foran did not. Major musical stars—notably Bing Crosby in *Rhythm on the Range* (1936) and Dick Powell in *Cowboy from Brooklyn* (1938)—kept fan favor in what were unquestioned dalliances as singing cowboys. But their big-studio efforts were unmistakably comedic, in contrast to the classic Autry-Rogers heroism, and firmly rooted in more-sophisticated 1930s sensibilities, with Westernized, as opposed to authentically Western, music to match.

The demand for Western stars who could sing even brought gender and racial diversity to the field. Herb Jeffries headlined four African American-cast oaters in the 1930s, and at the end of the decade, Dorothy Page became the screen's first "Singing Cowgirl." All kinds of folks, not just plain ones, liked singing cowb ... uh, cowpeople because they reflected a slowly diversifying society. In a 1938 letter to the National Association for the Advancement of Colored People, the black actor-writer Flournoy Miller asked for the organization's help to urge people to "reserve criticisms" about the first of Jeffries' films, *Harlem on the Prairie*, because "colored motion pictures are in an experimental stage" and that "criticism of these pictures should be constructive rather than destructive.... Major studios flatly refuse to give colored people a decent part or to produce a first class colored picture."[5] Miller further explained that the Jeffries films were "an entertaining and authentic" effort to glorify such black cowboys of the real West as Bill Pickett and Simeon Sheffield.[6] Well-purposed talk aside, in a business sense, we saw Jeffries and Page on the prairie because even the series Western needed to offer something different.

This section is reserved for 1930s Western novelties: the Autry-Levine chapterplay that propelled the singing cowpoke trend, plus titles with nontraditional Western principals—a famous baseball player, the Terrors of Tiny Town, trailblazers Jeffries and Page, and Crosby and Powell channeling Autry and Rogers. Oh ... and David Niven.

The Phantom Empire
(Mascot; February 23, 1935)

Directors: Otto Brower, B. Reeves Eason. Story: Wallace MacDonald, Gerald Geraghty, Hy Freedman. Continuity: John Rathmell, Armand Schaefer. Photography: Ernest Miller, William Nobles. Editor: Earl Turner. Sound: Terry Kellum. Special Effects: Jack Coyle, Howard Lydecker. Assistant Director: William Witney. Production Manager: Armand Schaefer. Running Times: 252 minutes (12-chapter serial), 70 minutes (feature-length re-release)

Chapter Titles: *The Singing Cowboy*; *The Thunder Riders*; *The Lightning Chamber*; *Phantom Broadcast*; *Beneath the Earth*; *Disaster from the Skies*; *From Death to Life*; *Jaws of Jeopardy*; *Prisoners of the Ray*; *The Rebellion*; *A Queen in Chains*; *The End of Murania*.

Cast: Gene Autry (Gene Autry. "Radio's Singing Cowboy"); Frankie Darro (Frankie Baxter); Betsy King Ross (Betsy Baxter); Dorothy Christy (Queen Tika); Wheeler Oakman (Lord Argo); Charles K. French (Mal); Warner Richmond (Rab); J. Frank Glendon (Professor Beetson); Lester "Smiley" Burnette (Oscar); William Moore [Peter Potter] (Pete); Edward Peil, Sr. (Cooper); Jack Carlyle (Saunders); Stanley Blystone (television operator); Frank Ellis, Wally Wales, Jay Wilsey (Thunder Guards); Richard Talmadge (Thunder Rider captain); Fred Burns (Muranian priest); Duke R. Lee (Tom Baxter); The Beverly Hillbillies (ranch band).

Songs: "I'm Getting a Moon's Eye View of the World" [Autry], "I'm Oscar, I'm Pete" [Autry, Burnette, Moore], "Just Come on Back" [Radio Rangers], "No Need to Worry" [Radio Rangers], "Uncle Henry" [Autry] (Gene Autry, Smiley Burnette); "Uncle Noah's Ark" [Autry, Burnette, band, twice] (Gene Autry, Smiley Burnette, Nick Manoloff); "My Cross-Eyed Gal" [Radio Rangers], "That Silver-Haired Daddy of Mine" [Autry, band] (Gene Autry, Jimmy Long).

Also Released As: *Men With Steel Faces*, *Radio Ranch* (titles of reissue feature).

Disc: Banner 33225, Conqueror 8296, Melotone 13192 ("That Silver-Haired Daddy of Mine," Gene Autry); Banner 33485 ("My Cross-Eyed Gal"/"Uncle Noah's Ark," Gene Autry and Smiley Burnette).

Home Video: Alpha DVD; Serial Squadron DVD; Sinister Cinema DVD; Timeless Media Group DVD; VCI Entertainment DVD.

The Story: Singing cowboy Gene Autry and business partner Tom Baxter own and operate Radio Ranch, the locale of a daily "Thunder Riders" live radio broadcast. If the broadcast doesn't begin on time at 2 p.m. each day, Gene will lose both his radio contract and the dude ranch. Gene's sidekicks, young siblings Frankie and Betsy Baxter, find evidence of mysterious signals coming from underground. Gene and the kids notify Professor Beetson, who secretly covets rich radium deposits below ground in the area, wants the ranch shut down, and frames Gene for the murder of the Baxters' father. Gene is kidnapped by "Thunder Riders" from the empire of Murania, which exists 25,000 feet below the surface and consists of the last survivors of a lost human tribe that was forced under the Earth's surface by long-ago glacial activity. The Muranians have built a futuristic city complete with robots, ray guns, and long-range television monitors outfitted with super-sound. Murania is led by Queen Tika, who believes her people will be imperiled by Beetson's plot. Gene returns to the surface, where Frankie and Betsy free him from Beetson's men, but he and the two kids are recaptured by the Muranians. As Lord Argo leads a rebellion against her, Tika condemns Gene to death, but he escapes the "death chamber" and is pursued by Argo. Gene escapes to the surface and survives a plane crash. Gene, Frankie, Betsy, and members of Frankie and Betsy's "Junior Thunder Riders" club take turns rescuing each other, and even Gene's stooges Oscar and Pete journey into the lost city. Tika avoids Argo's command that she enter the "Death Chamber" and forges an uneasy alliance with Gene. Still, the Muranian city is destroyed after Argo's men activate a deadly machine. Frankie uses Murania's futuristic technology to clear Gene's name—without anyone missing a broadcast.

In 1935, *The Phantom Empire* was a multi-faceted, unprecedented movie treat—the first mix of Western, science fiction, and musical formulas. A 12-chapter serial, it unfolded over weeks from shore to shore to excited audiences of all ages who could hardly imagine what they were going to see next. It made a household name—and the screen's first true singing cowboy—out of its leading man, who was out-acted by everyone else in the film but within a year or two could be legitimately argued as the world's most popular movie star.

If it all seemed like something out of a dream, well ... in a sense, it was. If you believe the account propagated by its studio, an inventive little company called Mascot Pictures, the story for *Phantom Empire* was thought up by its writer, Wallace MacDonald, while he was sedated for a tooth extraction. Mascot's president, Nat Levine, had been Hollywood's leading purveyor of serials—31 produced between 1927 and 1935. His chapterplays had been nudging filmgoers into increasing suspensions of disbelief, and he wanted an idea from MacDonald that would push the fantasy envelope further. As well, there were the occasional feature-length science-fiction musicals—Fox's weird *Just Imagine* and weirder *It's Great to Be Alive* [q.v.]—and a few cowboys who sang (as opposed to Singing Cowboys). Now, in the depths of the Depression, it was time for the audience to be toppled over a cliffhanger.

Levine found an unexpected collaborator in Gene Autry (1907–1998), who wasn't the studio chief's first choice for his sci-fi Western. That was Ken Maynard, the longtime sagebrush star, but Maynard had ridden in greener pastures at First National and Universal, and he chafed at Mascot's paltry production budgets. Levine didn't like Maynard's offscreen drinking, and the two parted ways. The Oklahoma- and Texas-bred Autry had debuted on screen, unbilled, in two 1934 Maynard Mascots—a feature, *In Old Santa Fe*, and a serial, *Mystery Mountain*, and he already was nationally known as a yodeling radio singer and top-selling recording artist. In retrospect, *In Old Santa Fe* and *Mystery Mountain* both yielded clues that the future of the B Western was in better hands with Autry than Maynard. In the latter, Autry didn't sing a note, but art hinted at life when his character was shown mistakenly shooting Maynard out of the saddle. *In Old Santa Fe* allowed Autry to sing two songs during a sequence set at a party, and that got noticed. In an opinion about *In Old Santa Fe* in *Motion Picture Herald*, a Florida exhibitor (female, by the way) hinted at what the Western with songs could do to the box office:

> It's above the average and will please not only western fans, but others more sophisticated. The plot is good, it has an historical glamor and some really delightful Gene Autry music to lift it out of the rut of the commonplace shooting and fighting.... Most folks (not decadent) like clean outdoor adventure, and with a little music and cowboy singing, westerns will go over well weekly in my town. And don't you ever think my western fans don't know the difference between these two types of westerns. The box office proves it conclusively.[7]

Autry, however, had an unimpressive physical presence and an awkward screen demeanor. Late in his life, he admitted that he didn't really feel that strongly about a film career, and that he had to be talked into considering one by his wife. Asked by Levine if he wanted to star for Mascot, Autry recalled replying, "I don't know if I want to do that or not—I don't think I'm ready to be a star in a picture yet."⁸ However, Levine remembered differently to historian Jon Tuska:

> For a period of six months [Autry] wrote to me continually, conveying that he would do anything for the opportunity…. Autry was completely raw material…. All my associates questioned my judgment in putting him under contract. They thought I was slipping.⁹

Levine signed Autry to a $100-a-week contract, added his song numbers to the serial, and protected him with a cast headed by longtime juvenile actor Frankie Darro (1917–1976) and teenaged "World Champion Trick Rider" Betsy King Ross (1921–1989). Darro was so well known for his roles in action pictures and other fare that some ads for *The Phantom Empire* listed him as the star. There also were veteran heavy Wheeler Oakman and ubiquitous beauty Dorothy Christy, whose depth of experience included work with Will Rogers, Buster Keaton, Maurice Chevalier, and Laurel and Hardy. Christy (1906–1977) was cast as the imperious ruler of Murania, a futuristic society whose lost city just happens to be hidden directly under a patch of lucrative range land near a vacation ranch where Gene Autry—or at least a fictionalized version—performs daily over the radio. All Autry had to do was sing pleasantly and not fall off his horse. And not ham it up—which he could not do anyway—and that would make him so ultimately iconic, because he was "one of us."

Mascot typically spent between $30,000 and $50,000 for its serials, but the budget for *Phantom Empire* was about $70,000, to accommodate special effects, elaborate underground-city sets, and the salaries of two directors, Otto Brower and B. Reeves "Breezy"

Gene Autry sidekick Smiley Burnette is imperiled by underground denizens in Chapter 11 ("A Queen in Chains") of the science-fiction Western musical serial *The Phantom Empire*.

Eason, the last move a common one in serials to streamline the production process.[10] Levine used his recently leased backlot at the former Mack Sennett Studio for interior shots, and the newly constructed Griffith Observatory in Los Angeles for exteriors of the Muranian city. The costumes of the Muranian servant robots seen in the serial were bought from a costume shop and were leftovers from the Joan Crawford-Clark Gable musical *Dancing Lady* (MGM, 1933).[11] It might be difficult for 21st century folk schooled in an age when fantasy elements are malleable with any kind of screen story—think *Abraham Lincoln: Vampire Hunter* or *Cowboys & Aliens*—to acknowledge that *The Phantom Empire* might be a hard sell. Mascot touted *The Phantom Empire* as a "could it be true?" tale inspired by fact—at least fact as presented by popular author James Churchward, who wrote three books about the Lost Continent of Mu, an ancient civilization that some believed once existed in what is now the Pacific Ocean.

And although the core fandom for serials and Westerns was children, this chapterplay turned out to be more than kid stuff in interest. For the young'uns, Mascot entered into tie-ups with makers of a dozen novelties—balloons, masks, toy airplanes, birds, and more—for use by exhibitors.[12] But many cities slotted *The Phantom Empire* in both kiddie matinees and evening shows. In Allentown, Pennsylvania, it was paired with the George Raft gangster musical *Stolen Harmony* at night and the Tom Mix serial *The Miracle Rider* in Saturday daytime slots. In Cumberland, Maryland, it was on the bill with Hoot Gibson's oater *Rainbow's End*, but in Honolulu, it was with the edgy crime drama *Scarface* and the racy war comedy *Cock of the Air*.

Theater owners liked the returns whenever *Phantom* played. In June 1935, in *Motion Picture Herald*'s "What the Picture Did for Me" feature, a Detroit neighborhood theater man reflected the consensus:

> Here is something different in serials, based on the fantastic ideas made popular by the comic strips such as Buck Rogers and Flash Gordon. Started this on a hot Sunday but it is building and holding those who started it. It is well done with more plot than most serials. Just showed the third episode. The producers deserve credit for this new idea in serials and the clever manner in which this has been produced.[13]

Not only did *The Phantom Empire* wake the B Western out of its esthetic slumber, it helped to prompt a burst of science fiction on screen. Besides the aforementioned Fox musicals, filmed American sci-fi consisted mainly of mad-doctor tales such as *Frankenstein*, *The Mask of Fu Manchu*, and *Murder at Dawn*. But the Universal invisible-robot serial *The Vanishing Shadow* of 1934, as well as *The Phantom Empire*, turned filmmakers toward the overtly fantastic. As Jon Tuska and others have noted, if not for *Phantom Empire*, we might not have had Universal's *Flash Gordon* chapterplay (and its $300,000 budget) of 1936 and its successors. In retrospect, we can see how much sense this made, right up until filmmakers like George Lucas changed film forever by using Western and serial tropes, Lucas throughout *Star Wars* and its follow-ups.

Although the eight songs in *The Phantom Empire* are delivered as little more than interludes in the action, they are keys in the subplot concerning Autry's necessity for putting on his regular radio broadcast despite all the distractions. This explained Autry singing "I'm Getting a Moon's Eye View of the World" from a remote hook-up while flying on a dynamited airplane soon to plummet toward Earth. Mere filler, a Hollywood musicals purist might sniff, but grownups who showed up for a Gene Autry movie, even in 1935, expected to see Autry sing. The numbers also showcased the talents of Lester "Smiley" Burnette, who was Autry's associate on radio's *National Barn Dance* show as early as 1933, followed him into the movies, and stayed with him as sidekick for the pair's first few years in pictures. Burnette co-wrote six of the songs in *Empire* and shows off his frog-like croak on a couple. The serial also found the time to fit in the Autry-composed favorite "That Silver-Haired Daddy of Mine." Burnette's assistance in music and dialogue, and the employment of pre-teen cohorts and an unkissed lead female, set the template for the canon of the Greatest Cowboy Star of Them All.

In May 1935, three months after the debut of *The Phantom Menace*, Autry signed with Levine to make eight more pictures, but in June, Mascot was merged into the newly formed Republic Pictures. Republic was created at the behest of Herbert J. Yates, president of the film processing laboratory Consolidated Film Industries, who serviced multiple Poverty Row concerns and sought to head one himself. As a creditor to these small firms, he united six of them—Mascot included—as a production and distribution entity; he also eased out Levine and assumed control over Autry and put him to work steadily in B Westerns. Starting with his first starring feature, *Tumbling Tumbleweeds* (1935), Autry grew more at ease before the camera, and the box office showed it. By 1937, as a newspaper feature writer stated, Autry was receiving "more fan mail every day in the year than Gable and [Robert] Taylor and Errol Flynn get together and makes more pictures than the three of them, also combined."[14] By 1939, Autry had crossed over, smack-dab into the *Motion Picture Herald*'s poll of the top 10 box-office attractions, at number four.

With Autry atop the Western world in 1940, *The Phantom Empire* was reissued in the form in which many modern Earthlings have seen it: at feature length. The initial 70-minute cut was unappealingly titled *Men with Steel Faces*, then improved to *Radio Ranch*. The short version worked better as the property made the rounds on early broadcast television, then into the public domain for releases to cable TV and home video. It also dropped some of the songs and offered considerably less comic relief from Smiley Burnette and fellow cut-up William Moore. Perhaps most regrettably, it lacked much of the exposition that explained the Muranian queen's antipathy toward the less-advanced, "childish" 1930s form of Earth-bound humanity.[15] It also seemed not to show Gene Autry being bailed out by his kid sidekicks as often as folks saw in 1935. (Eyebrows raised....)

Phantom Empire/Radio Ranch became a pop-culture property that inspired movie and TV-episode homages in the 1970s and '80s and, from Mexican writer Alejandro Perez Cervantes, a short-story collection in 2006. The serial was also viewed in some quarters as camp: In Australia in 1988, there were screenings with live, lip-synched comic dialogue in place of the real audio. "I love doing Gene Autry," the actor voicing the star told a Melbourne newspaper. "He's such an idiot ... but the nicest idiot around."[16] *The Phantom Empire* gained more plaudits in the 21st century, when VCI Entertainment issued a double-DVD digital restoration (2008) with plenty of extras, and Timeless Media Group distributed a three-DVD set (2011), the latter coming from Autry's personal film archives. They allowed enthusiasts to ditch their washed-out, worn-out videotapes and enabled new fans to visit Murania for the first time.

Palm Springs
(Walter Wanger/Paramount; June 5, 1936)

Director: Aubrey Scotto. Producer: Walter Wanger. Screenplay: Joseph Fields. Adaptation: Humphrey Pearson, based on the short story "Lady Smith" by Myles Connelly. Photography: James Van Trees. Editor: Robert Simpson. Art Direction: Alexander Toluboff. Sound: Earl Sitar. Music

Director: Boris Morros. Costumes: Helen Taylor. Assistant Director: George Blair. Running Time: 71 minutes.

Cast: Frances Langford (Joan Smyth aka Lady Sylvia Dustin); Sir Guy Standing (The Earl of Blythstone aka Captain Smyth); Ernest Cossart (Starkey); David Niven (George Brittel); Smith Ballew (Slim); E.E. Clive (Bruce Morgan); Spring Byington (Aunt Letty); Sterling Holloway (Oscar); Grady Sutton (Bud); Sarah Edwards (Miss Pinchon); Maidel Turner (Mrs. Baxter); David Worth (Leonard); Ann Doran, Margaret LaMarr, Mary Bovard, Jean Allen, Ruth Lamb, Maxine Westrom, June Horne, Ella McKenzie, Betty Auken (students); Annabelle Brudie, Marianne Brudie (twin girls); Grace Goodall (teacher); Lee Phelps (bartender); Eddie Tamblyn (soda clerk); Fred "Snowflake" Toones (porter); Fuzzy Knight (cowboy); Cyril Ring (reception clerk); Larry Steers (casino customer); Henry Iblings, Kirby Hoon, Marshall Sohl, Lewis Yoeskel (male quartet).

Songs: "The Hills of Old Wyoming" [Ballew, chorus; reprised by Langford, Ballew, chorus, then by Langford, Ballew], "I Don't Want to Make History, I Want to Make Love" [Langford, chorus; reprised by Langford] (Leo Robin, Ralph Rainger); "Will I Ever Know?" [Langford, chorus; reprised by Langford] (Mack Gordon, Harry Revel).

Also Known As: *Palm Springs Affair*.

Disc: Decca 663B ("Will I Ever Know?" Frances Langford with Victor Young Orchestra); Decca 783 ("The Hills of Old Wyoming"/"I Don't Want to Make History, I Want to Make Love," Frances Langford with Victor Young Orchestra).

The Story: The Earl of Blythstone is an English widower who travels the country as a professional gambler with his valet, Starkey, and poses as "Captain Smyth." He has kept his title, his livelihood, and his financial shortcomings a secret from his American-born daughter, Joan, whom he has installed in finishing school. Joan has rejected many marriage proposals from young men because she yearns to find the right match ("Will I Ever Know?"). Joan is expelled from school for gambling and goes to join her father in the California resort town of Palm Springs. She meets Slim, an easygoing cowboy who gives horse riding lessons to visitors, and George, a wealthy Englishman whose finances are controlled by his Aunt Letty. Slim charms Joan with his honesty and pleasing singing voice ("The Hills of Old Wyoming"). George warns Joan of an older man who is cheating at the gambling table, and Joan is shocked to learn he is talking about her father. Embarrassed, Joan decides to forsake her romantic ideals and marry for money ("I Don't Want to Make History, I Want to Make Love"). Letty remains suspicious of her nephew's new love interest, but George proposes to Joan and she accepts. Letty announces Joan and George's engagement, but Smyth uses the presence of an old friend, Morgan, to help expose his daughter, now pretending to be "Lady Sylvia," and keep her honest. Letty announces Joan and George's engagement, but her father reveals Joan's deception. Now convinced that love should trump social standing, Joan rejects George for Slim.

Neither a full-time Western nor a full-blooded musical, *Palm Springs* sports a title that promises an insider's look at the California resort town where millionaires and movie stars rub noses, but it doesn't really deliver. Save for a couple of good tunes sung by a pair of newcomers from radio, comely Frances Langford and cowboy Smith Ballew, plus the novelty of future star David Niven in an early (and non-singing) role, there isn't much to justify sitting through this romantic comedy trifle.

In the 1930s, most prospective viewers would have thought they knew what they would get from such an entertainment. Located 110 miles, or about three hours of travel, from Hollywood, Palm Springs was where moviedom's biggest and brightest could go to get away from it all. They were joined by kings of industry from the East, cattle barons from the West (which actually was to the east of the city), and various moneyed matrons and their kin. They drove over by car, yes, but many could afford to fly in by plane over the desert. Palm Springs was a state of mind, it was often said, and just to say you'd been there was to convey the fact that you'd relaxed and/or had fun.

So why—as producer Walter Wanger did in January 1936—make a movie called *Palm Springs* without genuine movie stars? Wanger had a distribution agreement with Paramount, and had successfully filmed the studio's first all-Technicolor release, *The Trail of the Lonesome Pine* (1936). He maintained a roster of stars that included Henry Fonda, Charles Boyer, Madeleine Carroll, Sylvia Sidney, and Walter Pidgeon, but now he had much more product than usual to grind out. Wanger functioned for decades as a producer with independence of varying degrees and subject matter of highly varying financial and aesthetic appeal. But a new contract he'd signed with Paramount, which demanded a new film every two months for $300,000, made him less his own man and more subject to studio demands on finances, casting, and scripts.[17] As a result, he was stretching his resources thinner than ever and may have felt the need to develop more of his own topliners.

For *Palm Springs*, this meant giving pop singer Frances Langford her first leading role. Wanger originally announced a film with that title in mid-1935, with Fonda and Ida Lupino attached. Somewhere in the process it became a musical as well as a comedy with Langford, a Florida-bred miss with a silky contralto. She had supported George Raft and Alice Faye in Wanger/Paramount's *Every Night at Eight* (1935)—in which she sang her signature tune, "I'm in the Mood for Love"—and had performed specialty numbers in *Broadway Melody of 1936* (MGM 1935) and *Collegiate* (Paramount 1936), but that was it for her in features to that point. More people knew Langford (1913–2005) for her singing on the radio shows of Louella Parsons, Rudy Vallee, and Dick Powell than for her screen work, but Wanger—who now had her under contract—hoped that would change.

Other key personnel for *Palm Springs* were unproven on film. Director Aubrey Scotto was a former operatic baritone and prolific maker of early sound shorts at Paramount who was now in features. In the "good-guy" male principal role was Ballew (1902–1984), a pop-jazz singer and bandleader who was getting a relatively late start in pictures at age 34. An erstwhile collaborator with Glenn Miller, Ted Fio-Rito, and the Dorsey brothers, Ballew didn't have the typical singing-cowboy tones, but he was from Texas and he was tall and handsome, compared to Gary Cooper in stature and Bing Crosby in voice tones. The ample height wasn't necessarily a springboard to stardom in 1936; media accounts speculated that, at 6 foot 4 inches, Ballew might tower too high in romantic scenes.[18] But he was on the rise in reputation, a newly acquired gig as host of the *Shell Chateau* radio show (replacing Al Jolson) providing evidence.

Niven, on the other hand, had a budding career that was being cultivated by loan-outs from Wanger's rival producer Samuel Goldwyn, to whom the young Englishman was under pact. Niven (1910–1983) already had experienced a lot. Trained in the English army service, he grew tired of the peacetime military and resigned his commission in favor of a new life in North America. After diversions in Atlantic City, Mexico, Cuba, and Bermuda, in activities as varied as whiskey sales and rodeo promotions, he was accepted in Hollywood by Central Casting as "Anglo-Saxon Type No. 2,008." Samuel Goldwyn signed him to a contract, and with each of his films, Niven was getting a little more to do. *Palm Springs* was only his fourth credited part, his first with any kind of extended dialogue. This left a rather unlikely sort—62-year-old British character actor Sir Guy Standing, who had been in movies only three years—in the second-billed spot of the cast. A former military officer, Standing had less-dignified aims in *Palm Springs* as the professional-gambler father of Langford's character, Joan Smyth (pronounced "Smythe" with a long "I").

Joan goes to the titular city to find her dad and ends up having to choose whom to love between two young men—played by Niven and Ballew—who represent opposite poles of her personality. She yearns to share the innocence of the horseman she meets in the hills above the town, but, once at ground level, she is drawn to a wealthier man as she leans toward the risk-taking gambler's attitude of her rascal father. But nothing in this triangle is very interesting: Neither Langford nor Ballew has much charisma; she's easy to root for and looks good in overalls, but she doesn't have enough glamour to carry even a minor musical like this, and the Gary Cooper look-alike is more glum than laconic. The concerns over Ballew's height remained, for until the finale, his romantic scenes with Langford show them either sitting down or atop horses. In only about 10 minutes on screen, Niven smiles a lot, shows his good nature, and unconvincingly tries to get in good with Langford by claiming he's "half English, half Texan." He's not a bad sort, but in this kind of story, he's not going to end up with the girl.

Amid unimpressive reviews of the film, *Modern Screen* was especially snide about Ballew: "He plays an honest cowboy ... like the hero of the senior class play."[19] Not surprisingly for someone so stalwart, Ballew became better known as a B Western lead; among his efforts was 1938's *Rawhide* [q.v.], in which his co-lead was "The Iron Horse" (baseball star Lou Gehrig) and not a real steed. Niven is likable but does nothing to distinguish himself from any other young actor with an English accent from Central Casting. In a cast heavy on British actors, Standing and fellow countryman Ernest Cossart do good work as a team of crooked gamblers, the latter working as the former's valet when they're not making trouble.[20] Their attempt to teach ditzy socialite Spring Byington how to make a proper poker face plays well, and E.E. Clive (also from the U.K.) contributes a scene-stealing bit as an explorer who unwittingly helps Langford keep up the charade of posing as a member of nobility. Actually, she really is a noble because of her father, except that she doesn't know it ... uh, never mind.

Palm Springs plays as if it could be set at any generic resort haven, and in fact Wanger chose not to shoot it in the real "Playground of the West," leaving the desert exteriors to be filmed closer to Los Angeles in Palmdale, California, and the indoor shots in Hollywood.[21] Among its mere three songs, Paramount songwriting reliables Leo Robin and Ralph Rainger contributed two that became much covered: "I Don't Want to Make History, I Just Want to Make Love," which Langford introduces as an intimate expression that segues to a bevy of datable schoolgirls sitting with beaux in parked cars, and "In the Hills of Old Wyoming," which Ballew and Langford (aided by a cowboy chorus) trade off as "their" song. Paramount gave these and *Palm Springs*' other selection, Mack Gordon and Harry Revel's "Will I Ever Know?," plenty of radio exposure prior and during the film's release, and it featured "I Don't Want to Make History, I Just Want to Make Love" in one of its "Talkartoons" cartoons with the Vincent Lopez Orchestra. Upon the release of *Palm Springs* in June, reviewers lauded the music while sharing *Variety*'s opinion that the film was "innocuous ... almost exclusively rudimentary."[22]

Palm Springs contributed to a bad stretch for Wanger, whose work was not enhanced by the increased studio influence. Made at a $328,000 cost, it lost more than $150,000 and joined a parade of money-losers for its producer; there would be seven in a row for Wanger at Paramount in the wake of *The Trail of the Lonesome Pine*.[23] Wanger transitioned to United Artists at the start of 1937. Niven's breakout roles, in David O. Selznick's *The Prisoner of Zenda* and Warner Bros.' *The Dawn Patrol*, were one and two years ahead, respectively, so he didn't have too much time to stew over his busman's holiday in the ersatz Palm Springs.

Rhythm on the Range
(Paramount; July 27, 1936)

Director: Norman Taurog. Producer: Benjamin Glazer. Executive Producer: William LeBaron. Screenplay: John C. Moffitt, Sidney Salkow, Walter DeLeon, Francis Martin. Story: Mervin J. Houser. Photography: Karl Struss. Film Editor: Ellsworth Hoagland. Sound: Eugene Merritt, Don Johnson. Art Direction: Hans Dreier, Robert Usher. Set Decoration: A.E. Freudeman. Music Director: Boris Morros. Visual Effects: Gordon Jennings, Dev Jennings. Costumes: Edith Head. Assistant Director: Joseph C. Youngerman. Running Time: 87 minutes.

Cast: Bing Crosby (Jeff Larabee); Frances Farmer (Doris Halloway); Bob Burns (Buck Eaton); Martha Raye (Emma); Samuel S. Hinds (Robert Halloway); Warren Hymer (Big Brain); Lucille Gleason (Penelope Ryland); George E. Stone (Shorty); James Burke (Wabash); Martha Sleeper (Constance Hyde); Clem Bevans (Gila Bend); Leonid Kinskey (Mischa); Charles Williams (Gopher); Beau Baldwin 50th ("Cuddles," a bull); Louis Prima (trumpeter); Emmett Vogan (clerk); Billy Bletcher (Shorty); John Eckert, Richard Powell, Ben Hendricks, Frank Sully, Eddie Dunn (cowboys); Eddy Waller (field judge); Dennis O'Keefe [Bud Flannigan] (sidewalk heckler); Duke York (police officer); James Blaine, Robert E. Homans, Edward LeSaint (train conductors); Herbert Ashley (brakeman); James "Slim" Thompson (porter); Jim Toney (oil station proprietor); Syd Saylor (Gus); Oscar Smith (waiter); Dorothy Tennant (dowager); Charles E. Arnt (steward); Harry C. Bradley (minister); Otto Yamaoka (Charlie); Ella Ethridge (seamstress); Bob McKenzie (uncooperative driver); Irving Bacon (announcer); Heinie Conklin (driver); Frank Dawson (butler); Jack Rice (man at train station); Helen Drew (party guest); Larry Steers (dining car passenger); The Sons of the Pioneers [including Roy Rogers].

Songs: "Drink It Down" [Crosby, Kinskey, Sons of the Pioneers] (Leo Robin, Ralph Rainger); "Empty Saddles (In the Old Corral)" [Crosby, chorus] (J. Keirn Brennan, Billy Hill); "I'm an Old Cowhand (From the Rio Grande)" [Crosby, Kinskey, Raye, Burns, Prima, Sons of the Pioneers] (Johnny Mercer); "I Can't Escape from You" [Crosby] (Leo Robin, Richard A. Whiting); "(If You Can't Sing It) You'll Have to Swing It (Mr. Paganini)" [Raye, Burns, Prima, Sons of the Pioneers] (Sam Coslow); "Roundup Lullaby" [Crosby] (Charles Badger Clark, Gertrude Ross).

Disc: Decca 870 ("Empty Saddles"/"Roundup Lullaby," Bing Crosby); Decca 871 ("I'm an Old Cowhand"/"I Can't Escape from You," Bing Crosby with Jimmy Dorsey Orchestra); Decca 11008 ("Empty Saddles"/"I'm an Old Cowhand," Bing Crosby); Decca 11009 ("I Can't Escape from You," Bing Crosby); Decca 2679A, Decca 25001 ("I'm an Old Cowhand," Bing Crosby with Jimmy Dorsey Orchestra); Decca 25346 ("Empty Saddles"/"Roundup Lullaby," Bing Crosby); Decca 5247 ("Empty Saddles"/"I'm an Old Cowhand," The Sons of the Pioneers).

Home Video: MCA Universal DVD/VHS.

The Story: Doris Halloway, daughter of one of the richest bankers in New York City, is talked out of an impending loveless marriage by her aunt, Arizona ranch owner Penelope "Penny" Ryland. At a rodeo at Madison Square Garden ("Empty Saddles"), money-shy cowboy/singer Jeff Larabee and his bazooka-playing pal, Buck, agree to travel West to work on Penny's ranch so they can earn enough for Jeff to keep his prized bull, Cuddles. To make the trip herself, Doris stows away on her aunt's boxcar, where she meets Jeff and Cuddles, but she hides her lofty lineage by pretending to be a cook. Penny and Buck get on board after the latter attracts the attention of Emma, a salesgirl headed to the ranch to visit her brother, but a mishap separates Jeff and Doris from the train and forces them to steal a car to ride West ("I Can't Escape from You"). Vagabond gangsters Big Brain, Shorty, and Wabash intercept a telegram from Doris to her father and plan to kidnap her and cash in. At Penny's Frying Pan Ranch, Buck declares his intent to marry Emma, who sings "Mr. Paganini" with a cowboy chorus. Buck encourages Jeff to propose marriage to Doris, amid more singing ("I'm an Old Cowhand [From the Rio Grande]," "Drink It Down") and partying at the ranch. Penny wrongly accuses Jeff of romancing Doris for her money. Jeff leaves the party in a huff, but he is reunited with Doris (and Cuddles) after fending off the kidnappers.

If anyone doubted that cowboy melodies were lassoing the cultural zeitgeist of the middle 1930s, they would have been hushed by the soothing tones of Bing Crosby, who placed the musical movie Western firmly into the mainstream with *Rhythm on the Range*. Crosby, always one to keep the customer satisfied, lately had been including cowboy songs in his prodigious recording-studio time, and a kindred addition to his movie career was inevitable. As a visual cowpoke, Crosby would be a bit loco in plausibility, but who cared? Certainly not the multitudes who made *Rhythm on the Range* one of the top-grossing movies of 1936.

By this time, Crosby had risen to the elite in cinema as well as music, and although his features at home studio Paramount weren't as technically elaborate as the spectacles at MGM and Warners, he was usually supplied with potent ingredients. For *Rhythm on the Range*, these included the guiding hand of reliable comedy director Norman Taurog and the creative talents of tried-and-true contract songwriters Richard Whiting, Leo Robin, Ralph Rainger, and Sam Coslow. A runaway-heiress-meets-rodeo-cowboy story was deemed sufficient to exploit the singing-cowhand fad, but the project really came together through less cinematically experienced folks. Bob Burns, a down-home, bazooka-playing comic monologist, already was exchanging zingers with Crosby on his weekly radio show. Martha Raye was a 19-year-old singer whom Taurog spotted in Hollywood's Trocadero nightclub and hired because he thought she could both clown and sing. Songster Johnny Mercer would supply *Range*'s most popular tune.

Mercer has passed into history as one of the greatest contributors to the Great American Songbook, but in 1936 he was smarting from merely moderate achievement as a radio writer and performer and, more painfully, from unremarkable appearances as an actor and singer in the minor RKO musicals *Old Man Rhythm* and *To Beat the Band* [both q.v.]. But if Mercer couldn't sing and act like Bing Crosby, he certainly could write for Crosby. That opportunity began to present itself as Mercer and his wife traveled by car from Hollywood to Mercer's boyhood home in Georgia, and Mercer noticed many people adorned in old-time cowboy hats and clothes while driving trucks and doing other modern activities. From these observations emerged "I'm an Old Cowhand (From the Rio Grande)"—a satirical song about an out-of-place modern cowboy who "never saw a cow" and can't rope a steer, cited by Mercer historian Philip Furia for a "satiric underside" that "vented some of Mercer's own bitter frustration with Hollywood."[24] That Crosby liked the tune, and sang it in his movie, was acknowledged by Mercer as having saved his Hollywood career, "because I began to get more offers after that."[25]

Crosby musical colleagues such as trumpeter-bandleader Louis Prima and Western song stylists The Sons of the Pioneers—with future Westerns icon Roy Rogers singing tenor—showed up briefly in *Rhythm on the Range*. But the female lead was no warbler, and new in pictures and not a typical Bing Girl besides. Frances Farmer (1913–1970) had made national headlines as a University of Washington co-ed for winning a trip to Moscow in a contest sponsored by a Communist newspaper. This did not flag Farmer's acting aspirations, for besides fervently claiming she was no Communist, she was also intelligent and beautiful—the latter asset primary to her gaining a Paramount contract in 1935. She married another young Paramount actor, Leif Erickson, but her discontent over her new life hinted at problems to come later. Before *Rhythm on the Range*, she had appeared only in two programmers, and she rode the *Range* only after Para's negotiations with Merle Oberon broke down. In her memoir, *Will There Really Be a Morning?*, Farmer recalled the Crosby movie as "absurd."

Art, as it were, was simply flushed down the drain, but strangely enough, the only movie I had fun making was *Rhythm*. The role was simple and undemanding and from a reserved distance, I enjoyed the people with whom I was working. But when the day was over, I fell back into my sullen despondency, bored with Hollywood and my husband.[26]

However inexperienced, Farmer bonded with Crosby on her first "A" picture, finding kinship as a fellow Washington state native, and he helped her work patiently through her nervousness, even as others on set, in Hollywood and the High Sierras hamlet of Lone Pine, California, in the spring of 1936, thought she was merely being arrogant.[27] Farmer recalled the filming as "a long sweet nightmare," but she was cheered for the rest of her life by the diamond necklace that Crosby gifted her at the end of shooting.[28] Farmer does not sing in the finished film, although a duet with Crosby on "The House That Jack Built for Jill" was cut just before release, a snipping that deprives the film's central romance of no little depth. *Range* still showcases Farmer favorably, her striking smartness and slight reserve nicely reflecting her character's upper-crust background even while showing a playfulness that meshed with the down-to-earth leading man. The film brought Farmer better roles, most notably in Samuel Goldwyn's *Come and Get It* (1936), but alcoholism, mental instability, and other personal problems derailed her career in the 1940s and led to her being institutionalized for a few years.

Farmer and friends help present Crosby to better advantage than in some of his immediately preceding pictures, and it was noted in some quarters that Bing helpfully had shed weight for this flick. Crosby's stocky physique, evident even in the '30s, didn't deter

Arizona rancher Lucille Gleason gets the goods on banker Samuel S. Hinds in the Bing Crosby-headed musical comedy Western *Rhythm on the Range*.

anyone from accepting him even though the star lacked the athleticism of the champion bull roper he was supposed to be. And even a hipster like Crosby could deliver another of the film's standout songs, "Empty Saddles (In the Old Corral)," without a lick of condescension while bringing citified audiences, and not just his on-screen rodeo mates, near to tears. Its composer, Billy Hill, had co-written "The Last Round-Up," a hit 1933 cowboy's lament that was recorded by Crosby and many others. "Empty Saddles" was in the same vein, a tribute to a disappearing classic West and Westerners. Such a sad song provided handy balance to the film that was perhaps more comedy than musical, a typical example of the former being a scared cow spraying milk into Der Bingle's face.[29]

Ever the good sport for the likes of milk sprays, Crosby also knew the value of spreading the comedy wealth. In Burns and Raye, Paramount found a mirthfully romantic duo that it reteamed for Crosby's *Waikiki Wedding* (1937) and in their own musical comedy, *Mountain Music* (1937) [q.v.], which upped the cornpone quotient. Raye's part had been added to *Range* so hastily that bits of her nightclub act—including a fake drunk act—had to be employed.[30] Nonetheless, her first feature earned Raye plenty of attention—her manic, chatterbox quality nicely contrasted Burns' slow talkin', self-effacing attitude.[31] The *New York Times* review by Frank S. Nugent focused mainly on Raye's presence as a "stridently funny comedienne with a Mammoth Cave, or early Joe E. Brown, mouth … and a chest which, in moments of burlesque aggressiveness, appears to expand fully ten inches."

> It is entirely possible that she had several clever lines of dialogue in the picture; we wouldn't know, because every time she opened her mouth the audience started laughing.… Hollywood has found a remarkable pantomimist, an actress who can glare in several languages, become lovelorn in Esperanto and register beatific delight in facial pothooks and flourishes. She sings, too; swing music in a voice with saxophonic overtones and an occasional trace of pure fog horn. Puzzling at first, but you grow accustomed to it.[32]

At the film's New York City premiere on July 29, 1936, Raye heard the audience break into applause halfway through her rendition of "(If You Can't Sing It) You'll Have to Swing It (Mr. Paganini)," written for Raye by Sam Coslow and a signature number over the next half-century of the performer's career. The response drove Raye to tears, "bawling so hard," she would recall, "that I didn't even see myself for the rest of the movie."[33] Paramount officials reacted by raising Raye's compensation from its original $1,300 per week.

It was left to Bob Burns to use his jest-folks notoriety for the world premiere of *Rhythm on the Range,* which rather than occurring in a Western locale, came to Burns' home-state stamping grounds in Little Rock, Arkansas, on July 27. Burns and his familiar bazooka highlighted a sold-out screening, which included appearances by the state's governor and a U.S. senator, by leading a four-block parade. "Instead of riding in a new Packard car, Burns made a hit with crowds when he led the parade in a rickety old Ford with worn out tires," *Film Daily* reported.[34] The festivities also included some 500 representatives from Burns' hometown of Van Buren, Arkansas—a hamlet frequently referenced in the performer's radio tales—and the showing of the film in Little Rock, 150 miles from Van Buren, was helpfully arranged as a matinee "to enable the Van Buren delegates to return home early."[35]

Boosted by heavy promotion on Crosby's *Kraft Music Hall* radio series and through ample record sales, *Rhythm on the Range* rapidly became what *Motion Picture Daily* called "Crosby's best work to date" and its studio touted as "Paramount's outstanding tune show of 1936."[36] It was remade, at the same company and by Taurog, in 1956 as *Pardners*, starring Dean Martin and Jerry Lewis. Crosby's only other Western was the 1966 remake of *Stagecoach*, in which he did not carry a tune. But once a singing cowboy, always a singing cowboy.

The Devil on Horseback
(Grand National; September 29, 1936)

Director: Crane Wilbur. Presented By: Edward L. Alperson. Producer: George A. Hirliman. Associate Producers: Louis Rantz, Charles Hunt. Story/Screenplay: Crane Wilbur. Assistant Directors: William O'Connor, Lou Merman. Photography: Mack Stengler. Supervising Editor: Joseph H. Lewis. Film Editor: Ralph Dixon. Sound: Hal Brumbaugh. Production Manager: Samuel Diege. Art Direction: Frank Sylos. Music Director: Hugo Riesenfeld. Musical Supervisor: Abe Meyer. Dance Director: Arthur Dreifuss. Costumes: Adrienne. Running Time: 70 minutes. Hirlicolor.

Cast: Lili Damita (Diane Corday); Fred Keating (Gary Owen); Blanca Vischer (Manuela Torres); Del Campo (Don Pedro "Pancho" Granero); Jean Chatburn (Jane Evans); Juan Torena (Juan Torres); Tiffany Thayer (Wilbur Hitchcock); Enrique De Rosas (Colonel Berea); Renee Torres (Rosamond); Carlos Montalban (Captain de Reana); Lucio Villegas (General Valdez); Ann Miller (hacienda dancer).

Songs: "The Love Fiesta" [Del Campo, chorus; danced by Vischer, chorus], "O Bella Mia" [Del Campo], "Out of the Hills (The Riding Song)" [Del Campo, chorus, twice], "So Divine" [Del Campo, twice] (Jack Stern, Harry Tobias).

Working Title: *Song of the Andes*.

Home Video: Alpha DVD; Sinister Cinema DVD.

The Story: In the South American country of Alturas, Pancho Granero is a wealthy landowner whose weaknesses are his hot temper—which has caused his exile by the government to his hacienda—and his admiration for film star Diane Corday ("So Divine"). Diane visits Alturas on a personal-appearance tour while accompanied by her American fiancée, coffee heir Gary Owen, who is an old friend of Pancho's. With them are Diane's press agent, Wilbur Hitchcock, and her bookish secretary, Jane. Pancho and his horsemen hijack the train on which the visitors are traveling so he can meet Diane, and Wilbur decides to drum up publicity by reporting the incident as an abduction by bandits. Pancho is thrilled to see Diane and be reunited with Gary, but the report of the "kidnapping" by the "Robin Hood of Alturas" puts Pancho in hot water with the authorities. At the villa, Pancho's assistant Juan attempts to soften Jane's edges, and Gary and Pancho compete for Diane's affection ("Love Fiesta," "O Bella Mia") as Juan's jealous sister, Manuela, seethes. Led by Colonel Berea, soldiers descend upon Granero's home but are deterred from further action after Gary and Diane assert that there was no kidnapping. The romantic conflicts are settled as well ("Out of the Hills").

An all-"natural color" musical Western, *The Devil on Horseback* was announced as the first release of independent Grand National Films. It quickly came and went through theaters—a casualty of poor reviews and audience apathy that found neither its Westernness nor its music and romantic comedy stylings particularly appealing. It has survived, albeit without the color process that added to the scorn against it more than 80 years ago.

Grand National was the brainchild of Edward L. Alperson, who in 1936 was transforming a company that distributed titles of American and British independent films in the United States into a full production studio. Alperson envisioned issuing both expensive and inexpensive in-house fare to showcase the company logo of a giant, futuristic clock and the slogan "It's Time to See a Grand National Release," and he acquired studio space from the declining Educational Pictures as a physical locale. Among GN's producers was the prolific quickie specialist George A. Hirliman, who in the middle '30s was juggling low-budget projects under various company names, including Western and non–Western action pictures starring George O'Brien for RKO release, Also planned were musical adventures featuring former Broadway baritone George Houston under Hirliman's own Regal banner, and dramas starring Conrad Nagel and Eleanor Hunt (Hirliman's new wife) under the Condor label.

Hirliman, who originally entered the film business as a seller of raw film stock, was interested in color productions, which in the mid-'30s were of increased interest because of the need to draw potential audiences away from their home radios. He envisioned his newly patented (and not-so-catchily titled) "Hirlicolor" as an affordable alternative to the big studios' Technicolor. The producer promised that his two-color method—an adaptation of the Cinecolor process, which involved a device attached to a standard camera instead of a special camera—would not require the extra lighting required by the three-color Technicolor. He expected Hirlicolor to reduce costs so significantly that within a year it would be nearly as low-priced as black-and-white.[37] This resulted in a deal to make color English-language features for GN release that also would be made into Spanish-language releases released by MGM.[38] The first of those was *The Devil on Horseback*, the English version of which was filmed in July 1936 at the RKO Pathe facility in Hollywood and then publicized as Grand National's debut.[39]

Written and directed by veteran Crane Wilbur, the South America-set, modern-dress *Devil on Horseback* offered an eclectic, international cast. Top-billed Lili Damita (1904–1994) was a French-born beauty who got her start in French and German productions before coming to Hollywood and making a splash as a saucy Latina miss in Fox's hit *The Cock-Eyed World* (1929). Unfortunately, her celebrity for her own talents lately had been eclipsed by her status as "Mrs. Errol Flynn," spouse of the newly risen Warner Bros. heartthrob. Male lead Fred Keating (1897–1961) was a New Yorker of Irish and Spanish parentage, and was transitioning to an acting career after a decade or more as a well-known stage magician.[40] A protégé and frequent collaborator of Tallulah Bankhead—she convinced him that he could act as well as prestidigitate—he had enough of a sense of humor to call his expensive new Hollywood Hills home "Casa Escrow." Further down the cast list were Guatemala-born Blanca Vischer, who had played many acting and dancing bits at Fox, and Philippines-bred Juan Torena, most of whose American work was in the Spanish-language realm and as part of Hirliman's stock company.

But the most exotic player in *Devil on Horseback* was its primary singer, billed only as Del Campo. His full name was Francisco Del Campo (1908?–?), and he was a tenor from Chile. Del Campo had debuted on the West Coast under his full name and established himself with extended runs at the Cocoanut Grove under the mentorship of songwriter Con Conrad. Lately, he had become famous, by his surname only, as CBS Radio's "Valentino of the Air," prompting Hirliman to give him a celluloid chance. (His only other film credit to that point was a 1936 uncredited singing role in Fox's *Ramona*.) Del Campo ably performs four songs in *Devil on Horseback*, the most romantic being "So Divine," which became a radio hit. He portrays a landowner and political exile in a fictional South American country whose fixation with an American movie star is so acute that he shoots up the screen in his local movie house whenever he sees his favorite gal in a kissing scene.

When Damita's femme shows up in said country, the result is a "kidnapping" concocted for the fan mags by the actress' pushy publicity man. Hirliman originally cast Fuzzy Knight as the flack, but out of the blue he installed the novelist Tiffany Thayer.[41] Thayer (1902–1959) was better known as the author of critically reviled but widely read books that became pulpy movies (*Call Her Savage*, *Thirteen Women*) and oddball science fiction. Thayer's singular film performance has been likened to the "sissy" characterizations of Franklin Pangborn and his ilk, but he's more like Fuzzy Knight without a drawl but with an energy jolt. Knight might have walked through this role, but Thayer puts some enthusiasm into a character saddled with silly lines like "Inspiration's got me; it's shaking me like a tin can on the end of a dog's tail!" and asked to brandish a gun as if a toy. In the film's big dance number, "Love Fiesta"—featuring a chorus of three-score that includes then-teen hoofer Ann

Miller—the main couples pair off, which leaves Thayer to ogle a chubby señora. It's almost too bad Thayer didn't get any more to do—or choose to do more—as a character actor ... if only to spare haters from his writings.

Another of the film's unusual figures is Damita's mannish secretary, played by starlet Jean Chatburn (1914–2007). Chatburn is seen with a severe haircut, horn-rimmed glasses, and business suits, and flatly remarks that she doesn't like men. Torena, playing the landowner's major domo, flat out asks the young woman whether she is a woman or a man (for he and his friends have been taking bets). "She looks like a man but walks like a woman!" he says in puzzlement. He shortly finds out which, as he encounters the secretary stripping down to her skivvies for a swim during a hike, and then seduces her: "You've got curves and you didn't even know it!" The woman, having been "rehabilitated," spends the rest of the film dressed more gender-appropriate for the 1930s. Still, true to the period, the Anglo secretary and her Latin boyfriend fail to end up together, for at the climax, all of the visitors from the north return there and all of the locals stay home.

For Del Campo, Thayer, Chatburn, and Vischer, this programmer represented as much acting exposure as they would get in any movie, and even Keating and Damita would get few future opportunities. For all the chance he got to sing, Del Campo's ensuing film career consisted of a single Universal 1938 short subject, *Latin Hi-Hattin'*.[42] Despite its isolated novelty factors, *The Devil on Horseback* stretches two reels of plot into 70 somewhat dull minutes. The filmmakers tried to sell the color angle and the big production number—with its "Diablero" South American devil dance—but the movie was panned. *The Film Daily* wrote that it "has practically everything that ever went into screen entertainment"—as one of the few thumbs-up verdicts, GN repeatedly used the quote in its promos. More of the reviews read closer to the one from *Harrison's Reports*, which criticized the "slow" action, "listless" performances, and "sickly" color quality.[43] Even nastier was the write-up from *The Hollywood Reporter*:

> Strong box office names in the leads might have lifted the production into the B class, but Lili Damita is so badly miscast that the director's intention to capture her beauty of face and hair for the glory of Hirlicolor results in nothing more than a demonstration that her hair is titian and her face white. Keating has little to do but look wise and dispiritedly fill the part of a jealous lover.[44]

Unfortunately, we can't tell you what we think of the Hirlicolor in *The Devil on Horseback* because color prints apparently no longer exist. The film was, in fact, believed lost until it resurfaced in a private collection in the 1980s; you can see it for free on YouTube and elsewhere now. George Hirliman went on making movies, but his most famous production—which was not in color and which did not become famous in his lifetime—was *Tell Your Children* (1938), an anti-drug melodrama. You might know it better as *Reefer Madness*.

Herb Jeffries—The Bronze Buckaroo:
Harlem on the Prairie

(Associated Features; December 9, 1937)

Director: Sam Newfield. Producer: Jed Buell. Associate Producers: Sabin W. Carr, Bert Sternbach. Story/Screenplay: Fred Myton. Additional Dialogue: Flournoy E. Miller. Photography: William Hyer. Editor: Robert Jahns. Sound: Hans Weeren. Music Director: Lew Porter. Music Supervisor: Abe Meyer. Production Supervisor: Maceo B. Sheffield. Running Time: 55 minutes.

Cast: Herbert Jeffries (Jeff Kincaid); Flournoy E. Miller (Crawfish); Mantan Moreland (Mistletoe); Connie Harris (Carolina Clayburn); Maceo B. Sheffield (Wolf Cain); Spencer Williams, Jr. (Doc Clayburn);

George Randol [Randall] (sheriff); Nathan Curry (henchman); The Four Tones; The Four Blackbirds.

Songs: "Harlem on the Prairie" [Jeffries, Four Tones, Four Blackbirds] (Lew Porter, Mary Schaeffer); "Romance in the Rain" [Jeffries, Four Tones, Four Blackbirds] (Lew Porter, Lyle Womack, Mary Schaeffer); "Albuquerque" [Jeffries] (Don Swander, June Hershey); "A New Range in Heaven" [Jeffries] (Fred Stryker, Johnny Lange); "Polkadoo" [Four Tones] (Ira Hardin); "Old Folks at Home" ("Swanee River") [Four Tones] (Stephen Foster).

Also Known As: *Bad Man of Harlem.*

The Story: Jeff Kincaid, an itinerant cowboy, protects medicine wagon operator Doc Clayburn and Doc's daughter, Carolina, from outlaw Wolf Cain, who wants to recover the stolen $50,000 in gold that Doc seeks to return as a repudiation of his former life in crime. In search of a map showing where the gold is hidden, Cain's men kill Doc, who before dying gets Jeff to return the gold and keep Carolina safe. Aided by hapless Crawfish and Mistletoe, Jeff finds the treasure, enables the capture of Cain and his henchmen, and saves Carolina from being kidnapped.

Two Gun Man from Harlem

(Merit Pictures/Sack Amusement Enterprises; May 1, 1938)

Director/Producer: Richard C. Kahn. Screenplay: Richard C. Kahn. Photography: Marcel LePicard, Harvey Gould. Editor: William Faris. Sound: Cliff Ruberg. Art Direction: Vin Taylor. Production Manager: Al Lane. Running Time: 66 minutes.

Cast: Herbert Jeffries (Bob Blake/The Deacon); Marguerite Whitten (Sally Thompson); Clarence Brooks (John Barker); Mantan Moreland (Bill); Matthew "Stymie" Beard (Jimmy Thompson); Spencer Williams, Jr. (Butch Carter); Mae Turner (Ruth Steel); Jesse Lee Brooks (sheriff); Rosa Lee Lincoln (Dolores); Tom Southern (John Steel); The Cats and the Fiddle; The Four Tones; Paul Blackman (himself); Faithful Mary (Mary).

Songs: "I'm a Happy Cowboy" [Jeffries, Four Tones] (Herbert Jeffries, Four Tones); others.

Home Video: Alpha DVD; Cascadia DVD; Desert Island Films DVD.

The Story: Bob Blake, who works at a Wyoming ranch owned by John Steel, discovers that Steel has been murdered by a unidentified man with whom Steel's wife, Ruth, had been having an affair. Ruth falsely implicates Bob by switching his gun with the killer's while Bob inspects the crime scene. Despite his budding friendship with Sally Thompson and her young brother, Jimmy, Bob evades arrest by hitchhiking cross-country to Harlem. There, he meets a killer and former preacher named "The Deacon" and is inspired to return to Wyoming in the guise of a church elder with the same nickname. Bob pretends to ally with miner Butch Carter, who has been paid by Steel's killer to kidnap and murder Ruth. Bob saves Sally from an attempt by Carter to foreclose on the Thompson ranch. He apprehends John Barker, who is revealed by Ruth as her husband's killer and her former lover. Bob and Sally are reunited.

The Bronze Buckaroo

(Hollywood Pictures/Sack Amusement Enterprises; January 1, 1939)

Director/Producer: Richard C. Kahn. Screenplay: Richard C. Kahn. Photography: Roland Price, Clark Ramsey. Sound: Cliff Ruberg. Art Direction: Vin Taylor. Production Manager: Dick L'Estrange. Running Time: 60 minutes.

Cast: Herbert Jeffries (Bob Blake); Lucius Brooks (Dusty); Artie Young (Betty Jackson); Flournoy E. Miller (Slim); Spencer Williams, Jr. (Pete); Clarence Brooks (Buck Thorn); Lee Calmes (Lee); Earl J. Morris (bartender); Rellie Hardin (Joe Jackson); Tom Southern (poker player); The Four Tones.

Songs: "Almost Time for Roundup" [chorus], "Git Along Mule" [Four Tones], "Got the Pay Day Blues"

[Jeffries, Four Tones; danced by Calmes] (Lew Porter, Johnny Lange); "I'm a Happy Cowboy" [Jeffries] (Herbert Jeffries, Four Tones).
Home Video: Alpha DVD; Image Entertainment DVD; Sinister Cinema DVD.

The Story: Texas cowboy Bob Blake journeys to Arizona to visit an old friend, Joe Jackson, after receiving a concerning letter from the rancher. Joe is absent from the ranch, and his sister, Betty, reveals that her brother has disappeared in the wake of the murder of their father. Meanwhile, Bob's sidekick, Dusty, is conned by ventriloquist ranch hand Slim into believing that the mule he has just bought can talk. A neighbor, Buck Thorn, bids to buy the Jackson ranch and, as the killer of the elder Jackson, takes advantage of Betty in Joe's absence. Bob learns the origin of Joe's letter and fears that his friend has been kidnapped. Blake attempts to rescue Joe but is waylaid by Thorn's men, led by Pete, who kidnap Betty and force her and her brother to sign over the deed to their ranch. Bob leads a posse to rescue Joe and Betty—and wins the latter. Dusty, meanwhile, gains revenge on the dishonest Slim.

Harlem Rides the Range
(Hollywood Pictures/Sack Amusement Enterprises; February 1, 1939)

Director/Producer: Richard C. Kahn. Screenplay: Spencer Williams, Jr., Flournoy E. Miller. Story: Spencer Williams, Jr. Photography: Roland Price, Clark Ramsey. Sound: Cliff Ruberg. Art Direction: Vin Taylor. Production Manager: Dick L'Estrange. Running Time: 56 minutes.
Cast: Herbert Jeffries (Bob Blake); Lucius Brooks (Dusty); Flournoy E. Miller (Slim Perkins); Artie Young (Margaret Dennison); Clarence Brooks (Bradley); Spencer Williams, Jr. (Watson); Tom Southern (Connors); Leonard Christmas (Dennison); Wade Dumas (sheriff); John Thomas (Cactus); The Four Tones.
Songs [all by Jeffries, Four Tones]: "Cowpokes Lullaby" (Herbert Jeffries, Spencer Williams, Jr.); "I'm a Happy Cowboy" (Herbert Jeffries, Four Tones); "Prairie Flower" (Lew Porter, Johnny Lange).
Working Title: *West of Harlem*.
Home Video: Alpha DVD; Echo Bridge DVD; Westlake Entertainment DVD.

The Story: Jim Dennison is threatened by fellow ranch owner Bradley, who seeks to claim the ranch—as well as Dennison's lucrative but secret radium mine. Itinerate cowboys Bob Blake and Slim Perkins go to work for another rancher, Watson, whose foreman, Connors, attracts Bob's suspicion. Watson fires Connors and replaces him with Bob. Bob is framed in connection to the disappearance of Dennison, who is feared dead. Dennison's daughter returns home and is threatened by Bradley before being rescued by Bob, who has fallen in love with the girl after borrowing her photograph. Dennison turns out not to be dead, but simply holed up in his mine.

It was a story that Herb Jeffries enjoyed telling—he told it often, and into his 100th year—in answering the inevitable question from a fan, reporter, or historian: Why star in the first all–African American Western? Jeffries would reply by telling of his meeting a black boy who was crying because other children "wouldn't let him play cowboy."[45]

> This was a chance to make something good out of something bad. Little children of dark skin—not just Negroes, but Puerto Ricans, Mexicans, everybody of color—had no heroes in the movies. I was so glad to give them something to identify with.[46]

There had been many black cowboys in the real West, so why not a new one in pictures? So Jeffries—a big-band baritone who enjoyed his most prestigious professional success as a hit-making soloist for Duke Ellington and others—became a singing cowboy movie star. His starring career lasted only through four dirt-cheap programmers mainly seen in segregated theaters. But he was a hero when minority audiences sorely lacked them in the movies. When Jeffries passed on, eight months into his second century, he was mourned not only as the last-surviving Golden Age singing cowboy but also as a pioneer whose influence belied the lowly stature of his Western "race movies."

Born into a mixed marriage as Umberto Balentino in Detroit, Jeffries (1913?–2014) dropped out of high school to earn a living as a singer. Jobs were hard to come by in the early '30s, but he found work with the Erskine Tate and Earl "Fatha" Hines orchestras after asserting that his Irish-Sicilian parentage also contained Ethiopian blood.[47] Jeffries' racial identity was always something of a mystery, as he told people at various times that he was white or black or mixed. Census information from 1920 listed him as "mulatto," but he classified himself as Caucasian on his marriage licenses. (He was married five times.)

Harlem on the Prairie (1937) was the first of the all-black Westerns with singer Herbert Jeffries.

Whatever his racial classification, Jeffries' yen for social equality in the movies led him to a quickie producer named Jed Buell. A former publicist for Mack Sennett, Buell had launched his own company, Spectrum Productions, to make an oater series (produced by closet Westerns fan Stan Laurel!) that starred operetta baritone Fred Scott. Scott could sing better then he could act, and the same was true with Jeffries, but Buell saw a novelty factor in the latter that he would later exploit more bizarrely in the all-midget Western *The Terror of Tiny Town* [q.v.]. Buell teamed with Sabin W. Carr, a former Olympic champion pole vaulter, to start Associated Features, a unit to produce a planned series of Jeffries films, and the first, *Harlem on the Prairie*, was filmed in October 1937 and released by year's end.

Buell employed some considerable talent for *Harlem on the Prairie*, which he purportedly made for between $20,000 and $70,000, but besides prolific B director Sam Newfield, not much of it was seasoned on the screen. Flournoy E. ("F.E.") Miller (1885–1971) was a vaudeville comic who also was a screenwriter and lyricist. He was joined by his current stage partner, Mantan Moreland (1902–1973), who was just starting in pictures but would become a popular actor in both "race" and mainstream features. Spencer Williams, Jr. (1893–1969) was returning to the screen after a three-year hiatus that followed a long and fruitful period as an actor-writer-filmmaker for both black and white companies. Even with a career that began in the silent-picture days, and praise from the African American press as the rightful "black daddy" of film, Williams is best known now for playing Andy in the 1950s TV version of *Amos 'n' Andy*. Fellow actors Connie Harris and Maceo Sheffield were a nightclub singer and L.A. club owner, respectively. A pair of vocal groups, The Four Tones and The Four Blackbirds, helped deliver the film's five songs, and the Tones' bass-singing leader, Lucius "Dusty" Harris, would get separate screen time in future Jeffries vehicles as a comic actor.

As much as he wanted to see a black Western made, Jeffries recalled years later that he landed the lead only because he could ride, act, and sing, the riding part acquired at his grandfather's farm in Michigan and honed via a three-month visit to a dude ranch.[48] The singing part came easier, as Jeffries delivered "Harlem on the Prairie" and "Romance in the Rain," co-written by veteran singing-Westerns composer Lew Porter. Six-foot-3 and handsome, Jeffries was not too light-skinned to perform in all-black bands, but Buell thought his star needed to show darker on the screen, and the singer did by applying makeup. "I'm glad to be the first to represent my race in musical Westerns," Jeffries was quoted in a 1937 newspaper article that stressed his modest beginnings and his good-guy nature. "…I'm not one who leaped to the top at one bound. My musical education came very slowly. It's been a struggle all my life to get the money for music lessons—often I've chosen the lessons instead of a meal—but it's worth it."[49]

The plot, typically rudimentary in the "B" tradition, concerned the hero's quest to recover stolen gold, but we can't be privy to specifics, because *Harlem on the Prairie* may have become a lost film, at least as of this writing. It did garner more media attention than the typical series Western, for becoming what trade publications reported as "the first 'all-colored' picture" to play in a first-run Broadway theater. Still, Jed Buell did not agree to any follow-ups, despite backhanded trade reviews that praised the film for its demographic appeal, if little else.

But in the African American press, the response was encouraging, and the approximately 800 black-audience theaters in the United States craved entertainment like *Harlem on the Prairie*. With that in mind, Jeffries made three more features with a pair of key white collaborators: producer-director-writer Richard C. Kahn, with Merit Pictures, and Dallas-based distributor Alfred Sack, whose Sack Entertainment Enterprises specially catered to the "race" picture audience. Playing a character named Bob Blake and billed more correctly as "Herbert Jeffrey"—Jeffrey was the last name of his stepfather—Jeffries again showed off his white Stetson (which he wore constantly to hide his brown hair), black clothing, and horse named "Stardusk." The actor's offscreen mode of transportation now was a Cadillac with steer horns on the hood, signifying his new professional identity.

Moreland, Williams, and the Four Tones returned for the first of the Kahn films, *Two Gun Man from Harlem*. As with all the Jeffries Westerns, it was filmed on a dude ranch near Victorville, California, that catered to black customers, so there were no concerns over the cast being welcome, and some of the real cowboys at the ranch ended up as bit actors. *Two Gun Man from Harlem* was a little less musical than the other Jeffries films, but its only full-length tune, "I'm a Happy Cowboy," became Jeffries' theme song. It also was a little less Western, with some of it being set in Harlem, which is depicted as an immoral geographic alternative to the flawed but purer West.

The film allows Jeffries to flex his burgeoning acting muscles in a dual role as the titular cowboy disguised as a preacher and the New York killer whose baleful presence inspires the hero's masquerade. The story partly concerns an extramarital affair—an unusually risqué departure from the standard series Western. As in the typical oater, there is comic relief, in Moreland, strangely cast as Jeffries' brother (despite being chubby and about a foot shorter) but who, as usual, lifts even weak material as found here. His unique interpretation of the biblical story of Job is a highlight. Other amusing interludes are supplied by Matthew "Stymie" Beard, who, three years removed from his regular role in "Our Gang" shorts, plays the kid brother of the female love interest. His mischievous antics, however, are more representative of a kid closer to Stymie's "Our Gang" age than his age at the time (which was 13).

Stymie's presence was warmly noted in newspaper ads for *Two Gun Man from Harlem*, and in at least some areas, the film drew interest from more than "race" audiences. A trade-publication report indicated that *Two Gun Man* was "a sensation in white theaters," citing results from houses in Texas, Oklahoma, and Arkansas.[50] In Jackson, Tennessee, the local newspaper ran an ad that excitedly noted that the local Paramount Theater, where the film had been playing to segregated audiences, was to be opened "to the white people for this attraction!"[51] Another drawing card, albeit minor, was the appearance in the film of one "Faithful Mary," who was enjoying fleeting real-life notoriety as a disenchanted follower of a controversial African American spiritual leader, Father (M.J.) Divine. Audiences were curious to see the rotund, matronly figure now in the news, but her footage is missing from surviving prints.

The final two Jeffries Westerns—*The Bronze Buckaroo* and *Harlem Rides the Range*—were shot back to back in October 1938 for release early the next year, and by now, segments of the "sepia" media were persuaded to take note. Earl J. Morris, movie editor for the *Pittsburgh Courier* newspaper, spent two weeks reporting from the set. Morris arrived in time to witness a visit by heavyweight boxing champion Joe Louis to the dude ranch—and to chronicle an unexpected challenge by a representative of the Screen Actors Guild, who asked that all the performers on the set leave the project because Kahn's company was not affiliated with the union. The request was strongly rejected, with Spencer Williams, according to the *Courier*, telling the SAG agent: "None of our actors will agree to leave this set…. Your white film concerns have ignored the dramatic ability of the Negro actor. He rarely ever receives any worthwhile employment."[52] Perhaps befitting the "let's put on a show" nature of these films' casting, Morris was given the small role of a bartender in *The Bronze Buckaroo*. Morris' movie debut provided more fodder for his "Grandtown Reporter" column: "I hope you will hiss when you see that mean bartender break a bottle over Herbert Jeffrey's head…. It is a good movie, even if I am not so hot as an actor."[53]

These last two features yielded mixed artistic results. *The Bronze Buckaroo* is quite watchable for its nearly equal reliance on music and comedy in comparison to riding and gunplay. "Dusty" Harris, promoted to sidekick, gets a lot to do with typically inane behavior that includes being fooled into thinking he's bought a talking mule and being cheated literally out of his clothes by a card shark. He's no Mantan or Stymie, but he'll do. Musical content is an improvement over *Two Gun Man from Harlem* in time spent and quality. There's a bizarre number, "Almost Time for Roundup," in which the singing by barroom cowboys is abruptly interrupted when a card player shoots another. The vocals stop for a couple of seconds, then continue to the end of the song, the body of the victim slumped over the card table. Justice is served to both main cowboys, the sidekick using newly acquired powers of ventriloquism to vanquish his tormentor (played by F.E. Miller) and the hero getting the girl and a closing song ("Git Along Mule," by Lew Porter).

The enjoyment factor is not as significant in *Harlem Rides the Range*, which is sluggishly paced and convoluted. There's a nice ballad, "Prairie Flower," which Jeffries sings to … no one. Instead, he's enamored with the photograph of the pretty daughter of a missing rancher; he hasn't met either of them yet. In fact, the female lead (Artie Young) doesn't appear in the flesh until the final 10 minutes of the hour-or-so movie, and even the most hardened action fan must admit there needs to be a little more mush in a singing Western. Despite some color-specific humor and language—which, in *The Bronze Buckaroo*, even includes the casual utterance of the N-word—the Jeffries films were intended to reflect the standard series Western. The novelty was not in what the actors were saying or doing, it's that they were saying and doing it at all.

Unlike the earlier Jed Buell feature that starred Jeffries, the Kahn films found little attention from reviewers partly due to the limited reach of distributor Sack Amusement Enterprises. Jeffries himself later referred to them as "C-minus" pictures. However, *The Film Daily* lauded the Kahn's work in *The Bronze Buckaroo* as "an all-around good job" and recognized its crossover appeal to white theaters.[54] Jeffries hit the road with The Four Tones for live performances of songs and rope trucks to tout their celluloid efforts, but a planned fourth Kahn-Jeffries feature went unmade, and Jeffries soon saw his career take an exciting new dimension. Jeffries attracted Duke Ellington's attention when the maestro's band played in live shows preceding Jeffries Westerns, and Ellington invited the singer-actor to join his unit.

Jeffries soloed on the 1940 Ellington hit "Flamingo" and a year later appeared in Ellington's all-black revue *Jump for Joy*. After Air Force service during World War II, Jeffries experienced a long career as a jazz recording artist and character actor, in Europe as well as the U.S. A profile of Jeffries in *Life* magazine in 1951 noted that he had been an $85-a-week singer six years before but was now earning more than $50,000 a year, mainly from record royalties and nightclub dates.[55] Jeffries moved to Los Angeles in the 1960s and worked steadily in clubs and theaters and in roles on TV shows such as *Hawaii Five-O* and *The Virginian*.

It was the recording field for which he was best known … that is, until scholars began researching the elusive history of blacks in film. Three of Jeffries' Westerns emerged from obscurity in a cache of old films found in Texas. As modestly as they were made, and as tattered as the surviving prints were, the movies verified their star's legacy as a cinematic pioneer, much to the delight of a grateful subject who sang grandly into his 90s. In 1995, he recorded an album, "The Bronze Buckaroo Rides Again," that revived the music from his movies, and a decade later, became the subject of a film documentary, *A Colored Life: The Herb Jeffries Story*. When Jeffries was asked about his racial identity, and that was often, he replied pretty much as he did in a 2008 newspaper interview: "I am colored, and I love it. I have a right to identify myself the way I do and if nobody likes it, what are they going to do? Kill my career?"[56]

No, that couldn't happen, even if Jeffries may have been born 50 years too early. "Herb was a sex symbol," the African American film historian Donald Bogle told the *Los Angeles Times Magazine* in 2003 in a profile of Jeffries. "With his wavy hair and Clark Gable mustache, he might have been a different kind of star had America been a different kind of place."[57]

Rawhide
(Principal/20th Century–Fox; March 23, 1938)

Director: Ray Taylor. Producer: Sol Lesser. Associate Producer: Lindsley Parsons. Screenplay: Daniel Jarrett, Jack Natteford. Story: Daniel Jarrett. Assistant Director: V.O. Smith. Photography: Allen Q.

Thompson. Editor: Robert Crandall. Art Direction: Lewis J. Rachmil. Sound: Tom Carmen. Music Director: Michael Breen. Running Time: 58 minutes.

Cast: Smith Ballew (Larry Kimball); Lou Gehrig (Lou Gehrig); Evalyn Knapp (Peggy Gehrig); Arthur Loft (Ed Saunders); Cy Kendall (Sheriff Kale); Dick Curtis (Butch); Si Jenks (Pop Mason); Carl Stockdale (Bascomb); Lafe McKee (L.G. McDonnell); Cecil Kellogg (Gilliam); Slim Whitaker (Biff); Tom Forman (Rudy); Cliff Parkinson (Pete); Harry Tenbrook (Rusty); Lee Shumway (Johnson); Ed Cassidy (Fuller); Charles Murphy (Pop); Edward Cecil (doctor); Ray Whitley and the Six-Bar Cowboys (band at party).

Songs: "A Cowboy's Life" [Ballew, Gehrig (?), chorus; reprised by Ballew] (Charles Rosoff, Eddie Cherkose); "Drifting" [Ballew, Whitley band] (Albert von Tilzer, Harry MacPherson); "That Old Washboard Band" [Whitley band] (Norman Phelps, Willie Phelps); "When a Cowboy Goes to Town" [Ballew] (Albert von Tilzer, Eddie Grant).

Working Titles: *Laughing Senor; Boots and Saddles.*

Home Video: Alpha DVD; Echo Bridge DVD; Synergy DVD.

The Story: Baseball star Lou Gehrig tells reporters he is retiring from the New York Yankees to seek peace and quiet at a ranch that his sister, Peggy, has bought near the Montana town of Rawhide. There, an unscrupulous group of businessmen has forced the citizenry to join the Ranchers Protective Association, which holds a monopoly on their spending for supplies and skims their profits. Young attorney Larry Kimball attempts to fight the extortionists' ringleader, Ed Saunders, who is slowly poisoning the fair-minded owner of the association, L.G. McDonnell. Lou and his sister arrive in town and join forces with Kimball to fight the association, which responds by damming the water flowing into the Gehrig ranch property. Kimball and the Gehrigs organize ranchers against the association and save McDonnell from being finished off by Saunders. With peace finally achieved, Gehrig gets a telegram asking him to report to spring training.

Short of Jed Buell's all-midget show in *The Terror of Tiny Town* [q.v.], the oddest example of stunt casting in the twin worlds of the Hollywood musical and the B Western was Lou Gehrig in *Rawhide*. No, not the 1960s TV show—this was a 1938 second feature that gave the New York Yankees' first baseman—then arguably the best baseball player on the planet—his only opportunity as an actor. It's a neat little novelty that wraps up in a little less than an hour (only a few seconds, thankfully, show Gehrig opening his mouth to sing), and the exercise itself is easily forgettable. To the modern-day viewer, the sad knowledge of what would soon happen to the film's doomed co-star may be harder to shake.

Baseball fans still revere Gehrig as "The Iron Horse"—the durable slugger who set a record for appearing in 2,130 consecutive regular-season games for the perennial champion Yankees between 1925 and 1939. Gehrig's prodigious home-run hitting never really got its due, as he played mainly in the shadows of outsized personalities such as teammates Babe Ruth and Joe DiMaggio. A native of Manhattan who had studied engineering at Columbia University, Gehrig was shy and easygoing off the field, not the gregarious type who would have sought the Hollywood spotlight. His engagement for *Rawhide* would seem to be attributable to the efforts of two strong marketing minds: Christy Walsh, Gehrig's innovative personal manager, and Sol Lesser, a prominent independent film producer.

Walsh was the sports industry's first super-agent, and counted Babe Ruth, boxer Jack Dempsey, and football coach Knute Rockne among his clients. Lesser had been making movies since the early '20s; among the scores of low-budget films on his resume were *Tarzan the Fearless* (1933), with Buster Crabbe, and a Bela Lugosi serial, *The Return of Chandu* (1934). He was riding high in the late '30s with a series of successful musicals starring child singing prodigy Bobby Breen, but Lesser, who owned screen rights to Tarzan sold to him by the character's creator, Edgar Rice Burroughs, sought to make another film featuring the jungle man for his Principal Productions. Hearing about Lesser's plans, Walsh contacted the

Baseball star Lou Gehrig went to bat before the cameras as a fictional version of himself in the B-Western musical *Rawhide* (with Evalyn Knapp).

producer and offered Gehrig's services. Whether Gehrig-as-Tarzan was meant as a serious proposition or not originally, a deal soon was to be forged for the Yankee to make a film for Lesser.[58] Only it wouldn't be a Tarzan flick: Lesser reportedly took one look at Gehrig's bony, unshapely knees and decided they wouldn't look good uncovered by a loincloth.[59] Lesser instead obtained another sports luminary, Olympic gold-medal decathlete Glenn Morris, to star in *Tarzan's Revenge* (1938).

Lesser did sign Gehrig anyway, in March 1937, to a contract for a reported $2,500 per week—not bad for a guy paid $36,000 per year on the diamond—to make a film immediately after the conclusion of that year's baseball season.[60] At first it was announced that Gehrig would play opposite Richard Arlen in a Western. Arlen was committed to making six for Lesser for 20th Century–Fox release, with the first, *Secret Valley* (1937), already shot. But Arlen suddenly became unavailable to Lesser for contractual reasons; Lesser couldn't come to terms on a loan-out from Arlen's home studio, Columbia. So Gehrig was passed down to Smith Ballew, the pop tenor-turned-actor and bandleader who had assumed Arlen's place in a series of Lesser Westerns—which didn't mean they were necessarily lesser Westerns.[61]

As months passed before the making of *Rawhide*, the combination of Walsh's press-agent puffery and Lesser's movie-flack hype made for a teaming as potent as any of Gehrig's Yankee teams. According to one probably apocryphal story, Gehrig, while in Hollywood for initial screen tests, refused to pose with a group of starlets so as not to displease his absent wife.[62] In a variation on this tale, Walsh obtained a stray nightshirt of Gehrig's, adorned it with the autographs of Joan Crawford, Jean Harlow, and other film glamour gals, and sent it to Mrs. Gehrig at her Connecticut home before her husband returned from his stay West. "Mrs. Gehrig inspected the nightshirt, seized a pen, scribbled her refusal to accept the shirt because it lacked Mae West's 'endorsement,' and airmailed it back to Mr. Walsh," read one columnist's account.[63] This not only depicted Eleanor Gehrig as having one heck of a sense of humor, but also was planted to assure young fans of Gehrig's virtuosity, with a Gene Autry–type kiss-the-horse-not-the-girl attitude.

After the Yanks won yet another World Series in the fall, Gehrig joined the Lesser troupe to shoot *Rawhide* in January 1938. A week or so into the filming, reporters were invited to the set to see the new movie star, who was described by a wire-service scribe on hand as "Hollywood's toughest—and strangest—cowpuncher."

> Two six-guns slung at his hips in typical Western fashion, this cowboy-homerun king pulled his horse to a halt, tipped a bullet-creased Stetson back on his curly head and dismounted in front of the Palace saloon in a rough-and-tough Cowtown a half-hour from Hollywood Boulevard.
>
> He swaggered to the door of the Palace, yawned and, Eastern accent and all, yelled: "Boy! This is more fun than even the World Series!"
>
> ... "I'm having the time of my life," Gehrig said. "Honestly, I haven't had so much fun since I was a kid."[64]

It helped that the newcomer was cast as a fictionalized version of Lou Gehrig, a New York Yankees great, but one who also has a ranch-owner sister, played by Evalyn Knapp, who needs help fending off extortionist merchants in her small town in Montana. (Since Knapp was playing Lou's sis and not his girl, the kissing quandary was solved.) Much of the pre-release chatter focused on whether Gehrig could be taught to ride, but a more glaring shortcoming is the player's inability to carry a tune. A verse of a song called "A Cowboy's Life"—in which Lou laments that "I seldom miss a fly I chased, but now the flies chase me"—is clearly dubbed. Predictably, *Rawhide* is loaded with references to Gehrig's real livelihood: "You're not in New York now!" snarls the heavy as he threatens the big-city interloper at a key juncture (or, if you will, an early inning). At two separate times, Gehrig gets the good guys out of jams with on-target southpaw throws—first, a series of cueballs during saloon fisticuffs, then in a later scene requisite for a movie like this, a baseball borrowed from a group of kids playing on the street and thrown through a window. The town's name was the presumed inspiration for the film's title, but "Ol' Rawhide" also was a favorite nickname for the durable Gehrig by the sporting press.

Film cowboy-composer Ray Whitley and his band also are on hand for authentic musical interludes. But the showcase performer, of course, is Ballew, who introduces himself by singing "When a Cowboy Goes to Town," a neatly worded description of his occupation (attorney) and clientele (townsmen). Gehrig couldn't sing, but he *was* Lou Gehrig, "Eastern accent" and all, and after viewing rushes and rough cuts of the film, Lesser decided to promote the ballplayer from featured status to co-star with Ballew billed above the title.[65] That's how the credits read when *Rawhide* made its world premiere, not in New York or Los Angeles but instead in St. Petersburg, Florida, the city where the Yankees did their spring training, on March 23. A parade including local marching bands and fireworks preceded a screening attended by city celebrities and members of the St. Louis Cardinals (the ball team that also trained in St. Pete). Gehrig's teammates diplomatically praised their man's performance, and according to one witness, "only occasionally did they yell rude remarks during the showing."[66] It was an especially good week for Gehrig, who had just signed a new one-year contract with the Yankees with a $3,000 raise, to $39,000, perhaps lessening any need to moonlight in the movies.

As he did with sportswriters, Gehrig played the publicity game while promoting *Rawhide* with the entertainment press, telling interviewers about his first time being on a horse and about the camera tricks used to make his steed move faster.[67] The good will he'd built up allowed his performance to be met with polite acceptance by movie pundits, and the film generally to be well praised. "Gehrig has a pleasant, easy-going manner, making one forget his shortcomings as an actor," *Harrison's Reports* wrote, and *Variety* lauded the film as "a fast-moving, well-produced mesa meller ... [with] the baseball star as more than window-dressing.... He has both the personality and the voice to insure the stamp of approval by producers as well as audiences."[68] Next to Gehrig's professional home, the *New York Times* was bullish on the film but not its celeb: "The Iron Man appears to be painfully conscious ... that acting is one of his lesser accomplishments ... [but] even without the Yankees' clean-up man as its star de resistance, *Rawhide* would be a better than average entertainment in its field."[69]

The *Variety* review cited above predicted that Gehrig might be developed into a William Boyd or Buck Jones sagebrush hero type should his baseball career come to an end, but we never got to find out if that could have happened. Early in the 1939 season, Gehrig was forced to retire after being diagnosed with amyotrophic lateral sclerosis, an incurable neuromuscular disorder now better known as ALS, or Lou Gehrig's disease. ALS claimed Gehrig's life in July 1941 at age 37, and he was honored by Hollywood a year later as the subject of the acclaimed biopic *The Pride of the Yankees*, starring Gary Cooper. When that film debuted, *Rawhide* with the real Gehrig was revived for theatergoers, and it was then that Eleanor Gehrig admitted to columnist Louella Parsons as to her and Lou's feelings on his Western foray. "Need we mention *Rawhide*? Lou didn't like it and I was greatly disappointed in the picture."[70]

In a postscript of sorts, two neurological scholars published a research paper in 2007 on the possible effects of ALS on Gehrig at the time of the making of *Rawhide*. After watching the film and comparing it to photographs of the ballplayer from both 1938 and 1939 (the latter the year of his official diagnosis), the writers concluded Gehrig was not exhibiting symptoms of the disorder in early 1938 and had "normal hand muscles and leg function."[71] Gehrig's heartfelt farewell speech at Yankee Stadium about being "the luckiest man on the face of the earth" surpassed anything he could have done as an actor, and even Cooper couldn't match the real thing in his re-enactment. *Rawhide* ended up as little more than a footnote in the life of this courageous man, and it also proved that this sports hero also could be a good sport.

Cowboy from Brooklyn
(Cosmopolitan/Warner Bros.; July 9, 1938)

Director: Lloyd Bacon. Associate Producer: Lou Edelman. Screenplay: Earl Baldwin, based on the play *Howdy Stranger* by Robert Sloane and Louis Pelletier, Jr. (New York opening, January 14, 1937; 77 performances). Photography: Arthur Edeson. Editor: James Gibbon. Art Director: Esdras Hartley. Sound: Dolph Thomas, Charles David Forrest. Music Director: Leo F. Forbstein. Orchestral Arrangements: Adolph Deutsch. Costumes: Milo Anderson. Assistant Director: Dick Mayberry. Running Time: 77 minutes.

Cast: Dick Powell (Elly Jordan aka "Wyoming" Steve Gibson); Pat O'Brien (Ray Chadwick); Priscilla Lane (Jane Hardy); Dick Foran (Sam Thorne); Ann Sheridan (Maxine Chadwick); Johnnie Davis (Jeff Hardy); Ronald Reagan (Pat "Speed" Dunn); Emma Dunn (Ma Hardy); Granville Bates (Pop Hardy); James Stephenson (Professor Landis); Hobart Cavanaugh (Mr. Jordan); Elisabeth Risdon (Mrs. Jordan); Dennie Moore (Abby Pitts); Rosella Towne (Panthea); May Boley (Mrs. Krinkenheim);

Harry Barris (Louie); Candy Candido (Spec); Donald Briggs (*Star* reporter); Jeffrey Lynn (*Chronicle* reporter); John Ridgely (*Beacon* reporter); William B. Davidson (Mr. Alvey); Mary Field (Myrle Semple); Monte Vandergrift, Eddy Chandler (brakemen); Cliff Saum (conductor); Sam Hayes (news commentator); Eddie Graham, Leyland Hodgson, Frank Mayo, Jack Wise (reporters); Olin Francis (radio contestant); Don Marion (bellboy); Jack Mower (station manager); John Harron (technician); Wendell Niles (announcer); John T. Murray (Colonel Rose); George Hickman (newsboy); Stuart Holmes (doorman); Ben Hendricks (judge); Emmett Vogan (rodeo announcer).

Songs: "Howdy Stranger" [Powell], "I've Got a Heartful of Music" [Powell, Barris, Candido], "I'll Dream Tonight" [Powell, twice], "Ride, Tenderfoot, Ride" [Powell, Lane; reprised by Powell, then by Powell, chorus] (Johnny Mercer, Richard A. Whiting); "Cowboy from Brooklyn" [instrumental] (Johnny Mercer, Harry Warren); "Git Along, Little Dogies" [Davis, chorus] (trad.).

Working Titles: *The Brooklyn Cowboy*; *Dude Rancher*; *Howdy Stranger*.

Disc: Decca 1820A ("Ride, Tenderfoot, Ride," Dick Powell with Harry Sosnik Orchestra).

Home Video: Warner Archive DVD.

The Story: Elly Jordan, a singer from Brooklyn, is en route with Louie and Spec, his two colleagues in a musical act, to California to try out for the movies ("I've Got a Heartful of Music"). They are thrown off a train near Two-Bit, Wyoming, and find their way to a dude ranch, run by Pa and Ma Hardy and their daughter, Jane. Desperate for work—and despite his fear of animals—Elly talks Jane into giving the three musicians jobs as entertainers at the ranch ("Ride, Tenderfoot, Ride"). Jane's brother, Jeff, is a singer himself ("Git Along, Little Dogies"), but their egotistical friend Sam Thorne, who fancies himself an accomplished vocalist, becomes jealous of Jane's attention to Elly. Broadway agent Ray Chadwick, vacationing with his publicity man, Pat "Speed" Dunn, hears Elly sing. Thinking the crooner is an authentic Westerner, Ray signs him to a contract as a singing cowboy under the name of "Wyoming" Steve Gibson. Hailed as a national find ("Howdy Stranger"), Elly arrives in New York, soon to be followed by the Hardys and Sam, as the latter is to be a contestant on Colonel Rose's radio talent show. Elly is assured by Ray that he is about to land a movie deal, but Ray's confidence becomes less certain when he learns that Elly is a non-cowboy who is from Brooklyn. When Sam threatens to expose Elly to the media, Ray enters Elly in a rodeo at Madison Square Garden, and Jane has Elly hypnotized by Professor Landis so he can gain the courage needed to compete. Despite Ray also being put under Landis' spell accidentally, Elly sets a world record at the rodeo and signs his movie contract.*

Roy Rogers was born near Cincinnati ... as in Ohio. Tim Holt was brought into the world in California ... in Beverly Hills. Tom Mix and Ken Maynard hailed from Pennsylvania and Indiana, respectively. Charles Starrett, Bob Allen, George Houston, and James Newill all were raised in the East ... and the first two Ivy Leagued it at Dartmouth. Nothing against these fine representatives of Old West cinema for not actually being from the West—they were, after all, *actors*. But whether one was a singing cowboy or a no-frills cowpoke, there was a certain stigma for a Western movie hero not being considered "authentic." In 1938, amid the craze for crooning cowboys on the screen, Warner Bros. satirized this idea with a comedy about a fellow from the least likely of buckaroo birth locales. The title: *Cowboy from Brooklyn*. The star: Dick Powell, from Flatbush on screen but actually born in Mountain View, Arkansas (OK ... could be worse).

In 1938, Dick Powell had bigger things to worry about than whether anyone from Brooklyn or Arkansas should be a Western star. He was still a busy film actor, but the fresh-faced co-star of *42nd Street*, *Gold Diggers of 1933*, *Dames*, and so many other popular musicals was falling into a career rut. Not wanting to do the same kind of singing juvenile roles over and over—especially now that he was entering his mid–30s—he petitioned his studio to allow him other kinds of assignments. But besides being placed in a couple of light comedies that weren't musicals, Powell wasn't finding satisfaction in what he saw as typecasting. This was not an uncommon concern for Hollywood stars—especially at Warners, where James Cagney had just returned after leaving the studio for more than a year, and where Bette Davis periodically sat out for more pay and better parts. The 1937 Powell-headlined musicals *Varsity Show* and *Hollywood Hotel* were both money-losers at the box office (although both were budgeted at more than $1.1 million, significantly higher than most of its WB predecessors).[72] Married to actress Joan Blondell and raising their two children, Powell had seen too many other talents wither from misuse, and he aired his concerns to an Associated Press reporter:

> I like to sing, always have, always will, but if I don't have a good reason when I sing on the screen, I can't blame the public for getting tired of it.
>
> As a family breadwinner, I'd like to keep my job in this business. Been around for six years and want to stay a lot longer. It seems to me I ought to demonstrate I can be interesting as an actor without having a song dragged in for me by the heels.[73]

In April 1938, with *Hollywood Hotel* in theaters and *Cowboy from Brooklyn* having just wrapped, Powell was placed on a 90-day suspension after declining a co-starring role in another musical, *Garden of the Moon*. Scuttlebutt was that Powell read the script for *Garden* and saw his role as much less meaty than that of co-star Pat O'Brien. Apparently he didn't have the same complaint about *Cowboy from Brooklyn*, which paired him with O'Brien—and Powell's *Varsity Show* sweetheart, pretty Priscilla Lane (1917–1995)—once Powell returned to WB after a month away. Based on an unremarkable Broadway play, *Cowboy from Brooklyn* saw Powell in the title role as an Easterner whose potential as a tough-but-tender cowhand crooner-actor is threatened by an abject fright over horses—and animals of every non-human sort.[74]

After a routine first half hour or so as a pleasant, leisurely paced romance of opposites—meaning Powell and Lane—the film is given a serious energy boost by O'Brien, sending up his fast-talking image as a "big theatrical man from New York" who will go to great ends to make Powell's tenderfoot a star. With a typical romanticized but condescending view of the West, its cowboys and their values, he has come West for a hiatus to "forget New York and all those phonies." But with one look at Powell, his promoter rat-a-tat-tat re-emerges: "I can picture you on a pinto pony coming out of the Lincoln Tunnel taking charge of Times Square!" He and his publicity man—played by Ronald Reagan in his sixth movie—raise their newest find to national headlines as "a Sensational Singing Cowboy" for no longer than a train trip from the big country to the Big Apple.

The musical numbers disappear for the last 20 minutes, which ramp up the pace to farcical levels that include identity confusion, mistaken hypnotism, and logic-stretching sporting feats. The overall result is silly but highly entertaining, and a definite cut above the typical late-1930s Dick Powell vehicle, even without the tunes. And why not? The director, Lloyd Bacon, knew his way around a comedy. Ann Sheridan, although underused, is an extra added attraction as O'Brien's gold-digging sister. And the songs are handed to composer Richard Whiting and lyricist Johnny Mercer, terrific enough in their separate careers and underrated as a duo.

Mercer already knew his way around Western pop: His self-penned "I'm an Old Cowhand (From the Rio Grande)" became a hit from the Bing Crosby film *Rhythm on the Range* [q.v.]—and if a Crosby film was parodying singing Westerns, it meant that singing Westerns had truly arrived. In *Cowboy from Brooklyn,* the last of their four cinematic collaborations, Whiting and Mercer produced a classic cowboy ballad, "Ride, Tenderfoot, Ride." It combines Whiting's horse-hoofing syncopation with Mercer's wordplay, in which tending one's castle and holding one's liquor is a succinct primer for any novice Westerner, and becomes something that a real cowboy wouldn't mind singing around a campfire. "I'll Dream Tonight," a more traditional Tin Pan Alley romantic ballad, is less striking but a good showcase for Powell. "Ride, Tenderfoot, Ride" was covered by Bing Crosby and Gene Autry (in his B Western of the same name), among many others, but it was the last composition for Whiting, who died of a heart attack just as he and Mercer were finishing their three songs for *Cowboy from Brooklyn*. Harry Warren was brought in to write the music for a title song, which is heard only in the underscoring.

Powell earned good reviews despite being ... uh, saddled with a character who requires a good bit of audience suspension of disbelief for his phobia about squirrels, canaries, and owls as well as horses, and his climatic rodeo scene, in which his character bulldogs a steer in record time, showed he could do physical comedy.[75] To maintain his prairie cred, "Wyoming Steve" engages in some entertaining double-talk to Manhattan reporters: "I reckon there's a heap of you city folks to do real herding," or something like that. Still, O'Brien (1899–1983) steals the film with his boisterous performance in which he waves six-guns around like toys and that yields the same kind of result Powell must have feared would happen with *Garden of the Moon*. One wonders what Dick Foran thought about the singing-cowboy parody. Foran—born in Flemington, New Jersey—was one of the sagebrush singing stars that *Cowboy from Brooklyn* was sending up. Foran (1910–1979), a dependable actor perhaps miscast in series Westerns because of his booming, operatic baritone, made B's for WB between 1935 and 1937. Here, in a role that requires him to rein in his vocal talents, he is entrusted to deliver little more than a few bars of "Home on the Range."

Warner Bros. promoted its two "great, new Western stars"—"Two-Gun" O'Brien and "Dead-Eye" Dick Powell, and the reception to *Cowboy from Brooklyn* from patrons and critics was generally positive. *Variety* thought "the phobia is laid on pretty thick ... [and] the actors take to clowning," but *The Film Daily* called it "an uproariously funny comedy that should pile up a heavy quota of laughs in any theater.... Pat O'Brien was never better."[76] For the record, the *Brooklyn Daily Eagle* called the film "unusually pleasant and diverting" and exalted that "good ol' Flatbush has found itself an important spot in the American cinema."[77] As ballyhoo for the New York premiere booking at the Strand Theatre in Manhattan, a wild West stagecoach including six cowboys—three dressed as authentic Westerners and three dressed as faux Brooklyn cowpokes—journeyed from Borough Hall in Brooklyn, crossed the Brooklyn Bridge, and went up Broadway to the theater. The coach was decorated with banners reading "We Are Cowboys from Brooklyn Invading Manhattan," and the "cowboys" on board distributed cards to onlookers reading "Are You Cowboys from Brooklyn? We Are Looking for You."[78] Business there turned out to be brisk.

Powell believed enough in the film that he embarked on a tour to visit exhibitors in a dozen major cities to get them interested in bookings. Unfortunately, *Cowboy from Brooklyn*, produced for $572,000—on the high side for a mid-level big-studio feature—lost $71,750 at the box office.[79] Warners spent roughly $150,000 on two costly sets—a dude ranch and, for the rodeo finale, a Madison Square Garden reproduction inside a soundstage.[80] Powell's career really didn't benefit in the long run, either; he made three more films before leaving Warners, the last being *Naughty but Nice* [q.v.].

Although his character was made to look foolish at times, Powell liked doing *Cowboy from Brooklyn*, surprisingly enough. In later years, Ronald Reagan would joke to Powell, a longtime friend, about how it was "one we'd both better forget." But actress June Allyson, Powell's second wife, disclosed that the actor was proud of making the film and secretly kept a stash of photographs of himself in cowboy garb.[81] Not bad for a kid from Arkansas.

The Terror of Tiny Town
(Principal/Columbia; December 1, 1938)

Director: Sam Newfield. Producers: Jed Buell, Sol Lesser. Associate Producers: Abe Meyer, Bert Sternbach. Screenplay: Fred Myton. Additional Dialogue: Clarence Marks. Story Editor: Helen Gurley. Assistant Director: Gordon Griffith. Photography: Mack Stengler. Editors: Martin G. Cohn, Richard G. Wray. Art Director: Fred Preble. Costumes: James Wade. Music Director: Lew Porter. Musical Background: Edward Kilenyi. Sound: Corson Jowett. Makeup Creations: Louis Phillipi. Running Time: 61 minutes.

Cast ("Jed Buell's Midgets"): Billy Curtis (The Hero [Buck Lawson]); Yvonne Moray [Bistany] (The Girl [Nancy Preston]); Little Billy [Rhodes] (The Villain [Bat Haines]); Bill Platt (The Rich Uncle [Jim "Tex" Preston]); John T. Bambury (The Ranch Owner [Pop Lawson]); Joseph Herbst (The Sheriff); Charles Becker (The Cook); Nita Krebs (The Vampire); George Ministeri (The Blacksmith); Karl Casitzky (The Barber); Johnnie Ferr [Fern Formica] (Diamond Dolly); W.H. O'Docharty (The Old Soak); John Winters (traveling salesman); John Leal (henchman); Clarence Swensen (preacher); "Henchmen, Cowhands and Citizens of Tiny Town."

Songs: "Down on the Sunset Trail" [Curtis], "Laugh Your Troubles Away" [chorus, reprised by Becker], "Mister Jack and Missus Jill" [Moray, reprised by Krebs, Ferr, chorus], "She's the Daughter of Sweet Caroline" [barbershop chorus] (Lew Porter); "Hey, Look Out (I'm Gonna Make Love to You)" [Ferr] (Lew Porter, Phil Stern).

Home Video: Alpha DVD; BFS Entertainment DVD; Mill Creek DVD; Sinister Cinema DVD; Synergy DVD.

The Story: After an onstage announcer introduces the film and the hero and villain interrupt him by bickering at each other, the scene shifts to the Old West village of Tiny Town ("Laugh Your Troubles Away"). The villainous Bat Haines is rustling cattle from the neighboring Lawson and Preston families and forging their brands so that each clan blames the other for the thefts. Haines is in league with the town's sheriff, thus thwarting the efforts of young hero Buck Lawson to solve the crimes. Nancy, the niece of ranch owner Tex Preston, arrives in town, and she and Buck become mutually attracted. The two begin meeting in secret ("Down on the Sunset Trail," "Mister Jack and Missus Jill"). Buck's investigation comes close to finding the culprit, so Haines responds by shooting "Tex" and spreading blame on Buck for the murder. Buck is nearly lynched by the angry townspeople. With unexpected help from Bat's spurned girlfriend, Buck tracks Lawson down in a remote cabin and engages in a fight to the finish—with explosive results.

"I must caution you not to take it too seriously," says the normal-sized, tuxedo-clad man shown standing on a stage in front of a microphone as he introduces *The Terror of Tiny Town*. As if to underscore his claim, the actors playing the hero and villain appear, then begin bickering over their importance during the hour that will follow this brief prologue. If the viewer doesn't know it already, this will not be like any other hour at the movies ... for said hero and villain are no more than 4 feet tall, and no one else in their picture will stand taller. *The Terror of Tiny Town* remains the only Hollywood motion picture with what, in the parlance of its release year of 1938, was an "all-midget cast." It was highly publicized enough to promise a trend of little-people movie novelties, but then sanity prevailed, and little people would have to wait until more enlightened times to become unquestionable entertainment attractions. Viewed in this new light, is *The Terror of Tiny Town* fully exploitative or partly affirming? The answer is obvious in the consensus of history, which places this bizarre offering among the worst movies ever made.

Why make a musical Western with an all-little cast? Why not? Or so thought Jed Buell, who had been making dirt-cheap, mainly musical Westerns since the mid-'30s. He ramped up the novelty factor with a 1937 all-black feature, *Harlem on the Prairie* [q.v.], starring big-band singer-turned-actor Herb Jeffries. Buell had been publicity chief for Mack Sennett

Studio once upon a time, and before that a theater manager, so he had learned to sell a good story. In May 1938, just as production began on *The Terror of Tiny Town*, he explained to a reporter that his inspiration for it was the result of a discussion with some colleagues: "One of the [prop men] cracked that if I kept on trying to keep expenses down, I'd probably use midgets for actors. That struck me as a good idea—and that's what I'm doing. Only the expenses are going up, not down."[82]

With about $35,000 to work with, Buell went on a national talent search to recruit actors, advertising "Big Salaries for Little People." At the time of the above interview, he had just secured the services of 16 members of the famous Singer Midgets troupe for his cast of 40 for about $150 per day for 12 days of shooting.[83] The Singer Midgets, founded in Vienna in 1912, had been based in the United States since after World War I and had become vaudeville favorites. Among its members was the performer cast as Buell's hero, Billy Curtis (1909–1988), an American who was just beginning a long movie career during which he rarely played the good guy. A former professional wrestler, Curtis had lately made headlines for marrying Lois de Fee, a 6-foot-4 nightclub bouncer from Miami, but a divorce was already pending, allegedly because Curtis grew weary of bouncing on his wife's knee.[84]

The "Terror" of the title, a troublemaker pitting two ranching families against each other, was played by scratchy-voiced "Little Billy" Rhodes (1895–1967). Rhodes had been in movies since the days of the silent, and early-musicals fans might recall him as "Major Tiny" in *Swing High* (Pathé 1930). Blond, full-figured Yvonne Moray (1917–1974) was a 21-year-old

Billy Curtis (as "The Hero") sings to Yvonne Moray in *The Terror of Tiny Town*.

New Yorker cast as the heroine, a Juliet to Curtis' Romeo. She was chaperoned on the set by her full-sized mother, and promotional material warned that her brother was a large-sized professional boxer, lest fans of any dimensions become too enamored. Moray had the misfortune to break her hand in a fall from a horse, but the good news was the tumble was merely from a Shetland pony. Key support players such as Nita Krebs (a Czechoslovakian import), Charles Becker (a native German), and 61-year-old Bill Platt came from the Singer troupe. Location shots were taken in the California hills near Chatsworth, about 50 miles from Hollywood, with interiors at the International Studios in L.A.

Director Sam Newfield was rushing through a filmmaking career that would include nearly 300 credits (including the '40s cult horrors *Dead Men Walk* and *The Mad Monster*), and he had *Tiny Town* just about finished within a couple of weeks in the spring of 1938. But the in-house buzz was building, and when Sol Lesser—another indie producer, but with many more resources than Buell, and relationships with major studios—viewed the rushes, he wanted in. Lesser's Principal Productions bought a half interest in the project, doubled the budget to $75,000, and funded additional scenes, emphasizing the comedic aspect that Lesser thought would be box-office boffo, to be written and shot in July.[85] Lesser was known for making children into stars—kiddie tenor Bobby Breen was his latest discovery—and he thought he might do the same for a different kind of little people.

Lesser had the film previewed for trade reviewers and potential distributors. Among what were mainly positive early reviews, the business-minded *Film Daily* was especially enthusiastic ("Properly exploited, it should do handsomely at the box office"), and so was Columbia, which picked up *Tiny Town* for a worldwide release to come in December.[86] With ballyhoo masters Buell and Lesser now double-teaming on promotion, news about the film—of greatly varying shades of accuracy and taste—was eagerly transmitted to the news media throughout 1938. Some examples:

- *The Film Daily*, April 27: Jed Buell has contracted for 40 Shetland ponies, "all of them trained for fast riding."[87] The producer later complained that too many of the *Terror of Tiny Town* actors were falling off the mini-ponies.
- Late May: Louella O. Parsons' Hearst Universal Service column describes seeing eight "little midgets" picketing in front of her home with signs reading "Parsons Unfair to Tiny Town," "We Want Bigger Breaks for Little People," and "If It's News When Gable Does It Why Can't We Get a Break?" Louella tells readers that the "publicity strike" was settled "over a 5-pound box of candy and a promise that I'd do better by them in the future."[88]
- June 6: "Why is it that there are no midget Indians?" asks *Los Angeles Times* columnist Lee Shippey in response to Buell's quest to find one for *Tiny Town*. "He has been told there is one in Colorado, but he can't locate him."[89] (Apparently, Buell never did track him down, for no Native Americans are seen in the film.)
- *The Film Daily*, June 18: "A miniature emergency hospital with physician and surgical equipment, accompanies on location the Liliputians [sic] appearing in *The Terror of Tiny Town*."[90]
- *Los Angeles Times*, June 19: Cast members of *Terror of Tiny Town* throw a party for Buell and their agent, Thelma Weisser, that includes a buffet supper and "songs, dances and the playing of scenes from the picture." The guest list—which includes actors Pat Gleason, Tempe Pigott, and Minerva Urecal and directors Erle C. Kenton and Louis (*Reefer Madness*) Gasnier—is not exactly A-list.[91]

- *Los Angeles Times*, June 26: "A growing animosity between midget leading man Billy Curtis and midget heavy Little Billy ... reached its height in the sensational fight scenes which took place in the outlaw's hideout.... Instead of boxing for camera effects, the two tiny persons turned upon each other and allowed accumulated grudges out in the form of swift rights to the jaw ..., Little Billy coming off with a sprained wrist and Billy Curtis with a badly bruised elbow and knee."[92]
- *Los Angeles Times*, August 4: "Little Billy, 3-foot 3-inch [sic] midget heavy in.... *The Terror of Tiny Town*, was glimpsed walking up the Vine Street hill with a huge box of flowers. He was calling on Nita Krebbs [sic], 3-foot 'Vamp' of the production."[93]
- *Los Angeles Times,* August 9: "Yvonne Moray, actress and old enough to vote, weighs only 46 pounds. But she is doing her darndest to reduce .... Among midget leading ladies ... one who gets much above 45 pounds may be considered lovely but—well, just a trifle on the buxom side."[94]
- September: *Variety* reports that Little Billy and the impresario of the Singer Midgets, Leo Singer, are "shopping around Hollywood" for a location in which to build "a Tom Thumb eatery and nitery with an all-runt cast."[95]

Variety noted that the club was being planned "with the studios going for midget productions in a big way"—this boast before most people had seen *The Terror of Tiny Town*. Either with foresight of a trend or a need to feed the publicity monster (certainly the latter), Buell and Lesser separately announced plans for further little-people projects. Buell declared he would follow *Tiny Town* with a lumber-camp picture with a cast of midgets surrounding a normal-sized Paul Bunyan.[96] Lesser announced that *Tiny Town* would be the first in a series of midget-acted burlesques of current hit films.[97]

Wow ... but as the cowboy said to his frisky horse: "Whoa!" There were no more pint-sized flicks to follow on the heels of *The Terror of Tiny Town*. It would be what showmen called "a freak attraction"—a one-shot fluke. It may seem difficult to believe 80 years later, but this was considered all-ages fare, not a whole lot different than Disney's animated *Snow White and the Seven Dwarfs*, which debuted in theaters only a few months earlier. Many towns played *Tiny Town* as a Christmas or New Year's treat for kiddies at the end of 1938 and '39. A Los Angeles newspaper reviewer speculated that "children especially will love this old-time ... story, set to a new twist—with midgets, who make it an ideal kids' movie."[98]

The Terror of Tiny Town remains difficult to defend, although once the viewer adjusts to a world in which everyone is 4 feet tall and rides Shetland ponies, it's possible to settle in with a minimum of discomfort. The size-based jokes are mixed in their propriety: Most of them are sight gags concerned with the small-sized actors interacting with full-sized props (beer steins, saloon doors, musical instruments, furniture), but except for a cry of "Everyone chin up to the bar!" not much of the dialogue explicitly makes fun. The villain's boast that he will be the "biggest man in the county" is something you'd hear from any B Western heavy, and that's really more to the point about the satire here. It's an "all-midget" movie, but it's just as much a gentle lampoon of sagebrush-on-a-budget tropes—thrilling chases, crooked sheriffs, stagecoach robberies, barroom brawls, and Fuzzy St. John-style comic relief (symbolized by Becker, who speaks in a European accent and spends much of his screen time chasing a duck in hopes of cutting it up for dinner).

And, of course, there's a singing cowboy. The good guy vocalizes only once in the film

("Down on the Sunset Trail"), and the other three Lew Porter-penned tunes are assigned to the heroine and others, most tolerably in a rendition of the modestly catchy "Mister Jack and Missus Jill." Led by the Marlene Dietrich–like vamp character portrayed by Krebs, the saloon-set number is positioned to relieve tension from an ongoing chase scene—a plotting strategy that is another musical-Western tradition. Krebs severely overshadows Moray among the female principals, but Curtis wins out as a thespian over Little Billy, whose overacting is out of step with the rest of the cast.[99] Most of the *Terror of Tiny Town* actors—Curtis, Moray, Rhodes, Krebs, Becker, and Mae West-lookalike Johnnie Fern among them—went from that film to MGM's *The Wizard of Oz*, thus traveling from the ridiculous to the sublime. Whatever lasting fame came to them over the years was from that movie, not this one.

Oz became perhaps the most loved musical of Hollywood's Golden Age; with apologies to *Golden Dawn*, *Hellzapoppin'*, and *The 5,000 Fingers of Dr. T*, Jed Buell's brainchild became (charitably, perhaps) the weirdest. Interest in *The Terror of Tiny Town* got a bump in 1978 with the publication of the best-selling book *The 50 Worst Films of All Time*, which hammered *Tiny Town* hard enough to make people curious to see it. In 1980, the brains behind the *50 Worst Films* book, brothers Harry and Michael Medved, took more shots at the film in a follow-up tome, *The Golden Turkey Awards*. That same year, the Medveds brought the now-public domain movie out of mothballs to play at their World's Worst Film Festival in New York.

The VCR revolution allowed viewers to retreat into the privacy of their own homes to watch the old-timey "dwarfs" interact, and nowadays you can take more time to read this sentence than to locate *The Terror of Tiny Town* on YouTube. In the meantime, the general interest in little people as entertainment accelerated in the 2010s through reality TV series such as *Little People, Big World*; *The Little Couple*; and *Little Women: LA*. They were praised despite walking the same kind of line between humanization and exploitation as did *Tiny Town*. But how much were the productions old and new driven by the same kind of almost-prurient curiosity the Medveds and others accused Jed Buell of propagating? The answer is not so clear-cut.

So, should *The Terror of Tiny Town* be justified or condemned? Its top-billed cast member, Billy Curtis, went on to act for 50 years in scores of movies. He became known for not taking the kind of demeaning roles too many performers of his physical stature were forced into. Interviewed late in his life, Curtis seemed to be bitter about the general treatment of little people in show business, but hardly resentful of *Tiny Town* and his role in it, reminding us that we might not have to be so nasty about that film.

> Small, in the minds of stupid people, is kiddie stuff. So first they try to exploit little people. Then they patronize you. And when the picture comes out, then the audience laughs at you. Why? Not because we were low budget, because most Westerns then were B's. Because we rode ponies. What would a person my size ride—a stallion? I played the good guy who put the bad guy behind bars at the end—just like John Wayne. And I kissed the pretty girl—just like he did. So what the hell's so funny?[100]

Dorothy Page—The Singing Cowgirl: *Ride 'Em Cowgirl*

(Grand National; January 20, 1939)

Director: Samuel Diege. Producer: Arthur Dreifuss. Associate Producer: Donald K. Lieberman. Executive Producer: George A. Hirliman. Screenplay: Arthur Hoerl. Photography: Mack Stengler. Editor: Guy

V. Thayer, Jr. Sound: William Wilmarth. Music Director: Ross DiMaggio. Special Effects: Howard A. Anderson. Production Manager: Joseph Boyle. Assistant Director: Robert Richards. Running Time: 52 minutes.

Cast: Dorothy Page (Helen Rickson); Milton Frome (Oliver Shea); Vince Barnett (Dan Haggerty); Lynn Mayberry (Belle); Frank Ellis (Sheriff Larson); Harrington Reynolds (Doyle); Stanley Price (Robert Weylan); Warner Richmond (Wiley); Lloyd Ingraham (judge); Joseph Girard ("Ruf" Rickson); Merrill McCormick, Fred Berhle (deputy sheriffs); Pat Henning (Lingstrom); Fred Cordova (Philbin); Eddie Gordon (Grigg); "Snowy" the horse.

Songs: "A Campfire, a Prairie Moon and You" [Page, reprised by Mayberry, then by Page, Frome], "I Love the Wide Open Spaces" [Page, Frome, Mayberry, Barnett, chorus] (Al Sherman, Walter Kent, Milton Drake).

Working Title: *Fury's in the Saddle*.

Home Video: Alpha DVD.

The Story: Doyle, an international crook, is smuggling silver from a mine across the Mexican border into the United States via the ranch of "Ruf" Rickson. Reynolds holds sway over Rickson's finances, cheating him at cards so he can seize control of the ranch. Rickson's daughter, Helen, seeks to help her father by competing for the $5,000 first prize in a local horse race. As treasurer of the local rodeo organizers, Helen is entrusted with keeping the money in a safe at the ranch, but the $5,000 is stolen and Ruf becomes the prime suspect. With the help of traveling telephone linemen Oliver Shea and Dan Haggerty, Helen goes into hiding to recover the money and clear her father's name. Helen enters the race at the last moment and wins. Oliver feigns interest in Doyle's scheme to claim the Rickson ranch, but is found out by the villain. Helen rescues Oliver, Dan, and her friend Belle from Doyle's clutches, and Oliver, now revealed as a federal agent, makes the arrest.

Water Rustlers

(Grand National; January 6, 1939)

Director: Samuel Diege. Producer: Donald K. Lieberman. Executive Producer: George A. Hirliman. Screenplay: Arthur Hoerl. Story: Lawrence Meade, Don Laurie. Photography: Mack Stengler. Editor: Guy V. Thayer, Jr. Set Decoration: Lou Diege. Sound: Hans Weeren. Musical Score: Ross DiMaggio. Music Supervisor: Lee Zahler. Special Effects: Howard A. Anderson. Production Manager: Joseph Boyle. Running Time: 54 minutes.

Cast: Dorothy Page (Shirley Martin); David [Dave] O'Brien (Bob Lawson); Vince Barnett (Mike); Stanley Price (Robert Weylan); Ethan Allen (Tim Martin); Leonard Trainor (Jurgens); Warner Richmond (Wiley); Eddie Gordon (Sherman); Edward Peil (lawyer); Lloyd Ingraham (judge); Merrill McCormick (sheriff).

Songs [all by Page]: "I Feel at Home in the Saddle," "Let's Go on Like This Forever," "When a Cowboy Sings a Dogie Lullaby" (Al Sherman, Walter Kent, Milton Drake).

Working Title: *The Last Barrier*.

Home Video: Alpha DVD; The Film Detective DVD; Grapevine Video DVD.

The Story: Unscrupulous businessman Robert Weylan builds a dam that diverts water from local ranchers who won't sell their land to his meatpacking syndicate. With his cattle dying on parched grazing lands, rancher Tim Martin attempts to drive them through to the water, but his foreman tips off Weylan and Martin is killed. Martin's daughter Shirley hires a new foreman, Bob Lawson, and the two conspire to thwart Weylan, who is intimidating ranchers from testifying against him in court.

The Singing Cowgirl
(Grand National; June 2, 1939)

Director: Samuel Diege. Producer: Donald K. Lieberman. Executive Producer: George A. Hirliman. Screenplay: Arthur Hoerl. Photography: Mack Stengler. Editor: Guy V. Thayer, Jr. Set Decoration: Lou Diege. Sound: Hans Weeren, Glen Glenn. Musical Score: Ross DiMaggio. Music Supervisor: Lee Zahler. Special Effects: Howard A. Anderson. Production Manager: Joseph Boyle. Running Time: 59 minutes.

Cast: Dorothy Page (Dorothy Hendrick); David [Dave] O'Brien (Dick Williams); Vince Barnett (Kewpie); Dorothy Short (Nora Pryde); Dix Davis (Billy Harkins); Stanley Price (John Tolen); Warner Richmond (Gunhand Garrick); Edward Piel (Tom Harkins); Paul Barrett (Rex Harkins); Lloyd Ingraham (Dr. Slocum); Ethan Allen (Sheriff Teasley); Eddie Gordon (Trigger Williams); Merrill McCormick (deputy sheriff).

Songs: "I Gotta Sing" [Page], "Let's Round Up Our Dreams" [Page, twice], "Prairie Boy" [Page, three times] (Al Sherman, Walter Kent, Milton Drake).

Working Title: *Lady Buckaroo*.

Home Video: AFA Entertainment DVD; Alpha DVD; Grapevine Video DVD; Tex Ralph's Westerns DVD.

The Story: Tom Harkins is the target of cattle rustlers led by Gunhand Garrick, but the rancher and his young son, Billy, find help from neighbor Dorothy Hendrick, her friend Kewpie and cowboy Dick Williams. Dick goes to work as a rider for attorney John Tolen, who is secretly in league with the cattle thieves. The elder Harkins and his wife are murdered by Garrick's henchmen, who are seeking gold on Harkins ranch, and Billy is left in Dorothy's care. The boy's uncle, Rex Harkins, arrives in town and falls for another newcomer—Tolen's niece, Nora Pryde. When he learns that they know about the gold, which is actually on Tolen's ranch, Garrick's men capture Nora, Billy, and Rex. Jolted by the kidnapping, Tolen confronts Garrick, and Dorothy and Dick capture the outlaws.

Grand National was a dying company as 1939 dawned, and what would become film's greatest year threatened to be that indie studio's final full annum. James Cagney wasn't going to walk back through GN's doors anytime soon, and the corporate optimism that had accompanied the elite actor's presence in *Something to Sing About* [q.v.] had long disappeared. Amid many months of money troubles, the original Grand National Films Inc. had gone bankrupt and been reorganized as Grand National Pictures under the presidency of E.W. Hammons, who had founded, and lately lost, the now-defunct Educational Pictures. Grand National was hanging by a thread releasing inexpensive action dramas and Westerns, and now part of its future was to rely on the looks, charm, vigor, and voice of a minor radio singer named Dorothy Page. The screen's first "Singing Cowgirl," Page made three unremarkable features that ended her film aspirations—and, not entirely coincidentally, Grand National's.

The desperation was palpable. Grand National had lost its top cowboy star, Tex Ritter, to not-quite-as-lowly Monogram, and for '39, it would have to be Page, bandleader-crooner Art Jarrett, boxing champion Max Baer, or obscure vocalist Tex Fletcher making good in proposed Western series. Page and GN had a no-win at the whims of the sagebrush fan base. The young, predominantly male audience liked their stars virile and their opposite-sex interactions beyond chaste ... so what to do with Dorothy Page? Presenting her as a "true" cowgal might come off as too butch; make her too feminine, and she'd be snickered off the screen.

Page (1904–1961) wasn't a bad choice—pretty and auburn-haired with a tallish, vaguely athletic physique that was low on cleavage. She was born, raised, and attended college in Pennsylvania, and although some reportage on her in the 1930s indicated ties to Texas, this does not appear to have been the case.[101] Publicity touted Page's cover-girl stint with the *Saturday Evening Post* and the silver cup she allegedly won as "the most beautiful girl in radio." Page ascended to the airwaves after winning a 1932 national talent contest tied to Paul Whiteman, with whose band she toured, and a regular gig on the radio show *Paducah Plantation*, hosted by humorist Irwin S. Cobb. The press was silent on less fan-favorable life details: Page was divorced, amid press rumors of marital infidelity, from a physician in Detroit, with their two children being raised by her ex-husband's parents in New England.

Page was singing at a Chicago hotel when a Universal bigwig heard her and arranged a successful screen test. The "U" featured her in two minor 1935 features with past-prime male leads: *Manhattan Moon* (Ricardo Cortez) and *King Solomon of Broadway* (Edmund Lowe). Page leased a Spanish-style home in Toluca Lake, California, where, she bragged, she often swam in the pool of Dick Powell, who lived across the street.[102]

Nightclub singer Dorothy Page donned Western garb as the "Singing Cowgirl" of the silver screen at the end of the 1930s.

But her Universal contract was allowed to expire, and in 1937, she was well down the cast list in Republic's *Mama Runs Wild*, in which she didn't sing at all. Hollywood stopped calling her for parts, and as the actress told a magazine reporter years later, "Suddenly I began to be a bit frightened."

> Waiting became rather terrible. I'd wake up in the morning, look at the clock and jerk myself up quickly, thinking, "I'll have to hurry or I'll be late on the set." And then I'd remember that I wasn't due on the set and there would be a sinking, frightening feeling…. Later, I was to learn that I had done all the wrong things. Rules are the reverse in Talkie Town. If you're frankly looking for a job, they think you can't be any good or you'd have one.[103]

Page returned to radio, but her picture days weren't over, even if Grand National was considered a bit of a comedown. She regained her on-camera contralto in what was planned as a run of six musicals for GN's Coronado production unit, which, under new director Samuel Diege, in five-day bursts between August and October of 1938, ground out *Ride 'Em Cowgirl*, *Water Rustlers*, and *The Singing Cowgirl*, in that order. The first two came to theaters almost simultaneously in January 1939 and, depending on where they played, were announced as the series debut. Advance flackery noted the presence of bald, big-eared, pint-sized Vince Barnett (1902–1977) as comic relief in all three pictures.

Theatergoers were advised to promote Page, in a nod to old-time action flickers, as a "singing Western star who can do all the stunts that Ruth Roland and the serial queens were famous for."[104] Page was very nearly not the first Roland or Pearl White of the sagebrush, however. Ruth Mix, the real-life daughter of Hollywood cowboy legend Tom Mix, was billed second to Rex Bell and Hoot Gibson in a few B Westerns, and there was talk at Grand National in 1937 about her getting a non-musical series, which did not pan out.[105] The genuine, premier chanteuse of 1930s Western song was Patsy Montana, who performed with Gene Autry on radio and recorded the 1935 million-seller "I Want to Be a Cowboy's Sweetheart," but Montana didn't make it to the movies until mid–1939's *Colorado Sunset*, and then only as support to Autry. By then, Page's starring pictures were making the small-town rounds.

Ride 'Em Cowgirl, as the first entry of the three actually filmed, has the most novelty value, not just in the presence of Page, who rides and shoots adequately with stuntperson help, but in the odd choice of its male lead. Viewers came to know Milton Frome as the chrome-domed, fast-talking actor who played numerous comic parts on '50s and '60s television (semi-regularly as a studio executive in *The Beverly Hillbillies*) and movies (*Bye Bye Birdie* and many Jerry Lewis films), but at age 30 he was a vaudeville comedian with a full head of hair and the second-most-prominent role in a Dorothy Page Western.

Singing also was part of Frome's live act, and as he recalled decades later, he paid a visit to the Page film's producers and its director, Samuel Diege, after hearing they needed a singing cowboy actor. "[A]fter we had a talk and they heard me sing a few notes, they decided I was their man."[106] It was that easy! After a period in the studio where Frome and Page pre-recorded a pair of songs for *Ride 'Em Cowgirl*, "A Campfire, a Prairie Moon and You" and "I Love the Wide Open Spaces," filming commenced in the small town of Kernville, east of Los Angeles.

Frome isn't permitted much more than a couple of longing glances at Page and all-too-short duets with her on the two songs, and *Ride 'Em Cowgirl* did nothing for his cinematic aspirations. The final-reel revelation that his character is a G-man from the East is intended to satisfy purists over the supposed miscasting. Still, Frome (1908–1989) holds his own, even with picture-buff viewers who might read the opening credits and think ... "Milton Frome?!" When Frome's character pretends to scheme with the bad guys to betray the cowgirl, the actor exudes just enough potential shadiness to make us think he might really mean it—then we remember that this is a B Western.

Meanwhile, Vince Barnett is paired a little more explicitly with a distaff counterpart in Patsy Kelly look-alike Lynn Mayberry; the two sing "I Love the Wide Open Spaces" while cuddling up in a car. Mayberry, a radio and stage comedienne cast as Page's stranded-actress sidekick, was known for harmonica playing astute enough to mimic a freight train, but we don't get to hear that here. Reviewers of *Ride 'Em Cowgirl* somehow missed the rather indifferent portrayal of the main villain by British actor Harrington Reynolds, whose baddie acts as if he'd rather be playing golf or cricket than smuggling silver.

After submitting *Ride 'Em Cowgirl* to the camera, the filmmakers may have gotten cold feet, for a less daring, more conventionally handsome cowboy, Dave O'Brien, was brought in to claim second billing in the other two pictures. O'Brien (1912–1969) has achieved posthumous notoriety in non–Westerns—mainly as the serials' Captain Midnight, as the drug-addled "fast! ... faster!" guy in *Reefer Madness* (1938), and as the klutzy Everyman of those '40s–'50s Pete Smith MGM shorts—but in 1939 he was just starting many years of stardom in budget oaters. A former stuntman and chorus dancer, O'Brien was well suited to action pictures, and he's romantically convincing enough to impress the *Water Rustlers* heroine with a compliment: "Even the nightingales stop singing so they could listen to you." In this unimaginatively titled middle picture, Page gets to show a little more femininity, taking off her hat and holster to reveal a comely dress and a curvy figure to sing "Let's Go on Like This Forever." But she remains at the forefront of the action, engaging in gunplay with outlaws and rescuing her man from surging dam waters to the reward of a halfhearted climactic clench that looks more like two buddies with arms around shoulders. As a ranch cook, Barnett readopts the Italian dialect he'd put on in the gangster epic *Scarface* (1932)—but with no female complement, as in *Ride 'Em Cowgirl.*

The third feature, *The Singing Cowgirl*, lived up to its title by allowing Page to sing more than in her previous quickies. Her most frequent number was "Prairie Boy," a downbeat ditty tied to the character of a 10-year-old-or-so boy (Dix Davis) whose parents are shot dead and is later laid up by a bullet himself. Page does all the vocalizing in another chaste pairing with O'Brien, but this seems like more his movie than hers, with him doing most of the dirty work in capturing an outlaw gang. Again, there's a secondary couple—a younger pair played by Dorothy Short (O'Brien's real-life wife) and Paul Barrett. At the finish, the younger couple embraces, Page and O'Brien stare at each other on opposite sides of a playground-sized merry-go-round, and Barnett and little Dix Davis are left to amuse themselves with the kid's toys. Behind the scenes, Grand National awaited the debut of their lady cowboy in movie houses.

Then came the dawn. *Ride 'Em Cowgirl* and *Water Rustlers* were issued to tepid to negative notices, although most downgraded the routine script and direction more than the concept of a lady buckaroo. "This girl Dorothy knows how to act, and she stands a strong chance to go over big with the action fans," praised *The Film Daily*, and the *Independent Exhibitors Film Bulletin* cited Page's "pulchritude" and "pleasing personality."[107] *Variety* was more dismissive: "[The] gag of putting a girl in the lead of an actioner sounds better for exploitation angles than it pans out."[108] With better resources, Page might have had a longer stint in Westerns, as long as her films didn't get too sappy for the fandom.

But by the time *The Singing Cowgirl* debuted at midyear of 1939, Grand National was doomed. Even its Westerns weren't working out: The Baer series failed to materialize, and the entries for Jarrett and "Lonely Cowboy" Fletcher stopped at one.[109] Diege, the director of the three Page Westerns, didn't even make it into the new decade. At age 37, he was the victim of a fatal heart attack in October 1939. His regular job was production manager of the Fine Arts studio, a Grand National production arm. As the year concluded, GN was limited to releasing British titles, and by January 1940, the money-starved company disappeared for good.

At least the "Singing Cowgirl" series spawned one Western star—it just happened to be Dave O'Brien and not Dorothy Page. Page endured worse setbacks than failed Westerns; her second husband, a California attorney and NBC executive, died of a heart attack in 1941 after one year of marriage. Her showbiz career gone, Page spent much of the rest of her life out West—operating, with her third spouse, a ranch in Fresno, California, and owning a 1,700-acre cotton farm in Texas—before succumbing to cancer in Florida at age 57.[110] There have been many strong females in Westerns in the decades since she rode the range, but Page deserves to be remembered as the only starring, and singing, heroine of the classic B Western.

5

Invasion of the Opera Singers, or: End of an Aria

The relationship between motion pictures and traditional opera has long been a tease, highlighted by periodic, awkward attempts of two culturally mismatched art forms—one seen as populist, one as elitist—to cooperate in harmony. For all except those who truly understand the power of opera on the live stage, it's not much of a simplification to claim that the movies have given opera sex, and that opera has given the movies class. But can the outsized personal appeal of operatic performers, singing or not, be adequately captured on the silver screen ... and do movie watchers in Peoria and Podunk really want them up there, despite what they say? History would indicate that those answers have generally been in the negative—but not for lack of trying.

Although opera in general was at its most populist during the Three Tenors phenomenon of the 1990s, in concert settings (halls and even arenas), television, and the recording studio, opera and the movies engaged at their hottest and heaviest in America during the mid- to late 1930s. There were earlier alliances, even some before screen audiences could hear a synchronized note. Historian Paul Fryer has asserted that by 1915, more than 70 operas appeared as silent films.[1] Cecil B. DeMille became enraptured enough with American soprano Geraldine Farrar to make six Paramount films with her, including *Carmen* (1915) and the spare-no-expense *Joan the Woman* (1916), in which the beautiful Farrar portrayed Joan of Arc. Farrar's rival Mary Garden and even the great Enrico Caruso dabbled in pictures as well. Opera-based silent films even were distributed with piano transcripts from opera in a short-lived attempt to convey it artificially. Most of these films were quite popular, as opera and opera performers were then more of a firmament of American culture as now. Their opulent, privileged lives were presented prominently in the mainstream media, and their music was more likely to be heard in the typical American home then as now, especially after the emergence of radio.

When sound came in, Warner Bros. brought back opera in bulk (no pun intended). Requiring talent for its Vitaphone shorts, many of which were being filmed in New York, the studio bought from the Metropolitan Opera the rights to bargain with its artists for screen appearances.[2] This brought a wealth of talent to Vitaphone one-reelers in which the stars duplicated excerpts from their greatest stage performances and/or appeared in no-frills concert settings. These shorts featured such luminaries as Giovanni Martinelli, Ernestine Schumann-Heink, Mary Lewis, Giuseppe DeLuca, Reinald Werrenrath, and Charles Hackett. It was no coincidence that the initial few Vitaphone theatrical programs, including the lid-lifter that preceded screenings of *Don Juan* in 1926, were strongly tied to opera, with solos by Martinelli (a sensational "Vesti la giubba"), Marion Talley ("Caro nome"), and Anna Case ("La Fiesta") in that first presentation alone. These simple films lent prestige that the studios couldn't buy elsewhere, as well as hinterlands exposure that opera might not get otherwise. Between 1926 and 1931, more than 50 operatic Vitaphone shorts were filmed, but as viewers sought snappier music, non-static settings, and semblances of plot, their disappearance went mainly unmourned.

More significant were the appearances in early talking feature films by prominent opera performers, as the operetta became a staple of early sound cinema. The most popular of these singers were two young Americans: Lawrence Tibbett and Grace Moore. Tibbett, a California-born baritone, starred in four films at MGM in 1930–31, the first being *The Rogue Song*, a box-office success that brought him an Academy Award nomination as best actor. Moore, the Met's soprano "Tennessee Nightingale," made two films at Metro—one of which, *New Moon* (1930), based on the show of "Lover, Come Back to Me" fame, co-starred Tibbett. By this time, audiences were already balking at the glut of musical films generally, and when their picture contracts were allowed to lapse, Tibbett, Moore, and their like returned to the stage, concert halls, and radio studios ... but not permanently.

When musicals re-emerged as Hollywood draws, it didn't take long for opera, or operetta, to take part. The catalyst was Grace Moore, or, perhaps more precisely, Harry Cohn. The Columbia studio chief was enamored enough with Moore to sign her for a lofty $25,000 a picture, reduce her sizable temperament (and her weight, which had been on the high side at MGM), and mold her into a real screen star. Cohn did just that in 1934 with a surprise hit, *One Night of Love*, which Richard Barrios has amusingly described as a "mix of Cinderella, Tosca, and Ruby Keeler."[3] Indeed, what housewife in Peoria wouldn't imagine herself in Moore's place as an aspiring American singer romanced abroad by a Italian voice teacher and a Yankee socialite? Along with another 1934 sleeper, *It Happened One Night*, Moore's European vacation lifted Columbia out of the Depression doldrums and nudged it further toward major-studio status. It earned Moore a best actress Oscar nomination and even managed to overshadow MGM's *The Merry Widow*, with its starring queen of operetta, Jeanette MacDonald (who had edged out Moore for the female lead opposite Maurice Chevalier).[4] Like her future screen partner, Nelson Eddy, MacDonald was essentially a film actress with modest operatic credentials. By 1935, MacDonald and Eddy would be united, and their reel classical voices would be challenged by a bevy of real classical tones.

And so they came: Gladys Swarthout, Nino Martini, Lily Pons, James Melton, Helen Jepson, Jan Kiepura, Mary Ellis, Michael Bartlett—and, back again after riding the first musical wave, Marion Talley, Everett Marshall, ... and Lawrence Tibbett. For the most part, these personalities—especially the women—had to be physically different than the typical opera favorites. The photogenic imports, declared a fan magazine, "have made avoirdupois an obsolete charm. Buxom Carmens are no longer tolerated. Audiences laugh at two-hundred-pound Manons, and any Madame Butterfly who cannot fit into a kimono designed for a girlish figure is taboo, no matter how golden her voice."[5]

This kind of talk about the weight of opera stars was frequent, as if somehow we could connect more with them by bringing them down to our level. Portly Paul in Maine or fleshy Flossie in Kansas could feel not so common in the knowledge that, however rich or famous you are, money can't buy you slimness. An example of this cultural obsession was a 1935 Associated Press roundup of weight-loss techniques by grand opera luminaries. Tibbett, the story asserted, "is taking a reducing roller along on his concert tours" and "guards against a 'bay window' by walking on his hands in his ... apartment." Readers ... uh, ate up this kind of stuff. The tenor Nino Martini, it was claimed, "exemplifies the new Hollywood opera chassis. He keeps his lithe lines by saying, 'Spaghetti? No thanks.'"[6] See, Flossie, that's how it's done.

But how to present these singers, weighty or not, on the screen? Viewers abroad were welcoming of opera, but American audiences had an uneasy relationship with the form. Some Yanks were genuine enthusiasts, but many others were more interested in (or tolerable of) exposure to operatic excerpts—the warhorse "greatest hits"—than full-length presentations. Whether or not the disconnect was mainly attributable to foreign-language barriers, opera was something more to be admired than enjoyed—enjoyed more, perhaps, when folks like the Marx Brothers sent it up. Thus, films about the backstage aspect of opera sought to find the proper balance between dialogue and music, and even between opera and pop tunes. Screwball comedy worked for many stars, so why not throw some in? Highbrow types shook their fingers at Hollywood for breaking faith with tradition by putting it in tights—by making Lily Pons into a bird-like "female Tarzan" or daring to show Gladys Swarthout being (fictionally) pelted with tomatoes while singing a famous aria.

Frank Nugent, the stuffy *New York Times* film critic, seemed especially offended by the intent of shaking the movie opera singer "from her pedestal and [bringing] her back to earth," although he was writing in the context of a discussion of the particularly egregious *Hitting a New High*, the above-mentioned (and below-featured) Pons folly. "There seems to be something about a soprano that brings out the worst in a script writer. …," Nugent opined. "Even if accepting it in the spirit of farce, the chances are that Miss Pons will not be able to go backstage at the Metropolitan without stirring a chorus of bird-calls."[7] Moviemakers responded to purists like Nugent by saying, in essence, that *you have no idea*. Boris Morros, who had a ball in both courts as a symphony conductor and an independent film producer, shared the latter sentiment in a wire-service interview:

> What the screen is doing for grand opera is to make it a vital art form to 100,000,000 persons instead of the toy of a handful of dilettantes, who are more concerned with its "society" aspects than its music. Visually, stage opera has always been pretty bad … but, after all, hearing is only one of the senses that we must play up to on the screen. First, we must please the eye.[8]

So, besides finding the best-looking people among opera's best, there was the strength-in-numbers idea: Put more than one opera star in an opera movie. Or bring in a big non-opera name—Cary Grant or, say, Busby Berkeley—for key support. Other pictures put their stars in unusual locales, as fish out of water, to make them seem more relatable. Of course, these highbrow artists, whose off-screen lives often were covered as closely as traditional film stars, did well at making themselves all too human. The movies accentuated their already substantial presences—but as their flawed lives away from the stage showed, they were not much so unlike us.

As much as people aspired to like high-rung entertainment—and wanted to feel the glow of doing so—Hollywood's mid-'30s opera performers didn't excel long, their pay-box returns declined, and the prosaic won out. Pons, Martini, and Ellis made it through three pictures; Bartlett did four films, Moore and Swarthout five, and others weren't half as fortunate. At decade's end, although opera had not disappeared from Hollywood films, it had returned to functioning as a complementary component—the Hollywood-developed MacDonald and Deanna Durbin aside. The operatic interlopers from the East Coast and the great cities of Europe returned home with small dents to their impressive egos, but also with greater exposure (read: bargaining power for future projects) and the knowledge that, in some small way, they had contributed to the democratization of their music.

The titles featured below are a cross-section of mainly less-valued (for reasons fair and unfair) films during this faddish period that showcased operatic figures: one-shot stars, titan couples, and, most conspicuously, pictures that brought their headliners' cinematic careers to screeching halts. Many of these entertainments proved that force of personality or prestige mattered less than the quality of material, no matter how fancy the presentation. They may have prompted their watchers to leave their theaters in dismay, and their stars to run figuratively screaming from Hollywood—preferably at a high C. If this chapter seems like a litany of dreary stories of high-minded folks embarrassing themselves, well, how often are there happy endings in grand opera?

I Live for Love
(Warner Bros.; September 28, 1935)

Director: Busby Berkeley. Producer: Bryan Foy. Story/Screenplay: Jerry Wald, Julius J. Epstein, Robert Hardy Andrews. Photography: George Barnes. Editing: Terry O. Morse. Art Direction: Esdras Hartley. Music Director: Leo F. Forbstein. Costumes: Orry-Kelly. Running Time: 63 minutes.

Cast: Everett Marshall (Roger Kerry aka Owen Jones); Dolores del Rio (Donna Alvarez); Guy Kibbee (George Henderson); Allen Jenkins (Jim "Mac" McNamara); Berton Churchill (Howard Fabian); Hobart Cavanaugh (Townsend C. Morgan); Eddie Conrad, [Al] Shaw and [Sam] Lee (street musicians); Don Alvarado (Rico Cesaro); Mary Treen (Clementine); Robert Greig (dancing nightclub patron); Mike Morita (Toyo); James Farley (stage doorman); Lester Dorr (Fabian aide); Frank Du Frane, Eddie Graham, Edward Morgan, Lottie Williams (actors at audition); Matty Roubert (newsboy); Emmett Vogan (radio announcer).

Songs: "I Live for Love" [Marshall], "I Wanna Play House with You" [Marshall?], "Mine Alone" [Marshall, three times], "Shaving Song" ("A Man Must Shave") [Marshall, Jenkins, Conrad, Shaw and Lee], "Silver Wings" [Marshall] (Mort Dixon, Allie Wrubel); "Oh Marie" [Marshall, Conrad, Shaw and Lee, twice] (Eduardo Di Capua).

Working Title: *Romance in a Glass House.*

Disc: Victor 25164 ("Silver Wings," Everett Marshall).

The Story: Donna Alvarez, the temperamental star of producer Howard Fabian's budding Broadway play, insists that her under-talented beau, Rico Cesaro, be cast as her leading man. To keep Rico away, Fabian plucks a newcomer, Roger Kerry, off the street and insists he already has his male lead. Posing as "Owen Jones," Kerry is derided by Donna during rehearsals as "a street singer trying to be an actor." Dismissed from the play, Roger takes up with a trio of street musicians. Henderson, who owns a soap company, hears Roger and hires him for his radio program, launching him to overnight stardom. Donna is booked to appear on Roger's program and is shocked to realize he and "Jones" are the same man. Donna insists on performing first, but when Roger leads off instead ("I Live for Love"), the two bicker over the air. On the opening night of Donna's latest play, Roger and his press agent, "Mac" McNamara, make a commotion that spoils the show. Smarting over his play's flop, Fabian conspires with his assistant, Morgan, and Henderson and Mac to bring Donna and Roger together, first by convincing Donna to accept an invitation to appear in a series of radio shows with Roger. Their plan takes a different tack after Donna and Roger ("Mine Alone") announce their intention to get married, potentially impairing their public popularity ... and the sales of Henderson's soap.

The second time was no charm for Everett Marshall. The erstwhile Metropolitan Opera regular was launched into pictures with an unsuccessful co-starring role in an RKO musical of 1930. Five years later, having fortified his renown via the Broadway stage and radio airwaves, he was signed by Warner Bros. for a return engagement before the camera. That the

Marshall of 1935 was a better screen actor than before hardly seemed to matter, and despite the directorial hand of Busby Berkeley, *I Live for Love* came and went quickly despite its male lead's sturdy baritone.

A tall, classically handsome, auburn-haired New Englander, Marshall (1900–1965) was trained in Europe with the sponsorship of prominent financier John J. Raskob. He sang secondary baritone roles at the Met through 1931 after debuting there at the unusually young age of 27. Marshall journeyed West in 1930 to appear with Bebe Daniels and the comedy duo of Bert Wheeler and Robert Woolsey in RKO's operetta *Dixiana*. This expensive film reunited Daniels, Wheeler, Woolsey, and comedienne Dorothy Lee from the studio's 1929 hit *Rio Rita*, with Marshall taking over, of sorts, for John Boles. But *Dixiana* was no reprise financially, losing $300,000 at the box office.[9] Worse for Marshall, his stiff performance was widely criticized, especially for his facial grimaces when he let loose in song; even his screen paramour, Daniels, considered him "disastrous" and said "[he] looked dreadful when he sang."[10] In a 1993 interview with this author, Dorothy Lee was only a little kinder:

> They were so mean to Everett Marshall, and that made us [actors] all mad because he was such a nice guy. But ... when he sang, he'd have to expand his lungs and [would] have to have elastic in the back of his vest and all. They had such a terrible time photographing him because he'd make such a face when he'd sing. He was a singer, not an actor. I don't think they did him justice....[11]

Marshall returned to the East, where he honed his skills on pop material on Broadway in *George White's Scandals* of 1931, the *Ziegfeld Follies of 1934*, and the revue *Calling*

Baritone Everett Marshall (left) got a second chance at cinematic renown with *I Live for Love*, with (from right) Don Alvarado, Dolores del Rio, and Allen Jenkins.

All Stars.¹² He also found substantial success on the radio as the classy host of the CBS *Broadway Varieties* show. It was this public acceptance, and not so much his operatic rep, that prompted WB to give Marshall a second chance at film. He was signed in early 1935 to co-star in a backstage musical comedy about bickering performers-turned-lovers called *Romance in a Glass House*, the title of which was changed near the end of filming in July to *I Live for Love*. Billed just behind Marshall was Dolores del Rio (1905–1983), the beautiful Mexican-born star who was, by now, underused by her home studio.¹³ Thanks to the artistry of cinematographer George Barnes and costumer Orry-Kelly, del Rio was displayed in soft-focus photography and an array of gowns that emphasized her beauty and made viewers not care that she was not singing so much as one note.

There seemed to be other issues with *I Live for Love*. Despite the presence of Berkeley—the most famous dance director around—this was a musical with nary a true dance number. Even before its release, there were indications of trouble. In late July, Warner Bros. let it slip that it was "predicting 'big things' for Everett Marshall after viewing the rushes."¹⁴ So, then, why did the studio, in early August, bring in director William McGann to supervise what *Variety* reported were "several days" of retakes?¹⁵ By the time *I Live for Love* opened in September, Berkeley was too seriously distracted to celebrate. He had been involved early that month in an auto accident that resulted in the deaths of three people; the director was tried for second-degree murder but would be acquitted in a third trial after the first two ended in hung juries.

The result was a routine *Taming of the Shrew* variation in which a South American actress (del Rio, overacting a bit) falls for the radio singer/would-be stage co-star she initially detests. Marshall, now much more at ease before the camera and reducing his funny singing faces, supplies straight-ahead, no-frills vocalizing that shows why he was such a class act on radio. But the script—by Jerry Wald, Julius J. Epstein, and Robert Hardy Andrews—is thoroughly predictable, and the pop songs—by Mort Dixon and Allie Wrubel—leave no impression.¹⁶ ("Mine Alone" is the best.) Even the comic relief supplied by vaudevillians Eddie Conrad and the team of Shaw and Lee doesn't add much. That threesome joins Marshall in a so-so novelty number, "A Man Must Shave," in which their more-silly-than-clever romping inside a hotel suite is the closest the film comes to requiring choreography. Besides Marshall's voice, the film's only other benefit is the snappy pace of a typical WB programmer, which brings it in at a compact 63 minutes.

The New York Times rightfully lauded Marshall's "lusty baritone ... and engaging personality," and *I Live for Love* earned more than a few approving, if not glowing, reviews.¹⁷ The theatergoing public did not respond in kind. According to *Motion Picture Herald*'s weekly surveys of theater managers, *I Live for Love* was dead on arrival. "I wanted to hide myself for a week after playing this one," wrote a house manager from Virginia.¹⁸ "One of those pictures that brings tears to the eyes ... of the exhibitor," reported someone from Kansas.¹⁹ A theater man from Indiana made sport of the title: "They need not have lived; they should have passed out and I and the audience would join the mourners and throw the last handful of sand on the grave."²⁰

Even as *I Live for Love* was in release, Marshall was hinting—in a mini-editorial published under his name in a trade newspaper—at reasons for his film failing:

> ...Motion picture executives certainly could improve on the type of script that is being given operatic singers. The stories ... are too light and frothy—the fact that the name of a Metropolitan star is flashed from the marquee is enough, the producers feel, to insure the patronage of the more serious audience.²¹

With a reaction such as that, it was no surprise that Marshall endured another one-and-done in the movies. No matter: He had plenty to do, and not just on the radio. In 1936, he appeared in Billy Rose's inaugural *Casa Manana* revue in Texas with bandleader Paul Whiteman, "bubble dancer" Sally Rand, and others. In 1939, amid a much-publicized divorce and child-custody battle with his first wife, he declared bankruptcy, then attempted to incorporate his voice in an attempt, his first spouse claimed, to avoid alimony payments.[22] A year later, he was back as the front man for an elaborate touring revue, *Stars Over Broadway*, billed in ads as "the Barnum & Bailey of all stage revues" and featuring "70 artists including 48 girls," among them Edna Strong, a dancer who was Marshall's second wife.[23] Marshall toured for years in mainstay operettas such as *The Student Prince* and *Blossom Time* and he pleased grateful audiences with favorite songs such as "The Night Is Young."

In 1949, the *Philadelphia Inquirer* caught up with the singer, a bit heavier in the waist but none the worse for wear, while on the road in his beloved role as Dr. Engel in *The Student Prince*. Marshall said he enjoyed bringing culture to the hinterlands: "The people have been treated to so many horror plays and 'hopeless' dramas in recent years, it is a joy giving them a fairy tale packed with reality. This play is just as appropriate today as it was a quarter of a century ago."[24]

Marshall was in Carmel-by-the-Sea, California, when he died in 1965. His demise, from a heart attack, went mainly unnoticed by obit writers. But whenever TCM brings *I Live for Love* or *Dixiana* out of the vaults, listeners can hear this trouper's golden tones again ... even if they merely tolerate him as an actor.

Here's to Romance
(Fox; October 4, 1935)

Director: Alfred E. Green. Producer: Jesse L. Lasky. Screenplay: Ernest Pascal, Arthur Richman. Story: Sonya Levien, Ernest Pascal. Photography: L. William O'Connell. Editing: Irene Morra. Art Direction: Max Parker. Music Director: Louis De Francesco. Ballets Produced By: Maria Gambarelli. Technical Advisor: Reginald LeBorg. Sound: Alfred Bruzlin. Costumes: René Hubert. Assistant Director: Jasper Blystone. Running Time: 86 minutes.

Cast: Nino Martini (Nino Donelli); Genevieve Tobin (Kathleen Gerard); Anita Louise (Lydia Lubov); Maria Gambarelli (Rosa); Mme. Ernestine Schumann-Heink (Mme. Schumann-Heink); Reginald Denny (Emery Gerard); Vicente Escudero (Spanish gypsy dancer); Adrian Rosley (Sandoval); Mathilde Comont (Viola); Elsa Buchanan (Enid); Miles Mander (Bert); Keye Luke (Saito); Pat Somerset (Fred); Albert Conti (Lefevre); Egon Brecher (Descartes); Orrin Burke (Carstairs); Armand Kaliz (Andriot); Leonard Carey (butler); Rudolph Amendt (violinist); Wilson Millar (piccolo player); Paul Portanova (guitarist); Carmita (Spanish dancer); Andre Cheron (café manager); Charles Locher [Jon Hall] (chauffeur); George Regas (Rosa's husband); Marcelle Corday (concierge); Maurice Brierre (waiter); Zaruhi Elmassian (singer); Jean De Briac (maître d'); Jacques Vanaire (maître d'); Alice Ardell (maid); Landers Stevens (stage manager); Edward McWade (stage doorman); Miguel Sandoval (orchestra leader); Stanley Andrews (father); Grace Goodall (mother); Charles Fallon (vendor); Jack Mulhall (secretary); Esther Muir (piano player).

Musical Selections: "Here's to Romance" [Martini; reprised as dance by Louise, chorus, then sung by Martini], "Midnight in Paris" [Martini, danced by Louise; reprised as dance by Escudero, Carmita] (Herb Magidson, Con Conrad); "Mattinata" [Martini], "Vesti la giubba" (from *I Pagliacci*) [Martini] (Ruggero Leoncavallo); "Delusione" [Martini] (Miguel Sandoval); "Il Principe de Firenze Serenade" [Martini] (Miguel Sandoval, Louis E. De Francesco); "E lucevan le stelle" (from *Tosca*) [Martini] (Giuseppe Giacosa, Luigi Illica, Giacomo Puccini); "The Hunkadola" [Martini] (Jack Yellen, Cliff Friend, Joseph Meyer); "I Carry You in My Pocket" [Martini] (Ralph L. Grosvenor); "Le rêve de des Grieux" (from *Manon*) [Martini] (Henri Meilhac, Philippe Gille, Jules Massenet); "Siciliana" (from

Cavalleria Rusticana) [Martini] (Guido Menasci, Giovanni Targioni-Tozzetti, Pietro Mascagni); "Le cygnet" ("The Swan," from *The Carnival of the Animals*) [danced by Gambarelli] (Camille Saint-Saëns); "Wiegenlied" ("Cradle Song") [Schumann-Heink] (Johannes Brahms).
Working Title: *Melody of Life.*
Home Video: 20th Century–Fox DVD.

The Story: Vying to make each other jealous, wealthy New York music patrons Kathleen and Emery Gerard encourage the careers of promising artists—she in tenor Nino Donelli and he in ballerina Rosa—by offering to send them to Paris to study for six months. Nino is encouraged by his voice teacher, Mme. Schumann-Heink, who believes no expense should be spared to promote him. In Paris, Nino falls in love with young ballerina Lydia Lubov ("Mattinata"). Emery discovers that Rosa is married and turns his attentions to Lydia. Lydia makes Nino promise he will reject Kathleen's help and instead build his career conventionally in the provinces. Kathleen schemes to secretly fund Nino's debut in Paris by paying his salary and buying out the house, but an upset Nino falters in his opening performance in "Cavalleria Rusticana" after he learns what Kathleen has done. Emery invites Lydia to come to America to perform, but she declines because she loves Nino. Nino goes to New York City, where he is reduced to singing "The Hunkadola" at the sheet music counter of a 5-and-10-cent store. Kathleen goes to Mme. Schumann-Heink for help in reviving Nino's fortunes. Lydia, touring in America on Emery's dime, arranges for producer Carstairs to hear Nino sing; from the store counter, the tenor passes his audition with an impassioned "Vesti la giubba." Nino ultimately triumphs in his "real" debut in "Tosca."

The Hollywood opera trend flowered too late on screen for some of the form's most revered figures. One of them was Ernestine Schumann-Heink, the German-Bohemian contralto whose brief but memorable performance in her only feature film, *Here's to Romance* (1935), hinted at a new direction in her career. Audiences stood and applauded when she was heard on the screen, and many reviewers praised her work in the movie as much or more as that of its star, the Italian tenor Nino Martini. Schumann-Heink was even discussed as a potential new film star amid a field of neophytes who were younger, slimmer, and flashier. Her cinematic services even became a bone of contention between two companies who took their fight all the way to the Hays Office. Not bad for a dame of 74.

Stout, graying, and grandmotherly, Schumann-Heink was already one of the most respected women in the world. She had worked tirelessly to entertain troops and raise money to help wounded Great War veterans (two of her seven children fought on opposite sides in that conflict). Although she was no beauty, she had great charisma and, despite her star status, a down-to-earth quality. She was pleasantly old-fashioned to her fans, and she was even known to include in one of her frequent concerts a curtain chat about her home life. For more than 20 years, there had been rumors that she would star in a picture; that one had not happened may have been for lack of popular demand for the Wagnerian characters that had brought the prima donna her greatest fame. Once sound arrived, in 1926–27, Schumann-Heink was captured for the first time on screen, singing high- and middle-brow numbers, from Schubert to "Danny Boy," in three of the initial batch of New York-shot Vitaphones. Her compensation was reported to be $3,500 per short—not Jolson or Jessel money, nor even the $4,500 given her operatic contemporary Giovanni Martinelli for singing "Vesti la giubba" in his sound debut, but nice coin by Vita standards.

The inertly filmed opera shorts ran their course quickly, and Schumann-Heink resumed central singing duties with the Metropolitan Opera Company and in recitals on the radio, where she made a Christmas tradition of performing "Silent Night" in both English and German and for a time earned her own regular NBC show. In mid–1930, there was talk that Elsie Janis, another adored music figure, was pushing Paramount to sign Schumann-Heink, and that Mary Pickford was similarly advocating for the singer.[25] By this time, however, musicals were temporarily going out of favor in the film capital, and the great lady would have to wait five more years before her acting bow.

The opportunity came through the efforts of one of Paramount's founders, Jesse L. Lasky, who in 1935 was producing on his own for Fox release in a cushy $3,000-per-week deal for six pictures a year. Lasky was a longtime opera enthusiast who had brought Geraldine Farrar and Enrico Caruso into films way back when. But he was preparing *Here's to Romance* without a star until he found one in a not-so-familiar tenor heard one night over the producer's car radio. Lasky should have known whom he was hearing: He had brought Martini to Paramount for an unsuccessful stint at the dawn of the '30s before the latter became a leading artist at the Met in New York. The producer called Martini's manager and was politely rebuffed with the excuse that the singer had a concert tour approaching. "I asked the manager to give Martini my kind regards and hung up," Lasky wrote in his autobiography. "[But] within an hour, the singer called back and said, 'Mr. Lasky, it is so good of you to come to me. If you think you can use me, I will be ready.'"[26] Lasky's intent was to star Martini in multiple pictures, but it was his mistake to connect with Schumann-Heink (1861–1936) for just this one.

One of the final Fox productions before the studio's merger with 20th Century Pic-

Legendary contralto Ernestine Schumann-Heink (left) appeared with Genevieve Tobin in her only feature, *Here's to Romance*, and was envisioned as another Marie Dressler: a grande dame with a flair for comedy.

tures, *Here's to Romance* ranks on the plus side among opera movies, despite the short, slender Martini's lack of sex appeal and knack for goofy grins that play better in the comedy scenes than the serious stuff. With a lesser screen ego than, say, Jan Kiepura, Martini goes down easy when he's not dazzling the audience in song. His rise-to-fame tale—a trek from disgrace in Paris to triumph in New York—offers few surprises, but the choice of music is astute, and reviewers of the time particularly liked Martini's delivery of the impassioned "Vesti" from *I Pagliacci*. This emotional peak comes at a point when the main character, who seemingly has blown his chance at success, is reduced to singing at the sheet music counter of a department store.[27]

Martini (1905–1976) is also heard in excerpts from *Tosca, Cavalleria Rusticana* and *Manon*, but it's not all about opera, as he adds "I Carry You in My Pocket," a recent radio hit of the tenor's, plus a couple of tunes written for the film by Herb Magidson and Con Conrad. Hollywood non-singing vets Reginald Denny and Genevieve Tobin are welcome sights as bickering society marrieds. She's Martini's amorous patron, and he's a dilettante whose claim to talent recognition is his incessant boast that "my father brought the great Pavlova to America." There is also musical novelty in the appearances of Italian ballerina Maria Gambarelli (both in her own part and as a dance double for ingénue Anita Louise) and Spanish flamenco dancer Vicente Escudero (in his film debut). Reactions were mixed. "Good for the classes, but only fair for the masses" was the succinct reaction from exhibitor-minded *Harrison's Reports*.[28] Written for readers from "the classes," the *New York Times* review was a bit too tough in dismissing *Here's to Romance* as "a dull entertainment which inspires fitfully between its high moments of song."[29]

But there was no disagreement over the quality of Schumann-Heink's work—even if she had to do little more than impersonate herself, and make herself understood despite her heavy accent, for a mere 8½ minutes of screen time. Using her real surname in portraying Martini's affectionately cranky, demanding voice teacher/press agent, she delightfully exhorts her pupil in the film's first reel that "an artist should care if a phone is ringing! ... A singer is good for nothing if the world don't [sic] hear him, and it is the duty of the singer that the world hears him—no matter whose money he spends!" Schumann-Heink's major highlight is not in dialogue, but in a touching rendition of Brahms' Lullaby, and although her presence by the end is reduced to reaction shots at Martini's ultimate performance of *Tosca*, she was not so easily set aside by viewers. Noting audience enthusiasm during preview screenings, *The Film Daily* noted that she "comes through with flying honors as an actress.... Fans will want more of her whimsical mannerisms."[30]

Lasky thought, or said he thought, that he had Schumann-Heink secured for future employment. In August 1935, with *Here's to Romance* in the can and awaiting release, he announced a partnership with Mary Pickford for three films a year through United Artists, with Schumann-Heink, Martini, and Francis Lederer on the acting roster. Lasky talked of Schumann-Heink becoming the next Marie Dressler, a grande dame with a flair for comedy. This came at a time when demand for opera-related movies was at a peak. Paramount, for example, was scrambling to find sufficient story material for what the trades called its "four canaries"—Gladys Swarthout, Mary Ellis, Helen Jepson, and the Austrian soprano Grete Natzler (the last two spent nary a minute in a film for that studio). And when *Here's to Romance* opened in October, one Hollywood correspondent for a big-city daily chanced to state that Schumann-Heink ranked with Eleanor Powell and Wini Shaw as three of the few examples of "startlingly new women prospects" for film stardom.[31]

Too bad for Lasky, because MGM—the studio that had lost Dressler with her death in 1934—had its own designs on Schumann-Heink. While Lasky was taking a train East to New York to put his deal with the singer in writing, an agent for MGM swooped in via air, got to her first and forged a three-year, $75,000-per-picture agreement. Lasky was incensed enough to cite a somewhat weak gentleman's agreement among producers against star-raiding, such as this was, and he took his protest to picture czar Will Hays. Contacted for an interview, Schumann-Heink reacted to the furor with her customary modesty: "It is very comic, ja. This quarreling among the motion-picture men who call me terrific, colossal and gigantic, I think I don't like that 'gigantic' very much, hah?"[32] The final ruling—headlined by *Variety* in its usual ideo-creative style ("Schumann-Heink to Square Lasky Wail")—was that the diva belonged to MGM but that she would be loaned to Lasky for one picture during the coming year.[33]

Sadly, neither Metro nor Lasky-Pickford would be able to exploit their "new" talent. MGM put Schumann-Heink through the publicity paces, photographing her with its kiddie star Freddie Bartholomew upon her anticipated arrival to the Coast, but dilly-dallied on script after announcing her for a musical to co-star Frances Langford, Harry Stockwell, and/or May Robson. Lasky wanted to put Schumann-Heink in a film based on her own life, but in the meantime, he had Martini star in two more pictures, *The Gay Desperado* (UA 1936) and *Music for Madame** (RKO 1937), to diminishing returns. In a story for *Photoplay*, the journalist Adele Rogers St. Johns bristled at the lack of consideration for the great lady as "the silliest mistake of the Hollywood season—the most sightless maneuver they have ever made for this woman."[34]

Mortality intervened before that mistake could be rectified, and on November 17, 1936, Schumann-Heink died of leukemia at her Los Angeles home. Whether she could have been a Dressler-level star or a Maria Ouspenskaya–type support player, her loss marked a missed opportunity, but at least we have 8½ minutes (or so) of her to cherish in *Here's to Romance*. As Lasky wrote in his memoirs: "She was the most spiritual, courageous, wonderful character I've ever met in show business.... I thought I had discovered a new film personality of the caliber of Marie Dressler, and with a celestial voice besides."[35]

Give Us This Night
(Paramount; March 8, 1936)

Director: Alexander Hall. Producer: William LeBaron. Executive Producer: Henry Herzbrun. Screenplay: Edwin Justus Mayer, Lynn Starling. Story: Jacques Bachrach. Photography: Victor Milner. Editing: Ellsworth Hoagland. Art Direction: Hans Dreier, Roland Anderson. Music Director: Erich Wolfgang Korngold. Costumes: Travis Banton. Set Decoration: A.E. Freudman. Sound: Harry Lindgren, John Cope. Special Photographic Effects: Gordon Jennings. Assistant Director: James Hogan. Running Time: 71 minutes.

Cast: Jan Kiepura (Antonio Belizza); Gladys Swarthout (Maria Severelli); Philip Merivale (Marcello Bonetti); Benny Baker (Tomasso); Alan Mowbray (Forcellini); Michelette Burani (Francesca); Sidney Toler (first carabiniere); Charles Judels (second carabiniere); William Collier, Sr. (priest); John Miltern (Vincente); Mattie Edwards (Elena); Chloe Douglas (Lucrezia); Maurice Cass (Guido); Franklin Pangborn (Forcellini's valet); Nick Thompson, Robert E. Milasch, Monte Carter, Constantine Romanoff, Sam Appel, Jack Raymond, Roger Joseph, Charles Stevens, Hank Mann, John Picorri, Jerry Mandy (fishermen); Jack Burdette, Harry Semels, Jules Cowles, Sidney D'Albrook, James Aubrey, Billy Franey (prisoners); Billy Gilbert (leader of claque); Frank Hall Crane (stage door man); Gaston Glass (usher); Frank Mayo (man); Frances Morris (woman); Allen Rogers (singing voice for Alan Mowbray).

Music: "Fisherman Song" [Kiepura, chorus], "I Mean to Say I Love You" [Kiepura, reprised by Swarthout], "Music in the Night (and Laughter in the Air)" [Swarthout, chorus], "My Love and I" [Kiepura, reprised twice by Kiepura, Swarthout], "Processional (Lift Up Your Voices/Religioso)" [Swarthout, Kiepura, chorus], "Softly Through the Heart of Night" (*Romeo and Juliet* Garden Scene) [Swarthout,

5. Invasion of the Opera Singers, or: End of an Aria

Rogers, reprised by Kiepura], "Sorrento Song" [Kiepura, reprised by him as "Morning Song in Naples"], "Sweet Melody of Night" [Kiepura, reprised by Swarthout, Rogers, Kiepura] (Oscar Hammerstein II, Erich Wolfgang Korngold); "Di quella pira" (from *Il Trovatore*) [Kiepura, chorus] (Giuseppe Verdi). Working Title: *Song of the Nile*.

The Story: Maria Severelli, ward and protégé of composer-conductor Marcello Bonetti, prepares to sing the leading female role in Bonetti's new "Romeo and Juliet" opera in Naples. She dislikes her intended co-star, the egotistical tenor Forcellini, who is pelted with eggs during a performance of "Il Trovatore" by opera-loving fisherman Antonio Belizza and his friend Tomasso. While attending church in Sorrento, Maria hears Antonio's impressive tenor ("Lift Up Your Voices") and encourages Bonetti and the show's producer, Vincente, to hire him in place of Forcellini. During rehearsals in Naples, Antonio enlists the help of Tomasso to learn the part of Romeo, but the homesick new actor feels uncertain on stage and Maria must coax him back to the production. Antonio falls in love with Maria ("My Love and I"), but he holds off on announcing their engagement because Bonetti confides in Antonio his own intent to ask for Maria's hand ("I Mean to Say I Love You"). Wracked with guilt, Antonio returns home and is hastily replaced by a drunken Forcellini. With help from his mother, who has so far discouraged her son's new career, Antonio has a change of plan, which involves upending Forcellini and recapturing Maria ("Sweet Melody of Night") during opening night of "Romeo and Juliet."

Not since Lawrence Tibbett and Grace Moore in *New Moon* was there such a heralded Hollywood pairing from grand opera as Jan Kiepura and Gladys Swarthout in *Give Us This Night*. However, through studio design or personal ego, theirs was an unequal partnership, with the stronger of the two personalities—and the louder of their two voices—far overshadowing the other. Despite quality contributors seen and unseen, this modestly plotted operetta generated as much off-screen drama as on, and enough of the public stayed away that some snobs in the press suggested that it should have been called "Give Us Something Else."

Paramount producer William LeBaron must have considered it a coup to land Kiepura (1902–1966), the Polish tenor making his American film debut, and Swarthout (1900–1969), the Kansas-born mezzo-soprano. Both were already well known here, she for her Met appearances (dating from 1929) and prolific radio schedule and he for European-made movies such as *Be Mine Tonight* (1932) and *My Heart Calls You* (1934) as well as ample stage work. She, as an American celebrity, was more of a fan favorite on these shores; he, acclaimed as "the Polish Caruso," was the bigger name worldwide. However, theirs was a teaming of opposites in personality, which was emphasized in how the

Polish tenor Jan Kiepura proved hard to handle away from the camera in his American film debut, *Give Us This Night*.

two were portrayed in the press. Stories about Swarthout concentrated on her cheerful disposition, her un-diva-like slim figure (and how she kept it that way), and her happy marriage (to singer Frank Chapman). In one interview, she modestly claimed she "never was a prima donna and never will be."[36] She was allowed to test her acting muscles with her first feature film, playing opposite John Boles as a Mexican miss who dresses as a female Zorro type in Paramount's *Rose of the Rancho*. It was finishing production just as *Give Us This Night* was starting up in October 1935.

The volatile Kiepura, on the other hand, seemed to earn every check mark on the list of opera-star stereotypes of self-importance, conceit, and general unpredictability. A former law student in his home country, he had a quick mind and business savvy to go with his golden tenor and unrelenting confidence. His contract with Paramount, which earned him more than $100,000 for *Give Us This Night*, allowed him much say into the content of his Hollywood debut, and he balked at the story of a lightweight tale of a lowly Italian fisherman who gets his big chance at fame. When Bing Crosby showed up in the recording studio to watch him, Kiepura demanded that the crooner douse his pipe. (Ah, to be a fly on *that* wall!) Not only did he not want any smoking on his set—a tall order for 1935—Kiepura also declared that he would not begin work before 10 a.m. on any morning. ("Studio hopes to change this habit," *Variety* dryly reported.)[37] To protect his pipes, he decided he would not talk to anyone for two hours before or after singing, which left director Alexander Hall and other crucial *Give Us This Night* personnel to be signaled by their leading man through smiles, nods, head shaking, gestures to the throat, and other sign language.[38] Swarthout was happily married and seemed more than willing to open up about it, but Kiepura couldn't be talked into revealing his marital relationship with Hungarian actress-singer Marta Eggerth.

Worst of his insecurities was Kiepura's insistence that he be the only singer in the picture, a declaration that led to production delays of several days and must have insulted his diplomatic co-star. Oscar Hammerstein II, the immortal librettist and lyricist who co-wrote the songs in *Give Us This Night*, was dispatched (uncredited) to beef up Swarthout's part but threw up his hands as the script was revised by multiple hands. "The book is getting worse every week," music director Erich Wolfgang Korngold told his wife. "By the time we start shooting, it will be unusable."[39] With Swarthout disinclined to depart—which Paramount wasn't going to allow to happen anyway, even as Kiepura refused to sing any duets—Kiepura declared he would simply sing louder than she. He could ... and did.

"Kiepura was always singing," sniped movie columnist Sidney Skolsky, who was not above exaggeration in his reporting, but whose accounts in this case of reverse snobbery matched most others.

> He would sing in his dressing room. He would sing while walking to the set. He would visit another performer's dressing room and sing.... Kiepura had the right to okay the singing takes.... He would sit in the projection room and applaud after the numbers. When someone else was on the screen, Kiepura would lean back in his chair and yawn.[40]

Whatever Paramount's attitude toward Kiepura's behavior, it could not have been accused of stinting on songster talent for *Give Us This Night*. Hammerstein's collaborator was the great Korngold, whose compositions for this was his first for the movies in America. Korngold had been brought to the United States from his native Austria to arrange Felix Mendelssohn's incidental music for director Max Reinhardt's screen version of *A Midsummer Night's Dream* at Warners. Korngold's film career would become established with his symphonic score for WB's *Captain Blood* later in '35, and when Korngold wasn't working on

Give Us This Night, he was spending evenings composing the music for the WB adventure that made Errol Flynn a star.

Kiepura had sung Korngold's works on the operetta stage in Europe, and the Korngold-Hammerstein team wrote for *Give Us This Night* what was promoted as the first original opera sequence created for film. Based on *Romeo and Juliet*, it was not the Gounod classic, but a new work. Paramount also spent a not-inconsiderable $30,000 on location shooting at Laguna Beach, southeast of Los Angeles, to stand in for the hero's Italian fishing village. The studio also beefed up the cast by including the distinguished British stage actor Philip Merivale to portray Swarthout's mentor (and would-be mate), and the positive publicity he garnered for his sound-film debut offset the bad press on Kiepura.

Still, audiences—and most reviewers—were not impressed upon the film's debut in March 1936. Exhibitor's friend *Harrison's Reports* declared *Give Us This Night* "not for mass consumption because it lacks glamorous romantic appeal, and has little comedy."[41] "Stilted and slow entertainment" was the verdict of *Variety*, which like many others derided a weak story.[42] Indeed, funnymen Alan Mowbray and Benny Baker don't make much of an impact, and Swarthout gets only one full-length number by herself. The lack of vocalizing by the female lead was not lost of Frank Nugent, the critic at *The New York Times*:

> Miss Swarthout probably found it easier to gaze rapidly at Mr. Kiepura's quivering tonsils than to admire Mr. Boles's [in *Rose of the Rancho*], but the process seems extravagantly wasteful. Almost any wide-eyed ingénue can register admiration of a tenor; it should not be necessary to hire an operatic mezzo for the job.[43]

Although he has one hell of a tenor voice to admire, Kiepura has limited he-man appeal, he's not very believable as a fisherman, and his Polish accent doesn't mesh well with the film's Italian setting. The leads have no mutual sizzle, in or out of melodic mode. For example, in a touching church processional meant to take place during Mass as the main characters meet, Swarthout and then Kiepura trade solos more in competition than revelation. Only on "My Love and I," the big show-within-a-show number, are their voices allowed to blend, and guess who clearly sings louder? *Give Us This Night* holds great appeal for opera diehards, especially today for those who have been able to see it, but it was niche entertainment even when it was new.

Give Us This Night also came up short in overseas support, a bad sign for a movie needing business in opera-friendly Europe. It was banned in Germany because of Korngold's Jewish heritage, and Italy threatened to withhold it because of its alleged Italian stereotypes, then relented on a threat to ban all Paramount product. No wonder *Variety* called the picture "a round-the-world headache."[44] Kiepura returned to Europe, and *Give Us This Night* was his only Hollywood credit. His co-star lacked overseas options, and *Give Us This Night* hadn't even been released before critics roasted Swarthout's *Rose of the Rancho*. Paramount balked at a third film for Swarthout before putting her in two middling musicals, *Champagne Waltz* (1937) [q.v.] and *Romance in the Dark* (1938, with John Boles again). She might have received a lift when, at one point, she was linked to what became *The Great Victor Herbert* [q.v.], but Paramount produced it in 1939 with Mary Martin as the female lead.

Instead, Swarthout completed her Paramount contract—and her movie career—in 1939 with *Ambush*, a crime thriller in which she did not sing a note. What greater dishonor could come to a singer of grand opera?

Fatal Lady
(Walter Wanger/Paramount; May 15, 1936)

Director: Edward Ludwig. Producer: Walter Wanger. Screenplay: Samuel Ornitz, Horace McCoy. Story: Harry Segall. Adaptation: William R. Lipman. Additional Dialogue: Tiffany Thayer. Photography: Leon Shamroy. Editing: Ernest Nims. Art Direction: Alexander Tolubofi. Set Direction: Howard Bristol. Musical Direction: Boris Morros. Operatic Numbers Staged By: Boris Petroff. Sound: William Fox. Costumes: Helen Taylor. Running Time: 72 minutes.

Cast: Mary Ellis (Marian Stuart/Maria Delasano/Malevo); Walter Pidgeon (David Roberts); John Halliday (Martan Fontes); Ruth Donnelly (Melba York); Alan Mowbray (Uberto Malla); Guy Bates Post (Feodor Glinka); Samuel S. Hinds (Guili Ruffano); Norman Foster (Philip Roberts); Edgar Kennedy (Rudolf Hochstetter); Frank Puglia (Felipe); Jean Rouverol (Anita); Irene Franklin (Russian countess); Mitchell Lewis (magistrate); Edward Van Sloan (French police official); Russell Hicks (opera house manager); Ward Bond (American stage manager); George Davis, Don Brodie (French waiters); Albert Conti (head waiter); Fred Vess, Peaches O'Neil, Eldon Jones (adagio team); Armand and Diana (dancers); Marshall Sohl (tenor); Harry Depp, Frank Hammond, Lucille Ward, Fern Emmett (American tourists); Robert Graves (French guide); Maurice Brierre (chauffeur); Russ Bell, Harry Oliver (cab drivers); Tudor Williams (grand duke); William Gilbert (major domo); Charles Fallon (impresario); Maurice Cass (prompter); Mario Dominici (stage manager); Lucio Villegas, Paul Ellis, Carlos San Martin, Enrique Acosta, Eva Dennison, Isabel LaMal (Paris café guests); William Pawley, Robert du Couedic, Eugene Borden, William B. Davidson (detectives); Frederic Roland (Anita's father); Laura Treadwell (Anita's mother); Jerry Mandy (proprietor); Mariska Aldrich, Virginia Ainsworth, Rosa Caprino, D'Arcy Corrigan, Catherine Courtney, Anna Demetrio, Antonio Filauri, Gaston Glass, Virginia Lee, Jacques Lory, Nina Matleva, Alex Melesh, Maria Melesh, Consuela Moreno, Manuel Paris, H.O. Perline, Maximo Pilo, Russ Powell, Elizabeth Rudnicki, Hector Sarno, Minerva Sherwood, Phil Sleeman, Genaro Spagnoli, Arturo Turich, Nina Visaroff, Marie Wells (Brazilian opera troupe).

Musical Selections: "Bal Masque" [Ellis, company, twice] (Leo Robin, Max Terr, Sam Coslow, Victor Young, Gerard Carbonara); "Isabelle" [Ellis, company] (Leo Robin, Max Terr, David Ormoni, Gerard Carbonara); "Je Vous Adore" [Ellis] (Sam Coslow, Victor Young); Overture from *William Tell* [Ellis, Sohl, company] (Gioachino Rossini).

Working Title: *Brazen*.

The Story: On the eve of her debut as an opera singer in New York, Marian Stuart is questioned by police after the death of a male acquaintance, and the performance is canceled when her nerves make her unable to sing. She travels to Brazil, where she changes her professional name to Maria Delasano and rebuilds her confidence under the direction of maestro Feodor Glinka, who urges her to forsake all for her career. Marian is courted by Philip Roberts, whose marriage proposals she turns down; Uberto Malla, a wealthy patron; and Martan Fontes, a Brazilian impresario. Philip's brother David, who runs a successful coffee company, is suspicious of Marian and encourages Philip to marry someone else. After Malla is murdered, Marian is believed responsible. She moves to Paris to sing in a café under the name Malevo, known as "the woman who is fatal to love." Marian urges Philip to return to Brazil as David and Martan re-enter her life, but the younger Roberts is found dead. David, who may or may not be falling for Marian, proposes they team up to find the real killer as Marian is booked for a comeback engagement at the Paris Opera.

In mid–1936, *Fatal Lady* could have been a description of the cinematic standing of its star, Mary Ellis, as well as the title of her third—and final—Hollywood musical. Perhaps it shouldn't have turned out that way for Ellis, an intelligent, attractive, versatile "singing actress" from the stages of New York and London who was now cast as someone whose mere presence brings misfortune to those around her. Ellis was a favorite of such formidables as Noël Coward, Ivor Novello, and Jerome Kern; sang at the Met with Enrico Caruso; originated the title role in the beloved operetta *Rose-Marie*; acted well into her 90s; and lived to be 105. She was acclaimed for her work in grand opera, light opera, musical com-

5. Invasion of the Opera Singers, or: End of an Aria

edy, and even Shakespeare. So if you want to cry for her, you need tear up only for the 70-minutes-and-change of *Fatal Lady*, a preposterous Paramount musical murder mystery in which Ellis' character (if not the actress herself) turns out not to be so bad after all.

Born in New York City of German-French parentage, Ellis (1897–2003) was a dark-haired beauty who introduced her stage name in 1918 at the outset of a three-season stint at the Metropolitan Opera, mainly in minor roles. But she proved she could act as well as sing, and the impresario David Belasco prevailed upon her to widen her scope by playing Nerissa in his 1922 Broadway staging of *The Merchant of Venice*. Her triumph in *Rose-Marie* came two years later. Still, Ellis wanted to do heavier fare, and she broke her contract for the Rudolf Friml operetta to satisfy that yen. In 1930, she and her husband, actor Basil Sydney, moved to London, where she became a bigger star than ever, mainly in comedy and drama but also by singing in Kern and Oscar Hammerstein's hit musical *Music in the Air*. Later in the '30s, she co-starred with Novello in a series of musical-stage romances, but before those came, she took a stab at the movies. Ellis began her film career with a non-musical British melodrama, *Bella Donna* (1934), then answered a call from Paramount to return to the nation of her birth—and to exercise her soprano.

Immediately, Ellis was promoted as a "woman of mystery," not just because of her reluctance to talk to interviewers about her private life (Sydney was husband number three) but for her insistence that, despite what her studio might have wanted, she wasn't just another Grace Moore clone. A wire-service reporter chatted with Ellis before the release of her first Hollywood picture and noted her desire to be known as a singing actress rather than

The sizable abilities of English singer Mary Ellis weren't enough to distinguish her final U.S. movie, Paramount's *Fatal Lady* (with Alan Mowbray).

an opera singer. "I never did want opera as a career," Ellis was quoted as saying. "I took it up as a ruse to get on the legitimate stage."[45] (Some work for that ruse!) Not surprisingly, a fan magazine headlined a 1935 Ellis feature story "Tornado in Leash," the implication of intensity being clear despite the mixed metaphors of the title. "In the theater and in the studio, Miss Ellis frequently terrifies people," the story read. "Many of them will break down and admit that they have never seen her fly into a rage, but they are not taking any chances on unleashing that dynamic energy. Somehow the impression is abroad that the Ellis temper is not one to trifle with."[46]

Ellis couldn't have helped but flash her temper at Hollywood by this point, for by the time the fan magazine followers were reading the above, she had been seen in two Paramount features—both frothy flops. The first, *All the King's Horses* (1935), saw her wasted in a role as a Ruritanian queen who is so self-deluded that she cannot recognize the movie actor who is posing as her monarch husband (Danish singing actor Carl Brisson had the dual role). Not even the directorial touch of Frank Tuttle, who had a flair for light comedy, could drum up interest in a would-be Maurice Chevalier-Jeanette MacDonald duo. This was followed by the Lewis Milestone-directed *Paris in Spring* (1935), a tale of two mismatched couples (and suicide!) in which a youthful, blond Ida Lupino was billed third behind Ellis and Tullio Carminati. In retrospect, both movies retain a certain charm and, despite unremarkable songs (save for the title tune of *Paris in Spring*), reveal Ellis' ample promise as a Hollywood star. But the window was small in 1935, and with so much product moving in and out of theaters, she had little time to make an impression. After shooting *All the King's Horses* and *Paris in Spring*, Ellis returned to London to appear in a play, then came back to California in February 1936 to make another movie. In the meantime, *Rose-Marie* was now arriving in movie houses courtesy of MGM, and MacDonald's presence in the role Ellis had created could not have improved the latter's mood.

Something different was needed for Ellis' next vehicle, and it came in the guise of independent producer Walter Wanger, then working through Paramount. Wanger was not averse to presenting musicals, as he'd recently made two: *Every Night at Eight* (1935), which made money, and *Palm Springs* [q.v.] (1936), which didn't. In 1925, as the New York–based general manager of Paramount, Wanger had been impressed enough with Ellis' personality to offer her a film contract, even though her rich voice would have had no value in the medium at the time. Wanger got his belated wish by aligning with her a decade later, as Ellis related in an interview that also included some un–Hollywoodian candor about the lack of quality of her previous efforts (the boldfacing is this author's):

> After more than 10 years, I finally am working for the man who was my first champion. I have seen him from time to time during those years and he always has expressed a desire to have me make a picture for him. Even **the last two mediocre productions** I made last Winter didn't shake his faith in me. That's why I'm back in Hollywood, glad to have the opportunity to make *Fatal Lady* for him.[47]

Unlike Ellis' first two Paramounts, *Fatal Lady* figured to display the serious side Ellis preferred to show—but by playing the diva role she no longer wanted in real life. Meant to widen her potential audience, this was a backstage murder mystery with an operatic background—including two "original operas" written for the film by Sam Coslow, Victor Young, and others—and semi-mystical elements. Wanger spent more than $400,000 on *Fatal Lady*—nearly $100,000 more than the average of the other 13 pictures he produced for Paramount release in 1935–36, and he took the time and trouble to stage the opera scenes with more than a thousand extras in the soon-to-be-razed Grand Opera House in Los Angeles.[48] However, he saddled the project with Edward Ludwig, a director of little repute. And no fewer than five writers were involved with the script, in which the recurring theme of fate determining the bad luck of the globe-trotting, man-attracting singer played by Ellis is hinted at in a series of cutaways to a horoscope chart, but is otherwise undeveloped.[49] Why is she such a femme fatale anyway?

To be a halfway attractive male in the cast of *Fatal Lady* is to become either a target of the murderer in its story or go under suspicion of being such. A dreary little number such as this was no career-booster for its leading men, which contributed to the film's air of desperation. Walter Pidgeon was under contract to Wanger but in the career doldrums that lasted throughout the 1930s. Norman Foster, a once-promising film juvenile, was now mired in bad parts that couldn't overshadow the notoriety of his marriage to the much-more-famous Claudette Colbert. Foster, playing a lovesick swain, is saddled with lines like "You're *wonderful!*"—which explains why he soon gave up acting to retreat behind the camera as a director-screenwriter. *Fatal Lady*, too, was the end of the line for Pidgeon as a Wanger contractee; he went on to Universal, then finally to more important projects at MGM and Fox.

Usually watchable support players such as John Halliday, Alan Mowbray, and Samuel S. Hinds—all portraying native South Americans without the slightest effort to sound South American—are wasted, and exasperated average-guy comic Edgar Kennedy seems out of place as part of Ellis' retinue. At least Kennedy wasn't miscast as the surprise killer, but the script cheats with its out-of-the-blue perpetrator, a minor character whose homicidal yen would at least explain why he/she would follow the heroine from the grand stages of New York and Brazil to a seedy Apache café in Paris. (We'll leave his/her identity a secret, to be enjoyed by anyone who might seek out *Fatal Lady*.)

Wanger took a bath on the film, which garnered mainly unfavorable reviews, finished more than $200,000 in the red, and portended the end of his tie-in with Paramount.[50] As often on the bottom of double bills as not, *Fatal Lady* was paired with similarly routine fare—the Fox-issued George O'Brien adventure *Whispering Smith Speaks* in Mason City, Iowa; Paramount's Charlie Ruggles-Mary Boland comedy *Early to Bed* in Salt Lake City; MGM's thriller *Absolute Quiet*, starring Lionel Atwill, in Oakland, California; and—in the ultimate Fatal Lady twin bill—Universal's horror entry *Dracula's Daughter* in St. Louis.

In her memoir, published in the 1980s, Mary Ellis showed some respect for her U.S. film finale. *Fatal Lady* was "a ghastly title," she wrote, but "it had quite a good story … and an outstanding opera sequence."[51] The rest of Ellis' movie credits, only a handful, were achieved in England, but she amassed a list of stage and small-screen credits that extended into Jeremy Brett-starring Sherlock Holmes TV episodes in the 1990s. Against her many triumphs, the failure of *Fatal Lady* ranks as a mere misstep.

Follow Your Heart

(Republic; August 11, 1936)

Director: Aubrey Scotto. Producer: Nat Levine. Executive Producer: Albert E. Levoy. Associate Producer: Leonard Fields. Screenplay: Lester Cole, Nathanael West, Samuel Ornitz. Story: Dana Burnet. Additional Dialogue: Olive Cooper. Photography: John Mescall, Allyn C. Jones. Editing: Murray Seldeen, Ernest J. Nims, Robert L. Simpson. Musical Supervision: Harry Grey. Music Settings: Hugo Riesenfeld. Sound: Terry Kellum, Harry Tribby. Dance Director: Larry Ceballos. Costumes: Eloise. Assistant Director: Jasper Blystone. Running Time: 82 minutes.

Cast: Marion Talley (Marian Forrester); Michael Bartlett (Michael Williams); Nigel Bruce (Henry Forrester); Luis Alberni (Tony Masetti); Henrietta Crosman (Madame Bovard); Vivienne Osborne (Gloria Forrester); Walter Catlett (Joe Shelton); Eunice Healey (specialty dancer); Ben Blue (himself);

Mickey Rentschler (Tommy Forrester); John Eldredge (Harrison Beecher); Margaret Irving (Louise Masetti); Si Jenks (Mr. Hawks); Josephine Whittell (Mrs. Plunkett); Clarence Muse (choir leader); Hall Johnson Choir.

Songs/Musical Selections: "Magnolias in the Moonlight" [Bartlett, chorus, danced by Blue, Healey; reprised by Bartlett, dancers], "Who Minds 'Bout Me?" [Muse, Hall Johnson Choir] (Walter Bullock, Victor Schertzinger); "Follow Your Heart" [Talley, Bartlett, chorus, three times] (Sidney D. Mitchell, Victor Schertzinger); "O ciel! Où courez-vous?" (from *Les Huguenots*) [Talley, Bartlett], "Vaga donna illustre e cara" ("Page's Song" from *Les Huguenots*) [Talley] (Giacomo Meyerbeer); "Ah! Che la morte ognora" (from *Il Trovatore*) [Talley] (Guiseppe Verdi); "Chi mi frena in tal momento" (sextet from *Lucia di Lammermoor*) [Bartlett, Alberni, Crosman, Irving, chorus] (Gaetano Donizetti); "Je suis Titania" (from *Mignon*) [Talley] (Ambroise Thomas); "The Hunt Is Up" [Talley, chorus] (William Gray); "Oh Marie" [Bartlett] (Eduardo Di Capua); "It's All Over Me" [Johnson Choir], "This Old Hammer Killed John Henry" [Johnson Choir]; "Work in the Morning" [Johnson Choir, danced by Healey] (trad.).

Working Titles: *My Old Kentucky Home*; *Spotlight*.

The Story: Marian Forrester resides on a Kentucky farm as the only level-headed member of an eccentric family that includes her soft-touch voice teacher father, Henry; spendthrift divorcee sister, Gloria; and horn-playing little brother, Tommy. Gloria borrows a significant amount of money from her father, which imperils the family's future. Marian's uncle Tony Masetti and his bickering actress wife, Louise, bring their small-time opera troupe to the Forrester home, with plans of staying until his next production is ready for staging. Among the troupers is a handsome tenor, Michael Williams, who notices and encourages Marian's impressive singing talent while falling in love with her. Marian, who is promised to fellow local Harrison Beecher, declines to sing professionally, but she is forced to perform in a big show staged by the troupe by producer Joe Shelton at the refurbished mansion. Despite Marian's reluctance, the performance is a success, and as the company prepares to depart on tour, Harrison gallantly gives up Marian, who joins Michael on the road.

Marion Talley was no run-of-the-mill opera singer, although not always for the right reasons. In a genre filled with performers from elsewhere, she was one of us—American-born and -raised. She made her debut at the Metropolitan Opera at the highly uncommon age of 19. And she shocked the nation by giving up her career at age 23 and retiring to a farm in Kansas. In this country, interest in the "Kansas City Canary" probably exceeded her stature in the opera world, but like many others of greater reputation, she gave Hollywood a go in the mid-'30s—this after her temporary rural departure. Her movie career consisted of only one feature, the 1936 Republic super-musical *Follow Your Heart*, which was super by Republic standards but clearly reveals why its lady did no further leading.

As quickly as her career descended after *Follow Your Heart*, Talley (1906–1983) rose meteorically to the top of her profession. The soprano garnered national, if not global, headlines in February 1926 when she emerged from the heartland to become the youngest prima donna to appear on the Met stage (as Gilda in *Rigoletto*). The occasion became such a big deal that a telegraph machine was set up backstage so that Talley's father could report news updates to his daughter's hometown and the rest of the country.[52] The Met distinction landed her a recording contract with Victor, a cover showcase in *Time* magazine, and a stint in the movies—in one of the earliest Vitaphone short subjects. Talley's performance of "Caro nome" from *Rigoletto* was included among seven musical performance shorts on the very first Vita program, preceding the synchronized Warner Bros. silent *Don Juan* for its opening in New York on August 6, 1926.

The program of mainly classical and operatic acts was widely praised; Talley's participation was not. In a review of the program headlined "Vitaphone Bow Is Hailed as Marvel," the writer lambasted a teenager who "failed to register and looked to be grimacing her way

Marion Talley, the mercurial "Kansas City Canary," paired with fellow opera star Michael Bartlett for her film comeback in Republic's *Follow Your Heart*.

through."[53] The fan magazine *Photoplay* was even less kind: "Long shots—and good, long ones—were just invented for that girl."[54] It may well have been that the quality of Talley's voice—as opposed to the way the attractive but mildly stout girl looked as she sang—could, as the historian Richard Koszarski has noted, be attributed to the film being projected out of sync, or to her coloratura registering beyond the range of the primitive sound system.[55] The "Caro nome" short was dropped from the Vitaphone program in many bookings, and Talley made only two other films for Warners, both operatic shorts.[56]

In 1929, Talley left the New York stage for the fields of Colby, Kansas, where, she said, "I am going to be just like the other farmers," and the Met vehemently denied rumors she'd left because her contract was about to be dropped.[57] Talley would later claim that she did no farming herself and did not even live on the land, which she said was a highly profitable investment.[58] Moreover, she never really stopped singing—she made occasional radio and concert appearances. In 1932, she married the German pianist Michael Raucheisen, although the union was annulled within months, allegedly because he would not satisfy a premarital agreement that her mother and sister live with them. In 1935, in what would turn out to be an even less sedate marital foray, Talley got hitched to her voice teacher, Adolph Eckstrom, who moved with her to Los Angeles when she was signed to a contract by Metro-Goldwyn-Mayer.[59] No sufficient properties could be found for her under the six-month MGM pact—although there might have been personal issues at play. Talley bided her time by headlining her own NBC radio show, until fledgling Republic Pictures, best known for making action movies, stepped up with an offer that became *Follow Your Heart*.

The project was directed by Aubrey Scotto, lately of Paramount's *Palm Springs* [q.v.], with three new songs by the esteemed Victor Schertzinger. It paired Talley with another American opera singer, tenor Michael Bartlett, who was having his own studio troubles with subpar exposure at Columbia. A handsome and athletic Massachusetts native, Bartlett (1903–1979) supported such talents as Grace Moore and Claudette Colbert but hadn't been given a male lead by himself and had been reduced to singing the pop novelty "The Music Goes 'Round and Around" in his most recent film.[60] Bartlett, who was not highly regarded as an actor, provides a dynamic performance that is one of the best assets of a strange mix of straight-faced operetta and *You Can't Take It with You* familial screwball. *Follow Your Heart* would be Bartlett's final Hollywood film, and second-to-last overall (followed only by a 1937 British operetta, *The Lilac Domino*), but for now, hopes were much higher for him and Talley at Republic.

The brain behind *Follow Your Heart* was Nat Levine, the former founder and operator of Poverty Row's Mascot Pictures, which was best known for action stuff but also made non-adventure fare. He was now president of Republic, formed in 1935 as a union of Mascot and five other indie companies (Chesterfield, Invincible, Liberty, Majestic, Monogram) under the financial thumb of Herbert J. Yates, president of the film processing laboratory Consolidated Film Industries. Among the new company's earliest releases were minor musicals—among them *Harmony Lane* (1935) [q.v.] and *The Old Homestead** (1935)—but now Republic was putting much of its immediate future in the allure of a plumpish Kansas diva. Levine trumpeted *Follow Your Heart* as one of its 1936–37 upper-tier "Jubilee Six" productions and its biggest release of the upcoming season. In asking for higher rentals from theater owners, he announced, somewhat prematurely, at Republic's national convention that "we are no longer considered an independent company. Our facilities and work are of major calibre."[61]

Shooting on *Follow Your Heart* was well underway at this point (June–July 1936), but one of the potential problems with its roly-poly star was solved. Talley had slimmed by somewhere between 25 and 60 pounds … and not without attention. Hollywood insiders alleged that it was closer to the latter; Talley's masseuse responded that the loss was no more than 10 or 12 pounds, down to 105 on the singer's 5-foot-3 frame.[62] Backed by her meticulously kept weight charts, Talley finally went public to announce the "official" reduction—26 pounds—in a report that wire services sped around the country. "When I signed a picture contract, it was necessary, of course, to reduce. They tell me you look bigger in pictures than you really are, so, to appear slender, you have to be very, very slender."[63] This reportage was great promotion not only for Talley's film but also for her new radio program, which happened to be sponsored by Ry-Krisp, the low-calorie rye-based cracker now cited as a major part of Talley's diet. Ry-Krisp print ads purported to tell "The True Story of Marion Talley's New HOLLYWOOD FIGURE" and advised readers to "Get the Hollywood Habit" by slimming down.

Republic reportedly made *Follow Your Heart* for a hefty (for Republic) $250,000. By comparison, however, Columbia spent an eye-popping $2 million around the same time on the Frank Capra-directed prestige drama *Lost Horizon* (which had a 3½-hour initial cut), and independent Grand National may have spent as much as $900,000 on its way-over-budget 1937 James Cagney musical, *Something to Sing About* [q.v.]. Unfortunately, the returns for the Talley film were not what Levine and company expected. An early indicator was the film's failure to last longer than a single week at the brand-new Criterion

Theatre in New York City, where Talley was billed under Bartlett on the marquee.[64] Much of the overall blame had to fall on Talley. Her singing voice is up to the task—she offers selections from *Mignon, Les Huguenots,* and *Il Trovatore*, plus the Schertzinger title song—and her slender figure brings out a previously hidden loveliness. But her nasal, monotonous Midwestern twang makes her no talent of talk. When she sings, she's an international star; when she speaks, she's the dowdy neighbor lady who lives down the street. The script gives a credible cast of support players—Nigel Bruce, Luis Alberni, and Walter Catlett among them—little to do, although the small dose of alleged comedian Ben Blue (on hand mainly for dance specialties) is about right.

Follow Your Heart was accused by some of being overly pretentious, but at least the music is rendered in amusing ways. We first see Talley's character singing "Ah! I Have Sighed to Rest Me" (from *Il Trovatore*) while cleaning out the family furnace—see, neighbor lady. Bartlett is introduced singing "Oh Marie" while sitting in the back of a truck tossing wieners to a pack of hunting dogs on the chase. "I'll get the sheriff!" yells one of the perturbed pursuing hunters. "I'll get the ASPCA!" replies the tenor in a reaction uncharacteristic of 1936. Most fun is the number involving the opening stanzas of the sextet from *Lucia di Lammermoor*, as the players prepare a big dinner. Bartlett sings while gazing lovingly at a glazed ham, Alberni's response is directed to what looks to be a garnished haddock, and so on. Later, we hear Talley present a down-home bit of *Les Huguenots* while in a hayloft, accompanied by a makeshift gramophone operated by her little brother as he toots a French horn.

The show-within-a-show finale, for which Republic constructed a life-sized mansion house and put on its front lawn a revolving stage to hold scores of performers, finds Bartlett doing more singing than Talley, both on the title song and a Southern-oriented number, "Magnolias in the Moonlight," both written for the film. There are also pleasing appearances by the renowned Hall Johnson Choir and actor-baritone Clarence Muse for cultural diversity, before a somewhat rushed resolution. Despite all the effort, and some backhanded positive reviews—*The Hollywood Reporter* praised it as "the tops of class entertainment *from an independent*" (italics by this book's author)—it stalled the cinema careers of its starring duo and deterred Republic from repeating such high-minded musical fare.[65] *Variety* was as blunt as could be about the leading lady: "She won't stay in films long.... Miss Talley doesn't photograph any too well."[66] And when Republic returned to bigger-budget musicals, in 1937 with *The Hit Parade** and *Manhattan Merry-Go-Round**, they had a more popular-song sensibility. By then, Nat Levine was gone from the company, frozen out by Herb Yates and his ambition to assume artistic control to go with his financial power.

Talley had her live dates and radio work to fall back on, but her show would be off the air by 1938 and an attempted concert hall comeback in 1940 never panned out. Soon, she would be out of show business for good, partly because of a bitter legal battle that involved a prominent figure from *Follow Your Heart*. In 1939, Talley admitted publicly that she was the mother of a 3-year-old child over whom she and husband Adolph Eckstrom were now vying for custody, and that she had not seen the girl since she was less than a year old. In 1941, with Talley having been awarded custody of the girl, Eckstrom filed a separate maintenance suit that alleged his wife had engaged in acts of misconduct with seven men—an eclectic roster that included a now-dead socialite, a prominent New York attorney, and, among others, ventriloquist Edgar Bergen, music teacher Arthur Rosenstein, actor Erik Rhodes (the comic-relief guy in Astaire-Rogers musicals), and ... Aubrey Scotto, the director of *Follow Your Heart*. Eckstrom stated that Talley had left him two months after their 1935 marriage, and Talley responded by accusing Eckstrom of blackmail and strongly implying they had married only because their child had been conceived out of wedlock.[67] Within weeks, Scotto's wife filed for divorce herself, accusing Talley of "immoral and improper acts" with her husband over the past five years, and attempted to testify on Eckstrom's behalf against Talley in his divorce trial.[68]

After a very ugly row that played out in newspapers nationwide, Talley won a divorce and permanent custody of her daughter in mid–1941, retired to the Los Angeles area, and lived in relative obscurity until her death at age 76. One might wonder if she ever caught *Follow Your Heart* during one of its frequent late-late show airings when television was as novel as her opera career had once been.

Under Your Spell
(20th Century–Fox; November 6, 1936)

Director: Otto [Ludwig] Preminger. Associate Producer: John Stone. Screenplay: Frances Hyland, Saul Elkins. Story: Bernice Mason, Sy Bartlett. Photography: Sidney Wagner. Editing: Fred Allen. Art Direction: Duncan Cramer. Music Director: Arthur Lange. Dance Director: Sammy Lee. Sound: Paul Neal, Harry M. Leonard. Costumes: Herschel. Assistant Director: Jack McEdwards. Running Time: 62 minutes.

Cast: Lawrence Tibbett (Anthony Allen); Wendy Barrie (Cynthia Drexel); Gregory Ratoff (Petroff); Arthur Treacher (Botts); Gregory Gaye (Count Raul du Rienne); Berton Churchill (judge); Jed Prouty (Mr. Twerp); Charles Richman (Uncle Bob); Claudia Coleman (Mrs. Twerp); Madge Bellamy (Miss Stafford); Nora Cecil (schoolteacher); Joyce Compton (secretary); Jack Mulhall (court clerk); Josef Swickard (amigo); Theodore von Eltz (Cynthia's attorney); Pierre Watkin (Allen's attorney); Edward Gargan (detective).

Songs: "Amigo" [Tibbett, chorus], "My Little Mule Wagon" [Tibbett], "Under Your Spell" [Tibbett, four times] (Howard Dietz, Arthur Schwartz) "Le veau d'or" (from *Faust*) [Tibbett, chorus] (Jules Barbier, Michel Carré, Charles Gounod).

Alternate Title: *Love Flight*.

The Story: New York–based opera baritone Anthony Allen chafes at the ridiculous, time-wasting publicity stunts concocted by his domineering manager, Petroff, such as judging flower shows and celebrity-lookalike contests. At a performance of "Faust" in Chicago, spoiled socialite Cynthia Drexel makes a deal with Petroff for Tony to sing at her party for $15,000, with the money tied to a bet she's made with Count Raul du Rienne so she doesn't have to marry him. After Petroff stages a particularly objectionable, scandalous stunt involving the singer and the "jealous husband" of a bogus love interest, Tony escapes to his hometown ranch in New Mexico with his valet, Botts, to find solitude. Drexel flies her private plane there and attempts to convince Tony to return to his career (and her party). Tony falls for Cynthia despite her impetuous nature, and he follows her back to the city under the pretense of returning her missing suitcase. Cynthia attempts to make Tony jealous by telling her of Raul's intentions, but Tony refuses to help Cynthia win the bet and prevent her wedding to the count. In response, she has the singer arrested for breach of contract. When the case goes to court, Tony talks the judge into dismissing the case, then convinces Cynthia to sign a marriage license after giving her—behind closed doors—the spanking he is told she has deserved all along.

Lawrence Tibbett's film career, which had started with a bang in 1930 with his Oscar-nominated performance in MGM's prestige release *The Rogue Song*, ended with a whimper in 1936 with a 20th Century–Fox "B," *Under Your Spell*. The 62-minute programmer was a movie nobody wanted to make, save for contractual obligations, and its only distinction—if only in retrospect—was that it marked the American directorial debut of Otto

Preminger. In terms of where their respective fortunes were headed, Tibbett and Preminger were two ships passing in the Hollywood night.

In August and September 1936, when *Under Your Spell* was being filmed, the artist then known as Otto Ludwig Preminger was a glorified apprentice filmmaker assigned to handle a star whom the studio no longer wanted. By "studio" we mean one of the movie industry's most powerful men: TCF production chief Darryl F. Zanuck. Noting the success enjoyed by Tibbett's contemporary Grace Moore at Columbia, Zanuck signed the beloved baritone in 1934 to a two-picture contract, at $100,000 per film.[69] Tibbett (1896–1960) had few good memories of his earlier stint in movies, as even *The Rogue Song* engendered so much pre-release uncertainty from MGM that the studio brought in Stan Laurel and Oliver Hardy to film comic-relief scenes. Tibbett's big voice in playing a Russian thief won over fans anyway—and earned him his Oscar nomination. Metro responded by putting Tibbett into *New Moon* (1930), a filming of the operetta that paired him with Moore but inexplicably jettisoned the libretto and most of the Oscar Hammerstein-Sigmund Romberg songs.[70] It was not a success, and neither was Tibbett's third Metro effort, *The Prodigal* (1931), in which he stretched his acting muscles as a shiftless antihero but failed to play to his base. A fourth feature, *Cuban Love Song* (1931), was a turgid soap opera that co-starred the attractive Lupe Velez; it made a profit for MGM, but the studio had better things to do by now.

So did Tibbett. He was as popular as ever in the mid '30s, and in a letter to the *Los Angeles Times,* he explained why he was returning to pictures. It wasn't, he said, for the better money that he would be passing up from radio and the concert and operatic stages.

> When I left Hollywood four years ago to rejoin the Metropolitan Opera, I pledged myself never to return. Now I am back and glad of it.... The truth is that four years ago, Hollywood had not advanced far enough in the handling of sound to do full justice to the operatic voice. Today, an amazing degree of perfection has been attained.[71]

Tibbett got to show off that perfection in *Metropolitan*, which premiered in November 1935 as the first 20th Century–Fox release, Zanuck's 20th Century Pictures having merged with Fox. The virile, handsome Tibbett, his voice as strong as always, was at ease before the camera and sang a varied collection of works, from "On the Road to Mandalay" to "The Glory Road" to excerpts from *Carmen, Faust, The Barber of Seville,* and *I Pagliacci.* Virginia Bruce, Alice Brady, Cesar Romero, and opera-film fixture Luis Alberni supported him in another of those behind-the-scenes yarns. Reviewers praised the film, but Tibbett's comeback picture lost $117,000 on a $536,000 negative cost.[72] This was at a time when the average feature-film production cost between $350,000 and $400,000. It probably didn't help that *Metropolitan* opened at around the same time as the Marx Brothers' popular opera spoof, *A Night at the Opera.*

Zanuck groused at having to use Tibbett in one more picture, but the singer would not agree to a buyout of his contract.[73] Before *Metropolitan* flopped, that next project was to be a musical remake of *The Mark of Zorro*, the Douglas Fairbanks swashbuckler, for which six Arthur Schwartz-Irving Caesar songs were written. In an intra-studio missive, Zanuck envisioned the *Mark of Zorro* remake as "a delightful romantic comedy of adventure and song" in the manner of MGM's *Rose-Marie*, and possibly to be filmed in Technicolor. But that was out, and now, Tibbett was placed under the directorial hand of Preminger, the Viennese stage director whose accomplishments in New York productions attracted Zanuck's attention.[74] Preminger had directed only one previous film, a minor Austrian drama (*Die Grosse Liebe*, in 1931), and *Under Your Spell* was to be an audition of sorts for him, even if it didn't seem like much of an assignment.

According to Preminger's memoir, Zanuck bad-mouthed Tibbett for not allowing a buyout of the singer's contract: "We're stuck with the son-of-a-bitch. There's no chance he'll ever be a success in films, so you go ahead and practice on him."[75] However, Tibbett was cordial with his new director, admitting he was making the picture for money's sake. "I'm sorry for you," Tibbett told Preminger, "since it isn't your fault, but I intend to work strictly according to my contract. It provides that I stop work at five o'clock. So be prepared. At five o'clock, I quit."[76] Nonetheless, the two men got along well, and Tibbett entertained the cast and crew between scenes by singing and playing piano.[77] Preminger—uncharacteristically, considering his later reputation for over-producing, brought in *Under Your Spell* on time and budget. Tibbett was playing an opera star again, this time being alternately in love and at odds with a spoiled debutante played by Wendy Barrie. But with only one full-fledged operatic excerpt—the star as Mephistopheles in "Le veau d'or" from *Faust* (in a part he'd never played on the live stage)—the emphasis was more on semi-screwball romantic comedy than high-falutin' melodies.[78]

Tibbett does the best he can with weak material, and one can imagine that, given his rural California roots, he must have liked that his character was a Western rancher-turned-opera star. But *Under Your Spell* suffers from a derivative, unconvincing central love story (unearthed from a Spanish-language comedy made by Fox a few years before), an annoyingly overbearing performance by Gregory Ratoff as the fictional singer's bossy agent, and an hour-and-change running time that reeks of routine and studio disrespect. Preminger's direction is competent but without a hint of his future expertise. The Howard Dietz-Arthur Schwartz title song is pleasing but threatens to be overused, with no less than four renditions. Arthur Treacher effectively does his usual manservant thing, but such is best in small portions. Ultimately, the attempt of *Under Your Spell* to disassociate itself from the "typical" opera movie backfires. Tibbett—a highly competent actor—is placed in comparison with someone like Clark Gable in the similarly plotted *It Happened One Night* as opposed to, say, Nino Martini or James Melton in anything else.

Tibbett knew what was up; he privately called his film *Under Your Smell*. In its initial New York City run at the RKO Palace Theater, it played at the bottom of a bill with an unremarkable Warner Bros. Kay Francis-George Brent soaper, *Give Me Your Heart*, to achieve a take *Variety* described as "mild." In Philadelphia at the Aldine, management withdrew the Tibbett film after only five days. On the opposite coast the same opening week, the results for *Under Your Spell* were "only satisfactory" in a solo booking at Fox's Four Star house in Los Angeles.[79] Such apathy in key major cities with opera-savvy audiences was bad enough; in fly-over country, the reaction was downright insulting. The comments by small-town exhibitors in the *Motion Picture Herald* reflected a sense of reverse snobbery—or maybe they were just calling a spade a spade. "I certainly must have been under Fox's spell when I booked this one," a Louisiana theater man said. "Lawrence Tibbett may suit the Metropolitan Opera directors, but not an audience bent on entertainment."[80] This from Michigan: "No one likes [Tibbett] here. Plenty of walkouts. No business."[81] An exhibitor from Florida was more rueful: "I could have wept when Lawrence Tibbett's glorious voice rang out to thrill a mere handful of people."[82]

Preminger was promoted to TCF's A-grade pictures after *Under Your Spell*, and by 1944, he was on top to stay with *Laura*. As for Tibbett, he still envisioned movies as part of his career—albeit, as he told *The New York Times* in 1936, "a single picture annually, with songs of wider and more instant appeal" than opera.[83] But there were no more pictures, for a long period of professional and personal setbacks—a decline in voice, a surplus of drink, a bout with arthritis—soon was to begin for him. Tibbett's misfortune included a fluky but tragic incident while *Under Your Spell* was in theaters. At the Met in January 1937, Tibbett was in a dress rehearsal for a scene from *Caponsacchi* in which he was to lunge with a dagger at a character being restrained by two thieves. The gilded, ornamental weapon inadvertently cut the hand of basso Joseph Sterzini, who was playing one of the thieves. Sterzini, a good friend of Tibbett, sustained a good deal of bleeding but left the rehearsal under his own power. However, he died five hours later. Officials ruled that Sterzini died of a heart ailment and not directly from the wound,[84] but the accident weighed heavily on Tibbett.

In the end, it is Tibbett's artistry that remains. Even the *Times*' B.R. Crisler, in his mainly negative review of *Under Your Spell*, was compelled to include what, regarding Tibbett in 1936, remained obvious: "His voice remains the richest, the most dramatic, the most beautifully controlled vocal instrument on the contemporary screen."[85]

When You're in Love
(Columbia; February 12, 1937)

Director: Robert Riskin; Harry Lachman (uncredited). Associate Producer: Everett Riskin. Screenplay: Robert Riskin, based on an idea by Ethel Hill and Cedric Worth. Photography: Joseph Walker. Editing: Gene Milford. Art Direction: Stephen Goosson. Costumes: Bernard Newman. Music Director: Alfred Newman. Sound: Lodge Cunningham. Production Ensembles Staged By: Leon Leonidoff. Arrangement of "Minnie the Moocher" By: Al Siegel. Assistant Director: Arthur S. Black. Running Time: 103 or 110 minutes.

Cast: Grace Moore (Louise Fuller); Cary Grant (Jimmy Hudson); Aline MacMahon (Marianne Woods); Henry Stephenson (Walter Mitchell); Thomas Mitchell (Hank Miller); Catharine Doucet (Jane Summers); Luis Alberni (Serge Vilnikoff); Gerald Oliver Smith (Gerald Meeker); Emma Dunn (Mrs. Hamilton); George C. Pearce (Mr. Hamilton); Frank Puglia (Carlos); Marcelle Corday (Marie); Enrique de Rosas (hotel manager); William Pawley, Don Rowan (bruisers in nightclub); Billy Gilbert (José); Dewey Robinson (photographer); Edward Keane (stage manager); Gene Morgan (dancer); Hector V. Sarno (jail guard); Antonio Vidal (justice of the peace); Soledad Jimenez (wife of justice of the peace); Lucille Ward (music teacher); Pat West, Harry Holman (Babbitt brothers); Scotty Beckett (crying boy); Robert McKenzie (Charlie Perkins); Henry Roquemore (travel agent); Manuel Paris (Mexican hotel clerk); C. Montague Shaw (attorney); Frank Leyva, Raul Lechuga (police officers); Romaine Callender, Jean De Briac, Gus Reed (waiters); Arthur Hoyt, May Wallace (shouting couple); Chuck Hamilton (Tony); Leyland Hodgson, Bess Flowers, Cyril Ring (festival patrons); Chris-Pin Martin (servant); Otto Fries (Otto); Louise Brooks (ballet dancer); Edgar Kennedy (Michael O'Brien); Barnett Parker (butler); Robert Emmett O'Connor, George Cooper (assistant immigration officers); Herbert Ashley (immigration chief); Arthur Stuart Hull (businessman); J.P. Lockney (doorman); Ann Doran (secretary); Emery D'Arcy (Scarpia).

Songs/Musical Selections: "Our Song" [Moore, reprised by Moore, chorus], "The Whistling Boy" [Moore, chorus] (Dorothy Fields, Jerome Kern); "Un bel di" (from *Madama Butterfly*) [Moore], "Vissi d'arte" (from *Tosca*) [Moore] (Giacomo Puccini); "In the Gloaming" [Moore] (Meta Orred, Annie Fortesque Harrison); "Minnie the Moocher" [Moore, chorus] (Cab Calloway, Clarence Gaskill, Irving Mills); "Serenade" [Moore, chorus] (Franz Schubert); "Siboney" [Moore, chorus] (Dolly Morse, Ernesto Lecuona); "Je veux vivre" ("The Waltz Song") (from *Romeo et Juliet*) [Moore] (Charles Gounod).

Working Title: *Interlude*.
Also Known As: *For You Alone*.
Disc: Decca 23023 ("Our Song"/"The Whistling Boy," Grace Moore and Victor Young Orchestra).

The Story: Australian opera singer Louise Fuller has overstayed her visa period in the United States and is forced to leave for Mexico despite a pending engagement to sing at a song festival run by her elderly uncle, Walter, a conductor and composer. Louise's friend Carlos suggests she obtain U.S. citizenship through an arranged marriage with an American. The singer meets an American artist, Jimmy Hudson, who is jailed for defending Louise's honor at a nightclub ("Siboney"). Louise bails Jimmy out of captivity and the two are wed in a quickie ceremony before immediately separating. They agree she will pay him $2,000 for the marriage on the condition he divorce her after they come to the United States. In New York to rehearse for her uncle's concert ("The Whistling Boy"), Louise gets reacquainted with her husband, who steals into her penthouse. She thinks he's returned to her for her money, but Jimmy is in love. He urges Louise to rid herself of her "sycophants"—Jane, Gerald, and Serge—and to sing for herself and not "for a paycheck." Jimmy courts Louise at the country home lived in by his surrogate parents, the Hamiltons, where she sings "Minnie the Moocher" with Jimmy's old musician friends. Jimmy turns down a lucrative offer to paint murals for a new concert so he can take Louise on a mountain getaway. Meanwhile, Louise's press agent, Hank Miller, finds the couple and reminds Louise that she must fulfill her festival commitment. Jimmy leaves the home in a huff when Hank and some newspapermen expose her secret marriage. On the day of the festival, Louise tells Hank and her secretary, Marianne, of her intent to divorce Jimmy—just as he prepares to deliver divorce papers of his own. At the festival, Louise sings Schubert's "Serenade" but is delivered the divorce documents at intermission by Jimmy. Word spreads through the audience that Louise will not return to the stage to finish her performance, but she and Jimmy hurriedly make up and the "Our Song" finale goes on.

In 2016, a 79-year-old Columbia musical called *When You're in Love* attracted attention in the blogosphere when a restored version resurfaced for airing on cable television. Headlines blared: The *Los Angeles Times* topped its story with "Restored Version of Rare Cary Grant Musical ... to Air," and the *Huffington Post* announced "GetTV Premieres Rare Cary Grant Film."[86] But how could anyone write about *When You're in Love* without highlighting the name of its star? Grant's enduring legend may have made it possible for the film to return to circulation, but Grace Moore's briefer renown was the reason it was made at all.

We'll forgive the short memories or regency bias, for *When You're in Love* deserves recognition, even in retrospect. It was the fourth of five pictures Moore (1898–1947) made at Columbia during her second cinematic sojourn. Her triumph in *One Night of Love* (1934) had started the push for opera in Hollywood, but her two ensuing pictures, *Love Me Forever* (1935) and *The King Steps Out* (1936), failed to match expectations. The first, although well-written, lacked a strong male lead; the second was a standard-issue mittel-Euro operetta.

"A Hollywood bounce, I soon learned, was a diva's nosedive," Moore wrote in her autobiography concerning this period.

> My picture failure cut disastrous inroads into my career. It removed the golden sheen from my Metropolitan debut and ... took me out of an established category. If I had continued solely with concert and operatic work, I should have had a tag ... now, what was I? Serious artist? ... Movie star? Hardly![87]

Moore needed something lighter, and the response was to rescue her film career with two key names: Grant, then a popular leading man on the brink of top-rank stardom, and screenwriter Robert Riskin, whose collaborations with director Frank Capra had brought him multiple Academy Award nominations, and an Oscar for his script for *It Happened One Night* (1934).

Grant (1904–1986) was entering a crucial period in his career. This debut at Columbia began a period of independence in choosing his own roles and studio ties after years under the yoke of Paramount. Three of his important early films—*Topper* (1937), *The Awful Truth* (1937) and *Bringing Up Baby* (1938), each made for separate companies—followed the Moore picture. Meanwhile, Columbia hoped that the same breezy comic touch that was

5. Invasion of the Opera Singers, or: End of an Aria   173

Despite Cary Grant's enduring stardom, Grace Moore was the undisputed top draw of When You're in Love when it premiered in 1937.

branded as "Capra magic" would translate to the first Riskin effort as a writer and director. Riskin was said to resent the imbalance of credit Capra sought and received for their teamings, so it seemed inevitable that the scribe go off on his own. Riskin biographer Ian Scott has written that Riskin seemed to lack confidence about developing a script for Moore from the original story, which came from "the back of Columbia's files," and worried about the overwork of both writing and directing.[88] Columbia's remedy seems to have been to give Riskin a co-director, Harry Lachman, who had been making minor features in Hollywood since 1933. It was no secret in the press that Lachman was key in the helming, but Columbia was clearly promoting the film as a Riskin solo.[89] Indeed, Riskin received the only directorial credit on screen.

Riskin the director was unhappy with the script by Riskin the writer. "Every scene I wrote seemed satisfactory," he said, while admitting, according to Scott, that he "missed the quality control and editorship" that Capra had provided.[90] Perhaps this was because Riskin's scenario seemed a rehashing of *It Happened One Night*, with Moore's singer-in-trouble likened to the earlier film's heiress-on-the-run played by Claudette Colbert. The troubling situation here is that the soprano, who is from Australia, needs to gain entry to the United States from Mexico, which she does by engaging Grant's talented but vagabond artist in a marriage of convenience. He spends most of the film trying to win her heart to go with her name on the license, sometimes sabotaging his efforts by emphasizing talk over action. Mainly, the seemingly unlikely pairing works—and, on a smaller-scale level, due to what has been famously said about a much more enduring screen couple, Fred Astaire and Ginger Rogers. Only here, it's she who gives him class and he who gives her sex. *When You're in Love* is the first film in which Moore is presented more as a woman than as a diva; she's more cute than condescending. In the 21st century, it is easy to watch this film and believe Grant runs away with it. Indeed, his was considered a strong performance at the time, and he remains the most interesting figure, on and off screen. But in 1937, more of the talk was about the person billed above the title as "Miss Grace Moore."

The humanizing of Moore isn't only in the choice of her Romeo, or even in the simplification of her dress (she dons overalls at one point). Audiences who liked *When You're in Love* most often cited Moore's choice of song, perhaps not so much in the two new Jerome Kern-Dorothy Fields compositions. "Our Song" is good-not-great Kern, and Moore's rendition, meant to symbolize her late-blooming love for Grant as the two court in the woods, is marred by reaction shots (!) of nearby animals. (Oh, look ... an owl ... and a badger!) Another new tune, "The Whistling Boy," comes off as too calculated as Moore sings it to a crowd of adoring children. No, what drew the most applause in 1937 comes two-thirds into the film after Louise is half-kiddingly asked to "audition" for her husband's former amateur band, the members of which know her only as their pal's new wife. A question arises: What about "Minnie the Moocher"? Grant smirks (and so does the audience), but Moore has a surprise for everybody. "What makes you think I wouldn't know it?" she replies, proving her hipness by rattling off the names of the blues song's composers. Moore handles the earthy lyrics—with the drug and sex references excised—with more zest than we might expect from an opera singer, with some trills to go with the scat.[91] Moore didn't want to do the number, but it was her effort that counted, and the preview house at New York's Radio City Music Hall applauded loudly at the novelty.

Moore was enthusiastic about working with Grant (whom she called "the handsomest star in Hollywood") and Riskin, but not so much about taking on Cab Calloway's "Minnie." "It took me two days to get up the courage to 'swing it,'" she admitted in her memoirs as she considered the impact of her film exposure on her live career,

> ... and with Cary at the piano I found it great fun when I really got it going. Of course later when I stood in a concert hall and heard from the balcony the cry, "C'mon, Grace, give us 'Minnie the Moocher,'" I realized how these separate lives impinge on one another. Keep them apart in your own mind and understanding, your public can't and won't.[92]

When You're in Love was filmed as *Interlude* in the fall of 1936, and it premiered the following February.[93] Many reviewers considered it on a par with *One Night of Love* as Moore's best film, with *Variety* writing of its "skillful manipulation of star, cast, and music values" and the *Hollywood Reporter* lauding "a signal triumph for the foremost diva of the screen.... Cary Grant should soar to stardom."[94] Also praised were ballet sequences in an "Our Song" reprise finale that were staged by Leon Leonidoff, producer of Radio City Music Hall's live dance extravaganzas. Louise Brooks, the former silent star now trying to claw her way back to Hollywood prominence, was somewhere among the ballet dancers. She had agreed to the uncredited bit on the condition she would be featured in another Columbia film, but the latter never got made.[95] A minority opinion among reviewers was raised by the *New York Times*' Frank Nugent, who in a bit of backhandedness wrote that the film "is little more than a glib reworking of an ancient operatic formula ... and there is no reason why it should not prove as entertaining today as it did five, ten, or twenty years ago."[96]

However insignificant in the Cary Grant iconography, *When You're in Love* was the only film Riskin ever directed, as he returned to writing (sometimes with Capra), and occasionally producing. As for Moore, she would make one final picture for Columbia, the more-explicitly operatic *I'll Take Romance*, which debuted at year's end in 1937. After starring in Abel Gance's 1939 French filming of the opera *Louise*, Moore concentrated on her live performances, and she was on a concert tour when she died in a Copenhagen plane crash at age 48. Moore's Columbia films received scant TV airings as decades passed, but Sony-Columbia digitally restored the original negative of *When You're in Love* in 2014. It showed at the TCM Classic Film Festival in 2016 and in May of that year, it debuted on the Sony-owned GetTV cable channel. TCM viewers got to see it for the first time on that channel the following November.

Hitting a New High
(RKO; December 24, 1937)

Director: Raoul Walsh. Producer: Jesse L. Lasky. Executive Producer: Samuel J. Briskin. Screenplay: Gertrude Purcell, John Twist. Story: Robert Harari, Maxwell Shane. Photography: J. Roy Hunt. Editing: Desmond Marquette. Art Director: Van Nest Polglase. Associate Art Director: Al Herman. Set Decoration: Darrell Silvera. Costumes: Edward Stevenson. Music Director: Andre Kostelanetz. Sound: Hugh McDowell, Jr. Assistant Director: J. Dewey Starkey. Running Time: 85 minutes.

Cast: Lily Pons (Suzette, aka Oogahunga, the Bird-Girl); Jack Oakie (Corny Davis); John Howard (Jimmie James); Eric Blore (Cedric Cosmo); Edward Everett Horton (Lucius B. Blynn); Eduardo Ciannelli (Andreas Mazzini); Luis Alberni (Luis Marlo); Jack Arnold [Vinton Hayworth] (Carter Haig); Leonard Carey (Jevons); Rolfe Sedan (photographer); Richard Lane (Chez Suzette owner); Larry Steers (party guest).

Songs/Musical Sequences: "I Hit a New High" [Pons, band, chorus], "Let's Give Love Another Chance" [chorus, reprised by Pons, then by Pons, Oakie, Horton, chorus], "This Never Happened Before" [Pons, chorus, band] (Harold Adamson, James McHugh); "Mad Scene" aria from *Lucia di Lammermoor* [Pons, chorus] (Salvatore Cammarano, Gaetano Donizetti); "Je suis Titania" (from *Mignon*) [Pons] (Jules Barbier, Michel Carré, Ambroise Thomas); "The Nightingale's Song" ("Le rossignol et la rose") (from *Parysatis*) [Pons] (Camille Saint-Saëns).

Working Titles: *Born to Sing*; *The Girl in a Cage*; *It Never Happened Before*.

Disc: Decca 23017 ("The Nightingale's Song," Lily Pons).

Home Video: Warner Archive DVD.

The Story: Suzette, a little-known French soprano, toils in a Paris nightclub ("This Never Happened Before") with a band led by her American boyfriend, Jimmie James, but she would rather sing opera. She attracts the attention of Corny Davis, press agent for wealthy opera backer Lucius B. Blynn, who has left for Africa on a big-game hunt. Davis schemes to get Suzette noticed by Blynn by concocting a tale of Oogahunga, a legendary sweet-voiced "bird-girl" in the African jungles ("The Nightingale's Song"). Blynn "captures" the girl—who is, of course, Suzette in disguise—and takes her to New York. He arranges a debut radio broadcast of "Titania" with which he plans to top Mazzini, his greatest rival as a benefactor, as New York is seized by "Ooga-mania." Now in the city himself, Jimmie convinces Corny to allow Suzette to sing at night at his new club ("I Hit a New High") under her real name if Jimmie will keep quiet about her true identity so she can continue her operatic aspirations in the daylight. The charade is imperiled when Mazzini and composer Haig want Suzette to sing in their proposed "jazz" opera. Mazzini learns that the bird-girl and Suzette are one and the same, then Blynn finally realizes that his discovery has been moonlighting. But by now Suzette has something else on her mind other than singing ("Let's Give Love Another Chance").

Hitting a New High hit a new low for Lily Pons—and for the continuing attempt to humanize opera's elite for the screen. The world's most famous coloratura soprano brought new meaning to the term "songbird"—and effectively ended her sojourn in Hollywood—with a ridiculously contrived comedy that was a big money-loser for RKO. It also helped ring down the curtain on the opera-musical-movie trend.

This was the third feature, all at Radio, for Pons (1898–1976). The French-born performer rose to fame in 1931 with her debut for the Metropolitan Opera, in *Lucia di Lammermoor*, for which she reportedly received 16 curtain calls. She inherited the virtuosic singing roles previously handled by Amelita Galli-Curci, but it wasn't just the delicacy of her voice that proved Pons was someone to be reckoned with. She was shrewd about keeping her name in the burgeoning news media. Pons accepted a full-grown jaguar from a fan, and her new pet attracted his own share of newspaper coverage. Later, she allowed a Maryland town to be named for her (as Lilypons) and, like clockwork, posted Christmas cards from there every year. A wordy *Los Angeles Times* headline of 1932 revealed in shorthand the strange brew of Pons' private and public lives: "Jaguar Guards Lily Pons Well/Gift of Argentine Admirer Scares Off Rivals/But Prima Donna Insists She Has No Time for Men/Garbo's Longing for Privacy Wins Her Sympathy."[97]

That Pons seemed game for anything made the movies an inevitable diversion, and in November 1935, RKO premiered her first feature, *I Dream Too Much*. The notices were respectable; as with most diva starrings, the paybox was less kind. Not even a then-callow Henry Fonda, in his third film, could contribute much as the struggling composer overshadowed by wife Pons' path to renown from street singer to singing star, and Lucille Ball brought even less in one of her first billings as support. RKO did Pons right with four Jerome Kern–Dorothy Fields songs to go with her opera cuts ("Caro nome" from *Rigoletto*

As "Oogahunga, the Bird-Girl," Lily Pons revealed a new side of her personality. Edward Everett Horton (left) and Jack Oakie can hardly believe what they see.

and the "Bell Song" from *Lakmé*). Next for Pons came *That Girl from Paris* (1936), a remake of Radio's early musical *Street Girl*, with the locale moved from the Big Apple to the City of Lights. Jack Oakie and Gene Raymond were the key males this time, and there was more of Lucille Ball. And, mon dieu! ... the film made money.

That Girl from Paris was more lighthearted than *I Dream Too Much*, and the thought must have been that the next Pons film (she was under contract for three) should lean to broad comedy. Oakie was brought back for *Hitting a New High*, and RKO contract funsters Edward Everett Horton and Eric Blore—who had backed many an Astaire-Rogers musical—joined the cast for this one. Producer Jesse L. Lasky, the erstwhile Paramount showman, had overseen Nino Martini's three operatic pictures, among them *Here's to Romance* [q.v.], but now he had a new singer to go with a new director: Raoul Walsh, who had helmed a few programmer-type musicals but was better experienced in straightforward action pictures. Lasky's quest to bring opera to the screen didn't just mean employing Pons and Martini. In the spring of 1937, while *Hitting a New High* was in pre-production, RKO floated a report that Lasky was also preparing to commit the first full-length grand opera to celluloid, but as an original creation, set in the United States, and not adapted from one of the classics.[98]

One of *Hitting a New High*'s working titles was *The Girl in a Cage*, a reference to the publicity stunt pulled by those close to a headstrong French soprano who is passed off as a chirping, trilling, tweeting "bird-girl" from the African jungle to attract the attention of a New York opera money man (Horton) who big-game-hunts as a hobby. The weak plot unfolds as the services of "Oogahunga"—with the voice of a bird and the body of a woman—are fought over by the benefactor, the press agent, her bandleader boyfriend (John Howard, borrowed from Paramount), and a rival producer (Eduardo Ciannelli). The parody of the publicity machine that brought the real Pons her renown was likely not lost on the singer, but the story becomes especially ridiculous when her character is tasked with compartmentalizing her career by singing opera by day and her sweetie's sweet jazz by night—all without her identity exposed.

At least if RKO was going to make a comedy about a shapely miss who could sing like a canary, it had the right Met alumna. Pons took heat in the media for being made into a "female Tarzan," but her petite, 5-foot-2 frame is more pleasing to the eye than a singer with a more-robust build might have. She looks nice in a white-feathered brassiere, exposing her midriff, and brief skirt of the same. She's especially fetching in a "I Hit a New High" cabaret number in which she's decked out in top hat, tails, and tights. The number is meant to meld grand opera with the more plebeian forms of screen entertainment, and as such, it is less forceful but less pretentious than the similarly intended title sequence in Jeanette MacDonald's *Broadway Serenade* [q.v.] in 1939. On the minus side for Pons: the mere absurdity in her chirpy alter ego (a parody of the Rima the Bird Girl character in the novel *Green Mansions*) taking Manhattan by storm, even if she is only pretending to be from the wilds, and the overall nonsense of the story. How else to explain that civilization's first glimpse of this sheltered jungle miss reveals a note-perfect knowledge of Saint-Saëns' "Nightingale's Song"? Even the dependable comics get little mileage amid the air of desperation. An episode in which Blore attempts to blackmail Oakie by pretending he is the bird-girl's long-lost father shows promise but goes nowhere, laugh-wise.

The filmmaking process could've been a lot worse for Pons, who enjoyed Oakie's joke-playing on the set during shooting in September and October of 1937. She also got to spend time next to her longtime fiancé, Andre Kostelanetz, the Russian-born conductor-arranger who was the music director for *Hitting a New High*. (The two married in 1938.) But Pons did raise a ruckus even before filming when she shot down rumors that she and Nino Martini star together now that Martini and his mentor Lasky were also at RKO. "One opera star in a picture is ee-nuff!" she exclaimed in a wire story that was predictably punctuated in her perceived Gallic accent.[99] And once she did get into her feather dress for the jungle-discovery scene, Pons had to endure more down time. It took 12 takes, according to a news report from the set, for her to descend into a stream and emerge with a bird perched on her finger. Then there was the part when Pons was coated in light-brown paint (to simulate a suntan) and the bird-girl is placed in a crate and lifted into Eddie Horton's yacht for shipping to the U.S.

> The [actors playing the] huntsmen … must do this time after time before Director Raoul Walsh is satisfied. Once when the cage bangs into [a] palm tree and Miss Pons almost cries in fright, the cameraman cracks: "Well, you said you wanted to be an actress!"
> That gives Lily a new grip on herself. She smiles and the hoisting continues. At last, the cage lands with a bump on the deck of the yacht.
> When finally the day's shooting is over, she rubs the paint off her body, she puts on her clothes again and says she intends to take a vacation in Connecticut as soon as the picture is finished.
> "Then I will go back in December to New York and the opera," she concludes, in a voice, which makes it seem doubtful whether Hollywood ever will get to do such things again to Lily Pons.[100]

In an interview decades later, Walsh recalled his own displeasure with—or, perhaps, apathy over—the Pons film: "I didn't know what the hell it was all about—this girl singing her head off. Andre Kostelanetz using footage and stuff. 'What the hell,' I said, 'let 'em do what they want. I don't know what's going on.'"[101]

Whoever was in charge, when *Hitting a New High* premiered in theaters at Christmas-time, it was common knowledge that Pons' RKO pact was not to be renewed. The film's failure—and that of Grace Moore's final American film, Columbia's *I'll Take Romance*, which debuted around the same time—marked the unofficial end of the opera-star fad. Lasky was out at Radio as well, which meant no full-length filmed opera. "Miss Pons should have known better and left the feathers to Sally Rand," Frank Nugent wrote in *The New York Times*.[102]

Some reviewers praised *Hitting a New High*, but an exhibitor from small-town Texas seemed to sum up the way the film was viewed by those of a less-cultured bent: "The world's worst. Pons and Oakie are ruined for life in this territory.… It sure was lucky that I had it for one day only. The cat wouldn't have come out to see it the second day."[103] Indeed, Hollywood wouldn't have Lily Pons to knock around anymore. Her only other film appearance was to sing the "Bell Song" in a guest shot in *Carnegie Hall* (1947), but the record of her great stage performances outlasts the mistakes that Pons made in pictures.

The Road to Reno

(Universal; September 23, 1938)

Director: S. Sylvan Simon. Associate Producer: Edmund Grainger. Assistant Director: Vernon Keays. Screenplay: Roy Chanslor, Adele Comandini. Adaptation: F. Hugh Herbert, Charles Kenyon, based on the *Saturday Evening Post* magazine story by I.A.R. Wylie. Additional Dialogue: Brian Marlow. Photography: George Robinson. Editing: Maurice Wright, Paul Landres. Art Direction: Jack Otterson. Set Direction: Russell A. Gausman. Sound: Bernard B. Brown. Musical Director: Charles Previn. Costumes: Vera West. Running Time: 69 minutes.

Cast: Randolph Scott (Stephen Fortness); Hope Hampton (Linda Halliday); Helen Broderick (Aunt Minerva); Alan Marshal (Walter Crawford); Glenda Farrell (Sylvia Shane); David Oliver (Salty); Samuel S. Hinds (Pierce, Sylvia's attorney); Spencer Charters (judge); Charles Murphy (Mike); Ted Osborne

(Graves, Linda's attorney); Dot Farley (Mrs. Brumleigh); Mira McKinney (Hannah); Renie Riano (bailiff); Lita Chevret (Gladys); Willie Fung (Lame Duck); Jack Clifford (Truckee).
Songs/Musical Sequences: "I Gave My Heart Away" [Hampton], "Ridin' Home" [Hampton, chorus], "Tonight Is the Night" [Hampton] (Harold Adamson, Jimmy McHugh); "Quando me'n vo" ("Musetta's Waltz" from *La Boheme*) [Hampton, chorus] (Giacomo Puccini).
Also Known As: *The Lady and the Ranger*.

The Story: Opera star Linda Halliday performs "La Boheme" on the New York stage before traveling to Reno, Nevada, where she plans to divorce her estranged husband, rancher Steve Fortress, to marry her socialite fiancé, Walter Crawford. On the trip West, she befriends Sylvia Shane, who is headed to Reno to get unhitched from her latest mate. Steve still loves Linda and not only will he not grant the divorce, but he also maintains that his ranch is domiciled across the border in California, so she cannot break with him without his consent. Steve's Aunt Minerva, who wants to see Linda and her nephew back together, conspires to turn Steve's spread into a dude ranch replete with divorcees, much to Steve's disgust. Linda has decided she doesn't want the divorce after all, but then Walter flies in from New York. When Steve's herd of horses stampedes, Steve, Linda, and Walter pursue the errant animals in Walter's plane. When the plane runs out of gas, Steve and Linda are left alone in a remote cabin, where Linda attempts to recapture Steve's attention by singing "I Gave My Heart Away." The two end up in court suing each other for divorce, but cooler heads prevail and the couple end up together.

Unlike the other operatic alumni featured in this section, Hope Hampton didn't travel the beaten path to 1930s Hollywood. For her, singing was a second career. A lead actress in silent features for a few years, she retired from the screen in the late 1920s and—with the substantial sponsorship of a wealthy, influential husband—was trained and performed in grand opera. She returned to the screen in 1938 for a single feature: *The Road to Reno*, a Universal musical-comedy-Western. After its unsuccessful reception, Hampton returned to her most comfortable pastime—which was being famous for the sake of being famous.

The real life of Hampton (1897–1982) was more interesting than anything she could portray in *The Road to Reno*. The Houston-born, Philadelphia-bred beauty was launched into the movies in 1920 by her manager and paramour—multimillionaire financier Jules Brulatour, a former motion-picture executive who, as U.S. distributor of motion-picture film for Eastman Kodak, was one of the most powerful figures in the cinema business. This would-be Svengali first spotted Hampton when she was a teenager at a drama school performance. Brulatour was nearly 30 years Hampton's senior—and was married to actress Dorothy Gibson when he met the younger woman. But this was no William Randolph Hearst-Marion Davies hookup; Brulatour divorced Gibson in 1923 to make it legal with Hampton. Known better for her looks than her acting ability, Hampton amassed nearly a score of film credits—among them *The Gold Diggers* (1923) and *The Light in the Dark* (1922) while working with such estimable talents as Lon Chaney, John Gilbert, and directors Maurice Tourneur and Clarence Brown. In *Star Dust* (1921), based on the Fannie Hurst novel, she played a small-town girl who endures personal tragedy to train as an opera singer—and make her big-town debut in *Thaïs*. Perhaps the impressive associations for Hampton were no surprise, as Brulatour was known to offer lucrative salaries to his partner's potential working colleagues.[104]

Away from films after 1926 but, as ever, devoted to garnering publicity, Hampton traveled the world with Brulatour when they weren't residing in their four-story New York City brownstone—from whence Hampton was known as "The Duchess of Park Avenue"—and faithfully attending Broadway premieres as two of their city's most faithful first-nighters.

"No one at a premiere could possibly miss seeing Hope Hampton," wrote newspaper columnist Arthur Pollock in 1938. "She dressed as if the first performance of each new play were the greatest moment of her life.... [Her] every entrance was a thing of majesty. Those who were not used to seeing her, and even some of those who were, craned their necks and whispered.... She made it an event."[105]

Hampton has been cited as an inspiration for the Susan Alexander Kane character in *Citizen Kane*—but unlike her fictional counterpart, she achieved some measure of success as a singer. After taking voice lessons, Hampton played in a 1927 Broadway operetta, *My Princess*, that lasted two weeks. To less-than-encouraging reviews, she toured with grand opera companies in Chicago, Los Angeles, and Philadelphia, as well as in Europe, allegedly for the Opera Comique in Paris, in the late 1920s and early '30s. In 1934, Brulatour admitted putting up $4,000 so that Thomas Nazaro, a Boston baker and opera impresario, would stage *Manon* and *La Boheme* there with Hampton in the lead roles; the endeavor lasted one week.[106] Hampton did not, contrary to some reports, perform at any point with the New York Metropolitan Opera, although in 1936 it was rumored that she and Brulatour would start an opera company in New York to rival the Met.[107] Instead, the two decided to give the flickers another go. "And why not?" was a question posed in a syndicated newspaper column that carried Hampton's byline in 1937:

> Opera, both in song and story, has been popular for centuries.... Operatic legend lends itself exquisitely to the medium of motion pictures. I hope to be part of this. I want to bring song and color to the screen. For certainly both are a part of life's beauty worthy to be mirrored in the movies.[108]

A brunette in her silent days but now a still-shapely blonde at age 40, Hampton was signed by Universal for her comeback in the spring of 1937. The "new" Universal, lately freed from Laemmle family control, had been finding audiences with the initial musicals of lyric soprano Deanna Durbin, and Hampton could anchor similarly middlebrow material. Hampton was first announced for a Jerome Kern-Dorothy Fields musical called *Riviera* that went unproduced, and the studio began negotiations with Cary Grant to co-star in Hampton's film.[109] But the talks fell through, and Universal instead assigned Grant's close friend, Randolph Scott, to portray the rancher whose refusal to grant his opera-star wife a quickie divorce in Nevada propels *The Road to Reno*.

There might have been a quid pro quo aspect to the backstory, given Universal's shaky finances and Brulator's wife-promoting, as historian Richard Griffith noted in his 1970 book *The Movie Stars*:

> Just ahead of bankruptcy, [Universal] found itself with a hit on its hands, Deanna Durbin's *One Hundred Men and a Girl*, but without sufficient ready cash to pay for the prints to send to theaters eagerly awaiting it. The company appealed to Mr. Brulator. He was willing to extend credit, but at a price. His wife ... must "return" to the talking screen. There was nothing to do but comply, and soon Universal was flooding the fan magazines with photographs of the "new star" Hope Hampton.... Actors at Universal began to plead flux, syncope, and brain fever to avoid appearing opposite Miss Hampton; Randolph Scott was finally tagged to bell the cat.[110]

Based on a *Saturday Evening Post* story by novelist I.A.R. Wylie, the *Reno* script had a somewhat troubled gestation. Austin Parker, the studio scenarist recently divorced from actress Miriam Hopkins, was working on it when he dropped dead from a brain hemorrhage in March 1938.[111] Parker was replaced by Roy Chanslor, who was plying his trade with routine fare like this before going on to write the Western novels that became *Cat Ballou* and *Johnny Guitar* on the screen. Chanslor was one of four writers to receive screen credit; a trade report asserted that one of the others, Charles Kenyon, journeyed to Reno "to collect

5. Invasion of the Opera Singers, or: End of an Aria

Randolph Scott drew the unlucky assignment of playing opposite actress-turned-opera singer Hope Hampton in *The Road to Reno*.

data on divorce court procedure there, spending a week at a dude ranch, and to search for interesting local characters."[112]

Kenyon and the others don't find enough of real interest in *The Road to Reno*, a weak would-be-screwball comedy that satirizes two kinds of opera—grand and horse. It also sends up the then-popular reputation of little Reno as a divorce mill where everyone is in on the game, including a cowhand (played by Jack Clifford) who is a $40-a-week dog-walker in the employ of a soon-to-be-unhitched society matron. Meanwhile, Hampton's Linda Halliday is, like her real-life counterpart, accustomed to being on the front pages. Linda spends most of *The Road to Reno* trying to decide between her uptown fiancé (Alan Marshal) and her estranged cowboy mate; the songs, three of them, by Harold Adamson and Jimmy McHugh, show to whom her true love lies. There's also a *La Boheme* extraction, there to show off Hampton as the real thing operatically.

Truth is, Hampton's singing isn't bad, but her speaking voice, heretofore unheard on film, betrays her. She eschews an accent of culture with hard vowels and a too-often monotone reading of lines. Hampton just doesn't sound like an opera star when she's not doing opera, and her lack of pizazz is especially evident in her scenes with snappier cast members Glenda Farrell and Helen Broderick. Motor-mouthed Farrell was on loan from Warner Bros. and Broderick, always good with a quip, had escaped RKO in search of better roles than the one here.

The divorce-court climax would be done with better pacing in a more-famous Randolph Scott screwballer, *My Favorite Wife* (1940), but Scott and Marshal get some of the best material in *Reno*. During their macho competition for the heroine's hand, the twist is that the rich dandy outswims the rancher and holds his own in horse riding. Marshal's dandy is a good pilot, too—good enough to guide his small plane through spins that upset his rival's stomach (some nice camera effects emphasize Scott's queasiness). Hampton attracted more pre-release ballyhoo, but Scott (1898–1987) was the bigger star and is co-billed in the starring credits; an interesting development was the de-emphasizing of Hampton in trade ads during the course of the film's release, from being paired with Scott (with equal-sized photos) to a "co-starring" label amid the second-tier players. Scott historian Robert Nott has noted that *Road to Reno* was budgeted at $350,000 but that delays in shooting upped the cost nearly $20,000 more, and that a weekly in-house status report declared that "this picture continues to be the worst headache we have to keep anywhere near the budget figure."[113] Nott also spots a key plot hole—the lack of explanation as to how the soprano and the rancher got together in the first place.

As soon as production ended on *The Road to Reno*, its director, S. Sylvan Simon, got a career boost by signing a long-term contract with MGM, where he would stay for the next nine years. He was elsewhere, then, when lukewarm reviews started to come in. *Variety* praised Hampton for picturing "very attractively," but knocked the "uninspired" direction and the script shortcomings, and the *New York Times* praised Hampton's talking and singing in what it called an "amusingly indoors slant on the Great Outdoors" while acknowledging a "thin" story.[114] A bigger problem was that the film didn't register enough to present Hampton with another chance at film stardom. A trade-publication report from an anonymous Pennsylvania theater owner may have summed up much of the hinterlands reaction: "Miss Hampton is no actress and whatever was saved from a total flop was done so by that great little actress, Glenda Farrell…. The leads … spoiled the picture."[115] The Reno angle in the title also hurt the film's appeal in religiously conservative areas; in some, the name was changed to *The Lady and the Ranger*.

While *The Road to Reno* was being filmed but before its release, Hampton received offers from at least three other studios to sing for them, it was reported.[116] But any chances at a lasting film career disappeared, first in the film's negative response and then in a bout of bad publicity for the actress and her husband while *The Road to Reno* was playing nationally. On January 22, 1939, Brulatour was shot in the neck in the couple's Park Avenue abode; he explained that he had shot himself accidentally while cleaning a pistol. The authorities attempted to question Hampton on the matter, but she refused to say a word. Brulatour paid a $500 fine—and avoided a 30-day jail stint—for carrying a gun, and he and his wife continued on their merry way. Or did they? A New York columnist wondered about that:

> After his convalescence from that mysterious shot of a few weeks ago, [the] millionaire film magnate and his … wife are resuming their public appearances.
> First glimpse I had of them was in the Biltmore [Hotel] lobby…. Hope was looking longingly at some sparkling knick-knacks in a jeweler's cabinet—but Brulatour shook his head in a gesture of "No."
> Before the mysterious shooting, he was never known to deny Hope anything.[117]

Brulatour died in 1946, leaving Hampton with his millions to begin the Norma Desmond phase of her life, only with more headlines. In 1951, her Park Avenue place was robbed, and she reportedly told police that she'd recently taken her valuables out of storage into her home because she feared a possible atomic bomb attack on New York City.[118] Three years later, newspaper accounts alleged that she was to test at MGM for a French musical farce, *Hello Paree*.[119] In 1961, Hampton actually did return to the movies, briefly and obscurely, in a bit as herself in a low-budget pop musical, *Hey, Let's Twist!*, in which she did the eponymous dance. Broadway producers and the Met were still known to hold their opening-night curtains until Hampton entered in her furs and fancy dresses, but her style was fading, In the late '70s, not long before age stopped her from stepping out, Hampton saw a young woman in dungarees at the opera, and said, "Glamour is finished; I don't want my picture in the papers next to a girl with jeans on."[120]

She never went to an opening night at the opera again, according to an anecdote delivered (by Hampton's longtime companion) in a *New York Times* obituary that followed her death from a heart attack. The article was headlined "Hope Hampton, Opera Singer and First-Nighter, Dies at 84." Hampton would've loved the "Opera Singer" bit.

The Great Waltz
(Metro-Goldwyn-Mayer; November 4, 1938)

Directors: Julien Duvivier; Victor Fleming, Josef von Sternberg (uncredited retakes). Producer: Bernard H. Hyman. Screenplay: Samuel Hoffenstein, Walter Reisch. Story: Gottfried Reinhardt. Photography: Joseph Ruttenberg. Editor: Tom Held. Sound: Douglas Shearer. Art Director: Cedric Gibbons. Associate Art Directors: Paul Groesse, Edwin B. Willis. Music Adapted and Arranged By: Dimitri Tiomkin. Musical Director: Artur Guttmann. Dance Director: Albertina Rasch. Costumes: Adrian. Hairstyles for Miss Korjus: Sydney Guilaroff. Assistant Director: Robert S. Golden. Running Time: 104 minutes.

Cast: Luise Rainer (Poldi Vogelhuber); Fernand Gravet [Gravey] (Johann "Schani" Strauss); Miliza Korjus (Carla Donner); Hugh Herbert (Julius Hofbauer); Lionel Atwill (Count Hohenfried); Curt Bois (Kienzl); Leonid Kinskey (Dudelman); Al Shean (cellist); Minna Gombell (Mrs. Hofbauer); George Houston (Fritz Schiller); Bert Roach (Vogelhuber); Greta Meyer (Mrs. Vogelhuber); Herman Bing (Dommayer); Alma Kruger (Mrs. Strauss); Henry Hull (Franz Josef); Sig Rumann (Wertheimer); Christian Rub (coachman); Ferdinand Munier (innkeeper); Bodil Rosing (innkeeper's wife); Gertrude Sutton (Freda); Sue Moore (Anna); Mira McKinney (Miss Dunkel); Eddie Conrad, Lester Sharpe, Hans Joby, Art Hamburger, Arno Frey, Loretta DeLone, Anthony Marlowe (musicians); Henry Victor (Otto); Paul Weigel (organ grinder); Wesley Giraud (groom); Joseph DeStefani, Howard Mitchell (headwaiters); Torben Meyer (ticket taker); Larry Steers (man in uniform); George Du Count (Russian); Philip Terry, Brent Sargent, Ben Lewis (students); Luke Cosgrove (bearded man); Sidney d'Albrook (stagehand); Roland Varno (orderly); Frank Mayo (ship's officer); Christian J. Frank (porter); Boyd Gilbert, Jerry Fletcher, Walter Sande, Harry von Zynda, John Merton, Max Hoffman, Jr., George Magrill (revolutionaries); Edward Keane (officer); Earl Covert, Ralph Leon (voice doubles for Fernand Gravey).

Musical Selections: "Die Fledermaus" ("The Bat," from the operetta *Die Fledermaus*) [Korjus, chorus], "I'm in Love with Vienna" [Houston, Bois, Shean, Kinskey, chorus, orchestra, reprised by chorus], "One Day When We Were Young" [Gravey, reprised by Korjus], "Only You" [Korjus, Houston, reprised by Korjus], "Revolutionary March" [chorus], "Tales of the Vienna Woods" [Korjus, Gravey, café orchestra, reprised by chorus], "There'll Come a Time" [Korjus] (Oscar Hammerstein II, Johann Strauss II); "An Artist's Life" [orchestra], "The Blue Danube" [orchestra, chorus], "Vienna Blood" [orchestra] (Johann Strauss II).

Alternate Title: *The Life of Johann Strauss.*
Academy Awards: Best Cinematography (Joseph Ruttenberg).
Academy Award Nominations: Best Supporting Actress (Miliza Korjus); Best Film Editing (Tom Held).
Home Video: Warner Archive DVD; Warner Home Video VHS.

The Story: In 1845 Vienna, Johann "Schani" Strauss pays more attention to writing music and playing the violin than working as a bank clerk, and he is discharged. The young man's sweetheart, baker's daughter Poldi Vogelhuber, encourages Schani to pursue his dream of leading his own orchestra. At a sparsely attended concert at Dommeyer's casino, Strauss and his orchestra are heard by Carla Donner, a prima donna for the Imperial Opera. Carla promotes Strauss' work in Vienna by singing one of his waltzes ("There'll Come a Time"). Carla is being courted by Count Hohenfried, who looks down on the composer and his music, and a crestfallen Schani returns home to marry Poldi. Hofbauer, a prominent music publisher, signs Strauss to a lucrative contract. Schani and Carla are taken into custody during a student uprising, but they escape on a coach from which they are inspired to create "Tales of the Vienna Woods." After the revolution succeeds and Franz Josef becomes emperor, Schani is hailed as a national hero. He is reunited with Poldi, but his thoughts of Carla strain his marriage. Schani and Poldi tell friends they plan to go on an extended vacation ("One Day When We Were Young"), but Carla reappears to announce that Schani has been commissioned to write a new opera for the national company, and Poldi sees that Carla and her husband are attracted. The opera premieres ("Only You"), but Poldi does not attend. Hohenfried comes to Poldi and verifies the rumors about the relationship between the soprano and the composer; the count advises Poldi to fight for her husband. Poldi goes to the opera and confronts Carla, but Schani intervenes and declares he will go away with Carla. As they are about to leave the city together, Carla gives up Schani for the love of his wife ("One Day When We Were Young"). As Carla's ship sails away, Schani, sitting on the docks, is inspired to pen "The Blue Danube." More than 40 years later, Schani is hailed as "The Waltz King" of Vienna by Emperor Franz Josef and the people of his city.

Many movie musical lovers only know *The Great Waltz* through the excerpt from it in the MGM musical compendium *That's Entertainment, Part II* (1976). The rhythmic chirping of birds, blowing of shepherds' horns, and clip-clop of horse hoofs inspires composer Johann Strauss II—with help from opera singer Carla Donner, his fellow passenger in a coach out in the country—to create the immortal "Tales of the Vienna Woods." It is perhaps the most eye-rolling "and then I wrote …" moment found in a motion picture, and its implausibility doesn't do much for the legacy of *The Great Waltz*. But take a closer look at that curvy blonde setting next to Strauss in that coach. Her real name is Miliza Korjus, and her Oscar-nominated performance—which evokes Mae West as much as it does Grace Moore—steals this film out from under her more-practiced co-stars.

In 1938, the novelty of grand opera in pictures had abated—oddly enough, just as MGM was finding this long-awaited operatic performer with genuine sex appeal to go with her big voice. A spare-no-expense biopic of Strauss, *The Great Waltz* brought its studio great prestige while showing off some interesting directorial touches (from multiple helmsmen) to go with its lush melodies. But the Polish-Estonian soprano with a surname that, Metro's ads helpfully reminded, "rhymes with 'gorgeous,'" is what keeps us transfixed. Not Fernand Gravey, the dashing Belgian-born Frenchman who made a more-than-adequate Strauss, the legendary "Waltz King" of Vienna.[121] And not even the picture's third headliner: German-born Luise Rainer, who at age 28 was already on the downside of a short but astonishing Hollywood career that brought her two Academy Awards.

According to lore, Korjus (1909–1980) wasn't even hired on her looks or acting ability. Already among the top singers in Europe, a coloratura dubbed as "The Berlin Nightingale," the film novice was signed by MGM after the German screenwriter (and future director) Gottfried Reinhardt played a record of her singing Strauss' "Voices of Spring" to Metro production supervisor Irving Thalberg during a telephone call from Europe.[122] Korjus had a pretty face and could act, but hers was a major catch when drawing from opera—she was way too heavy. She came to the U.S. with her husband and children in March 1936. Given MGM's largesse (and, at that point, the confidence Hollywood still had in opera crossovers), Korjus was given plenty of time and resources to get into shape for the cameras, be heard via radio to introduce herself to the American public—and get placed in the proper role.

Part of this process meant the revving of the Hollywood publicity machine, which was fed by columnist Jimmie Fidler in a fan magazine report:

Miliza Korjus (which, reminded MGM, "rhymes with 'gorgeous'") lost weight and then garnered an Oscar nomination for her performance in *The Great Waltz*.

> Meilza [sic] Korjus, the new Viennese soprano, is taking the town by storm. She travels everywhere with a femme bodyguard, wears flame colored tulle around her hair and a turned-up collar on her sealskin coat while rehearsing. Lost 20 pounds her first month in Hollywood, photographs excellently, MGM has signed her. Watch her picture career.[123]

Thalberg died in September 1936, more than a year before shooting began on the Strauss picture, but his colleague Bernie Hyman gave the project further esteem by employing the acclaimed French director Julien Duvivier, one of his country's "Big Five" classic filmmakers of the 1930s (ranking with Jean Renoir, René Clair, Jacques Feyder, and Marcel Carné). Duvivier had made Jean Gabin an international star with a gangster tale, *Pépé le Moko* (1937), and now he was giving Hollywood a try—albeit within a small window of time between projects back across the ocean. His Gabin this time was not the initially announced Nelson Eddy, but instead Gravey, who had made many films in Europe and had already appeared in two American pictures, *The King and the Chorus Girl* (1937) and *Fools for Scandal* (1938), at Warner Bros. The two screwball comedies were directed and produced by Mervyn LeRoy, who had Gravey under personal contract, so when LeRoy moved to MGM in 1938, Gravey (1905–1970) came with him.

That Gravey was not trusted to sing and Korjus had little command of English didn't matter much, for Rainer was to do the heavy lifting as an emoter. The petite, intense performer (1910–2014) had won a Best Actress Oscar as teary Anna Held in *The Great Ziegfeld* and was about to win a second for *The Good Earth*. Add new lyrics by Oscar Hammerstein II for appending to Strauss' familiar noteplay, music arrangements by Dimitri Tiomkin, ballet choreographed by Albertina Rasch, and the usual Metro assets, and *The Great Waltz* was earning a lot of attention already. The comparison to the earlier biopic was firmly established by MGM, which promoted its upcoming picture as "*The Great Ziegfeld* in Waltz Time."

In the wake of *The Great Ziegfeld*'s success, *The Great Waltz* was a highly appropriate follow-up. Johann Strauss II was still a significant figure in popular culture 40 years after his death, and not just on records and in ballrooms. Two films based on Strauss' life came from Germany, one a 1928 silent and the other a 1932 remake. No less a talent than Alfred Hitchcock directed *Waltzes from Vienna* (aka *Strauss' Great Waltz*), a 1934 British production starring Jessie Matthews and Edmund Gwenn; Hitchcock considered this the nadir of his career, but the film has been revived in recent years to some praise. In the United States, there was another *The Great Waltz*, not a motion picture but a similarly lavish stage operetta presented by impresario Max Gordon with a book by Moss Hart. Unlike MGM's film, it focused on the real-life rivalry between the father and son Johann Strausses over the son's greater talent.[124] American tenor Guy Robertson originated the junior Strauss role in New York in 1934 and played it in well over 1,000 performances across the country, but he was passed over for the movie.

As a biopic, MGM's *The Great Waltz* was about an inaccurate as the typical Hollywood effort. An opening title attempted to explain the depiction of Strauss and his times: "We have dramatized the spirit rather than the facts of his life, because it is his spirit that has lived—in his music." The elder Strauss is unseen, mentioned only once in the narrative for his wish that son "Schani" not take up a musical career. The other key characters are fictionalized, Carla Donner from scratch. The film became a love-triangle story, in which Carla becomes Strauss' muse although he is married to baker's daughter Poldi, that was infused with political elements, the latter as shown in 1840s Austrian student uprisings, of which Strauss is an artistic inspiration via his "Revolutionary March," in favor of a constitution and free speech.

MGM took 45 pounds off La Korjus before she was allowed to step before a camera, in May 1938, but the role was worth the wait, even if it was make-believe. Carla is a sexy tigress, described as "a woman of violent feelings, strange whims, irresistible impulses." And that's her lover saying that! She is full of suggestion, particularly for a Production Code-enforced MGM production, and is great fun. When Carla and Strauss meet for the first time, at a society soiree, she informs him that his foot is on her dress. He tries to free it, but it is snagged ... "caught," he says. "So soon?" she says with a wicked smile. Then she remedies the problem by simply tearing the entangled cloth. "We are going to explode a little bomb, you and I?" she says. In the short run, she's talking about her intended singing of a Strauss waltz, which just wasn't done in 1845 Vienna, but she could be foreshadowing their personal interaction. She sings "There'll Come a Time" to an audience that might as well be "Schani" alone, given her body language whenever she's in proximity to the composer, her clenched-toothed smile hinting at her intentions. She peers close to him at the piano, then leads him into a "quiet room" to share some wine. Schani will be married to Poldi very soon, but that won't be a deterrent for Carla.

Korjus' work, which earned an Academy nomination as best supporting actress, received extra oomph after Duvivier's departure from the uncompleted project at the end of June 1938 due to filmmaking commitments in Europe. To replace Duvivier, MGM brought in trusted house man Victor Fleming, and his reshoots—and script revisions by the likewise-uncredited John Lee Mahin—softened the political edges and beefed up Korjus' role. Now, the Schani-Carla relationship was unquestionably more central than

Schani-Poldi. This, Rainer recalled, came about "because they wanted to have more of Miliza Korjus.... I always jokingly said to my friends that after Duvivier had done the film, it was a film of Mrs. Strauss, not Mr. Strauss. Then he was replaced with Fleming, who made a film of Mr. Strauss."[125]

The reworking allows Korjus to emerge more favorably in contrast to her femme co-star. For Rainer, this was the kind of china-doll role that would kill her career in America, although the distractions of her marriage to volatile playwright Clifford Odets didn't help. After spending the film emoting in a drab, one-note manner, Rainer finally uncoils for her character's final confrontation with Carla backstage at *Die Fledermaus*. We know the deceived wife has taken a gun, but the final version undercuts the tension—and firmly asserts Carla as the aggressor—by deleting Poldi's line "I came here to kill you"—which we know exists because it survives as spoken by Rainer in the trailer. Another boost for Korjus is an added reprise of the affecting "One Day When We Were Young" as Carla and Schani part for good, she sacrificing for the sake of his marriage (and the Production Code).

Duvivier can be credited with what are perhaps the two most skillfully shot moments in the picture—an exhilarating early scene in which the Strauss orchestra's playing of the new waltz "An Artist's Life" spontaneously fills a casino dance floor with happy Viennese compelled to come in from off the streets, and a climactic series of camera cuts that mark the entrance of the forlorn Poldi into a cavernous, intimidating opera house and take her from a close-up view to being not much bigger than a dot. Duvivier received sole directorial credit on *The Grand Waltz* and was not recorded as showing discontent with the final product, although the finale was shot by yet a third director, Josef von Sternberg, as a montage showing the public adulation that verifies Strauss' waltz legend. (This sequence also helped Joseph Ruttenberg win an Oscar for cinematography.) Duvivier would return to Hollywood to direct again—most notably in the anthology films *Tales of Manhattan* (1942) and *Flesh and Fantasy* (1943)—but never with the force he had behind him at MGM.

Reviews for *The Great Waltz* were mainly positive, although the "Vienna Woods" scene did not escape derision and some writers considered the whole thing elephantine. It was not lost on perceptive viewers to compare the political aspects of the film to the current situation in Europe, despite MGM's intentions. The picture, made for an exorbitant $2.2 million, lost more than $700,000 for Metro, and Gravey headed back to France and Rainer (after further clashes with MGM over her assignments) to New York. Given the studio's advance good word on Korjus and her performance to match, reviewers were eager to talk her up as an operatic sexpot. "That's the first time I knew Mae West could sing like Jeanette MacDonald," one wag was heard to say after a preview screening.[126] But Korjus made no other American movies. She was rumored to co-star in *New Moon*—in the role eventually given to her friend MacDonald—but instead was penciled in for a film adaptation of the novel *Sándor Rózsa*. However, her MGM contract expired, and she reportedly entered negotiations with Warner Bros. to star in a remake of *The Desert Song*.[127] Before that could happen, in May 1940, Korjus was severely injured in an auto accident in Los Angeles; she broke a leg and was bedridden for six months.[128] Her leg was saved from amputation, but the delay kept Korjus away from public view all the longer. She made a film in Mexico not long after, and enjoyed a long recording and concert career, much of it back in the United States, but just not before the movie camera.

Many Americans lost touch with *The Great Waltz* until its fragmented appearance in *That's Entertainment, Part II*. The same was not said for the people of Russia, where prints sent before the outbreak of World War II stayed for the duration because of the restrictions of the conflict. With little new product coming in, *The Great Waltz* was played repeatedly through Soviet projectors, to an unforeseen result. According to historian Michael Sragow, Korjus was told that she was Joseph Stalin's favorite actress, and that whenever the autocrat, sitting in his screening room at the Kremlin, saw her sing "One Day When We Were Young" at the end of *The Great Waltz*, "he would rise from his seat, place his head against the wall, and weep like a baby."[129]

6

The Teenagers Are Restless

American youth wanted to go dancing in the mid–1930s, and the foxtrot just wasn't going to cut the rug. Disinterested in traditional pop fare as a respite from impending worldly economic reverses, the young demanded a new kind of escapist musical entertainment in an uncertain new era. Its answer came with swing, the potent mix of jazz and dance music that swept listeners away from their troubles with driving big-band rhythms and frenetic, responsive movement. Big-band jazz didn't just suddenly appear in 1935; it had existed for decades on the margins of popular entertainment, and in wider acceptance through the popularity of black bandleaders Duke Ellington, Cab Calloway, and others. But just as the rock 'n' roll revolution began a generation later when a core African American genre (rhythm and blues) was adapted for palatability by a majority-white audience, so went the transition from jazz to swing.

This time, the catalyst was the white jazz clarinetist Benny Goodman, who began his own band in 1934. Driven by the orchestrations of black bandleader and songwriter Fletcher Henderson and the guidance of visionary white producer John Hammond, the Goodman unit bridged the gap between the improvisational Dixieland-style jazz mainly created by blacks and the more-structured offbeat pop preferred by majority-white audiences. The band gained initial popularity through weekly engagements on NBC's *Let's Dance* radio show, but its real breakthrough came with a raucous, much-publicized live performance at the Palomar Ballroom in Los Angeles on August 21, 1935, that became known as the unofficial start of the "Swing Era." Besides his crowd-pleasing "hot music," Goodman impressed progressives and enlightened mainstream listeners with a racially integrated band that at points included such talented performers as drummer Gene Krupa, pianist Teddy Wilson, vibraphonist Lionel Hampton, and trumpeter Harry James, all of whom went on to lead their own orchestras. Newly christened the "King of Swing," Goodman's was not the first "swing" band, even by definition of that evolving term, which had more to do with a mode of performance than a new musical form. But his was the first to capitalize on the swing craze, breaking attendance records seemingly wherever it played.

Motion pictures could not replicate the energy of live swing—and of the frenetic practitioners of the jitterbug dancing that often accompanied it. But Hollywood could exploit the trend ... and did. This was a polarized entertainment world: Were you partial to swing music, or did you favor "sweet" bands, with their more sedate, less culturally threatening "country club music"? *Radio Mirror* magazine, for example, listed two separate categories of band reviews in its mid-'30s "Off the Record" feature. One list was topped by the headline "Some Like It Sweet" and the other by "Some Like It Swing." In 1936, the same publication debuted its annual "Facing the Music" band popularity poll, as determined by its subscribers. Its swing list was topped by Goodman's ensemble ("and without much argument"), followed "on the side of the hot licks" by Bob Crosby, Tommy and Jimmy Dorsey, Ben Pollack, Glen Gray and his Casa Loma Band, and—as if to prove the fluidity of such labels— the usually more-conservative Ozzie Nelson band.[1] On the other side were such names as Wayne King, Guy Lombardo, Ray Noble, and Henry King, and not far below them was the dubiously crowned "King of Jazz" of a decade prior, Paul Whiteman.

Psychologists and academics derided swing as immoral and emotionally disturbing, in a precursor of those who complained when Elvis Presley and Chuck Berry rocked in the 1950s and the reactionary disc jockeys who burned Beatles records in the wake of John Lennon's "more popular than Jesus" talk in the '60s. One of the most vocal detractors of the new music was Professor Arthur Cremin, director of the New York Schools of Music, who called swing "the greatest libel upon modern civilization that has ever been perpetrated … [from] its beginnings in the dark jungle of the early savage." Cremin claimed to have conducted "laboratory experiments" in which he placed a young male and female in a room. By his reckoning, the subjects became politely friendly as waltzes were piped in, but began to neck if swing were substituted.[2] "I appeal to all New Yorkers who are anxious to preserve really worthwhile music to join us in the fight against Benny Goodman and his kind," Cremin told the press.[3] Somewhere, Benny Goodman and his kind shrugged.

The jitterbug had its own hazards, Americans were told. "These dances are violent exercise and require as much training and as good physical condition as tennis, basketball, swimming and golf," a recent president of the American Osteopathic Association told The Associated Press in 1938. "The hysteria for swing music and the hopping, grimacing dances that go with it will pay its adherents with thick ankles, broken [and] maladjusted feet and an exhausted nervous system, unless they recognize its dangers."[4] A 1939 report that a young woman in New York City—"scantily clad," noted newspaper accounts, and "at a gay liquor party"—fell while jitterbugging, hit her head on a piece of furniture, and sustained a fatal brain hemorrhage failed to abate the fast moves.[5] Even the etiquette-minded columnist Emily Post felt compelled to chime in on jitterbug behavior in the dance space: "…Bad behavior is not permissible just because it is perpetuated in rhythm…. It is NOT all right to knock people down if you knock them down to rhythm!"[6]

Hollywood money men might have become annoyed at all the fuss, especially as live swing bands began to crowd out movie fare from many big-city theaters. A stuffy ex-film star like Mae Murray, with little of a career left to lose, could condemn swing in 1936 as "not in the hearts of those … who have a careful sense of music appreciation."[7] Star shapers and traditional movie-music figures had to pay lip service to the new style, however. Reacting to the strong public criticism of swing, screen songwriter Harry Warren looked ahead, not backward. "There's no doubt that swing music will liven the senses, but is there anything wrong with that?" he asked. "I think it does a lot of good when it sweeps cobwebs out of the brains of a lot of old fogeys."[8] With swing beginning to make Hollywood inroads, Warren wasn't about to dismiss future work opportunities—and he went on to write swing-style tunes for films.

It was easy to present swing acts in small portions with little to no attempts at characterizations, so short subjects were preferred, usually in early Vitaphone-style stand-and-perform mode. Less frequently, swing performers were integrated into features, but not very pleasingly. The movies were more comfortable with contrasting the emotional, instinctual jitterbugs with their deeper-thinking, older "superiors." For example, Oklahoma-bred singer-composer-bandleader Pinky Tomlin took time from playing hicks in his 1936–37 series of Poverty Row musicals (see Chapter 3) to appear in *Swing It Professor* [q.v.], in which his character, a sheltered college music teacher, is forced into poverty because the swing craze has killed demand for highbrow tunes. More often, perhaps, swinging got you in trouble. Between signal appearances in *Pigskin Parade* [q.v.] and *The Wizard of Oz*, Judy Garland's jazzy stylings got her expelled from a snooty private school, where she sings "Swing, Mr. Mendelssohn." This was in a minor MGM musical comedy, *Everybody Sing* (1938), in which everybody tries a little too hard to be eccentric, but when Judy tells her disapproving headmistress, "I can't help it.... I don't know why, but when I hear music it does something to me," folks could relate.

The demand for swing-specific performers became so great that the Harlem-based Whitey's Lindy Hoppers dance troupe was used as a specialty act in such films as *Strike Me Pink* (1936), *A Day at the Races* (1937), and *Manhattan Merry-Go-Round** (1937). An ensemble billed as "The National Jitterbug Champions" was shoehorned into a 1939 Warners musicomedy, *Naughty but Nice* (see below), and even a expectedly staid Jeanette MacDonald musical, *Broadway Serenade* [q.v.], was invaded by a troupe of masked jitterers. In contrast, with little entrusted to them on screen, Goodman and his boys got short shrift in features. Even at their collective creative and popular peak, all they landed were glorified specialty assignments in Paramount's star-filled *The Big Broadcast of 1937* and Warner Bros.' name-dropping *Hollywood Hotel*. What little swing we were seeing in pictures was coming in dribs and drabs—the Goodman numbers, Martha Raye singing "Mr. Paganini" in *Rhythm on the Range* [q.v.], or Fred MacMurray leading his band in "Tiger Rag" in Paramount's *Champagne Waltz*.

This seemed to leave hipper listeners wanting more, as was the case with the California-based writer of this letter to a movie fan magazine:

> I'm not trying to drag down the "finer music," but it's high time people began to admit they like those swing numbers. For the social minded, aren't there enough Grace Moores, Lily Ponses, Gladys Swarthouts, and even a Leopold Stokowski to state their type of music "without" their mournful wail of "too much" swing, when there is a scene or two of it in a picture?
>
> For my part, and I don't believe I'm the only one, I'm wondering why we can't have a real "swing" picture.[9]

DownBeat, a top jazz magazine, was more downbeat in its assessment of Hollywood swing, described in an editorial of December 1938: "Not only does it not swing—not only is it not jazz—it's even stinking as sweet music."[10]

These purists were not to get their way soon. It didn't help that some of swing's biggest performers weren't crazy about their movie sidelights. Louis Armstrong seemed to be all right with his 1938 comedic turn at Warner Bros.—a few years after, he referred to the picture as "that fine *Going Places*"[11]—but Benny Goodman grew dismissive of his own film forays. Artie Shaw, that most intellectual of jazz masters, agreed to lead his orchestra in an MGM romantic comedy of 1939, *Dancing Co-Ed*, then snobbishly complained that the picture was beneath him as the incensed crew, star Lana Turner testified, "plotted to drop an arc light on his head."[12] Shaw avoided a cranial calamity, ended up winning Turner (long enough for a seven-month marriage), and got his wish about screen exposure; his band was under-heard and Shaw barely got to act in the lackluster final product.

The only big-band leader to achieve semi-lasting headliner status in features was Kay Kyser, the colorful, folksy North Carolinian who was featured with his band in seven films, mainly at RKO, between 1939 and 1944, starting with *That's Right—You're Wrong*. Kyser was a safe choice in that although his ensemble could play "hot"—or at least with ample energy—it played more to a novelty angle than a swing-or-sweet hook. Kyser's band was also all-white, which kept certain other objectors at bay. Historian Krin Gabbard has made the interesting case that because Kyser's swing lacks the coolness factor among jazz purists (even though some in the less-discerning general public classified Kyser's output as jazz in its time), he and his band have been historically marginalized despite their sizable following. Rock 'n' roll's big tent has found room for Pat Boone and the Carpenters to stand alongside Lou Reed and the Grateful Dead, but its jazz counterpart is not as inclusionary.

Despite the popularity of his studio programmers, Kyser was certainly not the greatest film figure to emerge from the swing band era. That was Frank Sinatra, who made his movie debut in Paramount's 1941 musical *Las Vegas Nights* as an uncredited vocalist in the Tommy Dorsey band. By this time, we were seeing big bands much more favorably presented, as with Goodman's (finally) in 20th Century–Fox's *Sweet and Low-Down* (1944) and the Glenn Miller Orchestra's appearances in Fox's *Sun Valley Serenade* (1941) and *Orchestra Wives* (1942). Miller, whose band by then was the nation's most commercially popular, insisted during contract negotiations that the unit be integral to the films' plots.[13] Miller would have done more pictures, but the war (and accompanying tragedy) sadly intervened. His appearances fall outside the chronological purview of this book, and when we are left to consider swing-era acts in 1930s cinema, the pickings are much slimmer than in the decade thereafter. In this chapter, we will pick up some of those scraps.

The Big Broadcast of 1937
(Paramount; October 9, 1936)

and *Hollywood Hotel*
(Warner Bros.-First National; December 20, 1937)

The Big Broadcast of 1937

Director: Mitchell Leisen. Executive Producer: William LeBaron. Producer: Lewis E. Gensler. Screenplay: Walter DeLeon, Francis Martin. Story: Erwin S. Gelsey, Arthur Kober, Barry Trivers. Photography: Theodor Sparkuhl. Editor: Stuart Gilmore. Sound: Harold Lewis, Louis Mesenkop, Charles Althouse. Art Direction: Hans Dreier, Robert Usher. Set Decoration: A.E. Freudeman. Musical Director: Boris Morros. Dance Director: LeRoy Prinz. Special Photographic Effects: Gordon Jennings, Paul K. Lerpae. Assistant Director: Edgar Anderson. Running Time: 100 minutes.

Cast: Jack Benny (Jack Carson); George Burns (Mr. Platt); Gracie Allen (Mrs. Platt); Bob Burns (Bob Black); Martha Raye (Patsy); Shirley Ross (Gwen Holmes); Ray Milland (Bob Miller); Frank Forest (Frank Rossman); Benny Fields (himself); Sam Hearn (Schlepperman); Benny Goodman and His Band [including Gene Krupa] (themselves); Leopold Stokowski and His Symphony Orchestra (themselves); Larry Adler (specialty act); Louis Da Pron, Eleanore Whitney (dance specialty); Virginia Weidler (flower girl); David Holt, Billy Lee (train bearers); Ernest Cossart (radio "uncle"); Don Hulbert (page boy); Irving Bacon (property man); Billy Bletcher (property man); Harry Depp (studio assistant); Billie Bellport (Mrs. Peters); Helen "Cupid" Ainsworth (Penelope); Nora Cecil (romance program speaker); Terry Ray [Ellen Drew] (telephone operator); Murray Alper (taxi driver); William Arnold (Jones); Gino Corrado (violinist); Harrison Greene (Violinsky); Leonid Kinskey (Russian); Maurice Cass (science show host); Alexander Schoenberg (science show guest); Edward LeSaint (minister); Marjorie Reynolds (dancer); Matt McHugh (café diner); Dennis O'Keefe (man in radio station lobby); Gertrude Short (waitress); Pat West (stage manager); Mitchell Leisen (man in radio station hallway).

Musical Selections: "Heigh-Ho the Radio" [male trio], "Here's Love in Your Eyes" [Fields], "I'm Talking Through My Heart" [Ross], "La Bomba" [Forest, band, dancers], "Night in Manhattan" [opening instrumental], "Vote for Mr. Rhythm" [Raye, band], "You Came to My Rescue" [Forest, Ross] (Ralph Rainger, Leo Robin); "Bugle Call Rag" [Goodman band] (John Pettis, Billy Meyers, Elmer Schoebel);

"Fugue in G Minor" [Stokowski orchestra] (Johann Sebastian Bach); "You're a Minstrel Man" [Goodman band, female singers] (trad.).

Disc: Decca 23019 ("La Bomba," Frank Forest with Victor Young Orchestra); Victor 25467 ("Bugle Call Rag," Benny Goodman and His Band).

The Story: Jack Carson, manager of the National Networks Broadcasting Company, must placate golf ball manufacturer George Platt and his ditzy wife by hiring talent for the new radio program sponsored by the couple. Agent Bob Miller, the "Boy Bandit of Broadway," aggressively pushes his client, egotistical tenor Frank Rossman, into a featured spot on the show ("La Bomba"). Instead, Carson becomes interested in small-town disc jockey Gwen Holmes, who criticizes Rossman nightly on her show ("You Came to My Rescue"). Miller arranges to have Gwen signed to a contract by NNBC so she can be kept out of circulation to satisfy Rossman. Meanwhile, Arkansas rube Bob Black shows up at the studio with his homemade "bazooka" instrument and asks for an audition with famed conductor Leopold Stokowski. Miller's scheme is exposed in a prominent gossip column, and the Platts, with Carson's support, demand that Gwen be signed for their program. Miller responds by dating Gwen to distract her—they watch Benny Goodman and his band at a nightclub—as Gwen falls in love with him and Carson stews. Feeling betrayed as she learns about the effort to keep her under wraps, Gwen demands a sizable payment to appear on the air, as she receives encouragement from Carson's secretary, Patsy. Gwen sings "I'm Talking Through My Heart" on the Platt show, then begins a romance with Rossman that quickly helps her build a career. Jack offers to marry Gwen, but she declines because she still loves Miller. Jack promotes an on-the-air wedding of Gwen and Rossman, but Gwen goes missing on its eve and Rossman shows up in a drunken state. Patsy goes on instead and makes a hit by performing "Vote for Mr. Rhythm." Miller pleads over the air for Gwen's return, and she and Miller are married over the air.

Hollywood Hotel

Director: Busby Berkeley. Screenplay: Jerry Ward, Maurice Leo, Richard Macaulay. Story: Jerry Wald, Maurice Leo. Photography: Charles Rosher, George Barnes. Editor: George Amy. Sound: Oliver S. Garretson, David Forrest. Art Director: Robert Haas. Music Direction: Leo F. Forbstein. Orchestral Arrangements: Ray Heindorf. Costumes: Orry-Kelly. Dialogue Director: Gene Lewis. Running Time: 109 minutes.

Cast: Dick Powell (Ronnie Bowers); Rosemary Lane (Virginia Stanton); Lola Lane (Mona Marshall); Hugh Herbert (Chester Marshall); Ted Healy (Fuzzy); Glenda Farrell (Jonesy); Johnnie Davis (Georgia); Louella Parsons (herself); Alan Mowbray (Alexander DuPrey); Mabel Todd (Dot Marshall); Frances Langford (Alice Crane); Allyn Joslyn (Bernie Walton); Grant Mitchell (B.L. Paulkin); Edgar Kennedy (Callahan); Jerry Cooper (himself); Ken Niles (himself); Duane Thompson (herself); Raymond Paige and His Orchestra; Benny Goodman and His Orchestra [including Lionel Hampton, Harry James, Gene Krupa, Teddy Wilson]; Fritz Feld (The Russian); Curt Bois (dress designer); Perc Westmore (himself); Eddie Acuff (cameraman); Clinton Rosemond (colored man); William B. Davidson (Kelton); Wally Maher (Drew); Georgie Cooper (seamstress); Libby Taylor (Cleo); Joseph Romantini (waiter); Paul Irving (Bramwell); Ronald Reagan (radio announcer at premiere); Jack Mower (airport guard); Sonny Bupp, David Leo Tillotson (little boys); John Ridgely (hotel desk clerk); Billy Wayne (photographer); Harry Fox (shoe fitter); John Harron (radio official); Lester Dorr, George O'Hanlon (casting assistants); Jean Maddox (hotel maid); George Offerman, Jr. (elevator operator); George Guhl (police officer); Jerry Mandy, Demetris Emanuel (waiters); Carole Landis (hat check girl); John Sheehan (nightclub guest); Constantine Romanoff (falsetto-singing man at drive-in); Harrison Greene (drive-in customer with three boys).

Songs: "Hooray for Hollywood" [Davis, Langford, Goodman band, reprised by Davis, Rosemary Lane, Powell, Healy, Todd, chorus, Paige orchestra], "I'm Like a Fish Out of Water" [Powell, Rosemary Lane], "I've Got a Heartful of Music" [Goodman band, quartet]; "I've Hitched My Wagon to a Star" [Mowbray dubbed by Powell, then by Powell, Paige band], "Let That Be a Lesson to You" [Davis, Powell,

Rosemary Lane, Goodman band, Todd, Healy, chorus], "Silhouetted in the Moonlight" [Rosemary Lane, reprised by Cooper, Langford], "Sing, You Son of a Gun" [Powell, Davis, Langford, Rosemary Lane, Cooper, chorus] (Johnny Mercer, Richard A. Whiting); "Sing, Sing, Sing" [Goodman band] (Louis Prima); "Dark Eyes" ("Otchitchornya") [Paige band, chorus] (trad.).

Disc: Decca 1557 ("I've Hitched My Wagon to a Star," Dick Powell with Harry Sosnik Orchestra); Decca 1558 ("Silhouetted in the Moonlight," Frances Langford with Harry Sosnik Orchestra); Victor 25708 ("I've Hitched My Wagon to a Star"/"Let That Be a Lesson to You," Benny Goodman and His Band); Victor 25711 ("Let That Be a Lesson to You," Benny Goodman and His Band); Victor 25796 ("Sing, Sing, Sing," Benny Goodman and His Band); Victor 36205B ("Sing, Sing, Sing," Benny Goodman and His Band).

Home Video: Warner DVD.

The Story: *Ronnie Bowers, a singer and saxophone player with the Benny Goodman band, leaves the unit after being signed to a contract by All Star Pictures ("Hooray for Hollywood"). His arrival in Los Angeles is greeted by cynical studio public relations man Bernie Walton and photographer "Fuzzy." At the Hollywood Hotel, egotistical star Mona Marshall complains with leading man Alexander DuPrey about their lack of quality roles, and she refuses to attend an important premiere. Studio chief B.L. Paulkin hires Ronnie and Mona's look-alike stand-in, Virginia Stanton, to attend the premiere instead; as the two sing afterward, Mona's sister Dot sets her sights on Fuzzy ("I'm Like a Fish Out of Water"). Mona learns of the deception, and Ronnie is discharged. He learns that Virginia is actually a waitress, and the two court by visiting the Hollywood Bowl ("Silhouetted in the Moonlight"). Left with the inept Fuzzy as his agent, Ronnie is turned down by multiple casting agencies and stoops to work as a car hop at Callahan's drive-in as his old band opens at the Hollywood Hotel ("Let That Be a Lesson to You"). Kelton, a director at All Star, hears Ronnie sing at the drive-in and offers him work voice-doubling DuPrey in song numbers for his new film, "Love and Glory." Ronnie's voice helps make the movie a success at a preview ("I've Hitched My Wagon to a Star"), and DuPrey impulsively accepts columnist Louella Parsons' invitation to sing live on her "Hollywood Hotel" radio show. Meanwhile, during an unrelated rehearsal, Goodman's band performs "Sing, Sing, Sing" and "I've Got a Heartful of Music." With DuPrey's reputation at stake, Paulkin and Walton negotiate a deal with Virginia for Ronnie to dub for DuPrey on the radio. Ronnie, Virginia, Fuzzy, and Mona's eccentric father, Chester, conspire to kidnap DuPrey so Ronnie can sing for himself on Parsons' program. This Ronnie does ("Sing, You Son of a Gun," "Hooray for Hollywood"), and his stardom is assured.*

For their celluloid debut, Benny Goodman and his boys took time from their busy schedule to appear as part of a lineup of radio stars for the third of Paramount's "Big Broadcast" series. In *The Big Broadcast of 1937*—the first of the band's two 1930s feature-film appearances—Goodman (1909–1986) and company backed some of the picture's vocalists and was given an exciting showcase number.

The band's appearance in what was otherwise a predictable behind-the-scenes comic romance was less auspicious on screen than off. Goodman is introduced halfway through the picture as his band launches into a hot arrangement of "Bugle Call Rag," a Top 10 hit for them from 1934. The number is creatively photographed with process shots of individual sections of the band—most notably its intense, charismatic drummer, Gene Krupa—augmented by longer views of the entire unit. It is an effective way to kick off, although Goodman et al. are also heard earlier in a shortish rendition of "You're a Minstrel Man" during a sequence in which the characters played by Shirley Ross and Ray Milland survey the New York nightclub scene. Goodman's clarinet also gets in a few notes at the climax during a brief swing version of "Here Comes the Bride" as sung by the up-and-coming comedienne Martha Raye.

But Goodman's true value to *Big Broadcast of 1937* was as a mutually satisfying promotional vehicle to himself and Paramount. His unit was newly contracted for CBS's *Camel Caravan* radio show—for which the film provided conspicuous exposure of dance bands for non-swingers. Goodman balanced work on the set of *Big Broadcast* in June and July 1936 with the weekly *Camel Caravan* performances and nightly gigs at the Palomar Ballroom. And Paramount was enabled to push an epic battle of high energy versus high class, with Goodman and the august symphony conductor Leopold Stokowski—on hand to lead a Bach fugue in his own maiden film—both among the specialties. Stokie's appearance with the Philadelphia Symphony Orchestra in *Big Broadcast* is much more dramatic than Goodman's by design—with an opening close-up of the conductor's magic hands. This after Gracie Allen has characteristically introduced what she describes as the "hottest swing band in the world."

Even had Goodman's few minutes been excised, *Big Broadcast of 1937* wouldn't have suffered much at the box office; it was a significant moneymaker for Paramount. George Burns and Gracie Allen, singers Frank Forest and Benny Fields, harmonica man Larry Adler, and dialect comic Sam Hearn make brief appearances to fulfill the radio bona fides, and Bob Burns, hot off Para's *Rhythm on the Range*, wanders in and out as a bazooka-brandishing, storytelling hick hoping for an audition with Stokowski. (We are somehow let down that the two incongruous artists never appear in the same scene.)[14] The gist of the plot for director Mitchell Leisen concerns a romantic triangle between the characters played by Milland, Ross, and first-billed Jack Benny.

For Ross (1913–1975), who was called in to sub for original ingénue choice Jane Froman, this was a major career booster. Wearing a Chevalier-style straw hat, she puts across Leo Robin and Ralph Rainger's "I'm Talking Through My Heart" with notable gusto as what the *New York Times* called "a hitherto unobserved bit player who now moves pleasantly up the cinematic ladder."[15] The "bit player" label for Ross wasn't much of an exaggeration: Previous screen chances for the former Gus Arnheim band soloist were little other than uncredited song numbers in *Manhattan Melodrama* (in which she delivered the Rodgers-and-Hart tune that later became "Blue Moon") and the MGM flop *Hollywood Party*. But this *Big Broadcast* part earned her pairings with Bing Crosby (*Waikiki Wedding*) and Bob Hope (*The Big Broadcast of 1938* and more).

Benny Goodman brought his clarinet and his band to *The Big Broadcast of 1937* to support a starry cast that included Martha Raye.

Unlike MGM's simultaneous "Broadway Melody" series of musicals and most of Paramount's Bing Crosby musicals, three of the four "Big Broadcast" movies rarely have been revived for television of late. The exception, *The Big Broadcast of 1938*, was a necessity for home video, given the appearances therein of W.C. Fields and Bob ("Thanks for the Memory") Hope. Using the excuse of a Jack Benny tribute, Turner Classic Movies excavated *Big Broadcast of 1937* from the vault for a single showing on June 28, 2014.[16] Here's hoping for a few more looks.

Conversely, the Goodman band's return engagement, *Hollywood Hotel*, has aged well with the benefit of many small-screen showings—and the enduring quality of Johnny Mercer and Richard Whiting's "Hooray for Hollywood." That ironic, iconic song opens the Busby Berkeley-directed film and hints at Goodman and his band getting more screen time than they will be allowed. The band members are shown riding in convertibles featuring placards promoting movie stars real and imagined, as pretend band members Johnnie "Scat" Davis and Frances Langford are out front singing in an airport sendoff to their (fictional) Tinseltown-bound vocalist, Ronnie Bowers. Mercer's wonderfully tongue-in-cheek lyrics were inspired by his real-life difficulty in establishing himself in pictures a few years before (see Chapter 2). "Hollywood seemed to me like a big put-on, and I just tried to make a little fun of it," he would recall.[17]

"Hooray for Hollywood"—now a staple at award ceremonies and other respectful celebrations of American film—is actually a sly send-up of the industry, boasting of the ease with which any palooka from Paducah "can be a panic," yet we see Ronnie struggle to gain footing in his new career, despite his looking and sounding just like Dick Powell. When next we see Goodman, in a short dialogue scene in which he, Powell, Davis, and Langford are reunited on an L.A. street, Ronnie has found no better work than as a car hop, no more competent representation than his wisecracking hack of an agent (Ted Healy), and no more prestigious of a girlfriend than the double (Rosemary Lane) to a famous star (Lola Lane). The Lane sisters' similarity in look is a key part of the story, although the studio's first choice would have been to cast its resident diva, Bette Davis, in both parts.[18] Powell does his usual good work, although he was tiring of such frivolous roles.

Oblivious to the trials of their erstwhile colleague, Goodman leads his band in a truncated, two-minutes-and-change version of the dynamic signature song "Sing, Sing, Sing," with solos for Gene Krupa, Harry James, and himself. Goodman was already associated with the song, so it was a safe choice. Continuing what is depicted as a rehearsal session at the eponymous hotel, "I've Got a Heartful of Music" follows as performed by the integrated quartet of Goodman, Krupa, Teddy Wilson, and Lionel Hampton. Southern audiences were deprived of seeing this band-within-a-band in many places—pity on them—but the informal jam-session setting made the number more tolerable to some patrons than a "public" interracial performance. The end of the number reveals as much about Goodman's demanding personality as any movie audiences were going to get, as he reminds his charges, "That's all, and don't forget, let's be on time tonight!" According to Goodman lore, Warner Bros. attempted to synchronize a visual of "Scat" Davis, who was a trumpet player as well as an actor but not real a Goodman band member, with an actual solo by James in "Sing, Sing, Sing," but the bandleader threatened to pull out of the film if the studio got its way. Another version of the story states that Goodman complained about Warners' attempt to dub Davis' genuine trumpet work into the recording made by the band.[19]

At picture's end, Raymond Paige's less-interesting orchestra has replaced Goodman's at the hotel just as Ronnie/Powell is getting his big break, and the trademark patterned-dancing Berkeley spectacle number never comes, an ultimately tiresome Paige revival of "Dark Eyes" climaxing the film instead. At least we get a reprise of "Hooray for Hollywood" at the very close, but for Berkeley, and an increasingly budget-conscious Warner Bros., this was the last "big" musical of the decade.

Newspaper columnist, and purported "First Lady of Hollywood," Louella Parsons was the host of the CBS radio show *Hollywood Hotel*, which inspired the film's title and setting, and she was convinced by Warners to appear in the movie. It wasn't a great experience, as Parsons dared to relate during filming in September 1937 for the world to read in her column: Under the "all-seeing eye of the camera … you start getting an inferiority complex.… I won't say I am becoming an actress because I never will be one."[20] Parsons came off so stiff on screen that most of her footage was deleted, and she chose to blame Berkeley's well-known drinking problems for the middling box-office returns. Moreover, the radio program's sponsor, Campbell Soup, and the owners of the real Hollywood Hotel sued Warner Bros. over the studio's use of the hotel in the film's title.[21] Continuing the bad karma: Ted Healy's sudden, mysterious death from a heart attack (still whispered about as homicide), which occurred hours after he attended a preview of the film in Los Angeles.

Lost among the laugh generators in the cast—Hugh Herbert, Glenda Farrell, Alan Mowbray, and Martha Raye tooth-alike Mabel Todd—a serious (and uncredited) Ronald Reagan puts in a very early appearance as a red-carpet radio announcer. But it was Goodman and the gang whom many patrons came to see. *Hollywood Hotel* opened in New York City in January 1938 at the Strand Theatre, where swing kids hung out in anticipation of their favorite band. As *New York Times* critic Frank S. Nugent pointed out about his first look at this "perspiringly energetic" picture:

> We left sure of one thing, our sanity not necessarily excepted: it is that, next to Mr. Goodman's swing band, the noisiest thing in the world is an audience of Goodman admirers. Since the maestro is going to give a recital at Carnegie Hall this Sunday, we feel the management should be informed and advised to take whatever cover is available.… For Mr. Goodman could not so much as poke his clarinet into camera range yesterday without producing an ovation. …
>
> We could have done with a few less musical numbers …. But Benny Goodman's fans didn't seem to mind. They were yowling for more when we left.[22]

The recital to which Nugent refers turned out to be the high point of Goodman's long career—the orchestra's legendary Carnegie Hall performance on January 16, 1938. It did for jazz what Paul Whiteman's "Experiment in Modern Music" semi-classical concert at New York's Aeolian Hall in 1924 did for an earlier form of pop. Both presentations, 14 years apart, legitimatized the people's music to the nation's cultural gatekeepers. Goodman had feared his Carnegie Hall foray would be dismissed as a mere publicity gambit, but it came at the right time, just as *Hollywood Hotel*, which was viewed by the nation at the same time, preserves his unforgettable band at its apex.

Champagne Waltz
(Paramount; January 29, 1937)

Director: A. Edward Sutherland. Producer: Harlan Thompson. Screenplay: Frank Butler, Don Hartman. Story: Billy Wilder, H.S. Kraft. Photography: William C. Mellor. Special Photographic Effects: Gordon Jennings, Art Smith. Editor: Paul Weatherwax. Sound: John Cope, Harry D. Mills. Music Direction: Boris Morros. Arrangements: Phil Boutelje. Vocal Supervisor: Frank Chapman. Dance Direction: LeRoy Prinz. Art Direction: Hans Dreier, Ernst Fegté. Set Decoration: A.E. Freudeman. Costumes: Travis Banton. Assistant Director: Russell Matthews. Running Time: 88 minutes.
Cast: Gladys Swarthout (Elsa Strauss); Fred MacMurray (Buzzy Bellew); Jack Oakie (Happy Gallagher);

[Frank] Veloz (Larry); Yolanda [Casazza] (Anna); Herman Bing (Max Snellinek); Fritz Leiber (Franz Strauss); Vivienne Osborne (Countess Moriska); Frank Forest (Karl Lieberlich); Benny Baker (Flip); Ernest Cossart (Walter); James Burke (Mr. Scribner); Maude Eburne (Mrs. Scribner); Maurice Cass (Hugo); Guy Bates Post (Lumvedder); The California Collegians (Buzzy's band); Michael Visaroff (Ivanovich); Nora Cecil (train passenger); Ferdinand Munier (Mayor); Sam Savitsky (chief of police); Emil Hoch (chef); Henry Roquemore (first moustache); Russell Powell (second moustache); Ralph Fitzsimmons (Jiggs); Lillian Castle (Maggie); Stanley Price (Johann Strauss II); Rudolph Amendt (Franz Josef); Nick Lukats (young man); Alex Pollard (waiter); Henry Hanna (Heinrich); Tony Merlo (headwaiter); Raymond Brown (commissionaire); Mattie Edwards (old woman); Dorothy Vernon (woman patron); George Lloyd (Greek proprietor); Harold Minjir (clerk); Martha Bamattre (peasant); Alex Woloshin (peasant); Lois Kent (little girl); Tommy Bond (Otto); Richard Carle (postman); H.R. Brannum (man in elevator); Jerry Bergen (shooting gallery proprietor); Tom Brower (Texan); Harold Nelson (driver); Joaquin Garay (singer); Maenner Gesanges Verain (choral group); The Most Beautiful Girls (female orchestra).

Working Title: *Opera vs. Jazz.*

Songs: "Could I Be in Love?" [Swarthout, twice] (Leo Robin, William Daly); "The Merry-Go-Round" [Garay, Swarthout, Veloz and Yolanda, chorus, girls band] (Ann Ronell); "Paradise in Waltz Time" [Swarthout, orchestra, twice] (Sam Coslow, Frederick Hollander); "When Is a Kiss Not a Kiss?" [MacMurray, band, twice] (Ralph Freed, Burton Lane); "The Blue Danube" [orchestra, reprised by Swarthout, orchestra] (Johann Strauss II); "The Champagne Waltz" [danced by Veloz and Yolanda] (Milton Drake, Con Conrad, Ben Oakland); "Tiger Rag" [California Collegians, reprised by orchestra] (The Original Dixieland Jazz Band).

Disc: Decca 881B ("Paradise in Waltz Time," Victor Young Orchestra); Decca 23019 ("Could I Be in Love?" Frank Forest).

The Story: Violinist Franz Strauss, from the famous Viennese musical family, watches the business at his Vienna Waltz Palace decline, despite the singing talent of his granddaughter, Elsa ("Paradise in Waltz Time"). Next door, Max Snellink's newly opened Jazz Palace is thriving with American conductor Buzzy Bellew and his jazz band ("When Is a Kiss Not a Kiss?"). Elsa takes her complaints about the jazz club's noise to American consul Scribner, but Buzzy impersonates Scribner, and he and Elsa fall in love despite the mistaken identity. Happy Gallagher, Buzzy's publicist, is seduced by a jealous Russian countess. Still pretending to be the consul, Buzzy courts Elsa ("Could I Be in Love?"), teaching her how to enjoy the American delicacy of chewing gum. Snellink wants to tear down the waltz palace to create more room for the jazz palace, but Buzzy threatens to quit if the Strauss hall is closed. Elsa learns Buzzy's true identity after she visits the jazz club, which is expanded when the waltz club is closed. Gallagher and Snellink buy a club on Broadway, where they feature Elsa and Franz and their old-fashioned music, while Buzzy's career languishes. However, Elsa and Buzzy are reunited when Gallagher features them at a new combined waltz and jazz palace in New York, where the orchestras team to play "The Blue Danube" and "Tiger Rag."

"That's not music, that's noise," a Viennese waltz club owner in *Champagne Waltz* says ruefully about the sound so loud that it is coming through his walls. The noise is being made next door by a jazz band in this swing-vs.-sweet film standoff—assuming you extend the definition of "sweet" back to the lush, continental melodies of Johann Strauss II. The misleading title of this 1937 Paramount entry makes it sound like a generic, timeless Euro-operetta. Instead, we get a determinedly modern setting—eventually in New York and not Vienna—with 1930s cultural skirmishes fought by Fred MacMurray and Gladys Swarthout in a Billy Wilder-created story about the unlikely pairing of an American bandleader and an Austrian diva. As Wilder claimed to be, Paramount was disappointed in *Champagne Waltz*, on which the studio spent a lot of money with middling returns. A reappraisal of this forgotten but entertaining picture is merited, however.

Champagne Waltz was initially envisioned to star Olympic skating champion Sonja Henie—who in the spring of 1936 was fielding offers from multiple studios for her Hollywood debut—with George Raft.[23] But Henie signed with Fox, and Paramount turned to a replacement with little more screen experience: opera luminary Swarthout, who had debuted in that studio's *Rose of the Rancho* and *Give Us This Night* [q.v.]. Brown-haired and brown-eyed, and with some acting chops, contralto Swarthout held out for six months before agreeing to a screen test by Paramount. Her objections were for aesthetic reasons, as she told a newspaper interviewer in 1936:

> My reluctance to go to Hollywood was based, I believe, on my love for opera, for the personal touch, and the feeling that Hollywood was too "factory-like" in its methods, and too "canned." My attitude gradually changed. As I saw the number of people my music reached, I found a great deal of satisfaction in my work.
>
> Perhaps I have a tendency to proselyte as far as music is concerned.... Therefore, with all the ardor of a preacher spreading the gospel, I'm gratified by large audiences. And motion pictures do give me that.[24]

The early notices on her first two pictures weren't good, but Swarthout was still thought to have promise. Raft's replacement as leading man was Fred MacMurray, whom Paramount was developing much more smoothly in both comic and serious parts, most conspicuously in the Technicolor hit *The Trail of the Lonesome Pine* (1936). A former saxophone player and sometime vocalist with the Gus Arnheim Orchestra, MacMurray (1908–1991) was no great tune-carrier but could pass capably as the smart-aleck jazzman he was now assigned to play for comically inclined director Eddie Sutherland. MacMurray's musicians in *Champagne Waltz* were played by members of the California Collegians, an act for which the actor had played a few years before.

Champagne Waltz was developed from an original story, alternately titled *Vienna Hall* or *Moon Over Vienna*, that was co-written by Wilder in his first project for Paramount. Wilder had spent a couple of unremarkable years at Fox after initial success in Berlin, and while working with Broadway-imported scribe H.S. Kraft, he wrote the swing-in-Vienna scenario and attracted the interest of independent producer Lester Cowan, who bought it for $10,000. But after paying each of the two writers a $1,000 advance, Cowan could not get the project off the ground at Paramount. In lieu of owing Wilder the remainder of the payment of his fee, he arranged to get Wilder a job as a contract writer at the studio where the latter would build his filmmaking fame ... but not now. The script that became *Champagne Waltz* was fashioned by two other writers, and Wilder, who had hoped for better things, was unimpressed by the finished product.

Still, Wilder must have liked what he saw in the slight edge MacMurray brought to his character, who attempts to conquer Viennese music lovers while wooing a lovely descendant of waltz king Johann Strauss, for Wilder used MacMurray as a firmer heavy type in his classics *Double Indemnity* and *The Apartment*. The writer-director also echoed his *Champagne Waltz* story in a script he co-authored for his 1948 musical *The Emperor Waltz*, in which an American phonograph salesman (Bing Crosby) falls for an Austrian countess (Joan Fontaine). Wilder wasn't happy with that picture either, although it was a much bigger success than *Champagne Waltz*.

The latter didn't fall into complete obscurity. "Yeah, I sure remember *Champagne Waltz*," MacMurray told Wilder biographer Maurice Zolotow decades later,

> Yeah, it was where I chew gum all the time. I was a nice guy but fresh. That was how Paramount always cast me. Nice guy. But fresh.... I guess if it hadn't been for Billy, I'd still be playing nice fresh guys. He made me a villain.[25]

The gum thing attracted some attention, as MacMurray's not-quite-a-heel attempts to show Swarthout's character how to be an American by teaching her how to chew the stuff. The lesson in diplomacy (and cultural appropriation) becomes a running joke. The bandleader also pretends to be the American consul to Vienna so as not to let on that he's the reason her family business is crumbling. Swarthout, who hailed from Kansas, has some innate warmth to balance her prima-donna qualities, without the haughtiness that a contemporary like Grace Moore couldn't conceal. A little more seasoning in front of the cameras might have made her into an Irene Dunne–type personality with a dash of sass to go with class. She put more into her pictures than she got out of them.

The jazz club patrons here are of indeterminate age, not like the real "swing kids" of Europe, but they aren't stuffy enough to enjoy the bandsmen's on-stage hijinks pretending to be trained seals. Even the dignitaries who are assembled by manager Jack Oakie to welcome the American musicians are won over with a few bars of "Tiger Rag." By the end of the hour and a half, all that is left to be conquered by the bandleader is the Straussian beauty, an act for which we must wait until shortly before formerly dueling ensembles join together at the finish to play "The Blue Danube" and "Tiger Rag."

Opera luminary Gladys Swarthout touts old-timey Viennese music in *Champagne Waltz*.

The music helps carry us throughout, with a couple of appealing Swarthout showcases, "Could I Be in Love?" and "Paradise in Waltz Time," plus a lively, elaborate "The Merry-Go-Round" song-and-dance sequence set in a beer garden. The last features the renowned dance duo of Veloz and Yolanda, who perform to the title song in their more-familiar ballroom setting. Paramount relied strongly on repurposed music—besides "Champagne Waltz," a pop hit from 1934 offered to positive advantage, there was "The Merry-Go-Round," an obscure Ann Ronell-penned song that had been heard as early as 1934 and only in a couple of Radio City Music Hall trunk shows.[26] After dancing to it in *Champagne Waltz*, Veloz and Yolanda made the song a regular part of their act, although "The Merry-Go-Round" never became a standard.

Radio tenor Frank Forest is prominent among the supporting players but isn't heard singing a note. Ernest Cossart effectively complements the music with a comedic acting turn as an overly secretive waiter/spy who is in on the gum game—his small-dose, Brit-cultured humor is more welcome than Oakie's frequent, tiresome double takes, and the latter's dalliances with a potentially homicidal countess played by Vivienne Osborne.[27] Given its relative lack of availability, *Champagne Waltz* is rarely discussed in depth by historians. But author

Jacqueline Vansant, in her book *Austria Made in Hollywood*, contrasts the "invasion" of jazz in Vienna, "staged as a takeover" in the then-burgeoning European style, with the saving of the endangered traditional Viennese music by transporting it to New York in the film's latter stages—a serious message for those "seeking refuge in the United States from Hitler's tyranny" in "a call for acceptance of different cultures and a reminder of the belief that America was built on the idea of strength in diversity."[28] The Vienna of *Champagne Waltz* is somewhat romanticized, and as run by the fascistic government that predated Nazi annexation, it might have pushed back on an American-style jazz club much more strenuously than the comic opposition depicted on screen here.

For Swarthout, *Champagne Waltz* was one of her happiest experiences of a too-short film career. Her husband, singer Frank Chapman, was on the set as a vocal supervisor. She, MacMurray, and director Sutherland shared some amusement during a scene in which the 6-foot-3½ MacMurray attempted to climb under a small beer garden table for some intimate moments between the leads as they attempt to dine.[29] At another point, MacMurray half-kiddingly complained that "my feet feel as big as hams" as he and the leading lady posed for stills depicting waltz scenes.[30] Swarthout sang her songs for the film in five languages—French, German, Italian and Spanish as well as English—to increase the popularity of *Champagne Waltz* abroad.

In a generally positive review, *Variety* proclaimed *Champagne Waltz* "a box office middleweight."[31] This was not good news for Paramount, which had picked the film to commemorate its "Adolph Zukor Silver Jubilee"—the 25th anniversary of the mogul's founding of the studio—and arranged openings in 20 world capitals in January 1937.[32] The studio touted *Waltz* as the "finest musical comedy Paramount has ever made."[33] But the movie's above-average business in its initial Broadway run was dismissed in the trades as the impact of the Fred Waring band's accompanying live sets.[34] Despite an overall box office performance being rated as "good" by *Harrison's Reports*,[35] the film didn't quite connect, some seeing the film as too heavy-handed despite its frothy aspirations. A typical theater man's response was one from rural Oklahoma: "Good picture, wonderful settings, just a little too high class for our town."[36] Another, from Washington state: "Good picture, good names, poor draw."[37] By now, there was a public backlash against the overuse, or misuse, of operatic performers on the screen, and even an exception such as Swarthout, especially so long after Moore's success in *One Night of Love*, wasn't inclined to catch a break.

Too bad, for *Champagne Waltz* benefits from its appealing stars, elaborate production values, solid-if-not-spectacular music selections—and even a timely hands-across-the-music-world theme. It's still all right to like both "Blue Danube" and "Tiger Rag," isn't it?

Swing, Sister, Swing

(Universal; December 16, 1938)

Director: Joseph Santley. Associate Producer: Burt Kelly. Screenplay: Charles Grayson. Story: Burt Kelly. Photography: Elwood Bredell. Editor: Frank Gross. Sound: Bernard B. Brown. Art Directors: Jack Otterson, Ralph M. DeLacy. Dance Director: Matty King. Music Direction: Charles Previn. Set Decoration: Russell A. Gausman. Costumes: Vera West. Assistant Director: George Webster. Running Time: 67 minutes.

Cast: Ken Murray (Nap Sisler); Johnny Downs (Johnny Bennett); Kathryn Kane (Snookie Saunders); Eddie Quillan (Chick "Satchel Lips" Peters); Ernest Truex (Professor L. Orlando Beebee); Edna Sedgwick (Nona Tremayne); Nana Bryant (Hyacinth Hepburn); Esther Howard (Mrs. Fredericks); Herbert

Heywood (Mr. Beagle); Clara Blandick (Ma Sisler); Ted Weems and His Orchestra (themselves); Elmo Tanner (whistler with Weems band); Emmett Vogan (Murphy); John Ward (Nate Raymond); Hugh Stovall, LeRoy Atkins (black specialty act); Alan Davis (Stafford); Clara Blore (dancer); Alice Weaver (teen dancer); Art Yeoman (reporter); Lloyd Ingraham (station agent); Fern Emmett (store customer); Larry Steers (diner).

Songs: "Baltimore Bubble" [Downs, band, reprised in dance by Downs, Kane, then by Weems band, dancers, then by Downs, Kane, dancers, then by dancers, then by company], "Wasn't It You?" [Downs, reprised by Kane, orchestra]; "Gingham Gown," "Just a Bore," "Kaneski Waltz" (Charles Henderson, Frank Skinner); "I Love to Whistle" [Weems band, Tanner] (Harold Adamson, Jimmy McHugh); "Out of the Night" [Weems band, Tanner] (Walter Hirsch, Ted Weems, Harry Sosnik).

The Story: While visiting his hometown of Greenvale, Maryland, Broadway press agent Nap Sisler discovers Johnny Bennett and Snookie Saunders, who have created a jitterbug dance called "The Baltimore Bubble," and their trombone-playing pal, Chick Peters. Johnny works at a service station (and dreams of owning one), and Chick is stuck in a job as a grocery store clerk, but Nap convinces the youths to go to New York City to seek success. Nap publicizes the "Bubble" by claiming its invention by Professor L. Orlando Beebee, a once-famous dance instructor. A premiere performance of the dance on a bill with Ted Weems' orchestra at the Club Royale is a big hit, and Beebee's dance school is besieged with would-be students. Within weeks, the "Bubble" becomes a national craze, and Johnny, Snookie, and Chick go out on a national tour that fizzles as the dance falls out of style. Snookie, who loves Johnny despite Chick's interest in her, returns with Chick to Greenvale. Johnny stays in New York in hopes of reviving his success with dance partner Nona Tremayne, but their return engagement at the Club Royale with the new "Bennett bump" flops. Johnny returns home in disgrace, only to discover that Snookie and Chick have used Johnny's share of "Bubble" proceeds to purchase and renovate Johnny's old gas station. Meanwhile, Beebee moves to Greenvale to achieve a lifelong goal of becoming a dentist.

A long-forgotten Universal musical comedy, *Swing, Singer, Swing* was acknowledged as Hollywood's first direct response to the widening appeal of jitterbuggery. Made in a hurry and on the cheap in 1938, it made as little of an impact on the public as the temporal dances that it satirizes. *Motion Picture Herald* rightly declared that the film "neither glorifies nor scorns the jitterbug, but shows him to be a normal sort of modern youngster subject to the urges, influences, and incentives youth was always heir to."[38] But when it trolls for laughs, *Swing, Sister, Swing* treats its dancers as if they are living in an alternate universe with an alien language.

In the tale, written for the youth trade by a fortyish producer named Burt Kelly and thirtysomething scribe Charles Grayson and directed by former stage actor Joseph Santley, a vacationing press agent played by Ken Murray (1903–1988) learns about his mother's young neighbors when she gives him a primer on jive talk. Having been taught by them such phrases as "alligators" (swing lovers), "ickies" (swing haters), and "88s" (piano keys), mom (Clara Blandick, aka Auntie Em) tells us that "anyone who doesn't understand swing talk is strictly long underwear." The cigar-chomping agent thinks he'd seen it all in New York, but these Maryland kids will turn out to be a challenging group who will find out that fame can be fleeting.

Playing the kids' leader, Johnny Bennett, is Johnny Downs, the former Our Gang regular who made a musical career out of budget films such as this. Downs (1913–1994) grew out of his Gang youth by age 13 but honed his song-and-dance skills in vaudeville, which enabled him to return to film to stay. Downs signed with Paramount in 1935 but ended up appearing among all the major studios and many minors while being linked to various co-stars (Dixie Dunbar, Eleanore Whitney, even Our Gang alumna Mary Kornman) in the gossip columns. In 1938, so newspaper reports recounted, Downs was saying he was marriage-shy because of a premonition he only had through that October 10 to live. To which a Paramount executive responded: "Johnny Downs can't die, we've got him under a long-term contract."[39]

Come October, Downs' fate-worse-than-death was to be filming *Swing, Sister, Swing* with energy well exceeding that of a would-be corpse, as he leads a surefire group dance called the "Baltimore Bubble." Downs effectively pulls off this film's arm-thrusting signature "bubble" once Murray counter-intuitively brings him and his pals to the big town to work in the studio of a famous but decidedly unhip dance "professor" (Ernest Truex). Downs and co-star Kathryn Kane get plenty of dance practice, as the script calls for repeated renderings of the central tune with practically no inspiration or variation. No wonder the nation gets tired of the "Bubble," which goes out as the interchangeable "Squeegie Slide" comes in … or Downs' flop follow-up, the "Bennett Burp," in this world of disposable entertainment.

The third member of the threesome discovered by Murray is a "slush pumper"—er, trombone player—portrayed by Eddie Quillan. At age 31, Eddie no longer was an easy click with young viewers, but more mature watchers liked the "overaged" comic. Downs was growing into juvenile leads just as Quillan was aging out of them, and this was beginning to limit the latter's screen opportunities. "Glad to see Eddie Quillan on the screen again; Hollywood has neglected him sadly," noted one trade publication. "[H]e has been appearing but seldom."[40] Quillan doesn't try hard to sync his pretend wild trombone playing with the piped-in sound, but few watchers likely cared, and he and

Two young jitterbugs (Kathryn Kane and Johnny Downs) find that fame is only temporary in the Universal programmer *Swing, Sister, Swing*.

Downs were reteamed by Universal in a '39 musical, *Hawaiian Nights*. Quillan (1907–1990) continued a peaks-and-valleys career as a character actor well into the 1980s, although never succeeding as he had in the 1930s.

The two pretties of *Swing, Sister, Swing* remain obscurities, even to buffs. Kane, a Bonita Granville-lookalike, had a brief vogue as a radio vocalist and was billed for a time as "Sugar" Kane—presaging Marilyn Monroe's moniker in Billy Wilder's *Some Like It Hot*. Kane had been singing in film shorts and in even-less-occasional features. "I had to spend some time reforming … to get more dignified. Now I'm starting all over again," Kane, purportedly from New Orleans but actually a New York product, admitted to a reporter during the filming of *Swing, Sister, Swing*.[41] This miss was so gung-ho about her assignment that she supposedly changed her stage name to Kathryn Kane from Katherine Kane out of superstition, as the latter had an unlucky 13 letters.[42] Kathryn/Katherine (1919–2019) spent most of the rest of her career performing on the stage and teaching music, and the part in *SSS* was as good of a role as she ever got on screen. The same was also true for Edna Sedgwick, appearing as Kane's competition for Downs. Sedgwick (1915–2002) was a featured dancer from the stage who came to Hollywood for a specialty in the Fox musical *You're a Sweetheart* (1937). Her real-life pairings with handsome clubmen garnered more attention in the gossip columns than her uninspired line readings in *Swing, Sister, Swing* merited. Both Kane and Sedgwick later married wealthy figures within the industry, Kane to cafeteria heir Horace Boos, who co-founded the first newsreel theater in the Los Angeles area, and Sedgwick to war hero Henry G. Plitt, who founded a national chain of movie theaters.

Swing, Sister, Swing attempts to be topical by offering the presence of an actual famous swing band. This one, however, is led by Ted Weems (1901–1963), who was not the heppest choice, even in 1938. Weems' dance sound leaned more to Lawrence Welk–type sweetness than Goodman-like sass, but the bandleader dutifully gave a nod to the energetic wing of swing in a wire-service interview promoting the film.

> Weems … said that a few months ago he was firm in the belief that swing music and jitterbugging was a passing fad.
>
> "But I'm not so sure," he admitted. "What makes it look as if it might be permanent is the fact that doctors are beginning to complain. They're saying that an hour of jittering is equal to playing a full football game. They're claiming that swing is bad for the heart…. But people are perverse and when somebody tells them they shouldn't do something, they insist on doing it. That's why I'm beginning to think that the jitterbugs will be with us for quite a spell."[43]

If Weems' ensemble is recalled at all, it might be because Perry Como sang in it during the 1930s; unfortunately, Como is nowhere to be seen in *Swing, Sister, Swing*. The fullest number we hear from Weems and company instead features novelty whistler Elmo Tanner in "I Love to Whistle," a retread from a bigger, better Universal pic, Deanna Durbin's *Mad About Music*. The two signature numbers written for *Swing, Sister, Swing* by Charles Henderson and Frank Skinner were that tiresome "Baltimore Bubble" and a not-bad ballad sung by Downs and Kane, "Wasn't It You?," which should have received more play than the film's 67 minutes allowed. "Light and mildly entertaining," was the verdict from *Variety*, which is about as good as this curio could hope for, as box office returns were rated fair to poor.[44] In more than a few locales. *Swing, Sister, Swing* was double-billed with Universal's *Son of Frankenstein*, portending that studio's early-1940s bread-and-butter of monster rallies and B-musicals.

The "bubble" is just a lark for the kids in *Swing, Sister, Swing*, but the egghead professor doesn't quite get it right when he claims that "from now on, swing means only what a gate does!" The expectation of many in 1938 was that this would be only the first in a glut of features exploiting the jitterbug craze. The glut didn't happen, but we still celebrate the swing era, even after good-natured lampoons such as *Swing, Sister, Swing* have been long forsworn.

In an unexpected epilogue of sorts to the story of *Swing, Sister, Swing*, the film was mentioned prominently in an essay by novelist Jerome Weidman (*I Can Get It for You Wholesale*) in a short story, "Product of the Country," written for *Variety* in January 1942. The piece tells of a young American man in Java, Netherlands Indies (now Jakarta), reluctantly on a night out with a young Englishwoman and her aunt just before the outbreak of war in 1939. The movie they see is *Swing, Sister, Swing*, which the cynical Weidman turns into a metaphor for his country's cultural mediocrity in a time of global crisis. In the theater, his date and her aunt press him as to whether the movie accurately reflects America, and the young man goes on to decry *SSS* as "full of too much trucking on the streets and jiving on sidewalks, and ... practically overflowing with Ken Murray and a cigar of barber-pole dimensions. From the ominous silence around me I knew I was going to have trouble."[45]

Going Places
(Warner Bros.-First National; December 31, 1938)

and *Naughty but Nice*
(Warner Bros.; July 1, 1939)

Going Places

Director: Ray Enright. Screenplay: Sig Herzig, Jerry Wald, Maurice Leo, based on the play *The Hottentot* by Victor Mapes and William Collier, Sr. (New York opening, March 1, 1920; 113 performances). Dialogue: Earl Baldwin. Photography: Arthur L. Todd. Editor: Clarence Kolster. Art Director: Hugh Reticker. Sound: Robert B. Lee. Music Director: Leo F. Forbstein. Orchestral Arrangements: Ray Heindorf, Frank Perkins. Costumes: Howard Shoup. Dialogue Director: Hugh Cummings. Assistant Director: Jesse Hibbs. Running Time: 84 minutes.

Cast: Dick Powell (Peter Mason aka Peter Randall); Anita Louise (Ellen Parker); Allen Jenkins (Droopy); Ronald Reagan (Jack Withering); Walter Catlett (Franklin Dexter); Harold Huber (Maxie); Louis Armstrong (Gabe); Maxine Sullivan (specialty act); Larry Williams (Frank); Thurston Hall (Colonel Withering); Minna Gombell (Cora Withering); Joyce Compton (Joan); Robert Warwick (Frome); John Ridgely (desk clerk); Joe Cunningham (night clerk); Eddie ["Rochester"] Anderson (groom); George Reed (Sam); Ferdinand Munier (Mr. Beckman); Janet Shaw, Rosella Towne (young women); John Harron, Charlotte Treadway (guests); Jesse Graves (butler); Ward Bond, Eddy Chandler (police officers); The Dandridge Sisters (singers); Etta Jones (voice double for Anita Louise).

Songs: "Jeepers Creepers" [Armstrong, reprised by Armstrong, Powell, band], "Mutiny in the Nursery" [Armstrong, Sullivan, Powell, Louise, Dandridge Sisters, band, chorus], "Oh, What a Horse Was Charlie" [Powell, Catlett, Huber, Jenkins, reprised by Huber, Jenkins], "Say It with a Kiss" [Powell] (Johnny Mercer, Harry Warren).

Disc: Decca 2267A ("Jeepers Creepers," Louis Armstrong and His Orchestra); Victor 26124 ("Say It with a Kiss," Maxine Sullivan).

Academy Award Nomination: Best Original Song ("Jeepers Creepers," Johnny Mercer, Harry Warren).

The Story: Peter Mason, an ambitious salesman for a New York sporting goods store, sells hunting expedition merchandise to wealthy Marylander Colonel Withering, who needs the goods to conceal an extramarital affair. Peter is assigned to represent the store at the Maryland Steeplechase while posing as an Australian rider named Peter Randall. Peter's boss, Dexter, accompanies him to Maryland as his "valet." They soon meet pretty Ellen Parker, her cousin Jack, and her aunt Cora Withering (the colonel's wife), as well as track railbirds Maxie and Droopy. Maxie and Droopy want to bet on a temperamental horse, Jeepers Creepers, and they insist Peter ride the beast, who behaves only when he hears stableman Gabriel perform a song written (and named) for him. At a party held by the Witherings, the colonel threatens to expose the two imposters, but Peter accidentally lands on Jeepers Creepers and manages to ride him effectively. However, Peter and Ellen are falling in love, and he promises to ride her horse, Lady Ellen, in the steeplechase. On the night before the steeplechase, Maxie and Droopy kidnap Lady Ellen and force Peter—whose identity is exposed—to mount Jeepers Creepers. During the race, Peter and the balky horse are followed around the track during the race by Gabriel and a band playing "Jeepers Creepers." Despite some detours, Peter claims the race, gains a promotion, and wins Ellen. Maxie and Droopy aren't so lucky.

Naughty but Nice

Director: Ray Enright. Executive Producer: Hal B. Wallis. Associate Producer: Sam Bischoff. Screenplay: Richard Macaulay, Jerry Wald. Photography: Arthur L. Todd. Editor: Thomas Richards. Art Director: Max Parker. Sound: Francis J. Scheid, Charles David Forrest. Music Director: Leo F. Forbstein. Orchestral Arrangements: Ray Heindorf. Dialogue Director: Hugh Cummings. Assistant Director: Jesse Hibbs. Costumes: Howard Shoup. Running Time: 89 minutes.

Cast: Ann Sheridan (Zelda Manion); Dick Powell (Professor Donald Hardwick); Gale Page (Linda McKay); Helen Broderick (Aunt Martha); Ronald Reagan (Eddie Clark); Allen Jenkins (Joe Dirk); Zasu Pitts (Aunt Penelope); Maxie Rosenbloom (Killer); Jerry Colonna (Allie Gray); Luis Alberni (Stanislaus Pysinski); Vera Lewis (Aunt Annabella); Elizabeth Dunne (Aunt Henrietta); William B. Davidson (Sam Hudson); Granville Bates (Judge Walters); Halliwell Hobbes (Dean Burton); Peter Lind Hayes (bandleader); Bert Hanlon (Johnny Collins); John Ridgely (Hudson's assistant); Herbert Rawlinson (defense attorney); Selmer Jackson (plaintiff's attorney); Hobart Cavanaugh (piano tuner); Grady Sutton (Mankton); Sally Sage (Miss Danning); Elise Cavanna (aunts' maid); Daisy Bufford (Zelda's maid); Edward McWade (Professor Trill); Jack Mower, Wedgwood Nowell, Sidney Bracey (professors); Bobby Sherwood (nightclub announcer); Ernest Wood (headwaiter); Stuart Holmes (Captain Gregory Waddington-Smith); William Newell (transcriber); Garry Owen, Harrison Greene (bartenders); Al Herman, Jerry Mandy (waiters); Frank Mayo, William Gould (bailiffs); Cliff Saum (radio announcer); John Harron (court clerk); Maurice Cass (witness); David Newell (attorney); The National Jitterbug Champions.

Songs: "Corn Pickin'" [Sheridan, danced by the National Jitterbug Champions], "Hooray for Spinach" [Sheridan], "I'm Happy About the Whole Thing" [Powell, Page], "I Don't Believe in Signs" [Sheridan], "In a Moment of Weakness" [Sheridan, Page]; "Millions of Dreams Ago" (based on "I Dreamt I Dwelled in Marble Halls" from *The Bohemian Girl* by Michael William Balfe) [Page]; "Remember Dad on Mother's Day" (based on Symphony No. 8 in B minor, D.759, "Unfinished," by Franz Schubert) [Colonna, Jenkins] (Johnny Mercer, Harry Warren); "Liebestraum" No. 3 ("A Dream of Love") [pianist, band at party] (Franz Liszt).

Working Titles: *Always Leave Them Laughing*; *The Professor Steps Out*; *Words with Music*.

Disc: Decca 2387B ("In a Moment of Weakness," Dick Powell with Harry Sosnik Orchestra).

The Story: Donald Hardwick, a sedate music professor at Winfield College and an avowed hater of popular music, goes to New York City to get his symphony published. While visiting Don's Aunt Martha, a patron of swing, lyricist Linda McKay convinces publisher Eddie Clark to buy Don's symphony and introduce it as a pop melody, "Hooray for Spinach," sung by radio vocalist Zelda Manion. Don is upset, as are his spinster aunts Penelope, Annabella, and Henrietta back home, but his music, once given a pop treatment by Linda, begins climbing the charts and making big money ("I'm Happy About the Whole Thing"). Don also makes headlines with his unintentional imbibing of high-alcohol concoctions that loosen his inhibitions and draw him closer to Zelda ("Corn Pickin'"). This attracts the attention of a shady music publisher, Sam Hudson, and the hack songwriting duo of Joe Dirk and Allie Gray, who have made a living adapting long-ago classical tunes into pop hits. Hudson signs Don to a bogus contract, and Dirk puts Don's name on a "new" composition, "I

Don't Believe in Signs," that appears to have been plagiarized from a classical piece. Don is hauled into court, where, with the help of his aunts, he attempts to clear his name in hopes of returning to Linda.

It wasn't just about the dance halls for swing on film. Now, swing music was improving the Sport of Kings and upgrading academia. It was giving primo crossover publicity to jazz icon Louis Armstrong and enabling him to perform one of the biggest song hits of 1939. It was not, however, doing much to recharge the movie career of crooner Dick Powell, despite the less-than-best efforts of his home studio, Warner Bros.

Powell (1904–1963) had been complaining about the quality of his film roles and scripts for months before he took part in shooting *Going Places* in the late summer of 1938. For a month in the previous spring, the usually amiable tenor had gone on a short suspension from Warners—his professional home since 1932, a reminder that it had been a long time since *42nd Street*—over his rejection of a co-starring role in a musical titled *Garden of the Moon*. He was seen in theaters that summer playing the title role as a tenderfoot-turned-radio star in *Cowboy from Brooklyn* [q.v.], which gave him some good material but continued a string of underperforming pictures. Responding to Powell's pleas that all of his pictures didn't have to be musicals, WB put him in a straight comedy, *Hard to Get*, opposite Olivia de Havilland, but it too stalled at the box office.

Powell's next project, *Going Places*, emphasized comedy over music, but at least it had Armstrong (1901–1971) and an endearing, Oscar-nominated Johnny Mercer-Harry Warren song. "Jeepers Creepers" did not originate the titular phrase of "no kidding"-type incredulity, but those two words became a catchphrase in 1939 based on Mercer's lyric. Mercer saw

Dick Powell and Anita Louise are the romantic duo in *Going Places*, but it's Louis "Jeepers Creepers" Armstrong (not seen here) who steals the show.

it, as he recalled years later, as a sanitized version of the oath "Jesus Christ!" that could be put to good use.

> I think I heard Henry Fonda say something like "Jeepers Creepers" in a movie, and I thought it would be a cute idea for a song. I searched around quite a bit and then found that it fit so well as a title for that melody of Harry's. It was lucky casting that we got Louis Armstrong to sing it, although it wasn't written for him.[46]

The song was new; the context wasn't. For *Going Places*, Warners hauled out a durable (read: tired) property: a horse racing play called *The Hottentot*, which had been filmed in 1922, with Douglas MacLean as the neophyte steeplechase rider, and in 1929, with Edward Everett Horton audibly heard as the lead. (*The Hottentot* was unofficially resuscitated for Warners' *Polo Joe*, an unremarkable Joe E. Brown comedy of 1936.) The balky steed of that play provided the title of the original, but for this go-around, the screen animal was conveniently renamed Jeepers Creepers to match the pre-written song.[47] That tune, and the jazzman who sings it in the film, were pretty much all that lingered from *Going Places* in 1939. That remains the case for watchers 80 years hence, when the urge is to hit fast-forward when Armstrong isn't on screen.

This was Armstrong's first substantial role in his handful or so before the flicker cameras; heretofore, he'd played himself or horn-playing, band-leading versions thereof. He portrays the aptly named Gabriel, the stableman whose trumpet and/or singing tones are the only modes to soothe the tempestuous Jeepers Creepers, the favorite to win the prestigious Maryland Steeplechase. The impostor rider played by Powell can get around the track only if Gabe and his band are playing the horse's eponymous song. Armstrong's work, especially his love song to a horse, has been the subject of debate among historians, with Krin Gabbard condemning it as "stripped of all sexual menace whatsoever" and arguing that Armstrong was finding his way around Hollywood racial constraints by "subverting the racist program of the film by overplaying and Signifyin(g) on his presenters," the latter term a reference to the African American idea of criticizing or ridiculing the listener.[48] Gabriel is referred to as an "Uncle Tom" by one of the comic villains of *Going Places*, but he also gets to do some un–Satchmo-type things such as ride a fast scooter (in pursuit of the equine JC) and exchange some playful conversation with the hero played by Powell and the tout enacted by Allen Jenkins.

The only allusion to romance on Gabe's part is in a duet of sorts between him and a maid portrayed by African American singer Maxine Sullivan during the film's big song-and-dance number, "Mutiny in the Nursery," only they are not allowed to have physical contact as Powell and female lead Anita Louise share in the same number. Sullivan (1911–1987), who enjoyed a jazz career of nearly a half-century, was no bit performer at this point, having just scored with a "sweet swing" version of "Loch Lomond" that earned her prominence in many ads for *Going Places*. "Mutiny in the Nursery" is a high-energy jam session in Mother Goose rhyme; the reason for the kiddie focus is unclear, though Gabbard wonders if it were "perhaps to associate children's ditties with the infantilized black characters."[49] Among the multi-racial performers are white comedians Jenkins, Walter Catlett, and Harold Huber; the black Dandridge Sisters (including future star Dorothy); and what studio publicity touted as "a group of colored swingsters from Los Angeles' Central avenue." The number was praised in the press, although a grumpy scribe from the *Los Angeles Times* groused that it was "scarcely a surprise to discover certain of the critics giving their applause to the colored entertainers ... and dismissing the star, Dick Powell, in a few contemptuous phrases."[50] That was the case in many evaluations, as when the *Hollywood Spectator* lauded

Armstrong as "a very natural and expressive comedian."[51] The aforementioned *Times* man didn't bother to namecheck Ronald Reagan, cast in his callow-socialite mode and saddled with dialogue like "Look at that Jeepers Creepers go!" that at least was put across by experience from Reagan's previous vocation as a sports announcer.

By Warners' math, *Going Places*, which was budgeted at $571,000 (not cheap, but half of what Powell's *Hollywood Hotel* [q.v.] and *Varsity Show* were allotted), came in at a box-office loss of $144,000.[52] But that most folks even in the 21st century have stored the "creepers … peepers" rhyme of "Jeepers Creepers" in their heads is a tribute to the Mercer-Warren artistry, described by Mercer authority Philip Furia as "jovial pixiness."[53] "Jeepers Creepers" landed at number one on the *Billboard* magazine chart for five weeks, but with a version played by Al Donahue and His Orchestra. Armstrong's own 78 landed in the top 15, and the song was also notably covered at the time by Paul Whiteman, Ethel Waters, and the Gene Krupa and Larry Clinton bands. "JC" earned Mercer his first Academy Award nomination, but no one can quibble with it losing the Oscar to another enduring favorite, "Thanks for the Memory." The song's title was used by Warners for one of its cartoons, a ghost story starring Porky Pig, and by Republic Pictures for its Weaver family/Roy Rogers hillbilly musical comedy released late in 1939 (see Chapter 3 for more on that *Jeepers Creepers*).[54] If younger folk of the 2020s know "Jeepers Creepers," it's more likely due to the trio of horror films of that name, issued in 2001, 2003, and 2017, than anything from the song's heyday.

As *Going Places* opened nationally at the dawn of 1939, Powell had just taken the somewhat risky measure of opting out of his contract with Warner Bros. The last of his WB assignments, *Naughty but Nice*, sat on the shelf for months after Powell's exit before being indifferently released at midyear, shorn of Powell's star billing and burdened with a confusing title, an unimaginative script, unremarkable songs, and the waste of a good cast. Warners had floated reports of Powell being cast in more-prestigious material—stories based on works by "serious" authors Jerome Odlum (writer of the crime novels *Each Dawn I Die* and *Dust Be My Destiny*) and Louis Bromfield.[55] However, in December 1938, Powell and his wife, Joan Blondell, decided on a permanent vacation from Warners, announcing their intentions to free-lance for better roles and foregoing the few short months remaining on their respective studio contracts.

Columnist Jimmie Fidler echoed the opinions of most when he took WB to task for allowing the two stars to be let go:

> Warners had everything to gain if Dick and Joan emerged from experimental pictures as dramatic stars and, on the other hand, if they had failed to live up to their own convictions, their personal popularity would have guaranteed their pictures against heavy loss.
>
> As a fan, I regret the short-sightedness of those producers, for they are recklessly throwing away personalities that I have learned to like, and I know from disappointing experience that about eight out of ten of the substitutes they will offer me will prove unpalatable. I wish that the Warners would read that old fable about the dog and the bone..[56]

Fidler had just appeared in the Powell-rejected *Garden of the Moon*, so one must wonder if that colored his opinion here. He turned out to be right about Dick and Joan emerging as dramatic stars in the long run, but we are getting ahead of ourselves regarding *Naughty but Nice*, which Powell finished just before leaving Warners—and what must have been his final straw.

This was stale fare, a touch of the swing-vs.-classical music generational rivalry. The songs by Mercer and Warren are so-so, a mix of purely original works and some, within the framework of the plot constructed by writers Richard Macaulay and Jerry Wald, intended to closely echo ancient melodies. Powell plays the namby-pamby college professor—is there any other kind in the movies?—whose classical compositions are sped up into pop-chart hits and who then is framed into a plagiarism charge, all the while wondering why the lemonade he thirsts for keeps going down as a potent rum drink. The scholar must also choose between two women—his kind-hearted lyricist partner (Gale Page) and a sultry nightclub singer, played by one of the most publicized young actresses in Hollywood, Ann Sheridan.

Page was a pretty brunette, a former big-band vocalist who was best known for being the only non–Lane sister among the ingénues in Warners' *Four Daughters/Daughters Courageous/Four Wives/Four Mothers* series. *Naughty but Nice* was her sixth film, apparently never with a love scene before the script called for her and Powell to hook up for a kiss. To allay Page's nervousness, Joan Blondell—visiting the *NBN* set—interrupted her knitting to show the younger actress how the smooching should be done, then Page and Powell got the thumbs-up from director Ray Enright on the very first take.[57] Meanwhile, the constant ad-libbing of supporting player "Slapsie" Maxie Rosenbloom, the erstwhile boxing champ playing the unlikely housekeeper of socialite Helen Broderick, irked the already on-edge Powell and kept fellow comic actor Broderick on her acting toes. Zasu Pitts (doing her fluttery-old-maid thing), Allen Jenkins, Jerry Colonna, and Luis Alberni fill out a credentialed comic cast, and even Ronald Reagan doesn't seem out of place as a baby-faced music publisher.

Sheridan (1915–1967) required less assurance than Page in love-making technique. Recently designated as the movies' "Oomph Girl" at the time of *Naughty but Nice*, she had been rapidly climbing stardom's ladder at WB after a slower ascent through bits and small parts at Paramount a few years before. The native Texan proved she could handle musical numbers in the Western *Dodge City* (1938), and thus was handed four of the new songs in *Naughty but Nice*. That must have been fine with Powell, who had been complaining about having to sing so much on screen and was given only a brief duet with Page ("In a Moment of Weakness") in this picture. This kept Powell from having to sing semi-mediocrities such as "Corn Pickin'," a jitterbug showcase, and "Hooray for Spinach," which in the story is supposed to prove that even a song with intentionally awful lyrics and an egghead origin can make a radio splash. Much of the other music heard in the film is appropriated from melodies by such masters as Mozart, Bach, Liszt, and Richard Wagner, some of whom are credited (out of gratitude or guilt) in the opening titles.

Powell's pre-release departure from Warner Bros. left the studio with a marketing quandary on *Naughty but Nice*—which it solved by elevating Sheridan to an unmerited top billing once it finally put the film in theaters in July 1939. (It didn't help in marketability that the title really didn't hint at anything *Naughty but Nice* was about—save for the debatable contention that swing was somehow "naughty.") Bosley Crowther of *The New York Times* frequently failed to match the mass consensus in his reviews, but he got it right in his case:

> Staffed by a competent cast of pranksters, this item might be steady fun if it were any more than a batch of old gags stuffed together. Some of the more time-honored are good for sizable laughs, as they always have been, but the whole thing is pretty flat—even down to the "borrowed" music.[58]

The antipathy toward the film extended to showmen. *Motion Picture Herald* quoted advice from a theater manager from Indiana to "play it on Bargain Night.... A few like this and all Ann Sheridan's buildup will drop like a thud." A theater man from the same state advised that "your audience will go to sleep waiting for this to start and when they wake up, they won't have missed a thing.... I just can't conceive a producer turning out so weak a story."[59] Maybe it was because of overwork: Between them, Macaulay and Wald churned out nine screenplays for Warners' 1938–39 releases (among them the much better *Brother Rat* and *The Roaring Twenties*), and this one could've used a little more tightening and a couple fewer characters.

In retrospect, the cast and context lend *Naughty but Nice* a certain appeal in silliness. In its world, everyone thinks they can craft a song, from the crooked Tin Pan Alley lyric stealer played by Jenkins ("Are you accusing us of bigamy?" he asks when grilled about his plagiarism) to Granville Bates' judge in the climactic trial who will tell anyone who will listen that he once wrote a Hasty Pudding show at Harvard. But the film's timing was no good. By the time audiences were seeing it, Powell was contemplating his first post–WB-contract project, an ultimately forgettable romantic comedy with Blondell called *I Want a Divorce* (1940). At approximately $399,000, *Naughty but Nice* was, not surprisingly, the lowest-budgeted Powell film in four years—since *Broadway Gondolier* (1935)—but it came in at a loss of just over $26,000.[60]

For Powell, a career turnaround was ahead, albeit not until he made a striking transition to tough-guy dramatic roles with RKO's *Murder, My Sweet* (1944). It took some time, but this unexpectedly versatile actor finally proved his career had been sidetracked by bad material and not by bad performances.

Some Like It Hot
(Paramount; May 19, 1939)

Director: George Archainbaud. Executive Producer: William LeBaron. Producer: William C. Thomas. Screenplay: Lewis R. Foster, Wilkie C. Mahoney, based on the play *The Great Magoo* by Ben Hecht and Gene Fowler (New York opening, December 2, 1932; 11 performances). Photography: Karl Struss. Editor: Edward Dmytryk. Sound: George Dutton, Walter Oberst. Art Directors: Hans Dreier, Earl Hedrick. Musical Advisor: Arthur Franklin. Running Time: 64 minutes.

Cast: Bob Hope (Nicky Nelson); Shirley Ross (Lily Racquel); Una Merkel (Flo Saunders); Gene Krupa (himself); Rufe Davis (Stoney); Bernard Nedell (Stephen Hanratty); Frank Sully (Sailor Burke); Bernadene Hayes (Miss Marble); Richard Denning (Weems); Clarence H. Wilson (Ives), Dudley Dickerson (Sam); Harry Barris (Harry); Wayne "Tiny" Whitt (bassist); Edgar Dearing (MacCrady); Jack Smart [J. Scott Smart] (Joe); Nora Cecil (landlady); Pat West (Flo's partner); Byron Foulger (radio announcer); Russell Hopton (barker); Eddie Kane (man in waiting room); Jack Chapin (cook); Lillian Fitzgerald (woman); Sam Ash (man); Harry Bailey (man); The Gene Krupa Orchestra.

Songs: "Blue Rhythm Fantasy" [Krupa and band] (Gene Krupa); "The Lady's in Love with You" [Hope, Ross, reprised by Ross, Krupa and band, then by Hope, Ross] (Frank Loesser, Burton Lane); "Some Like It Hot" [Davis, Whitt, Barris, Krupa and band, reprised by Ross, Krupa and band] (Frank Loesser, Gene Krupa, Remo Biondi); "Wire Brush Stomp" [Krupa and band] (Gene Krupa, Remo Biondi, Ray Biondi).

Also Known As: *Rhythm Romance*.

Disc: Brunswick 8340 ("The Lady's in Love with You"/"Some Like It Hot," Gene Krupa Orchestra); Decca 2568A ("The Lady's in Love with You," Bob Hope and Shirley Ross); Okeh 5627 ("Blue Rhythm Fantasy," Gene Krupa Orchestra).

Home Video: MCA/Universal VHS (as *Rhythm Romance*).

The Story: On Atlantic City's boardwalk, small-time barker/showman Nicky Nelson sponsors "Living Corpse" Sailor Burke—who's been "buried alive" for two months—and a rundown wax museum. Nicky wants to get Gene Krupa's swing band to play the Paradise Dance Pavilion but must convince its owner, Hanratty. Nicky meets singer Lily Racquel in Hanratty's office. To get their act off the ground, they write "The Lady's in Love with You" and she gives Nicky a ring to pawn, but Nicky gambles away both to Hanratty. After hearing them perform "Some Like It Hot," Hanratty hires Lily to vocalize for Krupa's band. Lily and Nicky break up. Nicky works to win enough money to regain Lily's ring, and with Krupa's help, his fortunes turn.

Benny Goodman's band was going strong in 1938, but the biggest news of that year was that Gene Krupa was no longer part of it. The flashy drum master left the orchestra at the beginning of March, his relationship with his boss having become impossibly strained. There were some reports that Krupa believed he was underpaid, but there was more to it than this. Goodman disliked fans' burgeoning attraction to the handsome, energetic Krupa, whose magnetic presence was overshadowing that of the more professorial, audience-detached Goodman. Krupa drummed with such energy and violence that he was said to break an average of two dozen drumsticks per week and require five packs of gum daily, for all the mouth-moving that went with his playing. Fans at concerts often came to scream for Krupa, not Goodman or their fellow bandsmen, to play as the curtain prepared to rise, and the two men began to react to this adulation on stage. Krupa would become, according to his biographer Bruce Klauber, "increasingly unsubtle" in his stick work and Goodman, while Krupa was soloing, "seemed to go out of his way to appear half asleep."[61] Their inevitable break caused a public furor, and one overzealous columnist paralleled it to King Edward's abdication of the throne in England.[62]

In November 1938, Krupa and his own newly formed band were signed by Paramount to play themselves in a Bob Hope picture titled *Some Like It Hot*. With the "King of the Hide-Beaters" in his first legit acting role, *Some Like It Hot* was touted as

Now leading his own band, drummer Gene Krupa brings his trademark frenetic style to Paramount's *Some Like It Hot* (aka *Rhythm Romance*).

an attraction for younger fans in a period when upstart swing was dueling for sales and airplay with Tin Pan Alley. This battle became part of the plot, when a dance-hall entrepreneur (played by Bernard Nedell) balks at hiring Krupa and his boys, then is won over when he sees midway patrons dance wildly to the band's "Wire Brush Stomp." The sequence, filmed in February 1939, was worth the effort for its participants, according to a magazine report: "Pretty soft for those two hundred jitterbugs.... Instead of paying their own money to dance to Gene Krupa's swing band, the kids are actually getting paid for doing what they would rather do than eat!"[63] During its stay in Los Angeles, the Krupa band frequented the Palomar, a popular Hollywood dance spot, to entertain jitterbugs and movie-colony curiosity seekers.

Few remember *Some Like It Hot*, even for the presence of Krupa (1909–1973), and if Bob Hope would have had a say, it would never have been made. Hope made plenty of musicals, but few of his films of any sort were as bad as *Some Like It Hot*, if the comic himself was to be believed. Indeed, the Hope feature remains so obscure that no one stands to confuse it with the same-named Billy Wilder-directed comedy of 20 years later. The older film was so overshadowed, it was redubbed *Rhythm Romance* for reissues and a fleeting home video release.[64] Wilder's heat was generated by Jack Lemmon, Tony Curtis, and Marilyn Monroe in a Roaring Twenties tale that, beyond its name, had nothing in common with Hope's vehicle.

An emerging comic lead but not yet a big star in early 1939, the 35-year-old Hope was assigned by Paramount to a remake of its lackluster 1934 musical comedy *Shoot the Works** in which he inherited Jack Oakie's role as small-time carnival barker Nicky Nelson, who literally gambles away his greatest chance at fame. The whole thing was based on a flop Broadway play, *The Great Magoo*, which was written by Ben Hecht and Gene Fowler but is remembered now only for spawning the first version of the song standard "It's Only a Paper Moon." Hope (1903–2003) had debuted in features with Paramount's *The Big Broadcast of 1938*, in which he sang what would become his signature song, the Oscar-winning "Thanks for the Memory," to co-star Shirley Ross. Hope and Ross clicked, and the studio paired them again in a comedy, *Thanks for the Memory* (1938), in which they debuted the hit "Two Sleepy People." Then came *Some Like It Hot*, which gained most of its credibility from swing pup Krupa.

The rapid disappearance of *Shoot the Works* from public consciousness made a redo all the easier a mere five years later—with, given the intervening change in pop music styles, the band led by Krupa supplanting Ben Bernie's sweet melodies of the first film. The faintly condescending attitude toward swing, which was echoed in 1950s films like *The Girl Can't Help It* as rock 'n' roll was usurping the status quo, also showed up in reviews of *Some Like It Hot*, including the one in *Variety* upon the film's May 1939 release. "Here's one that was turned out deliberately to catch the jitterbug devotees with Gene Krupa and his swing band going to town for the rug-cutters," it read. "...Story itself is just an excuse on which to hang Krupa's musical display.... Aside from the frequent appearances of Krupa's band, picture has little to offer."[65] Extant trailers for *Some Like It Hot* mention Krupa's name before Hope's, and as one newspaper analyst put it, "Mr. Hope might just as well have been at home reading a book for all his presence in the film means to reviewers."[66]

Still, even with the youth appeal (or perhaps because of it), Paramount seemed to have little faith in the film, and for its Los Angeles premiere in May 1939, the studio paired *Some Like It Hot* at the Paramount Theater on a bill with the squaresville Continental Ice Revue, co-sponsored by the American Legion. Patrons saw the live skating first, then, as the *Los Angeles Times* understated, "When the screen is eventually lowered, it reflects a contrasting item."[67] Krupa and his boys adopted a more tried-and-true marketing push by timing an East Coast tour throughout the summer to exploit their new picture.

Even with Hope's fast talking and Ross's pleasing voice, *Some Like It Hot* has little to offer besides the Krupa band's renditions of four songs, with "The Lady's in Love with You" and a Frank Loesser-Burton Lane title tune promoted most heavily. Although the latter two tunes were recorded by Krupa on a double-sided 78 for Brunswick Records, it was the Glenn Miller Orchestra that hit the top of the charts with "Lady's in Love." Perhaps feeling upstaged, or maybe emboldened at no longer having to share laughs with the likes of Martha Raye or W.C. Fields, Hope wielded his power over director George Archainbaud by enlisting his chief radio gag writer, Wilkie Mahoney, to add material to Lewis Foster's screenplay. According to Hope biographer Lawrence J. Quirk, the comic "added many lines for himself, courtesy of Mahoney, which didn't sit well with the other cast members.... Hope, already bossing his sets, ... maintained that it was time to protect his interest and stake out his game."[68] One of those lines in *Some Like It Hot*, spoken by Hope's character to Ross's, that really sounded like a Hope original—"I can see our name in lights—Nicky Nelson and Company!"—actually was.

Hope generally considered *Some Like It Hot* to be not only a lowlight, but also "the rock-bottom point of my career," as was written in his book *The Road to Hollywood*.

> After that one, there was no place to go but up. For years afterward, Bing [Crosby] wouldn't let me forget it. Whenever I started to give him the needle about something, he came back with a rejoinder, something like, "By the way, can you come over to the house tonight, Bob? We're going to barbecue some steaks and then all sit down and watch *Some Like It Hot*." That shut me up in a hurry.[69]

Some Like It Hot cooled Hope's career momentum, but he was already at work on the movie that changed his career for good. The comedy/mystery/horror hit *The Cat and the Canary* came out that November (and solidified Hope's "brash coward" persona, making most of what he had made before on screen instantly forgettable). Once Hope was teamed with Bing Crosby for *Road to Singapore* (1940), his reputation as a comedian really took off. Meanwhile, Krupa appeared as himself in periodic pictures throughout the 1940s—*Ball of Fire* (1941), *Syncopation* (1942), and *Glamour Girl* (1948) among them—and paid a tribute of sorts to his long-estranged mentor with an appearance with the band led by star Steve Allen in the 1956 biopic *The Benny Goodman Story*.

That's Right—You're Wrong
(RKO; November 15, 1939)

Director/Producer: David Butler. Screenplay: William Conselman, James V. Kern. Story: David Butler, William Conselman. Photography: Russell Metty. Editor: Irene Morra. Sound: Earl A. Wolcott. Art Directors: Van Nest Polglase, Carroll Clark. Set Decoration: Darrell Silvera. Costumes: Edward Stevenson. Musical Arrangements: George Duning. Dance Direction: Eddie Prinz. Visual Effects: Vernon L. Walker. Assistant Director: Fred A. Fleck. Running Time: 93 minutes.

Cast: Kay Kyser (Kay); Adolphe Menjou (Stacey Delmore); May Robson (Grandma); Lucille Ball (Sandra Sand); Dennis O'Keefe (Chuck Deems); Edward Everett Horton (Tom Village); Roscoe Karns (Mal Stamp); Moroni Olsen (Jonathan Forbes); Hobart Cavanaugh (Dwight Cook); Kay Kyser's Band featuring Ginny Simms, Harry Babbitt, Sully Mason, and Ish Kabibble; Dorothy Lovett (Miss Cosgrove); Lillian West (Miss Brighton); Denis Tankard (Thomas); Jane Goude (Mrs. O'Connell); Kathryn Adams (Mrs. Ralston); Effie Parnell (Miss Mann); Vinton Hayworth (producer); Charles Judels (Luigi); Horace McMahon, Elliott Sullivan (hoods); Louis Natheaux (studio executive). As Themselves: Sheilah Graham, Hedda Hopper, Erskine Johnson, Jimmy Starr, Feg Murray, Frederick Othman, Charles Doehrer.

Songs: "The Answer Is Love" [Kyser band with Simms, Babbitt, Mason, Kabibble, reprised by Kyser band, chorus and danced by Kyser, Goude] (Charles Newman, Sam H. Stept); "Chatterbox" [Kyser band with Simms, Babbitt] (Allan Roberts, Jerome Brainin); "Fit to Be Tied" [Kyser band with Simms] (Walter Donaldson); "Happy Birthday to Love" [Simms] (Dave Franklin); "(I've Grown So Lonely) Thinking of You" [Kyser band] (Paul Ash, Walter Donaldson); "The Little Red Fox (N'ya, N'ya, You Can't Catch Me)" [Kyser and band with Simms, Babbitt, Mason, Kabibble; reprised by band] (James V. Kern, Johnny Lange. Hy Heath, Lew Porter).

Disc: Columbia 35238 ("The Answer Is Love"/"Happy Birthday to Love," Kay Kyser and His Orchestra); Columbia 35295 ("Fit to Be Tied"/"The Little Red Fox," Kay Kyser and His Orchestra); Columbia 35307 ("Chatterbox," Kay Kyser and His Orchestra).

The Story: With box office revenues waning, Four Star Pictures studio chief Jonathan Forbes vows that his company will give the public what it wants and offer "down-to-earth" entertainment. This involves the hiring of Kay Kyser, who hosts the "College of Musical Knowledge" radio show, and his band ("The Answer Is Love"). To cozy up to his boss, producer Stacey Delmore promises to Forbes that his writing team of Village and Cook will have a story ready for Kyser's first project. Despite the enthusiasm of his agent, Chuck Deems, and his bandmates, Kyser is reluctant to go to Hollywood, but he ultimately gives in. Chuck rents a mansion for the band, and imports Kay's feisty grandmother to run its kitchen, but key members Ginny Simms, Harry Babbitt, Sully Mason, and Ish Kabibble begin to "go Hollywood" with expensive hobbies and glamorous playthings. The story concocted by Village and Cook, about a handsome Venetian gondolier, is too romantic for Kyser's folksy image, and Forbes delivers an ultimatum to Delmore to get the story right. Delmore responds by pushing leading lady Sandra Sands to portray Kay's love interest in place of Ginny Simms. Kay turns the tables on Delmore by agreeing to portray the romantic gondolier, with an announcement to be made at a party filled with Hollywood journalists ("Fit to Be Tied," "Happy Birthday to Love"). The obvious miscasting prompts Delmore to cancel the picture and pay off Kay's contract. Convinced that Hollywood is no longer for them, the contrite band members arrange to have Kay kidnapped and returned home to resume their radio show ("Chatterbox").

Kay Kyser's success in the movies (seven of them!) reminds us that more folks may have experienced the swing era as filtered through his comedic, novelty-driven sound than the more urgent, primal tones of Goodman, Ellington, and Satchmo. Kyser's middle-of-the-road band was not in the vanguard creatively, and its peppy, genial leader was positioned more as a cheerleader than a musician, but they gave the public what many wanted: swing with edges sweetly honed. Given how this business plan worked on the live stage—and especially on the radio, where Kyser and band headlined a popular quiz show with music—film work seemed an inevitability for the gang led by the hyperactive "Ol' Professor" decked out in cap and gown for show.

Propelled by folksy catchphrases such as "Students!" and "C'mon, chillun! Let's dance!" and "That's right—you're wrong!" (and vice versa) uttered by Kyser, his *Kollege of Musical Knowledge* show zoomed up ratings charts after its 1937 debut as the band's records sold briskly and its live sets sold out at record paces. The unit also yielded celebrity from within, as tenor Harry Babbitt, scat singer Sully Mason, mop-topped comic foil Ish Kabibble, and, especially, classy songstress Ginny Simms attracted their own followings. Their roster of hit songs included, by mid–1939, "The Umbrella Man," "Chopsticks," and the unusually playful "Three Little Fishies" (as in "Boop-Boop Dit-Tem Dot-Tem What-Tem Chu!"). This was material that went down easy with all ages and races, and Kyser's act was among the nation's most popular musically.

Blond and bespectacled, North Carolina-born James Kern Kyser (1905–1985) had an exuberant professional personality to go with the gimmick that separated his band from all

On the way to potential movie stardom, bandleader Kay Kyser is waylaid by gangsters Elliott Sullivan (left) and Horace McMahon in RKO's *That's Right—You're Wrong*.

the others that swung. If he was no more a natural comic actor than he was a gifted instrumentalist (he skewed serious offstage, and could hardly play a note), it didn't seem obvious to RKO. In July 1939, the studio signed him to a contract as part of an agreement to include veteran filmmaker David Butler as director, producer, and co-writer.[70] The prolific Butler had ample experience in lightweight musicals and comedies, among which were multiple Bing Crosby, Will Rogers, and Shirley Temple features. Newly at liberty after many fruitful but taxing years at Fox, Butler was approached by Jules Stein, founder of the powerful booking agency Music Corporation of America, and asked to make a picture with Kyser and his band. Butler acceded, then holed up with the writing duo of William Counselman and James V. Kern (the latter of whom had lately left the pop ensemble Yacht Club Boys) and attempted to concoct a story to go with their *That's Right—You're Wrong* title. As Butler recalled in his memoir:

> We thought of fifteen different plots, and nothing happened. We worked about a week. Finally, one night I thought of the idea—why not take the thing such as it is and make a story about it? Here's a bandleader who's not the lover type at all. Have him get an offer to come to Hollywood because he's so popular and carry on from there. They thought it was great....[71]

The less-is-more strategy of screenwriting worked—audiences were perfectly content to sit through a story about Kay Kyser—or a fictionalized version thereof—trying to break into the movies. It also wasn't taxing for Kyser, Butler wrote.

> [H]e wasn't too much of an actor. We had to surround him with other people. None of the band had any experience in pictures. When they would walk into a scene, I'd tell them to take their places, They

didn't know where to stand or to look or anything else.... But it really was a pleasure because they were all wonderful boys....[72]

Kyser was smart enough to agree to send up his folksy persona, and the clued-in multitudes who tuned in to his radio program every Wednesday night on NBC made *That's Right—You're Wrong* all the more entertaining in 1939, if not as much now. Kyser's non-matinee-idol image makes the film's funniest sequence—a faux screen test in which the professorial bandleader "seduces" his stuck-up leading lady (Lucille Ball, still in her ingénue period) by pretending to be a pencil-mustached Venetian gondolier—worth the wait. When Ball makes KK's glasses steam up, it's a hoot for the audience of Kyser's new medium—and an early look at Ball's knack for playing comedy. Meanwhile, the biggest-name legit actor in the picture, Adolphe Menjou (1890–1963), is less refined than usual while playing the fictional counterpart of David Butler—and hams it up with dialogue such as "What have I done! What HAVE I DONE!" and "This is a TRAGEDY!" Distinguished trouper May Robson (1858–1942) is on hand as Kyser's grandmother, seen at what must have been her career nadir in a bathing suit atop a kiddie flotation device in the middle of the mansion swimming pool.[73] Director Butler offered to eliminate the shot, or to rearrange it with another swimmer, but as Robson later was quoted, "Nothing doing; it's in the script, and it's a good gag, and I've never yet refused to do anything my parts have called for."[74]

Edward Everett Horton and Hobart Cavanaugh play under-inspired studio scribes who insist on shoehorning Kyser into an operetta-type screenplay, and Menjou's character is quick to remind Kay that the pair "won the Academy Award last year." (*Variety* speculated that the characters were said to be inspired by RKO's writing team of Graham Baker and Gene Towne.)[75] Kyser, Mason, and friends add to the fun by dressing as farm animals for the production number "The Little Red Fox," one of five new songs for the picture (and a piece of frivolity that one could not have envisioned for Benny Goodman and friends). The "Red Fox" novelty number was the film's most challenging for Kyser and colleagues, given that they are called upon to act in pantomime during a band rehearsal. However, RKO made it easy for the act, with all the numbers in the picture set in a performance context, meaning that no one was called upon to break into song during a dialogue scene. If Simms looks a little plainer than in her later films at RKO and MGM, it's because she underwent facial surgery after this film to make her look more glamorous.

The proceedings also include cameos, at a lawn party tossed by Kyser, by a handful of Hollywood columnists—Sheilah Graham, Hedda Hopper, Erskine Johnson, Frederick Othman, and Jimmy Starr, plus cartoonist Feg Murray. Appearances such as theirs, which happened frequently in pictures, were part of the publicity quid pro quo between the studios and the most famous show-business journalists. The films garnered some publicity; the scribes were supplied with "insider" material, usually written in the most self-deprecating, press-correspondents-are-people-too way. Graham used her space to complain about the 5:30 a.m. on-the-set time while blaming an incident of "camera crowding" on a certain colleague "who shall remain nameless."[76] Hopper, weaponizing her decades of stage and screen experience as a character actress, dwelled on her on-set reminisces with "Dave" Butler and Adolphe Menjou and decreed that Kyser "has some Harold Lloyd and Will Rogers characteristics."[77] Johnson described a "terrifying experience" that included the memorization of two short lines of dialogue, then made a prediction that Kyser's national popularity "will make ... a smash hit at theater boxoffices everywhere."[78]

Johnson was right about the "smash hit." RKO was clued in early, when the November 15 world premiere of *That's Right—You're Wrong* attracted some 25,000 visitors in Kyser's hometown of Rocky Mount, North Carolina, for a day-long celebration that included a mile-long parade; a homecoming dance; appearances by the governors of North Carolina, South Carolina, and Virginia; and an NBC radio broadcast starring the bandleader and his "Kollege."[79] The film swept into theaters by doing the best business for an RKO picture since *Gunga Din* in January 1939.[80] *That's Right—You're Wrong* ranked among RKO's biggest grossers for 1939, making $219,000, behind only the Irene Dunne-Cary Grant screwball comedy *My Favorite Wife* and the Anna Neagle musical *Irene* in the studio's 1939–40 program—that in a season in which the company incurred an overall loss of $480,000.[81] Reviews were almost uniformly positive, and even the stingy *New York Times*, overplaying the Kyser pseudo-academic angle in its review by B.R. Crisler, granted this swing picture "a cautious and conservative passing grade. Something should be counted in its favor for worthiness of aim... ."[82]

That's Right—You're Wrong ends with the fictionalized Kyser rejecting his studio's entreaty to return to Hollywood from North Carolina, but the truth was that Kyser, savvy on the economic end, couldn't stay away. Not only that, but pollsters hired by RKO from the American Institute of Public Opinion—the George Gallup organization—urged the studio to hire Kyser and other acts that appealed to the burgeoning teen audience, which scored Kyser high in ARI surveys as it was buying a larger percentage of movie tickets than ever.[83] Kay and band returned in *You'll Find Out* (1940), a haunted-house tale with three screen baddies—Boris Karloff, Bela Lugosi, and Peter Lorre—who make the film more attractive to horror fans rather than musical mavens.

RKO starred Kyser three more times: *Playmates* (1941, co-star John Barrymore's film finale), *My Favorite Spy* (1942), and *Around the World* (1943). Kyser also was top-billed, with ensemble, in *Swing Fever* (MGM 1943) and *Carolina Blues* (Columbia 1944).[84] None of these had the energy and tongue-in-cheek humor of *That's Right—You're Wrong*. For his first movie outing, at least, Kay Kyser had beaten Hollywood at its own game.

7

Big Stars, Short Memories

Take more than a cursory look through 1930s film musical histories, and you likely won't read about Al Jolson spending an entire feature-length motion picture pretending to be black. Or Ginger Rogers going off the grid in spectacles and false teeth while Fred Astaire was making do with one of his least-graceful dance partners. Or Maurice Chevalier playing second fiddle to a dog.

For all the triumphs by great names in the Hollywood musical's first decade, there were some efforts that were worth forgetting entirely or meriting of the back burner. Let's not overthink this: There was product that had to be delivered by the American film-industry assembly line, and not all of it was top-of-the-conveyor. The films included here are a mix of outright oddities, misuses of time and talent, and halfway-good pictures that are worthy of closer examination. Maybe James Cagney was in the wrong place to hoof for *Something to Sing About*, but he proved he could do just fine as a dancer—and singer!—back at his home studio a few years later in *Yankee Doodle Dandy*. Alice Faye hadn't been allowed to shake her Jean Harlow rep when she made *365 Nights in Hollywood*, but in time she would become her own woman on screen, and in much bigger and better pictures. However well Bing Crosby sang in *Too Much Harmony*—and he always had good song material in the '30s—there was Too Little Script to work with. Other artists were on their way out at their longtime employers, so the studios may not have considered those stars high priority.

Then there was the strange case of Jeanette MacDonald and Nelson Eddy. They had just made what would become one of their biggest box office successes—*Sweethearts* (1938), in which they portrayed a singing-and-acting couple who are tricked into ending their popular professional (and personal) relationship—but only temporarily. Then, for professional (and possibly personal) reasons, the real actors were made to go their own ways—she in *Broadway Serenade* and he in *Let Freedom Ring*. Hollywood columnist Jimmie Fidler, after visiting the two actors on their respective sets, was left to complain to his ample audience: "Nelson Eddy without Jeanette MacDonald is like ham without eggs." And vice versa. Then the box office reports came in, and Fidler stood taller on his soapbox: "Mr. and Mrs. John Q. Public have turned in a hard-boiled verdict. They want Jeanette and Nelson as co-stars, and if they can't have them that way, they don't want them at all."[1]

Maybe the problem was that, given the demands of production, and for double bills at many movie houses, not all pictures could be good. Even Bing Crosby, ever so sunny in the public realm, bluntly (for him) admitted as much in a late-in-life interview about his 1930s films: "So much of what I did seems to run together.... A lot of those pictures were, dare I say, very similar."[2] We have one of those deservedly featured below.

Big Boy
(Warner Bros.; September 11, 1930)

Director: Alan Crosland. Adaptation/Dialogue: Perry Vekroff, William K. Wells, Rex Taylor. Based on the musical play by Harold Atteridge (New York opening, January 7, 1925; 48 performances). Photography: Hal Mohr. Editor: Ralph Dawson. Sound: Hal Brumbaugh. Costumes: Earl Luick. Running Time: 68 minutes.

Cast: Al Jolson (Gus); Claudia Dell (Annabel Bedford); Louise Closser Hale (Mrs. Bedford); Lloyd Hughes (Jack Bedford); Eddie Phillips (Coley Reed); Lew Harvey (Doc Wilbur); Franklyn Batie (Jim); John Harron (Joe Warren); Colin Campbell (Steve Leslie); Tom Wilson (Tucker); Noah Beery (Bully John Bagby); William L. Thorne (Wainwright); Eddie Kane (oyster-hating diner); Edna Bennett (Dolly Read); Ray Turner (stable hand); Bill Elliott (race fan wearing straw hat); The Monroe Jubilee Singers.

Songs: "Liza Lee" [Jolson, danced by chorus], "Tomorrow Is Another Day" [Jolson, three times] (Bud Green, Sam H. Stept); "Hooray for Baby and Me" [Jolson, band], "Little Sunshine" [Jolson] (Sidney Mitchell, Archie Gottler, George W. Meyer); "Dixie" [Monroe Jubilee Singers] (Daniel Decatur Emmett); "All God's Children Got Shoes" [Jolson, Jubilee Singers], "Go Down, Moses" [Jolson, Jubilee Singers] (trad.).

Home Video: Warner Archive DVD; MGM-UA Laserdisc.

The Story: Gus, an African American stable hand, cares for the horses at the Kentucky plantation of the Bedford family, as his ancestors have done for generations ("Liza Lee"). Gus is expected to ride the family's prize animal, Big Boy, in the Kentucky Derby ("Little Sunshine"). Siblings Annabel and Jack Bedford arrive from the big city, where Jack has befriended gamblers Coley Reed and Doc Wilbur. Annabel and Jack attempt to convince their mother to hire English jockey Steve Leslie to replace Gus in the derby, but she reminds them of the loyalty of Gus's family to the Bedfords, as the action flashes back to an 1870 incident in which Gus's grandfather preserved the family honor by thwarting the vicious "Bully" John Bagby ("Tomorrow Is Another Day"). Reed and Wilbur use incriminating information on the dissolute young heir to force the Bedfords to discharge Gus so Leslie can ride Big Boy and throw the race. Fired after a false accusation of tampering with Big Boy, Gus finds work as a waiter in a swank Lexington eatery ("Hooray for Baby and Me") where, on the eve of the big race and with the help of Annabel's beau, Joe Warren, he uncovers the gamblers' plot. Now reinstated, Gus rides Big Boy to victory in the Derby.

Big Boy was one of Al Jolson's greatest triumphs on stage—and, arguably, his biggest failure in the movies. The superstar singer whose talent catapulted the world into the talkie era with *The Jazz Singer* and *The Singing Fool* was wearing thin on the screen by 1930, and by the time the film version of *Big Boy* debuted, insiders knew it was to be the final picture in his history-making alliance with Warner Bros. *Big Boy* disappeared quickly. Today, however, the film is not recalled for the misfortune of its timing, but rather for the oddity of its casting. This was one of the last mainstream Hollywood films in which an explicitly African American central character was played by a white actor, and it is for that blackface novelty that *Big Boy* has become best known, if known at all.[3]

The Singing Fool (1928) was the first blockbuster box office hit of the talkie era, with a then-record $5 million-plus worldwide gross and a monster hit song in "Sonny Boy." Then, due to overexposure and rampant film-musical competition, Jolson's film fortunes began to falter. *Say It with Songs* (1929) unexpectedly started the downturn despite its reuniting of Jolie with Davey Lee, the sonny of "Sonny Boy," and *Fool*'s songwriting trio of Buddy De Sylva, Lew Brown, and Ray Henderson. The maudlin tale of a radio singer forced to leave his beloved "Little Pal" for prison on a murder charge was such a bummer that the Warners Theatre in Los Angeles withdrew it from its schedule on 48 hours' notice. The goodwill generated by the Jolson brand further declined for his next effort, *Mammy* (1930). It was partly shot in Technicolor and offered well-staged minstrel numbers to go with music by Irving Berlin, but the continued melodramatics—and Jolson's sledge-hammer acting style—yielded mixed reviews and indifferent attendance. The bottom line suffered as well, with Jolson's $500,000-per-picture compensation making it nearly impossible for his films to make money.[4]

Even before the release of *Mammy* in March 1930, the relationship between Jolson (1886–1950) and Warner Bros. had soured, and it became well known that Jolson's next movie under his Warners contract would be his last before a new alliance with his friend Joseph M. Schenck and United Artists. Schenck bought the movie rights to *Big Boy*, Jolson's Broadway hit of 1925, for the singer's UA debut. Warner Bros., meanwhile, was having troubles finding a story for Jolson's contract-fulfilling finale in advance of an April 1 deadline, and *Variety* reported that Jolson was about to offer to return the $50,000 advance from the studio for that picture and ask for his release ahead of schedule.[5] Warner Bros. solved the creative problem by buying the *Big Boy* rights from Schenck. Jolson's offer to return Warners' advance has been tied by some historians to disappointment over the reception to *Mammy*. However, although *Mammy* had been shot by this point, it hadn't yet been seen by the public.

Filmed in April and May of 1930, *Big Boy* did not pack Jolson off to the pokey or show him as a drunken derelict, as had been the case in his previous films. He was bringing back Gus, his trademark blackface character from the stage, this time as a happy-go-lucky but deceptively wily stable hand for a Kentucky horse-breeding clan. The most memorable of the songs in the *Big Boy* stage score was "If You Knew Susie" (which became more identified with Eddie Cantor), but the highlight of the show was its racing finale, staged with four live steeds running on a treadmill in Jolson's favorite Broadway theater, the Winter Garden. "Never before did all present seem so distinctly the property of the actor as they did last night," *The New York Times* wrote of the enthralled audience at its January 1925 stage premiere.[6] Jolson toured the world in *Big Boy* before his aspirations to conquer the moving picture field as he had Broadway kept the entertainer away from the musical footlights for some time, but not permanently apart from Gus. For the stable man's return, Jolson was reteamed for luck with *Jazz Singer* director Alan Crosland.

As a Kentucky stable hand, Al Jolson went blackface for virtually all of *Big Boy*, based on his Broadway triumph.

Big Boy was Jolson's first movie comedy—about time. As self-assured as ever, he evaluated his upcoming new/old role in a newspaper interview as filming began:

> ...I don't want to be a negro servant. I want to be Al Jolson in a servant role in blackface. And when they handed me the script to read, I found that about all the servant said was a few "Yes, suhs. No, suhs." We're working it all out, however.[7]

The star was smart enough to know that nobody would watch *Big Boy* and forget that Al Jolson was under the dark makeup. There weren't many "no, suhs," although Gus's unsophisticated way with language makes for ample comic fodder. Retained from the play was this exchange between Gus and a trainer (Franklyn Batie, from the Broadway cast) over the servant's aches and pains:

> JOLSON: "You know what I think is wrong with me?"
> BATIE: "No, what?"
> JOLSON: "I think I've got inferno complications."
> BATIE: "Inferno? ... No, you mean *internal* complications. Inferno means the lower regions."
> JOLSON: "The lower regions? Brother, that's where I've got 'em!"

Although Gus is a fool at times, he is permitted to insult some of his white counterparts, like the vacant-headed English jockey who laments to him over not getting to ride a jackass. "You oughta get on to yourself," Gus replies, putting his hand on the foreigner's shoulder in feigned sympathy. In an uncomfortable Reconstruction-era flashback sequence in which Jolson plays Gus's grandfather, he cowers before the real menace of a virulently racist gunman (Noah Beery), who calls his new acquaintance "alligator bait" and complains that he hasn't "killed a black man in three days." Then the black man—offscreen, unsurprisingly—quells the villain with horsemanship and unforeseen rope-tying skills. This kind of melodrama was considered heavy-handed in 1870, and even reviewers in 1930 derided the flashback as superfluous and overlong, even without thinking to play what would be termed later as the race card.

The flashback seems to exist primarily for two reasons, and one of them is so that nominal female lead Claudia Dell can get a little face time. Dell (1910–1977) was seen in *Big Boy* after having made an impression in the Warners operetta *Sweet Kitty Bellairs* (1930). A former showgirl who had appeared in Ziegfeld and Shubert productions on Broadway, she allegedly was chosen for *Big Boy* by Jolson after he had interviewed some 50 actresses for her role.[8] It shouldn't have mattered that much, for Dell's character is almost extraneous. The flashback also allows Jolson to reel off a few traditional spirituals—"Go Down, Moses" and others—to the accompaniment of the Monroe Jubilee Singers. The entire *Big Boy* stage song score was discarded for the spirituals and four new compositions by Warner Bros. house men, including the oft-rendered "Tomorrow Is Another Day." This was a shrewd, and hardly uncommon, business move, for profits from the use of the new songs would go to the WB-controlled music publishing firm M. Witmark & Sons.

Apart from the music, *Big Boy* is at its most watchable during a comedic portion set at a Louisville restaurant where Gus, working at a waiter after falling out of favor with his longtime employers, seeks to uncover a frame-up that has resulted in his estrangement from Big Boy. Gus cuts up with various unhappy diners, then reunites with an old friend (John Harron) to get the goods on the gamblers who have unseated him from riding Big Boy in the Kentucky Derby. This includes a lengthy exchange taking a dinner order from "the biggest bettin' man in Kentucky" (played by unbilled William H. Thorne) for Gus to wisecrack his way into obtaining key information on the chicanery. The money man waves a big bill at the waiter to get him to sing "Hooray for Baby and Me" because ... well, it's time for another number. Jolson seems to be enjoying this fanciful respite from playing pitiable down-and-outers on film, and even if this isn't his best material, he gives it boundless energy. "Seeing *Big Boy*," the Jolson biographer Michael Freedland has written, "is the nearest a modern audience could come to experiencing Jolson at his greatest."[9]

The afterglow of the inevitable Kentucky Derby victory transitions to a finale that astounds, absent of context. As Gus steps up to a microphone in the winner's circle, there's a fadeout to the real, Caucasian Jolson, who stands upon a stage surrounded by the other cast members, who stand silent as statues or chess pieces (or movie props). Jolson tells the on-screen audience that he hopes they enjoyed the picture, then he is asked to sing a song. One of the actors calls out to suggest the over-exposed "Sonny Boy," a request that causes the patrons to jeer and threaten to walk out. (An in-joke!) Jolson quiets the mob with a reprise of "Tomorrow Is Another Day." This bizarre final sequence was added for the final draft of the screenplay by original scripter Rex Taylor. Nervous Warner Bros. executives may have thought it prudent to add such a scene to a film in which a black character cracks numerous jokes at whites' expense—just to remind the customers that it was only their big pal Al all along.

The *Variety* reviewer offered this reasoning in his write-up, and the trade journal *Harrison's Reports* confirmed that even in 1930 there were concerns over the racial undertones of a film "which may cause riots if it were shown south of the Mason and Dixon line, and which will be resented by many of those who will see it in theaters north of that line."[10] But most media coverage of *Big Boy* ignored what 21st century commenters would have referred to as "whitewashing" in casting. A trade story of 1930 mocked censors in Chicago for ordering the cutting of the word "darky" from local showings of the movie: "Albert Howson, Warner scenario editor, is all a-puzzled trying to figure out the mental ratiocination of the ... censors who ordered the words cut ... because Chicago negroes might be offended by it. And Howson always thought it was an affectionate word."[11]

Big Boy "isn't any special artistic triumph for Jolson," wrote *Variety* in its review, "but it will please the Jolson following."[12] But did it? At the Winter Garden, where patrons had dished out a hefty $6.60 per head to see Jolson live in *Big Boy* five years before, the celluloid version, at $1 per ticket, made "almost a record minimum (*Variety*) of $12,000 in its first five days of release."[13] The film barely made it through two weeks there—three to five had been expected—before being replaced. The public fatigue over song pictures also limited interest. By now, after three film flops in a row, Jolson was on to other projects. First, there was a return to Broadway in *The Wonder Bar*, then the first (and only) of his UA releases, *Hallelujah, I'm a Bum* (1933), which was a bigger commercial failure than any of Jolie's Warner Bros. underachievements. It, writes biographer Herbert Goldman, "proved to be the biggest nail in [Jolson's] professional coffin. Hollywood producers no longer considered him a star of the first magnitude."[14] His per-picture payment considerably lowered from the earlier $500,000, Jolson returned to Warners to make three films, starting with a 1934 version of *Wonder Bar*, but as popular as he remained as a live act, he was never the towering figure on the screen that he had been. His final co-starring role on screen was in *Swanee River* [q.v.] in 1939.

With direction by Lewis Milestone and a Richard Rodgers-Lorenz Hart score, *Hallelujah, I'm a Bum* has been re-evaluated as a true classic, but *Big Boy* isn't likely to be so graced. It was seen only in infrequent repertory screenings for many years, and, apparently, not on TV until it debuted on Turner Network Television in November 1989. It since has been shown occasionally on TNT's sister channel Turner Classic Movies, but only once (at this writing) after 1998. For buffs and curio seekers, however, it has been made available on physical media, first as part of a Jolson collection on laserdisc in 1992 and then starting in 2009 (and with a photo of an un-blacked Jolson on the cover) as a stand-alone Warner Archive DVD. Despite the access we now have to it, *Big Boy* is more of a cultural document of an irreplaceable entertainer than a piece of timeless entertainment.

Too Much Harmony
(Paramount; September 15, 1933)

Director: Edward Sutherland. Producer: William LeBaron. Story: Joseph L. Mankiewicz. Dialogue: Harry Ruskin. Photography: Theodor Sparkuhl. Editor: Richard Currier. Art Directors: Hans Dreier, Robert Odell. Sound: J.A. Goodrich. Dance Director: LeRoy Prinz. Running Time: 76 minutes.

Cast: Bing Crosby (Eddie Bronson); Jack Oakie (Benny Day); Richard "Skeets" Gallagher (Johnny Dixon); Harry Green (Max Merlin); Judith Allen (Ruth Brown); Lilyan Tashman (Lucille Watkins); Ned Sparks (Lem Spawn); Kitty Kelly (Patsy Dugan); Grace Bradley (Verne La Mond); Mrs. Evelyn Offield Oakie (Mrs. Day); Henry Armetta (Mr. Gallotti); Anna Demetrio (Mrs. Gallotti); Dell Henderson (theater manager); Shirley Grey (Lilyan); Billy Bevan (stage director); Red Corcoran (baggage man); Sammy Cohen (dance director); Cyril Ring (assistant director); Oscar Smith (valet); Hobart Cavanaugh (piano tuner); Jack Raymond (Louie); Lona Andre, Verna Hillie, Toby Wing (chorus girls).

Songs: "Black Moonlight" [Kelly, chorus], "Boo-Boo-Boo" [Crosby, chorus], "Buckin' the Wind" [Crosby, chorus], "Cradle Me with a Hotcha Lullaby" [Bradley, chorus], "The Day You Came Along" [Allen, reprised by Crosby], "Thanks" [Crosby; reprised by Crosby, Allen; then by Crosby], "The Two Aristocrats" [Oakie, Gallagher, twice] (Sam Coslow, Arthur Johnston).

Disc: Banner 33160, Brunswick 6643, Conqueror 8363, Melotone 13127, Oriole 2962, Perfect 13034, Romeo 2336, Vocalion 2867 ("Black Moonlight," Bing Crosby); Banner 33165, Brunswick 6644, Conqueror 8368, Melotone 13132, Oriole 2967, Perfect 13039, Romeo 2341, Vocalion 2830 ("The Day You Came Along," Bing Crosby); Banner 33164, Brunswick 6643, Conqueror 8367, Melotone 13131, Oriole 2966, Perfect 13038, Romeo 2340, Vocalion 2870 ("Thanks," Bing Crosby).

The Story: After producer Max Merlin's revue "Cocktails of 1932" closes in Chicago, his company prepares to rehearse in New York for the next version. Traveling east by plane, the show's star singer, Eddie Bronson, is stranded in an Ohio town where singer Ruth Brown and the song-and-comedy team of Benny Day and Johnny Dixon are on stage as "Dixon, Day & Co." ("The Two Aristocrats"). Eddie invites Ruth to New York to be cast as the ingénue in Merlin's show; she agrees to go, but only if Day and Dixon can come as well, so the four journey east via train ("Boo-Boo-Boo"). In New York, Eddie talks high-strung Merlin into hiring all three for the show, and his attentions shift toward Ruth and away from his possessive socialite fiancée, Lucille Watkins ("The Day You Came Along"). Ruth is attracted to Eddie at the expense of her boyfriend, Benny ("Thanks"). Actresses Patsy and Verne distract Lucille by convincing Benny to pose as Southern tobacco millionaire "Charles W. Beaumont, Jr." "Cocktails of 1933" opens with performances of "Black Moonlight," "Cradle Me with a Hotcha Melody," and "Thanks." Lucille—smitten with Beaumont's supposed wealth—breaks her engagement with Eddie, then learns that her new beau is a fake. Benny graciously gives up Ruth to Eddie in time for the show's "Buckin' the Wind" finale.

    In cinematic terms, 1933 was for Bing Crosby what 1915 was for Charlie Chaplin or 1931 for Clark Gable—a calendar year of alighting to undeniable movie stardom. As his signal 12 months began, Crosby was already one of the nation's most popular vocalists, riding an incredible wave of celebrity that had taken him from Paul Whiteman adjunct to champion of the recording studio, nightclubs, and radio wavery. What he had not done yet was become a screen luminary, a status necessary to his crowning as a king of all media. Crosby took that step in 1933, mainly on the strength of three financially successful features: his first with top billing (*College Humor*), a prestigious MGM loan-out (*Going Hollywood*) …

and the least-praised, much-least-remembered *Too Much Harmony*. The last did little more than prove that his home studio, Paramount, could put Crosby in just about anything in '33 and do brisk business.

Crosby (1903–1977) had been flirting with the movies for some time, with limited success. In 1929, as a member of Whiteman's Rhythm Boys vocal trio, he came to Los Angeles with the band for the making of its first cinema showcase, the Universal "super-special" revue *King of Jazz*. Crosby sang effectively with the Rhythm Boys in the picture, but a drunken-driving incident deprived him of a valued solo performance of "Song of the Dawn," a hit handed instead to John Boles on screen. Myriad problems delayed filming—*KOJ* did not debut until April 1930—so Crosby found time to network with Hollywood folk, including his future wife, actress Dixie Lee. After *King of Jazz* was finished (and before it became a major money-loser), he tested for the juvenile lead in a Paramount musical, *Honey*, but someone else was hired.[15] Another solo shot was lost when *The March of Time*, an MGM musical for which Crosby had filmed two numbers, was permanently shelved, unfinished. Crosby continued as a Rhythm Boy and was heard as part of the trio in *Check and Double Check* (RKO 1930), *Confessions of a Co-ed* (Paramount 1931), and a Pathé two-reeler, *Two Plus Fours* (1930), the last inexplicably giving more attention to fellow Boy Harry Barris. Crosby appeared without the Boys to sing a song in *Reaching for the Moon*, a 1930 United Artists comedy that initially was intended as a musical, but it was only one number in a largely inconsequential picture.

Even as his reputation as a singer grew to the point that the Rhythm Boys left Whiteman before Crosby went out on his own, Crosby needed an unlikely benefactor for a jumpstart in pictures. Comedy producer Mack Sennett took note of the potentially potent mix of Crosby's jazzy singing voice and adept comic timing and signed him to star in six two-reel musical comedies, with names based on Der Bingle hit songs: *I Surrender, Dear*, *One More Chance*, and *Blue of the Night* among them. These modest but entertaining films were made for Paramount release in 1931–32, by which time Crosby had become the most popular singer in America.[16] Paramount took note by casting him—second-billed to Stuart Erwin—in *The Big Broadcast* (1932), an inventive radio revue that showcased some of that medium's biggest names and launched a series of similarly named films—and scores of imitations from other studios. Paramount followed quickly with *College Humor*, in which Crosby shared the screen with the more-experienced Richard Arlen, Jack Oakie, George Burns, and Gracie Allen and delivered the Sam Coslow-Arthur Johnston songs "Down the Old Ox Road," "Moonstruck," and "Learn to Croon." In many ways, *College Humor* failed to improve upon *The Big Broadcast*—the *New York Times* called it "unsteady … with a modest fund of humor"—but it found an ample audience in more firmly establishing Bing's jaunty, happy-go-lucky screen persona.[17] Now married to Dixie Lee, Crosby was putting down roots in Los Angeles, building his first family home and awaiting the birth of his first child.

Unlike his major crooning competition—Rudy Vallee, whose film work at this point was mainly confined to specialties, and Russ Columbo, a more classically handsome type with lesser acting chops—Crosby was exploited by rush orders. Even before *College Humor* opened, Paramount found its next Crosby feature in a project that had been held up because of a common malady—"story trouble." *Too Much Harmony* was intended as a sequel to Paramount's very first musical, *Close Harmony* (1929), in which Jack Oakie and Richard "Skeets" Gallagher appeared as an egotistical vaudeville duo and Jewish dialect comedian Harry Green played a comically excitable stage producer.[18] Those three—and *Close Harmony* director Eddie Sutherland—were linked to the follow-up by March 1933, but an acceptable script was wanting. This problem was solved in May with the attachment of Crosby, who signed a two-year contract calling for two films per annum.

Coslow and Johnston returned to provide the songs for Bing—another boost for their pocketbooks—and to build box office in the wake of *College Humor*'s strong opening in June. The *Close Harmony* story was built around the singer in a script written by Joseph L. Mankiewicz.[19] The future hyphenate of *All About Eve* and *A Letter to Three Wives* fame was a contract writer at Paramount who, with director Sutherland and producer William LeBaron, was called into the office of the studio's new production chief, Emanuel Cohen, on the morning that *Too Much Harmony* was to begin shooting. Cohen liked the script but told his visitors that filming would have to be halted: "You have made one terrible mistake. You have Crosby falling in love with the girl. The public will never accept that. You must make the girl fall in love with him!'"[20] A solution would have to be found.

As in *Big Broadcast*, Crosby played a fictionalized version of himself, a famous singer caught between "good" and "bad" girls, and was joined in the cast by some usual suspects, as the singer noted with characteristic self-deprecation in his autobiography, *Call Me Lucky*:

> *Too Much Harmony* was up to its ears in comedians. There were Jack Oakie, Skeets Gallagher, Harry Green, Ned Sparks, and I don't know how many others. I ran in the middle. I'll never forget the first day of shooting. About all I managed to get in was a few nods, and Oakie dubbed me "Old Hinge Neck." There was very little opportunity to get a word in edgewise, competing with such experienced comedians and ad-libbers.[21]

Jack wasn't the only member of his clan to challenge Crosby for attention. Also in *Too Much Harmony* was Oakie's 65-year-old mother, Evelyn Offield, playing the role of a lifetime: the mother of Jack Oakie's character. A nationally syndicated columnist, Harrison Carroll, held that Mr. Oakie and Mrs. Offield (who, to allay confusion, was billed on screen with her son's actual surname) were the "most devoted mother and son in Hollywood" when she was cast for her first and only film.[22]

Casting Crosby's love interest was a bigger challenge, and no one seemed to be sure about the choice as shooting on *Too Much Harmony* neared its start in July 1933. *The Hollywood Reporter* related that director Sutherland "has haunted nightclubs and radio stations … but the sum total so far is several tests which have proved disappointing."[23] For a time, it looked as if Sari Maritza, a blond, British Hollywood newcomer who had just appeared in Sutherland's musical comedy *International House**, would land the role, but it instead went to a brunette, Judith Allen, who had even less experience but who had the good fortune to have been "discovered" by Cecil B. DeMille for his latest film, *This Day and Age*. Allen was whispered to be … uh, linked to Paramount executive LeBaron, who just happened to be the producer of *Too Much Harmony*. Apparently, it didn't matter whether or not Allen could sing; she appears to be song-dubbed in the film, a detriment noted by multiple reviewers, and she does little more as a thespian than look pretty. Paramount also couldn't have been happy over an unexpected burst of publicity about Allen while she was making *Too Much Harmony*—and just before the release of *This Day and Age*. She was thought to be single—DeMille especially wanted it that way—but it was revealed that she had a secret husband, a well-known professional wrestler named "Dynamite" Gus Sonnenberg. He was tiring of the way his wife's social life with actors like Gary Cooper was being written about in gossip columns and admitted so publicly. The resulting headlines slowed the career momentum of Allen (1911–1996), whose slow professional decline would soon find her in Poverty Row Westerns.

For whatever reason, Crosby showed little growth as an actor in *Too Much Harmony*, a routine backstager with too many characters and too much slack plotting. Without the cool confidence he would develop over time on screen, and just short on his appealing insouciance, Crosby is uneasy and too often overshadowed by his comic compatriots. Ensuing Crosby films are also filled with humor specialists, but there is little doubt who's top dog in those. Here, when he's not opening his mouth to sing, Crosby is little more than a slightly overaged juvenile. The strong ensemble emphasis was partly his own design: He asked Paramount to not give him star billing for *Too Much Harmony* and instead, per usual, feature him below the title—here with eight (!) other names in the crowded opening credits card—with the rationale of avoiding a jinx of sorts. Many ads for *Too Much Harmony* did place Crosby at the top above the title, but others emphasized the reteaming of Oakie (1903–1978) and Gallagher (1891–1955) with Green (1892–1958).

O&G's Benny Day and Johnny Dixon and Green's Max Merlin get the best lines in Harry Ruskin's pungent, argot-laden dialogue, which emphasized the duo's incompetence in contrast to its dearth of talent ("If nerves were sex appeal, he'd be Mae West" describes Oakie's character) and the producer's uncultured language-mangling ("It's like the old saying, You buttered your bread, now you have to sleep in it").[24] Dixon and Day (or is it Day and Dixon?) constantly squabble over billing and threaten to derail their new Broadway revue with a wretched slapstick act in which one of the duo tears off some of his partner's clothes. To placate Emanuel Cohen, the script was altered to have Oakie's character impersonate a tobacco tycoon to steal Crosby's temporary fiancée (Lilyan Tashman), paving the way for Judith Allen to fall for the singer without him having the make the first move.

Too Much Harmony wrapped in August and was speeded into theaters the following month, and the haste shows in the mixed bag of music. Coslow and Johnston's "Thanks" is an inferior response to the earlier Crosby tune "Please," but at least Crosby gets to sing it, and three times. In contrast, two other songs written for *Too Much Harmony*, "Black Moonlight" and "I Guess It Had to Be That Way," aren't sung by Crosby in the movie. "Black Moonlight," with a Harlem motif, is filmed in the show-within-the-show mainly in static medium shot. White chorus girls change color to black partway through, and Kitty Kelly, playing a wisecracking Broadway actress, provides indifferent vocals that don't even match her lip movements in a number that comes up way short of the more-innovative work being done at Warner Bros. at the time. "I Guess It Had to Be That Way" didn't even make the final release print, although, like "Black Moonlight," "Thanks," and "The Day You Came Along," it was recorded by Crosby.

Patrons got their money's worth in some better numbers. In her debut in a film career that included many musicals (and marriage to William "Hopalong Cassidy" Boyd), Grace Bradley (1913–2010) sings "Cradle Me with a Hotcha Lullaby" with an assurance that belies her teenage status. The finale, "Buckin' the Wind," is appealingly pre–Code, full of gusty-weather effects that blow away the clothes of the choristers, leaving them covered by a banner reading "CENSORED." But the lingering musical moment in *Too Much Harmony* is more modest: "Boo-Boo-Boo," a pleasant sendup of the crooner craze, is sung by Crosby to Allen in a scene in the baggage car of a train. The tune with lyrics about dukes and peers and racketeers chasing the blues away attracts a car full of enthralled passengers singing the B-B-B word. It plays well 80-plus years later because of the context it sets for the musical era that marked the rise of a new strain of pop.[25]

The public responded with appropriate enthusiasm. By early October 1933, two weeks after its general release, *Too Much Harmony* was breaking box-office records at Paramount theaters nationwide—New York, Los Angeles, Boston, Kansas City, and many other locales reported a doubling or tripling of normal business.[26] Crosby was too busy to bask in the public praise, for even before *Too Much Harmony* debuted, he was at MGM filming *Going Hollywood,* a bigger-budgeted musical with Marion Davies (and Stu Erwin, too, now permanently billed below Bing). With its release in December, it would cap Crosby's big year. Like the majority of Crosby's 1930s films, *Going Hollywood* has received a home video release. The same can't be said (as of this writing) for *Too Much Harmony.*

The Way to Love
(Paramount; October 20, 1933)

Director: Norman Taurog. Associate Producer: Benjamin Glazer. Screenplay: Gene Fowler, Benjamin Glazer. Additional Dialogue: Claude Binyon, Frank Butler. Photography: Charles Lang. Editor: Hugh Bennett. Sound: Eugene Merritt. Art Director: Hans Dreier. Assistant Director: Jack Mintz. Running Time: 83 minutes.

Cast: Maurice Chevalier (François); Ann Dvorak (Madeleine); Edward Everett Horton (Professor Bibi); Minna Gombell (Suzanne); Arthur Pierson (Joe); Nydia Westman (Annette); John Miljan (Marco); Blanche Friderici (Rosalie); Sidney Toler (Pierre); Grace Bradley (sunburned lady); George Regas (Pedro); Douglass Dumbrille (Agent Chapusard); Arthur Housman (drunk customer); Billy Bevan (Prias); George Hagen (Wladek, the Mighty); Jason Robards (guide); Dick Dennis (street singer); Michael Mark (window washer); Kathleen Burke (secretary for Prias); Guy Usher (detective); Tom Ricketts (elderly man in "Lucky Guy" number); Mutt, a Dog (Casanova).

Songs: "I'm a Lover of Paree" [Chevalier, chorus], "In a One Room Flat" [Chevalier, reprised by Chevalier, Dvorak], "It's Oh! It's Ah! It's Wonderful" [played on piano], "There's a Lucky Guy" [Dennis, chorus] (Ralph Rainger, Leo Robin); "The Way to Love" [Dennis] (Arthur Johnston, Sam Coslow).

The Story: François aspires to become a professional guide in his beloved Paris ("I'm a Lover of Paree"). However, he is stuck walking the streets as a "sandwich-board" advertiser for Bibi, a "professor of love" who creates fake travel postcards so that adulterers can avoid suspicion from spouses. François meets Madeleine, an orphaned gypsy girl who is the target in a circus knife-throwing act led by her abusive guardian, Pedro. He also finds a friend in Casanova, a dog he rescues from authorities who believe the pooch to be rabid. Circus barker Marco offers to take Madeleine away from Pedro, but she declines his proposal. Madeleine runs away from the circus and is taken in by François and his neighbors: landlord Pierre, club singer Suzanne, and American composer Joe ("In a One Room Flat"). Madeleine shows her love for François by creating a puppet in his likeness, but he does not respond as she would like. Joe proposes marriage to Madeleine, but she declines. Pedro arranges with the police to reclaim Madeleine, and her friends decide that if she is married, she finally can be free of Pedro. François reluctantly agrees to marry Madeleine, who is upset because of the motive for the marriage. François is hired by travel agent Prias as a guide, and he prepares to tell Madeleine of the good news. But Bibi's wife, Rosalie, plans to have François take a "proper" wife—her love-starved niece, Annette, who has a substantial dowry. Rosalie convinces Madeleine to reject François, who is left to lament his fortunes to Casanova. To patch things up, Bibi hires François as a guide so the two can celebrate their solitude by getting drunk and clipping the neckties of strangers. The pair visit the circus, where François gets roped into taking on a brute in a wrestling match, which François somehow wins. With the prize money in hand, he is reunited with Madeleine, and they go off together after quelling Pedro.

A mix of romance, comedy, and music without nearly enough of any, *The Way to Love* proved that Maurice Chevalier made one too many pictures at Paramount. Chevalier disliked a script that recycled material from previous movies—his and others'. The top two choices for his leading lady rejected the project—one by fleeing all the way to Europe—with the actress who did get stuck in the role not seeming all that enthused. Audiences responded similarly, and a run at Paramount that began with the dawn of sound came to a dismal end for America's favorite Frenchman.

Chevalier (1888–1972) was already starting to show discontent toward Paramount brass. He allowed himself to be upstaged by 1-year-old Baby Le Roy in his previous film, *A Bedtime Story* (1933), a comedy directed by Norman Taurog with songs by Ralph Rainger and Leo Robin. The cute-kid factor gave *Bedtime Story* a happy ending at the box office, so the studio reunited star, director, composers, and supporting comedian Edward Everett Horton for another go. (The nominal replacement for Baby Le Roy was an Irish terrier placed into the story to maintain the cuteness factor.) Chevalier's negotiations for a new contract to begin after *The Way to Love* had flagged, however, and by the time shooting on that film began in May 1933, the general understanding was that it was to be Chevalier's finale for Paramount.[27] Chevalier was whispered to be starting talks with MGM to star in a musical version of *The Merry Widow*, giving *Way to Love* even more of a lame-duck feel.

The disjointed script, credited to Gene Fowler and the film's producer, Benjamin Glazer, was an unofficial rehash of the silent hit *Seventh Heaven*, with the Parisian hero rescuing from harm a gypsy circus girl instead of a prostitute, as before. Chevalier was to be his usual lively self, a vagabond type who aspired to little more than being hired as a tourist guide to his city. But who to play the gypsy? Initially, Carole Lombard was tied to the part in trade reports, but these might have been referring to *A Bedtime Story*, which was at first titled *The Way to Love*.[28] Lombard balked, and the assignment in the actual *Way to Love* went to Sylvia Sidney, the waif-like Paramount actress who was much more at home in drama than in comedy. Sidney spent a month playing the role before production, then supposedly two-thirds complete, was halted in mid–July over the news that the actress needed a throat operation.[29] Sidney went under the knife, then flew to Europe at the end of July to convalesce. Citing ethical violations, the studio filed charges with the Academy of Motion Picture Arts and Sciences, asking for Sidney's return after the filming of *L'amour guide*, the French-language version of *The Way to Love* that was being finished while the English version was in limbo.[30] Sidney asserted she was benefiting the studio by protecting her health. She soon settled her dispute with Paramount in lieu of an Academy hearing, and her scenes in *Way* would have to be reshot at a reported cost of $10,000.

Choice number three was

Maurice Chevalier had to share the screen with a scene-stealing mutt in the humor-shy musical comedy *The Way to Love*.

yet another recalcitrant performer, Ann Dvorak. She was borrowed from Warner Bros., with which she had been battling over money in the wake of praise over her breakout role, *Scarface* (1932), which she had played for Howard Hughes before being sold for cheap to Warners. Dvorak (1911–1979) had gone to London, ostensibly for her honeymoon, to escape WB's clutches. Now, in Paramount's fictional Paree, she was walking through her part with Chevalier—but completing it, at least. "Now that Ann's back," sneered a fan magazine in a typical reaction to Dvorak's relationship with Warners, "everything seems to be patched up between her and the studio ... and that old salary probably looks pretty good."[31] The loan-out to Paramount did nothing for her career, much less her professional pride; Dvorak later would be mildly amused when called upon to sign copies of sheet music for *The Way to Love* that had sneaked into the retail market adorned with Sidney's photo and not hers.[32]

With the otherwise talented Dvorak better at frowning than singing or comedy, Horton and the pooch played by "Mutt" were more reliable comedic partners for the star in an uneven production described by a *Vanity Fair* critic as "like a production from the joint studios of René Clair and Mack Sennett."[33] The laugh content was so paltry that director Taurog plundered a comedy two-reeler he'd made years before as a source for a protracted gag about pranksters (Chevalier and Horton) drunkenly cutting off the neckties of strangers.[34] Una Merkel look-alike Nydia Westman appears as a maiden whose fear of men manifests itself in screaming every time someone utters "marry" or "marriage"—also a laugh non-starter.

Worse, even, the songs in *The Way to Love* seem like afterthoughts, and the film disposes of most of the singing after the first reel. The opening "There's a Lucky Guy," during which anonymous Parisians of all walks of life riff on life's misfortunes, recalls the rhythmic photography of better sequences in *Love Me Tonight* and *Melody Cruise*.* This number was led not by Chevalier but by young radio tenor Dick Dennis, playing a mustached street troubadour/accordionist. It was the first film appearance for Dennis, who appeared occasionally in '30s and '40s films (among them *The Great Ziegfeld*, *Maytime* and *Babes in Arms*). Chevalier himself sings only two tunes, the better of them being "In a One Room Flat," the closest thing to a theme song in *The Way to Love*. The other, "I'm a Lover of Paree," is just another Chevalier-tailored number—like the ones that worked before the actor's novelty factor diminished.

In September 1933, even before the premiere of *The Way to Love*, MGM announced the signing of Chevalier for *The Merry Widow*. The actor's unhappiness with his old studio—against which he apparently had been conspiring all summer to go elsewhere—was magnified days later in a luncheon given in his honor by Paramount PR types in which he gave a speech that did not once mention his soon-to-be-released Paramount picture.[35] Upon that release, reviewers had little good to say anyway. Despite a live Jack Benny–led revue in support, *The Way to Love* opened sluggishly in New York at the Paramount Theater. In Los Angeles, its first-week take dropped 25 percent from the previous attraction at that city's Paramount Theater, the Bing Crosby starrer *Too Much Harmony* [q.v.].[36] *Harrison's Reports* deemed *The Way to Love* "poor" as a box office performer for the 1933–34 season, and *Variety* dismissed it as "the poorest of the Chevaliers.... Sylvia Sidney walked out and it becomes evident why a full-fledged star would balk at the relatively stooge assignment."[37]

Chevalier was handed much better material for his first two post–Paramount talkies: *The Merry Widow* (1934), with two former collaborators in director Ernst Lubitsch and co-star/off-screen adversary Jeanette MacDonald, and the underrated *Folies Bergére de*

Paris (1935), at 20th Century. Thereafter, he returned to Europe and did not appear in another Hollywood picture until 1957 (*Love in the Afternoon*). There is no record of how Mutt's career proceeded.

America got another look at man and dog when *The Way to Love* popped up on American Movie Classics in 1989 and 1990, during a period when that channel was excavating many early Paramounts from the vault. Now, it's back underground, and given its negative reputation, *The Way to Love* is unlikely to resurface soon.

Stingaree
(RKO; May 17, 1934)

Director: William A. Wellman. Presented by: Merian C. Cooper. Executive Producer: Pandro S. Berman. Associate Producer: David Lewis. Screenplay: Becky Gardiner. Adaptation: Lynn Riggs, Leonard Spigelgass, based on the novel (and other stories) by W.W. Hornung. Photography: James Van Trees. Editor: James B. Morley. Art Direction: Van Nest Polglase, Al Herman. Sound: John E. Tribby. Music Director: Max Steiner. Costumes: Walter Plunkett. Special Photographic Effects: Vernon L. Walker. Assistant Directors: Ivan Thomas, Dolph Zimmer. Running Time: 76 minutes.

Cast: Irene Dunne (Hilda Bouverie); Richard Dix (Stingaree aka Mr. Smithson); Mary Boland (Mrs. Clarkson); Conway Tearle (Sir Julian Kent); Andy Devine (Howie); Henry Stephenson (Mr. Clarkson); George Barraud (Radford); Una O'Connor (Annie); Snub Pollard (Victor); Reginald Owen (governor general); Billy Bevan (Mac); Robert Greig (innkeeper); Edgar Norton, Lionel Belmore (governor's aides); Luis Alberni (cheering man); Frank Baker, Ben Hendricks, Jr. (constables); Earl Covert (singer); Norma Adoree (flower girl); Adrienne d'Ambricourt (mother); Georges Renavent (marquis); Rolfe Sedan (couturier); Ferdinand Gottschalk (party guest).

Songs: "I Wish I Were a Fisherman" [Boland. twice], "Once You're Mine" [Dunne] (Edward Eliscu, Max Steiner); "Stingaree Ballad" [Covert], "Tonight Is Mine" [Dunne, Dix; reprised twice by Dunne] (Gus Kahn, W. Franke Harling); "Ah! Je ris de me voir si belle en se miroir" ("Jewel Song" from the opera *Faust*) [Dunne] (Jules Barbier, Michel Carré, Charles Gounod); "The Last Rose of Summer" (from *Martha*) [Dunne] (Thomas Moore, Friedrich von Flotow).

Home Video: Turner Classic Movies DVD; Kino Lorber DVD/Blu-ray.

The Story: In 1874, the notorious highwayman Stingaree evades capture in the outback of Australia, despite the efforts of police inspector Radford. Hilda, a housemaid for wealthy local sheep rancher Hugh Clarkson and his wife, is blessed with a beautiful singing voice, but it is the haughty, tone-deaf Mrs. Clarkson who aspires to have a music career and has invited a well-known London composer, Sir Julian Kent, to visit so she can audition for him ("I Wish I Were a Fisherman"). While posing as music box importer "Mr. Smithson," Stingaree kidnaps Sir Julian with the aid of his henchman, Howie. The music-loving outlaw pretends to be Sir Julian when he meets Hilda and becomes charmed by her and her voice ("Tonight Is Mine"). When the outlaw's identity is exposed, Stingaree abducts Hilda and, while in hiding, encourages her to better herself by "taking everything you want, and wanting everything." At gunpoint, Stingaree forces Sir Julian to hear her sing at a party given in the composer's honor. Sir Julian is impressed enough to take Hilda to London for voice training. Stingaree is shot and imprisoned. Hilda becomes a renowned opera singer and Sir Julian's fiancée. When she returns to her home country to give what she has decided will be her final concert, Stingaree—again at large—shows up to watch. Still in love with the bandit, Hilda goes away with him.

"Out of the wilderness rides 'Stingaree,' who feared neither death nor devil ... a price on his head ... a song in his heart ... a girl in his dreams ... to fire your blood with leaping thrills in a rash romance of danger!" Now, doesn't that describe a movie you just *have* to see? Unfortunately, that tantalizing advertising copy for *Stingaree*—an American-made, quasi-Western operetta set in colonial Australia—was prose that teased, because for seven decades after the film's initial issue in 1934, almost no one could see it.

Indeed, *Stingaree* was once something of a mystery for classics buffs. It marked the reteaming—highly anticipated—of Irene Dunne and Richard Dix, co-stars of *Cimarron*, the Oscar winner for best picture of 1931. The director of *Stingaree* was the highly respected William A. Wellman. It was a little bit of a tough sell, yet it was well reviewed and appreciated by patrons who were willing to try something a little different. But then *Stingaree* was withdrawn from circulation, per its rights holders, thus resisting re-evaluation. Happily, this "lost" film re-emerged—for, like the crafty outlaw of its title, it could not be locked away forever. It reminds us—as if we still needed validation after her work in *Roberta* (1935) and *Show Boat* (1936)—that Dunne had a darn good singing voice to go with her acting ability.

Despite the seeming obscurity of its title, *Stingaree* was based on the same-named 1905 novel by Ernest William Hornung, who was better known for his "Raffles" stories about a gentleman thief of Victorian England. A brother-in-law of Sherlock Holmes author Arthur Conan Doyle, Hornung returned to the charming-rogue concept for the Stingaree character and his Robin Hood–style thievery in the Australian outback. *Stingaree* had been filmed in the U.S. in 1915 as a serial by the Kalem company. RKO meant its adaptation as a vehicle for Dunne by signing her for the role in May 1933 with British actor Leslie Banks as a rumored co-star. By that fall, with Banks now under contract at Fox, the male lead was being linked to John Boles, Dunne's co-star in the popular *Back Street* (1932).[38] But as the new year dawned, word came of Dix's involvement.

To hear it from film fans, this was blockbuster news: The *Los Angeles Times* reported that RKO had received between 10,000 and 15,000 requests for Dix (1893–1949) and Dunne (1898–1990) to be reunited on film.[39] But the career arcs of the two actors had reversed somewhat from the time of their first screen experience together. When named to top the bill for *Cimarron*, an epic Western based on the Edna Ferber novel, Dix was the company's biggest male star, and RKO had bought the property for him. Dunne was a newcomer with only one film—a failed 1930 RKO musical comedy, *Leathernecking*—to her credit. Dunne was one of 50 aspirants to test for the *Cimarron* role, for which the dramatic ability required ran counter to her experience on the operetta and musical comedy stages. However, she landed the part with no little help from Dix, who was cognizant of Dunne's stage work and persuaded studio brass to look her way.[40] As Ferber's trailblazing Oklahoma frontier couple, both actors earned Oscar nominations, Dix won the best notices of his career, and Dunne was elevated to starring status.

In the intervening years, Dunne built a big following in a series of heavy dramas, among which were *Back Street*, *Symphony of Six Million*, and the retroactively weird thriller *Thirteen Women*. Meanwhile, Dix fell into a rut of adventure films—one was the Wellman-directed *The Conquerors*, in which Radio sought to replicate its *Cimarron* glory— that mostly exposed the virile, square-jawed actor's tendency to overact. Dunne and Dix nearly were reunited directly after *Cimarron* for an RKO musical, *Marcheta*, in which Dix was to portray a bullfighter and Dunne a Spanish dancer, but the decline of film musicals that began in 1930 and extended into 1931–32 led to the cancellation of the project.

That RKO thought of Dunne for *Stingaree*—and billed her appropriately—was no accident, and although Wellman had not directed a full-fledged musical (and would not again), his knack for helming action scenes made him a logical choice.[41] The director of the Oscar-winning action picture *Wings* was personally asked by RKO production chief Merian C. Cooper to make *Stingaree*, for which Wellman was borrowed from 20th Century Pictures.[42] Of the screenwriters, Becky Gardiner was known for writing strong roles for women (Norma Shearer and others) and Lynn Riggs was a male playwright and poet best remembered in retrospect for writing *Green Grow the Lilacs*, the off-Broadway play that was adapted as *Oklahoma!*

With musicals back in vogue as shooting on *Stingaree* took place in February and March of 1934, Dunne's lyric soprano was put to good use as she portrayed a young housemaid who is mentored and cherished by Dix's antihero when she emerges from the outback as a performer. Opera scenes shot on the *Phantom of the Opera* set at Universal showcased Dunne singing excerpts from *Faust* and *Martha*, but *Stingaree*'s showcase tune was Gus Kahn and W. Franke Harling's "Tonight Is Mine." The song is introduced as a duet of sorts. Dix's character—unexpectedly proficient at the piano for a crook, even a cultured one—plays the melody he has created, then "feeds" spoken lyrics to Dunne, who repeats the words with the melody. (In the middle of the song, he exclaims "Marvelous!" and she sings it back, not knowing his outburst is not part of the performance.) The scene effectively establishes their bond as lovers as well as teacher-student in a melo-romantic tale meant more to be bathed in than picked apart.

There is a little of a lot in this genre hybrid—operetta, amour, action, suspense, Western, and comedy, the last supplied mainly by Mary Boland as a rich middle-ager who thinks she can sing better than her hired help ... and, just to make sure, doesn't allow her to sing in public. Former silent star Conway Tearle is a welcome presence as Dix's romantic rival, and Andy Devine can be forgiven his miscasting as the thief's valet. Given such larger-than-life treatment, the highly romantic, chase-filled ending—very different than the outcome of the novel—is not only tolerable but also expected.[43] Leslie Banks or John Boles might have done better with an attempt at an Aussie or English accent, of which Dix makes none, but the American's usual ebullience—most aptly demonstrated when Stingaree is playing mind games with the resident authorities—is in tune with the robustness of the material.

Despite the male star's enjoyable performance, no doubt coaxed by craftsman Wellman, *Stingaree* was no great boost for Dix's career. However, it did earn many laudatory notices. The *New York Times*, not known for its leniency on musicals or Westerns, praised it as "a pleasant narration of a highly improbable fable…. Miss Dunne gives a charming performance and she sings several songs very agreeably."[44] *Variety* noted that Dix's performance "seemed to give entire satisfaction" to the opening-night audience at New York's Radio City Music Hall, but noted the film's emphasis on music over sagebrush: "[RKO] probably realized that the horse operas have done much to rub the bloom of youth from hard riding and gives [the picture] mostly to Miss Dunne, who ... rises above her dramatic work, since the authors have given her small opportunity, and she wisely does not steam it up."[45] The studio thought enough of *Stingaree* to give it a New York opening at the Radio City Music Hall, with initial screenings preceded live by the new, high-kicking Rockettes.

However, neither the less-than-catchy title nor the period/geographical locale aided exhibitors in the marketability of *Stingaree*. "This one fooled us. It's really a dandy picture and the musical background is wonderful," said a merchant from Missouri quoted in the *Motion Picture Herald*'s weekly survey of theater operators.[46] The film seemed to arrive with concerns over its success, but it left patrons satisfied. "Don't be afraid of this one; it will please," added a showman from Michigan.[47] Referencing cultural values of the Depression-era, pre–Code (barely, in terms of release date) period, the exhibitor-targeted publication *Harrison's Reports* noted potential thematic drawbacks: "Because of the fact that Dix is a bandit, the picture may not be suitable for children, adolescents, and Sundays. The sex relationship between hero and heroine is handled delicately."[48] The bandit angle may seem ridiculous for which to condemn this film, but at least that generally did not prevent people in the

U.S. from seeing it. Not so in New South Wales, Australia—the main setting of the fictional story—where even in the 1930s pictures about "bushrangers"—the highwaymen of Stingaree's day—were flat-out prohibited, and thus *Stingaree* may have lost as much as 25 percent of its potential audience Down Under.[49]

Budgeted at about $400,000, *Stingaree* lost $49,000 at the box office.[50] But its great triumph—beyond making some of its audience believe that a famous opera singer would forsake her career to go on the run with her beau in the bush—was bringing Dunne back to musicals. It had been so long since she had sung on screen that RKO saw fit to promote *Stingaree* in some quarters by offering $100,000 to anyone who could prove the voice on screen was anyone's but Dunne's own.[51] She followed this picture with some even zestier musicals: *Sweet Adeline* (1934); *Roberta*; *High, Wide and Handsome* (1936); and the sublime *Show Boat*. They showed that even if Dunne wasn't the flashiest, most-attention-seeking actress in pictures, she was among the most versatile and professional. Still, her work here was forgotten within months of its debut, and *Stingaree* disappeared from attention, just as its namesake had at the climax.

The reason for the film's 70-plus-year absence from public view had to do with RKO's relationship with Merian C. Cooper. Cooper, the adventurer and military hero who had co-directed and co-produced *King Kong*, led production at Radio for slightly more than a year in 1933–34. Cooper got into a dispute with the studio over the revenue he thought was owed him from movies produced during his tenure; to settle the issue, RKO in 1946 sold him the rights to six of those features—one of which was *Stingaree*. The other five were *Double Harness* (1933), *Living on Love* (1937), *A Man to Remember* (1938), *One Man's Journey* (1933), and *Rafter Romance* (1933). Due to other legal concerns—it turned out the films were being held by a third party as a tax shelter—the six were held out of public view, except for a brief late-1950s engagement of *Stingaree* and four of the others on a New York TV station.

When most of the rest of the RKO library was sold to Ted Turner in 1987 for his cable channels' expansive repertoire, the six Cooper-secured films were not involved and thus did not show on Turner Classic Movies or any of its sibling outlets. That status changed in 2006 when TCM—responding to an inquiry from a curious fan about why the channel never televised one of the six titles—began a painstaking search that resulted in the purchase of their rights. Because the original nitrate negatives and 1946 master prints had disappeared, the films were restored primarily from 35 mm copies made for the television package that were in the Merian C. Cooper Collection at Brigham Young University.[52] In April 2007, the sextet of titles premiered on TCM and were shown periodically on that channel thereafter. They also showed theatrically in New York and Los Angeles, and there was a DVD boxed set of the films, billed as "The Lost & Found RKO Collection," that was available for only a limited time before going out of print.

Fortunately, *Stingaree* returned to video in DVD and Blu-ray releases by Kino Lorber in 2018. The case of its temporary disappearance is one we should be happy was solved.

365 Nights in Hollywood
(Fox; October 12, 1934)

Director: George Marshall. Producer: Sol M. Wurtzel. Screenplay: William Conselman, Henry Johnson, inspired by the book by James A. Starr. Photography: Harry Jackson. Sound: Bernard Freericks. Music Director: Samuel Kaylin. Dance Director: Sammy Lee. Art Director: Duncan Cramer. Set Decoration: Albert Hogsett. Costumes: Royer. Running Time: 74 minutes.

7. Big Stars, Short Memories

Cast: James Dunn (Jimmie Dale); Alice Faye (Alice Perkins); Frank Mitchell (Percy); Jack Durant (Clarence); John Bradford (Adrian Almont); Grant Mitchell (J. Walter Delmar); Frank Melton (Frank Young); John Qualen (Professor Ellenbogen); Ray Cooke (Eddie); Tyler Brooke (casting director in "My Future Star" number); Frank Conroy (executive); Ernest Wood (agent); Addison Richards (assistant district attorney); Harry Fox (dance director); Carl Stockdale (bookkeeper); Paul McVey (cameraman); Frank Sully, Gay Seabrook, Dorothy Bay, James Conlin, Helen Gibson, Ben Hall (student actors); Richard A. Whiting (Dick); Perry Ivins (lyricist); Paul Schwegler (Tarzan look-alike); Gladys Johnson (Mae West look-alike); Harry Wilson, Betty Stockton (future stars); Bo Ling (Chinese girl); Gloria Roy, Ruth Peterson (waitresses); Brooks Benedict (nightclub patron); Nelson McDowell (thinking man in "My Future Star" number); Arthur Housman (drunk motorist); Gene Morgan (flirting motorist); Ethel Wales (Mrs. Lipke); Larry Fisher, Russ Clark (electricians); Al Klein (prop man); Jessie Pringle (Mrs. Carey); Enid Gray (old lady); Lorraine Rugg (Lorraine); Harrison Greene (boarder); Jay Eaton (effeminate man); Betty Bryson (ingénue); Lynn Bari (showgirl).
Songs: "My Future Star" [Faye, Dunn, Brooke, chorus], "Yes to You" [Faye, Bradford, chorus] (Sidney Clare, Richard A. Whiting); "Hold Your Man" [Faye] (Arthur Freed, Nacio Herb Brown).
Disc: Banner 33253, Fox Movietone F-119, Melotone 13220, Oriole 3033, Perfect 13080, Romeo 2407 ("My Future Star"/"Yes to You," Alice Faye).
Home Video: Image Entertainment DVD; Englewood Entertainment VHS.

The Story: Jimmie Dale, a washed-up former "boy wonder" film director, can find work only as the prime acting teacher at the small-time Delmar Academy of Motion Picture and Dramatic Arts in Hollywood. The school is run by the shady J. Walter Delmar, who has an agreement with a well-known film actor, Adrian Almont, to use the latter's name to promote the school and attract students. Accompanied by inept ice men Percy and Clarence, pretty blonde Alice Perkins arrives in Hollywood from Peoria, Illinois, and enrolls at the academy, where she attracts the attention of Jimmie and Adrian. While working as a carhop, Alice meets Frank Young, a newcomer from Alabama who has just come into a $75,000 inheritance. Delmar talks Frank into investing the money into a musical picture, "365 Nights in Hollywood," to be directed by Jimmie and to co-star Alice and Adrian. Delmar and Adrian plan to skim funds from the production budget and leave Jimmie legally responsible if they are found out. Alice shows real talent during rehearsals, especially in the "Yes to You" number, and Jimmie, in hopes of making a comeback, decides to cross up Delmar and Adrian by spending the full amount on the picture. Delmar responds by telling legal authorities that Jimmie is taking the money himself. Jimmie figures out that to stave off financial ruin, the picture can be completed with one more day's shooting on the climatic production number, "My Future Star." A drunken Adrian tries to sabotage the filming by taking Alice to his secluded home, but Percy and Clarence help her escape and force Adrian to the set. When Adrian refuses to work, he and Jimmie get into a fistfight that is captured on film by an alert cameraman. Jimmie takes Adrian's place for the "My Future Star" number, then makes amends with his new sweetheart.

In the few short years before Alice Faye became the queen of 20th Century–Fox musicals, she was just another platinum blonde aspiring to fame, singing or not, as plain-old-Fox's answer to Jean Harlow. Her fourth film, the modestly produced *365 Nights in Hollywood*, found her still in that mode, but showing enough of the ample song-and-dance talent that hinted at her more-individualistic future. This surprisingly downbeat program picture—a Tinseltown exposé misleadingly sold as a laugh-a-minute comedy—remains Faye's most obscure musical, in part because it was presumed lost for six decades before audiences were able to rediscover it.

Faye (1915–1998) traveled the fast lane during 1934, her first calendar year in pictures. The New York City-born teenager got her first break as a vocalist in Rudy Vallee's band and was set to perform a number in Vallee's Fox starrer *George White's Scandals*. But when initial female lead Lilian Harvey exited the project over her reported objections that the part was too small, Faye stepped in with a third-billed splash, propelled by a rendition of the saucy hit "Oh, You Nasty Man." Fox rewarded Faye with a contract but, apparently still uncertain of what it had, followed *Scandals* by putting her in two non-musicals. *Now I'll Tell* was a drama in which she played the sexy mistress of gangster Spencer Tracy and sang a torch song called "Foolin' with the Other Woman's Man." In *She Learned About Sailors*, a comedy with Lew Ayres and comics Frank Mitchell and Jack Durant, she played a nightclub singer and, again, sang only one song. Meanwhile, headlines had broken that Vallee's wife had named Faye as a co-respondent in a divorce action, and Fox responded by softening Faye's off-screen image, keeping her hair blonde and her eyebrows plucked to match the Harlow look. News sources played up Faye's lack of pretense, her youth, and that she lived quietly with her mother and brother as a "home girl" in a modest apartment even as they chronicled her nightclubbing, real and imagined, with Vallee, Lyle Talbot, and a young Fox contractee, Nick (aka Dick) Foran.

In August 1934, Faye shot *365 Nights in Hollywood* at Fox's B-unit Western Avenue facility in Hollywood (where she also had made *She Learned About Sailors*). Even if actors like Faye might have preferred to be elsewhere, the long hours did provide her with valuable experience. Faye biographer Jane Lenz Elder quotes Faye's childhood friend Betty King Scharf as saying that the actress's experience shooting *365 Nights in Hollywood* and *She Learned About Sailors* was so intense that Fox "didn't want Alice to get too tired. A couple of times they dressed me the same as her and did long shots of me dancing for her."[53] At one point

In 1934, Alice Faye was a Jean Harlow lookalike appearing opposite James Dunn in a Fox second-tier musical, *365 Nights in Hollywood*.

with *365 Nights*, the production provided some variety by moving outdoors for a scene in which Faye's character, working as a carhop at a drive-in restaurant, meets an amorous young man played by Frank Melton.[54] Their presence at an actual shop (McDonnell's) on Wilshire Avenue in L.A. attracted a crowd of about 500 spectators, making the two theater actors as well as celluloid thespians.

Faye landed *365 Nights* because tempestuous German-English star Harvey ended her contract with Fox, allegedly by "mutual consent." In scuttling her Hollywood career, the finicky Harvey bolstered those of Faye and starlet Pat Paterson, who was handed intended Harvey assignments in *Love Time* (1934) and *Lottery Lover** (1935), although neither did as much for Paterson as Harvey's reject boosted Faye. Perhaps seeing the error of its ways with the lack of song content in its rising star's previous two films, Fox advertised *365 Nights* by alerting fans: "Faye Sings Again…. Only More So!" Faye was allowed only three songs, although two came in lengthy production numbers.

Faye was paired with jaunty leading man James Dunn (1901–1967) and reunited with *She Learned About Sailors* director George Marshall, its screenwriters William Conselman and Henry Johnson, and—less gainfully—its comic duo of Mitchell and Durant. Mitchell and Durant's violently physical slapstick in *365 Nights* was meant to lighten the sleaze of a cautionary tale of crooked Hollywood talent schools, the title of which was the lone remnant from the credited source material, a 1926 book of semi-fictional short stories about Hollywood life by showbiz columnist Jimmy Starr.[55] The fraudulent institution in the film is run by predatory racketeer J. Walter Delmar—played with relish by old pro Grant Mitchell—who unctuously tailors fake background stories and chummy regional accents to each client. "Umm, umm—I smell MON-ey!" he exalts as he watches another sucker approach his door. In another deceitful affectation, Delmar refers to the house piano teacher (John Qualen) as "Professor Herr-MON Ellenbogen … imported from the University of Leipzig!"

A big part of Delmar's scheme is to pay off stock screen juve Adrian Almont, who is played by screen newcomer John Bradford with a pencil-thin moustache as if to emphasize his villainy. Almont effectively kidnaps the heroine in the final reel, belying Fox's ad boast of a "rollicking farce-comedy of Hollywood life and loves … [that] continues to roll up laughs by the hundreds." Bradford (1905–1983) appeared in only a handful of features and was out of pictures after 1937. Born Charles Bradford Coleman in West Virginia, he began his theatrical career, in vaudeville and musical comedy, in 1929 and changed his name for the movies to forestall confusion with another acting Charles Coleman. Bradford/Coleman's acting career was interrupted by U.S. Army service in World War II, and he returned to his native state after the war to become a television executive. Newspaper ads in West Virginia for *365 Nights in Hollywood* took care to bill the native son as "Charles Coleman, screen name John Bradford."

"I'm still up there and you're not … [you] can't even sweep the floors" is how the swarmy Almont taunts once-famous director Jimmie Dale (Dunn), who cites a bout with "Old John Barleycorn" as the reason he's reduced to mentoring Delmar's suckers and living in a rooming house. An alcohol-induced downfall would soon be in the cards for Dunn, but his career rebounded in 1945 with an Oscar-winning performance in *A Tree Grows in Brooklyn*. Meanwhile, as Clark Gable-Boris Karloff wannabes, the lame-brained, knock-about ice men played by Mitchell and Durant audition with bad ideas such as two wrestlers meeting on the street and rolling around on the ground beating each other up. The Mutt-and-Jeff funnymen teamed up initially in vaudeville in the late '20s, then in Broadway shows before transitioning to the movies in Fox's *Stand Up and Cheer!* (1934). They were deemed sufficient support to Faye to be paired with her again by Fox in 1935's *Music Is Magic*. Mitchell and

Durant remain easy marks for criticism, but the novelty of their physically raucous routines just couldn't generate the energy on celluloid as they could in live form.

In its regular survey of theater owners, *Motion Picture Herald* published an Indiana showman's unusually impassioned, unintentionally humorous reaction to the comics:

> Two nights was too long for this one [*365 Nights in Hollywood*].... This Mitchell and Durant are another pair of radio stars that when seen on the screen are very unfunny. In fact they are worse than that. They are an acute pain in the neck to every part of the anatomy that I know of ... [O]n the screen it is impossible to get out from under the punishment of two comedians that are not funny in a picture.[56]

Delmar's scheme, challenging even by 1934 movie-economics standards, is to make a feature-length musical for only $45,000 and then pocket the rest of the production funds.[57] The production numbers alone, even in a "B" film like the one depicted in *365 Nights*, would make such a small outlay inconceivable. The first number, "Yes to You," begins as Faye's fatigued character sings to piano accompaniment by the song's actual composer, Richard Whiting (in a rare film appearance), then transitions to her more-energetic honey contralto on the set as the actress, now gowned and waving an ostrich fan, warms up a bookish chorister (Bradford), who then dreams of seeing the girl in double exposure and pursues her around the globe in Dutch, French, and Chinese versions.

Faye builds on her increasing confidence in the film's finale, "My Future Star," about a director picking an ingénue out of a casting cattle call and deliberating about the kind of screen persona she will adopt. It's pretty watchable stuff, augmented by an interlude involving Mae West and Tarzan look-alikes. The kind of actress everyone thought Faye was at this point is summed up early in the film in her brief rendition of "Hold Your Man," which she, in a figurative wink to press and public, introduces as "my impression of Jean Harlow." (The original Platinum Blonde had sung it the year before in the MGM film of the same name as the tune.)

Given the generally indifferent material, *365 Nights in Hollywood* had a somewhat mixed response among reviewers and theater owners. But the public couldn't get enough of Faye, despite *The New York Times'* dismissal of the film as "unimportant if true" and its musical sequences as extraneous.[58] *Variety*'s report was even more touchier—"no punch and little appeal"—although it praised the two leads and, especially, a "suave" Grant Mitchell.[59] Faye left the Fox "B" lot for good after *365 Nights*, resuming her run at the first-string facility in a return pairing with Dunn in *George White's 1935 Scandals*. Within months, her image was retooled into the sweeter, more natural look that would make her a superstar.

By then, the public had pretty much forgotten about *365 Nights in Hollywood*, and for many years it was feared lost. However, it was preserved by film collector/distributor/producer Wade Williams from a 16 mm print formerly owned by Faye biographer W. Franklyn Moshier, and which was derived from an old 35 mm nitrate print from the Fox vaults. Williams was a friend of Moshier (and Faye) and when the author died, Williams bought Moshier's film, book, and poster collections from the latter's estate. As Williams told the author via e-mail in 2016:

> *365 Nights in Hollywood* was a "lost" film and had never been made available for TV because the 35 mm negative had decomposed before a fine grain composite was made.... This was the only copy of the film that was known. Fox had no intention of making it available for TV because they had no negative or good fine grain and did not want to use the old nitrate material as it was starting to decompose. Alice had not seen the film since its premiere and was excited to see it again.
>
> Needless to say, I am a Faye fan.... In my opinion, Alice was the finest song stylist ever to appear in the movies. She was a genuine and nice person.[60]

Williams released *365 Nights in Hollywood* on home video, first on VHS in 1998 and then on disc five years later. It also has been preserved by the UCLA Film and Television Archive. Thanks to these efforts, we're able to enjoy one more performance by one of the movies' most genuinely nice musical stars.

In Person
(RKO; November 22, 1935)

Director: William A. Seiter. Producer: Pandro S. Berman. Screenplay: Allan Scott, based on the novel by Samuel Hopkins Adams. Additional Dialogue: Glenn Tryon. Photography: Edward Cronjager. Editor: Arthur Schmidt. Sound: Clem A. Portman. Music Director: Roy Webb. Dance Director: Hermes Pan. Art Director: Van Nest Polglase. Costumes: Bernard Newman. Assistant Director: Jimmy Anderson. Running Time: 87 minutes.

Cast: Ginger Rogers (Carol Corliss aka Miss Colfax); George Brent (Emory Muir); Alan Mowbray (Jay Holmes); Grant Mitchell (Judge Thaddeus Parks); Samuel S. Hinds (Dr. Aaron Sylvester); Joan Breslau (Minna); Louis Mason (Sheriff Twing); Spencer Charters ("Parson" Calverton Lunk); Edgar Kennedy (doorman); Lew Kelly (mountain man); Bob McKenzie (theater manager); Lee Shumway (studio representative); William B. Davidson (Bill Sutter); George Davis (cab driver); Bud Jamison (man in elevator).

Songs [performed by Rogers]: "Don't Mention Love to Me," "Got a New Lease on Life," "Out of Sight, Out of Mind" (Dorothy Fields, Oscar Levant).

Working Titles: *Public Property*; *Tamed*.

Disc: Decca 638B ("Don't Mention Love to Me," Ginger Rogers and Johnny Mercer).

Home Video: Turner Home Entertainment VHS.

The Story: Carol Corliss is a top Hollywood star who is recovering from a nervous breakdown caused by her fear of crowds during personal appearances. Her psychiatrist, Dr. Aaron Sylvester, has suggested Carol go out in public in disguise (as "Miss Colfax") to conquer her problem. While in disguise, Carol meets amateur ornithologist Emory Muir, who happens to be a nephew of Judge Thaddeus Parks, a friend of Sylvester's. Emory is persuaded to take the young woman to Parks' mountain retreat, where the newly domesticated Carol seeks to reveal her true identity to Emory because she has fallen in love with him ("A New Lease on Life"). Emory, who sleeps in a separate cabin, learns who she is, but he won't let on. Carol's jealous, egotistical co-star, Jay Holmes, demands that Carol return to the city with him, but Emory chases him away. To convince Emory she is who she says she is, Carol takes him to a local theater where her latest picture is showing ("Don't Mention Love to Me") and conquers her affliction by interacting with the customers. Carol and Emory have a falling-out, so Carol schemes with Minna, a child who is the granddaughter of the local sheriff, to force Emory into a marriage ceremony. But complications over the lawman confusing Emory with Jay threaten to thwart the lovers' reunion, even after Carol returns to Hollywood to resume her career ("Out of Sight, Out of Mind").

"For every film I did with Fred Astaire, I did three to four without him," Ginger Rogers wrote in her autobiography about the pairing that made her legend. "Our partnership was a limited one only in his case, not in mine. Fred didn't have this luxury; he was a musical comedy star, period.... Though I loved the musicals..., I was just as happy appearing in comedies and dramas."[61]

Rogers (1911–1995) enjoyed many triumphs—and even won an Academy Award—without her legendary dance partner. But in 1935, not much more than a year into her fast-track rise from second-lead ingénue to upper-rank star, her appeal was firmly attached to his. *Motion Picture Herald*'s latest annual exhibitors poll of biggest money-making stars ranked Astaire and Rogers fourth (behind Shirley Temple, Will Rogers, and Clark Gable, in that order)—but *as a team*, pundits were quick to point out.[62] At midyear, Rogers was four musicals into her partnership with Astaire at RKO, but she had made movies before Fred and sought to prove that she, as a more versatile performer, could excel on her own. She asked for a salary hike, plus equal billing and promotion as Astaire. Her studio responded with her first true test as a solo headliner: *In Person*, a slight but pleasant romantic comedy without a strong reliance on music, but with enough song and dance to satisfy fan demand. Although no big favorite of reviewers, this underrated entry nicely showcased its star and performed strongly enough financially to prove Rogers correct.

RKO squeezed the filming of *In Person* between *Top Hat* and *Follow the Fleet* in late summer of 1935. Rogers had the time partly because of the perfectionism that kept Astaire overly busy on creating the dances for his projects.[63] *In Person*'s female-celebrity-on-the-run story—this one involving an agoraphobic film star—bore a strong resemblance to the Oscar-winning *It Happened One Night*, and was the creation of the same writer, Samuel Hopkins Adams, with RKO wordsmith (and frequent Astaire-Rogers scribe) Allan Scott doing the screenplay.[64] Dependable leading man George Brent was borrowed from Warner Bros.; he had made Bette Davis, Ruth Chatterton, and Barbara Stanwyck look good, so why not Ginger?

Rogers' character spends most of the first half hour of the film in a disguise with a veil, black wig, spectacles, and false teeth, before a scene in which the leading lady goes swimming near her handsome host's mountain cabin, and he sees her for the first time without the masquerading. During location filming in the Big Bear Lake region in the San Bernardino mountains 60 miles from Hollywood, director William A. Seiter asked Rogers to dive into freezing lake water, go under, and then come up after swimming 30 feet so that Brent's character could see her blond mane and comely teeth for the first time. Despite complaining about the temperature, Rogers dutifully did the swim, although the trunks of her two-piece swimsuit nearly fell off. The Hays Office put up a beef about the suit revealing too much flesh, but Rogers wore it anyway.

In her 1991 memoir, Rogers remembered Brent (1904–1979) as "a joy to work with" and supporting player Alan Mowbray, cast as her on-screen counterpart, as "just hammy enough," and Grant Mitchell for doing "double-takes that cause me to laugh, even now, when I see the film."[65] To beef up a role turned down by multiple RKO lady stars—including her chief rival, Katharine

Ginger Rogers strips from an evening gown into shorts in "Out of Sight, Out of Mind," a highlight Hermes Pan-choreographed number in RKO's *In Person*.

Hepburn—Rogers was given musical material as box-office insurance. Dorothy Fields and Oscar Levant were brought in to provide three songs, and dances for two of them were created by Rogers'—and Astaire's—favorite choreographer, Hermes Pan. While doing the Lily Pons musical *I Dream Too Much*—for which he was paid $250 for 2½ weeks of service—Pan was salaried for one week, at a paltry $100, to work his magic on *In Person*.[66]

Rogers doesn't sing or dance until the film is half over, until "A New Lease on Life," when she hears her voice on the radio. Hoping Brent will be convinced she's a film actress, she picks up the tune about "Popeye the sailor-girl" and compactly hoofs on the living-room floor, atop a dining table, and on a short set of stairs as he sits in his easy chair and pretends to be unimpressed. The other Pan-staged dance number, more complicated and near the finale, shows Rogers rehearsing "Out of Sight, Out of Mind" on a soundstage. Performing atop a revolving circular bar, she wields a cigarette and interacts seductively with a dinner-jacketed male chorus, at first singing only but then suddenly stripping from an evening gown into shorts for some strenuous tap. The effect betters as each of the men gives Rogers a ribbon that stretches to create a human-pinwheel effect.

The third Fields-Levant composition, the rueful "Don't Mention Love to Me," is presented as Rogers and Brent sit in a theater watching the actress (her) perform on screen. (The film within a film is amusingly titled *No Escape*.) We half expect Rogers to jump out of the audience and finish the song in person, similar to what she has done in "A New Lease on Life." Instead, the song is given the serious treatment it deserves, and only then does Rogers take the stage to face a houseful of autograph seekers who will shake her out of her fear of contact. Her character spends the film torn between the allure of celebrity—"I like being a myth!" she admits at one point—and wanting to be left alone to live a private, domestic life. (Off the screen, Rogers had something of the same dilemma, as her year-and-a-half marriage to Lew Ayres was falling apart at the time of this filming.)

In Person is a bit too leisurely paced in its middle section, as Rogers' character builds her relationship with Brent's and learns to master kitchen supplies. But it holds up as lightweight but highly entertaining fare in which Rogers parodies her screen image—her character is described as "charming enough, but not a very good actress," which was how many people thought of her in 1935. Her fictional co-star, played by Mowbray, is a clueless airhead who relies more on his profile than his acting craft—in other words, he's no Astaire, but that's part of the screwball. Crazy, too, is the rural sheriff's nonchalance at Rogers waving a gun at her co-star.

The film was sellable enough with Rogers' name, but the title did not come easily, even with its handy connection to the main character's fear of personal appearances. RKO filmed it as *In Person*, then dropped that title over potential confusion on theater marquees—was it "Ginger Rogers *In Person*" or "Ginger Rogers in Person"? The new name, *Tamed*, was even more ambiguous (and made this sound like a jungle documentary), and after a spell with a not-bad third title, *Public Property*, the picture was released in November with its original moniker. No matter what it was called, the film drew wildly mixed reviews. *Variety* dismissed it as "an unfortunate starring debut" for Rogers ... "formula and rarely convincing or believable," and *Life* magazine was even less kind, calling it "a pulp romance, and VERY dull."[67] Even Oscar Levant admitted he didn't like the film much after seeing a preview just before its opening, and over dinner, he told producer Pandro S. Berman so. Levant likely owed his assignment on *In Person* to Berman, who, as Levant related, "rose from the table in a rage, flung down his napkin and said, 'Who in hell are you to be disappointed?' The discussion of who had to be who to be disappointed took quite a long time."[68]

Still, *In Person* verified Rogers' faith in herself by making a profit of $147,000 (on a $493,000 budget—a healthy expenditure, albeit not as expensive as a typical Astaire-Rogers).[69] Some first-run theaters turned down booking the film, thinking its star could not go it alone, but the financial returns proved that it wasn't just Fred that people liked, it was Ginger, too. The dancing duo reunited for *Follow the Fleet* and other successes, but Rogers was on her way to becoming one of Hollywood's top comediennes. She knew her career would never be the same—in a good way.

Sing and Be Happy
(Fox; June 25, 1937)

Director: James Tinling. Producer: Sol M. Wurtzel. Associate Producer: Milton H. Feld. Screenplay: Ben Markson, Lou Breslow, John Patrick. Photography: Daniel B. Clark. Editor: Nick De Maggio. Sound: E. Clayton Ward, Harry M. Leonard. Music Director: Samuel Kaylin. Art Director: Lewis Creber. Costumes: Herschel. Assistant Director: Saul Wurtzel. Running Time: 64 minutes.

Cast: Anthony [Tony] Martin (Buzz Mason); Leah Ray (Ann Lane); Joan Davis (Myrtle); Helen Westley (Mrs. Henty); Allan Lane (Allan Howard); Dixie Dunbar (Della Dunn); Chick Chandler (Mike); Berton Churchill (John Mason); Andrew Tombes (Thomas Lane); Luis Alberni (Posini); Frank McGlynn Sr. (sheriff); Edward Cooper (Mason's butler); Harry Strang (mover); Allen Fox (elevator operator); Charles Williams (man with punch); Irving Bacon (Palmer); Bruce Warren (orchestra leader); Carroll Nye (announcer); Francis Sayles, Harrison Greene, Fred Kelsey, Sidney Fields (hecklers); Cullen Morris, Pauline James (dancers); Harry Semels (peddler); Joseph G. Tozer (Lane's butler); Lynn Bari (John Mason's secretary); Jane Gale (secretary); Charles Tannen (clerk); Arthur Rankin, Paul McVey (car passengers).

Songs: "Pickles" [Davis, Chandler], "Sing and Be Happy" [Martin, chorus], "Travelin' Light" [Martin, band], "What a Beautiful Beginning" [Martin, Ray; reprised by Martin], "When I Hear You Tell Me You Love Me" [Ray, Martin, Davis, Chandler, chorus] (Sidney Clare, Harry Akst).

Working Title: *Everybody Sing*.

The Story: Singer Buzz Mason and his Flying Aces band get into trouble while promoting a concert in a small town by performing a song ("Travelin' Light") over a loudspeaker from an airplane and causing thousands of dollars of damage. Buzz attempts to convince his father, advertising executive John Mason, to pay the debt, but the elder Mason insists that his son return home to work for him. The elder Mason is competing for the accounts of two important clients—a food company owned by Mrs. Henty and a hosiery maker run by Posini—with Thomas Lane's rival ad firm. Lane's daughter, Ann, is designing a campaign for the hosiery account, but her father's general manager, Allan Howard, is spying on her and her father's company on behalf of John Mason. Buzz, a former college classmate of Ann's, tries to rekindle his friendship with her when he reluctantly returns to work for his father. Meanwhile, two would-be songwriters, Mike and Myrtle, attempt to audition their tune ("Pickles") promoting Henty's wares but are instead hired as window washers. Allan takes Ann to a nightclub, but Buzz follows along and coerces Ann into singing a duet on stage ("What a Beautiful Beginning"). Ann considers a proposal from Allan for a business trip/honeymoon in Bermuda. Buzz fails to take his new office duties seriously, so his father forces him to work against Ann for the Posini account. Buzz's use of real models appropriating the concepts in Ann's hosiery sketches prompt her to accuse Buzz of stealing her ideas and to accept Allan's marriage proposal. John Mason attempts to sabotage Lane's audition for the Henty account, but with Mike and Myrtle's help, Buzz thwarts his father's plans by having his band perform "When I Hear You Tell Me You Love Me" as part of the show. Both companies end up sharing the Henty account, Buzz and Ann make up, and Mike and Myrtle go back to washing windows.

 A top crooner better known for his nightclub, recording, and radio work than his screen emoting, Tony Martin was a robust, solid, not-quite-top-rank star of both movie musicals and non-musicals. In 1937, while a second-lead-type at 20th Century–Fox, he was handed his first starring role in a completely forgettable B-unit musical comedy, *Sing and Be Happy*. The title promised more than the hour-and-change filler could deliver.

Born Alvin Morris in San Francisco, Martin (1913–2012) worked as a saxophonist in various bands before going off his own to act and sing in the movies. He worked his way up from unbilled roles to credited secondary parts and specialties in the likes of 1936's *Pigskin Parade* [q.v.] and *Banjo on My Knee**. In assignments that would foreshadow future events, the handsome tenor then billed as "Anthony" Martin appeared briefly in *Poor Little Rich Girl* and *Sing, Baby, Sing* (both 1936), which starred Fox musicals sovereign Alice Faye. Benefiting from exposure as the featured vocalist on George Burns' and Gracie Allen's radio show, Martin made enough of an impression in a Jane Withers comedy, *The Holy Terror* (1937), for Fox to put him and erstwhile band singer Leah Ray, his romantic partner from that film, atop the cast of *Sing and Be Happy*.

There was more to TCF's "promotion" of Martin than a jobs-well-done gesture, however, for even as *Sing and Be Happy* was being announced, Martin was being seriously linked to Alice Faye in the romance-obsessed entertainment media. Beginning in the late summer of 1936, and for months beyond, the country's top print gossip columnists did their best to inform eager readers of the status of the Faye-Martin relationship—so why shouldn't Fox, and savvy production chief Darryl F. Zanuck, capitalize by boosting Martin as a star (albeit one not in the same stratosphere as his paramour)? What follows is a sampling of the free publicity from writers major and minor:

- Sidney Skolsky, *Los Angeles Herald-Express*, September 29, 1936: "Alice Faye and Tony Martin are singing the same language."
- Skolsky, October 6: "Alice Faye rushing on the set for *Banjo on My Knee*, taking Tony Martin to a corner, giving him a nice kiss and then dating him for the nite."
- Louella Parsons, Hearst Universal Service, October 9: "Alice Faye surprising Tony Martin with a cigarette lighter bought with the money he paid her on a baseball bet."
- Parsons, October 15: "That kiss Alice Faye publicly gave Tony Martin [is] creating plenty of comment on the Twentieth Century–Fox lot."
- Paul Harrison, Newspaper Enterprise Association, November 2: "Friends expect am engagement announcement for Alice Faye and Tony Martin."
- Skolsky, December 31: "Alice Faye holding hands with Tony Martin in a movie theater, while they listen to Tony sing in *Pigskin Parade*."
- Parsons, January 12, 1937: "Our guess is that Alice Faye and Tony Martin will tell it to a preacher before 1938 rolls around."
- Read Kendall, *Los Angeles Times* ("Odd and Interesting"), February 7, 1937: "There are some who insist that Frances Langford still packs a torch for Tony Martin, currently romancing Alice Faye."
- Parsons, February 14: "It's really too bad about these two kids, Alice Faye and Tony Martin. They are so much in love, but I heard just recently that their romance may never reach the altar because of the differences in their religious faiths." (Faye was Episcopalian; Martin, Jewish.)
- Parsons, February 26: "Alice Faye and Tony Martin returning to the hand holding stage."

- Walter Winchell, *New York Daily Mirror*, February 28: "Alice Faye's mater will take her to Honolulu ... which will signal the end of the Tony Martin matter."
- Winchell, May 4: "Tony Martin and Alice Faye are staying up late again in the joints—probably to make the columnists look sillier."
- Parsons, May 11: "Alice Faye and Tony Martin denying those marriage rumors."
- Skolsky, May 21: "Alice Faye leaving Tony Martin on the dance floor at the Troc, and walking outside to get 'a little fresh air.'"
- Sheilah Graham, North American Newspaper Alliance, May 28: "The romance between Alice Faye and Tony Martin, hatched by a publicity wizard, will culminate shortly in an elopement."
- May Mann, *Ogden* (Utah) *Standard-Examiner*, July 20: "[Among] the most steadfast two-somes of the film colony are.... Alice Faye and Tony Martin (though Wayne Morris may change that)."
- Winchell, August 10: "The Alice Faye-Tony Martin thing is off, again—after another loud word war."
- Winchell, August 17: "Tony Martin and Alice Faye have patched up matters and he announces they will soon marry."

On September 4, 1937, Faye and Martin proved they had indeed "patched up matters" by eloping via air flight to Yuma, Arizona. *Sing and Be Happy* had been shot in April and was well into making the rounds in theaters nationwide. Not shockingly, Fox also placed Martin (albeit again down the cast list) in a Faye vehicle, *You Can't Have Everything*, which was filmed just after *Sing and Be Happy* and released in August. The newlyweds were put on nearer-to-equal footing in *Sally, Irene and Mary*, which was shot right after their wedding and reached the public in February 1938.[70] Never a dull moment.

But back to *Sing and Be Happy*, a tale of bitter-rival advertising agencies and the stormy romance between the offspring of their proprietors. Martin and Ray (1915–1999) have some appeal as a team, but their characters' bickering grows tiresome. The shoehorned characterization of Martin as a businessman's son who just happens to be a bandleader isn't terribly convincing either. Petite soubrette Dixie Dunbar (1919–1991) is totally wasted, and Allan Lane—the future B-Western headliner and voice of TV horse Mister Ed—makes little hay out of an early part. Dunbar, who at this point was gaining some momentum with good roles in Fox films such as *Pigskin Parade*, would grow disenchanted with the picture business and exit it after 1939, and Ray would last only through 1938, retiring into luxury (as the wife of sports-and-entertainment executive David "Sonny" Werblin).

Sing and Be Happy, from the second-string unit of studio producer Sol Wurtzel, is best enjoyed through its secondary players, especially Berton Churchill, doing his stock shady-businessman thing, and especially rubber-faced, rubber-legged comedienne Joan Davis. Davis (1912–1961) troupes through this feature without showing the effects of a back injury sustained during the filming of a scene in which she climbed through an office window.[71] For Davis, who excelled at physical humor, this kind of mishap—which put her in a hospital for a week—was part of her trade, and Fox used her bad fortune to publicize her as the "sickest girl in Hollywood" ... in a good way, of course.

Of the quintet of songs by Sidney Clare and Harry Akst, the best is "What a Beautiful Beginning," delivered twice by Martin, once of which in a nightclub duet with Ray. The title song, not heard until the final minutes, is little more than a setup for the kind of collective singalongs made popular on the radio in such shows as the *Gillette Community Sing*. At one point during the "Sing and Be Happy" finale, which includes interpolations of old favorites such as "Let Me Call You Sweetheart" and "Smiles," Martin breaks the fourth wall, looks into the camera and says, "You folks in the theater know these songs; c'mon, join in!"

The trade journal *Harrison's Reports*, which was targeted mainly for independent theater owners, reacted to the whole thing with its usual honesty: "Mild program entertainment. The plot is trite, the action slow, and the characterizations unpleasant."[72] At least Joan Davis was just getting started in the flickers, and better material was ahead. The same for Tony Martin, who by the time he died, 19 months short of his 100th birthday, had made "Sing and Be Happy" a maxim for his life rather than the title of one of the least of his movies.

Something to Sing About
(Grand National; September 20, 1937)

Director: Victor Schertzinger. Producer: Zion Myers. Presented By: Edward L. Alperson. Screenplay: Austin Parker. Story: Victor Schertzinger. Photography: John Stumar. Editor: Gene Milford. Sound: A.E. Kaye, Hal Bumbaugh. Art Directors: Robert E. Lee, Paul Murphy. Dance Director: Harland Dixon. Musical Director: C. [Constantin] Bakaleinikoff. Orchestral Arrangements: Myrl Alderman. Set Decoration: Walter E. Kline. Assistant Director: John Sherwood. Production Management: Gaston Glass, Harold Lewis. Running Time: 88 minutes.

Cast: James Cagney (Terry Rooney aka Thaddeus McGillicuddy); Evelyn Daw (Rita Wyatt); William Frawley (Hank Meyers); Mona Barrie (Stephanie Hajos); Gene Lockhart (Bennett O. "B.O." Regan); Philip Ahn (Ito); Marek Windheim (Farney); Dwight Frye (Easton); Johnny Arthur (Daviani); William B. Davidson (Richards); Richard Tucker (Blaine); Kathleen Lockhart (Miss Robbins); James Newill (Jimmy); Harry Barris (Pinky); Cully Richards (soloist); Candy Candido (Candy); Percy Launders, Paul McLarind (band members); Harland Dixon, Johnny Boyle, John "Skins" Miller, Buck Mack, Pat Moran, Joe Bennett, Eddie Allen (dancers in deck number); Kenneth Harlan (transportation manager); Herbert Rawlinson (studio attorney); Ernest Wood (Eddie Burns); Eddie Kane (theater manager); Chick Collins, Duke Green (men whom Terry fights); Bill Carey (singer); Frank Mills (cab driver); Larry Steers (studio official); Edward Hearn (studio guard); Marjorie "Babe" Kane (receptionist); Robert McKenzie (ship's captain); Alphonse Martel (headwaiter); Daisy Bufford (maid); Bo Peep Karlin, Eleanore Prentiss, Elinore Welz (girls); The Vagabonds (themselves); Pinkie and Pal (Arthur Nelson's Fighting Cats); Dottie Messmer, Virginia Lee Irwin, Dolly Waldorf (Three Shades of Blue).

Songs: "Any Old Love" [Cagney, Three Shades of Blue], "Loving You" [Daw, danced by Cagney, chorus], "Out of the Blue" [band, danced by Cagney; reprised twice by Daw, band], "Right or Wrong" [Daw, band, twice], "Something to Sing About" [Daw, Newill, Candido, Cagney; reprised by band] (Victor Schertzinger); "Bridal Chorus" from *Lohengrin* [band; danced by Cagney, Daw] (Richard Wagner).

Working Title: *When I'm With You.*
Reissue Title: *Battling Hoofer.*
Academy Award Nomination: Best Score (C. Bakaleinikoff).
Home Video: Various public-domain distributors.

The Story: New York bandleader/dancer Terry Rooney (real name: Thaddeus McGillicuddy) departs from his orchestra to go to Hollywood to play the lead in a movie, "Any Old Love," at Galor Pictures. His sweetheart, band vocalist Rita, is left behind as well. Studio head B.O. Regan is impressed by early rushes of Terry's work but hides his praise, so as not to spoil Terry as he has temperamental contractee Stephanie Hajos. Terry secretly marries Rita and departs on a honeymoon in the South Seas. "Any Old Love" and its title song becomes huge hits, and Terry returns to find he has become a major star. Rita is forced by the studio to hide their marriage and pose as his private secretary, and publicity man Hank Meyers builds up Stephanie as Terry's new on- and off-screen love interest. Terry and Rita realize they can't go on living a lie, but the situation becomes more complicated when Stephanie tells the press she and Terry are to be engaged. Rita returns to New York to rejoin her old bandmates ("Out of the Blue"), but Terry follows her back and is reunited with her during a performance at their old club ("Right or Wrong," "Something to Sing About").

How unhappy was James Cagney with his home studio in the middle 1930s? So unhappy that one of the biggest names in Hollywood quit Warner Bros.—where he was perennially displeased with his compensation and working conditions—for newly formed independent Grand National Pictures. Acquiring Cagney's services was a huge public relations coup for Grand National, for which the actor would make two films in 1936–37. Unfortunately, one of them was *Something to Sing About*, a costly musical that failed at the box office. For the actor, this tuneful sendup of Hollywood stars and star-making was a blip on a lengthy resume of successes; for Grand National, what promised to be a great reward sowed the seeds for an eventual demise.

What brought Cagney to his new partner? Freedom—financial and artistic. Warner-rostered since 1930, Cagney had grown restive over the quality of material in his recent films, which found him in his traditional crowd-pleasing tough-guy mold. He was cast as Bottom in Warners' ambitious filming of *A Midsummer Night's Dream* (1935), but more often, his vehicles were unchallenging, pre-packaged, and predictable. One of them, *Frisco Kid* (1935), was derided in the actor's autobiography as "catch-as-catch-can ... built the way a Ford sedan might have been."[73] Worried about overwork and overexposure, Cagney (1899–1986) smarted at the studio's demand he make five movies per year rather than the presently contracted four. In late 1935, he refused to start work on his next scheduled Warner Bros. picture, then sued for breach of contract—and won. He had broken the dominance of the Hollywood studio system, but which studio would next employ this unexpected free agent?

Meanwhile, Grand National was being built by former film exchange manager Edward L. Alperson, who had incorporated the company in early 1936 and was distributing Westerns—among them the color musical *The Devil on Horseback* [q.v.] and a series of Tex Ritter entries—and other action films produced separately. His quest for talent was rewarded in July 1936 with the bombshell signing of Cagney to a four-picture contract at $150,000 per. Among the GN projects linked to Cagney were stereotypically Irish subjects—the stories *Luck of the Irish* and *John L. Sullivan's Hat* and an adaptation of the novel *Studs Lonigan*.[74]

What got made first, however, and was premiered in December 1936 to much attention as Cagney's first film in roughly a year, was *Great Guy*. It sought to drum up dubious excitement for a hero from the New York Department of Weights and Measures battling crooked businessmen and politicians. For publicity value, Mae Clarke—Cagney's infamous grapefruit target from *The Public Enemy* and hair-pull victim from *Lady Killer*—was second-billed. As their new actioner began to make its way through theaters, Cagney and Grand National were slated to follow it up with *Dynamite*, an adventure set in the oil fields of Texas, but events were set in motion to bring the actor into his first musical in four years. In late 1936, GN formed a unit that paired veteran comedy producer Zion Myers with director and composer Victor Schertzinger, who was best known for helming the Oscar-nominated Grace Moore vehicle *One Night of Love* (1934) and writing hits such as "I Remember You" and "Tangerine." For their first project together, with songs and story by Schertzinger, opera star Helen Jepson was intended as the female lead, but a bigger fish was on the line. Cagney was hooked in May 1937, when Myers and Schertzinger secured his services and *Dynamite* was postponed.[75] So was a plan to film a gangster story, *Angels with Dirty Faces*—but more on that later.

Jepson was dropped, and the trades reported that Schertzinger was making screen tests of prospective female-star hopefuls for evaluation by representatives of Grand Nation-

James Cagney escaped Warner Bros. control long enough to make a high-budget musical comedy for little Grand National, *Something to Sing About*. Marek Windheim is at left.

al's theatrical exchanges.[76] In reality, Schertzinger had found his fresh face in Evelyn Daw, an unknown South Dakota-bred soprano who was discovered by the director while she was performing with the Los Angeles Philharmonic. No taker of shortcuts, Schertzinger made sure his latest protégée passed all the right tests during the audition and training processes. Informed that she needed to make the necessary impression on "those that mattered," Daw (1912–1970) told a trade magazine interviewer in 1937, "I honestly believe I sang for everybody that passed Mr. Schertzinger's office ... executives, directors, bookkeepers, stenographers and gardeners among the many whom he asked in to hear me."[77] Not requiring endorsement from the GN workforce, William Frawley (borrowed from Paramount) and Gene Lockhart were signed to bolster the comedy in a film shot during June and July of 1937.

Great Guy did not reveal that Grand National could out-Warner Warners in the action field, but Cagney's musical resume—which on screen then encompassed only *Footlight Parade* (1933)—must have given Schertzinger and Myers encouragement. An erstwhile stage chorister, Cagney considered himself a song-and-dance man at heart. He especially delighted in working with veteran hoofers Johnny Boyle and Harland Dixon. Boyle was Cagney's dance instructor in Hollywood, and Dixon, a longtime vaudevillian who had been Cagney's dance teacher in New York in the 1920s, was the dance director for *Something to Sing About*. Both men were showcased with Cagney in a "tap-off" set aboard the deck of a ship in *Something to Sing About*; the number included an all-star dance lineup that also boasted "Skins" Miller and Buck Mack, then known as the duo Miller and Mack; Pat Moran (of the team Clifford and Moran); Joe Bennett (of Bennett and Reynolds); and Eddie Allen. Of his idols Boyle and Dixon, Cagney wrote in his 1976 autobiography:

> I must cheerfully admit that I had stolen all kinds of steps from them both down through the years, and it made me very proud to think that I was literally following in their footsteps and with their footsteps. It was warming to feel that I was one of their kind—a song-and-dance man working in the great tradition set by the head of our clan, George M. Cohan.[78]

Cagney's stiff-legged dancing style became best known to filmgoers in his Oscar-winning performance as Cohan in *Yankee Doodle Dandy* (1942). But there is no lack of that style in *Something to Sing About*, in sequences that open and close the picture, as well as in the deck number midway through. There had to be a lot of dancing, for in the "song" part of song and dance, Cagney was no Crosby. *Something to Sing About* gets around this shortcoming by opening with Cagney's character, Hollywood-bound bandleader Terry Rooney, attempting to sing the title song solo but hearing it hijacked by various members of his orchestra. Cagney is permitted a brief solo on "Any Old Love," most of which he song-speaks anyway. Daw, whose operatic style seems out of place for a vocalist in a swing band, does most of the singing but makes little impression as an actress. She would make only one other feature.[79]

Something to Sing About is one of the most widely available of Cagney's films. Having fallen into the public domain, it survives in murky, slightly truncated prints that underrate the production values given by its smaller, indie studio. It may rank with its star's second-tier Warner Bros. productions—not least because it lacks a memorable song—but it has much to recommend it. Cagney's energy is fortified by the pleasure of playing an unabashed romantic lead, and studio-spoofing satire is delivered by top character actors like Frawley and Lockhart, the former as an overly protective studio flack and the latter as a money-minded studio chief.

Welcome supporting players Dwight Frye, Johnny Arthur, and Philip Ahn weren't getting as much screen time for the majors in 1937 as they do here, and Ahn's character—an aspiring actor reduced to playing Asian stereotypes to work as Cagney's covertly whip-smart servant—even reflects WB-style social conscience. English actress Mona Barrie—then one of Hollywood's foremost players of "other-woman" roles—scores as a heavily accented Garboesque diva. Her abjectly insincere facial expression as she exchanges cheek kisses with a gossip columnist (played by Kathleen Lockhart, Gene's wife) is priceless. Barrie also provided a bit of levity during the filming of a love scene with Cagney, to which she reacted with an emphatic "Whew! The boy has talent!" The line got enough of a laugh on the set for Schertzinger to have it written into the script.[80] Befitting her second-tier status, Barrie (1909–1964) jokingly liked to call herself "the heroine of the cutting-room floor," but not so much here.

Those who wanted some fisticuffs in a Cagney picture were placated with a scene in which Rooney punches unruly stuntmen in the movie within the movie, and a bout of disagreement over whether Cagney's character should sign a long-term studio contract had to have been meant to recall current events. In fact, as Cagney biographer Patrick McGilligan and others have noted, *Something to Sing About* symbolizes the star's discontent with Hollywood by all but attacking what McGilligan describes as a "propitiously timed ... even blunt, attack by Cagney" on "the entire movie star syndrome."[81]

"The King of He-Men Becomes the King of Swing!" Grand National asserted in its promotions for *Something to Sing About*, and bragged that none other than Fred Astaire had helped Cagney with his steps at the latter's home, and that dance-studio titan Arthur Murray had set about teaching said moves to thousands nationwide.[82] A newsreel trailer featuring Evelyn Daw and Victor Schertzinger was prepared for theaters. The film's estimated $450,000 budget was no pittance even by the majors' standards, and it was a huge investment by an outlet like GN, which may have ended up spending as much as $900,000.[83] The popular thought nowadays is that *Something to Sing About* was made on the cheap because it looks so, but it was widely praised upon its release, and not just because of pent-up clamor for Cagney. *New Republic* critic Otis Ferguson, no shill for the studios, called it "about the happiest experience we've got in the last few months, what with all the lavish splashes and worthy wordage."[84] Frank S. Nugent of *The New York Times*, while admitting it was "nothing to shout about," praised the film as "an amusing piece, sardonic and frolicsome," carried along "with gusty humor, a tune or two and the celebrated Cagney scowl."[85] *Variety*'s man lauded it as "first-class ... [lifted] out of the independent field into favorable comparison with the best output of similar type from the major studios."[86]

Grand National was never the same after *Something to Sing About*, but not for the right reasons. Without the vast theatrical distribution network of the majors, the studio lost money on the film, and although GN carried on until 1940, it could not make as ambitious a project again. Edward Finney, advertising chief for the studio, told historian Gene Fernett that a key mistake was GN following up *Great Guy* with the wrong story for Cagney. The company considered starring him in *Angels with Dirty Faces*, written by Rowland Brown, author of the previous Cagney film *The Doorway to Hell*. But it never happened for Alperson, as Finney recalled:

> Alperson had the foresight to buy.... *Angels with Dirty Faces*.... Instead, with that story on Alperson's desk, mind you, he allowed himself to be talked into making instead.... *Something to Sing About*. As it turned out for Cagney and First National, however, it should have been named *Something to Cry About*—for that film bankrupted the corporation—eventually wiped it out completely.
>
> Several of us had tried to reason with Alperson. "Look," we argued, "do *Angels With Dirty Faces* first. After all, you've tied up $25,000 for the rights to the story, which is a perfect one for Cagney's talents."[87]

Grand National did put *Angels with Dirty Faces* on the production schedule, but not until January 1938. Just before filming was to start, Cagney was ordered in court to return to Warner Bros., which signed him to a lucrative contract: $150,000 per film *plus* 10 percent of the gross. With GN out of the picture, Warners purchased *Angels* and turned it into one of Cagney's biggest hits—complete with his first Oscar-nominated performance. The time away from Warners didn't hurt Cagney at all; indeed, his Grand National stint proved he could play against tough-guy type.

Cagney did not forget this, either. When he was asked, not long before his death, about which of his movies—besides *Yankee Doodle Dandy*—that he'd most like to see again, he picked *Something to Sing About*. A print was provided for the actor to watch, and he didn't regret his choice. "I like the songs. They're damned cute," Cagney said.[88] That's something to think about regarding *Something to Sing About*.

A Damsel in Distress

(RKO; November 19, 1937)

Director: George Stevens. Producer: Pandro S. Berman. Executive Producer: Samuel J. Briskin. Screenplay: P.G. Wodehouse, Ernest Pagano, S.K. Lauren, based on the novel by Wodehouse. Photography: Joseph H. August. Editor: Henry Berman. Sound: Earl A. Wollcott. Music Director: Victor Baravalle. Orchestral Arrangements: Robert Russell Bennett. Additional Arrangements: Ray Noble, George

Bassman. Dance Director: Hermes Pan. Art Director: Van Nest Polglase. Associate Art Director: Carroll Clark. Set Decoration: Darrell Silvera. Costumes: Claire Cramer. Special Effects: Vernon L. Walker. Assistant Director: Argyle Nelson. Running Time: 100 minutes.

Cast: Fred Astaire (Jerry Halliday); George Burns (George); Gracie Allen (Gracie); Joan Fontaine (Lady Alyce Marshmorton); Reginald Gardiner (Keggs); Ray Noble (Reggie); Constance Collier (Lady Caroline); Montagu Love (Lord John Marshmorton); Harry Watson (Albert); Jan Duggan (Miss Ruggles); Pearl Amatore, Mary Dean, Jack George, Betty Rome (madrigal singers); Charles Bennett (carnival barker); Frank Benson (attendant); Thelma Hart (ticket seller); Max Linder, Jack Wynn (footmen); Mary Gordon (servant); Violet Seton (Alyce's maid); Joe Niemeyer (dancer); Fred Kelsey (tourist); Ben Jacobs (bus driver); Frank Moran (bobby); William O'Brien (chauffeur); James Clemens, James Fawcett, Ken Terrell, Jack Walkin (drunks in funhouse).

Songs: "A Foggy Day (in London Town)" [Astaire], "I Can't Be Bothered Now" [Astaire], "The Jolly Tar and the Milkmaid" [Astaire, madrigal singers], "Nice Work If You Can Get It" [Astaire, Dean, Duggan, Rome, chorus, reprised by Astaire, orchestra], "Put Me to the Test" [Astaire, Burns, Allen], "Sing of Spring" [madrigal singers], "Stiff Upper Lip" [Allen, danced by Astaire, Burns, chorus], "Things Are Looking Up" [Astaire, danced by Fontaine] (Ira Gershwin, George Gershwin); "Ah! Che a voi perdoni iddio" ("Ah! May Heaven to You Grant Pardon," from *Martha*) [Gardiner, dubbed by Mario Berini] (Friedrich Wilhelm Riese, Friedrich von Flotow).

Academy Award: Best Dance Direction (Hermes Pan).

Academy Award Nomination: Best Art Direction (Carroll Clark).

Disc: Brunswick 7982 ("A Foggy Day [in London Town]"/"I Can't Be Bothered Now," Fred Astaire with Ray Noble Orchestra); Brunswick 7983 ("Nice Work If You Can Get It"/"Things Are Looking Up," Fred Astaire with Ray Noble Orchestra).

Home Video: Warner Archive DVD; Turner Home Entertainment VHS.

The Story: Lady Alyce Marshmorton is in love, and the domestic staff at her family home in Totleigh Castle takes wagers on the identity of her beau. Keggs, the clan's head domestic, bets she will marry Reggie, the dullard stepson of Alyce's stern aunt, Caroline, but follows the girl around to find out who her real love is. Alyce, who is temporarily smitten with an American skier, has a chance meeting with another Yankee, musical comedy star Jerry Halliday. He is visiting London with his press agent, George, and George's stenographer, Gracie. Jerry wants to quit showbiz because he is tired of his public image as a Lothario ("I Can't Be Bothered Now"). Led to believe that Alyce has fallen for him, Jerry rents a bungalow next to the Marshmorton castle ("Put Me to the Test"). With the aid of Alyce's unpretentious father, Lord John, and a young servant, Albert, Jerry goes to a country fair ("Stiff Upper Lip") in an attempt to win Alyce's affections, which he soon does ("Things Are Looking Up"). Realizing he will lose the staff lottery because he has picked Reggie incorrectly as Alyce's intended, Keggs forces Albert into exchanging their betting slips. With his betting interest changed, Albert turns Alyce against Jerry by showing her a sensationalized gossip column about them, although Jerry's love for her has deepened ("A Foggy Day"). Keggs forces Albert into another betting switch, but Keggs is thwarted when Reggie shows an interest in Gracie. Meanwhile, Lord John brings Jerry and Alyce together with some sage advice to Jerry. Jerry celebrates his triumph with a drumming, dancing rendition of "Nice Work If You Can Get It."

Given their mutual desire not to be joined at the hip professionally, it was inevitable that Fred Astaire would star in a movie without Ginger Rogers. She had taken a break from their fabulous partnership to fly solo in the 1935 musical comedy *In Person* [q.v.] and a few non-musical features. He, however, had never had to carry a picture on his own—not until *A Damsel in Distress* in 1937.[89] Despite ample resources—a script adapted by renowned British humorist P.G. Wodehouse from his own novel, songs by George and Ira Gershwin, direction by future multiple Oscar winner George Stevens, and comedy support from George Burns and Gracie Allen—*Damsel* was the first Astaire film to lose money. It didn't help that the new leading lady was all wrong, although the film truly suffers only in comparison to the lofty Astaire-Rogers standard.

7. Big Stars, Short Memories

Prior to the filming of *A Damsel in Distress*, Astaire and Rogers had been teamed seven times by RKO—frequently enough for Astaire, who didn't want to be tied to any one dance partner on film any more than he previously had been linked to his sister, Adele, on stage. In 1936, Astaire (1899–1987) secured a new contract assuring that three of his next five pictures would not include Rogers, unless he consented otherwise.[90] Astaire was to be paid a salary of $4,000 per week, with a percentage of his films' profits—a big boost compared to the $1,500 weekly he was compensated to make the duo's first movie together, *Flying Down to Rio*, in 1933. Astaire also feared that the public was beginning to tire of the duo, possibly in the box office returns relative to their films' increasingly high costs. *Shall We Dance*, the most recent Fred-and-Ginger, had made money, but not as much as earlier films, and the starring duo fell from third to seventh in the 1936 *Motion Picture Herald* annual exhibitors poll of biggest money-making stars. As Astaire wrote in his autobiography:

> The signs that the cycle was running out its course were beginning to show.... I asked for, and all hands at the studio agreed to, a picture away from Ginger, to keep us from falling into a rut. Ginger was for it, too.... We had not announced any permanent dissolution; in fact, we had our next (film) all planned to follow this slight intermission.[91] (Astaire is referring to *Carefree*, their 1938 release.)

So who would be Astaire's new consort? Fans on both sides of the Atlantic wished for it to be the British musical star Jessie Matthews. Astaire supposedly had agreed to partner with Matthews in her feature *Evergreen* (1934), but RKO would not loan him out. With Astaire committed, the England-set *Damsel in Distress* would've been an ideal teaming, but Matthews could not appear, reportedly because of scheduling complications.[92] Media

A Damsel in Distress wasn't a top-shelf Fred Astaire musical, and it didn't help that he had a mismatched female lead in young Joan Fontaine.

reports linked Ruby Keeler and Carole Lombard to the female lead. But the role was given, with Astaire's reluctant approval, to Joan Fontaine, an RKO contract actress who could neither sing nor dance but who, as the Tokyo-born daughter of well-to-do English parents, didn't look out of place playing a noblewoman.

The sister of Warner Bros. star Olivia de Havilland, Fontaine (1917–2013) had scant film experience, mainly small roles in a handful of movies. At age 19, she was years ahead of what would be an impressive starring career. She was miscast opposite opera star Nino Martini in a second-tier RKO musical, *Music for Madame** (1937), which wrapped just before *Damsel* but hadn't yet opened, but interacting with the perfectionist Astaire would be an even bigger challenge. RKO wisely anticipated the name-value vacuum Fontaine would create by borrowing Burns and Allen from Paramount, albeit as characters that were absent from Wodehouse's novel and ensuing play. Still, what about the showcase romantic numbers? Fontaine prepped with daily tap lessons with Keeler's brother, a dance instructor, but she ultimately couldn't be trusted to do any more than glide through a few steps in a single number following Astaire's lead: "Things Are Looking Up," in which she was not trusted to sing so much as a single note.

As George Stevens recalled years later, he, dance director Hermes Pan, and cinematographer Joseph August conspired to stage the number by having Astaire and Fontaine dance through a succession of scenery pieces such as bridges, trees, and hedges in order to keep the viewer's eye distracted from her non-dancing.[93] On location at the RKO ranch, Fontaine, as she recalled in her autobiography, knew she was in peril:

> I danced blisters on my size-4 feet. The summer heat only added to my misery. All those ballet lessons I had taken in my early youth had not prepared me for duet dancing, for the leaps and lifts devised by Astaire and (dance director Hermes) Pan. I tripped over fences and stepping stones to the tune of "Things Are Looking Up."[94]

The tension would become so great, Stevens remembered many years later, that a few weeks into shooting, Astaire and producer Pandro S. Berman came to him and urged that Fontaine be replaced. "She was a girl with problems, you know; she cried and all that," remembered the director, who insisted Fontaine be kept although he knew Astaire and Berman were right.[95] Astaire had good reason to have top-flight collaborators besides Berman and Pan; Stevens had directed him in *Swing Time* (1936), and the actor had Victor Baravalle, the renowned Broadway conductor, brought in as *Damsel* musical director.

The Gershwins knew Astaire well professionally, having written scores for his Broadway hits *Lady, Be Good* and *Funny Face* and his Rogers vehicle *Shall We Dance* (which introduced "They Can't Take That Away from Me"). After *Shall We Dance*, George Gershwin convinced Berman to buy the rights to Wodehouse's story, and the brothers wrote songs for it while envisioning its premise as a songwriter looking for a damsel in distress to sweep off her feet.[96] Eight of the Gershwins' songs made the cut for the movie, but George Gershwin didn't live to see the result. He died of a brain tumor on July 11, 1937, shortly before filming began, and the final script turned out to be more conventional than his vision.[97]

By the time *Damsel in Distress* was released in November, many of the Gershwin songs already had become hits via airplay, and what a score this film had—with (at least) two unassailable standards in "A Foggy Day (in London Town)" and "Nice Work If You Can Get It." "Foggy Day" was revived most notably in the 1950s by Frank Sinatra, but it debuted in a solitary performance by Astaire, photographed beautifully by Joseph August as he danced in a fog outside a castle and the party going on without him therein, and ruminating on the uneasy status of his love affair. "Nice Work" is first heard in a nicely unexpected way, sung by a group of madrigal singers joined by Astaire, who reprises the tune in an extended dancing drum solo with a nod to swing. The latter rendition is simple but dynamic, with Astaire operating in a tight space with a variety of drum types from which the camera barely moves—and, per the Astaire technique, nary a reaction shot from outside.

"I Can't Be Bothered Now" is meant as a jaunty response by Astaire's music-star character on the suffocation of his celebrity, as he dances among a group of adoring fans on a London street, an umbrella acting as a useful prop in a too-brief but entertaining number.[98] Two even more inventive sequences team Astaire with Burns and Allen, who demonstrate how their years of hoofing in vaudeville honed their skills, and why their $10,000-a-week salary for this picture was well worth it for RKO. "Put Me to the Test," an instrumental sequence in which the three actors use whisk brooms in rhythm and brush each other off, was inspired by a number Burns had seen on the stage by an act called Evans and Evans. He bought the rights to the routine and auditioned it with his wife for Astaire and Pan. "I love it!" Astaire told Burns and Allen. "We'll do it in the picture just as it is."[99]

But the most memorable number in *Damsel in Distress* is performed to the song "Stiff Upper Lip," and its cleverness and high energy won Hermes Pan the Academy Award then awarded for dance direction. In a carnival fun house in which Astaire's character reunites-cute with Fontaine's, Astaire, Burns, and Allen take more than 10 minutes to dash through a series of stunts—involving treadmills, chutes, barrels, circular revolving floors, and, most strikingly, the optical illusions of an eccentric mirror that exaggerates the performers' dimensions. It proved that the Astaire team hadn't run out of dance ideas just because Rogers was absent. As Burns quipped decades later in one of his memoirs: "I wasn't going to lose a chance to work with Fred Astaire. Look what it did for Ginger Rogers."[100]

Another comedian, the more urbane Reginald Gardiner, scores with a rendition (lip-synched) to an operatic aria, the context being that this domestic maintains a secret love for highbrow music. (No doubt the number was meant to evoke Gardiner's cameo in the recent MGM musical *Born to Dance*, in which he was a Central Park policeman who pretends to conduct an invisible orchestra.) On the flip side is the other-man character played by popular bandleader-composer Ray Noble, who fights his musical impulses for dance music although he's a member of the nobility. Noble gained plaudits here for portraying the kind of dull, dimwitted Englishman he was for years on Edgar Bergen's radio show. Gardiner's juvenile partner in betting collusion is played by Harry Watson (of the prolific Watson kiddie acting family) in a role said to be initially intended for Mickey Rooney.[101]

But for all the assets of *Damsel in Distress*, there is the chasm at leading lady. In their films, Astaire and Rogers make love through dance, rather than via flowery talk or smooching, but there very little dancing by Astaire and Fontaine together—and when there is, he does all the work—and thus the secret sauce of the Fred-Ginger features is lost to hungry viewers. *A Damsel in Distress* lost $65,000 at the box office.[102] Most critics praised it, with *Variety*, for example, saluting "the usual sumptuous investiture accorded … to any Astaire picture," and *The New York Times* observing that, with the absence of Rogers, "Fred Astaire is bearing up astonishingly well."[103] Unfairly, perhaps, the distress of *Damsel* was compared relentlessly by critics and fans to the hit status of Rogers' then-current release, the non-singing comedy *Stage Door*. New York's Radio City Music Hall, which traditionally had premiered the Astaire-Rogers musicals, passed on Astaire's solo turn, infuriating the star.[104] It didn't help that there was no precedent to Astaire starring by himself on celluloid.

Most Astaire historians have at least grudging praise for *A Damsel in Distress*, and in his memoir, Astaire deigned to call it "a goodish picture [that] accomplished what we tried to do."[105] The retroactive enthusiasm was not shared by its creator/co-screenwriter. In a preface to a 1975 edition of his source novel, P.G. Wodehouse dismissed the film version as "a mess which for some reason is still shown occasionally on American television and causes sets to be switched off from the rockbound coasts of Maine to the Everglades of Florida…. They did their best by engaging Fred Astaire and giving him nobody to dance with, so that he had nine [sic] solo numbers." Wodehouse was known to be unhappy with changes made to the work for the screen, mainly alterations made to the hero's originally reticent personality, the progression of the love story, and the insertion of Burns and Allen.[106]

Poor Joan Fontaine was relegated to billing among the featured players apart from the main three actors who did not have the title role in *A Damsel in Distress*. Speaking nearly 40 years after the fact, Berman admitted Fontaine happened to be assigned "because she was under contract to the studio…. The mix of personalities was certainly not as good because there wasn't much energy and that pep that Ginger had, and that comedy. Joan was a quiet girl…. But it also turned out to be a bad idea because she couldn't dance … and [*A Damsel in Distress*] was the least successful of all the Astaire pictures [at RKO]."[107] That "quiet girl" had to subject herself to embarrassment while watching the film's Hollywood premiere, as Fontaine recalled: "The theatre darkened; the film began. During my number with Mr. Astaire, the lady behind me loudly exclaimed, 'Isn't she AWFUL!' I sank to the floor. I was consigned to 'B' pictures once more."[108]

Not for long, though, and even if *A Damsel in Distress* wasn't quite the triumph intended, Fontaine and "Mr. Astaire" both would see greater successes. Astaire, contract be damned, was reteamed with Rogers twice more, in *Carefree* (1938) and *The Story of Vernon and Irene Castle* (1939), before he went off on his own for good at MGM with *Broadway Melody of 1940*. By then, Fontaine was scoring big in Alfred Hitchcock's *Rebecca*, and neither she nor her reluctant leading man of three years prior had much need to look back.

Let Freedom Ring
(Metro-Goldwyn-Mayer; February 24, 1939)

and *Broadway Serenade*
(Metro-Goldwyn-Mayer; April 7, 1939)

Let Freedom Ring

Director: Jack Conway. Producer: Harry Rapf. Story/Screenplay: Ben Hecht. Photography: Sidney Wagner. Editor: Frederick Y. Smith. Musical Director: Arthur Lange. Orchestral Arrangements: Leonid Raab. Art Director: Cedric Gibbons. Associate Art Director: Daniel B. Cathcart. Recording Director: Douglas Shearer. Set Decoration: Edwin B. Willis. Costumes: Dolly Tree, Valles. Special Effects: John Hoffman. Makeup: Jack Dawn. Assistant Director: Horace Hough. Running Time: 87 minutes.

Cast: Nelson Eddy (Steve Logan); Virginia Bruce (Maggie Adams); Victor McLaglen (Chris Mulligan); Lionel Barrymore (Thomas Logan); Edward Arnold (Jim Knox); Guy Kibbee (David Bronson); Charles Butterworth ("The Mackerel"); H.B. Warner (Rutledge); Raymond Walburn (Underwood); Dick Rich ("Bumper" Jackson); Trevor Bardette (Gagan); George ["Gabby"] Hayes ("Pop" Wilkie); Louis Jean Heydt (Ned Wilkie); Sarah Padden ("Ma" Logan); Eddie Dunn (Curly); C.E. Anderson (Sheriff Hicks); Philo McCullough, Harry Fleischmann, Ralph Bushman [Francis X. Bushman, Jr.] (Gagan henchmen); Maude Allen (Hilda); Adia Kuznetzoff (Pole); Luis Alberni (Tony); Emory Parnell (Axel); Victor Potel (Ole); Tenen Holtz (Hunky); Mitchell Lewis (Joe); Constantine Romanoff (Russian); Lionel Royce (German); Billy Bevan (cockney); Syd Saylor, Ted Thompson (surveyors); Heinie Conklin (rancher).

Songs: "Dusty Road" [Eddy] (Otis René, Leon René); "Home, Sweet Home" [Eddy] (John Howard Payne,

Henry Bishop); "Love Serenade" [Eddy, Bruce, Allen, reprised by Eddy] (Bob Wright, Chet Forrest, Riccardo Drigo); "My Country, 'Tis of Thee" [Eddy, Bruce, McLaglen, chorus] (Samuel Francis Smith, Henry Carey); "Pat Sez He" [Eddy, McLaglen] (Marty Symes, Phil Ohman); "Ten Thousand Cattle Straying" [Eddy] (Owen Wister); "When Irish Eyes Are Smiling" [Eddy] (Chauncey Olcott, George Graff, Ernest R. Ball); "Where Else but Here?" [Eddy, chorus] (Edward Heyman, Sigmund Romberg); "I've Been Working on the Railroad" [chorus] (trad.).
Working Titles: *The Dusty Road*; *Song of the West*.
Home Video: Warner Archive DVD.

The Story: In the late 1860s, Clover City awaits the coming of the railroad as the "Iron Horse" stretches across the American West, but its arrival means trouble for the town's peaceful natives. New York financier Jim Knox dispatches his hooligans to acquire land needed for the rail route, even if it means burning the residents out. Among the ranchers whose property is in the rail's right of way is Thomas Logan, whose son, Steve, is returning home from law studies at Harvard. Instead of opposing Knox openly, Steve pretends to be the tycoon's ally, which angers his father as well as his longtime sweetheart, Maggie Adams. Under the name of "The Wasp," Steve secretly publishes a newspaper exposing Knox's crimes, preaches democratic values ("Where Else but Here?") to Knox's foreign-born workers, and pretends to befriend Knox's construction foreman, Mulligan. Maggie attempts to make Steve jealous by agreeing (temporarily) to marry Knox; his heartbroken response is to rally the workers by singing "Dusty Road." When his stolen press breaks down, Steve convinces Knox to start his own newspaper, then steals Knox's new press for his own aims—to prevent Knox-friendly judge Bronson from winning an upcoming town election. As Knox's men prepare to burn down the Logan ranch, Steve battles fistically with Mulligan and convinces him of Knox's misdeeds. Steve and Maggie rally the electorate ("My Country, 'Tis of Thee") to overthrow Knox and his minions and restore democracy to Clover City.

Broadway Serenade

Director/Producer: Robert Z. Leonard. Screenplay: Charles Lederer. Original Story: Lew Lipton, John Taintor Foote, Hans Kraly. Photography: Oliver T. Marsh. Editor: Harold F. Kress. Sound: Douglas Shearer. Music Director: Herbert Stothart. Musical Score: Herbert Stothart, Edward Ward. Vocal and Orchestral Collaboration: Leo Arnaud, Leonid Rabb. Musical Presentation: Merrill Pye. Dance Director for "Flyin' High" and *Madame Butterfly* Numbers: Seymour Felix. Dance Director for Finale: Busby Berkeley. Art Director: Cedric Gibbons. Associate Art Director: Joseph Wright. Set Decoration: Edwin B. Willis. Gowns: Adrian. Men's Costumes: Valles. Makeup: Jack Dawn. Montage Effects: John Hoffman. Assistant Director: Marvin Stuart. Running Time: 114 minutes.
Cast: Jeanette MacDonald (Mary Hale); Lew Ayres (James Geoffrey Seymour); Ian Hunter (Larry Bryant); Frank Morgan (Cornelius Collier, Jr.); Wally Vernon (Joey the Jinx); Rita Johnson (Judy Tyrrell); Virginia Grey (Pearl); William Gargan (Bill); Katharine Alexander (Harriet Ingalls); Al Shean (Herman); Esther Dale (Mrs. Olsen); Franklin Pangborn (Gene); E. Alyn Warren (Everett); Paul Hurst (Reynolds); Frank Orth (Mr. Fellowes); Esther Howard (Mrs. Fellowes); Leon Belasco (Squeaker); Kitty McHugh (Kitty); Kenneth Stevens (baritone); Ray Mayer (Woods); Edward Hearn (Frank); Ray Walker (Madison); Lawrence Wheat (accountant); W.E. Lawrence (Burke); William Tannen (assistant stage manager); Morgan Wallace (Parks); Arthur "Pop" Byron (Pat); Arthur Housman (Jonathan); Ted Oliver (Spike); Al Hill (Chuck); Barbara Bedford (secretary); Jack Carlton (cameraman); Mary Beth Hughes (girl at party); Tom Hanlon (radio announcer); Hans Joby (Hans); Bernard Siegel (Otto); Estelle Etterre, Patricia West (girls with Bryant); Lionel Royce (Bachspiegel); Bert Moorhouse, Don Brodie, Jack Luden, Charles Sherlock, Allen Fox (reporters); Ernie Alexander (photographer); Jack Hutchinson (chauffeur); Olaf Hytten (hotel host); Mary MacLaren (costumer); Claude King (hotel visitor); Bruce Mitchell (train conductor); Arthur Q. Bryan (Ingalls process server); Norman Willis (divorce process server); Paul Newlan (man with female voice); Jane Barnes, Gertrude Short, Marjorie "Babe" Kane, Jill Dennett (salesgirls); Mary Gordon (Annie); Delos Jewkes (music maker); Warren Lewis (baritone); Ken Darby's Octet, Six Hits and a Miss (singers in "High Flyin'" number); Mary Kent (contralto in "High Flyin'" number); Helen Seamon, Roy Lester (jitterbug dancers).

Songs: "For Ev'ry Lonely Heart (Broadway Serenade)" [MacDonald, twice, reprised twice by MacDonald, chorus] (Gus Kahn, Herbert Stothart, Edward Ward, Pyotr Ilyich Tchaikovsky); "High Flyin'" [Kent, reprised by MacDonald, Pangborn, then twice by MacDonald, chorus], "One Look at You" [MacDonald, twice, also by MacDonald, Stevens, chorus] (Chet Forrest, Bob Wright, Herbert Stothart, Edward Ward); "Musical Contract" [Ayres, Shean] (Herbert Stothart, Edward Ward); "No Time to Argue" [MacDonald, Stevens] (Gus Kahn, Sigmund Romberg); "Time Changes Everything" [MacDonald, chorus, twice] (Gus Kahn, Walter Donaldson); "Un bel di" (from *Madame Butterfly*) [MacDonald] (Luigi Illica, Giuseppe Giacosa, Giacomo Puccini). "Naughty Nineties" Nightclub Medley [MacDonald, chorus]: "Yip-I-Addy-I-Ay" (Will D. Cobb, John H. Flynn); "What You Goin' to Do When the Rent Comes 'Round (Rufus Rastus Johnson Brown)" (Andrew B. Sterling, Harry von Tilzer); "Hearts Win, You Lose" (Andrew B. Sterling).
Home Video: Warner Archive DVD.

The Story: Struggling, and secretly married, vaudeville duo Mary Hale and James Geoffrey "Jimmy" Seymour attempt to sell one of Jimmy's high-minded songs ("None but the Lonely Heart") to Broadway producer Cornelius Collier, who is uninterested in the song but signs Mary when she sings "High Flyin'" and "One Look at You" from his latest revue. With rehearsals in Atlantic City, Mary and Jimmy must separate, enabling wealthy backer Larry Bryant to horn in. Mary becomes a big success ("Time Changes Everything"), overshadowing the show's star, Harriet Ingalls, and is linked to Larry in the press. Jimmy stews back home with his musician friend Herman and is passed off to reporters as Mary's "brother." Harriet quits the revue and spreads scandalous talk about Mary and Larry, and Jimmy drunkenly parts from his wife as her stardom grows over the next two years ("Un bel di"). On Christmas Eve, Mary files for divorce. Jimmy is further embarrassed after a chance near-reunion with his wife ("One Look at You"), but Herman encourages Jimmy to become serious about his songwriting again. On the night of her farewell performance in the revue, Mary accepts Larry's marriage proposal. Mary prepares to leave the country for the wedding in Larry's native England, but Jimmy reappears, his new "Rhapsody" soon to be produced. Larry steps aside, and the estranged couple are reunited as Collier's "Broadway Serenade" show, penned by Jimmy, premieres.

When was an evening at the movies with Jeanette MacDonald and Nelson Eddy not a Mac-Eddy delight? When MGM dared make an experiment that did not work. In 1939, some filmgoers around the U.S. saw Hollywood's premier romantic operetta duo on the same bill—but separately, her in *Broadway Serenade* and him in *Let Freedom Ring*. MacDonald and Eddy starred in other films without each other during their mutual 1935–42 run, but none more than these two simultaneously produced and commercially disappointing releases quite so boldly established that they were at their best together, not apart.

After MacDonald (1903–1965) and Eddy (1901–1967) had starred together in five pictures—the most recent being the smash hit *Sweethearts*—MGM assigned both to separate projects. Depending on whom you believe—given the eternal controversy over the nature of their off-screen relationship—this happened either because the studio sought to exploit their box-office potential separately, or because Louis B. Mayer didn't want MacDonald to leave her husband, actor Gene Raymond, for Eddy. In any case, while MacDonald was spending the final weeks of 1938 and the outset of 1939 on the set of *Broadway Serenade*, Eddy was nearby making *Let Freedom Ring*. She'd headlined a few films without him, but rarely as an above-the-title talent. Eddy had made one previous film as a co-lead, *Rosalie* (1937), a teaming with standout dancer Eleanor Powell. This time he was on his own musically, although Metro amply complemented Eddy in this period Western with a roster of strong supporting players: Virginia Bruce, Lionel Barrymore, Victor McLaglen, Edward Arnold, Guy Kibbee, Charles Butterworth, and H.B. Warner.

With these vast resources, Metro had in mind more than just showcasing acting talent with *Let Freedom Ring*. Oscar-winning screenwriter/playwright/novelist Ben Hecht fashioned a script that used a post–Civil War setting in the West to promote values of pre–World War II Americanism. As the film's introductory title read: "The greatest battles for Liberty and Human Rights are not fought on the Battlefields of History but in the Hearts of a Nation's People." Here, the battle was for the "New West," between the industrialists who pushed through the Transcontinental Railroad and the common people whose land represented roadblocks to the rail's progress or who, as foreign-tongued newcomers, were exploited as cheap labor. The not-so-subtle message in 1939 was the promotion of support for a united Europe against Axis aggression, with the film's slick robber baron (played by Arnold) a stand-in for Hitler or Mussolini, forcing the local ethnic melting pot of railroad workers—and their champion, attorney Steve Logan (Eddy)—into fear and submission. Co-author of the mega-hit play *The Front Page* and writer of many popular screenplays (*Scarface, Nothing Sacred, Viva Villa!*) in a variety of genres, Hecht was becoming more activist in his writings as the world situation worsened. With *Let Freedom Ring*, he was, as biographer Jeffrey Brown Martin has written, presenting "the case for persecuted minorities" and "the power of propaganda and ideas to sow rebellion" in "the Hechtian version of *The Mark of Zorro*."[109]

Zorro … er, Robin Hood … er, Steve sings the commoners' way out of peril, or so it seems, even if the local judge, sheriff, and newspaper editor are all in the railroad boss's pocket and the prodigal son, newly returned from schooling in the East, must pretend to be a weakling for a while. In its review of *Let Freedom Ring, Variety* hailed it as "the first in the cycle of film offerings to stress the American type of democracy and freedom for the classes and masses."[110] Those masses include the railroad "hunkies," as *Variety* called them, about whom super-spy Eddy says: "If we can only get the truth to them, we might turn them into Americans." Part of "getting the truth to them" is singing about it, which Eddy does forcefully in the theme song "The Dusty Road." He is nominally commenting on his reaction to Bruce's character about to marry Arnold's ("straight ahead lies my destiny!"), but the words are about the nation's future, too. In "Where Else but Here?," Eddy reminds the collective band of townsmen that freedom is not to be squandered in the new land, then specifically exhorts certain ethnics (an Italian, a German, a Russian) that they can sing, smile, and dream—if only they'd take advantage.[111]

MGM seemed to waver as to the degree it would promote the film as a modern parable on freedom as opposed to a more traditional singing Western … although how "traditional" could a Nelson Eddy Western be? Early in production, the studio changed the title from *Let Freedom Ring* to *Song of the West*, then to *The Dusty Road*, after one of its key songs. The message slant won out when, just as filming wrapped in January 1939, *Let Freedom Ring* became the permanent name. Even with its mix of old-timey tunes and new fare from the MGM composing stable, *Let Freedom Ring* sought bona fides as an action film. In an attempt to make Eddy more of a he-man, the actor is shown going toe to toe in fisticuffs with tough-guy Victor McLaglen—and coming out the winner. It's easy to knock Eddy for his performance; he simply lacks the necessary pizazz and acting range, despite the resources surrounding him. (Barrymore, cast as the hero's father, is among those assets but doesn't have much to do.) But what is missing more is the most crucial ingredient: a leading lady with whom Eddy can engage in melodic byplay. Bruce is pretty and pleasing, but she lacks MacDonald's voice, literally and symbolically.

And despite its appeals to patriotism, and the encouraging comments of most reviewers, *Let Freedom Ring* proved a tough sell to consumers, with Western enthusiasts inclined to stay away from semi-operatic fare, and operetta snobs inevitably lamenting a duo divided. "[It is] the kind of entertainment that kept the backwoods theaters going during many a lean year," the *Motion Picture Herald* opined hopefully but inaccurately.[112] This was the kind of movie to salute for good intentions, but it was no must-see. In a screen year filled with memorable major-company Westerns (*Stagecoach, Destry Rides Again, Union Pacific, Jesse James, Drums Along the Mohawk*), and even Bogart, Cagney, and Errol Flynn on the prairie in 1939, *Let Freedom Ring* was rapidly forgotten. Despite re-emerging on TV and DVD in recent years, it exists as little more than a historical curio.

Infused with even more impressive production values than *Let Freedom Ring*, *Broadway Serenade* is a much bigger mess. Let's start with a minor problem: that of Lew Ayres, who trudges through his assignment as the Eddy surrogate. The film's premise of a showbiz couple split by professional pressures must have hit home for the actor, who not only had seen the same plot unfold in his most recent project, MGM's *Ice Follies of 1939**, but also, it was whispered, had a real-life parallel in his failed marriage to Ginger Rogers. *Ice Follies* had united Ayres (and Jimmy Stewart) with Joan Crawford, who unnecessarily belittled Ayres for showing up to the set 10 minutes late one day. Could another strong personality like MacDonald be worse? No, it turned out—Ayres (1908–1996) enjoyed this experience, as he recalled her "most delightfully whimsical sense of humor" to author James Robert Parish decades later. During a recording of one of the song numbers, Ayres said, MacDonald spotted Ayres making a "wry face" at an unusually loud playback of her voice, and she reacted kindly.

> When I knew she had seen me, I only hoped she would understand; explaining would have been too difficult. Nothing was said at the time, but an hour later, a package arrived on the set for me containing a carton of anti-noise ear stopples. Accompanying the [earplugs] was a … very charming note saying this was a service, normally and willingly provided by Miss MacDonald to anyone engaged on her productions. With a serious face, I passed them around and about half a dozen of us wore them that day … to the merriment of all … especially Jeanette.[113]

Despite Ayres' input, this was MacDonald's movie, and with the swing music craze ongoing, it was thought that *Broadway Serenade* should lower the elitist factor of her light opera and appeal more to the jitterbug crowd—after all, the world was changing (see *Let Freedom Ring*). Thus, we see her as a star of a fanciful revue filled with watered-down production numbers of little value to either end of the snob spectrum—"High Flyin'," for example, offers hip vocalists (Six Hits and a Miss from radio), a comic juggler straight out of vaudeville, and Jeanette's trademark trills. The star adds a *Madame Butterfly* excerpt and a Gay Nineties medley, just to cover all the demographic bases, but few went home happy. MacDonald didn't like the song selection and was irked at not being consulted by the studio about it; she also was tiring of musicals and wanted to do straight-ahead drama.

Undeterred, Metro sunk a lot of money into *Broadway Serenade*, the first official dual producing and directing assignment for Robert Z. Leonard, who'd helmed the über-musical *The Great Ziegfeld* and the MacDonald-Eddys *Maytime* and *The Girl of the Golden West*. *Great Ziegfeld* choreographer Seymour Felix directed most of the big dance numbers in *Broadway Serenade*, but to give the film the desired punch, Leonard brought in erstwhile Warner Bros. master Busby Berkeley to stage the finale, set to a modernized version of the Tchaikovsky romance "None but the Lonely Heart." The section has one of those music-across-the-ages motifs, starting with a simple shepherd boy playing a pipe inspiring Tchaikovsky to write his melody, sung by MacDonald accompanied by lines of black oilcloth-clad instrumentalists and vocalists in grotesque sculpted masks, the classical stuff giving way to modernistic song and dance even as MacDonald (who even puts on a mask herself) sticks close to her usual style. The number ends with a fancy but more traditional presentation with MacDonald, her mask removed, atop a circular platform 30 feet above the stage—and the high-/middlebrow stuff winning out over the new-school pop. The number is gaudy for the sake of being gaudy, which is explainable, given Berkeley's admission to Parish that MGM "wanted the thing created in short order because Jeanette had to leave" on a concert tour.[114]

Broadway Serenade possesses both the assets and liabilities of the MGM moviemaking machine. Patrons could be placated by the familiar mannerisms of studio regulars: befuddled Frank Morgan (just off *The Wizard of Oz*), Brit-charming Ian Hunter, fast-talking William Gargan, and wizened Al Shean. Yet Metro had a rep for overthinking, and this typically overwritten film is full of character bits likely shortened by the cutter's scissors. Comic Wally Vernon threatens a sizable presence as a pop-eyed, semi-menacing show "jinx" but disappears after one scene, only to reappear fleetingly with an unexplained patch over his "evil eye," and then-starlet Virginia Grey promises more than we see her deliver as a showgirl inclined to shed as many clothes as she can get away with. Flighty Franklin Pangborn is on hand as the composer/conductor of MacDonald's show, and he not only exceeds his usual dialogue quota but also gets to sing with the star and by himself. "I love music," Pangborn later reminisced about what he often cited as his favorite film. "I rehearsed with Jeanette when she was recording. The part had a lot of color."[115]

Diva Grace Moore—MacDonald's perceived archrival in the press—gave *Broadway Serenade* a bit of unwanted publicity by declaring it a knockoff of Moore's 5-year-old hit *One Night of Love,* only in worse taste. By this time, Moore had gone off to Europe to make pictures after her Hollywood fortunes dried up, so she could get away with being snooty. "I can't see much similarity," an MGM executive, not taking the bait, replied to columnist

Some newspapers sought to advertise Jeanette MacDonald and Nelson Eddy as a "team," even if they were in separate pictures in the spring of 1939.

Harrison Carroll, "except that," in *Broadway Serenade*, "Jeanette MacDonald also sang 'Madame Butterfly.'"[116]

Unfortunately for the aspirations of MacDonald and Eddy, *Broadway Serenade* and *Let Freedom Ring* both lost money for MGM. They competed directly against each other in theaters in many cities and sometimes were paired together—such as for lucky audiences in Ogden, Utah (where newspaper ads heralded "The King and Queen of Song!—in Two of the Season's Big Hits!") and North Adams, Massachusetts (where the daily screamed over "Your Singing Screen Sweethearts! We Couldn't Keep Them Apart!"). When the dust settled, the high grosses for *Sweethearts* conspired with the underwhelming solo efforts to reunite MacDonald and Eddy. MacDonald won a new Metro contract—and promises of non-singing roles—and she and Eddy earned a few more years of professional bliss in tandem.

Chapter Notes

Chapter 1

1. "And Now, What?" *Inside Facts of Stage and Screen*, July 5, 1930.
2. *Film Daily Year Book of Motion Pictures*, 1930, p. 21, and 1931, p. 33. *Disraeli*, the Warner Bros. historical drama starring George Arliss, topped the 1929 poll.
3. James Layton and David Pierce, *King of Jazz: Paul Whiteman's Technicolor Revue* (Severn, Md.: Media History Press, 2016), p. 54. The quote is from *The Reminiscences of Paul Fejos*, a 1962 interview with Fejos by John T. Mason, Jr., for Columbia University's Oral History Program.
4. "Gigantic Crane Built for *Broadway*," *Universal Weekly*, January 26, 1929.
5. Hal Mohr 1973 interview with Richard Koszarski, included as extra on the *Broadway* home video release.
6. Layton and Pierce, *King of Jazz*, p. 55. Hall also designed a large miniature of Times Square for the striking opening sequence of *Broadway*, in which a metaphorical, devilish reveler dominates the area's late-night landscape.
7. "*Broadway* on Screen," *New York Times*, May 19, 1929.
8. "The Screen: *Broadway* With Frills," *New York Times*, May 28, 1929.
9. Layton and Pierce, *King of Jazz*, p. 288.
10. Antti Alanen, "*Broadway* (1929) (2016 Print From Universal Pictures)," *Antti Alanen: Film Diary*, June 29, 2016. Archived at https://anttialanenfilmdiary.blogspot.com/2016/06/broadway-1929-2016-digital-restoration.html. Accessed June 15, 2018.
11. In another scurrilous use of a theme song, Jolson wannabe George Jessel performed the tear-inducing "My Mother's Eyes" no less than four times in the Tiffany-Stahl musical *Lucky Boy** (1929). Mack Sennett sent up this kind of stuff in a late-to-the-party two-reeler, *A Hollywood Theme Song*, released in December 1930.
12. "Sound and Fury," cited from *Tampa Times*, January 19, 1929, among others.
13. Joel McCrea was listed as a cast member in some early accounts, among them "West Coast Notes," *Variety*, September 4, 1929.
14. *Jazz Heaven*, *Motion Picture News*, November 2, 1929.
15. "*Jazz Heaven* Offers Novel Touches in Globe Premiere," *New York Daily News*, October 30, 1929.
16. "Joseph Cawthorn Awarded Long-Term RKO Contract," *Film Daily*, November 4, 1929.
17. A better, and earlier in release, talkie take-off was the 1929 Vitaphone short *Georgie Price in "Don't Get Nervous."* In the one-reeler, vaudeville singer-comedian Price (playing himself) complains to a Vita director, Bryan Foy (also playing himself), that he's uncomfortable working in the new sound medium. The Warner Bros. crew is shown dressing the set—and staring at poor Price as he sings two songs and tells a couple of jokes. Price asks Foy for a pay raise and observes that "when you want more money here, the synchronization is very, very bad."
18. The billing of the Goodman orchestra in *The Talk of Hollywood* refers to *Follow Thru*, the Broadway show that the band was performing with at the time.
19. "Fay Marbe Didn't Work," *Variety*, September 18, 1929, and "News From the Dailies—New York," *Variety*, September 25, 1929.
20. "Inside Stuff—Music: Won't Publish His Own," *Variety*, December 11, 1929.
21. "The Talk of Hollywood," *Motion Picture News*, December 21, 1929, and "Film Reviews: *Talk of Hollywood*," *Variety*, January 1, 1930.
22. Newspaper Enterprise Association story, February 1930.
23. "School of Cinemaland," *Los Angeles Times*, April 13, 1930.
24. "They Say That –," *Motion Picture News*, April 19, 1930.
25. "News From the Dailies," *Variety*, March 15, 1932.
26. "Beyond Footlights: Noted Performer Now Helping Others Learn to Speak in Public," *Fort Lauderdale* (Fla.) *News/Sun-Sentinel*, January 30, 1985.
27. "Episode 1: Birth of a Titan," *Hollywood: The Golden Years: The RKO Story*, BBC-TV, 1987. VHS, author's collection.
28. *Photoplay*, December 1929.
29. "Universal Cutting Down '30-'31 Product to 20 Features," *Variety*, April 2, 1930.
30. "Universal Will Produce 20 Specials at Average Cost of $500,000 Each," *Universal Weekly*, April 19, 1930.
31. Cadman wrote at least four songs for *Captain*

of the Guard: "Love Time," "My Silhouette," "Song of the Sword," and "With Blood and Fair."

32. Richard Koszarski, "Hal Mohr's Cinematography," *Film Comment*, September-October 1974.

33. "Fejos Quits 'U' After Clash with Laemmle, Jr." *Motion Picture News*, March 29, 1930.

34. Universal's house publication, *The Gold Mine*, also blamed theater operators' requests for the title change, claiming that exhibitors pointed out that the *La Marseillaise* name "would reduce the word-of-mouth advertising by at least fifty percent." See "Exhibitor Requests Caused Title Change on *La Marseillaise*," *The Gold Mine*, March 29, 1930.

35. "Reviews of the Latest Pictures in New York: *Captain of the Guard*," *The Billboard*, April 5, 1930; "Film Reviews: *Captain of the Guard*," *Variety*, April 2, 1930.

36. "Barrymore in Critics' Hit," *Los Angeles Times*, April 6, 1930; "The Screen in Review: *Captain of the Guard*," *Picture Play*, July 1930.

37. "*Capt. Guard* $99,700 and Held Over at Roxy...," *Variety*, April 9, 1930; "*Journey's End* in Smash Class...," *Variety*, April 16, 1930.

38. "L.A. Runs Fair Behind *Angel*'s 32 Grand Intake," *Motion Picture News*, June 21, 1930.

39. "Fejos quits 'U,'" *MPN*. Fejos directed foreign-language versions of MGM's prison drama *The Big House* (1930) but never made another English-language movie in America after *Captain of the Guard*. In keeping with his eclecticism, he became an anthropologist.

40. "Historical Liberties Keep *Guard* out of France," *Variety*. April 16, 1930. Perhaps not coincidentally, Stein left Universal within weeks of the film's release.

41. Layton and Pierce, *King of Jazz*, p. 273.

42. Another aborted Boles musical project was the screen adaptation of the spicy, Preston Sturges-penned stage comedy *Strictly Dishonorable*, the rights to which were bought by Universal for a lofty $125,000 in April 1930. Universal made the property into a film, but, as released in December 1931, it starred Paul Lukas, Lewis Stone, Sidney Fox, and George Meeker ... but not John Boles. For its musical connection, see "Universal Buys Noted Play," *Los Angeles Times*, April 15, 1930. *Strictly Dishonorable* didn't get a musical treatment until MGM remade it under the same title in 1951 with Janet Leigh and Met *basso* Ezio Pinza.

43. "The Shadow Stage," *Photoplay*, July 1930.

44. "*Fox Movietone Follies of 1930* Started," *Hollywood Filmograph*, January 25, 1930.

45. "*Follies* Finished," *Inside Facts of Stage and Screen*, April 3, 1930.

46. "Film House Reviews: Roxy," *Variety*, June 25, 1930.

47. "Service on Pictures: *Movietone Follies of 1930*," *Exhibitors Herald-World*, June 28, 1930.

48. Miriam Seegar, a petite blonde from Indiana, didn't make much of an impression during a four-year film acting career (1928–1932) but achieved success on the London stage. She retired from performing not long after marrying director Tim Whelan in 1931, began a career as an interior decorator that ended with her retirement in 1995 ... and lived to be 103.

49. "Cheer Up and Smile" became the title of a Fox musical comedy released later in 1930, although the song from *Movietone Follies* was not repeated among the numbers. Arthur Lake, Dixie Lee, Olga Baclanova, and "Whispering" Jack Smith starred, with an unknown John Wayne down the cast list.

50. "4 More in Preparation...," *Film Daily*, February 23, 1930, mentions Murray's planned participation in *Ladies in Love*.

51. "Peggy Wood Wants $3,600 From Shelved *Blackface*," *Variety*, April 24, 1929; "William Collier, Jr., in *The Melody Man*," *The Morning Call* (Allentown, Pa.), March 30, 1930. Collier and Day were the romantic duo in *Melody Man*, with Walker placed in a less important role.

52. "Film Reviews: *Ladies in Love*," *Variety*, June 18, 1930; "*Ladies in Love* Beacon's Talkie," *New York Daily News*, June 16, 1930.

53. "Imagine My Embarrassment," *Photoplay*, January 1929.

54. "Film Reviews: *Border Romance*," *Variety*, May 28, 1930.

55. "*Home James*, Comedy at Hip, Has Laura La Plante as Star," *New York Daily News*, September 11, 1928.

56. "*Kathleen Mavourneen*, New Talkie, Will Star Sally O'Neil," Universal Service column, cited from *San Francisco Examiner*, June 14, 1929. In this Louella Parsons entry, she claimed (probably falsely) that O'Neil had written a theme song titled "Terry" for the film.

57. "Inside Stuff—Pictures," *Variety*, July 10, 1929.

58. "*Kathleen Mavourneen*," *Film Daily*, July 20, 1930; "Brief Reviews of Current Pictures," *Photoplay*, October 1930.

59. "R-K-O Gives Sally O'Neal Lead," Universal Service column, cited from *Pittsburgh Post-Gazette*, November 1, 1929.

60. Cary O'Dell, "The Movie Star Next Door: Sally O'Neil," *Classic Images*, October 2016.

61. "Film Queens in Auto Target of Mystery Shot," United Press story, cited from *New York Daily News*, January 28, 1930.

62. "New Acts—Reviews: Sally O'Neil and Molly O'Day," *Variety*, June 4, 1930; "Reviews," *The Billboard*, June 14, 1930.

63. Donald Novis (1906–1966), an English-born, California-bred tenor from Pasadena, first attracted attention as the winner of the 1928 National Radio Audition, a youth singing contest. This earned him appearances in the 1929 features *Bulldog Drummond* and *New York Nights* ... and *Kathleen Mavourneen*. He went on to renown on the radio and specialty parts in several films (*The Big Broadcast*, *Monte Carlo*, *One Hour With You*).

64. Beatrice Lillie with James Brough, *Every Other Inch a Lady* (Garden City, N.Y.: Doubleday, 1972), p. 226; "Film Star Loses Suit for Damages," United Press story, cited from *Pittsburgh Press*, December 1, 1930.

65. Lillie, *Every Other Inch*, p. 215.

66. Lillie's train journey West was overshadowed by that of a more famous fellow passenger, opera diva

Grace Moore, who was en route to L.A. to make her first film, MGM's *A Lady's Morals* (1930).

67. "Langdon With Miss Lillie," *Los Angeles Times*, April 8, 1930; "News From the Dailies About Hollywood," *Variety*, March 26, 1930.

68. "Hollywood Gossip: Traffic Tragedy," *The Daily Republican* (Monongahela, Pa.), May 23, 1930.

69. Lillie, *Every Other Inch*, pp. 215–216.

70. "Microphone Hard to Face, Beatrice Lillie Admits," Consolidated Press Association report, cited from *The Post-Crescent* (Appleton, Wis.), April 5, 1930.

71. "New Product: *Are You There?*" *Exhibitors Herald-World*, December 6, 1930.

72. "Opinions on Pictures: *Are You There?*" *Motion Picture News*, November 29, 1930.

73. "*Are You There?*" *Harrison's Reports*, February 21, 1931. The film was shown in Canada (Lillie's native country) and in England, where London's *The Guardian* praised "a series of self-possessed turns by Beatrice Lillie as extremely amusing" ("Beatrice Lillie's New Talkie," January 5, 1931).

74. "Film Reviews: *Are You There?*" *Variety*, July 14, 1931.

75. Aubrey Solomon, *The Fox Film Corporation 1915–1935: A History and Filmography* (Jefferson, N.C.: McFarland, 2011), p. 155.

76. Anthony Slide, *The Encyclopedia of Vaudeville* (Westport, Conn.: Greenwood Press, 1994), p. 316.

77. "Screen: The Beatrice Lillie of 1930," *New York Times*, August 2, 1971.

78. "Musical Films as Tonic," *Variety*, January 10, 1933.

79. "84 Features With Music Available for Booking in the Next Few Months," *Motion Picture Herald*, May 20, 1933.

80. "17 to 20 Spanish Dialogue Features Planned by Fox," *Film Daily*, June 17, 1932.

81. "Spanish Musical in Work," *Film Daily*, October 4, 1932.

82. "Fox Pic Big in Madrid," *The Hollywood Reporter*, March 10, 1933.

83. Gregory William Mank, *Women in Horror Films, 1930s* (Jefferson, N.C.: McFarland, 2005), p. 140. Stuart thought so little of *It's Great to Be Alive* that her sole reference to it in her autobiography (1999, post *Titanic*) is in a list of "forgettable films" she made early on. Moreover, it is misidentified as a release from Universal, her home studio at the time. See Stuart with Sylvia Thompson, *Gloria Stuart: I Just Kept Hoping* (New York: Little, Brown), p. 57.

84. In March 1933, the title of the film was changed from *The Last Man on Earth* to *It's Great to Be Alive*, but only after Fox reached an agreement with songwriters Lew Brown and Ray Henderson, who had written an unrelated song titled "It's Great to Be Alive." A song written for the film necessarily had a slightly different title: "It's Great to Be the Only Man Alive." See "*It's Great to Be Alive*," AFI Catalog of Feature Films, 2017. Archived at https://catalog.afi.com/Catalog/MovieDetails/1294. Accessed August 16, 2018. Also see "Fox Title Changed," *The Hollywood Reporter*, March 17, 1933.

85. AFI Catalog.

86. *Ibid.*

87. "*Great to Be Alive* May Pass," *The Hollywood Reporter*, June 23, 1933.

88. "*It's Great to Be Alive*," *Film Daily*, July 8, 1933.

89. "Dave, the Egg Dodger, Luring 161/2G Nevertheless on Blistering Coast," *Variety*, August 1, 1933.

90. "What the Picture Did for Me," *Motion Picture Herald*, June 15, 1933; June 22, 1933; and January 30, 1934.

91. "The Screen: … *It's Great to Be Alive*," *New York Times*, July 8, 1933.

92. "Raul Roulien in Fox Musical Film," *Philadelphia Inquirer*, June 3, 1933.

93. "Roulien's Fox Tuner," *Variety*, June 6, 1933.

94. "Huston Settles in Auto Death," United Press report cited from *New York Daily News*, July 7, 1935.

95. *The Last Man on Earth* is even more outrageous than its sound remake in terms of the passage of time therein, as the main character isn't found until 1954! Grace Cunard, the serial heroine of the 'teens, played the head mobster role in the silent.

Chapter 2

1. Gary Giddins, *Natural Selection: Gary Giddins on Comedy, Film, Music, and Books* (New York: Oxford University Press, 2006), p. 221. Originally published in "Just One of Those Things," *Los Angeles Times*, August 8, 2004.

2. "Talking Shorts: *Song Writers' Revue*," *Variety*, January 8, 1930.

3. The *Sammy Fain* short, which exists today, is particularly cherished by musical buffs for the presence of Evelyn Hoey. Hoey sang and acted on Broadway in *Fifty Million Frenchmen* and *Good News* and co-starred in the unreleased 1930 movie musical *Leave It to Lester* but appeared otherwise on celluloid only in the Fain film. She died in 1935 at age 24 after a shooting that was controversially ruled a suicide.

4. As they did with Johann Strauss II (see Chapter 5), European filmmakers beat Hollywood to the punch on Schubert, with the German-made *Schubert's Frühlingstraum* [*Schubert's Dream of Spring*] (1931) and the Austrian-German release *Leise Flehen Meine Lieder* [*Gently My Songs Entreat*] (1933). Schubert was portrayed by the popular Austrian operatic tenor Richard Tauber in the British release *Blossom Time* (1934), based on the Sigmund Romberg stage operetta.

5. "Hollywood Cavalcade-Minded: Old Songs Take on New Values," *Variety*, August 17, 1938.

6. George F. Custen, *Twentieth Century's Fox: Darryl F. Zanuck and the Culture of Hollywood* (New York: Basic Books, 1998), p. 78.

7. One could make a case for *King of Jazz* (1930) as the first sound biopic of an American composer, but it's not a biography even in a broad sense, as too much of the song and comedy material is not tied to its titular figure, bandleader-songwriter Paul Whiteman. Early plans for it as a conventional bio were scuttled by Whiteman's unwillingness to act on camera. The film does include an animated sequence about how Whiteman came to be crowned the "king

of jazz," and another section introduces Whiteman's bandsmen. Also, a more-extended section about Whiteman's "rise to fame" was planned but not filmed; see Layton and Pierce, *King of Jazz*, p. 266.

8. Ken Emerson, *Doo-dah! Stephen Foster and the Rise of American Popular Culture* (New York: Simon & Schuster, 1997), p. 12.

9. William Frawley sings only one song in the final print of *Harmony Lane*, but he filmed at least one other, "De Camptown Races," which was presented in a minstrel show extract. The sequence was inserted into a Gene Autry/Republic Western, *The Singing Vagabond* (1935), in which it survives today—with Frawley uncredited and in blackface.

10. "*Harmony Lane* Is Tragic Film Life of Foster," *Chicago Tribune*, October 10, 1935.

11. "Along the Rialto" and "Reviews: Douglass Montgomery in *Harmony Lane*," *Film Daily*, August 15, 1935.

12. "I Heard a Man Cry in a Projection Room…," *Independent Exhibitors Film Bulletin*, August 21, 1935.

13. Jon Tuska, *The Vanishing Legion: A History of Mascot Pictures 1927–1935* (Jefferson, N.C.: McFarland, 1982), pp. 115–116.

14. "Cashing in on Naturalness," *Modern Screen*, April 1940.

15. Nancy Kelly, in her early Hollywood phase and stuck in period dress roles, was freed from her *Swanee River* assignment to play opposite Tyrone Power in a gangster drama, *Johnny Apollo*, but TCF instead put her in a routine comedy, *She Married His Wife* (1940), with Joel McCrea.

16. "Plan Foster Film," *Motion Picture Daily*, January 13, 1939.

17. "Screen Biogs on Marie Lloyd, Stephen Foster," *Variety*, June 7, 1939.

18. The image of Foster as firmly pro-Southern, however at odds with the truth, turned against his reputation in 2018, when a prominent statue of the composer in Pittsburgh was removed over protests of racism. The statue, created in 1900, depicts an African American man playing a stringed instrument at the feet of a standing Foster.

19. John C. Tibbetts, *Composers in the Movies: Studies in Musical Biography* (New Haven, Conn.: Yale University Press, 2008), p. 113.

20. "Zanuck Tones Down Foster's Liquor Bouts," United Press report, cited from *Tampa Bay Times*, January 2, 1940.

21. *The Hollywood Reporter*, December 20, 1939.

22. "Film Reviews: *Swanee River*," *Variety*, December 27, 1939.

23. "Thoughts at Random," *Harrison's Reports*, January 13, 1940.

24. Philip Furia, *Skylark: The Life and Times of Johnny Mercer* (New York: St. Martin's Press, 2003), p. 74.

25. The report on Mercer's contract is from "Johnny Mercer's Film Opportunity on Coast," *Variety*, February 12, 1935.

26. Rogers made two films in England just before *Old Man Rhythm*, but neither had been released in the U.S. Also see "'Buddy' Rogers Returns to Screen in New Musical," uncredited story, cited from *Lansing* (Mich.) *State Journal*, September 26, 1935.

27. Gene Lees, *Portrait of Johnny: The Life of John Herndon Mercer* (New York: Pantheon, 2004), p. 104.

28. A sixth Mercer-Gensler tune, "When You Are in My Arms," was sung by Rogers but cut from *Old Man Rhythm* before release.

29. "The Film Estimates," *The Educational Screen*, September 1935.

30. Lees, *Portrait of Johnny*, p. 104.

31. "Junior Hollywood," *The New Movie Magazine*, September 1935. The story's author, Henry Willson, would go on to locate many new "finds"—Rock Hudson, Tab Hunter, and Robert Wagner among them—as a top talent agent, so maybe he had a good eye.

32. "Reproof for Dissenters," *New York Times*, September 16, 1934.

33. Tony Villecco, *Silent Stars Speak: Interviews With Twelve Cinema Pioneers* (Jefferson, N.C.: McFarland, 2001), p. 180.

34. "Irene Hervey, Los Angeles Girl, Gets Big Film 'Break,'" *Los Angeles Times*, September 29, 1937.

35. "A 'Little' From Hollywood Lots," *Film Daily*, March 10, 1937, and April 5, 1937; "A Town Called Hollywood," *Los Angeles Times*, September 26, 1937.

36. "Hollywood: Grand National's Scoop!" *Independent Distributors Film Bulletin*, July 17, 1937.

37. "*The Girl Said No* Offers an Unusual Combination of Up-to-Date Romance and the Savoyard Operetta," *Washington Post*, July 15, 1937.

38. "Film Reviews: *The Girl Said No*," *Variety*, June 23, 1937; "*The Girl Said No* at Four Star Clever Feature," *Los Angeles Times*, September 23, 1937; "The Screen: *The Girl Said No*, with Irene Hervey, Opens at Globe," *New York Times*, October 18. 1937.

39. "Alperson Announces 65 Features for Grand National in 1937–38," *Variety*, May 22, 1937; "The Hollywood Scene: Hollywoodpulp," *Motion Picture News*, June 5, 1937.

40. "U's *Mikado* revives GN's *Girl Said No*, Also With G. & S. Tunes," *Variety*, July 26, 1939. The movie *Mikado*, distributed in the U.S. by Universal, was directed by an American, Victor Schertzinger, and co-starred Yankee singer Kenny Baker with an otherwise all-Brit cast.

41. Hayley Taylor Block; Alex Ben Block and Lucy Autrey Wilson, eds., *George Lucas's Blockbusting: A Decade-by-Decade Survey of Timeless Movies Including Untold Secrets of Their Financial and Cultural Success* (New York: HarperCollins, 2010), p. 213.

42. "Film Reviews: *Alexander's Ragtime Band*," *Variety*, June 1, 1938.

43. Rudy Behlmer, ed., *Memo From Darryl F. Zanuck: The Golden Years at Twentieth Century-Fox* (New York: Grove Press, 1995), p. 13.

44. Laurence Bergreen, *As Thousands Cheer: The Life of Irving Berlin* (New York: Viking, 1990), p. 360.

45. *Ibid.*, pp. 360–361.

46. Fred MacMurray was initially intended for the *Alexander* lead (Bergreen, p. 361). With the acutely handsome Power in MacMurray's stead, one can see why Zanuck wanted to play up the romance.

47. Jane Lenz Elder, *Alice Faye: A Life Beyond the*

Silver Screen (Jackson: University Press of Mississippi, 2002), p. 110.
  48. Behlmer, *Memo From Darryl F. Zanuck*, p. 14.
  49. "Heavy Coin to Irving Berlin, Colman on Straight % Deals Lure for Others," *Variety*, August 30, 1939.
  50. Caryl Flinn, *Brass Diva: The Life and Legends of Ethel Merman* (Berkeley: University of California Press, 2009), p. 43.
  51. Michael Freedland, *Irving Berlin* (New York: Stein and Day, 1974), p. 135.
  52. *The Hollywood Reporter*, May 25, 1938.
  53. "The Screen: The Roxy Plays Host to *Alexander's Ragtime Band*, a Twentieth Century Tribute to Irving Berlin," *New York Times*, August 5, 1938.
  54. "Along the Rialto," *Film Daily*, August 6, 1938; "Over 100 Holdovers for *Alexander's Ragtime Band*," *Film Daily*, August 31, 1938.
  55. "'Alex' Clicks Again," *Variety*, August 31, 1938; "*Alex* Sets Another Kind of Record," *Variety*, September 7, 1938.
  56. "Plagiarism Suit Against Film Company Ordered Dismissed on Appeal," *St. Louis Star and Times*, February 25, 1946; "Court Rules Film Not Based on Novel," Associated Press story, cited in *Los Angeles Times*, February 26, 1946.
  57. Abel Green and Joe Laurie, Jr., *Show Biz From Vaude to Video* (New York, Henry Holt, 1951), p. 45.
  58. "Charles R. Rogers to Produce on His Own on a High-Budget Scale," *Boxoffice*, August 27, 1938; "Rogers' Cavalcade Film Idea; Based on Life of Gus Edwards," *Variety*, August 31, 1938.
  59. "Paramount Signs Rogers," *Motion Picture Daily*, November 10, 1938.
  60. "Linda Ware, Child Singer, Is Grown Up," North American Newspaper Alliance report, cited in *Hartford Courant*, May 24, 1942.
  61. Louise Campbell (1911–1997) enjoyed a more fruitful life away from the movies as the longtime spouse of actor Horace McMahon. Her stage career lasted into the 1980s.
  62. "Pooh for Shirley: They're in the Movies Now, *EveryWeek Magazine* report, cited in *Arizona Republic*, June 25, 1939.
  63. Gary Giddins, *Bing Crosby: A Pocketful of Dreams—The Early Years 1903–1940* (New York: Little, Brown, 2001), p. 537.
  64. "The Star Maker," *Film Daily*, August 22, 1939.
  65. "The Screen: *The Star Maker*, Based on the Life of Gus Edwards, Runs Like an Edwards Revue at the Paramount," *New York Times*, August 31, 1939.
  66. "Testimonial Dinner Marks Gus Edwards' Anniversary," *Los Angeles Times*, August 19, 1939; "Gus Edwards Feted by His Old Friends," Associated Press report, cited in the Sioux Falls (S.D.) *Argus-Leader*, August 20, 1939. Crosby's absence is noted in Giddins, *Bing Crosby*, p. 539.
  67. "Little Miss Contrary," *Radio Romances Formerly Radio Mirror*, September 1945.
  68. "Aunt Wins Battle Over Girl Actor," United Press report, cited from *Salt Lake Telegram*, October 4, 1938.
  69. "Over the Nation—'Round the World," unsourced wire service report, cited in *Arizona Republic*, August 1, 1951.
  70. A few months before Edwards' death, Monogram Pictures acquired the rights to use some of his songs in *Sunbonnet Sue* (1945), named for one of Edwards' most well-known tunes. The Gay '90s-set musical starred Gale Storm and Phil Regan and opened on the week of Edwards' passing.
  71. Edward Arnold was initially mentioned for the Herbert role, with Fred MacMurray, Melvyn Douglas, and Irene Dunne discussed as the younger leads. For more, see Ronald L. Davis, *Mary Martin: Broadway Legend* (Norman: University of Oklahoma Press, 2008), p. 48.
  72. Neil Gould, *Victor Herbert: A Theatrical Life* (New York: Fordham University Press, 2008), pp. 542–543. Ella Herbert Bartlett informed Paramount via letter that the title *The Gay Life of Victor Herbert* was "misleading and untruthful" and "infers that there were licentious or racy incidents in father's life." Also see "Mary Martin P.a.ing [sic] With *Victor Herbert*, *Variety*, November 22, 1939. Interestingly, there is some evidence, via newspaper clippings, that the Stone film was advertised in some foreign markets with the *Gay* title.
  73. Numbers for *The Great Victor Herbert* are from David Kaufman, *Some Enchanted Evenings: The Glittering Life and Times of Mary Martin* (New York: St. Martin's, 2016), p. 38.
  74. "Herbert Music in New Setting: Studio Doesn't Have Operetta Rights," *Detroit Free Press*, January 16, 1940.
  75. "Victor Herbert Film Play to Thrill Music Lovers," United Press report, cited from *Pittsburgh Post-Gazette*, August 21, 1939.
  76. Mary Martin, *My Heart Belongs* (New York: Morrow, 1976), p. 84.
  77. "The Screen: *The Great Victor Herbert*, With Walter Connolly and a Sheaf of Melodies, Arrives at the Paramount," *New York Times*, December 7, 1939.
  78. Ibid.
  79. "Film Reviews: *The Great Victor Herbert*," *Variety*, November 29, 1939.
  80. "Newspaper Critics 69 Per Cent Wrong on Films, Survey Shows," *Motion Picture Herald*, June 1, 1940.
  81. "Oh Susanna!" *Modern Screen*, November 1941.
  82. "Filmdom: Hollywood and Home Base," uncredited report, cited from *Indianapolis Star*, May 9, 1939.
  83. In 1948, Foster married the baritone Wilbur Evans, who was Mary Martin's co-star in the original London production of *South Pacific* in 1951. Foster and Evans become embroiled in a fierce custody battle for their two children after their divorce in 1956, and Foster fell into obscurity and poverty. She died in 2009.
  84. Gould, *Victor Herbert*, p. 543.

Chapter 3

  1. J.W. Williamson, *Hillbillyland: What the Movies Did to the Mountains and What the Mountains Did to*

the Movies (Chapel Hill: University of North Carolina Press, 1995), p. 16.

2. Peter Stanfield, *Horse Opera: The Strange History of the 1930s Singing Cowboy* (Urbana: University of Illinois Press, 2002), p. 60.

3. "Mountain Music," *Variety*, June 23, 1937.

4. "Quigley Plaque Winners for June," *Motion Picture Herald*, July 24, 1937.

5. "It's the Way He Says It," *Photoplay*, October 1932.

6. Garland and Durbin were paired in an MGM musical short, *Every Sunday*, that opened in November 1936, well into the theatrical run of *Pigskin Parade* and shortly before the Christmas-week arrival of Durbin's breakout picture, *Three Smart Girls*. The earliest newspaper ads for *Every Sunday* touted Garland's tie to the hit football film while heralding Durbin not as Universal's newest star, but as a soloist for Eddie Cantor's radio show.

7. Fifteen-year-old Robert "Bobby" McClung was a West Virginia native who attracted the attention of Fox production chief Darryl Zanuck because he could cut up on the harmonica. McClung (1920–1945) became a nightclub and radio performer and occasional movie actor until his death from pneumonia at age 24.

8. John Fricke, *Judy: A Legendary Film Career* (Philadelphia: Running Press, 2010), p. 65.

9. David Butler with Irene Kahn Atkins, *David Butler: A Directors Guild of America Oral History* (Metuchen, N.J.: Scarecrow Press, 1993), p. 146. Garland's at-the-game presentation of "It's Love I'm After" would have made more sense in its original guise as a reprise of a Downs-Grable duet earlier in the film. But the duet was cut, leaving the singing output of the underused Grable near zero. The Grable-Downs version, as well as Garland's delivery of "Hold That Bulldog," also trimmed from *Pigskin Parade*, resurfaced on CD decades later.

10. Gerald Clarke, *Get Happy: The Life of Judy Garland* (New York: Random House, 2009), p. 74.

11. Butler with Atkins, *David Butler*, p. 146.

12. Another of the TSU students, seen off and on in the background, is an unbilled Alan Ladd, who can be spotted with minimum eye strain.

13. Relatively forgotten as the 21st century dawned, the Yacht Club Boys, alone among the film's principal players, were left off the cover design for the 2007 DVD debut of *Pigskin Parade*. The film was digitally restored for the disc, but the YCB probably deserved better treatment.

14. "The Screen: *Pigskin Parade*, a Seasonal Musical Comedy, Opens at the Roxy," *New York Times*, November 14, 1936.

15. "Film Reviews: *Pigskin Parade*," *Variety*, November 18, 1936. The *Los Angeles Times* later reported (August 15, 1937) that had *Pigskin Parade* been released in September or October 1936 rather than November, its box office may have been as much as 25 percent higher.

16. Aubrey Solomon, *Twentieth Century-Fox: A Corporate and Financial History* (Lanham, Md.: Rowman & Littlefield, 2002), p. 217.

17. *Jackson* (Tennessee) *Sun*, February 14, 1937.

18. Judy Cornes, *Stuart Erwin: The Invisible Actor* (Lanham, Md.: Scarecrow Press, 2001), p. 52.

19. "Original Funsters Sought for *Pigskin Parade* Sequels," *Los Angeles Times*, May 14, 1937.

20. "Avalanche of College Films Headed for Screen," *Los Angeles Times*, August 15, 1937.

21. Fricke, *Judy*, p. 7.

22. "Conn Signs Tomlin," *Motion Picture Daily*, April 27, 1936.

23. "Toby Wing Gets Pinky's Ring, He Blushes at Party," Associated Press report, cited in the *Fresno* (Calif.) *Bee*, November 14, 1936.

24. "Wing-Tomlin Romance Is Definitely 'Off,'" Associated Press report, cited in *Jefferson City* (Mo.) *Post-Tribune*, January 27, 1937.

25. "Conn Steps Out," *Independent Exhibitors Film Bulletin*, July 3, 1937; "Ambassador Schedules Million for 36 Films," *Motion Picture Herald*, September 4, 1937.

26. 'Youthful Maurice Conn Started His First Film Production with $1,000," *Independent Exhibitor Film Bulletin*, January 30, 1937.

27. Decades later, Tomlin thought he'd been ripped off himself when he sued Walt Disney Productions for $2.25 million, claiming Disney had stolen the title of his song "The Love Bug Will Bite You" for its movie *The Love Bug*, but he lost in court in 1970.

28. "*With Love and Kisses*," *Motion Picture Review Digest*, December 28, 1936.

29. "Theater," unsourced item, *Cumberland* (Md.) *Evening Times*, September 30, 1937.

30. Pinky Tomlin, with Lynette Wert, *The Object of My Affection: An Autobiography* (Norman: University of Oklahoma Press, 1981), pp. 112–113.

31. "Wing-Tomlin Romance Is Definitely 'Off,'" see above.

32. Tomlin, *Object of My Affection*, p. 113. In 1938, Tomlin married Joanne Alcorn, who was acknowledged as the singer's college sweetheart, and the inspiration for "The Object of My Affection."

33. As astonishing as it might seem for an all-ages Pinky Tomlin musical to run into trouble with the Hays Office, this apparently happened with *Thanks for Listening*. According to Production Code Administration files at the Academy of Motion Picture Arts & Sciences Library, PCA director Joseph Breen objected to the original script for its "excessive and unnecessary" drinking, sexually suggestive dialogue, and unnecessary gunplay. The filmmakers agreed to tone down the script, and eliminated a character, an alcoholic crook named "Blotto." This character, the files indicated, was changed to a ham actor (likely the one portrayed by Rafael Storm) and the gangster-like qualities of him and his partner in crime were altered. See "*Thanks for Listening*," AFI Catalog of Feature Films, 2017. Archived at https://catalog.afi.com/Catalog/MovieDetails/5411. Accessed July 14, 2018.

34. Wallace died with Carroll in a plane crash in 1948 at age 35.

35. "Showmen's Reviews: *Swing It Professor*," *Motion Picture Herald*, November 13, 1937.

36. "Reviews of the New Films: *Swing It Professor*," *Film Daily*, November 13, 1937.

37. "Conn to Make 16 for 1937–38," *Motion Picture Herald*, October 16, 1937.

38. "Conn's 77B to Stay Certain Creditors," *Variety*, November 24, 1937; "Amb Pix Fights Lab's Move to Liquidate Films," *Variety*, December 22, 1937.

39. "Conn May Retire His Two Indie Prod. Cos.," *Variety*, June 29, 1938.

40. *You Bet Your Life*, NBC-TV, originally aired February 27, 1958. Archived on https://www.youtube.com/watch?v=kaZWqs7CV8E. Accessed July 12, 2018.

41. Tomlin, *Object of My Affection*, p. 198.

42. "Meet the Man From Arkansas! Bazooka Put Bob Burns in Clover," *Chicago Tribune*, March 1, 1936.

43. Esquire Features syndicated column, May 15, 1937. Burns' column was picked up in such markets as Muscatine, Iowa; Harrisburg, Pennsylvania; Harlingen, Texas; and Rushville, Indiana, among its more than 200 newspapers.

44. "A New Yorker at Large" column, Associated Press, July 22, 1937; extracted from *The Sandusky (Ohio) Register*.

45. Brian Taves, *Robert Florey, the French Expressionist* (Metuchen, N.J.: Scarecrow Press, 1987), p. 224. It didn't hurt that it was on the *Mountain Music* set where Florey met his future wife, actress Virginia Dabney, who had a small role in the film.

46. "*Mt. Music* a Bonanza for Hillbilly Virtuosi," *Variety*, April 21, 1937.

47. "Good News," *Modern Screen*, July 1937.

48. The man-and-jackass bit of business is repeated, albeit less effectively, by Bert Wheeler and the very same U-No in Paramount's 1941 musical *Las Vegas Nights*.

49. Sam Coslow, *Cocktails for Two: The Many Lives of Giant Songwriter Sam Coslow* (New Rochelle, N.Y.: Arlington House, 1977), p. 206.

50. Prior to *Mountain Music*, Davis was featured in two Vitaphone comedy shorts, *The City's Slicker* (1936) and *Sound Defects* (1937), in which he put his talent for mimicry to good use.

51. "What the Picture Did for Me," *Motion Picture Herald*, September 18, 1937.

52. *Ibid*.

53. "What the Picture Did for Me," *Motion Picture Herald*, October 30, 1937.

54. *Ibid*., February 26, 1938.

55. "A Poor Movie Wastes Talent of Bob Burns," *Chicago Tribune*, June 22, 1937; "Going Places," *Variety*, June 30, 1937.

56. "Arkansas Butt of 'Hillbilly' Humor May Have the Last Laugh," *The Christian Science Monitor*, August 1, 1980.

57. Besides their work at Fox, the Ritz Brothers also were at the Samuel Goldwyn studio in the cast of the infamous Technicolor musical flop *The Goldwyn Follies* (1938).

58. 20th Century Fox legal records at UCLA Theater Arts Library, cited in "*Kentucky Moonshine*," AFI Catalog of Feature Films, 2017. Archived at https://catalog.afi.com/Catalog/moviedetails/7525. Accessed July 14, 2018.

59. Untitled United Press story, cited in *The Cincinnati Enquirer*, June 1, 1938.

60. Butler with Atkins, *David Butler*, pp. 162–163.

61. "Around Our Town," *Evening Review* (East Liverpool, Ohio), June 10, 1938.

62. "Reviews of New Films: *Kentucky Moonshine*," *Film Daily*, May 3, 1938.

63. "The Screen: The Roxy's *Kentucky Moonshine* Shines Exclusively on the Ritzes," *New York Times*, May 21, 1938.

64. "Ritzes' *Moonshine* in $1,050,000 Theft Suit," *Variety*, October 12, 1938.

65. See "*Kentucky Moonshine*," AFI Catalog of Feature Films, 2017. Archived at https://catalog.afi.com/Catalog/moviedetails/7525. Accessed July 14, 2018.

66. *Ibid*.

67. Leonard Maltin, *Movie Comedy Teams* (New York: Plume, 1985), p. 236.

68. "Female Hunter," uncredited story cited from *Cicero (Ill.) Life*, December 2, 1938. Storey became a contract player at Republic and was a frequent leading lady to Gene Autry.

69. "Film Reviews: *Down in 'Arkansas,'*" *Variety*, October 12, 1938.

70. "What the Picture Did for Me," *Motion Picture Herald*, February 3, 1940.

71. Maris Wrixon (1916–1999) was a magazine cover girl who advanced to contract-player status at Warner Bros., which lent her to Republic for *Jeepers Creepers*. Her career included roles in WB programmers such as *Bullets for O'Hara* (1941) and *Spy Ship* (1942), but she is best remembered as for playing opposite mad doctor Boris Karloff in Monogram's *The Ape* (1940). She was married for more than 50 years to Oscar-nominated film editor Rudi Fehr.

72. "Film Reviews: *Jeepers Creepers*," *Variety*, November 1, 1939.

73. "The Weaver Brothers and Elviry," *Classic Images*, March 2008.

Chapter 4

1. The first of Wayne's Westerns as a singer was *Riders of Destiny* (1933), in which he was most likely dubbed by Bill Bradbury, the twin brother of cowboy star Bob Steele.

2. Stanfield, *Horse Opera*, p. 79.

3. Anthony Harkins, *Hillbilly: A Cultural History of an American Icon* (New York: Oxford University Press, 2004), p. 96.

4. "Gene Autry," *The Telegraph* (London), October 5, 1998.

5. Letter from Flournoy Miller to Walter White, January 11, 1938, NAACP Collection, Library of Congress.

6. *Ibid*.

7. "What the Picture Did for Me," *Motion Picture Herald*, April 27, 1935.

8. Holly George-Warren, *Public Cowboy No. 1: The Life and Times of Gene Autry* (New York: Oxford University Press, 2007), p.130. The book attributes

the quote to an interview of Autry by filmmaker Len Morris around 1991.
9. Tuska, *Vanishing Legion*, p. 156.
10. The budget figures are from Jeffrey Richardson, "Cowboys and Robots: The Birth of the Science Fiction Western," CrossedGenres.com. Accessed July 8, 2017.
11. Ibid. Richardson notes that the robot costumes were revived for a 1951 Columbia serial, *Captain Video, Master of the Stratosphere*.
12. "Mascot Serials Get Wide Exploitation," *Film Daily*, April 12, 1935.
13. "What the Picture Did for Me," *Motion Picture Herald*, June 29, 1935.
14. "The World's Most Popular Movie Star," *St. Louis Post-Dispatch*, November 3, 1937.
15. Beware the 59-minute version of *Radio Ranch* released to video by Alpha Home Entertainment in 2009; the musical sequences are cut entirely.
16. "Doubly Mad 'Masterpieces,'" *The Age* (Melbourne, Australia), June 24, 1988.
17. Matthew Bernstein, *Walter Wanger: Hollywood Independent* (Minneapolis: University of Minnesota Press, 1994), p. 106.
18. "Romantic Stars Growing Taller," *Los Angeles Times*, July 5, 1936, is among the accounts speculating on Ballew's height.
19. "Reviews—A Tour of Today's Talkies: *Palm Springs*," *Modern Screen*, August 1936.
20. Standing (1873–1937) would be dead within months of *Palm Springs*' release, the victim of a heart attack (the cause often has been incorrectly reported as a poisonous snake bite). The date of his death—February 24, 1937—was the same as another sudden demise: *Palm Springs* co-screenwriter Humphrey Pearson, whose death by gunshot was ruled a suicide. Pearson died in Palm Springs, by the way.
21. According to Raoul Walsh biographer Marilyn Ann Moss, *Palm Springs* was partially reshot by Walsh at Wanger's behest. See Moss, *Raoul Walsh: The True Adventures of Hollywood's Legendary Director* (Lexington: University Press of Kentucky, 2011), p. 427.
22. "Film Reviews: *Palm Springs*," *Variety*, June 24, 1936.
23. The financial information is from Bernstein, *Walter Wanger*, pp. 436–437.
24. Furia, *Skylark*, p. 85.
25. Ibid., p. 88.
26. Frances Farmer, *Will There Really Be a Morning?* (New York: Putnam, 1972), pp. 117, 119.
27. Peter Shelley, *Frances Farmer: The Life and Films of a Troubled Star* (Jefferson, N.C.: McFarland, 2010), p. 13.
28. Giddins, *Bing Crosby*, p. 415.
29. Another *Rhythm on the Range* song from a non-Paramount source was "Roundup Lullaby," with a melody written by a Los Angeles music teacher, Gertrude Ross, and words taken from verse of the same name by South Dakota's "poet lariat," Charles Badger Clark. The song was chosen for the film after Paramount put out a call for new music from so-called "amateur" songsmiths ("Song Writing Amateurs Get Movie Break," *Los Angeles Times*, June 28, 1936).
30. David C. Tucker, *Martha Raye: Film and Television Clown* (Jefferson, N.C.: McFarland, 2016), p. 10.
31. Although *Rhythm on the Range* was the initial feature film for Raye, she had started in a short subject, Mentone's *A Nite in a Nite Club* (1934).
32. "The Screen: Salute a New Comedienne in *Rhythm on the Range*, at the Paramount," *New York Times*, July 30, 1936.
33. Jean Maddern Pitrone, *Take It From the Big Mouth: The Life of Martha Raye* (Lexington: University Press of Kentucky, 1999), p. 21.
34. "Exploiting Current Films: Ralph Noble's Campaign on *Rhythm on the Range*," *Film Daily*, July 30, 1936. Just as *Range* began to open nationally, Burns' wife died on August 2 in Los Angeles of unreported causes.
35. Ibid.
36. "*Rhythm on the Range*," *Motion Picture Daily*, July 16, 1936.
37. "Simplified Color Process Is Perfected by Hirliman," *Film Daily*, March 16, 1936; "Hirliman to Patent a New Color Process," *Motion Picture Herald*, March 28, 1936.
38. *El carnaval del diablo*, the Spanish-language version of *The Devil on Horseback*, was produced for MGM release by another of Hirliman's companies, Metropolitan Pictures, and shot at the same time as its English counterpart. Fortunio Bonanova, George Lewis, and Juan Torena—the last playing the same character as he did in *Devil on Horseback*—headed the cast.
39. *The Devil on Horseback* ended up being the second Grand National Pictures release. Its debut date was delayed in late summer 1936 to move up that of *In His Steps*, a drama starring Eric Linden and directed by Karl Brown. *In His Steps* was issued on September 22; *Devil* came out a week later. Among the initial batch of GN titles were *Hats Off*, a musical with Mae Clarke and a young John Payne, and *Great Guy*, in which the studio got to show off its most famous talent acquisition, James Cagney.
40. Keating, who was sometimes billed as "The Notorious Charlatan," was no minor magic man. He was known for routines in which he swallowed needles and thread and made a birdcage disappear.
41. "Thayer's Thesper," *Variety*, July 1, 1936.
42. Francisco Del Campo, the actor-singer in *Devil on Horseback*, was occasionally confused in newspaper accounts on the film, to Manuel del Campo, the Mexican socialite in the headlines for marrying much-older actress Mary Astor in February 1937. Astor's del Campo stayed in Hollywood after his 1942 divorce from the actress and became a film editor.
43. "*Devil on Horseback*, with Fred Keating, Del Campo and Lili Damita," *Harrison's Reports*, October 17, 1936.
44. *The Hollywood Reporter*, October 5, 1936.
45. "African-American Cowboy Crooner Herb Jeffries Dies," Associated Press article, cited from *San Diego Union-Tribune*, May 26, 2014.

46. "Back From the Saddle Again," *Los Angeles Times*, October 2, 1998.
47. Jeffries was vague about his age but said near the end of his life that his recently discovered birth certificate dated from 1913. For more, see "Herb Jeffries, 'Bronze Buckaroo' of Song and Screen, Dies at 100 (or So)," *New York Times*, May 26, 2014.
48. Mary A. Dempsey, "The Bronze Buckaroo Rides Again: Herb Jeffries Is Still Keepin' On," *American Visions*, August-September 1997, p. 23.
49. "Here Comes the 'Westerns' Again," Ledger Syndicate story, cited from the *Honolulu Star Advertiser*, December 26, 1937.
50. "White Theatres Book Sack's *Two-Gun Man*," *Boxoffice*, July 23, 1938.
51. *Jackson* (Tenn.) *Sun*, April 24, 1938.
52. "Screen Actors' Guild Agent Defied; Artists Refuse to Quit," *Pittsburgh Courier*, October 22, 1938.
53. "Earl J. Morris: Grandtown Day and Night," *Pittsburgh Courier*, November 19, 1938. Morris clunks Herb Jeffries over the head about two-thirds through the proceedings.
54. "Reviews of the New Films: *The Bronze Buckaroo*," *Film Daily*, January 21, 1939.
55. "He Wouldn't Cross the Line," *Life*, September 3, 1951.
56. "Q&A: Herb Jeffries, Actor, Pioneer Film Cowboy: 'I Am Colored, and I Love It,' " *Atlanta Journal-Constitution*, July 25, 2008.
57. "Golden Buckaroo," *Los Angeles Times Magazine*, April 6, 2003.
58. Speculation as to whether the Walsh offer to Lesser regarding Gehrig was a "gag" is mentioned in "Hollywood Flickers," *Independent Exhibitors Film Journal*, October 28, 1936.
59. "Tarzan Can't Have Knobby Knees—Lou Turns Cowboy," United Press report, cited in *Pittsburgh Press*, January 4, 1938.
60. "Lesser Signs Lou Gehrig," *Film Daily*, March 4, 1937; "Lou Gehrig Signed by Principal Prod.," *Motion Picture Daily*, March 4, 1937.
61. "Two-Gun Gehrig," *Variety*, June 9, 1937. Arlen began the Lesser series with *Secret Valley* (1937), and Ballew followed with *Western Gold* (1937), *Roll Along, Cowboy* (1937), and *Hawaiian Buckaroo* (1938) before *Rawhide*. Ballew completed the series with *Panamint's Bad Man* (1938).
62. "The Hollywood Scene," *Motion Picture Herald*, March 27, 1937.
63. "Asides and Interludes," *Motion Picture Herald*, April 24, 1937.
64. "Gehrig Routs Cattle Rustlers as He Did Hurlers Last Season," United Press report, cited in *Oakland* (Calif.) *Tribune*, January 30, 1938.
65. "Gehrig, Ballew Co-Star," *Motion Picture Daily*, February 7, 1938. Most people think of *Rawhide* as "the Lou Gehrig movie." For example, when Alpha Home Video issued it on DVD in 2004, its cover showed a reproduction of an image of Gehrig and Ballew from the film but ignored the latter in its headline boast of "Baseball Legend Lou Gehrig in *Rawhide*."
66. "Lou Gehrig's Movie Has Bizzare [sic] Opening," United Press report, cited in *Santa Ana* (Calif.) *Register*, March 24, 1938.
67. Ray Robinson, *Iron Horse: Lou Gehrig in His Time* (New York: W.W. Norton, 1990), p. 232.
68. "*Rawhide*," *Harrison's Reports*, April 23, 1938; "Film Reviews: *Rawhide*," *Variety*, April 6, 1938.
69. "The Screen: At the Globe," *New York Times*, April 25, 1938.
70. "*Rawhide*, Filmed in 1939 [sic] With Lou Gehrig, Will Be Revived," International News Service column, cited from *San Francisco Examiner*, September 1, 1942.
71. Melissa Lewis and Paul H. Gordon, M.D., "Lou Gehrig, *Rawhide*, and 1938," *Neurology* 68:8, February 20, 2007. Accessed from Neurology.org, July 24, 2016.
72. Tony Thomas, *The Dick Powell Story* (Burbank, Calif.: Riverwood Press, 1993), p. 175.
73. "Crooner Dick Powell, Soon to Be Papa, Raps Song Role," Associated Press report, cited from *The Bakersfield Californian*, June 23, 1938.
74. The source play, *Howdy Stranger*, which played on Broadway for two months in 1937, had tenor Frank Parker, then famous on radio, in the central role.
75. Dick Powell was no off-screen cowboy, but he was comfortable on a horse. He played polo for many years in Hollywood until Warner Bros. nixed that activity.
76. "Film Reviews: *Cowboy From Brooklyn*," *Variety*, June 15, 1938; "Reviews of New Films: *Cowboy From Brooklyn*," *Film Daily*, June 14, 1938.
77. "The Screen: *Cowboy From Brooklyn* at New York Strand," *Brooklyn Daily Eagle*, July 14, 1938.
78. "Exploitation," *Variety*, June 13, 1938.
79. Thomas, *Dick Powell Story*, p. 175.
80. "Behind the Makeup," Hearst Universal Service column, cited from *Wilkes-Barre* (Pa.) *Record*, June 28, 1938.
81. DickPowell.net; see above. *Cowboy From Brooklyn* was remade by Warners in 1948 as *Two Guys From Texas*, with Dennis Morgan (as the animal-phobic singer) and Jack Carson.
82. "Midgets Star in Cow Opera," United Press report, cited from *Detroit Free Press*, May 30, 1938.
83. Stephen Cox, *The Munchkins of Oz* (Nashville, Tenn.: Cumberland House, 1996), p. 11.
84. "Half-Pint Wears 10-Gallon Hat," *Oakland* (Calif.) *Tribune*, August 7, 1938.
85. "Sol Lesser Resumes Series With Midgets," *Motion Picture Daily*, June 10, 1938; "This Western Must Be a 'Pony' Opera," United Press report, cited from *Pittsburgh Press*, July 3, 1938.
86. "Reviews of the New Films: *Terror of Tiny Town*," *Film Daily*, July 19, 1938.
87. "A 'Little' From 'Lots,'" *Film Daily*, April 27, 1938.
88. "Story Prepared as Vehicle for Grace Moore," Hearst Universal Service column, cited in *Rochester* (N.Y.) *Democrat and Chronicle*, May 27, 1938.
89. "Lee Side o' L.A.," *Los Angeles Times*, June 6, 1938.
90. "Big News as Seen by the Press Agent," *Film Daily*, June 18, 1938.

91. "Midgets Give Party," *Los Angeles Times*, June 19, 1938.
92. "Midget Stars Produce Realistic Fight Scene," *Los Angeles Times*, June 26, 1938.
93. "Around and About in Hollywood," *Los Angeles Times*, August 4, 1938.
94. "Lee Side o' L.A.," *Los Angeles Times*, August 9, 1938.
95. "Little Billy to Open Midget Nitery in H'wood, Lower Case All the Way," *Variety*, September 21, 1938.
96. "Pee-Wees' to Make Series of Pictures," *Variety*, July 20, 1938; "Curtain Calls," *Oakland Tribune*, July 21, 1938. Buell also announced he would produce *Follies on Horseback*, with a cast of 40 females and a lone male ("Forty Beauties and One Man Reverse Western Film Theory," *Los Angeles Times*, June 26, 1938).
97. "Midgets in Pix Travesties," *Film Daily*, June 13, 1938; "Lesser Buys In," *Variety*, June 15, 1938; "Plans 6 Midget Pix," *Film Daily*, August 9, 1938.
98. "*Tiny Town* Picturized," *Los Angeles Times*, July 18, 1938.
99. Moray proved much more competent as a singer, dancer, and impressionist, billed as "Miss Dyna-Mite" and "The Miniature Sophie Tucker," in nightclubs well into the 1970s. Her 1974 obituary—she died in her native Yonkers—credits her with being a mentor to the comedienne Totie Fields. See "Yvonne Moray, Area Entertainer," *Camden* (N.J.) *Courier-Post*, October 26, 1974.
100. Richard Lamparski, *Whatever Became Of…? All-New Eleventh Series* (New York: Crown, 1989), p. 47.
101. Much background information on Page can be found in an article published in her hometown newspaper, *The Morning Call* of Allentown, Pa., upon her second marriage ("Dorothy Page, Northampton Girl, Now Film Star, Weds," January 7, 1940).
102. "Northampton's Movie Star," *The Morning Call* (Allentown, Pa.), July 13, 1997.
103. *Ibid.*
104. "*Ride 'Em Cowgirl* Novel Musical Western," *Independent Exhibitor Film Bulletin*, February 11, 1939.
105. "GN Signs Ruth Mix; 6 Pictures Start," *Motion Picture Herald*, November 6, 1937.
106. John Brooker, *The Happiest Trails* (CP Entertainment Books/Lulu.com, 2017), p. 336. From interview of Frome in *Screen Thrills Illustrated*, February 1964.
107. "Reviews of the New Films: *Ride 'Em Cowgirl*," *Film Daily*, January 19, 1939; "*Ride 'Em Cowgirl* Novel…," *Independent Exhibitor Film Bulletin*, February 11, 1939.
108. "Film Reviews: *Ride 'Em Cowgirl*," *Variety*, January 18, 1939.
109. Jarrett's lone Grand National flick was *Trigger Pals* (1939), and *Six-Gun Rhythm* (1939) was Fletcher's only film of any sort.
110. "Dorothy Page Dies; Ex-Film, Radio Star," *The Morning Call* (Allentown, Pa.), March 27, 1961.

Chapter 5

1. Paul Fryer, *The Opera Singer and the Silent Film* (Jefferson, N.C.: McFarland, 2005), p. 1.
2. William Shaman, *The Operatic Vitaphone Shorts*, ARSC (Association for Recorded Sound Collections) *Journal*, Vol. 22, No. 1, Spring 1991, p. 40. Accessed September 25, 2016, from: http://arsc-audio.org/journals/v22/v22n1p35-94.pdf
3. Richard Barrios, *A Song in the Dark: The Birth of the Musical Film* (New York: Oxford University Press, 2010), p. 415.
4. Moore signed with Columbia in October 1933. Media reports indicated that her failure to secure the *Merry Widow* role stemmed from MGM's concerns about her weight, or an impasse over billing with Maurice Chevalier (who apparently preferred her over his previous screen partner, Jeanette MacDonald, or Lily Pons or Joan Crawford, who both were also linked to the project). See "Love Child to Star Songbird," *Los Angeles Times*, October 3, 1933, and "Lily Pons Joins Competition for *Merry Widow* role," *Los Angeles Times*, December 9, 1933. Moore offered to waive her fee to play in *Widow*; see Richard Fawkes, *Opera on Film* (London: Duckworth, 2000), p. 54.
5. "Who Will Be Hollywood's Jenny Lind?" *Modern Screen*, January 1936.
6. "Grand Opera Stars Cut Weight for Eye Appeal," Associated Press article, cited from *Los Angeles Times*, October 22, 1935.
7. "Music Hath Alarms," *New York Times*, December 26, 1937.
8. "Hefty Divas Given Go-By But Decorative Stars Pull on Tights to Pack Appeal in Film Operas," North American Newspaper Alliance column, cited in *The Winnipeg Tribune*, October 30, 1937.
9. Richard Jewell, *RKO Film Grosses: 1931–1951*, *Historical Journal of Film Radio and Television*, Vol. 14, No. 1, 1994, p. 57.
10. John Kobal, *Gotta Sing Gotta Dance: A Pictorial History of Film Musicals* (London: Hamlyn, 1971), p. 31.
11. Dorothy Lee interview with author, March 5, 1993.
12. Marshall's failure in *Dixiana* may have deprived him of the male lead in a planned RKO filming of Victor Herbert's *Babes in Toyland*. The general decline in Hollywood musicals likely had more to do with the abortion of the project, which was intended to co-star another new studio talent, Irene Dunne. See "Singer Slated for R-K-O Stardom," *Los Angeles Times*, April 15, 1930.
13. Verree Teasdale was initially slated as the female lead. Also, the singer Jane Froman and actor William Gargan were announced early on to be in the cast, but they did not appear in the finished product.
14. "A Little From 'Lots,'" *Film Daily*, July 31, 1935.
15. "*Live* for Retakes," *Variety*, August 7, 1935.
16. There were five songs written for *I Live for Love*, but "I Wanna Play House With You" does not seem to be in surviving prints, although it is mentioned in the *New York Times* and *Variety* reviews of the film.

17. "The Screen: At the Brooklyn Strand," *New York Times*, October 19, 1935.
18. "What the Picture Did for Me," *Motion Picture Herald*, January 11, 1936.
19. "What the Picture Did for Me," *Motion Picture Herald*, November 2, 1935.
20. "What the Picture Did for Me," *Motion Picture Herald*, January 11, 1936.
21. "Screen Not Yet Ready for Full-Length Opera," *Film Daily*, November 8, 1935.
22. "His Alimony Ex Blasts Marshall Corp. as Fraud," *New York Daily News*, May 8, 1939.
23. Marshall's first wife, Caroline Segrera, was an Italian-born singer whom Marshall married in 1928. He and Edna Strong were divorced in 1944.
24. "Singing Star Would Be Song Writer," *The Philadelphia Inquirer*, October 30, 1949.
25. "Gossip of All the Studios," *Photoplay*, February 1930; "Mme. Schumann-Heink May Sing in Mother Film," *Film Daily*, June 8, 1930.
26. Jesse L. Lasky, *I Blow My Own Horn* (Garden City, N.Y.: Doubleday, 1957), p. 248.
27. Unfortunately, Martini's "Vesti la Giubba" is not included in the print of the *Here's to Romance* DVD that was released in the 20th Century-Fox Cinema Archives series in 2015. Heard in its place is "Delusione," written for the film by pianist-composer-conductor Miguel Sandoval, who was Martini's accompanist and who appears briefly as a conductor in *Here's to Romance*. Sandoval co-wrote "Il Principe de Firenze Serenade" for the film; it and "Delusione" were substituted for arias from *I Pagliacci* and *Cavalleria Rusticana* in prints for select foreign markets.
28. "Here's to Romance," *Harrison's Reports*, June 29, 1935.
29. "The Screen: Nino Martini and *Here's to Romance* at the Center," *New York Times*, October 3, 1935.
30. "Reviews of New Films: *Here's to Romance*," *Film Daily*, August 27, 1935.
31. "Studios Farm New Crop of Romantic Men," *St. Louis Post-Dispatch*, October 13, 1935.
32. "Hays Called in Film Row," *Los Angeles Times*, September 11, 1935.
33. "Schumann-Heink to Square Lasky Wail," *Variety*, October 30, 1935.
34. "Schumann-Heink: Why Is She So Neglected?" *Photoplay*, October 1936.
35. Lasky, *I Blow My Own Horn*, p. 248.
36. "Opera Stars Bring New Kind of Temperament to Cinema," *Los Angeles Times*, December 29, 1935.
37. "Inside Stuff—Pictures," *Variety*, October 9, 1935.
38. "Star Sneezes in Tenor Clef," Chicago Tribune Syndicate story, cited in *Detroit Free Press*, November 4, 1935.
39. Jessica Duchen, *Erich Wolfgang Korngold* (London: Phaidon Press, 1996), p. 159.
40. "Kiepura Flashes Temperament," *Los Angeles Herald-Examiner* column, cited in *Rochester* (N.Y.) *Democrat and Chronicle*, April 6, 1936.
41. "*Give Us This Night*," *Harrison's Reports*, March 21, 1936.
42. "Film Reviews: *Give Us This Night*," *Variety*, April 8, 1936.
43. "The Screen: *Give Us This Night*, a New Operatic Film at the Paramount," *New York Times*, April 6, 1936.
44. "Reich Censors Tough on U.S. Pix," *Variety*, June 3, 1936; "Italians No Like Par's *This Night* Pic," *Variety*, July 1, 1936.
45. "Mary Ellis, Singing Actress, Is New Star Rising on Hollywood's Horizon," United Press report, cited in the *Indianapolis Star*, February 20, 1935.
46. "Tornado in Leash," *Picture Play*, November 1935.
47. "With or Without a Voice," *Brooklyn Daily Eagle*, July 12, 1936.
48. Financial data on *Fatal Lady* is found in Bernstein, *Walter Wanger*, p. 437.
49. The horoscope motif may have been the inspiration of Tiffany Thayer, the novelist (*Thirteen Women, Call Her Savage*) and occult-inspired philosopher who received an "additional dialogue" credit in *Fatal Lady*. More on Thayer can be found under *The Devil on Horseback* in Chapter 4.
50. Bernstein, *Walter Wanger*, p. 437. According to the book, *Fatal Lady* cost $431,000 and grossed barely $200,000. Wanger's new deal with UA was announced before the release of *Fatal Lady*. At UA, he rebounded strongly with *You Only Live Once* (1937), a critical success, and *History Is Made at Night* (1937), his first picture in a year to finish out of the red.
51. Mary Ellis, *Those Dancing Years: An Autobiography* (London: John Murray, 1982), p. 93.
52. Alfred E. Twomey, in Lawrence O. Christensen, William E. Foley, Gary R. Kremer, and Kenneth H. Wynn, eds. *Dictionary of Missouri Biography* (Columbia: University of Missouri Press, 1999), p. 739.
53. "Vitaphone Bow Is Hailed as Marvel," *Variety*, August 11, 1926.
54. "Studio News & Gossip East and West," *Photoplay*, October 1926.
55. Richard Koszarski, *The Astoria Studio and Its Fabulous Films* (New York: Dover, 1983), p. 19.
56. Talley's other shorts for Warner Bros., both from 1927, were a duet with Beniamino Gigli on "Verranno a te sull'aura" from *Lucia di Lammermoor*, and a rendition of the Quartette from *Rigoletto* with Gigli, Giuseppe de Luca, and Jeanne Gordon. The *New York Times* praised Talley's work in its review (February 4, 1927) of the latter.
57. "Marion Talley, Prima Donna Four Seasons, Quits to Buy Farm and Live on Earnings," *New York Times*, April 12, 1929; "Marion Talley to Retire and Purchase Farm," Associated Press and International News Service reports, cited from the *Lincoln* (Nebraska) *Star*, April 12, 1929.
58. "Marion Talley Bidding for Movie Fame Now," North American Newspaper Alliance syndicated column, cited from *Milwaukee Journal*, July 26, 1936.
59. Ibid.
60. Columbia's *The Music Goes 'Round** (1936), starring Harry Richman. Like Talley, Bartlett came up empty with a major studio—he was signed by Fox

in 1931 to appear in a Janet Gaynor musical but did not appear in any film while under contract there.

61. "Republic to Ask for 100% Rental Boost," *Motion Picture Daily*, June 5, 1936. Of the other five of the "Jubilee Six," only the Phil Regan starrer *Happy Go Lucky* was a musical. The rest were "serious" stories (*Hearts in Bondage, Portia on Trial*) and action-oriented comedies (*Army Girl, Join the Marines*).

62. "Marion Talley Ends Controversy as to Weight by Describing Reduction," Associated Press report, cited in the *San Bernardino County* (Calif.) *Sun*, November 10, 1936.

63. Ibid.

64. "*Broadcast* Tops Field in New York," *Los Angeles Times*, November 1, 1936.

65. *The Hollywood Reporter*, August 7, 1936.

66. "Film Reviews: *Follow Your Heart*," *Variety*, October 28, 1936.

67. "Marion Talley Sued for Separation; Mate Accuses Seven Men," United Press report, cited from the *Milwaukee Journal*, January 18, 1941; "Miss Talley Says Husband Attempted Blackmail," United Press report, cited from the *St. Petersburg* (Fla.) *Times*, February 6, 1941; "Says Husband Used Daughter as Pawn in Extortion Plot," United Press report, cited from *Mason City* (Iowa) *Globe-Gazette*, May 21, 1941.

68. "Opera Star Charged With Misconduct in Divorce Complaint; Marion Talley Accused by Producer's Wife," United Press report, cited from the *Corpus Christi* (Texas) *Caller-Times*, March 25, 1941; "Testimony About Miss Talley Ruled Out in Custody Trial," *Los Angeles Times*, June 4, 1941.

69. Hertzel Weinstat and Bert Wechsler, *Dear Rogue: A Biography of the American Baritone Lawrence Tibbett* (Portland, Ore.: Amadeus Press, 1996), p. 143.

70. The 1930 *New Moon* movie shifted the operetta's locale from late 18th century France and Louisiana to early 20th century Russia. The French roots might explain why MGM, in seeking not to confuse viewers with its 1940 remake, carelessly renamed the original *Parisian Belle* when it was issued to television.

71. Weinstat and Wechsler, *Dear Rogue*, p. 141.

72. Aubrey Solomon, *The Fox Film Corporation 1915-1935: A History and Filmography* (Jefferson, N.C.: McFarland, 2011), p. 223.

73. Fawkes, *Opera on Film*, p. 60.

74. Behlmer, *Memo From Darryl F. Zanuck*, p. 65.

75. Otto Preminger, *Preminger: An Autobiography* (Garden City, N.J.: Doubleday, 1977), p. 15.

76. Ibid., p. 16.

77. Ibid.

78. Among the pieces left on the cutting room floor for *Under Your Spell* was Jacques Wolfe's "Hallelujah Rhythm." Besides the *Faust* spot, the only other opera sampling heard in the final cut is a few bars of "Largo al factotum" from *The Barber of Seville* in a brief sequence involving Tibbett, a toucan, and a bullfrog.

79. "B.O. Blues Come to B'way After Election…," "*Spell* 5G Brodie," and "L.A. Trade Just Over the Break…," *Variety*, November 11, 1936.

80. "What the Picture Did for Me," *Motion Picture Herald*, January 23, 1937.

81. "What the Picture Did for Me," *Motion Picture Herald*, January 16, 1937.

82. "What the Picture Did for Me," *Motion Picture Herald*, May 22, 1937.

83. "Film Gossip of the Week … Mr. Tibbett Previews His New Picture," *New York Times*, October 25, 1936.

84. "Singer Cut in Stage Fight by Tibbett Dies," United Press report, cited in *Tulare* (Calif.) *Advance-Register*, January 27, 1937; "Tibbett Cleared in Singer's Death," *New York Times*, January 28, 1937; "Ailment, Not Tibbett Knife, Killed Singer," *New York Daily News*, January 28, 1937. Also see Weinstat and Wechsler, *Dear Rogue*, pp. 150–151.

85. "The Screen: *Under Your Spell* at the Palace," *New York Times*, November 7, 1936.

86. "Restored Version of Rare Cary Grant Musical *When You're in Love* to Air," *Los Angeles Times* (www.latimes.com/entertainment/classichollywood/la-et-mn-restored-when-you-re-in-love-cary-grant-20160407-story.html), April 7, 2016. Accessed August 8, 2017; Thomas Gladysz, "GetTV Premieres Rare Cary Grant Film," Huffington Post (http://www.huffingtonpost.com/thomas-gladysz/gettv-premieres-rare-cary_b_9831946.html), May 4, 2016. Accessed August 8, 2017.

87. Grace Moore, *You're Only Human Once* (Garden City, N.Y.: Doubleday, Doran, 1944), p. 177.

88. Ian Scott, *In Capra's Shadow: The Life and Career of Screenwriter Robert Riskin* (Lexington: University Press of Kentucky, 2006), p. 122.

89. Lachman's participation was frequently cited as being "in association" with Riskin (as, for example, in "Robert Riskin, Ace Scenarist, Promoted to Directorial Post at Columbia," *Los Angeles Times*, August 26, 1936). Lachman was lured to Columbia by a long-term contract and the promise of choosing his own stories, but he sought his release after *When You're in Love* and two unimportant credited films ("Inside Stuff—Pictures," *Variety*, July 7, 1937). He returned to Fox, where he directed until 1942.

90. Scott, *In Capra's Shadow*, pp. 122–123.

91. The "Minnie" number was censored for prints of *When You're in Love* by the time it was initially released for television, possibly over rights issues, but it has been restored for its most recent airings.

92. Moore, *You're Only Human Once*, p. 212.

93. Early reviews complained about the overlength of *When You're in Love*, and Columbia trimmed it either before its New York debut or before general release. This would seem to explain the absence of press-confirmed cast members Edgar Kennedy, Barnett Parker, Robert Emmett O'Connor, Ann Doran, and others from the currently circulating 103-minute version. Some early reviews also listed an excerpt from *Romeo et Juliet* as being sung by Moore, but descriptions of the movie for its general release do not mention this music, and it is missing from the restored print.

94. "Film Reviews: *When You're in Love*," *Variety*, February 24, 1937; "Moore's *You're in Love* Swell; Star

at Her Best," *The Hollywood Reporter*, February 13, 1937.

95. Gladysz, "GetTV Premieres."

96. "The Screen: *When You're in Love* Opens at the Music Hall," *New York Times*, February 19, 1937.

97. "Jaguar Guards Lily Pons...," *Los Angeles Times*, October 9, 1932.

98. "A 'Little' From Lots," *Film Daily*, April 14, 1937.

99. "No, No, Nino, Nevaire! Lily Says One Opera Star Enuff for Movie," Associated Press story, taken from *The Evening Sun* (Hanover, Pa.), October 19, 1936.

100. "Lily Pons Stripped of Dignity for New Movie Role," United Press story, taken from *St. Louis Star and Times*, September 13, 1937.

101. Moss, *Raoul Walsh*, pp. 156–157. The interview is from the program for "The Films of Raoul Walsh," British Film Institute, National Film Theatre, London, November 1974.

102. "The Screen in Review: *Hitting a New High*, at the Rivoli," *New York Times*, December 27, 1937.

103. "What the Picture Did for Me," *Motion Picture Herald*, March 26, 1938.

104. Fryer, *The Opera Singer and the Silent Film*, p. 215.

105. "The Theaters in Season Soon to Begin Will Have to Get Along Without Most Dramatic Spectator, Hope Hampton," *Brooklyn Daily Eagle*, August 23, 1938.

106. "Movie Cameras Unreel Fortune for Multi-Millionaire," Newspaper Enterprise Association story, cited from *Hope* (Ark.) *Star*, February 20, 1939.

107. Ibid.

108. "George Tucker: Man About Manhattan," Associated Press column, cited from *Corsicana* (Texas) *Daily Sun*, October 30, 1937.

109. "Hope Hampton Awarded Termer," *Los Angeles Times*, May 13, 1937; "Cary Grant Is Wanted for Hope Hampton Film," *Detroit Free Press*, November 8, 1937.

110. Richard Griffith, *The Movie Stars* (Garden City, N.Y.: Doubleday, 1970), p. 48. Besides Cary Grant's alleged association with the role played by Scott, Louis Hayward was linked to the second-string male part that was filled by Alan Marshal.

111. "Chanslor Gets Reno," *Motion Picture Daily*, March 28, 1938.

112. "A 'Little' From Hollywood 'Lots,'" *Film Daily*, August 30, 1937.

113. Robert Nott, *The Films of Randolph Scott* (Jefferson, N.C.: McFarland, 2004), p. 75.

114. "Film Reviews: *The Road to Reno*," *Variety*, October 5, 1938; "The Screen: Universal's *The Road to Reno*, With Hope Hampton and Randolph Scott, Opens at the Globe," *New York Times*, October 3, 1938.

115. "What the Picture Did for Me," *Motion Picture Herald*, December 24, 1938.

116. "Odd and Interesting," *Los Angeles Times*, September 11, 1938.

117. "George Ross: New York," syndicated *New York World Telegram* column, cited in *Piqua* (Ohio) *Daily Call*, April 28, 1939.

118. "Hope Hampton Victim of $335,000 burglary," Associated Press story, cited in *Toledo* (Ohio) *Blade*, April 16, 1951.

119. "Hope Hampton, Glamor Gal of Roaring '20s, Is Set for Comeback," International News Service story, cited in *Lubbock* (Texas) *Evening Journal*, December 28, 1954.

120. "Hope Hampton, Opera Singer and First-Nighter, Dies at 84," *New York Times*, January 25, 1982.

121. Gravey's name was anglicized to "Gravet" for billing on his Hollywood projects, one suspects for reasons having to do with the perils of culinary pronunciation.

122. Michael Sragow, *Victor Fleming: An American Movie Master* (Lexington: University Press of Kentucky, 2013), p. 275.

123. "Behind the Hollywood Front," *Radio Mirror*, April 1938.

124. The stage *Great Waltz* was adapted into a 1955 made-for-television production starring Keith Andes, Patrice Munsel, and Bert Lahr. Strauss became further screen fodder in a 1963 Walt Disney TV production called *The Waltz King* (as played by Kerwin Mathews) that was released theatrically outside the United States. A 1972 theatrical film, *The Great Waltz*, was written and directed by Andrew L. Stone and starred Horst Buchholz.

125. Sragow, *Victor Fleming*, p. 277.

126. "Good News," *Modern Screen*, February 1939.

127. "Miliza Korjus Likely Lead in *Desert Song*," *Los Angeles Times*, April 11, 1940.

128. "Miliza Korjus Filed Suit Over Injuries in Auto Crash," *Los Angeles Times*, December 13, 1940.

129. Sragow, *Victor Fleming*, p. 281.

Chapter 6

1. "Facing the Music," *Radio Mirror*, November 1936.

2. "Scene on Broadway," *The Record* (Hackensack, N.J.), July 31, 1937; "Asides and Interludes," *Motion Picture Herald*, October 2, 1937.

3. Ibid.

4. "Jitterbugs Warned Dances Peril All But Athletes," Associated Press report, cited from *Los Angeles Times*, October 28, 1938.

5. "A Jitterbug Girl Dances to Death at Liquor Party," *Chicago Tribune*, April 4, 1939.

6. "Do Jitterbugs Need Traffic Rules?" The Bell Syndicate column, cited from *Los Angeles Times*, June 18, 1939.

7. "Swing Music Under Attack," Associated Press report, cited from *Iowa City* (Iowa) *Press-Citizen*, November 26, 1936.

8. "Song Writers Defend Swing Music 'Morals,'" Associated Press report, cited from *Indianapolis Star*, September 22, 1937.

9. "Our Readers Write: Swing It!" *Hollywood*, August 1937.

10. "Hollywood Is Jazz's Deadliest Enemy," *Down-Beat*, December 1938.

11. Louis Armstrong letter to Leonard Feather, 1941, from Armstrong, *Louis Armstrong, in His Own Words: Selected Writings* (New York: Oxford University Press, 1999), p. 147.

12. Lana Turner, *Lana—the Lady, the Legend, the Truth* (New York: Dutton, 1982), p. 48.

13. Dennis M. Spragg, "Glenn Miller and his Orchestra Sun Valley Serenade 75th Anniversary Commemoration," 2016, Glenn Miller Archive. Accessed May 13, 2019. https://www.dennismspragg.com/wp-content/uploads/2017/11/SUN-VALLEY-SERENADE.pdf

14. Those wanting to see Martha Raye and Bob Burns reunited in this *Big Broadcast* likely came away disappointed, as the comic pair from the recent hit *Rhythm on the Range* appear in nary a scene together.

15. "The Screen: Paramount Flouts the Calendar With *Big Broadcast of 1937*," *New York Times*, October 22, 1936.

16. Benny's rarely aired *College Holiday* showed the same evening on TCM.

17. Philip Furia and Michael L. Lasser, *America's Songs: The Stories Behind the Songs of Broadway, Hollywood, and Tin Pan Alley* (New York: Routledge, 2006), p. 146.

18. Studio communications indicate that Davis declined the *Hollywood Hotel* assignment. See Rudy Behlmer, *Inside Warner Bros., 1935–1951* (New York: Simon & Schuster, 1987), pp. 39–40.

19. D. Russell Connor, *Benny Goodman: Listen to His Legacy* (Metuchen, N.J., and London: Scarecrow Press and the Institute of Jazz Studies, 1988), p. 70.

20. "Hot from Hollywood," International News Service column, cited from *Princeton* (Ind.) *Daily Clarion*, September 25, 1937.

21. Jeffrey Spivak, *Buzz: The Life and Art of Busby Berkeley* (Lexington: University Press of Kentucky, 2011), p. 152.

22. "The Screen: Benny Goodman Starts a Jam Session at the Strand in the New Warner Musical, *Hollywood Hotel*," *New York Times*, January 13, 1938.

23. "Swarthout vs. Raft in Paris Tune Tiffer," *Variety*, May 15, 1936; "A 'Little' From 'Lots,'" *Film Daily*, May 8, 1936; "Out Hollywood Way," *Motion Picture Daily*, May 19, 1936.

24. "When a Famous Opera Singer Visits Movieland," Five Star Publishing syndicated article, cited from *The Capital Journal* (Salem, Ore.), October 3, 1936.

25. Maurice Zolotow, *Billy Wilder in Hollywood* (New York: Putnam, 1977), p. 61.

26. Tighe E. Zimmers, *Tin Pan Alley Girl: A Biography of Ann Ronell* (Jefferson, N.C.: McFarland, 2009), p. 16.

27. Osborne replaced the bubbly comedienne Lyda Roberti, who might have made a more interesting choice for the malevolent-femme role.

28. Jacqueline Vansant, *Austria Made in Hollywood* (Rochester, N.Y.: Boydell & Brewer, 2019), p. 53.

29. "When a Famous Opera Singer Visits Movieland."

30. *Ibid.*

31. "Film Reviews: *Champagne Waltz*," *Variety*, February 10, 1937.

32. "*Champagne Waltz* to Have 20 World Capital Openings," *Film Daily*, January 6, 1937.

33. "Champagne," *Paramount International News*, November 1, 1936.

34. "New York Tip-Off," *Independent Exhibitors Film Bulletin*, February 13, 1937.

35. "Box Office Performances of 1936–37 Season's Pictures," *Harrison's Reports*, March 13, 1937.

36. "What the Picture Did for Me," *Motion Picture Herald*, April 17, 1937.

37. "What the Picture Did for Me," *Motion Picture Herald*, May 29, 1937.

38. "Showmen's Reviews: *Swing, Sister, Swing*," *Motion Picture Herald*, December 17, 1938.

39. "Wedding Off, Star Claims: Sweetheart Thinks He's to Die Before 25, in October," *Ogden* (Utah) *Standard-Examiner*, April 3, 1938.

40. "Some Late Previews: *Swing, Sister, Swing*," *Hollywood Spectator*, December 24, 1938.

41. "Orchestra Is Silent on Film Studio Stage," United Press report, cited from *The Tampa Tribune*, November 11, 1938.

42. "Strand Books *Swing Sister*," *Longview* (Texas) *News Journal*, February 5, 1939.

43. "Orchestra Is Silent on Film Studio Stage."

44. "Film Reviews: *Swing, Sister, Swing*," *Variety*, December 14, 1938; "Box-Office Performances of 1938–39 Season's Pictures," *Harrison's Reports*, April 20, 1939.

45. Jerome Weidman, "Product of the Country," *Variety*, January 7, 1942.

46. Bob Bach and Ginger Mercer, *Our Huckleberry Friend: The Life, Times and Lyrics of Johnny Mercer* (Secaucus, N.J.: Lyle Stuart, 1982), p. 63.

47. Glenn T. Eskew, *Johnny Mercer: Southern Songwriter for the World* (Athens: University of Georgia Press, 2013), p. 126.

48. Krin Gabbard, "Actor and Musician: Louis Armstrong and His Films," from Joshua Berrett, ed., *The Louis Armstrong Companion: Eight Decades of Commentary* (New York: Schirmer, 1999), p. 216; Krin Gabbard, "Signifyin(g) the Phallus: Mo' Better Blues and Representations of the Jazz Trumpet," from *Representing Jazz*, Krin Gabbard, ed. (Durham, N.C.: Duke University Press, 1995), pp. 104–105.

49. Gabbard, in Berrett, *Louis Armstrong Companion*, p. 216.

50. "Tepid Film Fare Viewed," *Los Angeles Times*, January 19, 1939.

51. "Could Have Sung Another…," *Hollywood Spectator*, December 24, 1938.

52. Thomas, *Dick Powell Story*, p. 175.

53. Furia, *Skylark*, p. 118.

54. *Going Places* and *Jeepers Creepers* share a prominent cast member: Thurston Hall, who plays a domestically dishonest colonel in the former and an antagonistic coal magnate in the latter. Hall (1882–1958) specialized in such blustery but impeachable authority characters, usually for comic effect.

55. "Dramatic Parts Named for Dick Powell," *Los Angeles Times*, October 5, 1938; "Dick Powell to Star

in Bromfield Story," *Los Angeles Times*, November 5, 1938. *Each Dawn I Die* and *Dust Be My Destiny* both became 1939 WB features, the former starring James Cagney and George Raft and the latter with John Garfield and Priscilla Lane. The Bromfield story initially attached to Powell was *It All Came True*, a crime comedy-drama with music that starred Ann Sheridan, Humphrey Bogart, and (perhaps in the part Powell would have filled) Jeffrey Lynn.

56. "Dick Powell and Joan Blondell Join Free Lancers—Want Different Roles," McNaught Syndicate column, cited from *The Salt Lake Tribune* (Salt Lake City, Utah), December 21, 1938.

57. "Hollywood Newsreel," *Hollywood*, March 1939.

58. "The Screen: At the Palace," *New York Times*, June 23, 1939.

59. "What the Picture Did for Me," *Motion Picture Herald*, September 9, 1939.

60. Thomas, *Dick Powell Story*, p. 175.

61. Bruce Klauber, *World of Gene Krupa: That Legendary Drummin' Man* (Ventura, Calif.: Pathfinder Publishing, 1990), p. 31.

62. Connor, *Benny Goodman*, p. 83.

63. "Hollywood Radio Whispers," *Radio Mirror*, June 1939.

64. *Some Like It Hot* was issued, as *Rhythm Romance*, on a 1999 VHS that was part of a Bob Hope collection of films, but it fell back into obscurity when it was bypassed for DVD in 2017, even as the other movies in the package emerged on disc.

65. "Film Reviews: *Some Like It Hot*," *Variety*, May 10, 1939.

66. "New York Critics Find Much to Razz in Cinema," *Los Angeles Times*, June 5, 1939.

67. "Ice Revue Presented on Stage," *Los Angeles Times*, May 26, 1939.

68. Lawrence J. Quirk, *Bob Hope, The Road Well Traveled* (New York: Applause Books, 2000), pp. 122–123.

69. Bob Hope and Bob Thomas, *The Road to Hollywood* (New York: Doubleday, 1977), p. 28.

70. "RKO Signs Kay Kyser," *Film Daily*, July 20, 1939.

71. Butler with Atkins, *David Butler*, p. 177.

72. *David Butler*, pp. 178, 180.

73. Robson returned as Grandma Kyser in *Playmates* (1941) in one of her final film roles. The exterior scenes featuring the band's mansion were made at the Jay Paley estate in the Holmby Hills section of Beverly Hills. The mansion was owned by the sometime film producer who hailed from the family that founded CBS. (Jacob "Jay" Paley was an uncle of William S. Paley.)

74. "One Steamboat Plenty, But Not for This Studio," Newspaper Enterprise Association report, cited in *Ogden* (Utah) *Standard-Examiner*, November 12, 1939.

75. "Film Reviews: *That's Right—You're Wrong*," *Variety*, November 22, 1939.

76. "Sheilah Graham Decides Against Movie Career," North American Newspaper Alliance column, cited from *Atlanta Constitution*, October 13, 1939. Based on the party-scene shot described by Graham, the camera-hogging culprit was Hedda Hopper, who was up to her old acting tricks.

77. "Hedda Hopper's Hollywood," Jones Syndicate column, cited from *Los Angeles Times*, October 10, 1939.

78. "Behind the Make-up: Your Hollywood Reporter Makes His Film Debut," International News Service column, cited from the *Wilkes-Barre* (Pa.) *Record*, October 16, 1939.

79. "City Ready to Celebrate Kay Kyser Day Tomorrow," *Rocky Mount* (N.C.) *Telegram*, November 14, 1939; "RKO Takes Over N.C. Town for Opening of Kyser Pix," *Film Daily*, December 16, 1939; "Hometown Premiere for Kyser's Film," *Boxoffice*, November 18, 1939. Also see Raymond D. Hair and Jurgen Wolfer, *Thinking of You: The Story of Kay Kyser* (Albany, Ga.: BearManor Media, 2016), p. 131.

80. "100% Hold-Overs for Kyser Pix as Result of Heavy Biz," *Film Daily*, November 28, 1939.

81. Box office figure is from Richard B. Jewell, *RKO Radio Pictures: A Titan Is Born* (Berkeley: University of California Press, 2012), p. 203. In his memoir, David Butler stated that he, as director and producer, made the picture for a mere $253,000 and was paid with a salary and 25 percent of the film's grosses; see Butler with Atkins, *David Butler*, pp. 176–177.

82. "The Screen in Review: *That's Right—You're Wrong* Shown at Criterion," *New York Times*, November 30, 1939.

83. Susan Ohmer, *George Gallup in Hollywood* (New York: Columbia University Press, 2006), p. 132. In January 1941, Gallup noted in a report to RKO that patrons under age 30 bought 65 percent of all movie tickets, and people under 20 accounted for half of those.

84. Besides their seven top-of-the-credits efforts, Kyser and his band also appeared briefly in *Stage Door Canteen* (United Artists, 1943) and *Thousands Cheer* (MGM, 1943).

Chapter 7

1. "Jimmie Fidler in Hollywood," McNaught Syndicate columns, cited from *The Daily Town Talk* (Alexandria, La.), January 18, 1939, and the *Battle Creek* (Mich.) *Enquirer*, May 12, 1939.

2. Giddins, *Bing Crosby*, pp. 471–472.

3. RKO's semi-musical *Check and Double Check*, with two white actors as the comedy radio duo of Amos 'n' Andy, debuted mere weeks after *Big Boy*. In June 1930, Warner Bros. released *Golden Dawn*, the notoriously racist operetta with white actor Noah Beery—in a warmup of sorts for *Big Boy*—blacked up as an African heavy who inexplicably speaks in an American Southern dialect. (One might also include Herb Jeffries [see Chapter 4] as such a cross-over actor, depending how one reads his racial identity.)

4. The $500,000 figure is from Barrios, *A Song in the Dark*, p. 216.

5. "Storyless Jolson," *Variety*, January 22, 1930.

6. "Al Jolson Triumphs as Jockey in *Big Boy*," *New York Times*, January 8, 1925.

7. "This Man 'Started It All,'" *Los Angeles Times*, April 20, 1930.
8. "Ex-Follies Girl!" *Screenland*, November 1930.
9. Michael Freedland, *Jolson: The Story of Al Jolson* (Portland, Ore.: Valentine Mitchell, 2007), p. 153.
10. "Warner Bros. Pictures," *Harrison's Reports*, October 11, 1930.
11. "Dark Mystery," *Film Daily*, September 10, 1930. The word in question is spoken by a character played by Louise Closser Hale as she introduces the flashback sequence.
12. "Film Reviews: *Big Boy*," *Variety*, September 17, 1930.
13. "Disappointments Sweep B'way," *Variety*, September 17, 1930.
14. Herbert G. Goldman, *Jolson: The Legend Comes to Life* (New York: Oxford University Press, 1988), p. 212.
15. "Someone else" was Stanley Smith, a frequent juvenile in early movie musicals who was a surer acting commodity than Crosby at the time, but whose tenor could not match even Crosby's early-era baritone. That helps explain why we are writing about Bing Crosby in this book and not Stanley Smith (whose significant picture work ended after 1933 or so).
16. Crosby made two more shorts in the spring of 1933 for release by Paramount, both directed by comedy specialist Arvid Gillstrom, but the studio held up their debuts for fear of its star's overexposure. (Crosby was becoming too important a star to be "wasted" in short subjects.) *Please* wasn't issued until November, and *Just an Echo* was delayed until January 1934.
17. "The Screen: *College Humor*, A College Frolic," *New York Times*, June 23, 1933.
18. Buddy Rogers and Nancy Carroll were the romantic leads of the box-office hit *Close Harmony*, playing characters absent from *Too Much Harmony*.
19. "Harry Green to Para," *The Hollywood Reporter*, April 5, 1933; "*Too Much Harmony* Goes in With Crosby," Ibid., May 17, 1933; "Para. to Build Crosby Role in New Picture," Ibid., June 21, 1933.
20. "Joseph Mankiewicz Scales Hollywood Peak," *New York Times*, September 24, 1950.
21. Bing Crosby with Pete Martin, *Call Me Lucky* (New York: Simon & Schuster, 1953), p. 117. Crosby forgot to mention Sammy Cohen, the long-limbed, lengthy-nosed comic who appears in *Too Much Harmony* as a nerve-wracked dance director. No fewer than three blondes—Kitty Kelly, Grace Bradley, and Lilyan Tashman—add to the fun.
22. "Mother of Jack Oakie Be in Play" [sic], King Features Syndicate column, cited in *The Sedalia* (Mo.) *Democrat*, August 6, 1933. Sedalia was Oakie's hometown, and the foray into film by his mother, a former schoolteacher in Sedalia, was big news. The *Democrat* dutifully reported Evelyn Offield "making a decided hit" in a personal appearance tied to the New York City premiere of *Too Much Harmony*, with future PAs in Washington, D.C.; Detroit; and elsewhere ("Mrs. Offield Scores in Appearances," September 25, 1933, and "Mrs. Evelyn Offield Thrilled by Appearances With Her Talkie Picture," October 1, 1933). Mom Offield died in 1939 at age 70.
23. "Vocal Ingenue Sought," *The Hollywood Reporter*, June 7, 1933.
24. Oakie and Gallagher's Ben Day and Johnny Dixon were, for some reason, renamed from *Close Harmony*'s Ben Barney and Johnny Bay, and Green's character, dubbed Max Mindel in the earlier film, was now Max Merlin.
25. As a transitional reminder of Crosby's burgeoning screen success, the company opens *Too Much Harmony* by singing a few bars of Coslow and Johnston's "Learn to Croon," a big hit from *College Humor*.
26. "Many Theaters Report Records With *Harmony*," *Film Daily*, October 6, 1933.
27. "Chevalier Washed Up With Paramount," *The Hollywood Reporter*, June 23, 1933; "Chevalier-MGM Dicker for Merry Widow Spot," *The Hollywood Reporter*, June 30, 1933.
28. "Lombard-Hopkins Placed," *Variety*, December 20, 1932; "On the Dotted Line…," *Motion Picture Herald*, December 31, 1932.
29. Disciplining Asked for Sylvia Sidney," *Motion Picture Herald*, August 5, 1933.
30. *L'amour guide* was co-directed by Taurog and Jean Boyer, and featured Jacqueline Francell and Marcel Vallee in the roles played in English by Dvorak and Horton. Dvorak spoke French but was not called upon for the Gallic filming.
31. "What Every Fan Should Know—," *Modern Screen*, June 1933.
32. Christina Rice, *Ann Dvorak: Hollywood's Forgotten Rebel*. (Lexington: University Press of Kentucky, 2013), p. 118.
33. "More Gossip," *Silver Screen*, March 1934.
34. "Old Gags Again Feature Movies," uncredited report cited from *The Evening Standard* (Uniontown, Pa.), December 10, 1933.
35. "Along the Rialto," *Film Daily*, September 22, 1933.
36. "…Chevalier Drops to $14,000 From *Harmony*'s $19,600," *Variety*, October 10, 1933; "B'way Strikes a Hiatus in B.O. Pace…," *Variety*, November 14, 1933.
37. "Box Office Performances of the 1933–34 Pictures," *Harrison's Reports*, June 2, 1934; "Film Reviews: *The Way to Love*," *Variety*, November 14, 1933.
38. "*Stingaree* Bought for Irene Dunne," *The Hollywood Reporter*, May 25, 1933; "RKO Buys Two Stories; Three Names Are Signed," *Film Daily*, May 25, 1933; "A 'Little' From Hollywood 'Lots,'" *Film Daily*, October 17, 1933. There is a modern-day account of RKO being in talks with MGM about a loan-out of Jeanette MacDonald to star in *Stingaree*, but this does not appear to be the case.
39. "Dix and Dunne Teamed," *Los Angeles Times*, January 17, 1934.
40. Margie Schultz, *Irene Dunne: A Bio-Bibiliography* (Westport, Conn.: Greenwood, 1991), p. 7.
41. Wellman also directed a football comedy with songs, *Maybe It's Love* (First National, 1930),

that could be classified as a musical, based on how strictly you define the term.

42. William Wellman, Jr., *Wild Bill Wellman, Hollywood Rebel* (New York: Pantheon Books, 2015), pp. 309–310. Wellman might have remembered *Stingaree* for its timing in relation to his fourth, and long-lasting, marriage, to actress Dorothy Coonan on March 20, 1934, right at the end of shooting.

43. An angle promoted heavily by RKO was that the horse ridden by Dix's character was the same one Rudolph Valentino mounted in *The Sheik* a decade prior. (See, among many other national mentions, "Around and About in Hollywood," *Los Angeles Times*, February 19, 1934.)

44. "The Screen: Richard Dix, Irene Dunne and Conway Tearle in a Film Conception of E.W. Hornung's *Stingaree*," *New York Times*, May 18, 1934.

45. "Film Reviews: *Stingaree*," *Variety*, May 22, 1934.

46. "What the Picture Did for Me," *Motion Picture Herald*, November 3, 1934.

47. "What the Picture Did for Me," *Motion Picture Herald*, January 26, 1935.

48. "*Stingaree*, with Irene Dunne and Richard Dix," *Harrison's Reports*, May 19, 1934.

49. "N.S.W. Bans *Stingaree*," *Motion Picture Daily*, February 8, 1935; "Films Get Share of Australian Trade," *Motion Picture Herald*, April 27, 1935.

50. Richard Jewell, "RKO Film Grosses: 1931–1951," *Historical Journal of Film Radio and Television*, Vol. 14, No. 1, 1994, p. 57.

51. "Romantic *Stingaree* Gallops at Stanley," *Pittsburgh Press*, July 2, 1934.

52. "Back in the RKO Fold," *Los Angeles Times*, April 1, 2007. The post-1933 movies were remakes of earlier ones, and thus were subject to the same rights concerns. Unlike the other five titles, *A Man to Remember* was restored from a Dutch-subtitled print found in Amsterdam.

53. Elder, *Alice Faye*, p. 61. Betty King Scharf married the well-known composer-arranger Walter Scharf.

54. "*365 Nights in Hollywood*," unsourced newspaper item, cited from *Warren* (Pa.) *Times Mirror*, November 20, 1934.

55. A view of a fake newspaper clipping accompanied by a photograph of Starr is the closest the film comes to recognizing its literary "inspiration."

56. "What the Picture Did for Me," *Motion Picture Herald*, December 1, 1934.

57. A typical major-studio program musical in 1934 would have been budgeted at about $400,000, 10 times the proposed cost of the movie within the movie in *365 Nights in Hollywood*. However, Fox "B" product such as this might have come in for less.

58. "The Screen: *365 Nights in Hollywood*, at the Mayfair," *New York Times*, November 7, 1934.

59. "Film Reviews: *365 Nights in Hollywood*," *Variety*, November 13, 1934.

60. Wade Williams e-mail interview with author, July 9, 2016.

61. Ginger Rogers, *Ginger: My Story* (New York: HarperCollins, 1991), p. 129.

62. "Biggest Money Making Stars of 1934–35," *Motion Picture Herald*, December 28, 1935. As singular entries, Astaire and Rogers were ranked 13th and 14th, respectively.

63. *The Hollywood Reporter* announced on November 3, 1934, that Fred Astaire was RKO's first choice for the lead. Would this have been another Astaire-Rogers project?

64. Scott also wrote the screenplay for the 1938 Astaire-Rogers musical *Carefree*, which, like *In Person*, had Rogers playing a woman with psychiatric trouble, although in the later film, the trouble is little more than an inability to commit to Ralph Bellamy.

65. *Ginger: My Story*, p. 149. Besides the two leads, Mowbray, Mitchell, and Samuel S. Hinds, comic actor Edgar Kennedy was supposed to be prominent in the cast, but his part as a hotel doorman was cut prior to release. Kennedy can be seen only from a distance, but recognizably.

66. John Charles Franceschina, *Hermes Pan: The Man Who Danced With Fred Astaire* (New York: Oxford University Press, 2012), p. 68.

67. "Film Reviews: *In Person*," *Variety*, December 18, 1935; *Life*, February 1936.

68. Charlotte Greenspan, *Pick Yourself Up: Dorothy Fields and the American Musical* (New York: Oxford University Press, 2010), pp. 92–93.

69. Numbers are from Richard Jewell, *RKO Film Grosses 1931–1951*, *Historical Journal of Film, Radio and Television*, Vol. 14, No. 1, 1994, p. 55.

70. Martin and Faye stayed married only until March 1941. He found more lasting marital bliss with actress-dancer Cyd Charisse, in a union that lasted for 60 years until her death in 2008. Faye also ended up in a long-lasting marriage, with actor-singer-bandleader Phil Harris, from 1941 until his passing in 1995.

71. "Joan Davis Better," *Variety*, April 28, 1937; "Pert Joan Davis a Real 'Fall Girl,'" uncredited, cited from *Wisconsin State Journal* (Madison), January 23, 1938.

72. "*Sing and Be Happy*, with Anthony Martin and Leah Ray," *Harrison's Reports*, June 26, 1937.

73. James Cagney, *Cagney by Cagney* (Garden City, N.Y.: Doubleday, 1976), p. 68.

74. "Budget of $500,000 for Cagney's Films," *Motion Picture Daily*, July 25, 1936.

75. "Cagney Will Do Musical Pix for Grand National," *Film Daily*, May 4, 1937.

76. "Schertzinger Asks Exchanges' Advice on Casting Lead," *Film Daily*, April 20, 1937.

77. "Rocketed to Stardom," *The Pacific Coast Musician*, Volume 26, 1937.

78. Cagney, *Cagney by Cagney*, p. 70.

79. *Panamint's Bad Man* (Fox 1938), a singing Western co-starring Smith Ballew.

80. "The Sound Track: Introducing Mr. James Cagney in a New Vehicle, *Something to Sing About*, Which Opens Tomorrow," *Brooklyn Daily Eagle*, September 19, 1937.

81. Patrick McGilligan, *Cagney: The Actor as Auteur* (South Brunswick, N.J.: A.S. Barnes & Co., 1975), pp. 68, 70. The screenwriter for *Something to Sing About*—Austin Parker, the author, newspaperman, aviator, and second husband (among four) of

actress Miriam Hopkins—probably deserves more than the footnote he's getting here. Parker didn't survive long past the initial release of *Something to Sing About*, dying of a brain hemorrhage in 1938.

82. The Astaire reference, referring to Cagney practicing steps with the help of his professionally elegant neighbor, is from "Hollywood Rediscovers the 'Short' ... On Cagney and *Zamboanga*," *New York Times*, July 18, 1937.

83. Tuska, *Vanishing Legion*, p. 185.

84. Title unknown, *The New Republic*, October 13, 1937.

85. "The Screen: James Cagney Comes A-Hoofing in Grand National's *Something to Sing About* at the Globe," *New York Times*, September 21, 1937.

86. "Film Reviews: *Something to Sing About*," *Variety*, September 1, 1937.

87. Gene Fernett, *Hollywood's Poverty Row, 1930–1950* (Satellite Beach, Fla.: Coral Reef Publications, 1973), p. 48.

88. John McCabe, *Cagney* (New York: Knopf Doubleday, 2013), p. 155. *Something to Sing About* fell into the public domain in the 1960s and was issued by many home video purveyors, including Hal Roach Studios, which put out a colorized version in 1987.

89. Astaire's only pre-*Damsel in Distress* film appearance without Rogers was his first feature: *Dancing Lady* (MGM 1933), in which he appeared briefly but memorably to dance twice with star Joan Crawford.

90. Bob Thomas, *Astaire: The Man, the Dancer, the Life of Fred Astaire* (New York: St. Martin's, 1984), p. 119.

91. Fred Astaire, *Steps in Time* (New York: Harper, 1959), p. 229.

92. Jessie Matthews told entertainer Michael Feinstein in 1979 that she had wanted to make *A Damsel in Distress* but that her film company (Gaumont) wouldn't lend her out. Feinstein admitted, though, that "Jessie was prone to fantastic inventions." (See Michael Feinstein and Ian Jackman, *The Gershwins and Me: A Personal History in Twelve Songs* [New York: Simon & Schuster, 2012], p. 295.)

93. Marilyn Ann Moss, *Giant: George Stevens, a Life on Film* (Madison: University of Wisconsin Press, 2004), pp. 52–53. The quote is from a transcript of an interview of Stevens by historians Joseph McBride and Patrick McGilligan in 1974.

94. Joan Fontaine, *No Bed of Roses: An Autobiography* (New York: Morrow, 1978), p. 88.

95. Moss, *Giant*, p. 51, quoted from Stevens interview with McBride and McGilligan.

96. Brian Taves, *P.G. Wodehouse and Hollywood: Screenwriting, Satires and Adaptations* (Jefferson, N.C.: McFarland, 2006), p. 97. The Gershwins' concept was adapted in 1987 into a "new" Gershwin musical, *Reaching for the Moon*, which was renamed *A Foggy Day* for a 1988 run.

97. A ninth song, "Pay Some Attention to Me," was written for, but not used in, the film.

98. A dancer seen imitating Astaire's character just before the "Bothered" number is Joe Niemeyer, a vaudevillian who impressed Astaire so much that the star made Niemeyer his stand-in, which he was for the next two decades.

99. Thomas, *Astaire*, p. 146; John Mueller, *Astaire Dancing: The Musical Films* (New York: Knopf, 1985), p. 132. Ira Gershwin's lyrics to "Put Me to the Test," which were not used in *A Damsel in Distress*, were finally heard, set to a Jerome Kern melody and sung by Gene Kelly, in the 1944 Columbia musical *Cover Girl*.

100. Mueller, *Astaire Dancing*, p. 132.

101. "Juve Joins Astaire," *Variety*, August 4, 1937. The item states that Rooney had been "penciled in" for the role played by Watson.

102. Jewell, *A Titan Is Born*, p. 143.

103. "Film Reviews: *A Damsel in Distress*," *Variety*, November 24, 1937; "The Screen: Fred Astaire & Co. Rescue *A Damsel in Distress* at the Rivoli," *New York Times*, November 25, 1937.

104. Mueller, *Astaire Dancing*, p. 128.

105. Astaire, *Steps in Time*, p. 229.

106. Taves, *P.G. Wodehouse*, p. 95.

107. Pandro S. Berman interview, "Episode 2: Let's Face the Music and Dance," *Hollywood: The Golden Years: The RKO Story*, BBC-TV, 1987. VHS, author's collection.

108. Fontaine, *No Bed of Roses*, p. 89.

109. Jeffrey Brown Martin, *Ben Hecht: Hollywood Screenwriter* (Ann Arbor, Mich.: UMI Research Press, 1985), p. 142.

110. "Film Reviews: *Let Freedom Ring*," *Variety*, February 22, 1939.

111. Information contained in Motion Picture Producers and Distributors of America/Production Code Administration files indicates censorship of some of the film's touchier lines. German censors deleted song lyrics describing the U.S. as a land of freedom, and censors in Estonia erased part of a speech by Eddy in which he exhorted "You Germans, Italians, Jews, Russians.... All you who are oppressed ... here you are free."

112. "Showmen's Reviews: *Let Freedom Ring*," *Motion Picture Herald*, February 18, 1939.

113. James Robert Parish, *The Jeanette MacDonald Story* (New York: Mason/Charter, 1976), p. 120.

114. Ibid., p. 119.

115. Anthony Slide, *Eccentrics of Comedy* (Lanham, Md.: Scarecrow Press, 1998), p. 103.

116. "Behind the Scenes in Hollywood," King Features Syndicate column, cited from Vineland, N.J. *Evening Times*, May 8, 1939; "Jimmie Fidler in Hollywood," McNaught Syndicate column, May 1939.

Bibliography

The American Film Institute Catalog of Motion Pictures: Feature Films, 1921–30. New York: Bowker, 1971.
The American Film Institute Catalog of Motion Pictures: Feature Films, 1931–40. New York: Bowker, 1993.
Armstrong, Louis. *Louis Armstrong, in His Own Words: Selected Writings.* New York: Oxford University Press, 1999.
Astaire, Fred. *Steps in Time.* New York: Harper, 1959.
Bach, Bob, and Ginger Mercer. *Our Huckleberry Friend: The Life, Times and Lyrics of Johnny Mercer.* Secaucus, N.J.: Lyle Stuart, 1982.
Barrios, Richard. *A Song in the Dark: The Birth of the Musical Film.* New York: Oxford University Press, 1995, 2010.
Behlmer, Rudy, ed. *Inside Warner Bros., 1935–1951.* New York: Simon & Schuster, 1987.
_____. *Memo From Darryl F. Zanuck: The Golden Years at Twentieth Century-Fox.* New York: Grove Press, 1995.
Bergreen, Laurence. *As Thousands Cheer: The Life of Irving Berlin.* New York: Viking, 1990.
Bernstein, Matthew. *Walter Wanger: Hollywood Independent.* Minneapolis: University of Minnesota Press, 1994.
Berrett, Joshua, ed. *The Louis Armstrong Companion: Eight Decades of Commentary.* New York: Schirmer, 1999.
Block, Hayley Taylor, with Alex Ben Block and Lucy Autrey Wilson, eds. *George Lucas's Blockbusting: A Decade-by-Decade Survey of Timeless Movies Including Untold Secrets of Their Financial and Cultural Success.* New York: HarperCollins, 2010.
Bradley, Edwin M. *The First Hollywood Musicals: A Critical Filmography of 171 Features, 1927 Through 1932.* Jefferson, N.C.: McFarland, 1996.
_____. *The First Hollywood Sound Shorts, 1926–31.* Jefferson, N.C.: McFarland, 2005.
_____. *Unsung Hollywood Musicals of the Golden Era: 50 Overlooked Films and Their Stars, 1929–1939.* Jefferson, N.C.: McFarland, 2016.
Brooker, John. *The Happiest Trails.* CP Entertainment Books/Lulu.com, 2017.
Burton, Jack. *The Blue Book of Hollywood Musicals.* Watkins Glen, N.Y.: Century House, 1953.
Butler, David, with Irene Kahn Atkins. *David Butler: A Directors Guild of America Oral History.* Metuchen, N.J.: Scarecrow Press, 1993.
Cagney, James. *Cagney by Cagney.* Garden City, N.Y.: Doubleday, 1976.
Christensen, Lawrence O., with William E. Foley, Gary R. Kremer, and Kenneth H. Wynn, eds. *Dictionary of Missouri Biography.* Columbia: University of Missouri Press, 1999.
Clarke, Gerald. *Get Happy: The Life of Judy Garland.* New York: Random House, 2009.
Connor, D. Russell. *Benny Goodman: Listen to His Legacy.* Metuchen, N.J., and London: Scarecrow Press and the Institute of Jazz Studies, 1988.
Cornes, Judy. *Stuart Erwin: The Invisible Actor.* Lanham, Md.: Scarecrow Press, 2001.
Coslow, Sam. *Cocktails for Two: The Many Lives of Giant Songwriter Sam Coslow.* New Rochelle, N.Y.: Arlington House, 1977.
Cox, Stephen. *The Munchkins of Oz.* Nashville, Tenn.: Cumberland House, 1996.
Crosby, Bing, with Pete Martin. *Call Me Lucky.* New York: Simon & Schuster, 1953.
Custen, George F. *Twentieth Century's Fox: Darryl F. Zanuck and the Culture of Hollywood.* New York: Basic Books, 1998.
Davis, Ronald L. *Mary Martin: Broadway Legend.* Norman: University of Oklahoma Press, 2008.
Duchen, Jessica. *Erich Wolfgang Korngold.* London: Phaidon Press, 1996.
Elder, Jane Lenz. *Alice Faye: A Life Beyond the Silver Screen.* Oxford: University Press of Mississippi, 2002.
Ellis, Mary. *Those Dancing Years: An Autobiography.* London: John Murray, 1982.
Emerson, Ken. *Doo-dah! Stephen Foster and the Rise of American Popular Culture.* New York: Simon & Schuster, 1997.
Eskew, Glenn T. *Johnny Mercer: Southern Songwriter for the World.* Athens: University of Georgia Press, 2013.
Farmer, Frances. *Will There Really Be a Morning?* New York: Putnam, 1972.

Fawkes, Richard. *Opera on Film*. London: Duckworth, 2000.
Feinstein, Michael, and Ian Jackman. *The Gershwins and Me: A Personal History in Twelve Songs*. New York: Simon & Schuster, 2012.
Fernett, Gene. *Hollywood's Poverty Row, 1930–1950*. Satellite Beach, Fla.: Coral Reef Publications, 1973.
Firestone, Ross. *Swing, Swing, Swing: The Life and Times of Benny Goodman*. New York: W.W. Norton, 1993.
Flinn, Caryl. *Brass Diva: The Life and Legends of Ethel Merman*. Berkeley: University of California Press, 2009.
Fontaine, Joan. *No Bed of Roses: An Autobiography*. New York: Morrow, 1978.
Franceschina, John Charles. *Hermes Pan: The Man Who Danced With Fred Astaire*. New York: Oxford University Press, 2012.
Freedland, Michael. *Irving Berlin*. New York: Stein and Day, 1974.
_____. *Jolson: The Story of Al Jolson*. Portland, Ore.: Valentine Mitchell, 2007.
Fricke, John. *Judy: A Legendary Film Career*. Philadelphia: Running Press, 2010.
Fryer, Paul. *The Opera Singer and the Silent Film*. Jefferson, N.C.: McFarland, 2005.
Furia, Philip. *Skylark: The Life and Times of Johnny Mercer*. New York: Macmillan, 2004.
_____, and Michael L. Lasser. *America's Songs: The Stories Behind the Songs of Broadway, Hollywood, and Tin Pan Alley*. New York: Routledge, 2006.
Gabbard, Krin. *Jammin' at the Margins: Jazz and the American Cinema*. Chicago: University of Chicago Press, 1996.
_____, ed. *Representing Jazz*. Durham, N.C.: Duke University Press, 1995.
George-Warren, Holly. *Public Cowboy No. 1: The Life and Times of Gene Autry*. New York: Oxford University Press, 2007.
Giddins, Gary. *Bing Crosby: A Pocketful of Dreams: The Early Years, 1903–1940*. New York: Little, Brown, 2001.
_____. *Natural Selection: Gary Giddins on Comedy, Film, Music, and Books*. New York: Oxford University Press, 2006.
Goldman, Herbert G. *Jolson: The Legend Comes to Life*. New York: Oxford University Press, 1988.
Gould, Neil. *Victor Herbert: A Theatrical Life*. New York: Fordham University Press, 2008.
Green, Abel, and Joe Laurie, Jr. *Show Biz From Vaude to Video*. New York, Henry Holt, 1951.
Greenspan, Charlotte. *Pick Yourself Up: Dorothy Fields and the American Musical*. New York: Oxford University Press, 2010.
Griffith, Richard. *The Movie Stars*. Garden City, N.Y.: Doubleday, 1970.
Hair, Raymond D., and Jurgen Wolfer. *Thinking of You: The Story of Kay Kyser*. Albany, Ga.: BearManor Media, 2016.
Harkins, Anthony. *Hillbilly: A Cultural History of an American Icon*. New York: Oxford University Press, 2004.
Hirschhorn, Clive. *The Hollywood Musical*. New York: Crown, 1981.
Hope, Bob, and Bob Thomas. *The Road to Hollywood*. New York: Doubleday, 1977.
Jewell, Richard B. *RKO Radio Pictures: A Titan Is Born*. Berkeley, Calif.: University of California Press, 2012.
_____, with Vernon Harbin. *The RKO Story*. New York: Octopus Books, 1982.
Kaufman, David. *Some Enchanted Evenings: The Glittering Life and Times of Mary Martin*. New York: St. Martin's, 2016.
Klauber, Bruce. *World of Gene Krupa: That Legendary Drummin' Man*. Ventura, Calif.: Pathfinder Publishing, 1990.
Kobal, John. *Gotta Sing Gotta Dance: A Pictorial History of Film Musicals*. London: Hamlyn, 1971.
Koszarski, Richard. *The Astoria Studio and Its Fabulous Films*. New York: Dover, 1983.
Kreuger, Miles, ed. *The Movie Musical from Vitaphone to 42nd Street, as Reported in a Great Fan Magazine*. New York: Dover, 1975.
Lamparski, Richard. *Whatever Became Of …? All-New Eleventh Series*. New York: Crown, 1989.
Lasky, Jesse L. *I Blow My Own Horn*. Garden City, N.Y.: Doubleday, 1957.
Layton, James, and David Pierce, *King of Jazz: Paul Whiteman's Technicolor Revue*. Severn, Md.: Media History Press, 2016.
Lees, Gene. *Portrait of Johnny: The Life of John Herndon Mercer*. New York: Knopf Doubleday, 2009.
Liebman, Roy. *Vitaphone Films: A Catalogue of the Features and Shorts*. Jefferson, N.C.: McFarland, 2003.
Lillie, Beatrice, with James Brough. *Every Other Inch a Lady*. Garden City, N.Y.: Doubleday, 1972.
Maltin, Leonard. *The Great Movie Shorts*. New York: Bonanza, 1972.
_____. *Movie Comedy Teams*. New York: Plume, 1970.
Mank, Gregory William. *Women in Horror Films, 1930s*. Jefferson, N.C.: McFarland, 1999.
Martin, Jeffrey Brown. *Ben Hecht: Hollywood Screenwriter*. Ann Arbor, Mich.: UMI Research Press, 1985.
Martin, Mary. *My Heart Belongs*. New York: Morrow, 1976.
McCabe, John. *Cagney*. New York: Knopf Doubleday, 2013.
McGilligan, Patrick. *Cagney: The Actor as Auteur*. South Brunswick, N.J.: A.S. Barnes & Co., 1975.
Moore, Grace. *You're Only Human Once*. Garden City, N.Y.: Doubleday, Doran, 1944.
Moseley, Roy. *Evergreen: Victor Saville in His Own Words*. Carbondale: Southern Illinois University Press, 2000.
Moss, Marilyn Ann. *Giant: George Stevens, a Life on Film*. Madison: University of Wisconsin Press, 2004.
_____. *Raoul Walsh: The True Adventures of Hollywood's Legendary Director*. Lexington: University Press of Kentucky, 2011.

Mueller, John. *Astaire Dancing: The Musical Films.* New York: Knopf, 1985.
Nott, Robert. *The Films of Randolph Scott.* Jefferson, N.C.: McFarland, 2004.
Ohmer, Susan. *George Gallup in Hollywood.* New York: Columbia University Press, 2006.
Parish, James Robert. *The Jeanette MacDonald Story.* New York: Mason/Charter, 1976.
Pitrone, Jean Maddern. *Take It From the Big Mouth: The Life of Martha Raye.* Lexington: University Press of Kentucky, 1999.
Pitts, Michael R. *Poverty Row Studios, 1929–1940.* Jefferson, N.C.: McFarland, 1997.
Preminger, Otto. *Preminger: An Autobiography.* Garden City, N.J.: Doubleday, 1977.
Quirk, Lawrence J. *Bob Hope, The Road Well Traveled.* New York: Applause Books, 2000.
Rice, Christina. *Ann Dvorak: Hollywood's Forgotten Rebel.* Lexington: University Press of Kentucky, 2013.
Robinson, Ray. *Iron Horse: Lou Gehrig in His Time.* New York: W.W. Norton, 1990.
Rogers, Ginger. *Ginger: My Story.* New York: HarperCollins, 1991.
Schultz, Margie. *Irene Dunne: A Bio-Bibliography.* Westport, Conn.: Greenwood, 1991.
Scott, Ian. *In Capra's Shadow: The Life and Career of Screenwriter Robert Riskin.* Lexington: University Press of Kentucky, 2006.
Shelley, Peter. *Frances Farmer: The Life and Films of a Troubled Star.* Jefferson, N.C.: McFarland, 2010.
Slide, Anthony. *Eccentrics of Comedy.* Lanham, Md.: Scarecrow Press, 1998.
_____. *The Encyclopedia of Vaudeville.* Westport, Conn.: Greenwood, 1994.
Solomon, Aubrey. *The Fox Film Corporation, 1915–1935: A History and Filmography.* Jefferson, N.C.: McFarland, 2011.
_____. *Twentieth Century-Fox: A Corporate and Financial History.* Lanham, Md.: Rowman & Littlefield, 2002.
Spivak, Jeffrey. *Buzz: The Life and Art of Busby Berkeley.* Lexington: University Press of Kentucky, 2011.
Sragow, Michael. *Victor Fleming: An American Movie Master.* Lexington: University Press of Kentucky, 2013.
Stanfield, Peter. *Horse Opera: The Strange History of the 1930s Singing Cowboy.* Urbana: University of Illinois Press, 2002.
Stuart, Gloria, with Sylvia Thompson. *Gloria Stuart: I Just Kept Hoping.* New York: Little, Brown, 1999.
Taves, Brian. *P.G. Wodehouse and Hollywood: Screenwriting, Satires and Adaptations.* Jefferson, N.C.: McFarland, 2006.
_____. *Robert Florey: The French Expressionist.* Metuchen, N.J.: Scarecrow, 1987.
Thomas, Bob. *Astaire: The Man, the Dancer, the Life of Fred Astaire.* New York: St. Martin's, 1984.
Thomas, Tony. *The Dick Powell Story.* Burbank, Calif.: Riverwood Press, 1993.
Tibbetts, John C. *Composers in the Movies: Studies in Musical Biography.* New Haven, Conn.: Yale University Press, 2008.
Tomlin, Pinky, with Lynette Wert. *The Object of My Affection: An Autobiography.* Norman: University of Oklahoma Press, 1981.
Tucker, David C. *Martha Raye: Film and Television Clown.* Jefferson, N.C.: McFarland, 2016.
Turner, Lana. *Lana—the Lady, the Legend, the Truth.* New York: Dutton, 1982.
Tuska, Jon. *The Vanishing Legion: A History of Mascot Pictures 1927–1935.* Jefferson, N.C.: McFarland, 1982.
Vansant, Jacqueline. *Austria Made in Hollywood.* Rochester, N.Y.: Boydell & Brewer, 2019.
Villecco, Tony. *Silent Stars Speak: Interviews With Twelve Cinema Pioneers.* Jefferson, N.C.: McFarland, 2001.
Weinstat, Hertzel, and Bert Wechsler. *Dear Rogue: A Biography of the American Baritone Lawrence Tibbett.* Portland, Ore.: Amadeus Press, 1996.
Wellman, William Jr. *Wild Bill Wellman, Hollywood Rebel.* New York; Pantheon Books, 2015.
Williamson, J.W. *Hillbillyland: What the Movies Did to the Mountains and What the Mountains Did to the Movies.* Chapel Hill: University of North Carolina Press, 1995.
Young, William H., with Nancy K. Young. *Music of the Great Depression.* Westport, Conn.: Greenwood Press, 1995.
Zimmers, Tighe E. *Tin Pan Alley Girl: A Biography of Ann Ronell.* Jefferson, N.C.: McFarland, 2009.
Zolotow, Maurice. *Billy Wilder in Hollywood.* New York: Putnam, 1977.

Index

Unless otherwise indicated, titles listed in *italics* are films, and titles in "quotes" are music compositions/musical numbers. Numbers in ***bold italics*** refer to pages with photographs. Entries marked with an asterisk (*) are films featured in this book.

Abbott, George 7
Aborn, Milton 56
Abraham Lincoln: Vampire Hunter (2012) 111
Absolute Quiet (1936) 163
Acuff, Roy 105
Adams, Samuel Hopkins 240
Adamson, Harold 181
Adler, Larry 195
"Advice to Lovers" 35
"After the Ball" 42
After the Ball (1929) 42
Ager, Cecelia 95–96
"Ah! I Have Sighed to Rest Me" 167
Ahn, Philip 248
Air Mail (1932) 38
Akst, Harry 244
Alberni, Luis 167, 169, 210
Alda, Robert 41
"Alexander's Ragtime Band" 62, 64
Alexander's Ragtime Band (1938) 3, 43, 44, 49, 50, 59–65, ***61***, 67, 71
"Alice in Wonderland" 62
All About Eve (1950) 226
"All Alone" 63
All American Chump (1936) 82
All-American Co-ed (1941) 82
All Quiet on the Western Front (1930) 19, 20
All the King's Horses (1935) 162
Allen, Bob 133
Allen, Eddie 248
Allen, Gracie 195, 225, 243, 250, 253
Allen, Judith 226, 227
Allen, Steve 214
Allyson, June 135
"Almost Time for Roundup" 127
Alperson, Edward L. 57, 120, 246, 249
Alvarado, Don ***150***

Ambassador Pictures *see* Melody Pictures
Ambush (1939) 159
Ameche, Don 2, 44, 49, ***49***, 50, 61, ***61***, 62, 63, 64
Ames, Adrienne 47
Amos 'n' Andy (TV series) 126
Anderson, John Murray 5, 19
Andrews, Robert Hardy 151
Angels with Dirty Faces (1938) 249
Annie Get Your Gun (stage musical) 63
"Any Old Love" 248
The Apartment (1960) 199
"An Apple for the Teacher" 69
"April in My Heart" 59
Archainbaud, George 214
Archie Gottler, His Songs Are Sung in a Million Homes (1928) 42
Are You There?* (1930) 3, 31–36, ***33*
Arkansas Judge (1941) 105
Arledge, John 54
Arlen, Richard 130, 225
Armida 28
Armstrong, Louis "Satchmo" 2, 104, 191, 207, 208, 209, 215
Armstrong, Robert ***57***, 58
Arnheim, Gus (and Orchestra) 195, 199
Arnold, Edward 256
Around the World (1943) 218
Arthur, Al 99
Arthur, Jean 73
Arthur, Johnny 105, 248
"An Artist's Life" 187
Associated Features 122, 125
Astaire, Adele 251
Astaire, Fred 1, 16, 40, 52, 54, 55, 62, 167, 174, 177, 219, 239, 240, 241, 242, 248, 250–254, ***251***
Asther, Nils 43

Atkinson, Brooks 56
Atwill, Lionel 163
August, Joseph 252
Austin, Gene 91
Austria Made in Hollywood (book) 201
Autry, Gene 2, 3, 77, 104, 106, 107, 108, 109, 110, 111, 112, 131, 135, 144
The Awful Truth (1937) 172
Ayres, Lew 236, 241, 258

Babbitt, Harry 215
Babes in Arms (1939) 230
Babes in Toyland (stage musical) 71, 72
Baby Le Roy 229
Bach, J.S. 210
Back Street (1932) 232
Baclanova, Olga 33, 35
Bacon, Lloyd 134
Baer, Max 142, 145
"Bagdad Daddies" 35
Baker, Benny 159
Baker, Graham 217
"The Balboa" 81
Ball, Ernest R. 44
Ball, Lucille 54, 176, 177, 217
Ball of Fire (1941) 214
Ballew, Smith 107, 113, 114, 115, 130, 131
"Baltimore Bubble" 203, 204
Banjo on My Knee (1936) 243
Bankhead, Tallulah 121
Banks, Leslie 232, 233
Bara, Theda 30
Baravalle, Victor 252
The Barber of Seville (opera) 169
Barbier, George 53, 54
Barnes, Edwin N.C. 50
Barnes, George 151
Barnett, Vince 143, 144, 145
Barnum Was Right (1929) 10
Barrett, Paul 145

Index

The Barretts of Wimpole Street (1934) 76
Barrie, Mona 248
Barrie, Wendy 170
Barrios, Richard 147
Barris, Harry 225
Barry, Wesley 28
Barrymore, John 218
Barrymore, Lionel 256, 257
Bartholomew, Freddie 156
Bartlett, Ella Herbert 72, 73
Bartlett, Michael 147, 148, **165**, 166, 167
"Bashful" 24
Batcheller, George R. 26
Bates, Granville 211
Batie, Franklyn 222
A Battery of Songs (1930) 42
The Battle of Paris (1929) 94
Baxter, Warner 24, 77
Be Mine Tonight (1932) 157
Beahan, Charles 26
Beard, Matthew "Stymie" 127
Beatrice Lillie and Her Boy Friends (1929) 32
"Beautiful Dreamer" 50
Becker, Charles 138, 139, 140
A Bedtime Story (1933) 229
Beery, Noah 222
Belasco, David 161
Bell, Nelson B. 59
Bell, Rex 144
"Bell Song" 177, 178
Bella Donna (1934) 161
Bennett, Constance 13
Bennett, Joe 248
Benny, Jack 42, 195, 230
The Benny Goodman Story (1956) 214
Bergen, Edgar 167, 253
Bergreen, Laurence 62
Berkeley, Busby 1, 10, 148, 150, 151, 196, 197, 258, 259
Berlin, Irving 2, 41, 42, 43, 44, 61, 62, 63, 64, 65, 71, 220
Berman, Pandro S. 241, 252, 254
Bernie, Ben 213
Berry, Chuck 190
Bert, Flo 22
The Beverly Hillbillies (TV series) 77, 144
Bickford, Charles 11
Big Boy (1930) 220–224, **221**
Big Boy (stage musical) 221, 222, 223
The Big Broadcast (1932) 225, 226
*The Big Broadcast of 1937 (1936) 92, 191, 192–197, **195**
The Big Broadcast of 1938 (1938) 195, 196, 213
The Big Trail (1930) 28
Billboard (periodical) 19, 209
"Black Moonlight" 227

Blandick, Clara 202
Blane, Sally 12
Blaze o' Glory (1929) 57
Blondell, Joan 134, 209, 210, 211
Blore, Eric 53, 55, 177
Blue, Ben 167
The Blue Bird (1940) 50
"The Blue Danube" 200, 201
"Blue Moon" 195
Blue of the Night (1933) 225
A Blueprint for Murder (1953) 74
Blystone, John 22
Bogart, Humphrey 78, 102, 258
Bogle, Donald 128
La Boheme (opera) 180, 181
Boland, Mary 163, 233
Boles, John 6, 17, **18**, 20, 150, 158, 159, 225, 232, 233
Boone, Pat 192
Boos, Horace 204
*Border Romance (1930) 27–29, **28**, 106
Born to Dance (1936) 253
Boswell, Connee 69, 89
Boucicault, Dion 30, 31
Boyd, William 132, 227
Boyer, Charles 114
Boyle, Johnny 247
Bradford, John 237
Bradley, Grace 53, 54, 58, 91, 227
Brady, Alice 169
Branch, Houston 18, 19
"The Breakaway" 22
Breen, Bobby 2, 129, 138
Brendel, El 6, 21, 22, 23, **23**, 24, 99
Brennan, Walter 82
Brent, Evelyn **8**, 9, 10
Brent, George 170, 240, 241
Bressart, Felix 50
Brett, Jeremy 163
The Brian Sisters 89, 90, 98
Brice, Fanny 64
Bringing Up Baby (1938) 172
Brisson, Carl 162
*Broadway (1929) 6, 7–10, **8**, 18
Broadway (1942) 10
Broadway (play) 7, 8
Broadway Gondolier (1935) 211
The Broadway Melody (1929) 5
Broadway Melody of 1936 (1935) 114
Broadway Melody of 1938 (1937) 83
Broadway Melody of 1940 (1940) 254
Broadway Scandals (1929) 13, 30
*Broadway Serenade (1939) 177, 191, 219, 254–256, 258–260, **259**
Broadway Varieties (radio show) 151
"Broadway's Gone Hill-Billy" 77
Broderick, Helen 55, 181, 210

Brokenshire, Norman 41, 43
Bromfield, Louis 209
*The Bronze Buckaroo (1939) 123, 127, 128
"The Bronze Buckaroo Rides Again" (record album) 128
Brooklyn Daily Eagle (newspaper) 99, 135
Brooks, Louise 174
Brooks, Mel 97
Brophy, Edward 58
Brother Rat (1938) 211
Brower, Otto 110
Brown, Clarence 179
Brown, Joe E. 119, 208
Brown, Johnny [John] Mack 12, **12**, 13, 106
Brown, Lew 22, 220
Brown, Melville 13
Brown, Nacio Herb 42
Brown, Rowland 249
Bruce, Nigel 167
Bruce, Virginia 87, 169, 256
Brulatour, Jules 179, 180, 182
"Buckin' the Wind" 227
Buell, Jed 125, 128, 129, 136–137, 138, 139
"Bugle Call Rag" 194
Burgess, Dorothy *iv*, 38
Burlesque (stage musical) 13
Burnette, Lester "Smiley" **110**, 111–112
Burns, Bob 2, 42, 77, 78, 92, 93, **93**, 94, 95, 96, 117, 119, 195
Burns, George 195, 225, 243, 250, 253
Burroughs, Edgar Rice 129
Burtis, James 26
Burton, Val 29
Butler, David 22, 33, 81, 97, 98, 99, 216, 217
Butterworth, Charles 256
Buzzell, Eddie 26
"By the Light of the Silvery Moon" 66
Bye Bye Birdie (1963) 144
Byington, Spring 115
Byrd, Ralph 102

The Cabin Kids 77
Cadman, Charles Wakefield 18, 19
Caesar, Irving 169
Caesar, Sid 97
Cagney, James 41, 44, 134, 142, 166, 219, 246, 247, **247**, 248, 249, 258
The California Collegians 199
Call Her Savage (1932) 121
Call Me Lucky (book) 226
The Callahans and the Murphys (1927) 30
Calling All Stars (stage revue) 150–151

Calloway, Cab 89, 174, 189
Camel Caravan (radio show) 195
Campbell, Louise 67
"A Campfire, a Prairie Moon and You" 144
Campus Rhythm (1943) 82
Canova, Judy 81, 102, 105
Cantor, Eddie 64, 66, 87, 221
Caponsacchi (opera) 171
Capra, Frank 25, 166, 172, 173, 174
Captain Blood (1935) 158
Captain of the Guard (1930) 10, 17–20, **18**, 72
Carefree (1938) 251, 254
Carmen (1915) 146
Carmen (opera) 169
Carmichael, Hoagy 55, 59
Carminati, Tullio 162
Carné, Marcel 185
Carnegie Hall (1947) 178
"Caro nome" 147, 164, 176
Carol, Sue 22
Carolina Blues (1944) 218
The Carpenters 192
Carr, Alexander 16
Carr, Mary 26–27
Carr, Nat 14, 15, 16
Carr, Sabin W. 125
Carradine, John 63
Carroll, Earl 90
Carroll, Harrison 226, 260
Carroll, Madeleine 114
Carus, Emma 62
Caruso, Enrico 16, 42, 146, 154, 160
Casa Manana (stage revue) 152
Case, Anna 147
The Cat and the Canary (1939) 214
Cat Ballou (1965) 180
Catlett, Walter 22, 167, 208
Cats (stage musical) 42
Cavalleria Rusticana (opera) 155
Cavanaugh, Hobert 217
Cawthorn, Joseph 13, **47**, 48
CBS (Columbia Broadcasting System) 64, 121, 151, 195, 197, 218
Cervantes, Alejandro Perez 112
Champagne Waltz (1937) 159, 191, 197–201, **200**
Chandler, Lane 89
Chaney, Lon 67, 179
Chanslor, Roy 180
Chaplin, Charlie 224
Chapman, Frank 158, 201
Charlie Chan Carries On (1931) 37
"Charmaine" 11
Chasen, Dave 53
Chasing Rainbows (1930) 29
Chatburn, Jean 122
Chatterton, Ruth 240

Check and Double Check (1930) 225
"Cheer Up and Smile" 24
Chelsea Pictures *see* Melody Pictures
Chesterfield Motion Picture Corporation 25, 26, 166
Chevalier, Maurice 6, 38, 87, 110, 147, 162, 195, 219, 228–231, **229**
Chicago Tribune (newspaper) 48, 95
"Chopsticks" 215
Christy, Dorothy 110
Christy, Edwin P. 48, 50
Christy, Eileen 48
Churchill, Berton 244
Churchill, Winston 16
Churchward, James 111
Ciannelli, Eduardo 177
Cimarron (1931) 232
Citizen Kane (1941) 77, 180
Clair, René 185, 230
Claire, Bernice 20
Clare, Sidney 244
Clarke, Mae 246
Clifford and Moran *see* Moran, Pat
Clifford, Jack 181
Clinton, Larry 209
Clive, E.E. 115
Clooney, Rosemary 68
Close Harmony (1929) 225
Cobb, Irwin S. 143
Cock of the Air (1932) 111
The Cock-Eyed World (1929) 5, 22, 121
Coe, Charles Francis 27
Cohan, George M. 6, 41, 44, 248
Cohen, Emanuel 226, 227
Cohn, Harry 147
Colbert, Claudette 50, 72, 73, 163, 166, 173
College Holiday (1936) 82
College Humor (1933) 224, 225, 226
College Rhythm (1934) 43, 82
College Scandal (1935) 82
College Swing (1938) 96
Collegiate (1936) 43, 114
Collier, William, Jr. 24
Collyer, June 13
Colonna, Jerry 210
Colorado Sunset (1939) 144
A Colored Life: The Herb Jeffries Story (2008) 128
Columbia Broadcasting System *see* CBS
Columbia Pictures 25, 30, 31, 77, 82, 136, 138, 147, 166, 169, 171, 172, 173, 174, 175, 178, 218
Columbo, Russ 11, 225
Come and Get It (1936) 82, 118
"Comes the Revolution, Baby" 54

Como, Perry 204
Compson, Betty 15
Conan Doyle, Arthur 232
Condor Productions 120
Confessions of a Co-ed (1931) 225
Conn, Maurice 86–91
Conn Pictures *see* Melody Pictures
Connolly, Walter 72, **72**, 73, 74
The Conquerors (1932) 232
Conrad, Con 9, 121, 155
Conrad, Eddie 151
Conti, Albert 13
A Continental Evening (1930) 16
Coogan, Jackie 53, 87
Cook, Elisha, Jr. 81
Cook, Joe 53
Cooper, Gary 114, 115, 132, 226
Cooper, Merian C. 232, 233, 234
Coots, J. Fred 42
Coquette (1929) 13
"Corn Pickin'" 210
Cornes, Judy 82
Cortez, Ricardo 143
Coslow, Sam 77, 94, 95, 117, 119, 162, 225, 226, 227
Cosmopolitan Productions 132
Cossart, Ernest 115, 200
"Could I Be in Love?" 200
Counselman, William 216, 237
Cowan, Jerome 73
Cowan, Lester 199
Coward, Noël 54, 160
Cowboy from Brooklyn (1938) 107, 132–135, 207
Cowboys & Aliens (2011) 111
"A Cowboy's Life" 131
Crabbe, Buster 129
"Cradle Me with a Hotcha Lullaby" 227
Cramer, Duncan 34
Crawford, Joan 13, 28, 47, 106, 111, 131, 258
Creacy, Don 105
Cremin, Arthur 190
Crisler, B.R. 171, 218
Crosby, Bing 1, 2, 6, 16, 34, 41, 55, 66, 67, 68, **68**, 69, 92, 94, 107, 108, 114, 117, 118, 119, 134, 135, 158, 195, 199, 214, 216, 219, 224–228, 230, 248
Crosby, Bob 190
Crosland, Alan 221
Crouse, Russel 71, 94
The Crowd (1928) 7, 25
Crowther, Bosley 73, 74, 210
Cruise, Tom 49
Cruze, James 15
Cry Terror! (1958) 74
The Cuban Love Song (1931) 169
Cummings, Constance 38
Curtis, Billy 137, **137**, 138, 139, 140
Curtis, Tony 213

Curwood, James Oliver 87
Custen, George F. 44

Dailey, Dan 65
Dames (1934) 1, 133, 230
Damita, Lili 121, 122
Damrosch, Walter 68, **68**
A Damsel in Distress* (1937) 249–254, **251
The Dance of Life (1929) 13
Dancing Co-Ed (1939) 191
Dancing Lady (1933) 11
The Dandridge Sisters (with Dorothy Dandridge) 208
Danforth, William 56, 58
Daniels, Bebe 6, 150
Daniels, Danny 68
"Danny Boy" 153
Dare, Irene 2
"Dark Eyes" 196
"Darktown Strutters' Ball" 69
Darro, Frankie 86, 87, 110
Daughters Courageous (1939) 210
Davidson, Max 58
Davies, Marion 13, 228
Davis, Benny 43
Davis, Bette 134, 196, 240
Davis, Dix 145
Davis, Joan 98, 244, 245
Davis, Johnnie "Scat" 196
Davis, Rufe 95
d'Avril, Yola 24
Daw, Evelyn 247, 248, 249
The Dawn Patrol (1938) 115
Day, Alice 25, 26
Day, Marceline 26
A Day at the Races (1937) 191
"The Day You Came Along" 227
"Days of Wine and Roses" 55
Dead Men Walk (1943) 138
Decatur, Stephen 25
de Fee, Lois 137
de Havilland, Olivia 207, 252
Delaney, Charles 30
Del Campo, Francisco 121, 122
Delicious (1931) 37
Dell, Claudia 222
de l'Isle, Claude Joseph Rouget 18
Del Rio, Dolores 40, **150**, 151
Del Ruth, Roy 67
DeLuca, Giuseppe 146
DeMille, Cecil B. 11, 26, 146, 226
Dempsey, Jack 129
Dennis, Dick 230
Denny, Reginald 155
The Desert Song (1929) 17, 20, 187
Destry Rides Again (1939) 258
De Sylva, Buddy 22, 220
**The Devil on Horseback* (1936) 120–122, 246
Devine, Andy 233
Dick Tracy (1937) 102

"Did You Ever See a Dream Walking?" 43
Dieckhaus, Mrs. E. Marie Cooper Oehler 64
Diege, Samuel 143, 144, 145
Dietrich, Marlene 140
Dietz, Howard 170
DiMaggio, Joe 129
DiPaolo, Dante 68
Disney, Walt 64, 98
Divine, Father M.J. 127
Dix, Richard 13, 232, 233
Dixiana (1930) 150, 152
Dixon, Harland 247
Dixon, Mort 151
Dr. Rhythm (1938) 34
Dodge City (1938) 210
"Doin' the Raccoon" 42
Don Juan (1926) 147, 164
Don Winslow of the Coast Guard (1943) 29
Don Winslow of the Navy (1942) 29
Donahue, Al, and His Orchestra 209
Donahue, William "Red" 94
"Don't Mention Love to Me" 241
The Doorway to Hell (1930) 249
The Dorsey Brothers (Tommy and Jimmy) 114, 190, 192
Double Harness (1933) 234
Double Indemnity (1944) 199
Down in "Arkansaw"* (1938) 91, 100–103, **103, 104
"Down on the Sunset Trail" 140
"Down the Old Ox Road" 225
Down to Their Last Yacht (1934) 26
"Down with Everything" 81
DownBeat (magazine) 191
Downs, Johnny 79, 80, **80**, 82, 202, 203, **203**, 204
Doyle, Maxine 90
Dracula (1931) 20
Dracula's Daughter (1936) 163
Dresser, Paul 44
Dressler, Marie 30, 155, 156
Drums Along the Mohawk (1939) 50, 258
Dunbar, Dixie 79, 81, 202, 244
The Duncan Sisters 15, 66
Dunn, Emma 39
Dunn, James **236**, 237, 238
Dunne, Irene 200, 218, 232, 233, 234
Dunne, Philip 49
Dunning, Philip 7
Durante, Jimmy 88
Durbin, Deanna 2, 67, 69, 80, 148, 180, 204
Dust Be My Destiny (novel) 209
"The Dusty Road" 257
Duvivier, Julian 185, 186, 187

Dvorak, Ann 230
Dynamite (1929) 11

Each Dawn I Die (novel) 209
Eagle-Lion Pictures 91
Earl Carroll's Vanities (revue) 33
Early to Bed (1936) 163
Eason, B. Reeves "Breezy" 110–111
Eckstrom, Adolph 165, 167, 168
Eddy, Nelson 2, 72, 73, 82, 147, 185, 219, 256, 257, 258, 260
Educational Pictures 77, 142
The Educational Screen (periodical) 54
Edward III 212
Edwards, Gus 2, 28, 42, 43, 66, 67, 68, 69
Edwards, Joan 69
"Eeny, Meeny, Miney, Mo" 55
Eggerth, Marta 158
Elder, Jane Lenz 236
The Elegy (1927) 57
Ellington, Duke 41, 124, 128, 189, 215
Elliott, Gordon "Wild Bill" 89, 90
Elliott, Robert 30
Ellis, Mary 147, 148, 155, 160–163, **161**
Ellis, Robert **8**, 9
Emerson, Ken 46
Eminem 48
The Emperor Waltz (1948) 199
"Empty Saddles (In the Old Corral)" 119
Enright, Ray 210
Epstein, Julius J. 151
Eran trece (1931) 37
Erickson, Leif 117
Erwin, Stuart 59, 79, 80, **80**, 81, 82, 225, 227
Escudero, Vicente 155
Evans and Evans 253
Evergreen (1934) 251
Every Night at Eight (1935) 114, 162
"Every Other Inch a Lady" (book) 32
Everybody Sing (1938) 191
"Everybody Step" 63
Excellent Pictures 15
Exhibitors Herald and Moving Picture World (periodical) 3, 23, 34
Exit Smiling (1926) 32

Fain, Sammy 43
Fairbanks, Douglas 169
"Faithful Mary" (actor) 127
Farmer, Frances 94, 117
"The Farmer Is Not in the Dell" 103
Farrar, Geraldine 146, 154

Farrell, Charles 6, 22, 24, 37
Farrell, Glenda 181, 182, 197
Fatal Lady (1936) 3, 160–163, **161**
Faust (opera) 169, 170, 233
Fay, Frank 32
Faye, Alice 2, 61, **61**, 62, 63, 64, 65, 80, 87, 97, 100, 114, 219, 235–238, **236**, 243–244
Fazenda, Louise 32, 78, 102
Fejos, Paul 6, 7, 8, 9, 10, 17, 18, 19, 20
Felix, Seymour 258
Fenton, Leslie 9
Ferber, Edna 232
Ferguson, Otis 249
Fern, Johnnie 140
Fernett, Gene 249
Fetchit, Stepin 77
Feyder, Jacques 185
Fidler, Jimmie 184, 209, 219
Fields, Benny 195
Fields, Dorothy 174, 176, 180, 241
Fields, W.C. 68, 74, 196, 214
Fifty Million Frenchmen (1931) 5
The 50 Worst Films of All Time (book) 140
The Film Daily (periodical) 5, 30, 39, 48, 69, 90, 99, 122, 128, 135, 138, 145, 155
Fine Arts 145
Finney, Edward 249
Fio-Rito, Ted 53, 114
First National Pictures 30, 109; *see also* Warner Bros. Pictures
Fisher, Fred 42, 44
5,000 Fingers of Dr. T (1953) 140
"Flamingo" 128
Flash Gordon (1936) 111
Die Fledermaus (stage operetta) 59, 187
Fleming, Victor 186
Flesh and Fantasy (1943) 187
Fletcher, Tex 142, 145
Florey, Robert 94
Flying Down to Rio (1933) 1, 40, 251
Flynn, Elinor 26
Flynn, Errol 112, 121, 159, 258
"A Foggy Day (in London Town)" 252
Folies Bergère de Paris (1935) 260–261
Follow the Fleet (1936) 62, 240, 242
Follow Thru (1930) 6
Follow Your Heart (1936) 163–168, **165**
Fonda, Henry 50, 114, 176
Fontaine, Joan 199, **251**, 252, 253, 254
"Foolin' with the Other Woman's Man" 236
Fools for Scandal (1938) 185

Foote, John Taintor 49
Footlight Parade (1933) 1, 247
Foran, Dick (Nick) 107, 135, 236
Ford, John 38
Forest, Frank 195, 200
42nd Street (1933) 1, 37, 87, 133, 207
Foster, Lewis R. 214
Foster, Norman 25, 163
Foster, Stephen 2, 43, 44, 46, 47, 48, 49, 50, 64
Foster, Susanna 74
The Four Blackbirds 126
Four Daughters (1938) 210
Four Mothers (1941) 210
The Four Tones 126, 128
Four Wives (1939) 210
Fowler, Gene 213, 229
Fowley, Douglas 54
Fox, Sidney 26
Fox Film Corporation/20th Century-Fox 5, 6, 21, 22, 23, 24, 25, 30, 31, 33, 34, 35, 36, 37, 38, 40, 43, 44, 46, 48, 49, 50, 59, 61, 62, 64, 65, 67, 74, 77, 78, 79, 81, 82, 83, 87, 89, 91, 93, 96, 97, 98, 99, 100, 103, 109, 111, 121, 128, 130, 152, 154, 163, 168, 169, 170, 192, 199, 216, 232, 234, 235, 236, 237, 238, 242, 243, 244
Foxe, Earle 37
Francis, Kay 170
Francis, Noel 22, **23**, 24
Frankenstein (1931) 20, 111
Frawley, William 48, 247, 248
Freed, Arthur 42
Freedland, Michael 223
Friend, Cliff 43
Friml, Rudolf 161
Frisco Kid (1935) 246
Frisco Sally Levy (1927) 30
Froman, Jane 195
Frome, Milton 144
The Front Page (play) 257
Froos, Sylvia 77
Frye, Dwight 248
Fryer, Paul 146
Funny Face (stage musical) 252
Furia, Philip 117, 209

Gabbard, Krin 192, 208
Gabin, Jean 185
Gable, Clark 111, 112, 138, 170, 224, 237, 240
Gabriel, Gilbert 71
Gale, June 81
Gallagher, Richard "Skeets" 225, 226, 227
Galli-Curci, Amelita 176
Gallup, George 218
Gambarelli, Maria 155
Gance, Abel 175
Gangs, Inc. see *Paper Ballots* (1941)

Garbo, Greta 13
Garden, Mary 146
Garden of the Moon (1938) 134, 135, 207, 209
Gardiner, Becky 232
Gardiner, Reginald 253
Gargan, William 259
Garland, Judy 1, 2, 79, 80, **80**, 81, 82, 83, 191
Garrick, John 22, 33, 34, 35
Gasnier, Louis 138
Gay Desperado (1936) 156
The Gay Divorcee (1934) 52
Gaynor, Janet 6, 22, 37, 100
Gaynor, Mitzi 65
Gehrig, Eleanor 131, 132
Gehrig, Lou 115, 129–132, **130**
General Film Distributors 59
Gensler, Lewis 53, 55
Gentle, Alice 15
Gentleman George (play) 25
George White's 1935 Scandals (1935) 238
George White's Scandals (1931 stage musical) 63, 150
George White's Scandals (1934) 235, 236
Gershwin, George 13, 16, 37, 41, 63, 250, 252
Gershwin, Ira 250, 252
GetTV 172, 175
Gibson, Dorothy 179
Gibson, Hoot 18, 111, 144
Giddins, Gary 41, 68
Gilbert, John 39, 179
Gilbert, W.S. *see* Gilbert and Sullivan
Gilbert and Sullivan 44, 56, 57, 58, 59, 71
Gill, Florence 94
Gillette Community Sing (radio show) 244
The Girl Can't Help It (1956) 213
The Girl of the Golden West (1938) 67, 258
The Girl Said No (1937) 55–59, **57**, 71, 73
"Git Along Mule" 127
Give Me a Sailor (1938) 96
Give Me Your Heart (1936) 170
Give Us This Night (1936) 156–159, **157**, 199
Glamour Girl (1948) 214
Glazer, Benjamin 71, 94, 229
Gleason, Lucille **118**
Gleason, Pat 138
Glendon, J. Frank 29
"The Glory Road" 169
"Go Down, Moses" 222
Going Hollywood (1933) 224, 228
Going Places (1938) 104, 191, 205–209, **207**
The Gold Diggers (1923) 179

Gold Diggers of Broadway (1929) 5, 6
Gold Diggers of 1933 (1933) 133
Golden, Ray 98
Golden Dawn (1930) 140
The Golden Turkey Awards (book) 140
Goldman, Herbert 223
Goldwyn, Samuel 14, 114, 118
Gone with the Wind (1939) 49, 50
The Good Earth (1937) 185
"Good Morning" 95
Goodman, Al, and His "Follow Thru" Orchestra 15
Goodman, Benny (and His Orchestra) 2, 48, 189, 190, 191, 192, 194–197, **195**, 204, 212, 215, 217
Goodwins, Leslie 87
Goosson, Steven 34
Gordon, Huntley 24
Gordon, Mack 43, 115
Gordon, Max 186
Gottler, Archie 9, 42
Gould, Dorothy 26
Grable, Betty 53, 54, 79, 80, **80**, 83
Graham, Sheilah 67, 217, 244
Gran, Albert 6
Grand National Films/Grand National Pictures 55, 57, 59, 120, 121, 122, 140, 141, 142, 143, 145, 166, 245, 246, 247, 248, 249
Grand Ole Opry (1940) 105
The Grand Ole Opry (radio program) 76
Grant, Cary 41, 148, 172–175, **173**, 180, 218
Granville, Bonita 204
The Grateful Dead 192
Gravey [Gravet], Fernand 43, 184, 185, 187
Gray, Gilda 23
Gray, Glen, and the Casa Loma Orchestra 190
Gray, Lawrence 6, 42
Grayson, Charles 202
Great Guy (1936) 246, 249
The Great Magoo (play) 213
The Great Victor Herbert* (1939) 44, 59, 70–75, **72, 159
*The Great Waltz (1938) 43, 183–188, **185**
The Great Waltz (1972) 74
The Great Ziegfeld (1936) 43, 185, 186, 230, 258
Green, Harry 225, 226, 227
Green, Howard J. 99
Green, Mitzi 2
Green Grow the Lilacs (play) 233
Green Mansions (novel) 177
Greig, Robert 38

Grey, Virginia 259
Grieg, Edvard 74
Grier, Jimmie 87
Griffith, Richard 180
Grinde, Nick 102
Die Grosse Liebe (1931) 169
Grossmith, George 33, 34
Gunga Din (1939) 218
Gunnels, Chester 102, **103**
Gunsmoke (TV series) 90
Gwenn, Edmund 186

Hackett, Charles 146
Haley, Jack **61**, 63, 79, 80, **80**, 81, 98
Hall, Alexander 158
Hall, Charles D. 9
Hall, Mordaunt 10
Hall, Thurston 104, 105
Hallelujah! (1929) 5
Hallelujah, I'm a Bum (1933) 223
Halliday, John 163
Hamilton, Lloyd 32, 33, 35
Hamilton, Morris 33
Hammerstein, Oscar II 158, 159, 161, 169, 185
Hammond, John 189
Hammons, E.W. 142
Hampton, Hope 179–183, **181**
Hampton, Lionel 89, 189, 196
Happy Days (1930) 22
The Hard-Boiled Canary (1941) 74
Hard to Get (1938) 207
Harkins, Anthony 107
Harlan, Kenneth 29
"Harlem on the Prairie" 126
Harlem on the Prairie* (1937) 3, 107, 122, 125–126, **125, 136
**Harlem Rides the Range* (1939) 124, 127–128
Harling, W. Franke 233
Harlow, Jean 131, 219, 235, 236, 238
*Harmony Lane (1935) 43, 44–50, **47**, 166
Harris, Charles K. 42
Harris, Connie 126
Harris, Jed 8
Harris, Lucius "Dusty" 126, 127
Harrison, Paul 243
Harrison, P.S. 50
Harrison's Reports (periodical) 50, 99, 122, 132, 155, 159, 201, 223, 230, 233
Harron, John 222
Hart, Lorenz 2, 41, 42, 195, 223
Hart, Moss 186
Hart, Vivian 56, 58
Harvey, Lilian 43, 235, 237
Hawaii Five-O (TV series) 128
Hawaiian Nights (1939) 204
Hayes, George "Gabby" 94
Haymes, Dick 65

Hays, Will 156
Hayworth, Rita 87
Healy, Ted 196, 197
Hearn, Sam 195
Hearst, William Randolph 179
Heath, Al 90
Heaven's Gate (1980) 78
Hecht, Ben 213, 257
Hee-Haw (TV series) 94, 102
Held, Anna 185
Hello, Sister! (1933) 38
Hellzapoppin' (1941) 140
Henderson, Charles 204
Henderson, Fletcher 189
Henderson, Ray 22, 220
Henie, Sonja 198–199
Henry, Grace 33
Hepburn, Katharine 47, 240–241
Herbert, Hugh 55, 197
Herbert, Victor 44, 71, 72, 73, 74, 75
"Here Comes Emily Brown" 22–23
"Here Comes the Bride" 194
Here's to Romance* (1935) 152–156, **154, 177
Hersholt, Jean 63
Hervey, Irene **57**, 58
Hey, Let's Twist! (1961) 182
Hi Diddle Diddle (1944) 74
Hickman, Darryl 68
"High Flyin'" 258
High Hat (1936) 77
High, Wide and Handsome (1937) 90, 234
Highway 301 (1950) 74
Hill, Billy 119
Hillbilly Heart Throbs (radio program) 77
Hillbilly Love (1935) 77
Hilton, Daisy 16
Hilton, Violet 16
Hinds, Samuel S. **118**, 163
Hines, Earl "Fatha" 125
Hirliman, George A. 120, 121, 122
The Hit Parade (1937) 167
Hitchcock, Alfred 186, 254
Hitler, Adolf 201, 257
Hitting a New High* (1937) 148, 175–178, **176
H.M.S. Pinafore (stage operetta) 56, 58
Hodges, Joy 53, 54, 55
Hold Everything (1930) 30
Hold That Co-ed (1938) 82
"Hold Your Man" 238
Hold Your Man (1933) 238
Hollywood Cavalcade (1939) 50, 64
*Hollywood Hotel (1937) 134, 191, 192–197, 209
Hollywood Hotel (radio show) 197

Index

Hollywood Party (1934) 195
Hollywood Pictures 123, 124
The Hollywood Reporter (periodical) 39, 50, 64, 122, 167, 174, 226
The Hollywood Revue of 1929 (1929) 66–67
Hollywood Rhythm (1934) 43
Hollywood Spectator (periodical) 208
Holmes, Phillips 42
Holt, Tim 133
The Holy Terror (1937) 243
"Home on the Range" 135
Honey (1930) 225
"Hooray for Baby and Me" 222
"Hooray for Hollywood" 55, 196, 197
"Hooray for Spinach" 210
Hope, Bob 69, 96, 195, 196, 212
Hopkins, Miriam 180
Hopper, Hedda 217
Horne, Lena 74
Hornung, Ernest William 232
Horton, Edward Everett **176**, 177, 178, 208, 217, 229, 230
The Hottentot (play and 1922 and 1929 films) 208
"The House That Jack Built for Jill" 118
Houston, George 120, 133
"How Am I to Know?" 11
"How 'Ya Gonna Keep 'Em Down on the Farm (After They've Seen Paree)?" 89
Howard, John 94, 177
Howard, Joseph E. 42, 44
Howlin, Olin 94
Howson, Albert 223
Hoyt, Waite 42
Huber, Harold 208
Huffington Post (online news site) 172
Hughes, Howard 230
Les Huguenots (opera) 167
Hunt, Eleanor 120
Hunter, Ian 259
Hurst, Fannie 179
Huston, John 40
Huston, Walter 40
Hyman, Bernie 185

I Can Get It for You Wholesale (novel) 205
"I Can't Be Bothered Now" 253
"I Carry You in My Pocket" 155
"I Don't Want to Make History, I Just Want to Make Love" 115
I Dream of Jeanie (1952) 48
I Dream Too Much (1935) 176, 177, 241
"I Feel That Certain Feeling Coming On" 24

"I Guess It Had to Be That Way" 227
"I Hit a New High" 177
*I Live for Love (1935) 149–152, **150**
"I Love the Wide Open Spaces" 144
"I Love to Whistle" 204
"I Never Saw a Better Night" 54
I Pagliacci (opera) 98, 155, 169
"I Remember You" 246
"I Saw Her at Eight O'Clock" 55
I Surrender Dear (1931) 225
I Want a Divorce (1940) 211
"I Want to Be a Cowboy's Sweetheart" 144
"I Wonder Who's Kissing Her Now" 69
I Wonder Who's Kissing Her Now (1947) 44
Ice Follies of 1939 (1939) 258
"I'd Love to Be a Talking Picture Queen" 24
"If I Had a Million Dollars" 52
"If I Put My Heart in My Song" 95
"(If You Can't Sing It) You'll Have to Swing It (Mr. Paganini)" 119, 191
"If You Knew Susie" 221
"I'll Dream Tonight" 135
"I'll Take Manhattan" 42
I'll Take Romance (1937) 175, 178
"I'm a Happy Cowboy" 126
"I'm a Lover of Paree" 230
"I'm an Old Cowhand (from the Rio Grande)" 55, 117, 134
"I'm Building Up to an Awful Letdown" 55
"I'm Getting a Moon's Eye View of the World" 111
"I'm in the Mood for Love" 114
"I'm Just a Country Boy at Heart" 89
"I'm Talking Through My Heart" 195
"In a Moment of Weakness" 210
"In a One Room Flat" 230
"In My Merry Oldsmobile" 66
In Old Chicago (1938) 49, 62
In Old Santa Fe (1934) 109
*In Person (1935) 13, 239–242, **240**, 250
"In the Cool, Cool, Cool of the Evening" 55
"In the Heart of the City That Has No Heart" 102
"In the Hills of Old Wyoming" 115
Independent Exhibitors Film Bulletin (periodical) 48, 145
Ingram, Jack 89
Inside Facts of Stage and Screen (periodical) 5

International House (1933) 226
Invincible Pictures 166
The Invisible Man (1933) 38
Irene (1940) 218
Irish Eyes Are Smiling (1944) 44
"Irish Rhapsody" 71
Irving Berlin's Alexander's Ragtime Band see *Alexander's Ragtime Band*
Is Everybody Happy? (1929) 26
It Happened One Night (1934) 72, 147, 170, 172, 173, 240
"It Must Be the Iron in the Spinach" 35
*It's Great to Be Alive (1933) **iv**, 3, 36–40, 109
"It's Great to Be Necked" 22
"It's Great to Be the Only Man Alive" 39
"It's Love I'm After" 81
"It's Only a Paper Moon" 213
"I've Got a Heartful of Music" 196

Jackson, Thomas (E.) 9, 10
James, Harry 189, 196
Janis, Elsie 154
Jarrett, Art 142, 145
Jason, Sybil 2
Jason, Will 29
*Jazz Heaven (1929) 3, 10–14, **12**, 30
The Jazz Singer (1927) 8, 220, 221
Jean, Gloria 2
"Jeanie with the Light Brown Hair" 50
"Jeepers Creepers" 104, 207, 208, 209
*Jeepers Creepers (1939) 100–101, 104–105, 209
Jeffries, Herbert 3, 107, 108, 122–128, **125**, 136
Jenkins, Allen **150**, 208, 210
Jepson, Helen 147, 155, 246
Jernagan (play) 26
Jesse James (1939) 258
Jessel, George 44, 66
Joan the Woman (1916) 146
Johnny Guitar (1954) 180
Johnson, Chic 5, 6
Johnson, Erskine 217
Johnson, Hall, Choir 167
Johnson, Henry 237
Johnson, Kay 11
Johnston, Arthur 225, 226, 227
Jolson, Al 1, 2, 6, 11, **49**, 50, 64, 65, 94, 114, 219, 220–224
Jones, Allan 71, 73, 74
Jones, Buck 132
Jones, Elliot "Jonah" 89
Jordan, Dorothy 38
Joseph E. Howard, America's Popular Composer (1928) 42
Journey's End (1930) 28

Judge, Arline 79
Julie (1956) 74
Jump for Joy (stage revue) 128
Just Imagine (1930) 22, 24, 34, 109

Kabibble, Ish 215
Kahn, Gus 233
Kahn, Richard C. 126, 128
Kalem Company 232
Kaley, Charles 42
Kane, Helen 6
Kane, Kathryn 203, *203*, 204
Kane, Marjorie "Babe" 6, 26, 28
Kann, "Red" 13, 34
Kantor, MacKinlay 94
Karloff, Boris 218, 237
"Kathleen Mavourneen" 30
*Kathleen Mavourneen (1930) 29–31
Kathleen Mavourneen (1937) 31
Kay, Arthur 73
Kearns, Allen 6
Keating, Fred *53*, 55, 121, 122
Keaton, Buster 53, 110
Keeler, Ruby 147, 252
Keene, Richard 24
Keene, Tom 106
Kelly, Burt 202
Kelly, Kitty 227
Kelly, Patsy 79, 80, *80*, 144
Kendall, Read 243
Kennedy, Edgar 163
Kennedy, Merna 9, 10
Kent, Barbara 8, 53
Kenton, Erle C. 138
Kentucky (1938) 99
*Kentucky Moonshine (1938) 89, 96–100
"Kentucky Opera" 98
The Kentucky Ramblers *see* The Prairie Ramblers
Kenyon, Charles 180, 181
Kern, James V. 216
Kern, Jerome 15, 41, 160, 161, 174, 176, 180
Kernell, William 37
Kibbee, Guy 256
Kiepura, Jan 147, 155, 157, *157*, 158, 159
King, Henry (bandleader) 190
King, Henry (director) 49, 62
King, Wayne 190
The King and the Chorus Girl (1937) 185
King Kong (1933) 234
King of Jazz (1930) 3, 5, 10, 18, 19, 20, 64, 225
King Solomon of Broadway (1935) 143
The King Steps Out (1936) 172
"A Kiss in the Dark" 73
"Kiss Me Again" 74
Klauber, Bruce 212

Kleber, Henry 48, 50
Knapp, Evalyn **130**, 131
Knight, Fuzzy 89, 94, 121
Knights of the Round Table (1953) 29
Kollege of Musical Knowledge (radio show) 215
Korjus, Miliza 184–188, **185**
Korngold, Erich Wolfgang 158, 159
Kornman, Mary 90, 202
Kostelanetz, Andre 177, 178
Koszarski, Richard 9, 165
Kraft, H.S. 199
Kraft Music Hall (radio program) 92–93, 119
Krebs, Nita 138, 139, 140
Kreuger, Miles 35
Krupa, Gene 189, 194, 196, 209, 212, **212**, 213, 214
Kuller, Sid 98
Kusell, Maurice 9
Kyser, Kay 191, 192, 215–218, **216**

La La Land (2016) 1
Lachman, Harry 173
*Ladies in Love (1930) 25–27
Ladies of Leisure (1930) 25
The Lady and the Ranger see The Road to Reno
Lady, Be Good (stage musical) 252
"Lady Detectives" 34
Lady Killer (1933) 246
"The Lady's in Love with You" 214
Laemmle, Carl, Jr. 7, 8, 18, 19
Lakme (opera) 177
Lamont, Sonny 53, 54, 55
Lamour, Dorothy 96
L'amour guide (1933) 229
Lane, Allan 244
Lane, Burton 214
Lane, Lola 196
Lane, Priscilla 134
Lane, Rosemary 196
The Lane Sisters 66
Lanfield, Sidney 49
Langdon, Harry 33
Langford, Frances 113, 114, 115, 156, 196, 243
La Plante, Laura 17, 18, *18*, 20
Las Vegas Nights (1941) 192
Lasky, Jesse L. 154, 155, 156, 177, 178
The Last Man on Earth (1924) 37, 40
The Last Moment (1927) 7
The Last Performance (1929) 8, 10
"The Last Round-Up" 119
The Last Voyage (1960) 74
Latin Hi-Hattin' (1938) 122
Laura (1944) 170

Laurel, Stan 125
Laurel and Hardy 72, 110, 169
Lawrence, Muriel 48
Layton, James 3, 6
"Lazybones" 52
"Learn to Croon" 225
Leathernecking (1930) 232
Leave It to Me! (stage musical) 73
LeBaron, William 73, 157, 226
Lederer, Francis 155
Lee, Billy 104, 105
Lee, Connie 90
Lee, Davey 220
Lee, Dixie 24, 225
Lee, Dorothy 150
Lee, Sammy 38
Leeds, Andrea 49
Leisen, Mitchell 195
Lemmon, Jack 213
Leonard, Robert Z. 258
Leonidoff, Leon 174
LeRoux, Buddy 90
LeRoy, Mervyn 185
Lesser, Sol 129, 130, 138, 139
"Let a Smile Be Your Umbrella" 43
*Let Freedom Ring (1939) 219, 254–258, 260, **259**
"Let Me Call You Sweetheart" 245
Let's Dance (radio show) 189
"Let's Go on Like This Forever" 144
A Letter to Three Wives (1949) 226
Levant, Oscar 13, 55, 241
Levine, Nat 86, 106, 108, 109, 110, 111, 112, 166, 167
Lewis, Edgar 25, 26
Lewis, Jerry 97, 119, 144
Lewis, Mary 146
Lewis, Ted 26
Liberty Pictures 166
Life (magazine) 241
Life Begins in College (1937) 82, 97
The Light in the Dark (1922) 179
Lightner, Winnie 6
The Lilac Domino (1937) 166
Lillie, Beatrice 32–36, **33**
"Listen to Me" 90
Liszt, Franz 210
"Little Brown Jug" 104
Little Caesar (1931) 10
The Little Couple (TV series) 140
Little Johnny Jones (1929) 26
Little Miss Broadway (1938) 89
Little People, Big World (TV series) 140
"The Little Red Fox" 217
Little Women (1933) 47
Little Women: LA (TV series) 140

Index

Lively, Robert 71
Living on Love (1937) 234
Lloyd, Harold 217
"Loch Lomond" 208
Lockhart, Gene 247, 248
Lockhart, Kathleen 248
Loesser, Frank 73, 214
Loff, Jeanette 19, 20
Lombard, Carole 229, 252
Lombardo, Guy 190
"Lon Chaney's Going to Get You, If You Don't Watch Out" 67
Lonesome (1928) 7, 10, 18
Lopez, Vincent, and His Orchestra 115
Lord Byron of Broadway (1930) 41
Lorre, Peter 218
Los Angeles Herald Express (newspaper) 243
Los Angeles Times (newspaper) 19, 58, 59, 82, 128, 138, 139, 169, 172, 176, 208, 209, 213, 232, 243
Lost Horizon (1937) 166
Lottery Lover (1935) 237
Louise (1939) 175
Louise, Anita 155, **207**, 208
Love at First Sight (1930) 25
"The Love Bug Will Bite You (If You Don't Watch Out)" 86, 90
The Love Doctor (1929) 13
"Love Fiesta" 121
Love Girl (unpublished novel) 64
Love in the Afternoon (1957) 231
Love Me Forever (1935) 172
Love Me Tonight (1932) 230
Love Time (1934) 43, 237
"Lover, Come Back to Me" 147
Lowe, Edmund 24, 143
Lubitsch, Ernst 1, 6, 230
Lucas, George 111
Lucas, Nick 6
Luce, Claire 24
Lucia di Lammermoor (opera) 167, 176
Ludwig, Edward 53, 162
Lugosi, Bela 26, 90, 94, 129, 218
Lum and Abner 105
Lum and Abner (radio program) 76, 77
Lupino, Ida 114, 162
Luther, Frank 77
Lux Radio Theatre (radio program) 65
Lyman, Abe, and His Orchestra 106

Macaulay, Richard 209, 210
MacDonald, Jeanette 2, 6, 67, 72, 73, 147, 148, 162, 177, 187, 191, 219, 230, 256, 258, 259, 260
MacDonald, Wallace 109
MacFadden, Hamilton 33, 34

Mack, Buck 247
MacLean, Douglas 208
MacMurray, Fred 67, 191, 198, 199, 201
Macon, Uncle Dave 105
Mad About Music (1938) 204
The Mad Monster (1942) 138
Madame Butterfly (opera) 258, 260
Magidson, Herb 155
"Magnolias in the Moonlight" 167
Mahin, John Lee 186
Mahoney, Wilkie 214
Majestic Pictures 166
Makers of Melody (1929) 42
Malneck, Matt 52, 55
"Mama Don't Allow No Music Played in Here" 95
Mama Runs Wild (1937) 143
Mammy (1930) 62, 220, 221
"A Man and His Dream" 69
"A Man Must Shave" 151
A Man to Remember (1938) 234
Manhattan Melodrama (1934) 195
Manhattan Merry-Go-Round (1937) 167, 191
Manhattan Moon (1935) 143
Mankiewicz, Joseph L. 226
Mann, May 244
Manon (opera) 155, 180
Marbe, Fay 15, 16
Marbe, Gilbert 15
The March of Time (1930, unfinished) 5, 225
"Marching Along with Time" 63
Maritza, Sari 226
The Mark of Zorro (1920) 169, 257
"La Marseillaise" 18, 20
La Marseillaise see *Captain of the Guard*
Marsh, Joan 38, 39
Marshal, Alan 181, 182
Marshall, Everett 6, 147, 149–152, **150**
Marshall, George 237
Martan, Nita 29
Martha (opera) 233
Martin, Dean 119
Martin, Jeffrey Brown 257
Martin, Mary 71, **72**, 73, 74, 159
Martin, Tony 79, 81. 97, 98, 243–245
Martinelli, Giovanni 146, 147, 153
Martini, Nino 147, 148, 153, 154, 155, 156, 170, 177, 178, 252
Marx, Groucho 66, 91
Marx, Harpo 101
The Marx Brothers 16, 148, 169
Mascot Pictures 44, 46, 47, 48, 86, 106, 108, 109, 110, 111, 112, 166
The Mask of Fu Manchu (1932) 111
Mason, Sully 215, 217
Master Art Products 43
Matthews, Jessie 186, 251
Mayberry, Lynn 144
Mayer, Louis B. 15, 80, 256
Maynard, Ken 18, 86, 106, 109, 133
Maynard, Kermit 86, 87
Maytime (1937) 230, 258
McClung, Robert 80
McCormack, John 22
McGann, William 151
McGilligan, Patrick 248
McHugh, Jimmy 181
McLaglen, Victor 256, 257
McMahon, Horace **216**
Me, Gangster (1928) 27
Medved, Harry and Michael 140
Meek, Donald 53
"Meet My Sister" 30
Melody Cruise (1933) 16, 230
The Melody Man (1930) 25
Melody Pictures 83, 84, 85, 86, 87, 88, 90, 91, 103
Melton, Frank 237
Melton, James 147, 170
"Memory" 42
Men with Steel Faces see *The Phantom Empire*
Men with Wings (1938) 67
Mendelssohn, Felix 158
Menjou, Adolphe 217
Mercer, Johnny 2, 44, 52–55, **53**, 77, 104, 117, 134, 135, 196, 207–208, 209
The Merchant of Venice (play) 161
Merit Pictures 123, 126
Merivale, Philip 159
Merkel, Una 230
Merman, Ethel 54, 63, 64, 65, 73
"The Merry-Go-Round" 200
The Merry Widow (1934) 147, 229, 230
Meter, Harry von 29
Metro-Goldwyn-Mayer (MGM) 1, 5, 6, 11, 12, 13, 25, 30, 41, 42, 53, 58, 66, 67, 68, 72, 73, 74, 79, 80, 81, 82, 83, 87, 111, 114, 117, 121, 140, 144, 147, 155, 156, 162, 163, 165, 168, 169, 182, 183, 184, 185, 186, 187, 195, 196, 217, 218, 224, 225, 228, 253, 254, 256, 257, 258, 259, 260
Metropolitan (1935) 169
MGM see Metro-Goldwyn-Mayer
Middleton, Ray 48
A Midsummer Night's Dream (1935) 158, 246

Mignon (opera) 167
The Mikado (1939) 59
The Mikado (stage operetta) 56, 58
Milestone, Lewis 162, 223
Milland, Ray 67, 96, 194, 195
Miller, Ann 121–122
Miller, Flournoy 107, 125, 127
Miller, Glenn (and His Orchestra) 114, 192, 214
Miller, John "Skins" 77, 247
Miller and Mack *see* John "Skins" Miller and Buck Mack
"Mine Alone" 151
"Minnie the Moocher" 174
The Miracle Rider (1935) 111
"Mister Jack and Missus Jill" 140
Mr. Lemon of Orange (1931) 24
"Mr. Paganini" *see* "(If You Can't Sing It) You'll Have to Swing It (Mr. Paganini)"
Mitchell, Grant 237, 238, 240
Mitchell, Sidney 9, 81, 98
Mitchell and Durant (Frank Mitchell and Jack Durant) 97, 236, 237, 238
Mix, Ruth 143
Mix, Tom 111, 133, 143
Modern Screen (periodical) 95, 115
Mohr, Hal 8, 9
Mojica, José 37
Monogram Pictures 48, 87, 91, 142, 166
Monroe, Marilyn 65, 204, 213
Monroe Jubilee Singers 222
Montana, Patsy 144
Montana Moon (1930) 106
Montgomery, Douglass 47, *47*, 49
"Moon River" 55
Moonlight and Pretzels (1933) 20, 42
"Moonshine Over Kentucky" 98
"Moonstruck" 225
Moore, Colleen 30
Moore, Grace 2, 147, 148, 157, 161, 166, 168, 172–175, *173*, 178, 184, 191, 200, 201, 246, 259
Moore, William 112
Moran, Pat 248
Moran, Polly 30
Moray, Yvonne 137, *137*, 138, 139, 140
Moreland, Mantan 125, 126, 127
Moreno, Rosita 37
Morgan, Frank 259
Morris, Earl J. 127
Morris, Glenn 130
Morris, Wayne 244
Morros, Boris 148
Moshier, W. Franklyn 238
Motion Picture Daily (periodical) 119

Motion Picture Herald (periodical) 3, 74, 78, 90, 95, 109, 111, 112, 151, 170, 202, 210, 233, 238, 239, 251, 258
Motion Picture News (periodical) 13, 15, 34
Moulan, Frank 56, 58
Mountain Melody (1934) 77
Mountain Music (1937) 3, 77, 78, 91–96, **93**, 119
The Movie Stars (book) 180
Movietone Follies of 1930 (1930) 21–24, **23**, 33
Mowbray, Alan 159, **161**, 163, 197, 240, 241
Mozart, Wolfgang Amadeus 210
Mundin, Herbert 38, 39
Murder at Dawn (1932) 111
Murder, My Sweet (1944) 211
Murders in the Rue Morgue (1932) 26, 94
Murray, Arthur 248
Murray, Feg 217
Murray, J. Harold 6
Murray, James 25
Murray, Ken 202, 205
Murray, Mae 66, 190
Muse, Clarence 48, 167
Music for Madame (1937) 156, 252
"The Music Goes 'Round and Around" 166
Music in the Air (stage musical) 161
Music Is Magic (1935) 237
Music Is My Beat (TV show) 91
Mussolini, Benito 257
"Mutiny in the Nursery" 208
"My Blue Heaven" 91
My Favorite Spy (1942) 218
My Favorite Wife (1940) 181, 218
"My Future Star" 238
My Gal Sal (1942) 44
"My Heart Belongs to Daddy" 73
My Heart Calls You (1934) 157
"My Love and I" 159
"My Old Kentucky Home" 46, 50
My Princess (stage operetta) 180
"My Walking Stick" 63
Myers, Zion 52, 53, 54, 55, 246, 247
Myrt and Marge (1933) 20
Mystery Mountain (1934) 109
Mystery of Edwin Drood (1935) 47
Mystery of the Wax Museum (1933) 10

Nagel, Conrad 120
Nat Carr, Character Comedian (1927) 14
The National Barn Dance (radio program) 76, 107, 111

National Broadcasting Company *see* NBC
"The National Jitterbug Champions" 191
Natzler, Grete 155
*Naughty but Nice (1939) 135, 205–206, 209–211
Naughty Marietta (1935) 72
Naughty Marietta (stage musical) 71
Nazaro, Thomas 180
NBC (National Broadcasting Company) 68, 145, 153, 165, 189, 217s
Neagle, Anna 218
Near the Rainbow's End (1930) 106
Nedell, Bernard 213
Neilan, Marshall 89
Nelson, Ozzie 190
New Faces of 1937 (1937) 89
"A New Lease on Life" 241
New Moon (1930) 147, 157, 169
New Moon (1940) 187
New Movie Magazine (periodical) 55
New Movietone Follies of 1930 see Movietone Follies of 1930
New Republic (magazine) 249
New York Daily Mirror (newspaper) 244
New York Daily News (newspaper) 13, 16, 30
New York Times (newspaper) 9, 10, 36, 39, 56, 59, 64, 69, 73, 74, 82, 99, 119, 132, 148, 151, 155, 159, 170, 171, 174, 178, 182, 183, 195, 197, 210, 221, 225, 233, 238, 249, 253
Newfield, Sam 125, 138
Newill, James 89, 133
Newman, Alfred 64
"Nice Work If You Can Get It" 252
A Night at the Opera (1935) 169
"The Night Is Young" 152
Night Must Fall (1937) 29
"Nightingale's Song" 177
"Nitwit's Holiday" (unfilmed story) 99
Niven, David 108, 113, 114, 115
No dejes la Puerta abierta (1933) 37
Noble, Ray 190, 253
"None but the Lonely Heart" 258
Norman, Al "Rubber Legs" 106
Nothing Sacred (1937) 257
Nott, Robert 182
Novello, Ivor 160, 161
Novis, Donald 31, 91
Now I'll Tell (1934) 236
"Now It Can Be Told" 63, 64
Nugent, Frank S. 99, 119, 148, 159, 174, 178, 197, 249

Index

Oakie, Jack 6, 43, **176**, 177, 178, 200, 213, 225, 226, 227
Oakley, Annie 73
Oakman, Wheeler 110
Oberon, Merle 117
"The Object of My Affection" 86, 87, 91
O'Brien, Dave 144, 145
O'Brien, George 120, 163
O'Brien, Pat 10, 134, 135
O'Connor, Donald 65
O'Day, Molly 30, 31
Odets, Clifford 187
Odlum, Jerome 209
Offield, Evelyn 226
Ogden Standard-Examiner (newspaper) 244
Oh Boy! (stage musical) 15
"Oh! How I Hate to Get Up in the Morning" 63
"Oh, How I Love You" 26
"Oh Marie" 167
Oh, Sailor, Behave! (1930) 6
"Oh! Susanna" 80
Oh, You Beautiful Doll (1949) 44
"Oh, You Nasty Man" 236
Oklahoma! (stage musical) 233
"Old Black Joe" 48, 50
The Old Dark House (1932) 38
"Old Folks at Home" (aka "Swanee River") 46, 50
Old Gold (radio show) 19
The Old Homestead (1935) 166
Old Ironsides (1926) 25
*Old Man Rhythm (1935) 51–55, 117
Oliver, Edna May 37, 38
Oliver, Sherling 15
Olsen, Ole 5, 6
On the Avenue (1937) 62, 97
"On the Road to Mandalay" 169
On with the Show! (1929) 13
"One Day When We Were Young" 187, 188
One Hundred Men and a Girl (1937) 180
One in a Million (1936) 97
One Mad Kiss (1930) 37
One Man's Journey (1933) 234
One More Chance (1931) 225
One Night of Love (1934) 147, 172, 174, 201, 246, 259
O'Neil, Sally 12, **12**, 13, 30, 31
Orchestra Wives (1942) 192
Orry-Kelly 151
Osborne, Vivienne 200
O'Sullivan, Maureen 22, 33
Othman, Frederick 217
Our Gang Follies of 1936 (1935) 89
Our Gang Follies of 1938 (1937) 90
"Our Song" 174
Ouspenskaya, Maria 156

"Out of Sight, Out of Mind" 240, 241
Over the Hill to the Poor House (1920) 25, 26

"Pack Up Your Sins and Go to the Devil" 63
Paddy O'Day (1935) 87
Paducah Plantation (radio show) 143
The Pagan (1929) 11
"Pagan Love Song" 11
Page, Dorothy 107, 108, 140–145, **143**
Page, Gale 210
Paid (1930) 47
Paige, Raymond, and His Orchestra 196
*Palm Springs (1936) 112–115, 162, 166
Pan, Hermes 1, 54, 240, 241, 252, 253
Pangborn, Franklin 259
Paper Ballots (1941) 69
Paper Moon (1973) 91
Parade of the West (1930) 106
"Paradise in Waltz Time" 200
Paramount Pictures 6, 13, 22, 25, 42, 43, 44, 55, 57, 59, 65, 67, 69, 70, 71, 72, 73, 74, 77, 78, 79, 87, 90, 91, 92, 95, 96, 112, 114, 115, 116, 117, 119, 146, 155, 156, 157, 158, 159, 160, 161, 162, 163, 166, 172, 177, 191, 192, 194, 195, 196, 197, 198, 199, 200, 201, 202, 203, 210, 211, 212, 213, 214, 224, 225, 226, 227, 228, 229, 230, 247
Pardners (1956) 119
Pardon My Gun (1930) 106
"Pardon My Southern Accent" 52
Paris in Spring (1935) 162
Parish, James Robert 258, 259
Parker, Austin 180
Parker, Jean 73
Parsons, Louella 30, 64, 114, 132, 138, 197, 243
Paterson, Pat 237
Pathé Exchange 16, 106, 137, 225
Patience (stage operetta) 58
Pearl, Minnie 102
Pendleton, Nat 78, 102
Penn, Sean 49
Pépé le Moko (1937) 185
Peter Pan (stage musical) 73
Petticoat Junction (TV series) 95
*The Phantom Empire (1935) 3, 106, 108–112, **110**
Phantom of the Opera (1925) 223
Phantom of the Opera (1943) 74
The Phantom President (1932) 6
The Philadelphia Inquirer (newspaper) 39, 152

Photoplay (periodical) 21, 27, 156, 165
Piantadosi, Al 15
Pickett, Bill 108
Pickford, Mary 13, 89, 154, 155
Picture Play (periodical) 20
Pidgeon, Walter 114, 163
Pierce, David 3, 6
Pigott, Tempe 138
*Pigskin Parade (1936) 78–83, **80**, 97, 191, 243, 244
The Pirates of Penzance (stage operetta) 56, 58
Pitts, Zasu 210
Pittsburgh Courier (newspaper) 127
Platt, Bill 138
Playmates (1941) 218
"Please" 227
Pleasure Cruise (1933) 37
Plitt, Henry G. 204
Poe, Bonnie 53, **53**, 54, 55
Poe, Coy 87, 90
Pointed Heels (1929) 42
Pollack, Ben 190
Pollack, Lew 81, 98
Pollock, Arthur 180
Polo Joe (1936) 208
Pons, Lily 147, 148, 175–178, **176**, 191, 241
"Poor Little Buttercup" 58
Poor Little Rich Girl (1936) 243
Porcasi, Paul 10
Porter, Cole 5, 41, 73
Porter, Lew 126, 127, 140
Potel, Victor 28, 29
Powell, Dick 107, 108, 114, 133–134, 135, 143, 196, 207, **207**, 208, 209, 210, 211
Powell, Eleanor 1, 66, 155, 256
Powell, William 43
Power, Tyrone 2, 49, 61, **61**, 62, 63, 64, 65
"Prairie Boy" 145
"Prairie Flower" 128
The Prairie Ramblers 107
PRC (Producers Releasing Corporation) 69
Preminger, Otto [Ludwig] 168–170
Presley, Elvis 48, 190
"A Pretty Girl Is Like a Melody" 63
The Pride of the Yankees (1942) 132
Prima, Louis 117
Princess Ting Ah Ling (stage operetta) 58
Principal Productions 128, 129, 136, 138
Pringle, Aileen 89
Prinz, LeRoy 43, 68, 73
The Prisoner of Zenda (1937) 115
The Prisoner of Zenda (1952) 29

The Prodigal (1931) 169
Prudence Pictures 14, 15, 16
Pryor, Roger 42, **53**, 55
The Public Enemy (1931) 246
"Put Me to the Test" 253
Puttin' on the Ritz (1930) 62

Qualen, John 237
"Queen of the Hunt Am I" 35
Quillan, Eddie 203–204
Quirk, Lawrence J. 214

Radio City Revels (1938) 42, 96
Radio Mirror (periodical) 189
Radio Pictures *see* RKO
Radio Ranch *see* *The Phantom Empire*
Radio Scout (1934) 99
Raft, George 10, 111, 114, 199
Rafter Romance (1933) 234
Rainbow's End (1935) 111
Rainer, Luise 184, 185, 187
Rainger, Ralph 115, 117, 195, 229
Ramona (1928) 12
Ramona (1936) 121
Rand, Sally 152, 178
Rasch, Albertina 186
Raskob, John J. 150
Ratoff, Gregory 170
Raucheisen, Michael 165
*Rawhide (1938) 115, 128–132, **130**
Ray, Albert 30
Ray, Johnnie 65
Ray, Leah 243, 244
Ray, Mona 106
Raye, Martha 78, 92, 94, 95, 96, 117, 119, 191, 194, **195**, 197, 214
Raymond, Gene 40, 177, 256
Reaching for the Moon (1930) 225
Reagan, Ronald 54, 102, 134, 135, 197, 209, 210
Rebecca (1940) 254
"Recitations" 32
The Red Mill (stage musical) 71
Reed, George 50
Reed, Lou 192
Reefer Madness *see* *Tell Your Children*
Regal Distributing 120
Reinhardt, Gottfried 184
Reinhardt, Max 158
Reisner, Charles 94
"Remember" 63
Renoir, Jean 185
Republic Pictures 44, 47, 48, 78, 87, 90, 91, 100, 101, 102, 103, 104, 105, 112, 143, 163, 164, 165, 166, 167, 209
The Return of Chandu (1934) 129
"Reuben, Reuben, I've Been Swingin'" 98
Revel, Harry 43, 115

Reynolds, Harrington 144
"Rhapsody in Blue" 63
Rhodes, Erik 53, 167
Rhodes, "Little Billy" 137, 139, 140
The Rhythm Boys 225
Rhythm on the Range* (1936) 55, 92, 94, 107, 116–119, ***118*, 134, 191
Rhythm Romance *see* *Some Like It Hot*
Richardson, Frank 22, 23, 24
Richman, Harry 62
Richmond, Kane 86, 87
**Ride 'Em Cowgirl* (1939) 140, 143–145
"Ride, Tenderfoot, Ride" 134, 135
Riggs, Lynn 233
Rigoletto (opera) 164, 176
Ring of Fire (1961) 74
"Ring, Ring de Banjo" 50
Rio Rita (1929) 5, 17, 27, 106, 150
Ripley, Arthur 19
Riskin, Robert 172, 173, 174
Ritter, Tex 107, 142, 246
The Ritz Brothers (Al, Harry, Jimmy) 82, 97, 98, 99, 100
Riviera (unproduced stage musical) 180
RKO (Radio Pictures) 5, 6, 10, 11, 12, 13, 26, 40, 42, 44, 51, 52, 53, 54, 55, 67, 79, 89, 96, 99, 105, 120, 121, 149, 150, 156, 175, 176, 177, 178, 181, 191, 214, 216, 217, 218, 225, 231, 232, 233, 234, 239, 240, 241, 249, 251, 252, 253, 254
Roach, Bert 58
Roach, Hal 72, 89
The Road to Hollywood (book) 214
*The Road to Reno (1938) 178–183, ***181***
Road to Singapore (1940) 69, 214
The Roaring Twenties (1939) 211
Roberta (1935) 53, 232, 233
Roberti, Lyda 43
Robertson, Guy 186
Robertson, John S. 19, 20
Robin, Leo 115, 117, 195, 229
Robinson, Bill 1, 74
Robson, May 156, 217
Rockne, Knute 129
Rodeo Day (1935) 77
Rodgers, Jimmie 76, 77
Rodgers, Richard 2, 42, 195, 223
Rogers, Charles "Buddy" 53, 54, 55
Rogers, Charles R. 67, 69
Rogers, Ginger 16, 40, 52, 54, 55, 62, 167, 174, 177, 219, 239–242, **240**, 250, 251, 253, 254, 258
Rogers, Roy 2, 104, 105, 107, 108, 117, 133, 209

Rogers, Will 93, 110, 216, 217, 240
The Rogue Song (1930) 147, 168, 169
Roland, Ruth 143
Romance in the Dark (1938) 159
"Romance in the Rain" 126
Romanoff, Michael 89
Romberg, Sigmund 169
Romeo and Juliet (play) 159
Romero, Cesar 169
Ronell, Ann 200
Rooney, Mickey 1, 2, 41, 253
Roosevelt, Franklin, Jr. 87
Rosalie (1937) 82, 256
Rose, Billy 152
Rose-Marie (1936) 162, 169
Rose-Marie (stage operetta) 160, 161
The Rose of Algeria (stage musical) 73
Rose of the Rancho (1936) 158, 159, 199
Rose of Washington Square (1939) 64
Rosenbloom, "Slapsie" Maxie 210
Rosenstein, Arthur 167
Ross, Betsy King 110
Ross, Lanny 47
Ross, Shirley 194, 195, 213
Ross, Vera 56, 58
Roulien, Raul *iv*, 37, 38, 39, 40
Ruben, J. Walter 13
Ruddigore (stage operetta) 58
Ruggles, Charlie 163
Runyon, Damon 58
Ruskin, Harry 227
Russell, Rosalind 73
Ruth, Babe 129
Ruttenberg, Joseph 187

Sack, Alfred 126
Sack Amusement Enterprises 123, 124, 126, 128
St. John, Fuzzy 139
St. Johns, Adele Rogers 156
Saint-Saëns, Camille 177
Sally, Irene and Mary (1925) 13
Sally, Irene and Mary (1938) 89, 244
Samuel Goldwyn Productions 49
Sand, Jillian 33, 35
Sándor Rózsa (novel) 187
Sandrich, Mark 14, 16
Santley, Joseph 47, 202
The Saturday Evening Post (magazine) 143
"S-A-V-E-D" 104
Saxon, Marie 24
Say It in French (1938) 59
Say It with Songs (1929) 220
Scarface (1932) 111, 145, 230, 257

Index

The Scarlet Pimpernel (1934) 76
Scharf, Betty King 236
Schenck, Joseph M. 221
Schertzinger, Victor 166, 167, 246, 247, 248, 249
"School Days" 66, 69
Schubert, Franz 43
Schumann-Heink, Ernestine 146, 153–156, **154**
Schwartz, Arthur 169, 170
Scola, Kathryn 63
Scott, Allan 240
Scott, Fred 107, 125
Scott, Ian 173
Scott, Randolph 180, 181, **181**, 182
Scotto, Aubrey 114, 166, 167, 168
The Scoundrel (1935) 54
Secret Valley (1937) 130
Sedgwick, Edna 204
Seegar, Miriam 24
Seiter, William A. 240
Selznick, David O. 49, 115
Sennett, Mack 64, 111, 125, 136, 225, 230
Sensations of 1945 (1944) 74
Seventh Heaven (1927) 11, 229
Seyffertitz, Gustav von 33, 35
Shall We Dance (1937) 251, 252
Shaw, Artie 191
Shaw, Wini 155
Shaw and Lee 151
She Learned About Sailors (1934) 236, 237
Shean, Al 259
Shearer, Norma 13, 233
Sheffield, Maceo 126
Sheffield, Simeon 108
Shell Chateau (radio program) 114
Sheridan, Ann 134, 210
Sherman, Richard 62
Sherwood, Robert E. 11
"She's Way Up Thar" 77
Shippey, Lee 138
Shirley, Bill 48
Shoot the Works (1934) 213
Shore, Dinah 65
Short, Dorothy 145
Show Boat (1929) 8
Show Boat (1936) 1, 232, 234
The Show of Shows (1929) 26, 30, 32
Sidney, Sylvia 114, 229, 230
Siegel, Al 54, 95
"Silent Night" 153
Silverman, "Sime" 34
Simms, Ginny 215, 217
Simon, S. Sylvan 182
Sinatra, Frank 192, 252
"Sing a Song of Harvest" 98
"Sing and Be Happy" 244
Sing and Be Happy (1937) 242–245
Sing, Baby, Sing (1936) 97, 243

"Sing, Sing, Sing" 196
Sing While You're Able (1937) 84, 87, 88–89
Singer, Leo 139
The Singer Midgets 137, 139
Singin' in the Rain (1952) 14, 16
The Singing Cowgirl (1939) 142–145
The Singing Fool (1928) 11, 220
Singleton, Penny 102
Sisters (1930) 31
Sitting Pretty (1933) 43
Six Hits and a Miss 258
Skinner, Frank 204
Skinner Steps Out (1929) 10
Skolsky, Sidney 243
The Sky Hawk (1929) 22
Slater, Charles 17
"Smiles" 245
Smiling Irish Eyes (1929) 30
Smith, Pete 144
Smith, Stanley 6
Smith, W. Clyde 78
Smith, "Whispering" Jack 22
Snow White and the Seven Dwarfs (1937) 64, 99, 139
"So Divine" 121
So This Is Harris (1933) 16
Sombras de gloria (1930) 57
Some Like It Hot [aka *Rhythm Romance*] (1939) 211–214, **212**
Some Like It Hot (1959) 213
"Someone" 11, 13
Something to Sing About (1937) 142, 166, 219, 245–249, **247**
Son of Frankenstein (1939) 204
Son of the Sheik (1926) 26
Song o' My Heart (1930) 22
Song of Norway (1970) 74
"Song of the Dawn" 225
The Song of the Flame (1930) 20
Song of the West (1930) 17, 27, 106
The Song Writer (play) 42
The Song Writers' Revue (1930) 42
Sonnenberg, Gus 226
"Sonny Boy" 11, 220, 223
Sono Art–World Wide Pictures 14, 15
The Sons of the Pioneers 117
S.O.S. Coast Guard (1937) 90, 102
"Sound Effects Man" 95
Sousa, John Philip 44
Soussanin, Nicholas 33
South Pacific (stage musical) 73
Sparks, Ned 68, **68**, 226
Specht, Paul, and His Orchestra 25
Spectrum Productions 125
Spence, Ralph 99
Sragow, Michael 188
Stage Door (1937) 49, 253

Stagecoach (1966) 119
Stahl, John M. 30
Stalin, Joseph 188
Stand Up and Cheer! (1934) 77, 237
Standing, Sir Guy 114, 115
Stanwyck, Barbara 25, 240
Star Dust (1921) 179
The Star Maker (1939) 44, 65–69, **68**, 74
Star Wars (1977) 111
"Stardust" 68
Starr, Jimmy 217, 237
Starrett, Charles 133
Stars and Stripes Forever (1952) 44
Stars Over Broadway (stage revue) 152
Start Cheering (1938) 82
Steele, Bob 28, 106
Stein, Alexandre 20
Stein, Gertrude 34
Stein, Jules 216
Stept, Sammy 99
Sternberg, Josef von 187
Sterzini, Joseph 171
Stevens, George 250, 251
Stewart, James 258
"Stiff Upper Lip" 253
Stingaree (1934) 231–234
Stinnett, Jack 94
Stockwell, Harry 156
Stokowski, Leopold 191, 195
Stolen Harmony (1935) 111
Stolen Heaven (1938) 59
Stoloff, Benjamin 22, 55
Stone, Andrew L. 56, 57, 58, 59, 71, 72, 73, 74, 75
Stone, John 37, 38
Stone, Milburn 90
Stone, Paula 90
Stone, Virginia Lively 74
Storey, June 103
Stormy Weather (1943) 74
The Story of Alexander Graham Bell (1939) 49
The Story of Vernon and Irene Castle (1939) 254
Straight, Place and Show (1938) 99
Strang, Harry 89
Strauss, Johann II 43, 74, 184, 186, 187, 198, 199
Street Girl (1929) 13, 177
Strike Me Pink (1936) 191
Stroheim, Erich von 8, 38
Strong, Edna 152
Stuart, Gloria 38, 40
The Student Prince (stage operetta) 152
Studs Lonigan (novel) 246
Styne, Jule 98
Sullivan, Arthur *see* Gilbert and Sullivan

Sullivan, Elliott **216**
Sullivan, Maxine 208
Summerville, Slim 98
Sun Valley Serenade (1941) 192
"Sunbonnet Sue" 66
Sunnyside Up (1929) 21, 22, 33, 97
Sutherland, Eddie 199, 225, 226
Svenson's Big Night Out see *Movietone Follies of 1930*
Svenson's Wild Party see *Movietone Follies of 1930*
*Swanee River (1939) 44–50, **49**, 64, 223
"Swanee River" *see* "Old Folks at Home"
Swarthout, Gladys 2, 147, 148, 155, 157, 158, 159, 191, 198, 199, 200, **200**, 201
Sweet Adeline (1934) 234
Sweet and Low-Down (1944) 192
Sweet Kitty Bellairs (1930) 222
Sweethearts (1938) 72, 219, 256, 260
Sweetie (1929) 79
Swickard, Josef 58
Swing Fever (1943) 218
Swing High (1930) 137
**Swing It Professor* (1937) 85, 90–91, 191
Swing, Sister, Swing* (1938) 201–205, **203
Swing Time (1936) 252
Swing Your Lady (1938) 78, 102
Sydney, Basil 161
Symphony of Six Million (1932) 232
Syncopation (1942) 214

"T for Texas" 77
Talbot, Lyle 236
Tales of Manhattan (1942) 187
"Tales of the Vienna Woods" 184
**The Talk of Hollywood* (1929) 14–17
Talley, Marion 147, 164–168, **165**
Talmadge, Norma 11
The Taming of the Shrew (play) 151
"Tangerine" 246
Tanner, Elmo 204
Tarzan the Fearless (1933) 129
Tarzan's Revenge (1938) 130
Tashman, Lilyan 227
Tate, Erskine 125
Taurog, Norman 43, 94, 117, 119, 229
Taylor, Rex 223
Taylor, Robert 87, 112
Tchaikovsky, Pyotr Ilyich 258
TCM *see* Turner Classic Movies
Tearle, Conway 233
Tell Your Children [aka *Reefer Madness*] (1938) 122, 138, 144

Temple, Shirley 1, 2, 50, 80, 97, 216, 240
The Terror of Tiny Town* (1938) 125, 129, 136–140, **137
Terry, Don 27, 28, 29, 106
"The Texas Tornado" 81
Thaïs (opera) 179
Thalberg, Irving 184
"Thanks" 27
**Thanks for Listening* (1937) 84, 89–90
Thanks for the Memory (1938) 213
"Thanks for the Memory" 196, 209, 213
That Girl from Paris (1936) 177
That's Entertainment, Part II (1976) 184, 187
That's Right—You're Wrong* (1939) 191, 214–218, **216
"That Silver-Haired Daddy of Mine" 112
Thayer, Tiffany 121, 122
"There's a Lucky Guy" 230
There's No Business Like Show Business (1954) 65
"There's Nothing Like a College Education" 54
"There'll Come a Time" 186
"They Can't Take That Away from Me" 252
"Things Are Looking Up" 252
Thirer, Irene 13, 30
Thirteen Women (1932) 121, 232
This Day and Age (1933) 226
This Way, Please (1937) 95
Thomas, Harry H. 15
Thompson, Harlan 34
Thorne, William H. 222
Thoroughly Modern Millie (1967) 34
Thorpe, Richard 28, 29
365 Nights in Hollywood* (1934) 219, 234–239, **236
"Three Little Fishies" 215
The Three Musketeers (1939) 49
The Three Stooges 53, 97
The Three Tenors 146
Thru Different Eyes (1929) 22
Tibbett, Lawrence 2, 147, 157, 168–171
Tiffany Pictures/Tiffany-Stahl Pictures 16, 27, 28, 29, 30, 106
"Tiger Rag" 191, 200, 201
Timblin, Charles "Slim" 94
Time (magazine) 164
Times Square Lady (1935) 87
Tin Pan Alley (1940) 89
Tinling, James 37
Tiomkin, Dimitri 185
"Tip-Toe Through the Tulips" 6
TNT *see* Turner Network Television

*To Beat the Band (1935) 51–55, **53**, 117
"To the Land of My Romance" 74
Tobacco Road (play) 94
Tobin, Genevieve **154**, 155
Todd, Mabel 197
Tomlin, Pinky 2, 83–91, **86**, 103, 190
"Tomorrow Is Another Day" 222, 223
"Tonight Is Mine" 233
*Too Much Harmony (1933) 219, 224–228, 230
Top Hat (1935) 16, 54, 62, 240
Torena, Juan 121, 122
Tosca (opera) 155
Tourneur, Maurice 179
Towne, Gene 217
Tracy, Lee 8, 24
Tracy, Spencer 236
The Trail of the Lonesome Pine (1936) 114, 115, 199
Treacher, Arthur 170
A Tree Grows in Brooklyn (1945) 237
Trevor, Hugh 6, 12
Tropic Holiday (1938) 96
Trotti, Lamar 62
"The Trouble with Me Is You" 87
Il Trovatore (opera) 167
Truex, Ernest 203
Tryon, Glenn 8, 9, 10
Tucker, Richard **57**
Tucker, Sophie 64
Tumbling Tumbleweeds (1935) 112
Turner, Lana 191
Turner, Ted 234
Turner Classic Movies (TCM) 1, 6, 40, 65, 152, 175, 196, 223, 234
Turner Network Television (TNT) 223
Tuska, Jon 48, 110, 111
Tuttle, Frank 162
20th Century-Fox *see* Fox Film Corporation
20th Century Pictures 169, 231, 232
**Two Gun Man from Harlem* (1938) 123, 126–127
Two Plus Fours (1930) 16, 225
"Two Sleepy People" 213
Two Tickets to Broadway (1951) 98
Tyler, Harry 58

El Ultimo varon sobre la Tierra (1933) 37–38
"The Umbrella Man" 215
Under Montana Skies (1930) 29
*Under Your Spell (1936) 168–171
Union Pacific (1939) 258

United Artists (UA) 74, 155, 156, 221, 225
Universal Pictures 3, 5, 6, 7, 8, 9, 10, 17, 18, 19, 20, 42, 47, 58, 67, 73, 106, 109, 111, 143, 163, 178, 179, 180, 182, 201, 202, 204, 225, 233
Untamed (1929) 28
Urecal, Minerva 138

The Vagabond King (1930) 6
Valentino, Rudolph 26
Vallee, Rudy 92, 98, 114, 225, 235, 236
The Vanishing Shadow (1934) 111
Vanity Fair (periodical) 230
Vansant, Jacqueline 201
Van Sloan, Edward 39
Variety (periodical) 15, 19, 23, 26, 29, 34, 37, 39, 43, 50, 59, 61, 66, 74, 76, 77, 79, 82, 95, 103, 105, 132, 135, 139, 145, 151, 156, 158, 159, 167, 170, 174, 182, 201, 204, 213, 221, 223, 230, 233, 238, 249, 257
Varsity Show (1937) 82, 134, 209
"Le Veau d'Or" 170
Veidt, Conrad 8
Velez, Lupe 169
Veloz and Yolanda 200
Venable, Evelyn 47
Vernon, Wally **61**, 95, 98, 259
"Vesti la giubba" 147, 153, 155
Victor, Henry 33
Vidor, King 7
Viennese Nights (1930) 6
The Virginian (1923) 29
The Virginian (TV series) 128
Vischer, Blanca 121, 122
A Vitaphonic Nightmare (video) 17
Viva Villa! (1934) 257
The Voice of Hollywood (1929–1931 shorts series) 16, 27, 106
"Voices of Spring" 184

Wagner, Richard 210
Waikiki Wedding (1937) 92, 119, 195
"Wait for the Wagon" 104
"Waiting for a Train" 77
Wald, Jerry 151, 209, 210
Walker, Johnnie 25, 26, 27
Walker, Terry **93**, 94
"Walking with Susie" 22
Wallace, Beryl 90
Walsh, Christy 129, 131
Walsh, Raoul 27, 177, 178
Walt Disney Pictures 94, 99, 139
Waltzes from Vienna (1934) 186
Wanger, Walter 112, 114, 115, 160, 162, 163
Ware, Linda 67, **68**, 69, 74
Waring, Fred 201

Warner, H.B. 256
Warner Bros. Pictures 1, 5, 6, 13, 30, 32, 78, 82, 87, 97, 102, 104, 115, 117, 132, 133, 134, 135, 146, 149, 151, 158, 164, 165, 170, 181, 185, 187, 191, 192, 196, 197, 205, 207, 208, 209, 210, 211, 220, 221, 222, 223, 224, 227, 230, 240, 246, 247, 248, 249
Warren, Harry 104, 135, 190, 207, 209
Washington, Ned 99
Washington Post (newspaper) 59
"Wasn't It You?" 204
*Water Rustlers (1939) 141, 143–145
Waterloo Bridge (1931) 20
Waters, Ethel 209
Watson, Harry 253
Watters, George Manker 18
Wax, Mo 48
*The Way to Love (1933) 228–231, **229**
Wayne, John 28, 106
Weaver, Loretta 104
Weaver, Marjorie 97, 98
Weaver Brothers (Leon and Frank, aka Abner and Cicero) and Elviry (June) 2, 77, 78, 100–105, **103**, 209
Webber, Andrew Lloyd 42
"We'd Rather Be in College" 81
The Wedding March (1928) 8
Weems, Ted 204
Weidman, Jerome 205
Weisser, Thelma 138
Welk, Lawrence 204
Wellman, William A. 232, 233
Wells, William K. 24
Werblin, David "Sonny" 244
Werker, Alfred L. 38
Werrenrath, Reinald 146
West, Mae 131, 140, 184, 187, 227
Westman, Nydia 230
Westmore, Hamilton "Bud" 94
Whale, James 38
"What a Beautiful Beginning" 244
What Price Glory? (1926) 11
"What'll I Do?" 63
"What's the Reason (I'm Not Pleasin' You)?" 87
Wheeler, Bert 6, 150
"When a Cowboy Goes to Town" 131
When You're in Love* (1937) 171–175, **173
"Where Else but Here?" 257
Whispering Smith Speaks (1935) 163
"The Whistling Boy" 174
White, Alice 30
White, Marjorie 22, 23, **23**, 24

White, Pearl 143
White Christmas (1954) 68
Whiteman, Paul 5, 6, 10, 18, 19, 41, 52, 63, 92, 143, 152, 190, 197, 209, 224, 225
Whitey's Lindy Hoppers 191
Whiting, Margaret 65
Whiting, Richard 117, 134, 135, 196
Whitley, Ray, and the Six-Bar Cowboys 131
Whitney, Eleanore 202
Wilbur, Crane 121
Wilder, Billy 198, 199
"Will I Ever Know?" 115
Will There Really Be a Morning? (book) 117
William Fox Movietone Follies of 1929 (1929) 21–22
Williams, Spencer, Jr. 126, 127
Williams, Wade 238–239
Williamson, J.W. 76
Wills, Bob 107
Wilson, Teddy 189, 196
Winchell, Walter 66, 244
Windheim, Marek **247**
Wing, Toby 39, 87, 88
Wings (1927) 22, 232
"Wire Brush Stomp" 213
**With Love and Kisses* (1936) 83, 87–88, 89
Withers, Jane 2, 243
Witney, William 90
The Wizard of Oz (1939) 81, 140, 191, 259
Wodehouse, P.G. 250, 252, 254
The Woman Disputed (1928) 11
"Woman Disputed, I Love You" 11
Woman to Woman (1929) 28
"Women" 38
Wonder Bar (1934) 223
The Wonder Bar (stage musical) 223
"Woo! Woo!" 81
Wood, Cyrus 13
Wood, Peggy 25
Woolsey, Robert 6, 150
Wray, Fay 42
Wrixon, Maris 104
Wrubel, Allie 151
Wurtzel, Sol 38, 100, 244
Wylie, I.A.R. 180

The Yacht Club Boys 81, 216
Yankee Doodle Dandy (1942) 219, 248, 249
Yates, Herbert J. 112, 166, 167
"Yes to You" 238
Yesterday (2019) 1
Yip Yip Yaphank (stage musical) 63
"Yo Te Adoro (How I Adore You)" 28

You Bet Your Life (TV show) 91
"You Can Always Count on Me" 35
You Can't Have Everything (1937) 97, 244
You Can't Take It with You (play) 166
You'll Find Out (1940) 218

Young, Artie 128
Young, Victor 162
"Young and Healthy" 87
"Your Mother and Mine" 66
"You're a Minstrel Man" 194
You're a Sweetheart (1937) 204
"You're Slightly Terrific" 81

Zanuck, Darryl F. 43, 44, 49, 50, 62, 63, 64, 98, 99, 169, 243
Ziegfeld Follies (stage revues) 66, 71, 150
Zierler, Samuel 15, 16
Zolotow, Maurice 199
Zukor, Adolph 57, 59, 201

www.ingramcontent.com/pod-product-compliance
Lightning Source LLC
Chambersburg PA
CBHW080800300426
44114CB00020B/2780